OPEN YOUR EYES

A Nichiren Buddhist View of Awakening

By Reverend Michael Ryuei McCormick

Table of Contents

Copyright

Forward

This book is perhaps one of the most important English works ever written about Nichiren Buddhist teachings. A must read for every Nichiren practitioner, regardless of affiliation, or any student of Buddhism interested in the evolution of East Asian Buddhism; from India to China to Japan to the West.

While this book is not meant to be an introduction to Buddhism, it is a wonderful overview of Buddhist history, and an excellent guide to one of Nichiren Shōnin's five major writings: the *Opening of the Eyes* (*Kaimoku-shō*). Nichiren Shōnin can be a controversial figure, who makes even some Nichiren practitioners uncomfortable. However, there is broad agreement that Nichiren is one of the most important and influential Buddhist teachers in history. This book is a thoroughly researched and well sourced reference combining a historical look at the spread of Buddhism and illuminating Nichiren's thinking within it's context of medieval Japanese culture. It carefully explains why Nichiren expressed criticism of other Buddhist schools and his overarching motivation to ease the suffering of people in this world by returning emphasis to Śākyamuni Buddha's message that everyone regardless of gender, status, or circumstance can become a buddha in this very lifetime.

Rev. Ryuei McCormick's name is derived from two characters: "Ryu," meaning dragon; and "ei," meaning English language; taken together meaning: "Dragon-of-the-English-Language." An apt name indeed. He has deeply studied the entire Buddhist canon from the *tripiṭaka*, the "three baskets" of the Pāli canon, to Tiantai writings to the major works of various Japanese schools, how Buddhism evolved across various lands and eras, and how these teachings and practices can apply to today's cultural and religious thinking. What drives Ryuei's work is explaining

Buddhism in plain language, distilling Buddhism's core messages out of various religious and cultural settings, making Buddhism relevant and accessible today.

No Buddhist book has impacted me over my forty years as a Buddhist as much as this book. I wish I had read it when I first converted to Buddhism.

Mark White Lotus Herrick
Oakland, CA
2019

Introduction

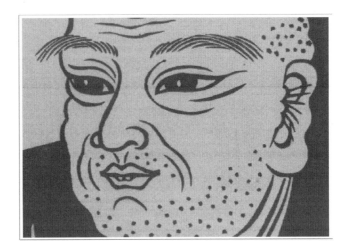

On September 12, 1271, Nichiren Shōnin was arrested and taken to the execution grounds on Tatsunokuchi beach. He was saved from death when a mysterious ball of light that flew through the sky frightened the executioner and the other samurai. A messenger from the regent arrived soon after with orders that Nichiren Shōnin was not to be executed in any case but exiled instead. On October 10, 1271, Nichiren Shōnin was sent into exile on Sado Island. At first, he lived in a small broken-down shrine in a graveyard called Tsukuhara. It was the hope of his enemies that Nichiren Shōnin would die in the harsh winter of Sado Island without any adequate shelter or provisions.

Many of Nichiren Shōnin's followers, like Nisshin and Nichirō had also been arrested and imprisoned. They wondered why they had not been protected from such persecution, so in order to resolve these doubts Nichiren Shōnin wrote the *Open Your Eyes to the Lotus Teaching* (*Kaimoku-shō*) in February 1272 and addressed it to Shijō Kingo, a samurai in Kamakura who was a staunch follower of Nichiren. Shockingly, Nichiren Shōnin wrote that he had been beheaded at Tatsunokuchi and it was his spirit that had come to Sado Island. This reflects Nichiren Shōnin's feelings that in a sense he had given up his life at the execution ground and had now begun a new life. At the same time, he was aware that he could still literally die in the harsh conditions of winter on Sado Island or that he might once again face execution. So he stated that the *Kaimoku-shō* was intended to be a memento and an expression of his true will if it should come to that. Throughout the work, Nichiren Shōnin states that the most important question is whether or not he really has been acting as the practitioner of the *Lotus Sūtra*; and, if so, why he and his followers have not received the blessings and protections of the buddhas, bodhisattvas and other divine protectors of the Dharma.

In the course of the *Kaimoku-shō* Nichiren Shōnin shows through a series of comparisons that only the teaching of the *Lotus Sūtra* can enable all people to attain buddhahood. He also shows that the *Lotus Sūtra* itself predicted that anyone propagating it in the Latter Age of the Dharma would be bound to encounter the kinds of hardships that Nichiren Shōnin and his disciples had already faced and would continue to face. Nichiren also discerned that of all the teachers in Japan at that time, he was the only one who was directing people to the *Lotus Sūtra* instead of away from it. Having reflected upon these things, Nichiren Shōnin states his determination in the form of a threefold vow to continue upholding the *Lotus Sūtra* for the sake of Japan, no matter what hardships he might have to face:

> *"...no matter how many great difficulties fall upon me, I will not submit to them until a man of wisdom defeats me by reason. Other difficulties are like dust in the wind. I will never break my vow to become the pillar of Japan, to become the eyes of Japan, and become a great vessel for Japan." (Hori 2002, p. 106; see also Murano 2000, p. 114; Gosho Translation Committee 1999, pp. 280-281)*

The *Kaimoku-shō* is one of the five major writings of Nichiren Shōnin. In it, Nichiren Shōnin reflects upon the course of his life and the nature of the hardships and persecutions that had beset him. In this work, Nichiren Shōnin clarifies his mission and renews his determination to work selflessly, even at the cost of his life, for the sake of Japan and by extension all sentient beings whose only salvation is in the universal promise of Buddhahood conveyed by the *Lotus Sūtra*.

Chapter 1 - Gratitude as the Motivation for Buddhist Practice

Writing of Nichiren Shōnin: Doctrine Vol. 2, pp. 30, 39-40, 91
Kaimoku-shō or Liberation from Blindness, pp. 7, 20-21, 92-93
The Writings of Nichiren Daishonin I, pp. 220, 228, 269

Nichiren begins the *Kaimoku-shō* with the following truism of East Asian culture: "All the people of the world should respect three kinds of persons: lords, teachers, and parents." (Murano 2000) Nichiren is talking about more than just respect and reverence however. The theme that he raises throughout *Kaimoku-shō* and other writings is that we owe these three kinds of people a huge debt of gratitude because life would not be possible if it were not for our parents who bring us into the world and nurture us when we are helpless; without educators to teach us the practical skills, traditions, and values that we need to learn; and without good and just rulers to maintain order and harmony in the country. In his other major writing, *Essay on Gratitude* (*Hōon-jō*), Nichiren says:

> *Those who learn and practice the teachings of the*
> *Buddha should never forget the kindness of their*
> *parents, masters, and sovereign. What is the best way*
> *for Buddhists to express their gratitude for the*
> *unfathomable kindness that they have received?*
> *Mastering Buddhism completely and to be sagacious in*
> *the Way. (Hori 2004, p. 2. See also Gosho Translation*
> *Committee 1999, p. 690).*

For Nichiren, the primary motivation for practicing Buddhism should not be a selfish desire to escape suffering on our own, or to gain supernatural powers, or to become detached meditators. Likewise, our aspiration to attain buddhahood and liberate all beings should not be a matter of condescending pity for suffering sentient beings. Rather, we should be motivated by gratitude for all that has been done for us by others, long before we were ever able to ask for such favors, much less be capable of earning such help as we received in our youth and throughout our life. We should have a heartfelt wish to do all we can to repay the great debt we owe others for the life that we have and all the assistance and blessings that we have received. This is not a matter of presuming to save others out of pity. It is a realization that others have already helped us and that our most authentic response is to repay that favor by following the Buddha Way for the sake of all.

Nichiren praises Confucianism for enabling people to recognize their filial obligations to their parents, but he criticizes it for not addressing how to fully repay those obligations. Nevertheless, Nichiren praises filial piety as the root virtue of all others. The obligation one has to one's parents is seen as the one that best represents all other obligations.

> *The purpose of the teachings of Confucianism, expounded in the texts of more than three thousand volumes, is to emphasize the importance of two virtues: filial piety or kō (hsiao), and loyalty to one's lord or chū (chung). A loyal subject grows out of a dutiful son. Filial piety is homonymic with kō (kao), meaning "high." The virtue of filial piety is higher in value than heaven. Filial piety is also homonymic with kō (hou) meaning "thickness." The virtue of filial piety is thicker in value than even the crust of the earth. Saints and sages of Confucianism were dutiful to their parents in their homes. Needless to say, we students of the teachings of the Buddha should know of the favors given by others and repay them. As far as we are disciples of the Buddha, we should acknowledge the four different kinds of favors and repay them. (Murano 2000, p 20. See also Hori 2002, p. 39, and Gosho Translation Committee 1999, p. 228)*

The four kinds of favors according to the *Contemplation of the Mind Ground Sūtra* are those received from parents, all living beings, the ruler, and the Three Treasures of Buddha, Dharma, and Sangha. There are variations however, and Nichiren sometimes speaks of them as parents, teachers, rulers, and the Three Treasures. However they are listed, the point of the four favors is that we all owe an incalculable debt to our parents who gave us birth and raised us (presumably), to all other beings who provide us with the means to live, with the teachers and rulers who guide us and help to maintain civilized life, and finally to the Three Treasures for providing all beings with a way to overcome suffering and attain buddhahood.

Nichiren criticizes those who follow the two vehicles of the *śrāvakas* (lit. "voice hearers" who are the Hīnayāna disciples of the Buddha) and the *pratyekabuddhas* (lit. "privately awakened ones" who contemplate dependent origination on their own) because these kinds of Buddhists attain liberation from the sufferings of this world of birth and death, but are unable to help anyone else, including their parents. Because of this, they fail to achieve the true purpose of the Buddha Dharma. Speaking of these Hīnayāna disciples, Nichiren says:

> *The purpose of becoming a monk by renouncing one's family is to save one's parents. Adherents of the two vehicles think that they can emancipate themselves from suffering. It may be true, but it is very difficult for them to benefit others. They may benefit others to some extent, but they will send their parents to the world where their parents can never become Buddhas. Therefore, I say that they do not know the favors of their parents. (Ibid, p. 21. See also Hori 2002, pp. 39-40, and Gosho Translation Committee 1999, p. 228)*

Nichiren's conclusion is that only the *Lotus Sūtra* has the power to enable our parents to attain buddhahood. Other Buddhist teachings and sūtras may state that in principle all beings can attain buddhahood, but only in the *Lotus Sūtra* is the buddhahood of all men and women guaranteed and even demonstrated. In the twelfth chapter, "Devadatta," the Buddha predicts that his treacherous cousin Devadatta will in time attain buddhahood; in that same chapter, the daughter of the dragon king attains buddhahood immediately after offering Śākyamuni Buddha a precious gem. Nichiren observes:

> *The filial piety of Confucian ethics is a virtue to be practiced only by those whose parents are still alive. Confucian saints and sages are such in name only*

because they cannot save their parents in the
afterworld. Brahmins know the past and future, but
they do not know how to save their parents in the
future. Buddhist saints and sages deserve to be called so
because they can save their parents in their future lives.
But it is difficult to attain even one's own Buddhahood
by following the Hīnayāna and Mahāyāna sūtras
expounded before the Lotus Sūtra. Needless to say, it is
more difficult to have one's parents attain Buddhahood.
The statement in some other sūtras that anyone can
attain Buddhahood is not confirmed in reality. When a
woman became a Buddha in the Lotus Sūtra, a mother's
attainment of Buddhahood was assured. When
Devadatta, the evil man, became a Buddha, a father's
attainment of Buddhahood was guaranteed. This sūtra
is the Book of Filial Piety (Kōkyō, Hsiao-ching) of
Buddhism. (Ibid, pp. 92-93. See also Hori 2002, p. 91,
and Gosho Translation Committee 1999, p. 269)

Therefore, the way to repay our debts of gratitude is by leading our parents
and all other people to faith in the *Lotus Sūtra* so that they can all attain
buddhahood. Only in this way do we truly fulfill the Buddha Way according to
Nichiren.

Though it is not discussed explicitly in *Kaimoku-shō*, reverence for parents,
teachers, and lords also meant reverence for the Eternal Śākyamuni Buddha
of the *Lotus Sūtra*. In the *Genealogical Chart of the Buddha's Lifetime
Teachings in Five Periods* (*Ichidai Goji Keizu*), Nichiren quotes Guanding (561-
632; aka Zhang'an), the second patriarch of the Tiantai school, who wrote,
"The one body of the Buddha is equipped with the three virtues of the lord,
teacher, and parent." (Hori 2004, p. 245 modified). In *A Treatise on the
Differences Between the Lotus School from the other Eight Schools* (*Hasshū
Imoku-shō*) Nichiren explains how the attribution of the three virtues of lord,
teacher, and parent to the Buddha was derived from passages in the *Lotus
Sūtra*:

Śākyamuni Buddha is quoted as declaring in the third
chapter, "A Parable," of the Lotus Sūtra, fascicle two,

13

"This triple world is my domain." This means that Śākyamuni Buddha has the virtue of being our lord, the king and the most respect worthy person in the world. His words, "All living beings therein are my children," means that the Buddha has the virtue of our parent; and "There are many sufferings in this world; only I can save all living beings," points out his virtue of being our teacher. In the 16th chapter, "The Life Span of the Buddha," of the Lotus Sūtra, the Buddha is quoted as declaring, "I am the father of the world. (Hori 2002, p. 17 modified. See also Gosho Translation Committee 2006, pp. 417-418)

Right after this passage Nichiren provides a diagram equating these three qualities with the "three bodies" (S. *trikāya*) of the Buddha: the Dharma-body (S. *dharmakāya*), reward-body (S. *sambhogakaya*), and accommodative-body (S. *nirmanakāya*). The quality of a ruler is equated with the reward-body, the quality of a teacher is equated with the accommodative-body, and the quality of a parent is equated with the Dharma-body. What does this mean? Briefly, the three bodies are a way of highlighting three different aspects of the Buddha. In other forms of Buddhism they are often viewed as different kinds of buddhas, but in Tiantai and Nichiren Buddhism these three aspects are all the properties of the Eternal Śākyamuni Buddha. But to understand them and how they relate to the parents, teachers, and rulers let's look at them one at a time.

The reward-body is an idealized buddha who resides in an ideal world called a pure land where all the conditions of that world make it easy to attain awakening. One of the most popular reward-body buddhas is Amitābha Buddha of the Pure Land School. The reward-body is a kind of personification of all the meritorious qualities of the Buddha that manifest themselves in the form of the thirty-two marks of a "great man" (the legendary "wheel-turning kings" or universal emperors and also certain classes of Vedic deities also had these marks). The reward-body, also called an "enjoyment-body," also personifies the bliss of the Buddha's awakening that only advanced bodhisattvas are able to perceive. A Buddha of the reward-body is like a ruler because he possesses these superior lordly marks and qualities and presides over a pure land where the faithful can be reborn after they die and there easily attain buddhahood.

The accommodative-body is the Buddha as a historical person. The historical Śākyamuni Buddha was born on a certain day, died on a certain day, and in between he was subject to aging, sickness, and infirmity, and had to eat, sleep, and relieve himself like the rest of us. This was the Buddha who spent fifty years of his life teaching others how to free themselves of suffering by attaining the same awakening that he did. For this reason the accommodative-body is related to the quality of a teacher.

The Dharma-body is the true nature of reality. In early Buddhism the term either referred to the Buddha's body of teachings or to the fivefold Dharma-body of practice and liberation: morality, concentration, wisdom, liberation, and knowledge of liberation. In Mahāyāna Buddhism, the Dharma-body came to mean true reality itself and was personified by cosmic buddhas like Mahāvairocana Tathagata (J. Dainichi Nyorai, which translates as "Great Sun Tathagata"). Because the true nature of reality is what makes all things possible, including the attainment of buddhahood, the Dharma-body is said to be like a parent, and we are all the children of this Buddha who is the true nature of our lives.

More will be said about the three bodies of the Buddha in later chapters. For now, the important thing is to know that Nichiren and his Tiantai predecessors viewed all three bodies and their qualities as aspects of the Eternal Śākyamuni Buddha of the *Lotus Sūtra*. For Nichiren, Śākyamuni Buddha surpasses our worldly rulers, teachers, and parents, because he is the lord who presides over our awakening, the teacher who leads us to awakening, and the parent who sees us as his children and who are the inheritors of his awakening.

> *Śākyamuni Buddha is equipped with the three virtues of a lord, master, and parent. As a lord, he protects the people; as a teacher he guides the people; and as a parent, he loves the people. It is only he who is perfectly equipped with these three virtues. (Hori 2004, p. 244 modified. See also Gosho Translation Committee 2006, p. 1039)*

When Nichiren spoke of repaying debts of gratitude to our rulers, teachers, and parents, he also means that we must realize and requite our debt of gratitude to the Eternal Śākyamuni Buddha above all, and in doing so repay the worldly debts as well.

Sources

Gosho Translation Committee, editor-translator. *The Writings of Nichiren Daishonin*. Tokyo: Soka Gakkai, 1999.

_____. *The Writings of Nichiren Daishonin Volume II*. Tokyo: Soka Gakkai, 2006.

Hori, Kyotsu, comp. *Writings of Nichiren Shonin: Doctrine Volume 2*. Tokyo: Nichiren Shu Overseas Propagation Promotion Association, 2002.

_____. *Writings of Nichiren Shonin: Doctrine Volume 3*. Tokyo: Nichiren Shu Overseas Propagation Promotion Association, 2004.

Murano, Senchu. *Kaimokusho or Liberation from Blindness*. Berkeley: Numata Center for Buddhist Translation and Research, 2000.

Williams, Paul. *Mahayana Buddhism: The Doctrinal Foundations*. New York: Routledge, 1989.

Chapter 2 - Scope of Time as the Criteria for Evaluating Religions

Writings of Nichiren Shōnin Doctrine 2, pp. 30
Kaimoku-shō or Liberation from Blindness, p. 7
The Writings of Nichiren Daishonin I, pp. 220
The Long Discourses of the Buddha, pp. 67-90

After stating who people should fundamentally respect, Nichiren states that people should study world religions (or at least those known to East Asians in the 13th century): "They should study three [religions]: Confucianism, Brahmanism, and Buddhism." (Murano 2000, p. 7) He then discusses each of these religions in turn, explaining their merits and also limitations and how each teaching in turn takes account of a larger span of time and so achieves a more complete perspective. This might seem like a novel way to evaluate different religious traditions, but it is not peculiar to Nichiren. Śākyamuni Buddha himself used this method in the *Supreme Net Discourse* (Pali *Brahmajāla-sutta*).

In the *Supreme Net Discourse*, the Buddha critiques sixty-two different kinds of wrong views that are like a net with sixty-two parts (later writings would expand this to ninety-five or ninety-six possible wrong views). He teaches his monks that the Buddha is truly praiseworthy not because of his moral practice (though that is also praiseworthy) but because he has understood all of these views, knows how they arise, knows where they lead to, and has no attachment to any of them. The Buddha is truly praiseworthy because has escaped the net of views and gone beyond them to perfect peace and liberation.

The sixty-two views are broken down in the following way: There are eighteen views arising from speculations based on past experiences and forty-four views arising from speculations about future experience based on present experiences.

Of the eighteen based on past experience there are four relating to belief that things are eternal. Then there are four relating to belief that some things are eternal and other things are not. Then there are four relating to beliefs about whether the world-system is finite or infinite. Then there are four variations of what is called "eel-wriggling" whereby the pundit in question only gives evasive answers for different reasons. Then there are two versions of those who believe that things come about by chance.

Of the forty-four speculations about the future there are thirty-two involving the belief that life persists after death in some form. Then there are seven versions of the belief that life does eventually come to a total end, though all but the first involve some temporary form of life after death. Then there are five different views about what constitutes nirvāṇa, that is to say: freedom from suffering.

In all of these sixty-two cases of wrong views, the Buddha traces the view back to some felt experience that leads to attachment and eventually to suffering. Some of the views are based on present material experience, some on a meditative absorption or attainment, some are based on the recovery of past life memories through meditation, and some are based on metaphysical speculations using logic and reasoning. What they all have in common is that the holders of these views have taken hold of something (a concept, a felt material experience, a meditative state) as proof of a particular view about life. The Buddha, however, is not trying to set up a conceptual scheme or metaphysical system to be an object of clinging. He is not trying to establish some partial experience as representative of some greater whole. Rather, the Buddha is trying to show that true freedom from suffering can only occur when one no longer clings to passing experiences or even conceptual constructs. By not clinging, one escapes the net of views and instead awakens to the Net of Brahmā that is the Supreme Net of the interdependent nature of reality that is selfless and free of suffering.

A few examples should help to see how this method works and how it is relevant to Nichiren's critique. The fifty-eighth wrong view is that nirvāṇa, total freedom from suffering, can be found through indulging in sensual pleasure. Of course, this shortsighted view overlooks the fact that sensual pleasures are unstable and impermanent. The fifty-first wrong view is that of the materialists who believe that the self is only material and is annihilated at death. This view overlooks the testimony of those like the Buddha who claim to have remembered past lives and have established that there is such a thing as rebirth, and this view also discounts those who have had brief glimpses of heavenly states in this life as evidence of future existences. In the Buddha's time, such a glimpse might come about as the result of yogic meditative practice, whereas in our day such glimpses might come from NDEs or Near-Death Experiences. To be fair, the materialists of our day also do not take such testimony as reliable evidence of any life past physical death. In any case, the Buddha viewed those who insisted that this life is the only one or that true happiness can be found through indulgence in sensual pleasures as being caught in the net of wrong views because they were making assumptions based on present experiences and clinging to those assumptions.

The "eel-wrigglers" or "endless equivocators" (see Maurice Walsh's comment on the Pali pun on p. 541 n. 58 of his translation *The Long Discourses of the Buddha*) all refuse to give definitive answers to philosophical and metaphysical questions. There are four kinds because there are four reasons for evasion: some because they do not wish to talk about what they don't know, some because they want to avoid attachment or aversion in regard to various opinions, some because they want to avoid debates, and some because they do not wish to reveal their ignorance. According to the Buddha, their attempt to avoid holding views is itself a kind of viewpoint and so they too are caught in the net of views.

Though the Buddha criticized the materialists and those who believed that life is eventually annihilated, he also criticized those who speculate on the eternity of life based on past life memories. They too are jumping to a conclusion based on limited experience. Even though they may recall hundreds of thousands of past lives or even innumerable lives over many periods of the cyclic expansion and decay of universes, this is not evidence of an eternal unchanging independent self. Though the *Supreme Net Discourse* does not go into it, in other discourses the Buddha explains that these many lives are not a single unchanging self but a continuum of flowing causes and conditions that only appears to have consistent unchanging qualities. If observed long enough it would be seen that even these qualities are not intrinsic but are caused and conditioned and the result of interdependent origination. It is a matter of scope. In the course of a week, a month, a year, or even a century a mountain might seem permanent, but in the scope of geological time even mountains arise and fall. So those who believe that life is eternal, independent, and unchanging based on past life memories are also caught in the net of views.

Of those who believe that some things are eternal, and some are not, the first view is described in terms of a fable explaining the arising of theism from within the framework of the Mt. Sumeru cosmology of ancient India. According to the Buddha's explanation, when this world system (i.e. our world with its various realms or sub-worlds for hell-dwellers, hungry ghosts, animals, fighting demons, humans, and deities) is in a period of contraction all the lower realms from the lowest hells all the way up to the Heaven of Radiant Sound (S. Ābhāsvara) will dissolve as their inhabitants are either all born into higher heavens or the truly incorrigible are reborn in the lower realms of other world systems. When the karma of beings is such that it is time for them to leave the higher heavens, the rest of the world begins to unfold once more. In the empty palace of the Great Brahmā Heaven the first being to be reborn there becomes the new Great Brahmā. This new god then becomes lonely and soon the other beings are reborn in the Great Brahmā Heaven as his companions. He believes himself to be their creator who willed them into being and they in turn believe that Brahmā is the great creator god. They have no memory of their past existences as other beings. Then, inevitably, some of those beings will fall from that heaven into lower realms and they forget all about their previous lives as part of the entourage of Brahmā in the Great Brahmā Heaven. Some ascetics in the human realm, through yogic discipline, later recover the memory of their past life serving Brahmā in the Great Brahmā Heaven. They conclude, based on those memories, that Brahmā is eternal and unchanging and that it is they who are therefore corruptible and changing or they would not have fallen away from that heaven and the presence of the creator god, Brahmā. These ascetics then teach others how to practice yoga and live in a meritorious way so that they can be reborn in the Great Brahmā Heaven and reunited with Brahmā for eternity. Of course, this view is also a false view based on a limited perspective and those who take it up are also caught in the net of views.

What these views all hold in common is that those holding them have taken up a particular speculative view about life based on some limited experience of conditioned existence. Those who don't look past the physical continuity of their present body take up materialistic views. Those who recall a few past lives might come to believe that they have a fixed identity or selfhood that reincarnates over many lifetimes. Others might recall larger spans of time in a heavenly existence and come to believe that such a heavenly existence is eternal whereas life in this mundane world is what is impermanent. In each case, the span of time becomes larger, but always there seems to be a more subtle level of impermanence that is not detected. In a hundred years all those alive today will be deceased, in millions of years even mountains crumble away, in billions of years even stars die. The Buddha is pointing out in this discourse that one cannot circumscribe a set period of time and draw a conclusion about conditioned phenomena. You can always widen the scope to reveal an even bigger picture.

Though the particularities of these sixty-two views and even the particulars of the Buddha's criticisms might strike us as odd, irrelevant, or unscientific, the main point the Buddha makes is one that I believe is still valid. If we wish to become free of the entanglement of speculative views, we need to stop trying to pin down the nature of the big picture based on transient experiences or finite points of view. Instead, we need to look directly at the causal nature of experience itself and how it arises and passes away based on causes and conditions. Looking ever more deeply into the causal and interdependent nature of conditioned phenomena is what brings about insight into the futility of selfish attachment. Without selfish attachment there can be an awakening to the unconditioned life of selfless compassion that is buddhahood. Of course, this too may sound like a view that one can make into an object of attachment or aversion, but the Buddha did not intend for it to be a conceptual doctrine. Rather, he was recommending that we let go of speculative views about conditioned phenomena and put his teachings into practice so that we can awaken to the unconditioned true nature of life for ourselves.

Sources

Gosho Translation Committee, editor-translator. *The Writings of Nichiren Daishonin*. Tokyo: Soka Gakkai, 1999.

Hori, Kyotsu, comp. *Writings of Nichiren Shonin: Doctrine Volume 2*. Tokyo: Nichiren Shu Overseas Propagation Promotion Association, 2002.

Murano, Senchu. *Kaimokusho or Liberation from Blindness*. Berkeley: Numata Center for Buddhist Translation and Research, 2000.

Walshe, Maurice, trans. *The Long Discourses of the Buddha: A Translation of the Digha Nikaya*. Boston: Wisdom Publications, 1995.

Chapter 3 - The Five Comparisons

Writings of Nichiren Shōnin: Doctrine 2, pp. 33-34, 44-45, 48, 77-78
Kaimoku-shō or Liberation from Blindness, pp. 11-12, 26-28, 32-34, 73-74
The Writings of Nichiren Daishonin I, pp. 222-223, 231-233, 235, 258-259

In Nichiren Buddhism it is understood that in the *Kaimoku-shō* Nichiren made five comparisons between various religious teachings in order to reveal the highest teaching. Nichiren himself does not ever use the term "five comparisons" and the fifth comparison is not as clear in *Kaimoku-shō* as it is in other writings. Nevertheless, *Kaimoku-shō* is regarded as the source of the five comparisons. I would now like to go over these five comparisons briefly in order to show how Nichiren uses similar reasoning to that used by the Buddha in the *Supreme Net Discourse* to make his case.

1. Buddhism is Superior to Non-Buddhism

The first comparison that comes up is between Buddhism and non-Buddhist teachings. Nichiren does in fact acknowledge the positive aspects of the religions and philosophies that predated Buddhism in both India and China, especially in regard to morality, ethics, and culture. In fact, like many of his East Asian contemporaries, Nichiren asserts that these were necessary precursors to Buddhism and were even a part of the Buddha's skillful teachings. The positive contributions of these teachings will be covered in more detail in the following sections.

The problem with the non-Buddhist teachings is that many of them, like Confucianism and some of the materialistic Indian philosophies, do not say anything about life after death, either regarding it as an unsolvable mystery or going so far as to assert that there is no life after death. Other Indian philosophies might teach that there is a process of rebirth but do not acknowledge the workings of causality over many lifetimes. Some believe that through either good deeds or the cultivation of meditation one can be reborn in a heavenly realm and then enjoy eternal life from that point on, not realizing that in the fullness of time even the gods exhaust their karmic merit and pass away.

Of all the non-Buddhist teachers Nichiren says, "Although they are called sages, they are as ignorant as infants in that they do not know causality." (Murano 2000) This is essentially the same critique the Buddha makes of the sixty-two false views in the *Supreme Net Discourse*. None of the sixty-two views takes into account the causal and interdependent nature of life. They tend to assert either a form of eternalism, wherein all or at least some beings enjoy an eternal unchanging existence, or they assert some form of annihilationism, wherein phenomena disappear without a trace, or they try to equivocate in some way.

The Buddha saw the views of eternalism and annihilationism as assumptions based on limited experience. The extreme of eternalism grasped at the idea of an eternal unchanging independent self that could at some point enjoy an eternal liberation from this world of change. The extreme of annihilationism despaired that there was any form of personal continuity and this became the rationale for nihilistic or hedonistic approaches to life. Neither eternalism nor annihilationism could provide a good basis for morality because if there were an eternal unchanging selfhood that could be found, then our moral actions for good or bad would not affect that unchanging entity, and if annihilation was to be our fate than nothing we do would matter anyway.

The Buddha pointed to the Middle Way between these extremes. If all life is caused and conditioned, then this means that there is no eternal unchanging self. At the same time, within the workings of universal causality there is the cycle of birth and death, and in that cycle the causes we make carry over from lifetime to lifetime. A fixed independent self may not be found, but a dynamic interdependent self is responsible for its actions, will reap the causes it sows, and can either further entangle itself in the sufferings of birth and death or untangle itself by making good causes and ultimately realizing the selfless nature of phenomena. Realizing the ultimately selfless nature of phenomena is to awaken to the unconditioned, or nirvāṇa, and thereby escape the cycle of birth and death.

This is why Nichiren declares that Buddhism is superior to non-Buddhism, because the Buddha "eliminated the cause of birth and death." (Ibid, p. 12) People need not fear annihilation of self, but neither do they need to cling to the false hope of an eternal heavenly existence that is not actually exempt from the continuing cycle of birth and death. The Buddha revealed the limitations of impermanent contingent phenomena so that people would let go of their attachments and aversions, become free of anxiety and wishful thinking, disentangle themselves from the cycle of birth and death, and awaken to nirvāṇa, the freedom of the unconditioned.

2. Mahāyāna is Superior to Hīnayāna

The next comparison is between Hīnayāna and Mahāyāna. "Hīnayāna" means "Small Vehicle" and is what Mahāyāna or "Great Vehicle" followers call those forms of Buddhism which teach that the highest possible goal of Buddhism is to become an arhat or "worthy one" by cutting off all the greed, hatred, and delusion that keep us entangled in the process of birth and death. An arhat is one who is forever free of the cycle of birth and death. Though Hīnayāna Buddhism admits that it might be possible to make vows to attain buddhahood, this is seen as an unrealistic goal. In fact, even becoming an arhat is really only possible for monastics. Householders have to settle for making merit by supporting the monastic Sangha, and thereby earning a rebirth in a heavenly realm or a future life as a monk or nun. Because the arhats only save themselves from the sufferings of birth and death through their own personal spiritual cultivation, this form of Buddhism was compared to a small raft by which only one person could cross over from one side of a river to another, thus it was a "Small Vehicle."

There are two kinds of practitioners who are regarded as Hīnayāna. There are the *śrāvakas* (lit. "voice-hearers") who listen to the Buddha's teachings and strive to become arhats. Then there are the *pratyekabuddhas* (lit. "privately awakened ones") who attain liberation from the cycle of birth and death through their own solitary contemplations. These two ways of practicing for one's own liberation are called the "two vehicles" and both are considered forms of Hīnayāna Buddhism.

Just as Buddhism is superior to non-Buddhism because it takes a greater perspective that goes beyond one lifetime or even many lifetimes to reveal the causal processes underlying even the births and deaths of the gods in the heavenly realms, Mahāyāna is superior to Hīnayāna because its perspective is vast enough to see that beyond the limited goal of nirvāṇa as an escape from the cycle of birth and death it is possible for people to raise their aspirations by taking the vows of a bodhisattva and thence embarking on the path to attain buddhahood, even if it takes an incalculably long time to do so. Another difference in perspective is that whereas the Hīnayāna only teaches that there are six worlds of rebirth (realms of hell-dwellers, hungry ghosts, animals, fighting demons, humans, and gods) and nothing more besides the

negation of rebirth in the six worlds known as nirvāṇa, Mahāyāna teaches that in fact there are many pure lands throughout the universe. The pure lands are realms where all the conditions are perfect for attaining buddhahood and each is presided over by its own buddha who is assisted by many bodhisattvas. With the help of the buddhas and bodhisattvas, sentient beings can be reborn in these pure lands in order to attain buddhahood. Nichiren says that the Mahāyāna sutras:

> ...were expounded for the purpose of criticizing
> adherents of the two vehicles who relied on the
> Hīnayāna sūtras. In these Mahāyāna sūtras, the Pure
> Lands of the Buddhas were established in the worlds of
> the ten quarters in order to encourage ordinary men
> and bodhisattvas to be born there. This troubled
> adherents of the two vehicles. (Ibid, p. 26)

So the perspective of the Mahāyāna is vast enough to show that even the attainment of buddhahood is an achievable goal given enough time to build up merit, serve innumerable buddhas and other bodhisattvas, and find the proper conditions to do so as in the pure lands. The Mahāyāna uses its vaster perspective to raise the aspirations of its adherents and to encourage them in their efforts.

3. True Mahāyāna of the *Lotus Sūtra* is Superior to Provisional Mahāyāna

Not all Mahāyāna sūtras are equally hopeful about the spiritual prospects of all beings, however. Some sūtras consider certain groups of people forever cut off from the possibility of attaining buddhahood. Women are sometimes considered incapable of attaining buddhahood. The *icchanitikas* or "incorrigible disbelievers" were beings said to be devoid of buddha-nature. They were supposedly so faithless and immoral that they would never be able to plant the good roots within their lives that would enable them to attain liberation from the cycle of birth and death, let alone buddhahood. Other Mahāyāna sūtras, however, did assert that buddha-nature was universal, so even women and *icchantikas* could theoretically attain buddhahood.

The arhats and the pratyekabuddhas were the hardest cases of all, even though they were considered to be virtuous and had already attained liberation from birth and death. That was the problem actually. Precisely because they had cut themselves off from the cycle of birth and death, they could no longer enter the world to help other beings and accumulate the wisdom and merit needed to attain buddhahood. They could not raise their aspirations because they had renounced any and all further intentional activity. Their liberation was in actuality a spiritual dead end. They had removed themselves from further consideration. The flaw of the other Mahāyāna sūtras besides the *Lotus Sūtra* is that they took the position that the people of the two vehicles who had left the cycle of birth and death could never attain buddhahood. Their spiritual journey was over, the processes of their lives complete and finished.

In the Lotus Sūtra, however, the Buddha reveals that the three vehicles he taught to the śrāvakas, pratyekabuddhas, and bodhisattvas are actually just partial aspects of the One Vehicle that leads all alike to buddhahood. The Buddha even makes a series of predictions that in future ages his major disciples and all the other members of the assembly will attain buddhahood. If it were not for the *Lotus Sūtra* then the major disciples who had become arhats would have no hope of attaining buddhahood. "But if the earlier sutras are more attractive [and more valuable], Śāriputra and other adherents of the two vehicles would have lost a chance to become Buddhas forever." (Ibid, p. 28) The other sūtras are considered provisional because they do not reveal this larger perspective that grants buddhahood even to śrāvakas and pratyekabuddhas and so they are not fully inclusive of all beings. The *Lotus Sūtra* alone should be considered the true Mahāyāna because it makes it clear that all beings can attain buddhahood without exception. This is the reason why the *Lotus Sūtra* is superior to the other Mahāyāna sutras.

4. The Original Gate is superior to the Trace Gate

Even within the *Lotus Sūtra* a comparison can be made between the first half of the sutra, which is called the Trace Gate (J. *Shakumon*) and the latter half, which is called the Original Gate (J. *Honmon*). Nichiren asserts that the Original

Gate provides a much larger and more radical perspective than even the Trace Gate.

The Trace Gate consists of the first fourteen chapters of the *Lotus Sūtra* in which the Buddha is still seen as the historical Śākyamuni Buddha who attained awakening two thousand five hundred years ago. It is called the Trace Gate because it covers the teaching of the One Vehicle by the historical Buddha as described above, and these teachings are the traces or imprints of the teaching of the Eternal Śākyamuni Buddha. The historical life of the Buddha and his teachings is like a print made in soft wax by a seal, or like traces left in the sand by a person walking on the beach. The Trace Gate is also referred to as the theoretical section of the *Lotus Sūtra* because it is in this part of the sūtra that the Buddha teaches that in theory all people are capable of attaining buddhahood.

The Original Gate consists of the latter fourteen chapters of the *Lotus Sūtra* in which the Buddha is the timeless ultimate truth and an ever-present reality leading all people to their own buddhahood. The Original Gate is also referred to as the essential section of the *Lotus Sūtra* because it is in this part of the sūtra that the Buddha reveals the transcendent nature of buddhahood and that it is an active and present part of our lives already, we only need the faith to realize it. From this point on, buddhahood is no longer a theory, but the essential truth informing all the other teachings.

The Original Gate, therefore, surpasses the more limited view of the Trace Gate that Śākyamuni Buddha attained awakening for the first time at the age of thirty (or thirty-five according to other sources) under the Bodhi Tree forty years before the time when he taught the *Lotus Sūtra*. From the perspective taken in the Original Gate, Śākyamuni Buddha's awakening occurred in a past time so remote that it is often just glossed as "eternal." Nichiren says,

> *"In the Original Gate of the Lotus Sūtra, it was revealed that the Buddha had attained perfect enlightenment in the remote past, making it untenable to assert that he had attained Buddhahood for the first time in this world." (Hori 2002)*

This is important because it means that even when the Buddha was demonstrating bodhisattva conduct in previous lives he was actually not trying to attain buddhahood but was demonstrating it in a progressively more complete way until he revealed the fullness of buddhahood as Śākyamuni Buddha in India 2,500 years ago. This means that buddhahood was always present and even after the passing away of the historical Buddha, Śākyamuni Buddha as the Eternal Buddha will remain present. The full meaning of this will be discussed later in terms of the Tiantai teaching of the "3,000 realms in a single thought-moment."

5. Buddhism of Sowing Superior to Harvest – Introspection over Doctrine

There is one final comparison that Nichiren makes in his teachings, though it is not set forth as clearly in *Kaimoku-shō* as it is in other writings. This is the comparison between the essential teaching of the *Lotus Sūtra* as a discourse given by Śākyamuni Buddha 2,500 years ago in India and the essential teaching of the *Lotus Sūtra* as spiritual contemplation for those in the present.

Nichiren identifies the spiritual contemplation of the essential teaching of the *Lotus Sūtra* with the Tiantai teaching of the "three thousand realms in a single thought-moment" that will be explained later. According to Nichiren, "The 'three thousand realms in a single thought-moment' doctrine is hidden between the lines of the sixteenth chapter on 'The Life Span of the Tathāgata' in the Original Gate of the *Lotus Sūtra*." (Ibid, p. 34 modified) Nichiren identifies the three thousand realms in a single thought-moment doctrine as the seed of buddhahood. "Based on the concept of the seed of buddhahood preached in the *Lotus Sūtra*, Bodhisattva Vasubandhu insisted on the 'supremacy of the seed' in his *Discourse on the Lotus Sūtra*. This later became the 'three thousand realms in a single thought-moment' doctrine of Grand Master Tiantai." (Ibid, p. 78 modified)

One of the things Nichiren criticizes the other teachings for is that their perspective is not grand enough to encompass the whole process of attaining buddhahood, beginning with the all-important step of sowing the seed of buddhahood.

> *The sutras of the True Word and Flower Garland schools*
> *do not mention even the names of the three steps of*

29

emanation: (1) to sow the seed of Buddhahood, (2) to grow the plant of Buddhahood, and (3) to develop Buddhahood into emancipation. Needless to say, those sutras do not explain these steps. (Murano 2000, p. 73 adapted).

Sākyamuni Buddha gave the Original Gate discourse to his disciples two thousand five hundred years ago in India at a time when their understanding was ripe and they could awaken to the fullest implications of what they were being told. The 'three thousand realms in a single thought-moment' is the Tiantai way of expressing the contemplative insight that is implied by the Original Gate of the *Lotus Sūtra*. Therefore, it is called the seed of buddhahood. In other writings, particularly *Treatise on Spiritual Contemplation and the Focus of Devotion* (*Kanjin Honzon-shō*), Nichiren identifies this seed with the *Odaimoku* (Sacred Title) of the five characters of the *Lotus Sūtra*: *myō*, *hō*, *ren*, *ge*, and *kyō*. Nichiren sees the present age as the time in which to sow this seed of buddhahood. Because of this seed, buddhahood is something that is not only found in the past or the future but is a reality that can be sown in our lives in the present moment.

The conclusion of the five comparisons is that *Lotus Sūtra* is the teaching that truly encompasses all time, from the remotest past, to the farthest future. In this perspective all beings are able to attain buddhahood in the fullness of time. More importantly, the perspective of the *Lotus Sūtra* provides assurance that buddhahood is a present actuality for all beings. Nichiren makes this point clear in *A Letter to the People of Seichōji Temple* (*Seichōji Daishū-chū*), a letter he wrote to Seichoji Temple in 1276:

> *The Lotus Sūtra preaches that Śākyamuni Buddha had attained buddhahood already 500 (million) dust particle kalpa in the past and that even those of the two vehicles such as Śāriputra, who are considered incapable of becoming buddhas, will inevitably attain buddhahood in the future... It is the Lotus Sūtra that explains the past and future with precision, and upholding this sutra is the way to attain buddhahood. (Hori 2008, p. 177 adapted; see also Gosho Translation Committee 1999, p. 652)*

Sources

Gosho Translation Committee, editor-translator. *The Writings of Nichiren Daishonin*. Tokyo: Soka Gakkai, 1999.

Hori, Kyotsu, comp. *Writings of Nichiren Shonin: Doctrine Volume 2*. Tokyo: Nichiren Shu Overseas Propagation Promotion Association, 2002.

_____. *Writings of Nichiren Shonin: Biography and Disciples Volume 5.* Tokyo: Nichiren Shu Overseas Propagation Promotion Association, 2008.

Murano, Senchu. *Kaimokusho or Liberation from Blindness*. Berkeley: Numata Center for Buddhist Translation and Research, 2000.

Chapter 4 - Chinese Learning: Confucianism

Writings of Nichiren Shōnin: Doctrine 2, pp. 30-32
Kaimoku-shō or Liberation from Blindness, pp. 7-10
The Writings of Nichiren Daishonin I, pp. 220-221

Confucianism is the first to be evaluated, though in fact it is not just Confucianism that Nichiren discusses. He actually refers to the tradition called *ju* by the Chinese. *Ju* is a word that means "scholar" and is usually a reference to Confucian scholars. *Ju* may, however, refer to the larger tradition of Chinese scholarship and learning. It is evident that in *Kaimoku-shō* Nichiren is using the term to encompass the teachings of the Taoists Laozi and Zhuangzi as well as Confucius.

In order to understand the tradition of Chinese learning as Nichiren understood it, we should begin with Confucius. It is no exaggeration to say that the worldview and values of China, Korea, Vietnam, and Japan were formed or at least clearly articulated by Confucius (551-479 BCE). Confucius is the Latinized name of Kong Fuzi. He was the son of an aristocrat who was born in the state of Lu during the declining years of the Zhou dynasty. His father died when he was only three, but his mother raised him with a great love of learning. He married at nineteen and soon had a son. As a young man he was employed in what would today be called middle management positions. He eventually attained the post of police commissioner. He later quit that post and traveled throughout China as an itinerant teacher. At that time China was little more than a patchwork of feudal kingdoms whose allegiance to the Zhou dynasty was nominal at best. The conflicting ambitions of the many feudal lords and scheming ministers led to frequent warfare and social upheaval. Confucius hoped to be given the chance to implement his ideas for a model government, but none of the rulers of the various states of China were interested in his reforms. He contented himself with studying the already ancient classics of poetry, history, and ritual and teaching his many disciples so that his vision of a harmonious society could be passed down and someday realized.

Confucius did not claim that he was teaching anything original. In fact, he insisted that he was trying to pass on the heritage of the idealized sage-rulers of the legendary golden age of China's past. These sage-rulers were the Three Sovereigns, Five Emperors, and Three Kings. The Three Sovereigns were the mythical prehistoric tribal rulers credited with the beginnings of civilization. They were: Fu Xi (c. 2852 BCE) who invented cooking, hunting, and the domestication of animals while his wife "discovered" marriage and family; Shennong (c. 2737 BCE) who is credited with the invention of the plow and agriculture, tea drinking, and herbal medicine; and Huangdi (c. 2607 BCE), the Yellow Emperor who invented pottery, houses, carts, and boats while his wife discovered how to gather and weave silk. A member of the court of the Yellow Emperor is even credited with the creation of the Chinese ideograms. The Yellow Emperor also organized the first army and used it to conquer the fertile land around the Yellow River. The legendary Five Emperors succeeded The Yellow Emperor: Shaohao, Zhuanxu, Di Ku, Yao (r. 2356-2347 BCE), and Shun (r. 2244-2205 BCE). Yao and Shun were particularly revered as ideal rulers who instituted many of the rites that Confucius believed were at the heart of civilized life. The Three Kings were the founders of the first three dynasties to rule China. The first was the Xia dynasty (c. 2205-1751 BCE) founded by Yu, the engineer who was the first to succeed in bringing the flooding of the Yellow River under control. The second was the Shang or Yin dynasty (c. 1751-1112 BCE) founded by a feudal prince named Cheng Tang who rose up against the corrupt and evil Emperor Jie. History repeated itself when King Wu Wang founded the Zhou dynasty (c. 1111-249 BCE) by overthrowing the corrupt Emperor Zhou Xin. King Wu was a model of filial piety, and so he attributed the founding of the new dynasty to his father King Wen. When King Wu died, his brother, the Duke of Zhou, ruled as regent until King Wu's son came of age. The Duke of Zhou proved to be an excellent ruler; nevertheless, he quietly stepped aside when it was time to do so. Confucius regarded the Duke of Zhou as a paragon of virtue and strove to emulate him. Confucius believed that these sage-rulers had left behind a blueprint for a model civilization in texts that Confucius designated as the "six classics." The six classics are:

1. *The Book of Changes* (*Yi Jing*): a book of divination with various layers of commentary centered on a series of sixty-four hexagrams composed of broken and unbroken lines viewed in a state of dynamic transition from one to another. These hexagrams and their components represent the various cosmological forces the Chinese believed made the world the way it is, most notably the receptive and nourishing element known as yin and the dynamic and creative element known as yang that are represented by the broken and unbroken lines respectively. This ancient method of divination utilized the

casting of yarrow stalks in order to discover which hexagram and its transitions applied to any given situation. Each hexagram and its transitions would reveal the underlying dynamics of a situation and provide appropriate advice. The ancient sage-ruler Fu Xi is credited with creating the eight trigrams that compose the hexagrams of the *Book of Changes*. King Wen received the credit for combining the trigrams into hexagrams and writing the short judgments associated with each one. The Duke of Zhou is credited with writing the text associated with the individual changing lines for each hexagram. In fact, the *Book of Changes* is sometimes called the *Changes of Zhou* (*Zhou-yi*) for this reason. The ten "wings" of commentary that compose the rest of the *Book of Changes* are attributed to Confucius himself though scholars have found that the various strata of commentary originate from different periods of time.

2. *The Book of Poetry*, also known as the *Book of Odes or Book of Songs*, is a collection of three hundred and five poems dating from the beginning of the Zhou dynasty to around 600 BCE. These poems described the ideal conditions of life in a harmonious society. Confucius summarized the teachings of these poems with the saying, "Swerving not from the right path." (Lau 1979, p. 63)

3. *The Book of History* or *Book of Documents* is a historical record of the Xia, Shang, and Zhou dynasties. It contains conversations between various kings and their ministers and is therefore held to be a repository of guidance on good government, morality, ethics, and religion.

4. *The Book of Rites* is a collection of writings that according to tradition describe the ancient rituals and ceremonies adhered to by the founders of the Zhou dynasty as collected and interpreted by Confucius and his disciples. These writings deal with matters of propriety in all matters, from public sacrifices to Heaven and the ancestors to the proper way of conducting oneself in all affairs of daily life.

5. *The Spring and Autumn Annals* are the court records of the state of Lu from 722-481 BCE. These records provided Confucius with a standard of virtue and good government by which to measure one's conduct. Confucius is even reported to have said, "Those who understand me will do so through the *Spring and Autumn Annals*; those who condemn me will also do so because of the *Spring and Autumn Annals*." (Lau 2003, p. 141)

6. Unfortunately, the *Book of Music* was lost during the persecution of Confucianism and the burning of Confucian literature by the short lived but brutal Qin dynasty (221-206 BCE). Confucius valued music that could exalt the mind and heart and convey an appreciation for harmonious living. He considered the teaching of the rites of propriety and music the twin pillars of culture and civilization. Confucius once said, "Be stimulated by the Odes, take your stand on the rites and be perfected by music." (Lau 1979, p. 93)

With the six classics as the basis of his curriculum, Confucius taught his disciples the Tao or Way that human beings should follow in order to become genuinely human and bring peace and harmony to their families, their society, and ultimately the world. Confucius teachings were composed of four main subjects: culture, right conduct, doing one's best for others, and trustworthiness. He told his disciples that his many teachings were strung on one main thread: benevolence. Confucius' concept of benevolence encompassed the values of filial piety, generosity, treating others as one would want to be treated oneself, doing one's best for others, and many other virtues. Many of the teachings and sayings of Confucius were recorded for posterity in a collection called *The Analects of Confucius*.

After the death of Confucius, the tradition continued to develop, and several important works appeared. One was the *Book of Filial Piety* by Zengzi (505-435 BCE), who was a disciple of Confucius. Zengzi is also credited as the transmitter of the *Great Learning*, an important work that was incorporated in the *Book of Rites*. Zengzi was also the teacher of Zisi (483-402 BCE), the grandson of Confucius. Zengzi is credited with compiling the *Doctrine of the Mean* that was also incorporated into the *Book of Rites*. One of Zengzi's disciples would become the teacher of Mencius, the second great Confucian sage. *The Great Learning* and the *Doctrine of the Mean* became very important as Confucianism developed. Both teach that self-cultivation is the key to a harmonious society. *The Great Learning* emphasizes the investigation of things and the extension of knowledge as the basis of personal cultivation that in turn leads to peace in the family, then the state, and ultimately world peace. The *Doctrine of the Mean* in particular teaches the cultivation of personal integrity and harmony in one's conduct as the middle way beyond unbalanced extremes that leads to a mystical integration with Heaven and Earth, in other words "all that is."

Mencius (372-289 BCE) was the second great sage of Confucianism. Mencius is the Latinized name of Mengzi. He lived during the Warring States period (480-222 BCE) of Chinese history when the Zhou dynasty was nothing more than a name and the princes of all the various states vied with each other over who would get to become the founder of a new dynasty. Despite the chaos and bloodshed, Mencius believed that through self-cultivation in accordance with the Confucian teachings people could manifest and develop their innate goodness and thereby bring about a peaceful and unified empire united by moral virtue rather than force of arms. His teachings were collected into a work called simply the *Book of Mencius*. Two passages from the *Book of Mencius* should be noted as they relate two very important themes in the Confucian tradition. The first passage relates the "four beginnings" which are the innate seeds of good all people possess:

> *"As far as what is genuinely in him is concerned, a man is capable of becoming good," said Mencius. "This is what I meant by good. As for his becoming bad, that is not the fault of his native endowment. The heart of compassion is possessed by all men alike; likewise the heart of shame, the heart of respect, and the heart of [knowing the difference between] right and wrong. The heart of compassion pertains to benevolence, the heart of shame to righteousness, the heart of respect to propriety, and heart of [discerning] right and wrong to knowledge. Benevolence, righteousness, propriety, and knowledge do not give me a luster from the outside, they are in me originally. Only this has never dawned on me. That is why it is said, 'Seek and you will get it; let go and you will lose it.' (Lau 2003, p. 247 modified)*

In the next passage, Mencius relates the ideal pattern of human relationships in terms of the five relations set forth by the Sage Emperor Shun:

> *According to the way of man, if they are well fed, warmly clothed, and comfortably lodged but without education, they will become almost like animals. The Sage (emperor Shun) worried about it and he appointed*

Hsieh to be minister of education and teach people human relations, that between father and son, there should be affection; between ruler and minister, there should be righteousness; between husband and wife, there should be attention to their separate functions; between old and young, there should be proper order; and between friends there should be faithfulness. (Chan 1963, pp. 69-70)

Unfortunately, despite the efforts of Confucius and Mencius and their followers, force of arms triumphed over moral virtue for a time and the ruthless King Zheng of Qin became Shi Huang Di, the first emperor of the ruthlessly totalitarian but mercifully brief Qin dynasty. Incidentally, the English name "China" was derived from the name of this dynasty, the first to truly unify China under imperial rule. The ruling philosophy of this dynasty was Legalism. Legalism taught that humanity was innately evil and that the only way to unify and control the empire was through the impartial administration of strict and harsh laws. The Qin dynasty tolerated no ideological rivals to Legalism and banned all other schools of thought. They particularly despised Confucianism and did their best to eradicate it by burning the Confucian classics and either executing or banishing the Confucianists themselves. In the end, the successors of Shi Huang Di fell victim to their own arrogance and corruption and the dynasty soon gave way to both peasant revolutions and the rebellion of the former feudal lords.

Confucianism revived during the Western or Former Han dynasty (206 BCE–8 CE). Under the Emperor Wu (r. 140-87 BCE) Confucianism became the state orthodoxy. A meritocracy under the emperor was established on the basis of a civil service examination that tested applicants on their knowledge of the five classics (the six discussed above minus the *Book of Music* lost during the Qin dynasty). The leading light of Confucianism at this time was Dong Zhongshu (179-104 BCE). Dong Zhongshu, consolidated and systematized Confucianism so that it could serve as the ideological underpinning of a united empire. When Nichiren speaks about Confucianism in his writings, it is most often the Confucianism of Dong Zhongshu that he is referring to.

Dong Zhongshu's approach was rather eclectic and he fused certain aspects of Legalist authoritarianism and the cosmology of the Naturalists (a.k.a. the Yin

Yang school) of early Chinese metaphysics with the humanism of Confucius and Mencius in order to create a more comprehensive ideology for the Han rulers. In particular, he believed that the forces of yin and yang govern the processes of nature and human life. The interplay between yin and yang bring about the succession of the five primary elements or agents: metal, wood, water, fire, and earth. Dong Zhongshu believed that a correspondence could be found between these five agents that compose and govern the world and other categories of five such as the five relations (as taught by Mencius in the passage cited above) and what he termed the five constant virtues: benevolence (C. *ren*), righteousness (C. *yi*), propriety (C. *li*), knowledge (C. *zhi*), and trustworthiness (C. *xin*). Mencius had taught that the first four of these were inborn in all people, at least in nascent form. Trustworthiness was a quality often emphasized by Confucius in relation to doing one's best for others and other aspects of benevolent conduct. The five constant virtues taught by Dong Zhongshu thereafter become a useful summary of Confucian values.

At this point, let us turn from the history of Confucianism to an examination of Confucian thought and values as Nichiren understood them, starting with the five constant virtues. The first and most important is benevolence. Benevolence was the one thread that Confucius insisted held together all his teachings. Benevolence means much more than just a general feeling of well-wishing towards others. Confucius held it out as an almost impossible to attain ideal of admirable and inspiring conduct. He taught that it was rooted in the love and respect that it is hoped one naturally feels towards one's parents and elder siblings and in the kindness and tolerance one ideally feels towards one's younger siblings and other family members. It also includes one's sense of dignity and self-respect. Extended beyond the family, it becomes generosity and kindness towards those one is responsible for, and an attitude of respect and deference towards one's elders and social superiors such as the ruler. The benevolent person always tries to put themselves in the others place so they can act as they would have others act towards them – the so-called golden rule. On this basis they always try to do their best for others at all times. The benevolent person is not an obedient automaton or a simpleton, however. They balance their kind-heartedness with learning and discernment and have the courage to remonstrate with their superiors if need be. Under no circumstances will they give in to wrongdoing nor do they value profit over virtue. The benevolent person is someone who has overcome selfishness and through personal example inspires and instructs others. Confucius believed that all people had the capacity to be benevolent but that few lived up to, or even tried to live up to, their potential. Mencius taught that the natural feelings of compassion people feel in the face of suffering, esp. of children or innocents, is the nascent form of benevolence.

The other four virtues support benevolence and complete it. The second is righteousness, the virtue of knowing how to act appropriately in all circumstances. Righteousness is having the self-restraint to resist temptation and the fortitude to do one's duty. Standing up for what is right also involves courage. Above all righteousness is about preserving one's integrity. Mencius taught that people's natural feeling of shame in regard to wrongdoing is the nascent form of righteousness.

Propriety refers to "ritual propriety." It is the virtue of knowing and acting in accord with the rites handed down from ancient times. These rites involved court manners, the proper way to perform ceremonies like sacrifices to Heaven or the ancestors, funerals, weddings, and other occasions, and matters of etiquette in various social situations. The rites governed social relationships and the mutual duties, responsibilities, and expectations between people. They set the standard but also set limits so that people could act in a way that was mutually beneficial and not exploitative. Confucius saw the rites as integral to culture along with music. They directed benevolence and righteousness in specific and concrete ways and refined one's character. Confucius was not inflexible about them, however. He recognized that the rites had changed over time from the Xia to the Shang to the Zhou dynasty. He preferred frugality and sincere expressions of feeling in regard to them and approved of changes along those lines. However, he was also concerned when standards were allowed to slide or when those not entitled to perform certain rites or to initiate changes in the rites presumed to do so. This was a sign of decadence and social disintegration. Above all, it would seem that for Confucius, ritual propriety was rooted in natural human feelings and mutually beneficial relationships and the goal was harmony both within oneself and between people and ultimately between Heaven and Earth and humankind. Mencius taught that the natural wish to be courteous and modest is the nascent form of propriety.

Knowledge is primarily the virtue of discerning right from wrong. In a sense it precedes the others because without knowledge one will have no sense of ethics, or social skills, or even just the plain common sense the other virtues require for guidance. Knowledge, however, does not rate as highly as the others because it is sometimes spoken of as though it involved only what is good or bad for oneself. In other words, this is the knowledge of enlightened self-interest and not cosmic awareness or esoteric knowledge. Mencius taught that people's instinctual ability to distinguish right from wrong is the nascent form of knowledge.

The final virtue is trustworthiness, sometimes called "faithfulness." Confucius praised this virtue many times and spoke of it as the mainstay along with doing one's best for others. Trustworthiness means not only being honest and sincere, but also being able to live up to one's word. The trustworthy person is the person who can be relied upon in all things. On one occasion Confucius stated that this virtue was close to righteousness. On another he stated that it was the consummation of other virtues.

A student of the Tao or Way, according to Confucianism, aims at becoming a person of nobility (C. *junzi*) who can guide others by exemplifying these five constant virtues. A noble person is a person of refinement and integrity. They are impeccable in their actions, fair and just in their dealing with others, and above all full of loving-kindness. Confucius confessed that in his own estimation he had not accomplished much in the way of the person of nobility. Beyond even the noble person is the sage whose virtue benefits all people and whose conduct can serve as the model for future generations. The sage's virtue and wisdom is so great that they are at one with Heaven and Earth. Incidentally, the title "shōnin" that is given to Nichiren is the Japanese pronunciation of the Chinese word for "sage."

Only the virtuous are fit to receive the Mandate of Heaven according to the political vision of Confucianism. The term "Heaven" is not any easy one to define. Sometimes it can mean the collective will of the ancestors and sage-rulers of the past who have ascended to the status of gods, becoming a kind of celestial bureaucracy under the Supreme Emperor of Heaven. At other times, Heaven can indicate the laws of nature or the supreme but impersonal metaphysical principle that gives rise to all life and all life-sustaining patterns and relationships. In any case, the Mandate of Heaven refers to a divine commission given to a nobleman worthy enough to serve as the Son of Heaven. The Son of Heaven rules China (the entire civilized world as far as the Chinese were concerned) as the emperor and in doing so serves to unite Heaven and Earth by fulfilling the will of Heaven in this world through benevolent leadership and the performance of the proper rituals and sacrifices. However, if the rulers do not fulfill their obligations and maintain their virtue, the Mandate of Heaven can be rescinded. In such a case, the corrupt dynasty will fall to anarchy and revolution and a new dynasty will receive the Mandate of Heaven in its place, as happened when the villainous emperors Jie and Zhou were overthrown by Cheng Tang and King Wu respectively.

Sources

Ames, Roger T. & Rosemont, Henry Jr., translators. *The Analects of Confucius: A Philosophical Translation*. New York: Ballantine Books, 1998.

Chan, Wing-tsit, trans. *A Source Book in Chinese Philosophy*. Princeton: Princeton University Press, 1963.

de Bar, Wm. Theodore and Bloom, Irene. *Sources of Chinese Tradition Volume One: From Earliest Times to 1600*. New York: Columbia University Press, 1999.

Gosho Translation Committee, editor-translator. *The Writings of Nichiren Daishonin*. Tokyo: Soka Gakkai, 1999.

Hori, Kyotsu, comp. *Writings of Nichiren Shonin: Doctrine Volume 2*. Tokyo: Nichiren Shu Overseas Propagation Promotion Association, 2002.

Lau, D.C., translator. *Confucius: The Analects*. New York: Penguin Books, 1979.

_____. *Mencius: A Bilingual Edition*. Hong Kong: The Chinese University Press, 2003.

Legge, James, translator. *The Four Books*. Taipei: Culture Books Co., 1992.

Liu, Shu-hsien. *Understanding Confucian Philosophy: Classical and Sung-Ming*. Westport: Praeger Publishing, 1998.

Lynn, Richard John trans. *The Classic of Changes: A New Translation of the I Ching as Interpreted by Wang Bi*. New York: Columbia University Press, 1994.

Murano, Senchu. *Kaimokusho or Liberation from Blindness*. Berkeley: Numata Center for Buddhist Translation and Research, 2000.

Plaks, Andrew, trans. *Ta Hsueh and Chung Yung*. New York: Penguin Books, 2003.

Simpkins, Alexander C. and Simpkins, Annellen. *Simple Confucianism: A Guide to Living Virtuously*. Boston: Tuttle Publishing, 2000.

Yao, Xinzhong. *An Introduction to Confucianism*. New York: Cambridge University Press, 2000.

Yasuo, Yamamoto. *The Structure of Oriental Values and Education*.

http://www.crvp.org/book/Series03/III-11/chapter_xxiii.htm

Yu-lan, Fung. *A Short History of Chinese Philosophy*. New York: The Free Press, 1966.

Chapter 5 - Chinese Learning: Taoism

Writings of Nichiren Shōnin: Doctrine 2, pp. 30-32
Kaimoku-shō or Liberation from Blindness, pp. 7-10
The Writings of Nichiren Daishonin I, pp. 220-221

When Confucius passed away in 479 BCE, China had entered the time that would afterwards be known as Warring States period (480 – 222 BCE) during which the strongest of the remaining feudal kingdoms battled to see who would be able to establish a new dynasty that would unite China. As we saw in the last chapter, this period ended with the rise and fall of the Qin dynasty and the ascendancy of the Han dynasty. During the Warring States period there were many itinerant philosophers and would-be statesmen who went from kingdom to kingdom searching for royal patronage. These wandering philosophers gave rise to what has been referred to as "one hundred schools of thought" and each offered a method or way (C. *dao*, anglicized as "tao") whereby their patrons could become "a sage within and a king without." By following the way of these itinerant philosopher-statesmen the ruler would be able to achieve both inner peace and practical success in realizing their worldly ambitions. Of these so-called "hundred schools," six are now remembered: the Confucianists, Legalists, Naturalists (a.k.a. the Yin Yang school), Mohists, Terminologists (a.k.a. the Logicians), and Taoists.

Confucianism, Legalism, and the Naturalists have already been discussed. The Mohists were the followers of Mozi (fl. 479-438) who taught a doctrine of universal love, utilitarian ethics, austere living, and non-aggression (though the Mohists were known to assist in the defense of feudal states that were under attack). Mozi also gave a much more explicitly theistic interpretation to the Will of Heaven than his rivals. Mozi's puritanical lifestyle and high ideals were never embraced by the mainstream of Chinese thought, and so Mohism as an active school of thought disappeared after the 3rd century BCE, eclipsed by the Han dynasty synthesis of Confucian pragmatism, Legalist authoritarianism, and Naturalist cosmology.

The Terminologists were a group of Chinese thinkers who were particularly interested in how to make sure that words match the realities that they refer to. This got them into issues involving semantics, logic, and even metaphysics. They would become famous, or perhaps infamous, for their debating skills. They were also notorious for their paradoxes and confounding rhetoric. The Terminologists subscribed to the ideal of universal love that the Mohists did, and the followers of Mozi also developed their own system of logic to defend their teachings. One of the Terminologists, Hui Shi (380-305 BCE?), was a debating partner and good friend of the Taoist sage Zhuangzi, who will be introduced below. Like the Mohists, the Terminologists also disappeared as an active school after the 3rd century BCE, as Chinese thinkers opted for the less abstract approach of Confucianism and the more mystical and intuitive approach of Taoism.

Taoism achieved much greater success and is still very much alive today as a philosophy, a religion, and a system for promoting health and longevity through various regimens of diet and exercise. Taoism is such a broad, multifaceted, and amorphous movement that it is hard to decide where even to begin. In fact, the major text of philosophical Taoism, the *Tao Te Ching*, warns us that, "He who knows does not speak. He who speaks does not know." (Chan, p. 166)

Nevertheless, if one is to talk about Taoism at all it is probably best to start with the *Tao Te Ching*, whose title can be translated as the *Classic of the Way and Its Virtue*. The *Tao Te Ching* is also called the *Laozi*, after the name of its legendary author. Legend holds that Laozi (the name means "Old Master") was a native of the southern state of Chu in present Henan province and that he was a librarian in the imperial archives and also a soothsayer. Laozi may have been the heir of a long legacy of southern Chinese shamanistic traditions. There is a story that in 518 BCE Confucius called upon him to inquire about the rites. Several versions of this story can be found in the *Zhuangzi*. Laozi later retired from the world and so journeyed past the western frontier, riding off into the sunset as it were. Before he left, the gatekeeper requested that he write a book for him. Laozi responded to the request by writing the *Tao Te Ching*. This story, while charming, has no credibility among textual scholars and the *Tao Te Ching* is believed to be the work of many hands that was probably compiled into its present form of eighty-one short chapters of prose and verse during the fourth century BCE. The *Tao Te Ching* is now one of the most beloved and popular works of wisdom literature in the world and has been translated countless times in many languages.

Though many believe that the *Tao Te Ching* teaches a philosophy of peaceful withdrawal from the world of affairs, it is actually intended to be a book of advice for rulers, so that they may preside over a peaceful and happy kingdom. The *Tao Te Ching* points to a life of non-attachment, contentment, simplicity, humility, receptivity, openness, tranquility, and a laissez-faire approach to governing. On the other hand, it also teaches that the ruler should keep his people free of cleverness and ambition as well, for if the people are simple-minded and content with their lot then they will not create trouble for each other, the rulers, or other countries. The ruler should learn the art of "acting without acting" (Ch. *wu-wei*, lit. not-acting) by refraining from forcing things or acting in an intrusive way. By not interfering with the natural flow of life things will proceed smoothly and efficiently according to their natural rhythms. The ruler should also "think without thinking" (Ch. *wu-xin*, lit. no-mind) by meeting life in a direct and unmediated way instead of relying on secondhand knowledge or theories about how things are or should be. The best way to live is to return to what is natural and authentic. The cultivation of the Confucian virtues is seen as a pretense that arises when authentic natural virtue has been lost. In the *Tao Te Ching*, the Tao is no longer simply a way or a method for people to follow for worldly success. The Tao of the *Tao Te Ching* is the formless, empty, and nameless One that is the source of all that is. The Te of the *Tao Te Ching* is the cosmic virtue of returning to the Tao and uniting with its uncontrived natural benevolence.

The second great philosophical work of Taoism is the *Zhuangzi*, likewise, named after its legendary author. Zhuangzi (369 – 286 BCE) was a native of the town of Meng, in the present-day Anhui Province. For a time, he was an official at a place called the "Lacquer Garden" and then became a hermit. The text called the *Zhuangzi* is a compilation of humorous and paradoxical anecdotes and essays in thirty-three chapters, of which perhaps only the first seven chapters (the so called "Inner Chapters") are thought to actually be the work of Zhuangzi himself.

Unlike the *Tao Te Ching*, the Zhuangzi is not primarily a book of advice for a feudal ruler (though such can be found in it as well). It is the *Zhuangzi* that more often than not praises the life of total withdrawal from society. Commenting on *Laozi* and *Zhuangzi*, Neo-Confucian scholar Zhu Xi (1130-1200) said, "Lao Tzu still wanted to do something, but Chuang Tzu did not want to do anything at all. He even said that he knew what to do but just did not want to do it." (Ibid, p. 178) Indeed, unlike Confucius and his followers who were always seeking some position whereby they could apply their methods, Zhuangzi refused such a position when it was offered to him:

> *Chuang Tzu was one day fishing in the Pu River when the King of Chu dispatched two senior officials to visit him with a message. The message said, 'I would like to trouble you to administer my lands.'*
>
> *Chuang Tzu kept a firm grip on his fishing rod and said, 'I hear that in Chu there is a sacred tortoise which died three thousand years ago. The King keeps this in his ancestral temple, wrapped and enclosed. Tell me, would this tortoise have wanted to die and leave his shell to be venerated? Or would he rather have lived and continued to crawl about in the mud?'*
>
> *The two senior officials said, 'It would rather have lived and continued to crawl about in the mud.'*
>
> *Chuang Tzu said, 'Shove off, then! I will continue to crawl about in the mud!' (Palmer, pp. 146-147)*

The *Zhuangzi*, particularly in the seven Inner Chapters, provides us with a view of life wherein all things are moving and changing. Any perspective or stance one might take can only be limited and biased. True happiness can be found if one lets go of all preferences and disputes to be open and accepting of life's changes and transformations. A particularly famous illustration of Zhuangzi's attitude and wit can be found in his recounting of a dream wherein he became a butterfly.

> *Once upon a time, I, Chuang Tzu, dreamt that I was a butterfly, flitting around and enjoying myself. I had no idea I was Chuang Tzu. Then suddenly I woke up and was Chuang Tzu again. But I could not tell, had I been Chuang Tzu dreaming I was a butterfly, or a butterfly dreaming I was now Chuang Tzu? However, there must be some sort of difference between Chuang Tzu and a*

butterfly! We call this the transformation of things.
(Ibid, p. 20)

Zhuangzi's view of the sage was far more transcendental than the one held by the Confucianists. The Confucian sage would be one who could govern humanity with benevolence and the strength of his personal example. The Taoist sage according to Zhuangzi is beyond politics or human society but is one with all of nature and to ordinary people appears to be quite useless.

> *How can the wise one sit beside the sun and moon and embrace the universe? Because he brings all things together in harmony, he rejects difference and confusion and ignores status and power. While ordinary people rush busily around, the sage seems stupid and ignorant, but to him all life is one and united. All life is simply what it is and all appear to him to be doing what they should. (Ibid, pp. 18-19)*

The teachings of Laozi were very popular during the early part of the Western Han dynasty. Laozi's teachings were then linked with traditions attributed to the Huang Di, the Yellow Emperor, and so this movement was named Huang-Lao. It concerned itself with the joys of the simple life, governing best by governing least, and the alchemical quest for an elixir of immortality. The Huang-Lao movement fell out of disfavor during the ascendancy of Confucianism, but it did not disappear, and starting from around the second century BCE the movement came to be known as Taoism.

During the Eastern or Latter Han dynasty (25-220 CE), Taoism developed into a religion with its own ceremonies, liturgies, divinely revealed scriptures, and even a hereditary high priesthood. In 150 CE the Han emperor dedicated a shrine to Laozi, divinized as the Great Lord on High. Around this time, a work called the *Classic of Great Peace* appeared which purported to have been revealed by Heaven to show humanity how to avoid calamity and bring about a utopia. In 142 a man named Zhang Daoling claimed that Laozi as the Great Lord on High had appeared to him and given him a new teaching. This was the beginning of the movement that would come to be known as the Celestial Masters or the Central Orthodox School of Taoism. Zhang Daoling's descendants would thereafter be the high priests of this form of religious Taoism, though it would in time come to be overshadowed by other mystical and religious movements.

Nichiren was not concerned with religious Taoism or Taoist alchemical traditions, and so it is to philosophical Taoism that we must turn back our attention. The collapse of the Eastern Han dynasty brought about a great disillusionment among the literati with the ideals and institutions of that dynasty. They turned away from Confucianism and began to engage in what they called "pure conversation" (C. *qingtan*). They indulged in wine, women, poetry, song, and other escapist pursuits. An example of their wit and flouting of social conventions can be seen in the following story:

> *In the Shih-shuo we have a story about Liu Ling (c. 221 – c. 300), one of the Seven Worthies of the Bamboo Grove (seven "famous scholars" who gathered for frequent convivial conversations in a certain bamboo grove). This story tells us that Liu evoked criticism through his habit of remaining completely naked when in his room. To his critics he rejoined: "I take the whole universe as my house, and my own room as my clothing. Why, then, do you enter here into my trousers?" (Ch. 23). Thus Liu Ling, though he sought for pleasure, had a feeling of what lies beyond the world, i.e., the universe. (Yu-lan, p. 235)*

These disaffected literati also engaged in metaphysical speculation. In particular they liked to talk about what they called the Mysterious or Dark Learning (C. *xuanxueh*), in reference to the first chapter of the *Tao Te Ching*:

> *The Tao (Way) that can be told is not the eternal Tao;*
>
> *The name that can be named is not the eternal name.*
>
> *The Nameless is the origin of Heaven and Earth;*
>
> *The Named is the mother of all things.*

Therefore, let there always be non-being so we may see their subtlety,

And let there always be being so we may see their outcome.

The two are the same,

But after they are produced, they have different names.

They both may be called deep and profound (hsüan).

Deeper and more profound,

The door of all subtleties!

(Chan, p. 139)

Those involved in the Dark Learning movement during the time of the Wei (220-265) and Chin (265-420) dynasties have come to be known as the Neo-Taoists, though in fact the many of them were syncretists who were trying to find a way to harmonize Confucian values with what they saw as the bigger picture of the Taoist insight into the natural order and therefore humankind's true nature. They viewed Confucius as the perfect sage who exemplified his interior realization in the nobility of his daily conduct, but they rejected the scholastic formalism that Dong Zhongshu's version of Confucianism had become mired in. The Neo-Taoists turned instead to the study of three texts: The *Book of Changes* that they associated with the investigation of being, the *Tao Te Ching* that emphasized non-being, and the *Chuangzi* that upheld both being and non-being.

The *Book of Changes* (also known as the *Changes of Zhou*) has been discussed already in connection with Confucianism. It is a work that deals with the changes and transformations of beings and their circumstances and therefore it is particularly associated with the various modes of being. As it says in chapter eleven of the "Appended Remarks Part 1" (one of the ten wings that compose it):

The Changes deals with the way things start up and
how matters reach completion and represents the Tao

that envelops the entire world. If one puts it like this,
nothing more can be said about it. Therefore the sages
use it to penetrate the aspirations of all the people in
the world, to settle the great affairs of the world, and to
resolve all doubtful matters in the world. (Lynn, pp. 63-
64 adapted)

A little further in that chapter it is written how the Great Ultimate (Ch. *taiji*) generates the forces of yin and yang and how these in turn generate the four forms of major and minor yin and yang, which in turn generate the eight trigrams that in turn determine all fortune and misfortune. The Great Ultimate is a name for all potential existence and its transformations. It is the undifferentiated state of primal chaos before the manifestations of yin and yang. Today we are familiar with the Great Ultimate as the symbol of a circle divided into a teardrop shaped yang or bright half with a yin circle in the middle and a teardrop shaped yin or dark half with a yang circle in the middle.

The Neo-Taoist thinker, Wang Bi (226-249) wrote one of the first philosophical commentaries on the *Book of Changes*. He also wrote an introductory essay called the *General Remarks on the Changes of the Zhou*. In this latter work Wang Bi wrote, "No thing ever behaves haphazardly but necessarily follows its own principle. To unite things, there is a fundamental regulator; to integrate them, there is a primordial generator. Therefore, things are complex but not chaotic, multitudinous but not confused." (Ibid, p. 25) Wang Bi believed that by using the *Book of Changes* one could discern the ruling principle at work in every moment of time and the changes that characterize each moment. With that knowledge one will know how to act (or not act as the case may be) in every situation. To Wang Bi, existence is about change and change occurs in accordance with natural laws or principles, and these in turn derive from the

One. But what is the One? Wang Bi found his answer to that question in the *Tao Te Ching*.

The *Tao Te Ching* points not to a primal chaos as the ultimate origin of existence or being, but to non-being (C. *wuji*). Speaking of the origin of things, the *Tao Te Ching* says, "Reversion is the action of Tao. Weakness is the function of Tao. All things in the world come from being. And being comes from non-being." (Chan, p. 160) The source of all beings cannot itself be a being; the source of all things must be no-thing. The ultimate source of being must be formless and empty of anything that would define or limit it, because otherwise it would belong to the world of beings and their transformations. Therefore, the ultimate source is non-being. If the Great Ultimate is the stirring of primal chaos that gives rise to all things, then non-being is the stillness that precedes the stirrings.

Wang Bi taught that the original substance (C. *ben-ti*) of all things is none other than original non-being (C. *ben-wu*). In his *Commentary on the Laozi* he wrote the following about the opening chapter of the *Tao Te Ching*:

> *All being originated from non-being. The time before*
> *physical forms and names appeared was the beginning*
> *of the myriad things. After forms and names appear,*
> *Tao (the Way) develops them, nourishes them, and*
> *places them in peace and order; that is, it becomes their*
> *Mother. This means that Tao produces and completes*
> *things with the formless and nameless. Thus they are*
> *produced and completed but do not know why. Indeed*
> *it is the mystery of mysteries. (Ibid, p. 321)*

Zhuangzi, in his typically whimsical way, takes a more dialectical approach to being and non-being, thereby putting them on par with one another. He has no wish to take sides in giving precedence to being or non-being and does not at all seem to be afraid of an infinite regress as one transforms into another depending on changing circumstances and one's point of view. In fact, Zhuangzi seems to reduce all such speculations about being and non-being to mere word play that one should not get too caught up in. It is better to learn acceptance of whatever arises or does not arise. In Zhuangzi's words:

There is a beginning. There is no beginning of that beginning. There is no beginning of that no beginning of beginning. There is something. There is nothing. There is something before the beginning of something and nothing, and something before that. Suddenly there is something and nothing. But between something and nothing, I still don't really know which is something and which is nothing. Now, I've just said something, but I don't really know whether I've said anything or not. (Feng 1974, p. 35)

Guo Xiang (d. 312) was the Neo-Taoist who is responsible for editing the redaction of the *Zhuangzi* that is known today. Incorporating an earlier commentary by Xian Xiu (fl. 250), Guo Xiang wrote what became the most famous and definitive commentary on the Zhuangzi. Guo Xiang emphasized Nature (C. *ziran*) and spontaneity rather than non-being. In his view all things are produced spontaneously by Nature without any self-conscious deliberation. This is the impersonal working of Heaven or Nature. In his *Commentary on the Zhuangzi* he wrote the following:

The music of Nature is not an entity existing outside of things. The different apertures, the pipes and flutes and the like, in combination with all living beings, together constitute Nature. Since non-being is non-being, it cannot produce being. Before being itself is produced, it cannot produce other beings. Then by whom are things produced? They spontaneously reproduce themselves; that is all. By this is not meant that there is an "I" to produce. The "I" is self-existent. Because it is so by itself, we call it natural. Everything is what it is by nature, not through taking any action. Therefore [Chuang-tzu] speaks in terms of Nature. The term Nature (literally "Heaven") is used to explain that all things are what they are spontaneously, and not to mean the blue sky. But someone says that the music of Nature makes all things serve or obey it. Now, Nature cannot even possess itself. How can it possess things? Nature is the general name for all things. Nature does not set its mind

for or against anything. Who is the master to make
things obey? Therefore all things exist by themselves
and come from nature. This is the Way of Heaven.
(Chan, pp. 328-329)

In all of these discussions of the origination of various forces like yin and yang and the various transformations that they take on (whether the five elements or the eight trigrams) there is an assumption that behind and beneath these changes is a substratum called *qi*. *Qi* is has been variously translated as "vital force", "matter-energy", "breath" and other things depending on the context and the understanding of the person using the term. It is not really matter or spirit for it is the life force that precedes such distinctions. *Qi* is pure potential and therefore the content of the Great Ultimate, but *qi* is also the basic energy or building block of all that exists. A living being or existent thing only persists for as long as its *qi* maintains that particular configuration. As the existence of things comes to an end the *qi* that composed them returns to a state of undifferentiated potential. In this view, life and death is a matter of the coalescence and dissipation of *qi*. Han Kangbo (d. 385), who was a latter-day disciple of Wang Bi, explains this in his comments on the *Book of Changes*: "When material force consolidates into essence, it meshes together, and with this coalescence a person is formed. When such coalescence reaches its end, disintegration occurs, and with the dissipation of one's spirit, change occurs." (Lynn, p. 52)

The teachings, exercises, and meditative disciplines of Taoism aim at stabilizing and preserving the *qi* that has been allotted to one for the sake of a long and happy life. The Taoist sage avoids stirring up trouble by leaving the world alone and working on his own self-cultivation. He (or she) influences the world in a positive way by not intervening in the natural cycles of life but simply by being one with all things and allowing them to find their own harmony and natural simplicity. Unlike the Confucian image of the sage who actively sets the world in order, the Taoist sage leaves things alone so that one and all may find their own natural order that is the Tao or Way appropriate to them.

Taoism began as a counterpoint to Confucianism, which constantly exhorted its followers to cultivate benevolence and righteousness and to refine themselves by conformity to the rites and the study of literature and the arts.

Laozi saw this as pretense and even hypocrisy. Confucianism was not the true way or Tao, but rather a symptom of the loss of the Tao. "When the great Tao declined, the doctrines of humanity and righteousness arose. When knowledge and wisdom appeared, there emerged great hypocrisy." (Chan, p. 158) Laozi recommended a return to the unadorned authentic nature of the Tao. "Display a genuineness like raw silk and embrace a simplicity like unworked wood, lessen your concern for yourself and reduce your desires." (Ames 2003, p. 104)

The criticisms and lampoons of Confucianism found in the Zhuangzi could be even harsher. In one passage the Confucianists are even blamed for people's loss of the virtue of the Tao.

> In the time of perfect Virtue, people live side by side
> with the birds and beasts, sharing the world in common
> with all life. No one knows of distinctions such as nobles
> and the peasantry! Totally without wisdom but with
> virtue which does not disappear; totally without desire
> they are known as truly simple. If people are truly
> simple, they can follow their true nature. Then the
> perfect sage comes, going on about benevolence,
> straining for self-righteousness, and suddenly everyone
> begins to have doubts. They start to fuss over the music,
> cutting and trimming the rituals, and thus the whole
> world is disturbed. (Palmer, p. 73)

In other passages, the Confucian teachings and precepts are put into the mouths of robbers and tyrants and used as justification for their crimes and tyranny.

> A member of Robber Zhi's gang asked him, 'Is there a
> Tao for the thief?' Zhi replied, 'What profession is there
> without its Tao? The robber works out what is worth
> stealing: this shows he is a sage; his courage is shown
> by being the first to break in; his righteousness is shown
> by being last to leave; his understanding is shown by
> deciding whether the raid is possible; his benevolence is

shown by his dividing the spoils equally. Without these five attributes, no one in the world could become such a great thief.' (Ibid, p. 77)

Granted that many of the critiques found in the Zhuangzi are similarly facetious, the point was made that Confucianism's virtues were more than capable of being twisted and used by a clever and ambitious elite to justify themselves and keep those with less power under control. Several stories in the Zhuangzi portray an ambitious and meddlesome Confucius who is overawed when he meets a true sage like Laozi, or even someone like Robber Zhi who sees right through the pretenses of Confucian teachings and precepts. There are other stories, probably by later more syncretistic writers, that present Confucius in a more favorable light, but even those passages subsume Confucius into the larger context and concerns of Taoism.

The Neo-Taoists like Wang Bi and Guo Xiang took a different view of the relative merits of Confucius and Laozi. As mentioned before, they both saw Confucius as the true sage, whereas Laozi and Zhuangzi were lacking in comparison. There is even an account of a fellow minister who asked Wang Bi for an explanation as to why Confucius, if he was the greater sage, did not speak about the profundities of non-being whereas Laozi did speak of it.

At the time when P'ei Hui was serving as Director of the Ministry of Personnel, Wang Pi, who then had not yet been capped [i.e. had not yet reached the age of maturity at twenty], went to pay him a visit. As soon as Pei saw him, he knew that this was an extraordinary person, so he asked him, "Nonbeing is, in truth, what the myriad things depend on for existence, yet the Sage [Confucius] was unwilling to talk about it, while Master Lao expounded upon it endlessly. Why is that?" Wang Pi replied, "The Sage embodied nonbeing, so he also knew that it could not be explained in words. Thus he did not talk about it. Master Lao, by contrast, operated on the level of being. This is why he constantly discussed nonbeing; he had to, for what he said about it always fell short. (Lynn, p. 11 adapted)

This view, though at odds with the mainstream of the Taoist tradition before and after them is strangely in keeping with Laozi's own view that "He who knows does not speak. He who speaks does not know." Wang Bi and Guo Xiang saw Confucius as the one who truly knew the Tao and so did not discuss it but simply embodied it through his teachings on mundane matters and his exemplary conduct in daily life. Wang Bi and Guo Xiang believed that the true sage was one who could function with equal facility in both the mundane and the transcendental worlds. Let us end, then, with Guo Xiang's words on this from his commentary on Zhuangzi:

> *Therefore principle has its ultimate, and the transcendental and the mundane world are in silent harmony with each other. There has never been a person who roamed over the transcendental world to the utmost who was not silently in harmony with the mundane world, nor has there ever been anyone who was silently in harmony with the mundane world and yet did not roam over the transcendental world. Therefore the sage always roams in the transcendental world. By having no deliberate mind of his own, he is in accord with all things. (Chan, p. 333)*

Sources

Ames, Roger T. & Rosemont, Henry Jr., translators. *Dao De Jing "Making This Life Significant": A Philosophical Translation*. New York: Ballantine Books, 2003.

Chan, Wing-tsit, trans. *A Source Book in Chinese Philosophy*. Princeton: Princeton University Press, 1963.

de Bar, Wm. Theodore and Bloom, Irene. *Sources of Chinese Tradition Volume One: From Earliest Times to 1600*. New York: Columbia University Press, 1999.

Feng, Gia-fu, and English, Jane trans. *Chuang Tsu: Inner Chapters*. New York: Vintage Books, 1974.

Feng, Gia-fu, and English, Jane trans. *Lao Tsu: Tao Te Ching*. New York: Vintage Books, 1972.

Gosho Translation Committee, editor-translator. *The Writings of Nichiren Daishonin*. Tokyo: Soka Gakkai, 1999.

Gregory, Peter N., trans. *Inquiry Into the Origin of Humanity*. Honolulu: Kuroda Institute, 1995.

Hori, Kyotsu, comp. *Writings of Nichiren Shonin: Doctrine Volume 2*. Tokyo: Nichiren Shu Overseas Propagation Promotion Association, 2002.

Kohn, Livia. *Early Chinese Mysticism: Philosophy and Soteriology in the Taoist Tradition*. Princeton: Princeton University Press, 1992.

Lau, D.C., translator. *Lao Tzu: Tao Te Ching*. New York: Penguin Books, 1963.

Liu, Shu-hsien. *Understanding Confucian Philosophy: Classical and Sung-Ming*. Westport: Praeger Publishing, 1998.

Lynn, Richard John trans. *The Classic of Changes: A New Translation of the I Ching as Interpreted by Wang Bi*. New York: Columbia University Press, 1994.

Murano, Senchu. *Kaimokusho or Liberation from Blindness*. Berkeley: Numata Center for Buddhist Translation and Research, 2000.

Palmer, Martin, trans. *The Book of Chuang Tzu*. New York: Penguin Books, 2006.

Robinet, Isabelle auth. Brooks, Phyllis trans. *Taoism: Growth of a Religion*. Stanford: Stanford University Press, 1997.

Wong, Eva. *The Shambhala Guide to Taoism*. Boston: Shambhala Publications Inc., 1997.

Yao, Xinzhong. *An Introduction to Confucianism*. New York: Cambridge University Press, 2000.

Yu-lan, Fung. *A Short History of Chinese Philosophy*. New York: The Free Press, 1966.

Chapter 6 – The Chinese Reception of Buddhism

Writings of Nichiren Shōnin: Doctrine 2, pp. 30-32
Kaimoku-shō or Liberation from Blindness, pp. 7-10
The Writings of Nichiren Daishonin I, pp. 220-221

The Chinese Emperor Ming (28-75 CE), the second emperor of the Later Han dynasty (25-220 CE), supposedly dreamed of a golden man floating over his garden. His counselors told him that in the western region (India) a great sage had been born many hundreds of years ago called the Buddha. The emperor sent eighteen envoys to India to bring back the Buddha's teachings and in response two monks returned with Buddhist sūtras and images on the back of a white horse in the year 67 CE. As a commemoration of this the emperor established the White Horse Temple. This legend is a romanticized version of the introduction of Buddhism to China in the first century. Buddhist merchants and maybe even monks may have unofficially been traveling into China along the Silk Road long before then. There may have even been Buddhist enclaves among foreigners in China already at the time this story supposedly took place, though there would be no significant numbers of Chinese Buddhist lay devotees or ordained monks until the fourth century.

In the following passage from his book Buddhism in Chinese History, Arthur F. Wright describes the early reception of Buddhism in China during the first three centuries and surveys the linguistic and cultural obstacles it faced:

> In these early years of its slow penetration, Buddhism
> did not influence the major social and intellectual
> movements we have described. There is no evidence
> that the great thinkers of neo-Taoism knew of it, and
> the religious Taoism which spread among the
> disaffected masses was wholly of Chinese origin. Early
> Chinese princes and emperors who gave Buddhism
> limited patronage were persuaded for a time that this
> Buddha might be a divinity of sufficient power to be
> worth propitiating, and he is often called Huang-lao

fou-t'u – a name which suggests that his worshippers saw him as part of the growing pantheon of religious Taoism. The range of the early imperfect translations of Buddhist writings indicates that few Chinese who became interested in the foreign religion were attracted by its novel formulas for the attainment of supernatural powers, immortality, or salvation and not by its ideas. This early Buddhism was generally regarded as a sect of religious Taoism. And, indeed, as Maspero suggested, Taoist communities may have served to spread certain Buddhist symbols and cults, thus playing a role somewhat analogous to that of the Jewish communities which helped spread early Christianity in the Roman world.

Keeping in mind these rather unpropitious beginnings, we might pause to consider the cultural gulf which had to be bridged before this Indian religion could be made intelligible to the Chinese. No languages are more different than those of China and India. Chinese is uninflected, logographic, and (in its written form) largely monosyllabic; Indian languages are highly inflected, alphabetic, polysyllabic. Chinese has no systematized grammar; Indian languages, particularly Sanskrit, have a formal and highly elaborated grammatical system. When we turn to literary modes, we find that the Chinese preference is for terseness, for metaphors from familiar nature, for the concrete image, whereas Indian literature tends to be discursive, hyperbolic in its metaphors, and full of abstractions. The imaginative range expressed in Chinese literature – even in the Taoist classics – is far more limited, more earthbound, than in the colorful writings of the Indian tradition.

In their attitudes toward the individual the two traditions were poles apart at the beginnings of the invasion of Buddhism. The Chinese had shown little disposition to analyze the personality into its components, while India had a highly developed science of psychological analysis. In concepts of time and space there were also striking differences. The Chinese tended to think of both as finite and to reckon time in life-spans, generations, or political eras; the Indians, on the other hand, conceived of time and space as infinite and tended to think of cosmic eons rather than of units of terrestrial life.

The two traditions diverged most critically in their social and political values. Familism and particularistic ethics continued to be influential among the Chinese even in an age of cataclysmic change, while Mahayana Buddhism taught a universal ethic and a doctrine of salvation outside the family. Whereas Chinese thinkers had long concentrated their efforts on formulas for the good society, Indian and Buddhist thought had laid particular stress upon the pursuit of other-worldly goals.

It was in the third century – when the certainty of the Chinese about their ideas and values was progressively undermined – that these cultural gulfs began to be bridged. It was in that period that there began in earnest the long process of adapting Buddhism to Chinese culture, preparing it for a wider and fuller acceptance among Chinese of all classes. (Wright, pp. 32-34)

As Arthur Wright points out, during the Later Han dynasty Buddhism was seen as just another form of Taoism, a kind of foreign variation. The buddhas and arhats who lived apart from the secular world and cultivated various supernatural powers through the practice of meditation seemed very much like Taoist hermits and immortals. Buddhist fasts and vegetarianism, devotional services, and contemplative practices focusing on mindfulness of the breath all seemed very similar to Taoist practices. It would be centuries before there were reliable translations of Buddhist sūtras, vinaya, abhidharma, or commentarial literature from India and so the Han Chinese did not have a very clear idea of what Buddhism was all about. Consequently, they saw the Buddha as another supernatural being like the divinized Laozi and Huang Di and so enshrined the Buddha with them. At first this was helpful, it allowed Buddhism to seem less foreign and more familiar, and therefore more welcome. The problem was that the Taoists began to claim that Buddhism was simply a derivative of Taoism. The story even circulated that Laozi, after leaving China for the west to convert the barbarians there, had become the tutor of Prince Siddhartha. This story became the basis of the apocryphal *Conversion of the Barbarians Sūtra* (*Hua Hu Jing*) said to have been composed in the fourth century by Wang Fu (265-316). The *Hua Hu Jing* recounts the teachings of Laozi to an Indian prince who is supposed to be Prince Siddhārtha before he became known as Śākyamuni Buddha.

Further blurring the distinction between Buddhism and Taoism was the method of translation known as "matching concepts" (C. *geyi*). Buddhist teachers and translators tried to explain Buddhist concepts in terms that would be familiar to their Chinese audience. They drew upon words and concepts from the Chinese classics, but especially Taoist works, for instance, the Buddha Dharma became the Tao, while nirvāṇa was equated with "acting without acting" (C. *wu-wei*). Buddhist emptiness and Taoist non-being were also equated, even though emptiness in Buddhism refers to the lack of a fixed, independent, substantial self within the process of dependent origination and not to a primordial field or basis out of which things emerge and to which they return. Buddhism teaches that all phenomena are empty as they are because all phenomena are temporary conglomerations of causes and conditions empty of a fixed selfhood, not that emptiness or non-being is some kind of ineffable metaphysical essence underlying manifest reality. To be fair, not all Taoists or Neo-Taoists thought of non-being this way, but many Taoists and early Chinese Buddhists (and even many later East Asian Buddhists) thought in these terms. Though it may have been necessary in the early phase of the introduction of Buddhism to China, by the fifth century it became clear that the method of matching concepts was distorting and not clarifying the Buddhist teachings. With the translation efforts of Kumārajīva (344-413) the method of matching concepts was finally discarded, and Buddhism was no longer dependent on Taoism but could present itself on its own terms and in its own terms.

The Confucian elite of the Han dynasty, on the other hand, did not look upon Buddhism favorably. They viewed it as a foreign superstition whose teachings about rebirth and karma were outlandish. They could see no reason to bow down before what they saw as a foreign god. In particular they criticized the Buddha for abandoning his family to become a vagabond and a beggar. They were skeptical about Buddhist claims regarding the afterlife and the process of rebirth. There were no such teachings in China. They were especially scandalized by Buddhist monasticism. The teaching that one should leave home and abandon one's filial duties in order to pursue the ephemeral goal of "awakening" struck them as appalling. Buddhists in China from the beginning have had to defend the validity of the Dharma and show that it was not trying to undermine Confucian values but rather supported them even as it claimed to transcend them.

One of the ways this was done was though the claims of apocryphal sūtras written in China, like the *Practicing the Pure Dharma Sūtra*, that claimed the Buddha himself had commissioned three bodhisattvas with the task of appearing in China as the three sages Confucius (551-479 BCE), his favored disciple Yan Hui (c. 521-481 BCE), and Laozi (6th century BCE?) the legendary founder of Taoism. According to the sūtra, the Buddha did so to ensure that secular virtues and civilized arts would be taught to the Chinese so they would be receptive to the Dharma.

The *Trapusa and Bhallika Sūtra*, another apocryphal Chinese sūtra composed in the year 460 by a monk named Tan-jing, equated the five major precepts of Buddhism that enable one to be reborn as a human being with the five constant virtues of Han Confucianism. This became a popular theme taken up by later East Asian Buddhist writers. In the ninth century work *Inquiry Into the Origin of Humanity* by Zongmi (780-841) the equation of the five precepts and five constant virtues is put forth in the following formula: "Not killing is benevolence, not stealing is righteousness, not committing adultery is propriety, not lying is trustworthiness, and, by neither drinking wine nor eating meat, the spirit is purified and one increases in wisdom." (Gregory, p. 117) Nichiren also assumed this equivalence and alluded to it in works such as The *Cause of Misfortunes* (*Sainan Kōki Yurai*), considered a trial essay for *Risshō Ankoku-ron*:

> *Prior to Buddhism being introduced in China sage rulers*
> *such as the Yellow Emperor governed their kingdoms by*
> *means of the five virtues. After the introduction of*
> *Buddhism we can see these five virtues are the same as*

the five precepts of Buddhism prohibiting killing,
stealing, adultery, lying, and drinking liquor. Ancient
Chinese sages such as Lao-tzu and Confucius are the
three sages whom the Buddha dispatched to China in
order to propagate a Buddhism adapted to suit the land
in the distant future. Therefore, the loss of kingdoms by
such rulers as King Chieh of Hsia, King Chou Hsin of Yin,
and King Yu of Chou through violating the five virtues
equals violating the five precepts.

Also, to be fortunate in being born a human being and
becoming a king is due to the merit of having observed
the five precepts and the ten virtuous acts. Although
non-Buddhist scriptures are superficial in teaching, not
preaching the cause-and-effect relationship between
merits in the past and rewards in the future, those who
observed the five precepts and ten virtuous acts became
kings. Accordingly, when people transgress the five
virtues, heavenly calamities and terrestrial disasters will
occur in succession. (Hori 2003, p. 82)

As far as Nichiren and other East Asian Buddhists like Zongmi, or the Tiantai patriarchs Zhiyi and Zhanran were concerned, the reality behind the Confucian teaching of the Mandate of Heaven was not the collective will of the ancestors or the inscrutable workings of nature, but the unfolding of the law of cause and effect. Cause and effect operate according to the nature of one's deeds for better or worse. In Buddhism wholesome and unwholesome causes have been taught in terms of the five major precepts or the ten courses of wholesome conduct: not killing, not stealing, not committing adultery, not lying, not engaging in malicious speech, not engaging in harsh speech, not engaging in idle chatter (or gossip), not giving in to covetousness, not giving in to ill will, and not holding wrong views. From the Buddhist perspective, the five constant virtues and the Mandate of Heaven taught by Confucianism is just another way of presenting the five precepts or ten courses of wholesome conduct but without the explanation of the subtle workings of karma. Confucian teachings and values therefore are still upheld, but now they are subsumed within the skillful methods used by the Buddha and the bodhisattvas to prepare sentient beings for the Wonderful Dharma. Nichiren in the *Kaimoku-shō*, even attributes an awareness of Confucianism as a skillful means to introduce Buddhism to Confucius himself. Nichiren says of him, "He regarded Confucianism as a preliminary to Buddhism. In order to have people understand more easily the meaning of the [three] Buddhist disciplines – precepts, meditation, and wisdom – Confucius taught them rituals (*li, rei*), music (*yūeh, gaku*), and so on." (Murano 2000, p. 9)

The Confucianists, and Taoists as well, did not accept that the founders of their traditions were simply incognito bodhisattvas sent to prepare the way for Buddhism. As mentioned, the Taoists had even claimed that Laozi had been the Buddha's teacher. It was also argued that the birth of the Buddha had been an inauspicious sign that signaled a series of short-lived dynasties in China.

> *After Buddhism has been introduced and established in China, Chinese critics often charged that the religion tended to shorten the duration of the ruling houses supporting it. As evidence of this, they pointed to the short-lived dynasties of Later Ch'in, Later Chao, Sung, and Ch'i, which lasted only 33, 24, 59, and 23 years respectively. To counteract these criticisms, the Buddhists forged texts purporting to show that the religion was introduced into China during the early years of the Chou Dynasty (ca. 1100-256 B.C.). The motive for assigning the date of introduction to the early Chou Dynasty is very clear, for the Chou lasted over eight hundred years and provided just the answer needed to refute the anti-Buddhist critics. As fitting accompaniments to the birth and death of such a famous sage as the Buddha, many anomalies and unnatural events, such as earthquakes, violent winds, and a rainbow with twelve color bands which did not vanish even at night, were listed in the forged texts and were said to have been observed by the Chou ruler. (Wright, p. 29)*

One such forged work claiming that the Buddha's birth auspiciously heralded the foundation of the Zhou dynasty was the *Record of Wonders in the Book of Zhou*. It appeared sometime before the early 6th century but is no longer extant. It was much quoted in other works as a source of information about the life of the Buddha. According to this work the Buddha was born on the eighth day of the fourth month of 1029 BCE and died on the fifteenth day of the second month of 949 BCE. The Confucians saw the early years of the Zhou dynasty as a golden age, and so making the Buddha's life coincide with it was a way of underscoring the auspiciousness of his appearance and teachings. In addition, this was long before the time of Laozi, and so it refuted the claim that Laozi could have been the Buddha's teacher. One negative consequence of setting the Buddha's life during the early Zhou dynasty was that because the Buddha predicted that the Latter Age of the Dharma would begin two thousand years after his passing the Buddhists of East Asia came to believe that the Latter Age began in 1052 CE.

If Taoists claimed that Buddhism was nothing more than a foreign derivative of their own teachings, and Confucians sharply rejected Buddhist monasticism and metaphysical claims, how was it that Buddhism became accepted into China at all? What did Buddhism offer that China's own indigenous traditions did not? One thing that Confucianism and Taoism did not offer was any teaching about life after death. Confucius was quite blunt in his refusal to involve himself in metaphysical speculations or anything other than practical humanistic concerns, as the following passages from the *Analects* make clear:

> *5.13 Tzu-kung said, 'One can get to hear about the Master's accomplishments, but one cannot get to hear his views on human nature and the Way of Heaven.'*
>
> *6.22 Fan Ch'ih asked about wisdom. The Master said, 'To work for the things the common people have a right to and to keep one's distance from the gods and spirits while showing them reverence can be called wisdom.'*
>
> *7.21 The topics the Master did not speak of were prodigies, force, disorder, and gods.*
>
> *11.12 Chi-lu asked how the spirits of the dead and the gods should be served. The Master said, 'You are not able even to serve man. How can you serve the spirits?'*
>
> *'May I ask about death?'*

'You do not understand even life. How can you understand death?'

(Lau 1979, pp. 78, 84, 88, 107)

When Confucius' most talented disciple Yen Yuan (also known as Yen Hui, or in Pinyin transliterated as Yan Yuan or Yan Hui) passed away, Confucius himself lamented that death had cut short such a life of promise. There is no hint that there can be any further development or unfolding of the causes one makes in life beyond the grave.

> *9.21 The Master said of Yen Yuan, 'I watched him making progress, but I did not see him realize his capacity to the full. What a pity!'*
>
> *9.22 The Master said, 'There are, are there not, young plants that fail to produce blossoms, and blossoms that fail to produce fruit?'*
>
> *(Ibid, p. 99)*

Taoism, or at least philosophical Taoism, did address the issue of birth and death, but it viewed life and death as two parts of a mysterious process of transformation and counseled acceptance rather than trying to provide any clear-cut answers about what will happen after one dies. The following three passages from the *Zhuangzi* are illustrative of this. Note that the last passage is in the form of a dialogue between Confucius and Yan Hui, as were many passages in the *Zhuangzi*.

> *The true man of old did not hold on to life, nor did he fear death. He arrived without expectation and left without resistance. He went calmly, he came calmly and that was that. He did not set out to forget his origin, nor was he interested in what would become of him. He loved to receive anything but also forgot what he had received and gave it away. He did not give precedence to the heart but to the Tao, nor did he prefer the way of*

humanity to those of Heaven. This is what is known as a true man. (Palmer, pp. 47-48)

Death and birth are fixed. They are as certain as the dawn that comes after the night, established by the decree of Heaven. This is beyond the control of humanity, this is just how things are. (Ibid, p. 49)

Yen Hui asked Confucius, 'When Meng Sun Tsai's mother died, he cried without tears, there was no distress in his heart. When he mourned there was no sorrow. Although he was deficient on these three points, nevertheless he is renowned throughout the state of Lu for his excellence as a mourner. Is it possible to obtain such a reputation, even when there is nothing to substantiate it? I find this very surprising.'

'Master Meng Sun Tsai did what was right,' said Confucius. 'He was far beyond mundane understanding. He could have restricted his actions even more but that was not really feasible. Nevertheless, he did cut out a great deal. Meng Sun Tsai does not know how he came to be born, nor how he will die. He just knows enough not to want one or the other. He doesn't know why he should continue, he just follows what happens without understanding! As we are all in a process of change, how can we know what unknown thing we will be changed into? As what we are changing into has not yet happened, how can we understand what change is? Perhaps you and I are in a dream from which we are yet to awake! In Meng Sun Tsai's case the body changes but this does not affect his heart. His body, housing his soul, may be affected, but his emotions are not harmed. Meng Sun Tsai alone has awoken. People cry, so he cries. He considers everything as his own being. How could he know that others call something their own particular self? You dream that you are a bird and rise into the Heavens. You dream that you are a fish and swim down deep into the lake. We cannot tell now if the speaker is awake or asleep. Contentment produces a

smile; a genuine smile cannot be forced. Don't struggle,
go with the flow and you will find yourself at one with
the vastness of the void of Heaven.' (Ibid, p. 56)

Those attracted to Buddhism were not content to leave the question of what lies beyond death (or before birth) unanswered. They were deeply dissatisfied by Confucian agnosticism and Taoist fatalism regarding why we are born, where (if anywhere) we go when we die, why there is so much injustice in the world, and whether our moral and spiritual strivings mean anything in the face of death's inevitability. The humanism of the indigenous Chinese traditions was very realistic and practical, but it tended to leave an existential void that Buddhism seemed better able to respond to with its teachings of rebirth and the process of sowing and reaping the effects of one's causes over many lifetimes. Though imperfectly understood, at least at first, Buddhism gave people a sense of hope, responsibility, and meaning by teaching that life did not end at death and that the course of our lives is not random or the product of some arbitrary fate (whether endowed by Heaven or the Tao) but is determined by our own actions in sowing the seeds of good or ill that will come to fruition in present or future lifetimes.

Nichiren, like many other Buddhist teachers in East Asia before and after him, praises the humanistic virtues and civilized arts that the Confucians and Taoists taught, but in the end he too finds that their teachings are limited to only the present lifetime and that they do not address the debts owed from previous lives nor do they teach anything pertaining to the lives to come.

They may be called saints as far as their teachings for
our present lives are concerned, but they cannot be
called saints when we see that they know nothing about
our previous or future lives. They are not different from
ordinary men who cannot look at their backs or blind
men who cannot see even their fronts… But they are not
true saints because they do not know the past and
future. They cannot save the future lives of their
parents, lords, and teachers. Therefore, we can say that
they do not know the favors given to them by their seniors.
(Murano 2000, pp. 8-9)

Reflecting back on the previous themes of gratitude and the sixty-two false views, the Chinese tradition of *ju* or Confucian scholarship as well as the Taoist or Neo-Taoist tradition is as limited as the view of the materialists that this life is the only one. Because of this limited scope those who do not go beyond such teachings are limited in the help they can offer those to whom they owe debts of gratitude. These teachings do not provide any kind of hope of a better life after the present one inevitably comes to an end. They do teach a virtuous way of life, but with no guarantee that such virtue will bring any reward or recognition, and only uncertainty regarding the life to come. By teaching about the law of causality and the process of rebirth, Buddhism looks beyond just a single lifetime and thereby provides a deeper and more comprehensive basis for refraining from evil, doing good, and striving for liberation from suffering both for oneself and others, especially those to whom one owes a debt of gratitude.

Sources

Chan, Wing-tsit, trans. *A Source Book in Chinese Philosophy*. Princeton: Princeton University Press, 1963.

Ch'en, Kenneth. *Buddhism in China: A Historical Survey*. Princeton: Princeton University Press, 1964.

de Bar, Wm. Theodore and Bloom, Irene. *Sources of Chinese Tradition Volume One: From Earliest Times to 1600*. New York: Columbia University Press, 1999.

Gosho Translation Committee, editor-translator. *The Writings of Nichiren Daishonin*. Tokyo: Soka Gakkai, 1999.

_____. *The Writings of Nichiren Daishonin Volume II*. Tokyo: Soka Gakkai, 2006.

Gregory, Peter N., trans. *Inquiry Into the Origin of Humanity*. Honolulu: Kuroda Institute, 1995.

Hori, Kyotsu, comp. *Writings of Nichiren Shonin: Doctrine Volume 2*. Tokyo: Nichiren Shu Overseas Propagation Promotion Association, 2002.

_____. *Writings of Nichiren Shonin: Doctrine Volume 1*. Tokyo: Nichiren Shu Overseas Propagation Promotion Association, 2003.

Kohn, Livia. Early *Chinese Mysticism: Philosophy and Soteriology in the Taoist Tradition*. Princeton: Princeton University Press, 1992.

Lau, D.C., translator. *Confucius: The Analects*. New York: Penguin Books, 1979.

Murano, Senchu. *Kaimokusho or Liberation from Blindness*. Berkeley: Numata Center for Buddhist Translation and Research, 2000.

Palmer, Martin, trans. *The Book of Chuang Tzu*. New York: Penguin Books, 2006.

Robinet, Isabelle auth. Brooks, Phyllis trans. *Taoism: Growth of a Religion*. Stanford: Stanford University Press, 1997.

Wong, Eva. *The Shambhala Guide to Taoism*. Boston: Shambhala Publications Inc., 1997.

Wright, Arthur F. *Buddhism in Chinese History*. Stanford: Stanford University Press, 1959.

Yu-lan, Fung. *A Short History of Chinese Philosophy*. New York: The Free Press, 1966.

Chapter 7 – Indian Religion

Writings of Nichiren Shōnin: Doctrine 2, pp. 32-33
Kaimoku-shō or Liberation from Blindness, pp. 10-12
The Writings of Nichiren Daishonin I, pp. 221-223

The religions and philosophies of India rate higher than the Chinese traditions in Nichiren's evaluation because some of them did teach the law of cause and effect, rebirth in the six paths of transmigration, and the need to strive for rebirth in the heavens through the cultivation of morality and meditative disciplines. Nichiren does not actually use the word "Brahmanism" to refer to them, but instead the Chinese character for "outside" in reference to all the teachings in India that Buddhists considered the "outside way" in contrast to the Buddha Dharma. In this outside way he is encompassing both the teachings of the brahmins who followed the Vedic revelation and the ascetics whose teachings rejected the Vedas. As discussed previously, the *Supreme Net Discourse* summarized their teachings in terms of the sixty-two false views. Later Buddhist traditions enumerated ninety-five or ninety-six. None of the enumerated views are in full accord with the Buddhist teachings of interdependence and causality, nor do they teach the way to attain liberation from transmigration in the six worlds. Of them Nichiren says, "But none of these brahmins, good or evil, of the ninety-five schools can get rid of birth and death." (Murano 2000, p. 11)

Some may wonder why the term "Hindu" or "Hinduism" is not used here to refer to the religions of India. To start with, the term "Hindu" is a very vague and problematic term that originally had more to do with geography than religion.

> *The actual term 'hindu' first occurs as a Persian*
> *geographical term for the people who lived beyond the*
> *river Indus (Sanskrit: sindhu). In Arabic texts, Al-Hind is a*
> *term for the people of modern-day India and 'Hindu', or*
> *'Hindoo', was used towards the end of the eighteenth*
> *century by the British to refer to the people of*

'Hindustan', the area of northwest India. Eventually
'Hindu' became virtually equivalent to an 'Indian' who
was not a Muslim, Sikh, Jain or Christian, thereby
encompassing a range of religious beliefs and practices.
The '-ism' was added to 'Hindu' in around 1830 to
denote the culture and religion of the high-caste
Brahmins in contrast to other religions, and the term
was soon appropriated by Indians themselves in the
context of establishing a national identity as opposed to
colonialism, though the term 'Hindu' was used in
Sanskrit and Bengali hagiographic texts in contrast to
'Yavana' or Muslim, as early as the sixteenth century.
(Flood, p. 6)

In referring to the "outside way," Nichiren and his contemporaries in East Asia were not referring to what we think of as Hinduism in the modern sense. They were referring to Brahmanism (the tradition that would eventually give rise to those forms of religiosity we now think of as Hinduism) and the movements founded by six teachers contemporaneous with the Buddha who all rejected the orthodox (S. *āstika*) teachings of Brahmanism founded upon the Vedic revelation and so were considered unorthodox (S. *nāstika*) by the brahmin priests of India. From the Buddhist point of view both Brahmanism and the teachings of these six teachers were the "outside way" because they either denied or misinterpreted the law of cause and effect as well as the Buddha's teachings concerning the ultimate goal of liberation from birth and death.

To understand the variety of spiritual practices and teachings in India both prior to Buddhism and those which developed afterwards, it is best to begin with the Vedas. The Vedas are the sacred hymns and teachings of the Āryans that were brought into India when they migrated into the sub-continent around 1500 BCE. The Vedas were not a written text at that time, and even today are passed on as an oral transmission. They were believed to be a revelation (S. *śruti* – "what is heard") given to the ancient seers (S. *ṛṣi*) and passed on to the brahmins, the priests of the Āryan people. There are four Vedas: the *Rig Veda*, the *Sāma Veda*, the *Yajur Veda*, and the *Atharva Veda*.

These nomads in the Punjab composed poems in an ancient form of Sanskrit; the oldest collection is called the *Rig Veda* ("Knowledge of Verses")

The Rig Veda consists of 1,028 poems, often called mantras ("incantations") grouped into ten "circles" ("mandalas"). (It is generally agreed that the first and last books are later additions, subsequent bookends around books 2-9.) The verses were rearranged for chanting as the Sama Veda ("Knowledge of Songs") and, with additional prose passages, for ritual use as the Yajur Veda ("Knowledge of Sacrifice"); together they are known as the three Vedas. A fourth, the Atharva Veda ("Knowledge of the Fire Priest"), devoted primarily to practical, worldly matters, and spells to deal with them, was composed later, sharing some poems with the latest parts of the Rig Veda. (Doniger 2009, pp. 104-105)

The Vedas express the wonder, hopes, and fears of the Ārayans. They were the poetic link that made it possible for people to commune with the divine order of the universe and its representatives. This intent is fully expressed in the Mantra Gāyatrī, one of the most famous of the verses in the *Rig Veda*, which can be translated as: "Let us bring our minds to rest in/The glory of Divine Truth/May Truth inspire our reflection." (Le Mee, p. 4) The spirit of inquiry and openness to unknowable mystery found in some of the Vedic hymns are quite remarkable. The following verses ask whether it is possible to know how or why there is anything at all:

Who really knows? Who will here proclaim it? Whence was it produced? Whence is this creation? The gods came afterwards, with the creation of this universe. Who then knows whence it has arisen?

Whence this creation has arisen – perhaps it formed itself, or perhaps it did not – the one who looks down on it, in the highest heaven, only he knows – or perhaps he does not know. (Doniger 1981, pp. 25-26)

As the verses just cited indicate, the gods of the Vedas did not create the world but came into being later. They were not omnipotent or omniscient. Since they personified the awe-inspiring and often capricious powers of the natural world, they were not even necessarily benevolent. Nevertheless, they were offered praise and sacrifices for the protection and blessings they could provide.

> *Not one of you, gods, is small, not one a little child; all of you are truly great.*
>
> *Therefore you are worthy of praise and sacrifice, you thirty-three gods of Manu, arrogant and powerful.*
>
> *Protect us, help us and speak for us; do not lead us into the distance far away from the path of our father Manu.*
>
> *You gods who are all here and who belong to all men, give far-reaching shelter to us and to our cows and horses. (Ibid, p. 22)*

The thirty-three gods referred to in the Vedas consisted of a group of eight gods called the Vasus, eleven gods called the Rudras, twelve gods called the Ādityas, and finally Indra and Prajāpati (See Olivelle, pp. 46-47). The eight Vasus represent the powers of fire (the god Agni), earth, wind (the god Vāyu), the space between earth and sky, the sun (the god Sūrya), the sky, the moon (the god Sóma who also personified the nectar of immortality), and the stars. The eleven Rudras are fearsome storm gods who also represent the vital powers of the five physical senses, five kinds of breath within the body, and the *ātman* (a reflexive pronoun that can mean a living body or the spiritual essence of a person or just "oneself"). The Ādityas represent the twelve months of the year and also personify things such as law, tradition, craftsmanship, knowledge, honor, and so on. Indra is the thunder god and chief of the others. Prajāpati is the first being. He emerged from a cosmic egg as the primordial man (Skt. *puruṣa*) who created all other beings including the other gods. In the time of the Buddha, Indra and the first thirty-two gods were believed to dwell in the Heaven of the Thirty-three Gods atop Mt. Sumeru at the center of the world. Prajāpati was more commonly known as Brahmā, and he dwelled in the Great Brahmā Heaven far above Mt. Sumeru.

Eventually, the Vedas were used to manipulate the gods or at least *Brahman*, the divine power that the gods were aspects of. It was believed that the gods could be addressed, appeased, flattered, and even controlled through the performance of the proper hymns and sacrifices in order to stave off disaster and gain good fortune as in the following verse addressing Prajāpati:

> *Let him not harm us, he who fathered the earth and*
> *created the sky, whose laws are true, who created the*
> *high, shining waters. Who is the god whom we should*
> *worship with the oblation?*
>
> *O Prajāpati, lord of progeny, no one but you embraces*
> *all these creatures. Grant us the desires for which we*
> *offer you oblation. Let us be lords of riches." (Doniger*
> *1981, p. 28)*

The Vedas also sanctified the Āryan social order. According to the *Rig Veda*, the gods sacrificed and divided the primeval cosmic man so that his parts became the four classes (Skt. *varṇa*) of Vedic society.

> *When they divided the Man, into how many parts did*
> *they apportion him? What do they call his mouth, his*
> *two arms and thighs and feet?*
>
> *His mouth became the Brahmin; his arms were made*
> *into the Warrior, his thighs the People, and from his feet*
> *the Servants were born. (Ibid, p. 31)*

The "Brahmin" refers to the priests (there are different ways of transliterating this in English – I use 'brahmins') who offered sacrifices for the next two castes. The "Warrior" refers to the *kṣatriya* who were the warriors and rulers. The "People" refers to the *vaiśya*, who were the commoners composed of merchants and landowners. Finally, the "Servants" refers to the *śūdra* who served the first three castes. A later compendium of Brahmanical laws and customs, The *Laws of Manu*, states the duties of these four castes as set by the primeval cosmic man:

> But to protect this whole creation, the lustrous one
> made separate innate activities for those born of his
> mouth, arms, thighs, and feet. For priests, he ordained
> teaching and learning, sacrificing for themselves and
> sacrificing for others, giving and receiving. Protecting
> his subjects, giving, having sacrifices performed,
> studying, and remaining unaddicted to the sensory
> objects are, in summary, for a ruler. Protecting his
> livestock, giving, having sacrifices performed, studying,
> trading, lending money, and farming the land are for a
> commoner. The Lord assigned only one activity to a
> servant: serving those (other) classes without
> resentment. (Doniger 1991, pp. 12-13)

Ideally, these four classes are an attempt to organize society according to the inclinations of the individual. Each person should take up one of those four roles in accordance with their talents and desires. In reality, heredity (S. *jāti* lit. "birth") came to decide which class a person belonged to, and naturally the Āryans belonged to the first three classes. These first three classes are known as the "twice-born" because their members are all "born again" when they undergo an initiation ceremony whereupon they become full members of Vedic society and receive a sacred thread to signify their status. The indigenous population became the servants (who were not permitted to study the Vedas or participate in Vedic sacrifices).

In addition to the servants, many other groups came to be excluded from Vedic ceremonies and learning, and thus were disenfranchised and marginalized. Wendy Doniger provides the following explanation of them and the many terms they are known by:

> There have been countless terms coined to designate
> the lowest castes, the dispossessed or underprivileged
> or marginalized groups, including the tribal peoples.

These are the people the Sanskrit texts named by specific castes (Chandala, Chamara, Pulkasa, etc.) or called Low or Excluded (Apasadas) or Born Last (or Worst, Antyajas) or Dog-Cookers (Shva-Pakas), because caste Hindus thought that these people ate dogs, who in turn ate anything and everything, and in Hinduism, you are what you eat. Much later the British called them Untouchables, the Criminal Castes, the Scheduled (they pronounced it SHED-yuled) Castes, Pariahs (a Tamil word that has found its way into English), the Depressed Classes, and Outcastes. Gandhi called them Harijans ("the People of God"). The members of these castes (beginning in the 1930's and 1940's and continuing now) called themselves Dalits (using the Marathi/Hindi word for "oppressed" or "broken" to translate the British "Depressed"). B. R. Ambedkar (in the 1950s), himself a Dalit, tried, with partial success, to convert some of them to Buddhism. Postcolonial scholars call them (and other low castes) Subalterns. Another important group of oppressed peoples is constituted by the Adivasis ("original inhabitants"), the so-called tribal peoples of India, on the margins both geographically and ideologically, sometimes constituting a low caste (such as Nishadas), sometimes remaining outside the caste system altogether.

It is important to distinguish among Dalits and Adivasis and Shudras, all of whom have very different relationships with upper-caste Hindus, though many Sanksrit texts confuse them. So too, the Backward Castes, a sneering name that the British once gave to the excluded castes in general, are now regarded as castes separate from, and occasionally in conflict with, certain other Dalit castes; the Glossary of Human Rights Watch defines Backward Castes as "those whose ritual rank and occupational status are above 'untouchables' but who themselves remain socially and economically depressed. Also referred to as Other Backward Classes (OBCs) or Shudras," though in actual practice the OBCs

often distinguish themselves from both Dalits and
Shudras. All these groups are alike only in being treated
very badly by the upper castes; precisely how they are
treated, and what they do about it, differs greatly from
group to group. All in all, when we refer to all the
disenfranchised castes below the three upper classes
known as twice born, it is convenient to designate them
by the catchall term of Pariah (a Tamil word − for the
caste that beat leather-topped drums − that find finds
its way into English) up until the twentieth century and
then to call them Dalits. (Doniger 2009, pp. 37-39)

Aside from providing a divine narrative to explain or justify the social organization of this life, the Vedas provided for a happy afterlife in a heavenly realm with the ancestors who had gone before. This heavenly realm comes to be associated with the moon. In Buddhist cosmology the Yama Heaven is one of the heavens situated above the Heaven of the Thirty-three Gods atop Mt. Sumeru but below the Great Brahmā Heaven. The most prominent of the revered ancestors who dwell there is King Yama who is said to have been the first mortal to die and who therefore becomes the pathfinder for the dead, their judge, and their king. In the *Rig Veda*, the funeral hymn instructs the recently deceased to go to Yama's realm and enjoy the rewards of their sacrifices and good deeds.

Unite with the father, with Yama, with the rewards of
your sacrifices and good deeds, in the highest heaven.
Leaving behind all imperfections, go back home again;
merge with a glorious body. (Doniger 1981, p. 44)

By the time of the Buddha, the fifth or fourth century BCE, many people wanted something more than the passing benefits of material gain that the sacrifices were said to bring. In order to satisfy their spiritual thirst they retired to the forest in their later years, and looked for sages who could help them. A new paradigm of four life stages (S. *āśrama*) resulted from this, a paradigm all but institutionalized by the time of the Buddha. In youth, the religion of the Vedas would be studied under the guidance of the brahmins. Following this, a young man would become a householder, which meant having a family and

81

fulfilling one's social duties. During the householder stage one was to pursue the three aims of life: pleasure, profit, and duty. He was also to repay the three debts to his teachers, his ancestors, and the gods. This would be followed in middle or old age by a retreat into the forest. As a forest-dweller, he would meditate and reflect upon the spiritual significance of life. The final stage was the life of the wandering mendicant; wherein the world is renounced and spiritual liberation (*mokṣa*) is achieved.

As Vedic society evolved, so did the Vedas. Or rather, the Vedas grew as new materials were added that could accommodate the new ideas and insights that came to be associated with the Vedic hymns and rituals. The four strata of the Vedas are: the hymns or Samhitā composed between 1700 and 900 BCE; the Brāhmanas composed between 800 and 600 BCE; the Āranyakas composed between 600 and 500 BCE; and finally the Upanishads that began to appear in the fourth century BCE and continued to be composed into the twelfth century CE.

> *One of the primary vedic distinctions for its own literature is between mantra, verses used in liturgy which make up the collection of texts called Samhitā, and Brāhmana, texts of ritual exegesis. The Brāhmanas are texts describing rules for ritual and explanations about it concerning its meaning and purpose. They contain etiological myths, posit elaborate correspondences (bandhu) between the rite and the cosmos, and even maintain that the sacrifice ensures the continuity of the cosmos. The Āranyakas, texts composed in the forest, form the concluding part of several Brāhmanas. They are concerned with ritual and its interpretation and form a transitional link between the Brāhmanas and the Upanishads. The Upanishads develop the concerns of the Āranyakas, explaining the true nature and meaning of ritual. (Flood, p. 36)*

In the Upanishads, one finds an earnest quest for the deepest and most liberating truth. This spirit can perhaps be summed up by the prayer of the patron of the sacrifice as reported in the *Brihadāranyaka Upanishad*: "From the unreal lead me to the real! From the darkness lead me to the light! From death lead me to immortality!" (Olivelle, pp. 12-13) The Upanishads are a record of the dialogues of the kings, brahmins, and sages (including women sages), who all attempt to express their insights regarding the ultimate liberating truth.

It was clear to these sages that material gain and even long life as promised by the Vedic rituals were impermanent. They must all ultimately end in death at some point. Even the promise of rebirth in the heavenly realm of the ancestors might only be temporary and lead in turn to rebirth somewhere else in accordance with the nature of one's stored up actions (karma) and desires.

> *Hence there is this saying: "He's made of this. He's made of that." What a man turns out to be depends on how he acts and on how he conducts himself. If his actions are good, he will turn into something good. If his actions are bad, he will turn into something bad. A man turns into something good by good action and into something bad by bad action. And so people say: "A person here consists simply of desire." A man resolves in accordance with desire, acts in accordance with his resolve, and turns out to be in accordance with his action. On this point there is the following verse:*
>
> *A man who's attached goes with his action.*
>
> *to that very place to which*
>
> *his mind and character cling.*
>
> *Reaching the end of his action,*
>
> *of whatever he has done in this world –*
>
> *From that world he returns*
>
> *back to this world,*
>
> *back to action.*
>
> *This is the course of a man who desires. (Ibid, p. 65)*

They asked themselves to what ends their actions should be directed: to mere worldly prosperity and rebirth in the heaven of the ancestors for a time? Or should they seek a different path to discover the true nature of the self (*ātman*) and an end to the painful cycle of rebirth?

> *Prajāpati is the year. It has two courses, the southern and the northern. Now, those who venerate thus: "The best action is offerings to gods and priests!" win only the lunar world. They are the ones who return again. Therefore, the seers here who yearn for children proceed along the southern course. This course of the fathers, clearly, is substance.*
>
> *Those who seek the self by means of austerity, chastity, faith, and knowledge, on the other hand, proceed by the northern course and win the sun. Clearly, it is the abode of life breaths; it is the immortal, free from fear; it is the highest course; from it they do not return; and so, it is the final stoppage. (Ibid, pp. 279-280)*

The identity of the true self or Ātman with the divine power or Brahman is the key insight of the Upanishads and the goal of its spiritual inquiries and methods of practice. The Ātman is not like anything else in the world, it is the spiritual essence of a person and in fact of all things. It is ungraspable and untouched by suffering. It is itself Brahman, the true reality from which all else in the world springs. Knowing the Ātman one no longer needs anything else.

> *As a spider sends forth its thread, and as tiny sparks spring forth from a fire, so indeed do all the vital functions (prāna), all the worlds, all the gods, and all beings spring from this self (ātman). Its hidden name (upanishad) is: 'The real behind the real.' for the real consists of the vital functions, and the self is the real behind the vital functions. (Ibid, p. 26)*
>
> *This immense, unborn self is none other than the one consisting of perception here among the vital functions*

84

*(prāna). There, in that space within the heart, he lies –
the controller of all, the lord of all, the ruler of all! He
does not become more by good actions or in any way
less by bad actions. He is the lord of all! He is the ruler
of creatures! He is the guardian of creatures! He is the
dike separating these worlds so they would not mingle
with each other. It is he that Brahmins seek to know by
means of vedic recitation, sacrifice, gift giving,
austerity, and fasting. It is he, on knowing whom, a man
becomes a sage. It is when they desire him as their
world that wandering ascetics undertake the ascetic life
of wandering.*

*It was when they knew this that men of old did not
desire offspring, reasoning: "Ours is this self, and it is
our world. What then is the use of offspring for us?" So
they gave up the desire for sons, the desire for wealth,
and the desire for worlds, and undertook the mendicant
life. The desire for sons, after all, is the same as the
desire for wealth, and the desire for wealth is the same
as the desire for worlds – both are simply desires.*

*About this self (ātman), one can only say "not _____,
not _____". He is ungraspable, for he cannot be
grasped. He is undecaying, for he is not subject to
decay. He has nothing sticking to him, for he does not
stick to anything. He is not bound; yet he neither
trembles in fear nor suffers injury." (Ibid, pp. 67-68)*

*A man who know this, therefore, becomes calm,
composed, cool, patient, and collected. He sees the self
(ātman) in just himself (ātman) and all things as the
self. Evil does not pass across him, and he passes across
all evil. He is not burnt by evil; he burns up all evil. He
becomes a Brahmin – free from evil, free from stain,
free from doubt. (Ibid, p. 68)*

*Now, this is the immense and unborn self, the eater of
food and the giver of wealth. A man who knows this
finds wealth. And this is the immense and unborn self,*

unageing, undying, immortal, free from fear – the
Brahman. Brahman surely, is free from fear, and a man
who knows this undoubtedly become Brahman that is
free from fear. (Ibid, p. 68)

How does one accomplish this realization of the Ātman? The sages of the Upanishads recognized that realization of the Ātman required something more than the Vedic sacrifices and other forms of knowledge directed to worldly ends.

Two types of knowledge a man should learn – those
who know Brahman tell us – the higher and the lower.
The lower of the two consists of the Rigveda, the
Yajurveda, the Sāmaveda, the Atharvaveda, phonetics,
the ritual science, grammar, etymology, metrics, and
astronomy; whereas the higher is that by which one
grasps the imperishable. (Ibid, p. 268)

The chanting of the sacred syllable "Om" and the
discipline of yoga are the two methods put forward by
the Upanishads to accomplish the transcendence of
worldly desires and the realization of the Ātman. With
regard to "Om" it is the verbal expression of Brahman
used in Vedic rituals. "Brahman is OM. This whole world
is OM." (Ibid, p. 182) It is also the Ātman and the way to
realize the Ātman. "Accordingly the very self (ātman) is
OM. Anyone who knows this enters the self (ātman) by
himself (ātman). (Ibid, p. 290)

The discipline of yoga as a spiritual practice is something that may have roots in India's Dravidian past, long before the Āryans rode out of the northern steppes. Today many people are familiar with Hatha Yoga, which has to do with physical postures, stretching, and breathing exercises. The ancient discipline of yoga spoken of in the Upanishads, however, has to do with sitting in stillness and silence in order to transcend the senses, overcome desires, still the mind, and realize the Ātman. The *Katha Upanishad* provides the following description of this kind of yogic discipline:

When the five perceptions are stilled,

together with the mind,

And not even reason bestirs itself;

they call it the highest state.

When senses are firmly reined in,

that is Yoga, so people think.

From distractions a man is then free,

for Yoga is the coming-into-being,

as well as the ceasing-to-be.

Not by speech, not by the mind,

not by sight can he be grasped.

How else can that be perceived,

other than by saying 'He is!'

In just two ways can he be perceived:

by saying that 'He is',

To one who perceives him as 'He is'.

it becomes clear that he is real.

When they are all banished,

those desires lurking in one's heart;

Then a mortal becomes immortal,

and attain Brahman in this world. (Ibid, p. 246)

In later Upanishads a more theistic approach emerges, wherein Ātman and Brahman are identified as a Supreme Lord or God (Īśvara). In the *Śvetāśvatara Upanishad* both meditation on the syllable Om and the practice of yoga are directed to the realization of the Supreme God who is called Rudra or Śiva (known in Buddhism as Maheśvara, the Great Freedom God).

> *When he keeps his body straight, with the three sections erect, and draws the senses together with the mind into his heart, a wise man shall cross all the frightful rivers with the boat consisting of the formulation (Brahman). (Ibid, p. 255)*

> *When, by means of the true nature of self, which resembles a lamp, a man practicing yogic restraint sees here the true nature of Brahman, he is freed from all fetters, because he has known God, unborn, unchanging, and unsullied by all objects. (Ibid, p. 256)*

> *That God, the maker of all, the immense self (ātman), is always residing in the hearts of people. With the heart, with insight, with thought has he been contemplated. Those who know this become immortal. (Ibid, p. 260)*

The theistic or devotional approach to liberation becomes even more pronounced in the two great epics of Indian literature the *Rāmāyana* and the *Mahābhārata*, and in the devotional narratives called the Purānas. Though these works are not considered divine revelation like the Vedas, they are highly revered as part of a sacred tradition (S. *smṛti* – "what is remembered"). These works are seen as a commentary on the Vedas or sometimes even as a fifth Veda. The *Rāmāyana* deals with a legendary hero named Rāma, a human avatar of the god Vishnu, who fights a demon named Rāvana who had kidnapped his wife Sītā. Various versions of it were composed between 200 BCE and 200 CE. The *Mahābhārata* deals with a fratricidal and apocalyptic war fought in India around 950 BCE. It was composed between 300 BCE and 300 CE. A multitude of Purānas were composed over a long period of time with the earliest appearing in the fourth century and the latest in the twelfth century.

One section of the *Mahabharata* is the well-known *Bhagavad Gītā*, wherein the hero-king Krishna (another avatar of Vishnu) becomes the spiritual teacher of one of the five main protagonists of the epic, a prince named Arjuna. Krishna instructs Arjuna in three different types of yoga, the yoga of spiritual knowledge (*jñana-yoga*), the yoga of acting to fulfilling one's duties while renouncing the fruits of action (*karma-yoga*), and the yoga of devotion to Krishna as the supreme God (*bhakti-yoga*). The *Bhagavad Gītā* brings together a great many of the teachings and methods of the Upanishads as well as other strains of Vedic thought. Its purpose is to show that all these spiritual teachings and methods culminate in Krishna and/or Vishnu (depending on one's interpretation) as the ultimate goal personified. The following passage is a sample of Krishna's teaching to Arjuna in the *Bhagavad Gītā*:

Closing the gates of the body,

And confining the mind in the heart,

Having placed the vital breath in the head,

Established in yoga concentration,

Uttering the single-syllable "Om" Brahman

Meditating on Me,

He who goes forth, renouncing the body,

Goes to the supreme goal.

He who thinks of Me constantly,

Whose mind does not ever go elsewhere,

For him, the yogin who is constantly devoted,

I am easy to reach, Arjuna.

Approaching Me, those whose souls are great,

Who have gone to the supreme perfection,

Do not incur rebirth,

That impermanent home of misfortune.

Up to Brahma's realm of being,

The worlds are subject to successive rebirths, Arjuna;

But he who reaches Me

Is not reborn. (Sargeant, pp. 360-364)

Starting around the time of the Buddha the religion of the Vedas, with their sacrifices to the gods of Mt. Sumeru for worldly success and an afterlife in a heavenly realm with one's ancestors, gave way to the sectarian movements centered on either Vishnu or Śiva, formerly minor deities from the Vedas. The Vaishnavas or devotees of Vishnu (aka Nārāyana or Bhagavān) or one of his avatars (Krishna or Rāma in particular) became the largest group, while the Śaivas or devotees of Śiva (aka Rudra or Maheśvara) were the next most popular. Nichiren was quite correct to say, "According to the Brahmanism of India, the two gods Maheśvara and Vishnu are regarded as the compassionate parents, gods, and lords of all living beings." (Murano 2000, p. 10) In time, the Goddess Devī (aka Durgā, Kālī, or Śakti and many other names) would also have her own devotees known as Śaktas. Unlike the earlier Vedic rituals whose performance and benefits were only for the upper three castes, the sectarian movements promised liberation to all, including women and outcastes. Most religious Hindus today are actually Vaishnavas, Śaivas, or Śaktas. There are other gods who are still popular in modern Hinduism, like Hanumān (the general of an army of monkeys who helped Rāma) or Ganeśa (the elephant headed Lord of Obstacles who is the son of Śiva's wife Pārvatī), but these deities themselves are subordinate to either Vishnu or Śiva. There is also the Smārta tradition based on the Purānas wherein the five deities Vishnu, Śiva, Devī, Ganeśa, and Sūrya (the sun god) are all worshipped as aspects of Brahman.

Some people today believe that the Hindus worship Brahmā, Vishnu, and Śiva as a kind of Hindu trinity. Wendy Doniger explains why this is a fallacy:

The tensions between the worshippers of Vishnu and
Shiva were relatively mild but important enough to be
explicitly addressed in narratives. The concept of a

trinity, a triumvirate of Brahma, Vishnu, and Shiva (the Trimurti [Triple Form]), which both Kalidasa and the Markandeya Purana mention, is a misleading convention. (The triumvirate may have been sustained, though not invented, in response to the Christian trinity.) The idea that Brahma is responsible for creation, Vishnu for preservation or maintenance, and Shiva for destruction does not correspond in any way to the mythology, in which both Vishnu and Shiva are responsible for both creation and destruction and Brahma was not worshipped as the other two were. (Doniger 2009, p. 384)

In these devotional (S. *bhakti*) movements, the chosen deity is the subject of worship services (S. *pūjā*) and offered flowers, candlelight, incense, water, and food. It is believed that through the grace of the chosen deity, viewed as the Supreme Being who is one without a second, the devotee will achieve liberation and attain union with God (or the Goddess as the case may be) in a heavenly realm that transcends the cycle of rebirth. As the devotional movements centered on Vishnu, Śiva, or Devī rose in popularity, the old Vedic sacrifices and the gods Brahmā, Indra, Agni, and Sóma became more and more marginalized. In time, they were demoted to the status of mere demigods or celestial servitors who were dependent on God (or the Goddess) for liberation from the cycle of birth and death. The old sacrifices were never completely forgotten, but for the great majority of people they were no longer needed if salvation could be achieved through devotion to God (or the Goddess), the ultimate truth and personal source of liberation.

Sources

Danielou, Alain. *The Myths and Gods of India*. Rochester: Inner Traditions International, 1991.

Dasgupta, Surendranath. *A History of Indian Philosophy Volume 1*. New Delhi: Motilal Banarsidass, 1997.

Doniger, Wendy, trans. *The Rig Veda*. New York: Penguin Books, 1981.

_____. *The Laws of Manu*. New York: Penguin Books, 1991.

_____. *The Hindus: An Alternative History*. New York: The Penguin Press, 2009.

Flood, Gavin. *An Introduction to Hinduism*. New York: Cambridge University Press, 1996.

Gosho Translation Committee, editor-translator. *The Writings of Nichiren Daishonin*. Tokyo: Soka Gakkai, 1999.

Hori, Kyotsu, comp. *Writings of Nichiren Shonin: Doctrine Volume 2*. Tokyo: Nichiren Shu Overseas Propagation Promotion Association, 2002.

Le Mee, Jean Marie Alexandre, trans., *Hymns from the Rig Veda*. New York: Alfred A. Knopf, Inc., 1975.

Murano, Senchu, trans. *Kaimokusho or Liberation from Blindness*. Berkeley: Numata Center for Buddhist Translation and Research, 2000.

Olivelle, Patrick, trans. *Upanishads*. Oxford: Oxford University Press, 1996.

Prabhavananda, Swami. *The Spiritual Heritage of India: A Clear Summary of Indian Philosophy and Religion*. Hollywood: Vedanta Press, 1979.

Sadataka, Akira. *Buddhist Cosmology: Philosophy and Origins*. Tokyo: Kosei Publishing Co., 2004.

Sargeant, Winthrop. *The Bhagavad Gita*. New York: State University of New York Press, 1994.

Chapter 8 – Indian Philosophy

Writings of Nichiren Shōnin: Doctrine 2, pp. 32-33
Kaimoku-shō or Liberation from Blindness, pp. 10-12
The Writings of Nichiren Daishonin I, pp. 221-223

Nichiren speaks of Three Seers named Kapila, Uluka, and Rishabha whom he credits with expounding the four Vedas some eight centuries before the time of the Buddha (whom East Asian Buddhist tradition dated 1029 – 949 BCE). He also asserts that at the time of the Buddha there were six non-Buddhist teachers who taught the Vedas and the six schools they founded later split in ninety-five or ninety-six schools. He then says that all these teachings can be summarized in terms of three different views of causality: (1) that the effect can be found within the cause, (2) that the effect cannot be found within the cause, and (3) that the effect does and does not exist within the cause. This was Nichiren's understanding of the non-Buddhist teachings of India at the time of the Buddha. Nichiren did not, of course, have any firsthand knowledge of India or Indian philosophy and religion, and it would seem as though his sources were not very accurate. In this chapter I hope to present a more accurate view of the Indian philosophical and spiritual tradition.

To begin with, the Brahman tradition believes that the Vedas were revealed to seven primordial seers (S. *ṛṣi*). "According to the *Śatapatha Brāhmana*, the seers are the authors of the Vedic hymns. Their names are Gautama, Bharadvāja, Viśvāmitra, Jamadagni, Vasishtha, Kaśyapa, and Atri." (Danielou, p. 317) The number and names of these sages differs in other texts, but Kapila, Uluka, and Rishabha are not among them. So who are these three "seers" that Nichiren mentions?

Kapila was the legendary founder of the Sāmkhya School who may have lived as early as the seventh century BCE. Sāmkhya is a system of analysis whose purpose is to show how the spiritual person (S. *puruṣa*) is separate from nature (S. *prakṛti*). Purusha is much like the Vedic Ātman except that there may be a plurality of them. Prakriti is sometimes translated as "matter" but in fact it includes things like mind, ego, and intellect as well as all the five sense organs; their corresponding objects; the physical organs of speaking, grasping, walking, excreting, and procreating; and the five elements of earth, air, fire, water, and space. Prakriti is in turn composed of three qualities (S. *guṇa*): (1) tranquility (S. *sattva*), (2) passion (S. *rajas*), and (3) inertia (S. *tamas*). These three qualities are present in varying proportions in everything that is of the natural world according to Sāmkhya. Sāmkhya would in time become the philosophical basis of the Yoga school.

Uluka or Kanāda was the founder of the Vaiśeshika school who lived in the 3rd century BCE. The Vaiśeshika is also a system of philosophical analysis that attempts to discern the ultimate realities of life in order to end ignorance and bring about liberation from the cycle of birth and death. In this school of thought a distinction is made between the individual self (S. *jīvātman*) that suffers the cycle of birth and death and the Supreme Self (S. *paramātman*) that is God. Vaiśeshika became associated with the Nyāya school of Gautama (c. 3rd century BCE) that concerns itself with logic and epistemology.

By the twelfth century CE, Sāmkhya, Yoga, Vaiśeshika, and Nyāya were grouped with the Mīmāmsā and Vedānta schools as the Six Darśanas or Six Views. The Six Darśanas are the six schools of Indian philosophy that are considered orthodox (S. *āstika*) by the brahmins because they all accept the Vedas as a divine revelation. Wendy Doniger provides the following summary of these six schools:

1. Mimamsa ("Critical Inquiry") began with Jaimini (c. 400 BCE) and was devoted to the interpretation of the Vedas, taking the Vedas as the authority for dharma and karma. Jaimini guaranteed the sacrificer life in heaven after death and decreed that women could sacrifice but Shudras could not.
2. Vaisheshika began with Kanada (c. third century BCE), who presented an atomic cosmology, according to which all material objects are made of atoms of the nine elements: the four material elements – earth, water, fire, and air – plus five more abstract elements – space, time, ether, mind, and soul. In this view, god created the world, but not ex nihilo; he simply imposed order on pre-existing atoms. Shankara called the Vaisheshikas half nihilists.

3. Logic and reasoning began with Gautama (c. second century BCE, no relation to the Buddhist Gautama) and was an analytical philosophy basic not only to all later Hindu philosophy but to the scientific literature of the shastras.
4. Patanjali's Yoga-Sutras (c. 150 BCE) codified yogic practices that had been in place for centuries. Yoga assumes a personal god who controls the process of periodic creation and dissolution and is omniscient and omnipotent. This school emphasized exercises of the mind and the body, "including the very difficult exercise of not exercising them at all." It believed that moksha came not from knowledge but from concentration and discipline of the mind and the body.
5. Sankhya as a philosophy has roots that date from the time of the Upanishads and are important in the Mahabharata (especially in the Gita) but were first formally codified by Ishvarakrishna (c. third century CE). Sankhya is dualistic, dividing the universe into a male purusha (spirit, self, or person) and a female prakriti (matter, nature). There are an infinite number of similar but separate purushas, no one superior to another. Early Sankhya philosophers argued that god may or may not exist but is not needed to explain the universe; later Sankhya philosophers assumed that god does exist.
6. And then comes Vedanta, the philosophical school that reads the Upanishads through the lens of the unity of the self (atman) and the cosmic principle (Brahman). Often expressed in the form of commentaries on the Upanishads, on the Gita, and on Badrayana's Vedanta-Sutras (c. 400 BCE), different branches of Vedanta tend to relegate the phenomenal world to the status of an epistemological error (*avidya*), a psychological imposition (*adhyaya*), or a metaphysical illusion (*maya*). Evil, too, which the myths struggle to deal with, and, especially, death turn out to be nothing but an illusion. (Doniger 2009, pp. 504-505)

Rishabha was a sage who is considered by the Jains to have been the first of twenty-four teachers of Jainism in the present era of the world.

During each motion of the wheel, twenty-four teachers, the fordmakers (tīrthankara), appear in succession who activate the Three Jewels, the uncreated Jain teachings of right faith, right knowledge and right practice, and who found a community of ascetic and lay followers which serves as a spiritual ford (tīrtha) for human beings over the ocean of rebirth. The pattern of the careers of these fordmakers is essentially identical. Always born into a family of the warrior class, they are generally awakened by the gods (in Jainism, beings who are subject like humans to the laws of rebirth but who cannot attain enlightenment in their divine state) to their destinies as great spiritual teachers and then renounce the world of the householder to become wandering mendicants. After an obligatory period in the practice of physical and mental austerities, facilitated by their uniquely powerful physical structure, in order to effect the burning away of the karma they have accumulated over innumerable existences, they attain the enlightenment which the Jains define as full omniscience. Finally, having engaged in a period of preaching and conversion, they die in meditation and their souls, freed from their bodies, travel to the top of the universe to abide in a state of bliss and pure consciousness along with the other liberated souls. (Dundas, p. 20)

As the first fordmaker, Rishabha is inevitably allotted a great deal of space in the Universal History. He was born not, as would be expected, at the very beginning of the avasarpinī, but near the end of its third spoke. Up to this point the needs of human beings had been satisfied by miraculous wishing trees but, as the efficacy of these decreased, society slowly became unstructured and incapable of self-maintenance. One of Rishabha's roles prior to his renunciation of the world was the patriarchal one of inculcating social skills such as the preparation of food, the kindling of fire, agriculture, writing, marriage, and organized system of society and

*so on. The nature of the vital institution of giving
(dāna), whereby a layman gives alms to an ascetic and
through that action gains merit, was articulated for the
first time when a king, Śreyāmsa, poured sugarcane
juice into Rishabha's cupped hands to break the
fordmaker's first fast as a renouncer. Rishabha can thus
be viewed as unique among the fordmakers in that he is
not just a spiritual teacher but a form of culture hero.
(Ibid, p. 21)*

Though Rishabha is mentioned in the *Rig Veda*, the *Bhagavad Gītā* and the Purānas, Jainism is considered by the Brahmans to be an unorthodox (*nāstika*) movement that rejects the authority of the Vedas. At the time of the Buddha there were six unorthodox teachers, aside from the Buddha, including the then current teacher of the Jains. These six teachers were Pūrana Kāśyapa, who denied the law of cause and effect; Maskarin Gośāli, who taught that everything is predestined; Samjayin Vairatīputra the skeptic; Ajita Keśakambala the materialist; Kakuda Kātyāyana the pluralist, who taught that the elements that make up life disperse at death with no continuity; and Nigrantha Jñatiputra, the teacher of Jainism, who taught that our actions bind us to suffering regardless of our intentions and that only complete inaction and nonviolence can lead to liberation. These six teachers were part of a large movement of people known as "strivers" (*śramanas*) who renounced the household for a life of mendicancy and asceticism in order to attain liberation from the cycle of birth and death.

*From about 800 to 400 BCE Sanskrit and Prakrit texts
bear witness to the emergence of the new ideology of
renunciation, in which knowledge (jñāna) is given
precedence over action (karma), and detachment from
the material and social world is cultivated through
ascetic practices (tapas), celibacy, poverty, and methods
of mental training (yoga). The purpose of such training
is the cultivation of altered or higher states of
consciousness which will culminate in the blissful
mystical experience of final liberation from the bonds of
action and rebirth. While the renouncer of śramana
traditions differ on points of doctrine and method, they*

*generally agree that life is characterized by suffering
(duhkha) and adhere to a teaching in which liberation
(moksha, nirvāna) from suffering is a form of spiritual
knowledge or gnosis (jñāna, vidyā). The spread of
disease among the new urban population may have
contributed to the growth of ascetic movements and
added poignancy to the doctrine of life as suffering. In
these new ascetic ideologies, spiritual salvation cannot
be attained simply due to high-caste birth, but only by
liberating insight or understanding the nature of
existence. The true Brahman, according to the Buddha,
is not someone born to a particular mother, but a
person whose conduct is pure and moral. Personal
experience in this way is placed above the received
knowledge of the vedic revelation. At an early period,
during the formation of the Upanishads and the rise of
Buddhism and Jainism, we must envisage a common
heritage of meditation and mental discipline practiced
by renouncers with varying affiliations to non-orthodox
(Veda-rejecting) and orthodox (Veda-accepting)
traditions. (Flood, p. 81-82)*

There are many things that Buddhism holds in common with these traditions.
The traditional story of the Buddha's life even states that he was initially
inspired by the sight of a *śramana* to leave the palace, and he later trained
with two teachers of yoga and afterwards practiced asceticism. During his
teaching career he entered into dialogues and debates with brahmins and
followers of the other six teachers. I will discuss the continuities and
discontinuities between the Buddha's teachings and both Brahmanism and
the unorthodox *śramana* movement in the next chapter.

Nichiren says that these six teachers gave rise to ninety-five or ninety-six
schools that all come down to three views regarding causation. Why does he
say this? As discussed previously, the numbers ninety-five or ninety-six are
found in various sūtras to simply indicate the great variety of views that were
held or potentially could be held by the Buddha's contemporaries. The
Supreme Net Discourse puts the number at sixty-two by combining different
metaphysical positions regarding past, present, and future, the finite or

99

infinite nature of the world, whether or not there is life after death and so on. As shown in a previous chapter, these sixty-two false views were all based on speculations about the nature of life based on a limited view of time, and thus a limited view of the workings of causes and conditions. I imagine that the ninety-five or ninety-six schools expressed more of the same. As far as Nichiren and his contemporaries were concerned, these myriad views of causality held by the non-Buddhists of India all boiled down to the following three views: (1) the effect can be found within the cause, (2) the effect cannot be found within the cause, and (3) the effect does and does not exist within the cause. These views concerning causality are important because they are denials of the law of cause and effect as taught by the Buddha, and the law of cause and effect taught by the Buddha relates to right view and right practice that leads to awakening.

In the *Outline of All the Holy Teachings of the Buddha* (*Ichidai Shōgyō Tai-i*), Nichiren associates Kapila with the view that effects are the transformations of the cause that is their substance or self-nature. This is justified in that Sāmkhya teaches that an effect exists as a potential within a cause and is produced when the cause transforms itself. For example, it is like clay (the cause) being shaped into a jar (the effect). The clay remains clay, though it has become a jar. In this view nothing is ever really created or destroyed, there are only transformations of what has always and will always exist. Cause and effect are identified as simply two different modes of an eternal unchanging substance. This is the view that Buddhism calls "eternalism."

Uluka is associated with the view that effects are generated by external causes. This is justified in that the Vaiśeshika held that the cause gives rise to the effect, but the cause does not enter into the being of the effect. The effect then becomes a cause for something else and in turn passes away. For example, once the moist lump of clay has been shaped by the potter and fired in the kiln it is no longer clay but a jar. In this view the cause disappears when the effect comes into existence and the effect itself disappears when it becomes the cause for some other effect. Cause and effect are denied any underlying substantial identity as the former vanishes without a trace when the latter comes into being. Buddhism calls this view "annihilationism."

Rishabha is associated with the view that effects are the product of causes external and internal to them. This is consistent with the Jain teaching of relativity in respect to conceptual statements. In other words, one should grant the relative truth of a variety of positions if one is not to fall into one-sided or partial views. Due to their teaching of relativity, the Buddhists attributed to Rishabha the position that a cause may in some respects transform into its effect but in other respects the cause and effect are distinct entities. Using the example of clay being turned into a jug: in some respects, the clay remains as the basis of the jug, but in other respects the jar has qualities the lump of clay did not have in terms of its shape, firmness, and ability to function as a container. Cause and effect are thereby identical in terms of some qualities but separate entities in terms of others.

Finally, the materialists are associated with the view that chance or fate governs the appearance and disappearance of phenomena and that there are no causal relations, that is to say no causes or effects. This is the view that things just happen without any rhyme or reason.

The *Ichidai Shōgyō Tai-i* passage (Hori 2004, p. 91) that aligns the thinkers of India in terms of four alternatives uses the tetralemma, a Buddhist way of presenting two alternatives, their combination, and the negation of both alternatives. The tetralemma supposedly exhausts all the possible solutions to a question. The present tetralemma about the relationship between cause and effect is often taken in Buddhism to really be about the relationship between the one who acts and the one who experiences the karmic fruition of that act either within the same lifetime or in some future lifetime. In other words, is the person who makes the cause the same as the person who will experience the effect? Kapila would say yes, Uluka would say no, Rishabha would say that both Kapila and Uluka are correct in some sense, and the materialists would deny any kind of causal connection. All four alternatives, however, contain an assumption that the Buddha did not share: that causes and effects are substantial entities that do or do not endure through time. Furthermore, the Buddha denied that there is an unchanging, independent, "self" that performs causes and suffers effects. Without that assumption, none of the proposals makes any sense.

The Buddha did teach that things have a provisional (though not intrinsic) existence based on causes and conditions. This is the teaching of dependent origination, the Middle Way between eternalism and annihilationism. Dependent origination means that all physical and mental phenomena are the arising and ceasing of causes and conditions and not substantial entities. The causes and conditions of phenomena depend upon other causes and conditions, and so on. Therefore, one who is following the Middle Way of the Buddha will think in terms of causes and conditions, and not the existence or non-existence of a substantial thing. For the follower of the Middle Way there are no immutable categories or boundaries, nor is there any question of absolute identity or absolute difference between entities. Dependent origination is the awareness of causality and the interdependence of all things. Awakening to the flow of causality gives rise to an authentic sense of responsibility for the causes we make and the effects we have set in motion. Awakening to interdependence gives rise to genuine love and compassion as we realize our connection with all that is.

The following discussion with the ascetic Kāśyapa shows how the Buddha rejected all four alternatives in terms of the connection between the suffering one experiences (an effect) and the one who made the cause that brought it about.

"How is it, Master Gautama: is suffering created by oneself?"

"Not so, Kāśyapa," the Blessed One said.

"Then, Master Gautama, is suffering created by another?"

"Not so, Kāśyapa," the Blessed One said.

"How is it then, Master Gautama: is suffering created both by oneself and by another?"

"Not so, Kāśyapa," the Blessed One said.

"Then, Master Gautama, has suffering arisen fortuitously, being created neither by oneself nor by another"

"Not so, Kāśyapa," the Blessed One said.

"How is it then, Master Gautama: is there no suffering?"

"It is not that there is no suffering, Kāśyapa; there is suffering."

"Then is it that Master Gautama does not know and see suffering?"

"It is not that I do not know and see suffering, Kāśyapa. I know suffering, I see suffering."

[Kāśyapa then reiterates his questions and the Buddha's responses by way of review and finally asks:]
"Venerable sir, let the Blessed One explain suffering to me. Let the Blessed One teach me about suffering."

"Kāśyapa, [if one thinks,] 'The one who acts is the same as the one who experiences [the result],' [then one asserts] with reference to one existing from the beginning: 'Suffering is created by oneself.' When one asserts thus, this amounts to eternalism. But, Kāśyapa, [if one thinks,] 'The one who acts is one, the one who experiences [the result] is another,' [then one asserts] with reference to one stricken by feeling: 'Suffering is created by another.' When one asserts thus, this amounts to annihilationism. Without veering towards either of these extremes, the Tathagata teaches Dharma by the middle: 'With ignorance as condition, volitional formations [come to be]; with volitional formations as conditions, consciousness.... Such is the origin of this whole mass of suffering. But with the remainderless fading away and cessation of ignorance comes cessation of volitional formations; with the cessation of volitional formations, cessation of consciousness.... Such is the cessation of this whole mass of suffering." (Bodhi 2000, pp. 546-547)

The Buddha dismisses the first alternative as representing the extreme of eternalism. This is because it assumes that the one who did the deed can be completely identified with the person who will experience the result. In other words, the person stays the same throughout the whole process of cause and effect, as though they were untouched by it. The second alternative is dismissed as representative of the extreme of annihilationism, because it assumes that the one who committed the initial deed will be entirely gone by the time it comes to fruition and that there is no connection at all with the person who will have to suffer the result. In other words, there is no personal continuity of any kind within the process of cause and effect. The third alternative states that the person both remains unchanged and has no personal continuity throughout the process of cause and effect. This alternative is dismissed because it is an attempt to bring together both extremes that is not only contradictory but contains the liabilities of both. The fourth alternative denies both eternalism and annihilationism but proposes that the process of cause and effect is arbitrary and a matter of luck or fate with no responsible parties. In denying all four alternatives, the Buddha seems to be denying any possible way of explaining the connection between the individual and the process of cause and effect. The Buddha does have an explanation, but it is one that Kāśyapa had not considered: dependent origination, the Middle Way between eternalism and annihilationism.

In his answer to Kāśyapa, the Buddha states that he teaches the "Dharma by the middle," in other words the Middle Way, and then proceeds to expound the twelve-fold chain of dependent origination (abridged in the translation cited). Dependent origination puts forth the view that one cannot abstract an unchanging person or even discontinuous persons from the process of cause and effect. The person is the process and changes along with it. There is no unchanging entity that suffers the effects of its own deeds, nor is there a disconnection between the one who acts and the one who experiences the result. In fact, there is no entity except in a provisional sense; there is simply the process wherein one thing leads to another. This is the Middle Way because it shows that there is change, as opposed to eternalism; and that within that change there is continuity, as opposed to annihilationism.

The Middle Way also steers clear of an unsatisfactory combination of the extremes or the equally unsatisfactory denial of any connection between persons and the process of cause and effect. In the Middle Way of dependent origination, there is no question of identity or lack of identity between the one who makes the cause and the one who suffers the effect, because the stream of cause and effect itself accounts for both the change and continuity of personal experience. Change and continuity within the process itself maintains the subjectivity of individual experience and personal responsibility for actions and their consequences. This is different from the Jain view that proposes a substantial entity that is changed in some aspects but remains the same in other respects. The flow of causes and conditions in the process of dependent origination does not assert any graspable "self" at all even as the process gives rise to a subjective sense of self. Likewise, though dependent origination does deny any substantiality to causes and effects it refutes the materialist view that there is no personal connection between actions and their consequences.

All of this can sound very abstruse. What it comes down to, however, is actually very practical. The Buddha's primary concern was to help people free themselves of false views that obscure the dynamic interdependent nature of reality and undermine the motivation to practice. If effects are nothing more than a rearrangement of what is already present, then we cannot really change ourselves, we can only work within the limitations of what we start with. If causes disappear as they give rise to effects, then again, we can bring about change but we will be negated in the process. The combination of those alternatives brings together the contradictory and not very happy idea that in bringing about change we cannot really change ourselves and in that only apparent change we will disappear. To deny causality altogether means that it does not matter what we do. Each of these views is disempowering and undercuts our sense of responsibility.

The Buddhist view is that what we do does matter. We are not fixed unchanging blocks. We are beings whose existence is a flow of causes and conditions connected to the causal flow of all other beings and the world we live in. When we make causes, the effects of those causes change our lives and the lives of everyone else for better or for worse. We are free to perpetuate the same old unwholesome patterns or to create new wholesome ones and these patterns of causes and their effects change the quality of the flow of life. Recognizing this, the Buddha taught that by making good causes it is possible to awaken to the dynamic interdependent nature of life and thereby let go of a narrow selfish view and instead live a life of selfless compassion that brings an end to suffering and is the basis of true happiness.

Sources

Bodhi, Bhikkhu, trans. *The Connected Discourses of the Buddha: A New Translation of the Samyutta Nikaya*. Boston: Wisdom Publications, 2000.

Bryant, Edwin F., trans. *The Yoga Sutras of Patanjali*. New York: North Point Press, 2009.

Dasgupta, Surendranath. *A History of Indian Philosophy Volume 1*. New Delhi: Motilal Banarsidass, 1997.

Doniger, Wendy. *The Hindus: An Alternative History*. New York: The Penguin Press, 2009.

Dundas, Paul. *The Jains*. New York: Routledge, 2002.

Flood, Gavin. *An Introduction to Hinduism*. New York: Cambridge University Press, 1996.

Gosho Translation Committee, editor-translator. *The Writings of Nichiren Daishonin*. Tokyo: Soka Gakkai, 1999.

_____. *The Writings of Nichiren Daishonin Volume II*. Tokyo: Soka Gakkai, 2006.

Hartranft, Chip, trans. *The Yoga-Sutra of Patanjali*. Boston: Shambhala, 2003.

Hori, Kyotsu, comp. *Writings of Nichiren Shonin: Doctrine Volume 2*. Tokyo: Nichiren Shu Overseas Propagation Promotion Association, 2002.

_____. *Writings of Nichiren Shonin: Doctrine Volume 3*. Tokyo: Nichiren Shu Overseas Propagation Promotion Association, 2004.

Murano, Senchu, trans. *Kaimokusho or Liberation from Blindness*. Berkeley: Numata Center for Buddhist Translation and Research, 2000.

Olivelle, Patrick, trans. *Upanishads*. Oxford: Oxford University Press, 1996.

Prabhavananda, Swami. *The Spiritual Heritage of India: A Clear Summary of Indian Philosophy and Religion*. Hollywood: Vedanta Press, 1979.

Sargeant, Winthrop. *The Bhagavad Gita*. New York: State University of New York Press, 1994.

Chapter 9 – The Buddha's Critical Assimilation of Brahmanism

Writings of Nichiren Shōnin: Doctrine 2, pp. 32-33, 65-66
Kaimoku-shō or Liberation from Blindness, pp. 10-12, 58
The Writings of Nichiren Daishonin I, pp. 221-223, 249

In regard to the actual practices of Indian spirituality, Nichiren says that some brahmins teach the five precepts and ten good precepts (i.e. the ten courses of wholesome conduct) that lead to rebirth in the heavens (a temporary respite in the cycle of birth and death), while other brahmins teach ascetic practices that only lead to rebirth in the three evil realms of the hells, hungry ghosts, and animals. We can see from this that in some ways Buddhism assimilated the methods and worldview of his predecessors but in other ways he departed from these ideas and methods based on his own experience and awakening.

If the Buddha lived from 463 – 383 BCE, then the earliest Upanishads like the *Brihadāranyaka* and the *Chāndogya* had already been composed and were being passed on orally from master to disciple. However, nowhere in the Buddha's discourses does he refer to Upanishads or the teaching of the oneness of Ātman and Brahman, the major theme of the Upanishads. Yet, the Buddha does draw upon many of the same values, ideas, and even figures of speech used in the Upanishads. Two particular images may be found throughout the Buddha's discourses and in the *Lotus Sūtra* in particular. The first is the image of someone's head shattering because they cannot answer a question put to them. "If you will not tell me that, your head will shatter apart," (Olivelle, p. 51) threatens the sage Yājñavalkya after asking the brahmin Śākalya a question about the Ātman. This strikingly violent image seems to be a metaphor for the consternation felt by a disputant who is backed into a corner and is unable to admit defeat or make a proper response. In chapter twenty-six of the *Lotus Sūtra*, the ten *rākshasīs*, the demon daughters of the Mother-of-Devils (J. Kishimojin), bestow spells called *dhāranīs* for the protection of the practitioners of the *Lotus Sūtra* and announce, "Anyone who does not keep our spells but troubles the expounder of the Dharma shall have his head split into seven pieces just as the branches of the arjaka-tree are split." (Murano 2012, p. 335). The other image is that of the lotus flower used to represent the purity of a spiritually awakened person who is in the world but no longer of it. "When someone knows [the Ātman] bad actions do not stick to him, just as water does not stick to a lotus leaf." (Olivelle, p. 134) In chapter fifteen of the *Lotus Sūtra* the Bodhisattvas from Underground are compared to lotus flowers. "They are not defiled by worldliness just as the lotus-flower is not defiled by water." (Murano 2012, p. 244) From these two examples it can be seen how the same images were shared in both Brahmanism and Buddhism.

In the life story of the Buddha it is said that the young prince Siddhārtha made four excursions in his chariot to see the city of Kapilavastu and that on the first three he saw an old man, a sick man, and a funeral procession. On the last excursion he encountered a wandering ascetic. As early as the *Rig Veda*, there are reports of wandering ascetics, some naked and some even wearing red robes (the Buddha would later garb himself and his monks in patchwork robes of saffron). "These ascetics, swathed in wind, put dirty red rags on." (Doniger 1981, p. 137) Some people have wondered how Siddhārtha could have encountered a monk in patchwork robes before he had established the Sangha, but the fact is that the presence of wandering monks wearing patchwork robes of red or saffron predate the Buddha by hundreds of years, perhaps even a thousand or more.

After Siddhārtha left the palace and took up the way of the wandering mendicant himself, he studied with two great masters of the yogic meditation tradition that predated Buddhism (it may have even predated the Āryan migrations) and would later be codified after the time of the Buddha by Patañjali in his *Yoga Sūtras* in the mid-second century BCE. The first yoga instructor was Ārāda Kālāma, who had attained a state wherein one experiences freedom from the material world in the state of nothingness. Siddhārtha rapidly achieved this state as well under Ārāda Kālāma's instruction, but he found that it was not the final end of suffering but only a temporary altered state of consciousness. He then studied with Rudraka Rāmaputra, who was able to enter into a state wherein there is neither perception nor non-perception. This was also a temporary state. Siddhārtha saw that altered states of consciousness brought about by yogic discipline could not change one's life or provide any meaningful answers to life's problems. By the same token, the heavenly realms that were supposed to correspond to these meditative states were also only temporary, though those born into them as the fruit of their spiritual practice might reside in those heavens for millions of years in worldly terms. As Nichiren says, even those who followed good teachers could at most attain the highest heavens for only two or three lives before falling back into the evil realms of the hells, hungry ghosts, and animals when they had exhausted the merit gained from their previous meritorious practice.

Having tried yoga, Siddhārtha then joined a band of five ascetics and lived a very austere and reclusive life for six years. He had hoped that a life of self-denial and severe discipline would give him the clarity he needed to find an answer. Nichiren mentions such ascetic practices as bathing repeatedly in the Ganges River in cold weather, pulling out one's hair, jumping off rocks, setting one's body on fire, and living naked. Siddhārtha took up the practice of fasting, to the point where he was eating only one grain of rice a day.

After six years of this, the Buddha was so weakened from fasting that he was close to death and still no closer to his goal. In fact, he passed out by the side of the Nairañjanā River while trying to get some water. A village woman named Sujātā, who was stirred by compassion for him, nursed him back to health with rice-gruel and saved him from death. Siddhārtha realized that the self-denial practiced by many bands of ascetics and also the Jains is as much of a hindrance to achieving spiritual awakening as self-indulgence. It was then that he realized the Middle Way between self-indulgence and self-denial and sat beneath the Bodhi Tree to utilize the method of concentrating his mind and then focusing his awareness on the present reality in order to gain insight. It was in this way that he attained perfect and complete awakening.

When the Buddha attained awakening beneath the Bodhi Tree, Brahmā, the Vedic creator god, entreated him to roll the Wheel of the Dharma out of compassion for all beings. Throughout the Buddha's discourses there are references to the Buddha interacting with and even teaching the gods of the Vedas. The Buddha speaks of the presence of these gods at his awakening in the following passage of the *Lotus Sūtra*:

> "On that occasion King Brahmā
>
> Heavenly King Śakra,

The four heavenly world-guardian kings,

Great-Freedom God, and other gods [of each world],

And thousands and millions of their attendants

Joined their hands together [towards me] respectfully,

Bowed to me,

And asked me to turn the wheel of the Dharma."
(Murano 2012, p. 46)

Once the Buddha set out to teach, he would often give a discourse on what he called the "progressive teachings" which consists of a review of those spiritual teachings and values that he shared with Brahmanism: generosity, self-discipline, and aspiration for the heavenly realms, as well as the dangers of sensual pleasures and the benefits of renunciation. For instance, in the following example, the Buddha taught a young man named Yasa the progressive instruction in order to prepare him for the unique insight of the four noble truths:

> *The Blessed One gave him progressive instruction, that is to say, talk on giving, on virtue, on the heavens; he explained the dangers, the vanity and the defilement in sensual pleasures and the blessings in renunciation. When he saw that Yasa's mind was ready, receptive, free from hindrance, eager and trustful, he expounded to him the teaching peculiar to the Buddhas: suffering, its origin, its cessation, and the path to its cessation. Just as a clean cloth with all marks removed would take dye evenly, so too while Yasa sat there the spotless, immaculate vision of the Dharma arose in him: All that is subject to arising is subject to cessation. (Ñānamoli, p. 49)*

The progressive instruction prepares people for the teaching special to the Buddhas by going over those things already familiar to the Buddha's contemporaries and with which the Buddha was in agreement. The talk on giving covered the merit to be gained from giving donations, offerings and sacrifices, especially to support the needy or virtuous. The talk on virtue covered the belief in the fruit of good and bad actions, and the gratitude and respect due to one's parents as well as the dangers of greed, hate, and delusion. The talk on the heavens covered the rewards received in the next world (i.e. the afterlife) for actions done in this one, including rebirth in the heavens.

Nichiren even attributes the five major precepts for laypeople (not to kill, not to steal, not to engage in sexual misconduct, not to lie, not to indulge in intoxicants) and the ten good precepts (a.k.a. the ten courses of wholesome action: not to kill, not to steal, not to engage in sexual misconduct, not to lie, not to engage in malicious speech, not to engage in harsh speech, not to engage in idle chatter, not to give in to covetousness, not to give in to ill will, not to hold wrong views) to the good brahmins. In fact, the ten courses of wholesome conduct can be found in the *Laws of Manu*, a treatise on legal and social codes from the first century C.E. The following passage lists the ten things that people should watch out for and discipline themselves against:

> *The three kinds of mental action are thinking too much about things that belong to others, meditating in one's mind-and-heart about what is undesirable, and adhering to falsehoods. The four kinds of speech (acts) are verbal abuse, lies, slander of all sorts, and unbridled chatter. The three kinds of bodily (action) are traditionally said to be taking things that have not been given, committing violence against the law, and having sex with another man's wife. (Doniger 1991, p. 278)*

There is also much in the Vedic worldview that carries over into Buddhism. The law of karma carries over, though the Buddha refined it and put the emphasis on the intentions behind purposeful action when determining whether a given act is wholesome or unwholesome. The various beings and worlds of the Vedic cosmology carried over and this eventually became the six paths of rebirth in Buddhism (the hell-dwellers, hungry ghosts, animals, fighting demons, humans, and heavenly beings), though the Buddha would propose a way to escape the round of rebirth among these six worlds. The Buddha certainly agreed with the Upanishadic sages that the benefits of the

Vedic sacrifices, worldly wealth and rebirth in the heavens, were temporary at best and that a more transcendental goal was needed.

Not everything carried over, however. The Buddha did not agree with the system of the four classes (what became the basis of the caste system) and frequently argued with brahmins who believed that they were superior simply by virtue of being born as brahmins, whereas the Buddha pointed out that it is only by virtuous deeds that one could claim to be pure and worthy of honor. The Buddha also did away with the more extreme and harmful forms of asceticism like wearing no clothes, fasting to the point of starvation, or subjecting oneself to the five fires (sitting in the middle of four bonfires with the hot summer sun overhead as the fifth fire). Instead he proposed a set of *dhūta* (lit. "shaking off"), twelve relatively mild austerities such as keeping only three robes, or only eating once a day, or sleeping under the open sky. The *dhūta* were a voluntary practice for those monks and nuns who felt the need for such extra discipline to help shake off the habits of self-indulgence. Note that in the *Lotus Sūtra* it says that one who keeps the sūtra even for a moment "should be considered to have already observed the precepts and practiced the *dhūta*." (Murano 2012, p. 198) Finally, although the Buddha did teach the methods of yogic concentration that he had learned from Ārāda Kālāma and Rudraka Rāmaputra, he taught the yogic methods only to provide a means to concentrate the mind in preparation for the distinctive Buddhist practice of "insight" (Skt. *vipaśyanā*; Ch. *kuan*; J. *kan*) meditation and as a form of peaceful abiding for the arhats. By itself, the yogic discipline only leads to the meditative absorptions known as the four *dhyānas* (Ch. *ch'an*; J. *zen*) and other states of deep concentration. These states were only temporary respites as were the heavenly rebirths that corresponded to their cultivation. This has been discussed in regard to the wrong views relating to eternity in the Buddha's *Supreme Net Discourse*.

The most important and far-reaching difference between the Buddha and Brahmanism is that he did not speak of Ātman and Brahman, but instead taught the doctrine of *anātman* or no-self. Instead of teaching people to discern a permanent, fixed, independent selfhood, the Buddha taught how to relinquish attachment to self by pointing out that the self is just a label given to the five ever changing and mutually interdependent aggregates of form, feeling, perception, mental formations, and consciousness. The Buddha pointed out that none of these five aggregates has any permanence. They all function in a constant state of flux. Additionally, they must all function in tandem. Any one of the five aggregates would be unable to exist without the other four. This lack of a stable basis for existence precludes any kind of peace or security that depends on something substantial and abiding. The life of the five aggregates is a dynamic interrelated process, and one who seeks some uninterrupted satisfaction from this process will only find suffering instead. Because the five aggregates are impermanent and lead to suffering, they are said to be without a self. Specifically, this means that one cannot attribute to them the permanently abiding and happy self that was the goal of the religious sages and mystics of the Upanishads. A provisional self can be attributed in an abstract way to the life process, but an actual thing or substance called a self cannot be found within the process. Nor can one meaningfully talk about a self apart from the five aggregates because such a self would be a mere abstraction with no substance or empirical reality to back it up. The conclusion is that the five aggregates of form, feeling, perception, mental formations, and consciousness are characterized by the three marks of impermanence, suffering and non-self. In this way, the Buddha revealed the vanity of the idea of a permanently abiding happy self. Once one ceases to think in terms of such a self, then one is free from all the compulsions, fears and desires that go along with the assumption that there is such a self to find, protect, or appease. One then becomes an arhat, or "worthy one," who will no longer suffer from the cycle of birth and death.

As was the case with Confucianism, East Asian Buddhists viewed Brahmanism as a precursor to Buddhism. They saw it as a teaching set up by the buddhas and the bodhisattvas to serve as a skillful means of entry to the Buddha Dharma. As Nichiren says in *Kaimoku-shō*:

> *After all, the most important thing for non-Buddhist teachings is, like Confucianism, to prepare the way to Buddhism. This is why some non-Buddhists maintain that the Buddha will be born 1,000 years later, while others insist on 100 years later. It is said, therefore, in the Nirvāna Sūtra that what is written in all the non-Buddhist scriptures is nothing but the teaching of the Buddha. Again, it is said in the Lotus Sūtra, chapter eight, "Assurance of Future Buddhahood," that disciples of the Buddha sometimes pretend to be contaminated with the three poisons of greed, anger, and ignorance*

or show the heretic view denying the law of cause and effect as an expedient means to save the people. (Hori 2002, p. 33)

Sources

Bodhi, Bhikkhu, ed., *In the Buddha's Words: An Anthology of Discourses from the Pali Canon*. Boston: Wisdom Publications, 2005.

Bryant, Edwin F., trans. *The Yoga Sūtras of Patanjali*. New York: North Point Press, 2009.

Danielou, Alain. *The Myths and Gods of India*. Rochester: Inner Traditions International, 1991.

Dasgupta, Surendranath. *A History of Indian Philosophy Volume 1*. New Delhi: Motilal Banarsidass, 1997.

Doniger, Wendy, trans. *The Rig Veda*. New York: Penguin Books, 1981.

_____. *The Laws of Manu*. New York: Penguin Books, 1991.

_____. *The Hindus: An Alternative History*. New York: The Penguin Press, 2009.

Dundas, Paul. *The Jains*. New York: Routledge, 2002.

Flood, Gavin. *An Introduction to Hinduism*. New York: Cambridge University Press, 1996.

Gosho Translation Committee, editor-translator. *The Writings of Nichiren Daishonin*. Tokyo: Soka Gakkai, 1999.

Hartranft, Chip, trans. *The Yoga-Sūtra of Patanjali*. Boston: Shambhala, 2003.

Hori, Kyōtsū, comp. *Writings of Nichiren Shonin: Doctrine Volume 2*. Tokyo: Nichiren Shu Overseas Propagation Promotion Association, 2002.

Le Mee, Jean Marie Alexandre, trans., *Hymns from the Rig Veda*. New York: Alfred A. Knopf, Inc., 1975.

Murano, Senchū, trans. *The Lotus Sūtra*. Hayward: Nichiren Buddhist International Center, 1012.

_____, trans. *Kaimokushō or Liberation from Blindness*. Berkeley: Numata Center for Buddhist Translation and Research, 2000.

Ñānamoli, Bhikkhu, trans. *The Life of the Buddha*. Seattle: Buddhist Publication Society Pariyatti Editions, 2001.

Olivelle, Patrick, trans. *Upanishads*. Oxford: Oxford University Press, 1996.

Prabhavananda, Swami. *The Spiritual Heritage of India: A Clear Summary of Indian Philosophy and Religion*. Hollywood: Vedanta Press, 1979.

Sadataka, Akira. *Buddhist Cosmology: Philosophy and Origins*. Tokyo: Kosei Publishing Co., 2004.

Sargeant, Winthrop. *The Bhagavad Gita*. New York: State University of New York Press, 1994.

Chapter 10 – Western Monotheism and other Problematic Views

Long Discourses of the Buddha, pp. 67-90, 187-195
Middle Length Discourses of the Buddha, pp. 506-519, 618-628
Numerical Discourses of the Buddha, pp. 61-64, 64-67

Nichiren knew nothing about Judaism, Christianity, or Islam. Knowledge of these religions had not reached Japan in Nichiren's time. If he had known about them, would he have included them among Brahmanism, Confucianism, and Buddhism as religions that all people should study? And how would he have evaluated them in comparison with the other religions. We can only speculate, but I think we can make an educated guess based on the criteria Nichiren has already used to evaluate the non-Buddhist religions.

Nichiren may indeed have included the three major forms of Western monotheism if he had known about them, as he seems to have wanted to account for all the major religions in the world. I also believe that he would have evaluated them using the same method of comparison in terms of the scope of time scales. To review: just as the Buddha criticized the sixty-two (or ninety-five) views of his contemporaries who drew dogmatic conclusions about the nature of life based on limited experiences either in this life or even from past-life recall, Nichiren evaluated Confucianism, Taoism, Brahmanism, Buddhism, and other philosophies and religions based on how limited or vast a scope of time their teachings accounted for. Confucianism fares the worst for not even attempting to account for life before birth or after death but limiting itself to teaching morality only in terms of the present lifetime. Brahmanism fares better for it does teach that there is a cycle of rebirth that unfolds according to the law of karma, and thus accounts for a much greater scope of time. In fact, Brahman cosmology teaches that there are whole cycles wherein world systems are created, maintained, and then destroyed over the course of eons and within those cycles beings are reborn continually until they can attain one of the heavenly realms. The Upanishads taught that those who realized the Ātman or True Self would be forever liberated from these cycles, but the Buddhist sūtras do not mention the Upanishads nor does Nichiren.

From the Buddhist point of view, however, in the course of time even those reborn in the heavens will exhaust their merit and they will have to be reborn elsewhere depending on what causes are able to come into fruition. From the Buddhist perspective even the vast amounts of time spent in a hell-realm or a heavenly-realm is still a finite period of time because all caused and conditioned states will eventually come to an end. Such is the universal law of the impermanence of all conditioned phenomena.

Coming back to Western monotheism, I think it would be fair to say that the mainstream view held by Jews, Christians, and Muslims is that there is only this one lifetime on earth to be followed by some form of last judgment by God, wherein those who have obeyed God's laws or accepted God's offer of salvation will live an eternal life in heaven (and/or a renewed earth), while those who are condemned will be cast into some form of hell or oblivion. Those who are saved will live as resurrected beings in a kind of glorified or spiritualized body. This is, of course, an oversimplification. Many Jews, Christians, and Muslims have different interpretations of what things like the "last judgment" or "resurrection" or "heaven and hell" might really mean. Judaism, in particular, does not make any dogmatic claims about the afterlife, and the doctrine of the resurrection came late in its development and has never been entirely uncontested or universally believed. There are also esoteric strains of each of these three traditions that do subscribe to some form of reincarnation. The important thing is that the mainstream view posits only one lifetime to be followed by an eternal afterlife of some sort. Going by Nichiren's criteria, I think he would perhaps have placed Western monotheism ahead of the agnostic Chinese schools of thought because it at least provides for some kind of afterlife wherein the causes one makes in this life will come to fruition for good or for ill. On the other hand, I think he would not have put Western monotheism on the level of Brahmanism, as the latter accounts for many lifetimes and its understanding of the unfolding of cause and effect over many lifetimes is more developed. From a Brahmanist point of view, one might live in heaven or hell for thousands or millions of years, but it is not actually an eternity though mistaken as such by those who don't see larger time scale. I stress, again, that this is my guess based on how Nichiren evaluated the other non-Buddhist traditions.

Aside from how small or how great a period of time is accounted for, there is the issue of monotheism itself. Setting aside the historical development of Judaism, or the Trinity of Christianity, the core teaching of Judaism,

Christianity, and Islam as they now stand is that there is only one God. There are no other gods, though there are angels that serve God and perhaps other spiritual beings who are not allied with God and may even be at odds with God but who are in no way on par with God. This one God is said to be the transcendent creator of all things. God brought forth the entire universe and all that lives from out of nothing. God cannot be compared to anything created and so cannot and must not be depicted. At the same time, however, these traditions teach that humankind was made in God's likeness and image (in a spiritual and not a physical sense), and that God is also immanent and present in a deep and unfathomable way always and everywhere. God is also omniscient, omnipotent, and all loving. Through the revelation of angels, prophets, and inspired scripture (and in the case of Christianity his "Son," Jesus Christ) God makes it known that he wishes humankind to live a life of justice and compassion for one another, but he allows humankind free will so that each person may choose to obey or disobey God. Because God knows that humankind will fail again and again, God offers forgiveness, grace, and ultimately salvation (though how salvation is attained differs in each tradition).

The God of monotheism is very different from the amorphous and impersonal Heaven of Confucianism, though similar in that both are the source of all worldly created things and of the ethical imperatives that should be followed in order to lead a good life. The God of Western monotheism is also different from the Brahmā of Brahmanism, in that Brahmā did not create the world out of nothing and in fact is the first being of many beings. As Hinduism developed out of Brahmanism, Brahmā became a kind of sub-creator, whose actions are ultimately inspired and guided by Vishnu or Śiva or the Goddess (depending on the sectarian tradition telling the story). Brahmā is also definitely male, not above being depicted in anthropomorphic form, and often shown to be far from omnipotent or omniscient. The sectarian traditions of Hinduism do often present Vishnu, or Śiva, or the Goddess in monotheistic terms, but even they are unlike the God of Western monotheism in that they are depicted anthropomorphically, and though they are qualitatively different than the other gods (in terms of being omnipotent, omniscient, and not only liberated from birth and death but the source of the cycle of birth and death and also the source of liberation from it) they still take their place among the other gods in the stories and epics. The God of Western monotheism may perhaps be more like the supreme reality called Brahman, and yet God is always presented in the Western traditions as personal and in a relationship with creation and particularly humankind and never as an impersonal monistic principle, which is how Brahman is presented in non-dualistic forms of Vedanta. The God of Western monotheism may justifiably be considered a unique conception.

Nichiren and his contemporaries did not have the chance to ponder the uniqueness of Western monotheism. Most of us, however, are more familiar with it than we are with the Confucian Heaven, the Brahmā of the Vedas, the Brahman of the Upanishads, or Krishna of the Puranas. We might wonder if Buddhism itself has anything to say about monotheism or religion based upon revelation and salvation by a transcendent God. Actually, throughout the Pāli canon, the Buddha did teach a lot of things that are relevant to the claims of Western monotheism. To begin with, the three Western monotheistic traditions all base themselves upon some form of revelation wherein God speaks to humanity. The Buddha, however, saw all teachings based on revelation, tradition, hearsay, or any other system of authority not based on direct experience as doubtful. The Buddha's teachings about this were famously expressed in the following exchange between himself and the Kalama people of the town of Kesaputta:

> "There are, Lord, some ascetics and brahmins who come to Kesaputta. They explain and elucidate their own doctrines, but disparage, debunk, revile and vilify the doctrines of others. But then some other ascetics and brahmins come to Kesaputta, and they too explain and elucidate their own doctrines, but disparage, debunk, revile and vilify the doctrines of others. For us, Lord, there is perplexity and doubt as to which of these good ascetics speak truth and which speak falsehood?"

> "It is fitting for you to be perplexed, O Kalamas, it is fitting for you to be in doubt. Doubt has arisen in you about a perplexing matter. Come, Kalamas. Do not go by oral tradition, by lineage of teaching, by hearsay, by a collection of scriptures, by logical reasoning, by inferential reasoning, by a reflection on reasons, by the acceptance of a view after pondering it, by the seeming competence of a speaker, or because you think: 'The ascetic is our teacher.' But when you know for

> *yourselves, 'These things are unwholesome, these*
> *things are blamable; these things are censured by the*
> *wise; these things if undertaken and practiced lead to*
> *harm and suffering', then you should abandon them."*
> *(Nyanaponika, p. 65)*

As for whether there is or can be such an omnipotent, omniscient, omnipresent, benevolent god of creation and salvation, the Buddha neither confirms nor denies such a Supreme Being. He does deflate the idea of Brahmā as being this kind of Supreme Being in the *Supreme Net Discourse* as discussed previously. In that discourse, the Buddha portrays Brahmā as making the very claims for himself that Western monotheism makes for God, and yet his claims are based on Brahmā not understanding the bigger picture that he is a part of.

> *"There are, monks, some ascetics and Brahmins who*
> *are partly Eternalists and partly Non-Eternalists, who*
> *proclaim the partial eternity and the partial non-*
> *eternity of the self and the world in four ways. On what*
> *grounds?*
>
> *"There comes a time, monks, sooner or later after a*
> *long period when this world contracts. At the time of*
> *contraction, beings are mostly born in the Abhassara*
> *Brahmā world. And there they dwell, mind-made,*
> *feeding on delight, self-luminous, moving through the*
> *air, glorious – and they stay like that for a very long*
> *time.*
>
> *"But the time comes, sooner or later after a long period,*
> *when this world begins to expand. In this expanding*
> *world an empty palace of Brahmā appears. And then*
> *one being, from exhaustion of his lifespan or of his*
> *merits, falls from the Abhassara world and arises in the*
> *empty Brahmā-palace. And there he dwells, mind-*
> *made, feeding on delight, self-luminous, moving*
> *through the air, glorious – and he stays like that for a*
> *very long time.*

"Then in this being who has been alone for so long there arises unrest, discontent and worry, and he thinks: "Oh, if only some other beings would come here!" And other beings, from exhaustion of their lifespan or of their merits, fall from the Abhassara world and arise in the Brahmā-palace as companions for this being. And there they dwell, mind-made, ... and they stay like that for a very long time.

"And then, monks, that being who first arose there thinks: 'I am Brahmā, the Great Brahmā, the Conqueror, the Unconquered, the All-Seeing, the All-Powerful, the Lord, the Maker and Creator, Ruler, Appointer and Orderer, Father of All That Have Been and Shall Be. These beings were created by me. How so? Because I first had this thought: 'Oh, if only some other beings would come here!' That was my wish, and then these beings came into existence!' But those beings who arose subsequently think: 'This, friends, is Brahmā, Great Brahmā, the Conqueror, the Unconquered, the All-Seeing, the All-Powerful, the Lord, the Maker and Creator, Ruler, Appointer and Orderer, Father of All That Have Been and Shall Be. How so? We have seen that he was here first, and that we arose after him.'

"And this being that arose first is longer lived, more beautiful and more powerful than they are. And it may happen that some being falls from that realm and arises in this world. Having arisen in this world, he goes forth from the household life into homelessness. Having gone forth, he by means of effort, exertion, application, earnestness and right attention attains to such a degree of mental concentration that he thereby recalls his last existence, but recalls none before that. And he thinks: 'That Brahmā, ... he made us, and he is permanent, stable, eternal, not subject to change, the same for ever and ever. But we who were created by that Brahmā, we are impermanent, unstable, short-lived, fated to fall away, and we have come to this world.' This is the first

case whereby some ascetics and Brahmins are partly
Eternalists and partly Non-Eternalists." (Walshe, pp. 75
– 77)

This story was probably not told to make fun of Brahmā so much as to make fun of the claims the brahmins were making for Brahmā. The point here is that if Brahmā or God is conceived as a being among beings, then he will be subject to the same law of causation as all other beings. Even as the preeminent or first being among beings, God is still a part of the process and cannot be apart from it. All of God's transcendent qualities, then, are simply ironic. They are simply false assumptions based upon a limited point of view. I have already shown, however, that the God of Western monotheism is not like Brahmā but an attempt at a much more sublime conception. Still, even in the case of those subtler and more sophisticated concepts, one is still left with a personal entity distinguishable in some manner from ordinary phenomena. Once again, one finds that God is presented as a being that stands outside creation and can enter into a relationship with created beings. Whatever the reality or unreality of God, the conception of such a God falls into the trap of appearing to be a being among beings, even if it is a Supreme Being who can make transcendent claims. Whether such a transcendent (and immanent) Supreme Being actually exists comes down to a matter of philosophical speculation and/or faith.

In any case, the Buddha was sharply critical of those who presumed to teach the way to union with God based on revelations or traditions. In the *Tevijja Sutta* the Buddha meets two young brahmins who are confused by conflicting opinions in regard to the way to achieve union with Brahmā. To resolve their doubts the brahmin Vāsettha asks the Buddha his opinion in regard to the conflicting truth claims. The Buddha, however, gets Vāsettha to admit that none of the supposed authorities or founders of the various traditions had any real knowledge of what they were talking about. The Buddha even compares them to the blind leading the blind.

> *'So, Vāsettha, not one of these Brahmins learned in the*
> *Three Vedas has seen Brahmā face to face, nor has one*
> *of their teachers, or teacher's teachers, nor even the*
> *ancestor seven generations back of one of their*
> *teachers. Nor could any of the early sages say: 'We*
> *know and see when, how and where Brahmā appears.'*

*So what these Brahmins learned in the Three Vedas are
saying is: 'We teach this path to union with Brahmā
that we do not know or see, this is the only straight
path, this is the direct path, the path of salvation that
leads one who follows it to union with Brahmā.' What
do you think, Vāsettha? Such being the case, does not
what these Brahmins declare turn out to be ill-
founded?" "Yes indeed, Reverend Gautama."*

*"Well, Vāsettha, when these Brahmins learned in the
Three Vedas teach a path that they do not know or see,
saying: 'This is the only straight path...', this cannot
possibly be right. Just as a file of blind men go on,
clinging to each other, and the first one sees nothing,
the middle one sees nothing, and the last one sees
nothing – so it is with the talk of the Brahmins learned
in the Three Vedas; the first one sees nothing, the
middle one sees nothing, the last one sees nothing. The
talk of these Brahmins learned in the Three Vedas turns
out to be laughable, mere words, empty and vain."*
(Ibid, pp. 188-189)

Now it could be objected that in Western monotheism the founders did claim
to have had personal contact with God. In the end, it must be admitted that
believing these claims are a matter of faith. In the final analysis, the Buddha
would say that the claims of Judaism. Christianity, and Islam are all based on
hearsay that one must either accept or reject on faith.

The Buddha then compares the learned brahmins to those who fall in love
with a woman they have never seen, or to those who build a stairway for a
palace that has not been built or to those who try to cross a river by calling out
to the other bank in the hope that it will come over to them. With these
similes, the Buddha points out to the young brahmins the foolishness of trying
to achieve union with a God that no one has ever known or seen for
themselves, or of trying to teach methods to attain something whose
existence is only speculation or of trying to achieve transcendence through
the mere chanting of mantras and supplications without trying to transform
themselves so as to be worthy of the goal.

The Buddha does teach the young brahmins the value of renunciation, the purification of the mind from ill-will and hatred, and the practice of the four divine abodes of loving-kindness, compassion, sympathetic joy, and equanimity. In this way, he tells them, they may be united with Brahmā at death by embodying the qualities of Brahmā while living and thus becoming capable of communion with Brahmā. In this way, the Buddha taught the brahmins what they wanted to know as far as communion with Brahmā or God. What is interesting about this is that while the Buddha criticized their naïve faith and assumptions, he did not try to dissuade them from belief in God and in fact taught them a better way to achieve their goals in terms that they would understand.

The Buddha was not concerned with affirming or denying any kind of God. What the Buddha constantly taught was for the purpose of helping people understand suffering, cut off the causes of suffering, realize the cessation of suffering, and follow the path to the cessation of suffering. Anything within the six worlds of transmigration, including the heavenly realms where gods of varying degrees of sublimity reside, was still within the purview of suffering and its causes. While union with God is looked upon as a worthy and attainable goal, it is not the final goal, for it is still involved in the impermanent flow of causes and conditions. Only the unconditioned peace of nirvāṇa can provide true peace according to the Buddha.

When the Buddha did criticize other teachings, it was almost always because those teachings negated or undermined the law of karma. The Buddha rejects such teachings because he saw that to dismiss the law of karma would in turn undermine morality and spiritual cultivation. In the following discourse the Buddha criticizes three beliefs, including a particular belief about God, that lead to what he calls "the doctrine of inaction", by which he means the doctrine that our present actions, the karmic causes we make, do not have any bearing on the development of our lives either now or in any future lifetime.

> *"There are, O monks, three sectarian tenets which, if they are fully examined, investigated and discussed, will end in a doctrine of inaction, even if adopted because of tradition. What are these three tenets?*

126

"There are, monks, some ascetics and brahmins who teach and hold this view: 'Whatever a person experiences, be it pleasure, pain or a neutral feeling, all that is caused by past action.' There are others who teach and hold this view: 'Whatever a person experiences ... all that is caused by God's creation.' And there are still other ascetics and brahmins who teach and hold this view: 'Whatever a person experiences ... is uncaused and unconditioned.'

"Now, monks, I approached those ascetics and brahmins (holding the first view) and said to them: 'Is it true, as they say, that you venerable ones teach and hold the view that whatever a person experiences ... all that is caused by past action?' When they affirmed it, I said to them: 'If that is so, venerable sirs, then it is due to past action (done in a former life) that people kill, steal, and engage in sexual misconduct; that they speak falsehood, utter malicious words, speak harshly and indulge in idle talk; that they are covetous and malevolent and hold false views. But those who have recourse to past action as the decisive factor will lack the impulse and effort for doing this or not doing that. Since they have no real valid ground for asserting this or that ought to be done or ought not to be done, the term "ascetics" does not rightly apply to them, living without mindfulness and self-control.'

"This monks, is my first justified rebuke to those ascetics and brahmins who teach and hold such a view.

"Again, monks, I approached those ascetics and brahmins (holding the second view) and said to them: 'Is it true, as they say, that you venerable ones teach and hold the view that whatever a person experiences ... all that is caused by God's creation?' When they affirmed it, I said to them: 'If that is so, venerable sirs, then it is due to God's creation that people kill ... and hold false views. But those who have recourse to God's creation as the decisive factor will lack the impulse and

effort for doing this or not doing that. Since they have no real valid ground for asserting this or that ought to be done or ought not to be done, the term "ascetics" does not rightly apply to them, living without mindfulness and self-control.'

"This monks, is my second justified rebuke to those ascetics and brahmins who teach and hold such a view.

"Again, monks, I approached those ascetics and brahmins (holding the third view) and said to them: 'Is it true, as they say, that you venerable ones teach and hold the view that whatever a person experiences ... all that is uncaused and unconditioned?' When they affirmed it, I said to them: 'If that is so, venerable sirs, then it is without causes and conditions that people kill ... and hold false views. But those who have recourse to an uncaused and unconditioned (order of events) as the decisive factor will lack the impulse and effort for doing this or not doing that. Since they have no real valid ground for asserting this or that ought to be done or ought not to be done, the term "ascetics" does not rightly apply to them, living without mindfulness and self-control.'

"This monks, is my third justified rebuke to those ascetics and brahmins who teach and hold such a view.

"These monks, are the three sectarian tenets which, if fully examined, investigated, and discussed, will end in a doctrine of inaction, even if adopted because of tradition." (Nyanaponika, pp. 61-63)

The first tenet is a view of karma that is so extreme it becomes a form of determinism, wherein people only have to blame the past for anything they do or fail to do in the present and there is no real freedom to choose one's course of action in the present. The second tenet is a form of predestination, wherein people can blame God for anything they do or fail to do. The last tenet is a form of nihilism that denies causality altogether. The Buddha points out that all of these beliefs have in common the undermining of personal responsibility for one's actions and the consequences of those actions. If everything is already determined by the past, or by God, or there is no causal efficacy, then there is no real reason to try to refrain from unwholesome actions or cultivate wholesome actions. Any efforts to attain liberation would be futile because we would be powerless to change anything – even ourselves.

In the *Apannaka Sutta* of the *Majjhima Nikaya* (Nanamoli & Bodhi, pp. 506-519), the Buddha similarly rejects those doctrines that deny what the Buddha called "mundane right view" (because it had to do with the workings of karma and rebirth) consisting of the affirmation of the efficacy of generosity, the fruition of good and bad actions, the reality of this life and the afterlife, respect for parents, the spontaneous rebirth of beings in the hells and heavens, and that there are those who have had direct knowledge of causality and the afterlife. He does so using an argument similar to what would later be called "Pascal's Wager" concerning the existence of God, except in this case it is the law karma that is at issue. The Buddha argued that one who denies the law of karma will fall into the lower realms, or even hell, if they are wrong; but even if they are right they will gain nothing and be censured by the wise. However, if someone affirms the law of karma and they are right then they will attain rebirth in the higher realms or even heaven; but even if they are wrong, they will have lost nothing and will be praised by the wise.

In the *Sandaka Sutta* of the *Majjhima Nikaya*, Ānanda conveys the Buddha's teachings regarding four ways that negate the holy life to the wanderer Sandaka. The first way is the nihilistic view that negates mundane right view on the basis of materialism:

> *"Giving is a doctrine of fools. When anyone asserts the doctrine that there is [giving and the like], it is empty, false prattle. Fools and the wise are alike cut off and annihilated with the dissolution of the body; after death they do not exist." (Ibid, pp. 619-620)*

The second way is the denial that actions have any necessary consequences:

"If, with a razor-rimmed wheel, one were to make living beings on this earth into one mass of flesh, into one heap of flesh, because of this there would be no evil and no outcome of evil. If one were to go along the south bank of the Ganges killing and slaughtering, mutilating and making other mutilate, torturing and making others inflict torture, because of this there would be no evil and no outcome of evil. If one were to go along the north bank of the Ganges giving gifts and making others give gifts, making offerings and making others make offerings, because of this there would be no merit and no outcome of merit. By giving, by taming, oneself, by restraint, by speaking truth, there is no merit and no outcome of merit." (Ibid, pp. 620-621)

The third way is the doctrine that denies any kind of causal power in beings:

"There is no cause or condition for the defilement of beings; beings are defiled without cause or condition. There is no cause or condition for the purification of beings; beings are purified without cause or condition. There is no power, no energy, no manly strength, no manly endurance. All beings, all living things, all creatures, all souls are without mastery, power, and energy; molded by destiny, circumstance, and nature, they experience pleasure and pain in the six classes."
(Ibid, p. 621)

The fourth way is a fatalistic doctrine that destiny must run its course and there is nothing we can do to change it:

"There is none of this 'By this virtue or observance or asceticism or holy life I shall make unripened action ripen or annihilate ripened action as it comes.' Pleasure and pain are meted out. The round of rebirths is limited; there is no shortening or extending it, no increasing or

130

decreasing it. Just as a ball of string when thrown goes
as far as the string unwinds, so too, by running and
wandering through the round of rebirths, fools and the
wise both will make an end of suffering." (Ibid, pp. 622-
623)

In each of these four ways the holy life is negated because according to these views there is no benefit to be gained by cultivating self-restraint or virtuous qualities. In fact, to do so would be to miss out on worldly pleasures and advantages for no good reason. Either death will bring an end to everything, or one's causes will not follow one into whatever next life there might be, or things happen for no reason, or destiny will determine one's fate regardless of one's actions. Each of these views undermines any motivation people might have for following the holy life or even for the mere cultivation of worldly virtue.

Ānanda goes on to explain that there are also four kinds of holy life without consolation that have been taught by the Buddha. These kinds of holy life are based on teachings that have a false or unreliable basis. The first is based on claims of omniscience on the part of a teacher even though those making such claims still had to ask questions about everyday things and still ran into misfortune. The "omniscient" teachers would explain this away by saying they were simply following necessity. The second is based on traditional teachings found either in oral traditions, legends, or scriptures. However, these traditions may or may not be passed down correctly, and even if handed down correctly they may have no factual basis in the first place. The third is based on reasoning and inquiry, but this too is open to criticism on the grounds that even what is well reasoned may not match actual facts. The fourth is based on what the Buddha calls "eel-wriggling" and basically amounts to radical skepticism or an agnostic noncommittal attitude towards any truth claims. None of these four ways can lead to any reliable knowledge about the law of karma, much less to the consolation of liberation from suffering.

After hearing about the Buddha's critique of the four ways that negate the holy life and the four kinds of holy life without consolation from Ānanda, Sandaka asks, "But Master Ānanda, what does that teacher assert, what does he declare, wherein a wise man certainly would live the holy life, and while

131

living it would attain the true way, the Dharma that is wholesome?" (Ibid, p. 625) Ānanda responds by describing the appearance of the Buddha, and the path taken up by one who comes to have faith in the Buddha, Dharma, and Sangha and thereby enters into Buddhist practice. This culminates in the practice of meditation that leads to the three types of true knowledge the Buddha realized for himself under the Bodhi Tree: the recollection of past lives, the divine eye that perceives the passing away and rebirth of other beings, and the knowledge of the destruction of the taints. Unlike those who follow the four ways that negate the holy life or the four kinds of holy life without consolation, the disciple who follows the Buddha's teaching will attain direct knowledge of the law of karma and the cycle of rebirth and what lies beyond karmic entanglement and rebirth, and will be able to live in accord with that direct knowledge and realize for themselves freedom from suffering. In this way, Ānanda criticizes the shortcomings of those teachings which negate karma and rebirth or that are incapable of providing reliable direct knowledge of such things and he goes on to point out the correct way to realize the law of karma and the cycle of rebirth and the way to be liberated from rebirth through Buddhist practice.

Now that we have reviewed the different ways that Buddhism evaluates and critiques non-Buddhist teachings and how Nichiren himself ranked them in order of increasing profundity, we are ready to see how Nichiren evaluates and ranks different teachings and traditions of Buddhism.

Sources

Nanamoli, Bhikkhu and Bodhi, Bhikkhu, trans. *The Middle Length Discourses of the Buddha: A New Translation of the Majjhima Nikaya*. Botson: Wisdom Publications, 1995.

Nyanaponika, Thera and Bodhi, Bhikkhu trans. & ed., *Numerical Discourses of the Buddha: An Anthology of Suttas from the Anguttara Nikaya*. Walnut Creek: AltaMira Press, 1999.

Walshe, Maurice, trans. *The Long Discourses of the Buddha: A Translation of the Digha Nikaya.* Boston: Wisdom Publications, 1995.

Chapter 11 – The Life and Teachings of Shakyamuni Buddha

Writings of Nichiren Shōnin Doctrine 2, pp. 33-34, 45-46, 75
Kaimoku-shō or Liberation from Blindness, pp. 12-13, 29, 71
The Writings of Nichiren Daishōnin I, pp. 223, 233, 257

After his review of Chinese and Indian religions and philosophies, Nichiren turns to Śākyamuni Buddha and praises him as far greater than any who had come before. Those who have grown up in a Buddhist culture would be familiar with the terms that Nichiren uses to praise the Buddha, but Nichiren also relies upon a distinct interpretation of the life and significance of the Buddha and his accomplishments that comes from the Tiantai school of Buddhism that Nichiren was ordained and trained in from an early age. This Tiantai view of the Buddha is itself inspired by the *Lotus Sūtra.* Because Nichiren relies upon this particular understanding of the Buddha throughout the rest of *Kaimoku-shō,* this would be a good place to go over the basics of the Buddha's life and teachings as Nichiren understood them.

Some scholars, notably Hajime Nakamura (1912-1999), estimate that the historical Siddhārtha Gautama, the young man who would become Śākyamuni Buddha, was born in the year 463 BCE. According to the accounts in the Pāli canon he left home at the age of twenty-nine to practice yoga and asceticism for six years and then attained buddhahood under the Bodhi Tree at the age of thirty-five. He passed away at the age of eighty in the year 383 BCE. Some scholars might push these dates back as far as a century. Nichiren and his contemporaries, however, going by a text called the *Record of Wonders in the Book of Zhou,* believed that the Buddha was born on the eighth day of the fourth month of 1029 BCE and died on the fifteenth day of the second month of 949 BCE. Furthermore, Nichiren and his East Asian contemporaries accepted the timeline of the Buddha's life taken from the *Great Perfection of Wisdom Treatise* attributed to Nāgārjuna (but possibly written by its ostensible translator Kumārajīva). In that treatise, Siddhārtha left home at the age of nineteen, spent twelve years practicing asceticism in the Himalayas (counting the year that he was nineteen) and attained awakening under the Bodhi Tree at the age of thirty. He then spent the next fifty years teaching, culminating in the expounding of the *Lotus Sūtra*. At the age of eighty he passed away (or attained final nirvāṇa).

According to the basic story, which is to say the pre-*Lotus Sūtra* story, the Buddha's path to awakening actually began countless lifetimes before his birth as Siddhārtha Gautama. Up to a certain point, the sentient being that would someday become Śākyamuni Buddha was a wanderer, like us, among the six worlds of rebirth (the hell-dwellers, hungry ghosts, animals, fighting demons, humans, and heavenly beings). In order to escape the round of rebirth, there were three options that could be taken. One way was to encounter a buddha or "awakened one" and become a *śrāvaka* (lit. voice-hearer) or disciple of that buddha, follow the Buddha Dharma, and extinguish all the defilements that lead to rebirth. A disciple of a buddha who attained liberation in this way would be called an arhat (lit. worthy one). Another way would be to contemplate causes and conditions directly and attain awakening, becoming a *pratyekabuddha* (lit. private-buddha). A pratyekabuddha, like an arhat, is also liberated from the cycle of rebirth. Together, these first two options would become known as the "two vehicles" that lead to liberation from rebirth. The third option was to make the determination to take up the path of a bodhisattva and someday attain buddhahood, thereby liberating not only oneself but also providing the means whereby others could attain liberation.

Three innumerable eons ago, the bodhisattva who would become Śākyamuni Buddha aroused the "awakening mind" (S. *bodhicitta*) that aspires to attain spiritual awakening for the sake of oneself and others. From that point on, for lifetime after lifetime, he sought wisdom and accumulated merit through countless deeds of compassionate self-sacrifice. One innumerable eon ago, the bodhisattva encountered a Buddha named Burning Light (S. Dīpaṃkara). In the presence of Burning Light Buddha the bodhisattva made his vow to attain buddhahood and Burning Light Buddha conferred upon him the prediction that he would someday attain perfect complete awakening and be known as Śākyamuni Buddha.

Assured of attaining buddhahood, the bodhisattva continued to strive to overcome what in Tiantai Buddhism are called the three categories of delusions. First, he overcame the delusions of views and attitudes that bind

135

sentient beings to the cycle of birth and death (S. *saṃsāra*) amid the six worlds. These deluded views and attitudes consist of the ten following defilements:

1. greed
2. hatred
3. delusion
4. pride
5. doubt (the kind that hinders or undermines practice)
6. view that there is a real personality (an independent, fixed self)
7. extreme views of eternalism or annihilationism
8. wrong views that deny causality
9. seizing upon views
10. seizing upon rules and rituals

Having overcome these defilements, the bodhisattva was able to overcome what the Tiantai school calls "transmigration with differences and limitations", in other words he was free of compulsory rebirth within the six worlds wherein sentient beings are differentiated and limited by the effects of their positive and negative karma. By overcoming deluded views and attitudes the bodhisattva was able to see that the "self" is empty of any fixed, independent substance. Knowing for himself the emptiness of the self and all conditioned phenomena, the bodhisattva was able to relinquish all those selfish and deluded habits of mind and heart that bind sentient beings to the ups and downs of the transient, disappointing, and painful conditions of life within the six worlds.

The bodhisattva then overcame the delusions innumerable as grains of sand. Though no longer bound to the six worlds, the bodhisattva still appeared within them in accordance with his vows to save all sentient beings and not abandon them until he had attained buddhahood. He thereby provided teachings that would enable others to liberate themselves from suffering. Delusions innumerable as grains of sand refer to those that obscure a bodhisattva's ability to deal appropriately with any and every particular situation that may arise. Though the emptiness of self and phenomena has been realized, phenomena still exist in terms of the interdependent flow of causes and conditions. The bodhisattva had to learn to accurately assess and minister to these causes and conditions: knowing when to give wealth, or when to withhold it, knowing when the time is ripe to give instruction in renunciation, knowing what method of meditation to teach particular people in accordance with their abilities and interests, meeting every situation with courage, loving-kindness, and a selfless spirit of compassion. By overcoming delusions innumerable as grains of sand the bodhisattva was able to remain engaged with the world in a positive way for the sake of all sentient beings.

The final delusion overcome by the bodhisattva was fundamental ignorance. Fundamental ignorance obscures the true reality that is the Middle Way that encompasses both the empty nature of phenomena and its contingent provisional existence. The Middle Way is ungraspable and inconceivable, yet it is also the dynamic and spontaneous source of all virtuous qualities. As the bodhisattva progressed, he saw that the empty and provisional nature of phenomena were not two separate things but two aspects of the true reality that is the Middle Way. Emptiness is not a thing but the true nature of phenomena that is provisionally existent in accord with causes and conditions. Provisional existence is thoroughly empty of any fixed, independent substance. The Middle Way is the total mutual implication of emptiness and provisional existence as the liberating and dynamic true nature of reality. By overcoming fundamental ignorance the bodhisattva attained buddhahood and transcended even the "transmigration with change and advance" that characterizes the rebirths taken by the bodhisattvas and even the arhats and pratyekabuddhas (who believe themselves to be exempt from rebirth but in fact find themselves taking up the way of the bodhisattva according to the One Vehicle teaching of the *Lotus Sūtra*). What this means, in terms of the basic understanding of Buddhism, is that upon attaining perfect and complete awakening the Buddha no longer needed to take rebirth to accumulate merit and wisdom because he had attained the goal that he started out for three innumerable eons before.

Nichiren sometimes alludes to the eight phases of Śākyamuni Buddha's life. This is a way of summing up the story of the Buddha in the following eight events:

1. Descent from the Tushita Heaven – Before his last earthly rebirth, the future Buddha lived in the Heaven of Contentment (Skt. Tuṣita) awaiting the right time, place and family for his final rebirth.

137

2. Entering Queen Māyā's womb – When the right conditions arose Queen Māyā of Kapilavastu had a most singular dream. She dreamed that a six tusked white elephant holding a white lotus flower in its trunk circled around her three times and then entered into her womb. At that moment Queen Māyā conceived the bodhisattva.

3. Emerging from Queen Māyā's womb – Queen Māyā gave birth to him painlessly while standing up and holding onto a sal tree branch while visiting the Lumbinī Garden near Kapilavastu. The legend states that immediately upon entering the world, the young Prince Siddhārtha took seven steps and made the following statement: "I am born for awakening for the good of the world; this is my last birth in the world of phenomena." (*Asvaghosa's Buddhacarita*, part II, p. 4)

4. Leaving home – After witnessing an old man, a sick man, a funeral procession, and a religious mendicant, Prince Siddhārtha left his family (his father King Śuddhodana, his wife Yaśodharā, and his son Rahula) and became an forest ascetic.

5. Overcoming Māra – After turning away from asceticism, the bodhisattva sat beneath the Bodhi Tree at Bodhgaya and overcame temptations and distractions of the demon Māra.

6. Attaining the Way – As the morning star (Venus?) rose in the morning sky, the bodhisattva attained buddhahood and henceforth became known as Śākyamuni Buddha.

7. Turning the Wheel of the Dharma – Starting at the Deer Park near the city of Vārānasī, the Buddha began to teach the Dharma and continued to do so for fifty years.

8. Entering final nirvāṇa – At the age of eighty, the Buddha passed away beneath the twin sal trees near the city of Kuśinagara.

9.

The Tiantai school divided the Buddha's fifty years of teaching into five periods of varying degrees of profundity. The first period occurred during the first few weeks that Śākyamuni Buddha sat beneath the Bodhi Tree. During that time, he taught the *Flower Garland Sūtra*, although Nichiren points out later in *Kaimoku-shō* that it would be more accurate to say that it was the bodhisattvas who were present that actually did the teaching. Starting with the discourse on the Four Noble Truths taught at the Deer Park to the five ascetics, Śākyamuni Buddha spent twelve years teaching the pre-Mahāyāna (aka Hīnayāna) teachings found in the Āgama sūtras. After that he spent eight years teaching the preliminary Mahāyāna teachings of the Vaipulya or

Expanded sūtras. He taught the Perfection of Wisdom sūtras during the twenty-two years that followed that. For the last eight years of his life, the Buddha taught the *Lotus Sūtra*. On the very last day and night of his life the Buddha taught the *Mahāyāna Mahāparinirvāna Sūtra*. It should be noted that even Nichiren points out in other writings that these time spans are uncertain. In any case, modern textual scholarship would dismiss all of this as arbitrary, especially since the Mahāyāna sūtras are now seen as compositions arising after the Buddha's lifetime. Nevertheless, Mahāyāna Buddhism accepts these sūtras as embodying the word of the Buddha in the sense that they convey the full depths of the Buddha's insight and compassion. The Tiantai system of classifying the sūtras into five periods of teaching can still be seen as a useful way of approaching the sūtras in terms of how they build upon one another and lead those who put them into practice into deeper and subtler insights.

Nichiren states that any of the teachings of the Buddha's fifty years of teaching are a great vehicle of salvation compared to the non-Buddhist teachings. This is because the other teachings either do not teach about karma and rebirth in the six worlds or they do not show how to thoroughly extinguish the greed, hatred, delusion and other defilements that perpetuate the cycle of rebirth. At the same time, there are differences in degrees of profundity even among the Buddha's teachings between Mahāyāna and Hīnayāna, exoteric and esoteric, accommodating and confrontational rhetoric, and between provisional and final statements of truth. Nichiren asserts that the highest truth can only be found in the *Lotus Sūtra*, and he cites the testimony of Śākyamuni Buddha, Many Treasures Buddha, and the buddhas of the ten direction in the *Lotus Sūtra* itself as confirmation of this.

Sources

Chappel, David, ed., and Masao Ichishima, comp. Trans. Buddhist Translation Seminar of Hawaii. *T'ien-t'ai Buddhism: An Outline of the Fourfold Teachings*. Tokyo: Shobo, 1983.

Gosho Translation Committee, editor-translator. *The Writings of Nichiren Daishonin*. Tokyo: Soka Gakkai, 1999.

Hori, Kyōtsū, comp. *Writings of Nichiren Shōnin: Doctrine Volume 2*. Tokyo: Nichiren Shu Overseas Propagation Promotion Association, 2002.

Hurvitz, Leon. *Chih-i: An Introduction to the Life and Ideas of a Chinese Buddhist Monk*. Melanges chinois et bouddhiques 12 (1960-62): 1-372. Brussels: l'Institute Belge des Hautes Etudes Chinoises.

Murano, Senchū, trans. *Kaimokushō or Liberation from Blindness*. Berkeley: Numata Center for Buddhist Translation and Research, 2000.

Sasaki, Konen. "When Did Life of Śākyamuni Begin and End?" [Part 1]. Nichiren Shū News, April 1, 2000, p. 1.

_____. "When Did Life of Śākyamuni Begin and End?" [Part 2]. Nichiren Shū News, June 1, 2000, p. 1.

Shen, Haiyan. *The Profound Meaning of the Lotus Sūtra: T'ien-t'ai Philosophy of Buddhism volumes I and II*. Delhi: Originals, 2005.

Swanson, Paul. *Foundations of T'ien-tai Philosophy: The Flowering of the Two Truths Theory in Chinese Buddhism*. Berkeley: Asian Humanities Press, 1989.

_____, trans. *The Collected Teachings of the Tendai School*. Berkeley: Numata Center for Buddhist Translation and Research, 1995.

Chapter 12 – The Wonders of the Lotus Sutra

Writings of Nichiren Shōnin Doctrine 2, pp. 34-35
Kaimoku-shō or Liberation from Blindness, pp. 13-14
The Writings of Nichiren Daishonin I, pp. 224

Why is the *Lotus Sūtra* considered the highest teaching of Śākyamuni Buddha? Kyōtsū Hori's translation of *Kaimoku-shō* has Nichiren state, "Twenty important doctrines are in this *Lotus Sūtra*." (Hori 2002, p. 34) Senchū Murano's version states, "The Buddha expounds two important teachings in this sūtra." (Murano 2000, p. 13). Nichiren does not immediately say what these twenty (or two) doctrines are, but instead begins to praise the Tiantai doctrine of the "three thousand realms in a single thought-moment" (J. *ichinen sanzen*) that can only be found between the lines of chapter sixteen, the "Lifespan of the Tathāgata," of the *Lotus Sūtra*. Nichiren goes on to say that while great Buddhist patriarchs like Nāgārjuna and Vasubandhu knew of the three thousand realms in a single thought-moment, only the Great Master Tiantai (aka Zhiyi) actually taught it.

Before explaining what the three thousand realms in a single thought-moment is all about, we should know what Nichiren means by the two or twenty important teachings in the *Lotus Sūtra*. Some editions of *Kaimoku-shō* apparently cite "twenty" while others have "two" as the number indicated, but both are clear references to the Tiantai teachings about the *Lotus Sūtra*. The twenty important doctrines can be found in the commentary *Profound Meaning of the Lotus Sūtra* by Zhiyi. In that work Zhiyi states that there are ten "wonders" or "subtleties" (he uses the Chinese word *miao*, which is *myō* in Japanese) that can be found in the Trace Gate (J. *Shakumon*) comprised of the first fourteen chapters of the *Lotus Sūtra*, and there are another ten wonders that can be found in the Original Gate (J. *Honmon*) comprised of the last fourteen chapters of the *Lotus Sūtra*. The two important teachings are the One Vehicle teaching expounded in the Trace Gate and the Buddha's revelation of the true extent of his lifespan expounded in the Original Gate.

The Trace Gate is called such because in the first half of the *Lotus Sūtra* the teacher is the historical Śākyamuni Buddha whose life and teachings are a phenomenal trace or imprint of the Original Buddha (or Eternal Buddha) to be revealed in the Original Gate. In the Trace Gate, the historical Śākyamuni Buddha speaks primarily to his historical disciples (Śāriputra, Ānanda, Mahākāśyapa and others) and assures them that all his teachings lead to the same awakening that he attained forty years before under the Bodhi Tree. In other words, despite having been given many different teachings appropriate to their limited aspirations, the Buddha actually had all along been teaching everyone the One Vehicle that leads to buddhahood. Nichiren discusses this at length further on in *Kaimoku-shō*. As for the ten wonders of the Trace Gate they involve the causes and effects of buddhahood understood from the perspective of the teaching of the historical Buddha and are as follows:

1. The Wonder of Objects: The wondrous objective realities that the Buddha taught such as the four noble truths, the twelve-fold chain of dependent origination, the ten suchnesses from chapter two of the *Lotus Sūtra*, the two truths (the conventional and the ultimate), the threefold truth (of the empty, the provisional and the Middle Way), and the one truth of ultimate reality itself are all wondrous because they lead to and express the subtle and perfect teaching of the *Lotus Sūtra*.

2. The Wonder of Knowledges: The deepening knowledge (or gnosis) of ordinary beings, śrāvakas, pratyekabuddhas, and bodhisattvas who awaken to the aforementioned objects are wondrous because they all ultimately lead to buddhahood.

3. The Wonder of Practices: All practices, including concentration and insight; the threefold training of morality, concentration, and wisdom; and the six perfections of the bodhisattva, are wondrous because they all lead ultimately to buddhahood.

4. The Wonder of Stages: All the stages of attainment that ultimately lead to buddhahood, from the stage of those who only strive for rebirth as a human being or in the heavens, to those stages of śrāvaka practice leading to arhatship, all the way up to the advanced stages of bodhisattva practice are wondrous.

5. The Wonder of the Threefold Dharma: All of the above leads to buddhahood, which is the wondrous fulfillment of the threefold Dharma or three tracks: the track of real nature, the track of contemplative illumination of wisdom, and the track of fulfilling potential as the accomplishment of meritorious deeds.

6. The Wonder of Receptivity and Response: The Buddha's wholesome influence and assistance given in response to the needs of sentient beings in accord with their receptivity to his teachings is wondrous.

7. The Wonder of Supernatural Powers: The power of the Buddha to assist sentient beings with supernatural mastery over his own body, clairaudience, mind reading, past life recall, clairvoyance, and knowledge of the destruction of the taints is wondrous.

8. The Wonder of Expounding the Dharma: The Buddha's ability to expound the Dharma in the form of sūtras (prose discourses), verse restatements of the prose (S. *gāthā*), original verse teachings (S. *geya*), expansive discourses (S. *vaipulya*), prophecies to his disciples concerning their attainment of buddhahood, short sayings, tales of causality, parables, stories of his disciples past lives, stories of his own past lives, tales of auspicious occasions, and dialogues is wondrous.

9. The Wonder of Attendants: The variety of relationships that sentient beings have with the Buddha depending on either the universality of buddha-nature or specific causes or the vows they have made is wondrous.

10. The Wonder of Merits and Benefits: The final wonder of the Trace Gate is the boundless merit enjoyed by the Buddha and the great benefit he confers upon all sentient beings when they encounter the Buddha, hear the Dharma, and put it into practice so that they also may attain buddhahood.

The Original Gate is called such because in the latter half of the *Lotus Sūtra*, Śākyamuni Buddha reveals that his awakened life has no quantifiable

beginning or end. The birth, awakening, and passing away into final nirvāṇa displayed by the historical Buddha were all skillful means of awakening all sentient beings to their own buddhahood. From the perspective of the Original Gate, the Eternal Buddha's awakening transcends any particular time or location and is a reality that can be realized through a single moment of faith and rejoicing anytime and anywhere. Nichiren will also discuss this at length further on in *Kaimoku-shō*. As for the ten wonders of the Original Gate they involve the causes and effects of buddhahood from the perspective of the Eternal Buddha and are as follows:

1. The Wonder of Original Cause: The Eternal Buddha's practice of the bodhisattva path occurred in the incalculably remote past and thereby puts the previous wonders of knowledges, practices, and stages of the Trace Gate in a timeless perspective.
2. The Wonder of Original Effect: Likewise the Eternal Buddha's attainment of buddhahood occurred in the remote past, and thus the wonder of the threefold Dharma is put into this timeless perspective.
3. The Wonder of the Original Land: Since the time of the Eternal Buddha's attainment of buddhahood in the remote past he has remained in this world of Endurance (Skt. *sahā*) teaching sentient beings. This world is, therefore, the true Pure Land of Eternally Tranquil Light of the Eternal Buddha.
4. The Wonder of Original Receptivity and Response: The wonder of receptivity and response is now shown to have begun in the remote past.
5. The Wonder of Original Supernatural Powers: The wonder of the Eternal Buddha's use of supernatural powers is now shown to have begun in the remote past.
6. The Wonder of the Original Expounding of the Dharma: The wonder of the Eternal Buddha's expounding of the Dharma is now shown to have begun in the remote past.
7. The Wonder of Original Attendants: The wonder of the Eternal Buddha's relationship with sentient beings and fostering of bodhisattvas is now shown to have begun in the remote past.
8. The Wonder of the Original Nirvāṇa: This is the wonder of the Eternal Buddha's actual abiding in nirvāṇa since the remote past, though he repeatedly displays the attainment of nirvāṇa with remainder (the extinction of greed, hatred, and delusion in life) and final nirvāṇa or nirvāṇa without remainder (physical extinction) in order to inspire sentient beings.
9. The Wonder of the Original Lifespan: This is the wonder of the Eternal Buddha's unborn and deathless life-span, though he takes on various transient lives in the world in order to teach, guide, and inspire sentient beings.

10. The Wonder of Original Benefits: The wonder of the Eternal Buddha's merit and beneficial influence on sentient beings is now shown to have begun in the remote past.

Nichiren does not discuss the ten wonders of the Trace Gate or the Ten Wonders of the Original Gate in *Kaimoku-shō*. Instead, he will go on to highlight the two main teachings of the *Lotus Sūtra* in terms of the One Vehicle and the Eternality of the Buddha's lifespan. I will explain the full significance of these in upcoming chapters. Underlying both of those teachings, however, is the principle of the "three thousand realms in a single thought-moment" taught by Zhiyi. Nichiren will return to it again and again throughout the *Kaimoku-shō*. Nichiren does not, however, explain this doctrine in *Kaimoku-shō*, assuming familiarity with it on the part of those he sent it to. In the next chapter I will clarify what is meant by the "three thousand realms in a single thought-moment."

Sources

Chappel, David, ed., and Masao Ichishima, comp. Trans. Buddhist Translation Seminar of Hawaii. *T'ien-t'ai Buddhism: An Outline of the Fourfold Teachings*. Tokyo: Shobo, 1983.

Gosho Translation Committee, editor-translator. *The Writings of Nichiren Daishonin*. Tokyo: Soka Gakkai, 1999.

Hori, Kyōtsū, comp. *Writings of Nichiren Shonin: Doctrine Volume 2*. Tokyo: Nichiren Shu Overseas Propagation Promotion Association, 2002.

Hurvitz, Leon. *Chih-i: An Introduction to the Life and Ideas of a Chinese Buddhist Monk*. Melanges chinois et bouddhiques 12 (1960-62): 1-372. Brussels: l'Institute Belge des Hautes Etudes Chinoises.

Murano, Senchū, trans. *Kaimokusho or Liberation from Blindness*. Berkeley: Numata Center for Buddhist Translation and Research, 2000.

Shen, Haiyan. *The Profound Meaning of the Lotus Sūtra: T'ien-t'ai Philosophy of Buddhism volumes I and II*. Delhi: Originals, 2005.

Swanson, Paul. *Foundations of T'ien-tai Philosophy: The Flowering of the Two Truths Theory in Chinese Buddhism*. Berkeley: Asian Humanities Press, 1989.

_____, trans. *The Collected Teachings of the Tendai School*. Berkeley: Numata Center for Buddhist Translation and Research, 1995.

Chapter 13 – The three Thousand Realms in a Single Thought-Moment

Writings of Nichiren Shōnin Doctrine 2, pp. 34-35
Kaimoku-shō or Liberation from Blindness, pp. 13-14
The Writings of Nichiren Daishonin I, pp. 224

The "three thousand realms in a single thought-moment" is the doctrine taught by Zhiyi in his magnum opus, the *Great Calming and Contemplation*. It was his way of giving expression to the inconceivable true nature of reality to which the Buddha had awakened. Nichiren states that this doctrine was hidden between the lines of chapter 16 in the Original Gate section of the *Lotus Sūtra*. Nichiren goes on to say that the "three thousand realms in a single thought-moment" is based upon the "mutual possession of the ten realms." What are the ten realms? And how do you arrive at three thousand realms altogether? And what does it mean to say that all of this is found in a single thought-moment?

Let's begin with the ten realms. As we have seen, there are the six paths of rebirth in Buddhism: the hell-dwellers, hungry ghosts, animals, fighting demons, humans, and heavenly beings. It should be noted that sometimes the world of fighting demons is left out, so some sūtras or commentaries only speak of five paths. Nevertheless, in Tiantai Buddhism, six paths are counted, and these six paths comprise the six lower realms. Four realms are added to these: the realms of the śrāvakas (lit. voice-hearers), pratyekabuddhas (lit. privately awakened ones), bodhisattvas, and buddhas. These are four noble states of liberation from the compulsive cycle of rebirth among the six lower realms. The first two of these are also called the two vehicles that only lead to liberation for the individual practitioner; however, the two vehicles together with the bodhisattva vehicle are all subsumed by the One Vehicle that leads to buddhahood according to the *Lotus Sūtra*. These ten (or at least the six lower realms) have traditionally been viewed as actual realms or forms of life that one can be reborn into depending upon one's karma (for the lower six worlds) or stage of awakening (for the four noble states), but they can also be viewed as metaphors for states of being that we can find ourselves in from moment to moment. Let's briefly review these ten realms:

- The realm of the hell-dwellers is the lowest of the realms. Those who willfully commit the ten evil acts are reborn as hell-dwellers as the fruition of their deeds. Likewise, those who commit one of the five grave offences (killing one's father, killing one's mother, killing an arhat, injuring the Buddha, causing a schism in the Sangha) will immediately be reborn in the lowest hell in their next life. The hot hells and cold hells (perhaps for the passionately unrestrained and the cold-hearted respectively) are the abode of those so consumed with hatred, bitterness, and despair that their only wish is to destroy themselves and others out of spite and the desire to end their miserable existence.

- The realm of the hungry ghosts is only slightly better. Those who commit the ten evil acts primarily motivated by selfish craving are reborn as hungry ghosts as the fruition of their deeds. Hungry ghosts are said to have large mouths and bellies, but only tiny throats. Hungry ghosts can never be satisfied and are consumed by craving. This is the state of those who suffer from addictions that control and dominate their lives. These addictions can be to drugs, alcohol, sex, gambling, power, work, entertainment, or even religion.

- The realm of animals is the state of cunning, primitive aggression, and instinctive desires. Those who unthinkingly commit the ten evil acts are reborn as animals. It is a state of mind that does not look beyond immediate gratification and pays no heed to consequences or long-term benefit. Here, pleasure and pain reign supreme over reason amid the brute struggle for survival as the strong prey upon the weak. Though not as inherently painful as the two previous worlds, those who are in this state will inevitably meet with frustration and confusion, if not outright pain and suffering.

- The realm of the fighting demons is the realm of arrogant demons who are obsessed with issues of status and power and whose ambition is to overthrow the gods of heaven. Those who follow the five precepts or even the five constant virtues (of Confucianism) but with ulterior motives and in a spirit of hypocrisy and self-righteousness are reborn as fighting demons. Those in this state are full of pride and arrogance and are extremely competitive and envious. They can never rest or feel secure because they must constantly strive to maintain and improve their position and prestige, no matter how well off they may actually be.

- The realm of humanity is, of course, the realm we are most familiar with. Those who follow the five constant virtues or who take refuge in the Three Treasures (Buddha, Dharma, and Sangha) and follow the five precepts are able to be reborn as humans. In the human world, suffering is recognized for what it is, and morality and reason are called upon to improve the human condition. At this point, civilized life can truly begin. The human state is considered a very fortunate one, because the suffering and striving of the previous four realms does not overcome reason, nor is there the complacency brought about by the pleasures of the heavens. From this realm of humanity, one can find the opportunity to encounter the Three Treasures, take up the teachings, put them into practice, and attain liberation.

- The realm of the heavenly beings is where the gods make their abode. Those who take refuge in the Three Treasures, follow the ten good acts, and give generously to worthy people and causes are able to be reborn in the heavens of desire. Those who follow the ten good acts and also go on to cultivate states of meditative absorption to overcome all inner disturbance and negativity are able to be reborn in the more refined heavens of form or formlessness, which correspond to the states of concentration they attained. The heavens are temporary (though long lasting) realms of spiritual bliss of increasing subtlety and refinement.

- The realm of the śrāvakas is the first of the four noble states. Śrāvakas are those who hear the teachings of the Buddha, specifically the four noble truths, and put them into practice by becoming monks or nuns and taking up a life of strict discipline and rigorous contemplative practices in order to awaken to the fact that all conditioned things are ultimately unsatisfactory, impermanent, selfless, and empty of any fixed unchanging essence. This awakening is their attainment of nirvāṇa. Nirvāṇa, for them, is the elimination of the fetters of greed, hatred, and false views that bind them to rebirth among the six lower realms.

Upon attaining nirvāṇa, śrāvakas are known as arhats (lit. worthy ones), who are worthy to receive offerings. Though this is called a realm, arhats do not exist in a separate realm apart from the world of humanity. Arhats are invariably human beings who attain nirvāṇa and upon their deaths (which is called final nirvāṇa) they are no longer to be found anywhere, much like a fire that has been extinguished.

- The world of the pratyekabuddhas is the second of the four noble states. Pratyekabuddhas are the ascetics and hermits who live in a time and place where Buddhism is unknown but attain liberation by contemplating causes and conditions and awakening to the unsatisfactory, impermanent, selfless, and empty nature of all conditioned phenomena. Unlike buddhas, they do not afterwards try to teach others how to awaken. Like the arhats they are invariably human beings who have eliminated greed, hatred, and false views. They too have realized nirvāṇa and are no longer bound to be reborn among the six lower realms. Sometimes pratyekabuddhas are not viewed as hermits who awaken on their own apart from Buddhism. Sometimes they are thought to be those Buddhist practitioners who live as forest-hermits and attain nirvāṇa by contemplating the twelve-fold chain of dependent origination taught by the Buddha to provide a deeper understanding of causes and conditions. In this case they are known as "cause-knowers" (J. *engaku*).

- The realm of the bodhisattvas is the third of the four noble states. Bodhisattvas are those who aspire to attain buddhahood so that they too can lead all sentient beings to liberation. To do this they make vows, for instance the four great vows of the bodhisattva (to save all being, quench all defilements, know all the teachings, and attain the path to buddhahood), and take up the practice of the six perfections (of generosity, morality, patience, energy, meditative absorption, and wisdom). Bodhisattvas sometimes reside in the pure lands of the buddhas of the ten directions but can just as often be found taking rebirth among those in the six worlds in accordance with their vows so that they can help sentient beings, cultivate wisdom, and accrue the merit needed to attain buddhahood.

- The world of the buddhas is the fourth of the four noble states. Buddhahood is the state characterized by purity, bliss, eternity, and self (or authenticity). With perfect wisdom and great compassion, the buddhas spontaneously and unselfconsciously respond to the spiritual needs of all sentient beings. They reside in the pure lands but also appear in the world of humanity as a person who attains buddhahood, teaches the Dharma, and establishes the Sangha.

Each of these ten realms contains the causes and conditions of all ten within themselves. This means that any of the ten contains the potential to manifest any of the others. This is the mutual possession of the ten realms. One might say that the lower realms contain the higher realms as seeds of their future growth and maturity, while the higher realms embrace the lower realms insofar as they are perspectives that have been outgrown and yet assimilated. These are not ten separate realms lined up alongside each other, but rather ten different subjective modes of the interplay of causes and conditions. This means that if you change the causes and conditions you can also change the kind of realm that is or will be experienced. This also means that the realm of buddhahood is accessible to all the other realms and conversely the realm of buddhahood is able to compassionately interact with the lower realms.

What exactly do the ten realms hold in common that allows for their mutual interpenetration? In short, one can answer, "causes and conditions." Zhiyi, however, specified ten suchnesses (or factors of life) that he derived from the beginning of the second chapter of the *Lotus Sūtra* wherein the Buddha talks about the reality of all things in terms of their appearance, nature, entity, power, activity, cause, condition, effect, recompense, and the ultimate equality of all of these factors from beginning to end. The mutual possession of the ten realms is possible because the ten realms all possess the ten suchnesses in common. These ten suchnesses are the ways in which each of the ten realms can be viewed as the manifestation of a dynamic interdependent process. Let's look at each of them:

- Appearance refers to external or objective phenomena. That which is seen, heard, smelled, touched, or tasted is included in this factor. Appearance involves the way phenomena are encountered in their various changing expressions and objective relations. For instance, the hell-dwellers have the appearance of undergoing various painful experiences such as being boiled in oil; on the other hand, heavenly beings have the appearance of pleasure and ease in their palaces and gardens. The two vehicles of the śrāvakas and pratyekabuddhas have peaceful demeanors as they have transcended suffering by realizing nirvāṇa. The bodhisattvas can be observed cultivating the six perfections, realizing nirvāṇa, and attaining virtuous qualities. The liberating activities of a buddha are the appearance of a buddha.

- Nature refers to internal or subjective phenomena. This factor focuses on inner thoughts and feelings. Nature is about the subjective side of life, the conscious and felt nature of experience. It also refers to the inner qualities that remain for a time even as external appearances, expressions, and relations change. For instance, hell-dwellers are constantly dwelling on the perpetration of unwholesome actions that they believe will benefit them, whereas heavenly beings dwell on the performance of wholesome actions in order to gain benefit. The two vehicles are no longer attached to notions of gaining benefit through wholesome or unwholesome actions. The nature of a bodhisattva is either that of heavenly deeds or undefiled wisdom or the determination to remain in the six lower realms to save all sentient beings. The wisdom that illuminates the true nature of reality is the nature of a buddha.

- Entity is the causal nexus that expresses itself in both internal and external phenomena. Internal and external can never really be separated because both are nothing more than partial aspects of an integral whole. The integral whole is the contingent entity whose qualities have an objective and subjective dimension. For instance, the entity of hell-dwellers is characterized by torment, but the entity of heavenly beings is characterized by the temporary transcendence of disturbance. The entity of the two vehicles is the fivefold Dharma-body of morality, concentration, wisdom, liberation, and knowledge of liberation manifest in their actions and attitudes. The entity of the bodhisattvas is that of the 32 marks of greatness and later the ability to transform into whatever is needed to save sentient beings. The entity of the buddha is the true nature of reality.

- Power is the ability of phenomena to effect and undergo change. Whereas the first three factors analyze phenomena in terms of internal and external relations and their integral unity, this factor and the next point out that phenomena do not stand still as they are actually not static things but causes and conditions in a constant process of mutual influence and transformation. Any phenomenon is a causal entity that has the power to affect the world in myriad ways. For instance, hell-dwellers have the power to enter into states of suffering while the heavenly beings have the power to attain pleasure. The power of the two vehicles is to be in the world but no longer of it. The power of the buddhas and bodhisattvas is expressed in the four great vows.

- Activity is the actual change brought about through the function of the aforementioned power. It should be pointed out that phenomena depend upon cooperative conditions in order to have an actual effect on the world. Just because something or someone has the power to do something doesn't mean that it will actually exert that power. When the right circumstances are met with, then that power will be activated. For instance, the hell-dwellers actively commit the ten evil acts, whereas the heavenly beings are generous and actively abide by the ten good acts. The activity of the two vehicles is to strive diligently to progress on the path to liberation. The performance of the six perfections is the activity of buddhas and bodhisattvas.

- Causes are those intentional actions of moral import made in the present. This factor and the next three directly refer to the moral law of cause and effect or karma. Cause, in this context, refers to all of our thoughts, words, and deeds, which become karmic seeds in the depths of our lives. These seeds are the habit-patterns that determine the ways in which our life will unfold. In fact, the dominant realm or state of mind that is our usual state of being is the fruition of these very seeds. Therefore, it is very important that we plant as many goods seeds in our life as possible. For instance, the hell-dwellers make bad causes of unwholesome thoughts, words, and deeds; the heavenly beings make good causes through wholesome thoughts, words, and deeds. The two vehicles make the cause of coming to know for themselves non-defilement. As the bodhisattvas progress, they initially make the same causes as the heavenly beings, then the same causes as the two-vehicles, and then the perfecting of wisdom becomes their primary cause. The perfection of wisdom is the cause made by the buddhas.

- Conditions are the secondary or environmental causes that allow the primary causes to bear fruit. The seeds we have planted in our life through our own actions require the proper circumstances before they come to fruition. Even when they do come to fruition, the exact ways in which they manifest can be influenced by the conditions that surround them. The causes we have made can be inhibited, distorted, modified, mitigated, or even amplified, depending upon the other causes that we have planted and the circumstances in which we find ourselves. For instance, the hell-dwellers find themselves in wretched circumstances and have unwholesome views and attitudes that drive them to greater desperation and even worse evils; whereas the heavenly beings find themselves in pleasant circumstances that put them at ease and inspire wholesome past times and benevolent attitudes. The two vehicles have as their conditions the practice of eliminating defilements. The bodhisattvas initially take the passions that bind beings to rebirth as their conditions but then move on to the practices and contemplations that reveal the truths of emptiness, provisional existence, and the Middle Way. The buddhas have the adornment of virtuous qualities as their conditions.

- Effects are the immediate consequences of the causes we make. Whenever we act, speak, or even think about something, there is an immediate effect upon our lives. That effect might be so minuscule as to be hardly noticeable. However, effects primarily refer to the planting of a new karmic seed in the depths of our lives, not just the immediate change in our consciousness or external circumstances. The importance of this is that everything we do has, at the very least, a subtle effect on our lives, and even more importantly contributes to the formation of our whole character. For instance, the hell-dwellers fall into bad habits as the effect of the causes they have made, whereas the heavenly beings cultivate good habits because they strive to make good causes. The two vehicles progressive elimination of the fetters that bind them to rebirth and their attainment of nirvāṇa is the effect

resulting from the causes and conditions, though nirvāṇa is not actually the effect of a cause but what is realized when the fetters are undone. The bodhisattvas initially eliminate deluded views and attitudes and later eliminate the delusions as innumerable as grains of sand as the effects of their continuing efforts. The buddhas realize perfect and complete awakening as the effect of the perfection of wisdom.

- Recompenses are the future manifest results of present causes. This refers to the perhaps unforeseen long-term effects of the causes we have set in motion. In one manner or another the karmic seeds planted in the depths of our lives come to fruition under the right conditions. For instance, the unwholesome actions of the hell-dwellers will lead to future rebirths in the lower realms, whereas the wholesome actions of the heavenly beings will lead to future rebirths in the heavens or at least the human realm. The two vehicles believe that there will be no future suffering of recompense for past karma because they have ended the process of rebirth, but from the perspective of the One Vehicle they are still subject to "transmigration of change and advance" until they overcome fundamental ignorance and attain buddhahood. The bodhisattvas likewise do not suffer the consequences of karmic recompense after they have matured in their practice and cultivation, but they do engage in "transmigration with change and advance" in accordance with their vows. The realization of the true nirvāṇa of purity, bliss, eternity, and self that is neither

identical to nor distinct from saṃsāra can be said to be the result enjoyed by the buddhas as a recompense of their cultivation of the One Vehicle.

- Beginning and end ultimately equal refers to the non-duality of all phenomena despite these differing aspects. Even though the ten realms can be distinguished due to their differing appearances, natures, and so on, they are all united and equal in that these differing aspects are all empty of any fixed independent substance, all temporary manifestations of causes and conditions, and all exemplify the Middle Way that embraces both emptiness and provisional existence.

I must confess that some of the application of the ten suchnesses to the ten realms seem arbitrary or forced. In particular the world of buddhahood at least would seem to transcend the causes and conditions of the ten suchnesses insofar as the buddhas awaken to the unconditioned. On the other hand, the unconditioned is the true nature of the conditioned, and so not apart from causes and effects. In order to show that the world of buddhahood also possesses the ten suchnesses and so is part of the same reality as the other nine realms, Zhiyi applied the ten suchnesses to it as well.

Likewise, those in the four noble states do not make the same kind of causes as those in the six lower realms, nor are they subject to effects and consequences in the same way. The causes made by those in the six lower realms are karmic causes, which is to say they are actions defiled by greed, hatred, and delusion that perpetuate the process of rebirth as they seek to reap the fruits of their activities but more often than not reap disappointment and suffering as the immediate effects and long-term consequences of the karmic actions they have sown. Karma, then, includes both wholesome and unwholesome actions of thought, word, and deed that are tainted by some degree of self-seeking. Those in the four noble states have realized that there is no unchanging separate self and are no longer motivated by self-interest (though neither are they motivated by self-neglect). Instead, through the power of compassionate vows they remain engaged with all sentient beings. The effects and recompenses they encounter are the results of these compassionate activities. As already mentioned, even the arhats and pratyekabuddhas who are believed to no longer generate recompenses in the form of future rebirths actually transition onto the bodhisattva path and make their own compassionate vows. Nevertheless, all the ten realms manifest by way of causes and conditions and are therefore united by holding the ten factors in common.

When each of the ten realms is multiplied by the ten realms again due to the mutual possession of the ten realms one arrives at a hundred realms. Since each of the hundred realms has ten suchnesses there are said to be one thousand realms. In addition to all this, Zhiyi taught that there are three categories of existence that must be taken into account. These categories are the five aggregates (form, feeling, perception, mental formations, and consciousness); the sentient beings of the ten realms; and the environments in which they live. These three categories show that the one thousand realms are present in and manifest themselves in terms of the components of each beings, the sentient beings themselves as a whole, and the environments inhabited by them. The one thousand realms multiplied by the three categories brings the final total up to three thousand realms that are operative in every single thought-moment.

The single thought-moment is nothing other than each singular moment of conscious awareness that comprises the here and now of our life. Each moment of awareness contains all three thousand realms. The single thought-moment and the three thousand realms arise simultaneously. There is never a single moment of awareness without all the realms present within and all the realms are always united in a single moment of awareness. In support of this idea, in his *Great Calming and Contemplation*, Zhiyi cited the following verse from the *Flower Garland Sūtra* to show that all these realms are manifest by the mind:

> *Mind is like an artist,*
>
> *Able to paint the worlds:*
>
> *The five aggregates all are born thence;*
>
> *There's nothing it doesn't make. (Cleary, p. 452 adapted)*

The idea here is that the realm or world we experience is nothing but the transformations of the mind itself, and apart from mind, the single moment of awareness, there would be nothing at all. It is the mind that determines the coloration of our experience. It is mind that makes causes and reacts to conditions and then suffers or enjoys the effects and consequences of the actions it initiates. It is by coming to know the nature of mind that one can awaken to the three thousand realms that are the mind's palette. It is by awakening to the three thousand realms in every moment of awareness that one realizes that buddhahood is there as well, available to us as the most authentic and liberated stance that realizes and actualizes the true nature of the whole.

Nichiren will discuss the three thousand realms in a single thought-moment from the perspective of the Trace Gate and the Original Gate of the *Lotus Sūtra* in later sections of the *Kaimoku-shō*. For now, it might be instructive to read the other verses from the *Flower Garland Sūtra* that the above verse was taken from. In these verses, Forest of Awareness Bodhisattva teaches that coming to know the mind leads to knowing the Buddha as well.

> *It's like a painter*
>
> *Spreading the various colors:*
>
> *Delusion grasps different forms*
>
> *But the elements have no distinctions.*
>
> *In the elements there's no form.*
>
> *And no form in the elements;*
>
> *And yet apart from the elements*
>
> *No form can be found.*
>
> *In the mind there is no painting.*
>
> *In painting there is no mind;*
>
> *Yet apart from mind*
>
> *Is any painting to be found?*

The mind never stops.

Manifesting all forms.

Countless, inconceivably many,

Unknown to one another.

Just as a painter

Can't know his own mind

Yet paints due to the mind,

So is the nature of all things.

Mind is like an artist,

Able to paint the worlds:

The five aggregates all are born thence;

There's nothing it doesn't make.

As is the mind, so is the Buddha;

As the Buddha, so living beings:

Know that Buddha and mind

Are in essence inexhaustible.

If people know the actions of mind

Create all the worlds,

They will see the Buddha

And understand Buddha's true nature.

Mind does not stay in the body,

Nor body stay in mind:

Yet it's able to perform the Buddha-work

Freely, without precedent.

If people want to really know

All Buddhas of all times,

They should contemplate the nature of the cosmos:

All is but mental construction. (Ibid, pp. 451 – 452)

Sources

Chappel, David, ed., and Masao Ichishima, comp. Trans. Buddhist Translation Seminar of Hawaii. *T'ien-t'ai Buddhism: An Outline of the Fourfold Teachings*. Tokyo: Shobo, 1983.

Cleary, Thomas, trans. *The Flower Ornament Scripture: A Translation of the Avatamsaka Sūtra*. Boston: Shambhala, 1993.

Gosho Translation Committee, editor-translator. *The Writings of Nichiren Daishonin*. Tokyo: Soka Gakkai, 1999.

Hori, Kyōtsū, comp. *Writings of Nichiren Shonin: Doctrine Volume 2*. Tokyo: Nichiren Shu Overseas Propagation Promotion Association, 2002.

Hurvitz, Leon. *Chih-i: An Introduction to the Life and Ideas of a Chinese Buddhist Monk*. Melanges chinois et bouddhiques 12 (1960-62): 1-372. Brussels: l'Institute Belge des Hautes Etudes Chinoises.

Murano, Senchū, trans. *Kaimokusho or Liberation from Blindness*. Berkeley: Numata Center for Buddhist Translation and Research, 2000.

Shen, Haiyan. *The Profound Meaning of the Lotus Sūtra: T'ien-t'ai Philosophy of Buddhism volumes I and II*. Delhi: Originals, 2005.

Swanson, Paul. *Foundations of T'ien-tai Philosophy: The Flowering of the Two Truths Theory in Chinese Buddhism*. Berkeley: Asian Humanities Press, 1989.

_____, trans. *The Collected Teachings of the Tendai School*. Berkeley: Numata Center for Buddhist Translation and Research, 1995.

Chapter 14 – Hinayana Buddhism: The Four Noble Truths

Writings of Nichiren Shōnin Doctrine 2, pp. 34-35
Kaimoku-shō or Liberation from Blindness, pp. 13-14
The Writings of Nichiren Daishonin I, pp. 224
In the Buddha's Words, pp. 75-78, 239-240

As mentioned in a previous chapter, the doctrine of the five comparisons is not explicitly taught in the *Kaimoku-shō* in those terms. Nevertheless, the five comparisons are derived from it. The first of the five comparisons are between Buddhism generally and non-Buddhism. We have already surveyed the non-Buddhist teachings that Nichiren was aware of and even commented upon how Western monotheism might compare to them using the criteria used by Śākyamuni Buddha and Nichiren Shōnin. Of them, Nichiren says that their sages were like infants compared to the Buddha in that they were ignorant of causality. The Buddha, on the other hand, was able to show the way to liberation from saṃsāra, the cycle of birth and death amid the six worlds.

Escaping saṃsāra, the cycle of birth and death, is actually the accomplishment of the arhats and the pratyekabuddhas. These are the people of the two vehicles, the first two of the four noble states. The śrāvakas and pratyekabuddhas, by following the four noble truths or contemplating the twelve-fold chain of dependent origination respectively, are able to break free of the six lower realms and attain liberation for themselves. This is considered an advance over those who seek respectability and prosperity in this life or who aim to be reborn in the heavenly realms, because these goals are both considered transient conditioned rewards that leave one enmeshed within the passions and delusions of the six lower realms. By having a greater insight into causality, those of the two vehicles transcend the six lower realms by cutting off their delusions of views and attitudes and when they die their bodies are burned to ashes and their consciousness is annihilated so that they are forever beyond the reach of any kind of suffering. In East Asian Buddhism, this is what is understood to be Hīnayāna Buddhism.

I would like to clarify here what is meant by the term "Hīnayāna." The term means "Small Vehicle" whereas Mahāyāna means "Great Vehicle." The Mahāyānists referred to those Buddhists who rejected the Mahāyāna sūtras as Hīnayāna Buddhists. The so-called Hīnayāna Buddhists believed that the Buddha's teachings could only be found in a closed canonical collection called the Three Baskets (S. *tripiṭka*) composed of the sūtras that are the Buddha's discourses, the monastic rules and procedures (S. *vinaya*), and the "Higher Dharma" (S. *abhidharma*) treatises that systematized the teachings in the discourses. The southern recension of these discourses is called the Pāli canon, since it was recorded in the Pāli language. It is composed of five Nikāyas or "Collections." The northern recension of these discourses was in Sanskrit. They were called the Āgamas or "Sources" and exist now in Chinese translation. Today the Theravādin schools of SE Asia and Sri Lanka continue to uphold the Pāli canon as the only authoritative canonical collection of the Buddha's teachings. The Sarvāstivādin and other northern schools that upheld the Āgama sūtras have long since disappeared in India. Because the term Hīnayāna is a disparaging epithet and not the proper name of a school, it is best to use the term Theravāda and not Hīnayāna when referring to the Buddhism of SE Asia. Calling the Āgama sūtras, their teachings, and the schools that rely upon them Hīnayāna, as they are by East Asian Buddhists to this day, is problematic for a couple of reasons. The first is that, as Nichiren points out, those who study these teachings or who belong to these schools may have actually adopted Mahāyāna views. The second problem is that, according to Zhiyi, the teachings introduced in the Āgama sūtras can themselves express the perspective of the Mahāyāna if understood more deeply. Nevertheless, the term Hīnayāna can be understood to refer to those teachings and schools that confine themselves to pre-Mahāyāna teachings, perspectives, and motivations, for that is how Nichiren uses the term in *Kaimoku-shō*.

In Japan, three schools of Buddhism upheld the Hīnayāna teachings: The Kusha and Jōjitsu schools that were based on different abhidharma treatises, and the Ritsu or Vinaya school that taught, conferred, and practiced the monastic precepts. Even by Nichiren's time these were not really separate schools of Buddhism but more like curriculums of study taken up by monks and nuns who were actually Mahāyāna adherents. Of these schools, Nichiren said:

> The Kusha, Jōjitsu, and Ritsu schools were founded on the Āgama sutras. These sects knew only six worlds, not the other four. They said that there is only one Buddha in the worlds of the ten directions. They did not go so far as to say that there are any buddhas in the worlds of the ten directions. Furthermore, they did not say that all living beings have Buddha-nature. They said that no one other than the Buddha had Buddha-nature. But nowadays they say that there are Buddhas in the worlds of the ten directions, and that all living beings have the Buddha-nature. It seems that some scholars of these schools, who appeared after the extinction of the Buddha, took these teachings from the Mahāyāna and put them into their own schools. (Murano 2000, p. 14 adapted)

In later chapters I will provide a survey of the schools of Buddhism that existed in Nichiren's time and also address Nichiren's accusation that these schools misappropriated the Mahāyāna teachings. For now, let us set aside these things and look at what kind of teachings and practices are understood to be Hīnayāna in nature, beginning with the four noble truths that the Buddha taught in his first discourse at the Deer Park in Vārānasī by revealing the Middle Way:

> "Monks, these two extremes should not be followed by one who has gone forth into homelessness. What two? The pursuit of sensual happiness in sensual pleasures, which is low, vulgar, the way of worldlings, ignoble, unbeneficial; and the pursuit of self-mortification, which is painful, ignoble, unbeneficial. Without veering towards either of these extremes, the Tathāgata has awakened to the Middle Way, which gives rise to vision, which gives rise to knowledge, which leads to peace, to direct knowledge, to enlightenment, to nirvāna.

"And what, monks, is that Middle Way awakened to by the Tathāgata? It is this noble eightfold path; that is, right view, right intention, right speech, right action, right livelihood, right effort, right mindfulness, right concentration. This, monks, is that Middle Way awakened to by the Tathāgata, which gives rise to vision, which gives rise to knowledge, and leads to peace, to direct knowledge, to enlightenment, to nirvāṇa." (Bodhi 2005, pp. 75-76)

The Middle Way as taught here by Śākyamuni Buddha is the Middle Way between self-indulgence and self-denial, both of which perpetuate the self-absorption that generates craving for worldly and otherworldly gain and is reinforced by deluded views. The Middle Way is in fact none other than the eightfold path that is the fourth of the four noble truths that the Buddha then proceeds to expound. Here is the first of the four:

"Now this, monks, is the noble truth of suffering: birth is suffering, aging is suffering, illness is suffering, death is suffering; union with what is displeasing is suffering; separation from what is pleasing is suffering; not to get what one wants is suffering; in brief, the five aggregates subject to clinging are suffering." (Ibid, p. 76)

The first noble truth of suffering means that conditioned phenomena are incapable of providing real lasting happiness. This does not mean that there is no happiness at all, but it does mean that even when we do get what we hoped for the happiness never lasts. In terms of the six lower realms, the worlds of the hell-dwellers, hungry ghosts, animals, and fighting demons are full of pain, ceaseless torment, and strife. Human life is naturally subject to old age, sickness, and death as well as the other sufferings enumerated. Even those who make wholesome causes and find themselves in heavenly circumstances will find that eventually the causes and conditions that put them there will change and they will find themselves forced to take birth into a new situation. In the six lower realms happiness is rare and fleeting whereas painful circumstances are abundant and insecurity is pervasive.

The Buddha concludes his observations of life's unsatisfactory nature by stating that, "the five aggregates subject to clinging are suffering." This refers to the Buddha's analysis of the five basic components of human life and experience, which Zhiyi used as one of the three realms in the doctrine of the "three thousand realms in a single thought-moment." In brief, they are form, feeling, perception, mental formation, and consciousness. It is from these five that we derive our notion of existence and especially our idea of selfhood. Unfortunately, none of these components of the self provide a basis for an eternal, independent, or completely fulfilled existence. What seems to be a "self" striving for eternal happiness or final satisfaction is in actuality the constant interplay of these five aggregates that require constant change and stimulation just to continue functioning. Therefore, the idea of an independent, changeless, or fully satisfied self is the result of mistaking a process for a substance. Such a self could not be a product of the five aggregates, and apart from the aggregates there is nothing that can meaningfully be called a self. Stated simply, the Buddha's analysis of life reveals that existence is process, and process provides no basis for an unchanging happiness.

Next, the Buddha taught the causes and conditions which bring about suffering and dissatisfaction:

> *"Now this, monks, is the noble truth of the origin of suffering: it is this craving that leads to renewed existence, accompanied by delight and lust, seeking delight here and there; that is, craving for sensual pleasures, craving for existence, craving for extermination." (Ibid, p. 76)*

The second noble truth teaches that the true root of suffering is the craving for happiness itself. This craving is the result of the unrealistic expectation that life should be a source of unchangeable happiness as discussed under the first noble truth. Craving is what transforms the occasionally painful process of life into an ongoing cycle of agony and unbearable suffering at worst or a life of subtle agitation and anxiety at best. Thus, while external circumstances can indeed bring about uncomfortable or tragic experiences, it is the internal craving that turns mere pain into suffering. Indeed, craving can even spoil

166

pleasant circumstances with its incessant demands and impoverished outlook on life. All of this is not to deny or denigrate the experiences of those who have or are experiencing affliction, exploitation, or tragedy. The point is that when one lets craving compound painful circumstances with emotional suffering or lets craving spoil even pleasant circumstances, then one has truly given up one's power and is destined for a life determined by the forces of greed, anger and ignorance which are naturally generated in reaction to suffering.

Looking at the six lower realms, it is craving to find real lasting happiness that motivates people to commit wholesome and unwholesome acts of thought, word, and deed. The human condition is rife with what Buddhism calls defilements: greed, hatred, ignorance, arrogance, mistaken views and so on. The other five of the six lower realms besides humanity put a spotlight on particular deluded views and attitudes. Those in the hells put themselves there with their destructive rage and by holding to false views whereby they try to deny responsibility for their actions and blame others for the problems they have created. The hungry ghosts doom themselves with their selfish cravings and addictions. The animals act without thought for long-term consequences. The fighting demons are full of arrogance and ambitions that constantly puts them at odds with others. Even the beings in the heavenly realms are not without fault as they are so engrossed in their pleasures or states of meditative absorption that they become complacent and forget that eventually they will have to leave their heavenly abiding for one of the other five worlds in accordance with their karma.

The Buddha then discusses three particular objects of craving, namely: sense-pleasures, existence, and non-existence. Sense pleasures are a pretty obvious and common way of appeasing craving, so no real comment needs to be made. The craving for existence and becoming refers not only to the desire to extend one's life into eternity in the pursuit or enjoyment of one's goals, but it is also a craving for a stable, abiding, and fulfilled self that does not have to undergo change and is self-sufficient. Finally, the craving for non-existence is the nihilistic desire to find peace by destroying the impermanent self and any other entities that one is disappointed or frustrated with. In each case, a means to avoid the impermanence and instability of the five aggregates that make up existence is sought. Since there is nothing that exists apart from the aggregates, the effort is doomed to failure and only leads to increased frustration.

At this point, the Buddha teaches the possibility of liberation from suffering and incessant craving:

> "Now this, monks, is the noble truth of the cessation of suffering: it is the remainderless fading away and cessation of that same craving, the giving up and relinquishing of it, freedom from it, nonattachment."
> (Ibid, p. 76)

Once one sees the true nature of life and the futility of craving, the next step is to realize that if craving were given up then one would be free from suffering. This is the true meaning of nirvāṇa, the extinguishing of the flames of passionate greed or craving. Zhiyi spoke of this as the elimination of deluded views and attitudes that puts an end to transmigration within the six lower realms. From the perspective of the Hīnayāna teachings, the arhats, pratyekabuddhas and even the buddhas who accomplish this are not reborn anywhere after death, not even in a pure land. They are simply gone, beyond the reach of conditioned existence and suffering. In life they attain nirvāṇa, the extinction of the greed, hatred, and delusion, and upon death they are said to attain *parinirvāṇa* or "final nirvāna" whereby they are no longer even subject to physical pain and infirmity. While there may be śrāvakas, pratyekabuddhas, bodhisattvas, and buddhas as individuals, they have no lands or worlds of their own, but simply live in the human world (or some of the others in the case of bodhisattvas) until they attain final nirvāṇa. Then they are gone forever. This is why the attainment of final nirvāna is referred to as reducing the body to ashes and annihilating consciousness and also why the Hīnayāna teachings are only said to expound the six lower realms and not the realms of the four noble states.

In the Hīnayāna teachings the attainment of buddhahood is not presented as the goal of Buddhist practice, so the bodhisattva vehicle is also not presented as something that can be taken up by ordinary people. The Hīnayāna teachings state that there can only be one buddha on any given world at a time. Furthermore, the time between the appearances of a buddha is vast. Each time a buddha appears they set in motion the Wheel of the Dharma (i.e.

they expound the Buddha Dharma), and after a buddha's final nirvāna the teachings may last for a period of time known as the Age of the True Dharma, linger on in a corrupted form during a period of time known as the Age of the Semblance of the Dharma, and finally they begin to disappear during a Latter Age of Degeneration that can last for ten thousand years or more until the Dharma is completely forgotten. There may then be a period of millions of years before another buddha rolls the Wheel of Dharma again. The Hīnayāna teachings do not speak of buddhas in other regions of the universe. The only two bodhisattvas who are recognized are the bodhisattva who became Śākyamuni Buddha, and Maitreya Bodhisattva who resides in the Tushita Heaven awaiting his time to become the next buddha in the distant future after Śākyamuni Buddha's Dharma has completely disappeared. Bodhisattvas are therefore rare and extraordinary beings. What all of this means is that the attainment of buddhahood is not presented as an even remotely realistic goal. The Hīnayāna teaches that the only feasible way to attain cessation from

suffering and escape saṃsāra is to take up one the two vehicles of the śrāvaka or pratyekabuddha, with the former being the easier as the śrāvakas can rely upon the four noble truths and the Middle Way taught by Śākyamuni Buddha.

So how does one live the Middle Way in order to put an end to craving? The fourth noble truth is an outline of the noble eightfold path:

> *"Now this, monks, is the noble truth of the way leading to the cessation of suffering: it is this noble eightfold path; that is, right view, right intention, right speech, right action, right livelihood, right effort, right mindfulness, right concentration." (Ibid, p. 76)*

As already stated, following the noble eightfold path is to live in accordance with the Middle Way. Basically, they are the eight aspects of a life free of self-interest or craving. In each case, "right" refers to the ability to live in a perfect or complete way, so that self-centeredness is extinguished, and one lives in accordance with reality in thought, word and deed. The specific meaning of each part of the noble eightfold path is explained by the Buddha as follows:

"Monks, I will teach you the noble eightfold path, and I will analyze it for you. Listen and attend closely; I will speak."

"Yes, venerable sir," those monks replied. The Blessed One said this:

"And what, monks, is the noble eightfold path? Right view, right intention, right speech, right action, right livelihood, right effort, right mindfulness, and right concentration.

"And what, monks, is right view? Knowledge of suffering, knowledge of the origin of suffering, knowledge of the cessation of suffering, knowledge of the way leading to the cessation of suffering: this is called right view.

"And what, monks, is right intention? Intention of renunciation, intention of non-ill will, intention of harmlessness: this is called right intention.

"And what, monks, is right speech? Abstinence from false speech, abstinence from malicious speech, abstinence from harsh speech, abstinence from idle chatter: this is called right speech.

"And what, monks, is right action? Abstinence from the destruction of life, abstinence from taking what is not given, abstinence from sexual misconduct: this is called right action.

"And what, monks, is right livelihood? Here a noble disciple, having abandoned a wrong mode of livelihood, earns his living by a right livelihood: this is called right livelihood.

"And what, monks, is right effort? Here, monks, a monk generates desire for the nonarising of evil unwholesome states; he makes an effort, arouses energy, applies his mind, and strives. He generates desire for the *abandoning of arisen evil unwholesome states… He generates desire for the arising of unarisen wholesome states… He generates desire for the continuation of arisen wholesome states, for their nondecline, increase, expansion, and fulfillment by development; he makes an effort, arouses energy, applies his mind, and strives. This is called right effort.*

"And what, monks, is right mindfulness? Here, monks, a monk dwells contemplating the body in the body, ardent, clearly comprehending, mindful, having removed longing and dejection in regard to the world. He dwells contemplating feelings in feelings, ardent, clearly comprehending, mindful, having removed longing and dejection in regard to the world. He dwells contemplating mind in mind, ardent, clearly comprehending, mindful, having removed longing and dejection in regard to the world. He dwells contemplating phenomena in phenomena, ardent, clearly comprehending, mindful, having removed longing and dejection in regard to the world. This is called right mindfulness.

"And what, monks, is right concentration? Here, monks, secluded from sensual pleasures, secluded from unwholesome states, a monk enters and dwells in the first dhyāna, which is accompanied by thought and examination, with rapture and happiness born of seclusion. With the subsiding of thought and examination, he enters and dwells in the second dhyāna, which has internal confidence and unification of mind, is without thought and examination, and has rapture and happiness born of concentration. With the fading away as well of rapture, he dwells equanimous and, mindful and clearly comprehending, he experiences happiness with the body; he enters and dwells in the third dhyāna of which the noble ones declare: 'He is equanimous, mindful, one who dwells happily.' With the abandoning of pleasure and pain, and with the previous

171

*passing away of joy and dejection, he enters and dwells
in the fourth dhyāna, which is neither painful nor
pleasant and includes purification of mindfulness by
equanimity. This is called right concentration." (Ibid, pp.
239-240)*

The noble eightfold path has also been restated as the threefold training, consisting of morality, concentration, and wisdom. Morality pertains to the ethical demands of right speech, right action and right livelihood. Specifically, the practice of morality can refer to the five precepts taken by laypeople, the ten virtuous precepts (i.e. the ten good acts), the ten precepts for novices, or even the full monastic precepts taken by monks and nuns. Concentration refers to the cultivation of the mind covered by right effort, right mindfulness and right concentration. Wisdom refers to the acquisition of right view and right intention. The Buddha taught that when morality, concentration, and wisdom are cultivated together, one is able to shake loose the bonds of craving and ignorance and attain the liberation of nirvāṇa.

More specifically, the practice of the eightfold path or the threefold training leads to four fruitions of the holy life. These four fruitions are referred to as "paths" when one first enters such a state and "fruits" when one realizes the benefits from the path attained. Specifically, the benefits of the four fruitions refers to our progressive liberation from ten fetters which keep us trapped in the ordinary life of birth and death and all the suffering, fear and anxiety which makes up that life.

The first class is that of the stream-enterer who is liberated from the first three of the ten fetters. The first fetter is the view that there is a self. This is the notion that there is a substantial, autonomous, unchanging, and independent self that must be protected and appeased. The next fetter is debilitating doubt in regard to the Three Treasures of Buddha, the Dharma and the Sangha. This does not refer to a healthy sense of doubt that can motivate us to find out the truth for ourselves; rather, it refers to lack of trust, either in oneself or in the Three Treasures, which can prevent one from following the path at all. Finally, there is the fetter of seizing upon rules and rituals. This refers to the belief that rules or ritual observances of themselves can bring about salvation or ensure good fortune or safeguard against misfortune. This kind of superstition engenders a false security and a dependency which blocks the way to following the true path to liberation as taught by the Buddha. It should be noted that these three fetters primarily deal with beliefs and opinions that prevent one from following the Dharma. These three fetters keep one preoccupied with one's own welfare and the maintenance of the status quo, which then becomes a distrust of the Three Treasures. The stream-enterer is firmly convinced that only by trusting the Three Treasures and taking up the five precepts (at least) can they escape from the constant bondage of self-concern and false security and thereby attain liberation. The stream-enterer enters the stream of the true teaching, follows the precepts perfectly and, at most, will only undergo seven more rebirths as a human or heavenly being in the realm of desire before realizing nirvāṇa.

The second class is that of the once-returner. The once-returner has partially overcome the fetters of sensual desire and ill-will. Such feelings may still occur, but they no longer hold sway over them. Not only are the once-returner's ideas and behavior in accord with the Dharma, even his or her emotional life has been tamed. As the name indicates, the once-returner will only undergo one more rebirth as a human or heavenly being in the realm of desire before achieving nirvāṇa.

The third class is that of the non-returner. The non-returner is completely liberated from the fetters of sensual craving and ill-will. These negative emotions no longer arise at all. For the non-returner, nirvāṇa will be attained either within their present lifetime or after being reborn in the pure abodes among the heavens in the realm of form.

The final class of holiness is that of the arhat. The arhat is one who has overcome even the more subtle forms of clinging that are the last five of the ten fetters. The sixth fetter is the desire for form realm existence. This is the notion of a continued existence in a spiritual body in a refined heavenly existence. The seventh fetter is the desire for formless realm existence. This is the notion of a continued existence as a pure thought form. Both of these are simply more subtle cases of a desire to immortalize an unchanging autonomous self and show a preoccupation with continued existence. It is still self-attachment, though in a much more refined and sophisticated form. The eighth fetter is pride, which refers to conceit arising from one's accomplishments on the path. Though not necessarily craving, this fetter still betrays a lingering self-preoccupation. The ninth fetter is restlessness. Restlessness is the residual need to accomplish something and make one's mark upon the world. It is the habitual need to assert a self in the midst of the world's demands and temptations. Finally, there is the fetter of ignorance. This is the fetter that obscures the selfless true nature of reality that is revealed by the Dharma. It is not the mere intellectual ignorance or delusion that is broken through by the stream-enterer. This is the root ignorance that views the self as a substantial reality and gives rise to all the habits, emotions and ideas that stem from the inability to come to terms with the selfless ungraspable nature of reality. The arhat has seen through all this, and has liberated himself from all passions, fixations and false views. The arhat is one who has achieved the freedom of nirvāṇa.

The *Lotus Sūtra* states that the Buddha taught the four noble truths for the sake of the śrāvakas. "To those who were seeking Śrāvakahood, he expounded the teaching of the four truths, a teaching suitable for them, saved them from birth, old age, disease, and death, and caused them to attain Nirvāṇa." (Murano 2012, p. 14) This would indicate that the four noble truths are a Hīnayāna teaching. Zhiyi, however, taught that the four noble truths could be understood on increasingly profounder levels as the four noble truths as arising and ceasing of conditioned phenomena, as the four noble truths as non-arising and non-ceasing of phenomena (since they are empty of a substance that can arise), as the four noble truths as immeasurable variety of provisional existence, and finally as the four noble truths as uncontrived expression of the inconceivable reality of the Middle Way. I will not attempt to explain what Zhiyi meant by all this, but it is good to keep in mind that while the four noble truths are in one sense a Hīnayāna teaching meant for voice-hearers, they are also capable of expressing much deeper perspectives.

Sources

Bodhi, Bhikkhu, ed., *In the Buddha's Words: An Anthology of Discourses from the Pali Canon*. Boston: Wisdom Publications, 2005.

Gosho Translation Committee, editor-translator. *The Writings of Nichiren Daishonin*. Tokyo: Soka Gakkai, 1999.

Hori, Kyotsu, comp. *Writings of Nichiren Shonin: Doctrine Volume 2*. Tokyo: Nichiren Shu Overseas Propagation Promotion Association, 2002.

Murano, Senchu, trans. *The Lotus Sutra*. Hayward: Nichiren Buddhist International Center, 2012.

_____. *Kaimokusho or Liberation from Blindness*. Berkeley: Numata Center for Buddhist Translation and Research, 2000.

Chapter 15 – Hinayana Buddhism: The Twelve-fold Chain of Dependent Origination

Writings of Nichiren Shōnin Doctrine 2, pp. 34-35
Kaimoku-shō or Liberation from Blindness, pp. 13-14
The Writings of Nichiren Daishonin I, pp. 224
In the Buddha's Words, pp. 353, 356-357
Connected Discourses of the Buddha, pp. 534-536

Dependent origination is a teaching whose importance cannot be overstated. The Buddha even went so far as to equate the Dharma itself with dependent origination. "Now this has been said by the Blessed One: 'One who sees dependent origination sees the Dharma; one who sees the Dharma sees dependent origination.'" (Nanamoli & Bodhi 1995, p. 284) An understanding of dependent origination is integral to having a clear understanding of Buddhism.

Put simply, dependent origination means that all phenomena arise as the result of conditions and cease when those conditions change. The Buddha taught the general theory of dependent origination as follows: "When this exists, that comes to be; with the arising of this, that arises. When this does not exist, that does not come to be; with the cessation of this, that ceases." (Bodhi 2000, p. 575) So there are no static isolated entities in existence. Everything arises and ceases depending on causes and conditions that arise due to yet other causes and conditions. There is no ultimate ground or primordial cause, but a network of causes and conditions. This undercuts the view of a metaphysical selfhood, fixed entity, or substance underlying the constant change that is life.

There are many ways in which the principle of dependent origination is applied to the specifics of human life, or life in general, in the Buddha's teachings. The four noble truths are one such application. The first two of the four noble truths explain the origin of suffering dependent on selfish craving for its cause. The third and fourth of the four noble truths describe the cessation of suffering by eradicating the causes upon which it depends. Unlike the many forms of fatalism, theism, or materialism taught by the Buddha's contemporaries, the Buddha taught there is a rational order of causes and conditions that we can awaken to and work with rather than against. Furthermore, the conditioned nature of all things is not something apart from who we are. Rather, conditionality is the way we are. Negatively, this means there is nothing permanent to grasp or cling to either outside of or within ourselves, but positively it means that we are not stuck or fixed in any one state and that we have the power to unbind ourselves from suffering and to experience the boundless joy of freedom from suffering and its causes. We may be the products of causality, but we are also the producers of the very causes that will determine whether we perpetuate suffering or attain liberation. The Buddhist vision of dependent origination is a vision in which sentient beings are not determined by forces beyond their control, but rather are fully integrated in the co-arising of all things and as such are able to take responsibility for themselves and create better conditions for themselves and others by making better causes informed by an awareness of the way things arise in mutual dependence.

Dependent origination is the Middle Way between the extremes of existence and non-existence. The view of existence, or "eternalism," imagines that fixed entities, independent of conditions and immune from change, can be found underlying the phenomena that do change. The view of non-existence, or "annihilationism," imagines there is no continuity at all within change and the entities that do arise will eventually vanish completely without a trace. Dependent origination is the Middle Way which cuts through those views by pointing out the ceaseless interplay of causes and conditions, which is the process of becoming, rather than the eternalism of being or the nihilism of non-being. The Middle Way points out that while there are no fixed entities there is a flow of continuity within the process of change. In the following sermon, the Buddha expounds the teaching of the Middle Way to Kātyāyana:

> *"This world, Kātyāyana, for the most part depends upon a duality – upon the idea of existence and the idea of nonexistence. But for one who sees the origin of the world as it really is with correct wisdom, there is no idea of nonexistence in regard to the world. And for one who sees the cessation of the world as it really is with correct*

wisdom, there is no idea of existence in regard to the world.

"This world, Kātyāyana, is for the most part shackled by engagement, clinging, and adherence. But this one [with right view] does not become engaged and cling through that engagement and clinging, mental standpoint, adherence, underlying tendency; he does not take a stand about 'my self.' He has no perplexity or doubt that what arises is only suffering arising, what ceases is only suffering ceasing. His knowledge about this is independent of others. It is in this way, Kātyāyana, that there is right view.

"'All exists': Kātyāyana, this is one extreme. 'All does not exist': this is the second extreme. Without veering towards either of these extremes, the Tathāgata teaches the Dharma by the middle." (Bodhi 2005, p. 356-357)

The extreme of existence is an attempt to attribute intrinsic entities to the flow of causes and conditions. It does not see the interdependence, flux and relativity of all phenomena. In the end it results in an absolutism that fixes things in rigid categories in defiance of the actual contingency of life. From this rigidity springs all kinds of evils, such as classism, racism, nationalism and religious fundamentalism. Compassion is effectively banished through the projection of fixed boundaries of self and other upon the dynamic flow and interdependence of the life process. Finally, the view of eternalism assumes that there is a self that is immutable and therefore immune to the law of cause and effect.

The extreme of non-existence is a refusal to accept any kind of meaning or value, since it assumes there are no entities of any kind to have any regard for. Life is reduced to chaos, absurdity or illusion. Ultimately, it is the negation of life itself; which is very different from the Buddha's liberation from the illusion of self. According to the Buddha, selfish craving is the cause of suffering, not life itself. In Buddhism, the goal is to become liberated from the delusion of self through the cultivation of the eightfold path. Nihilism only leads to irresponsible despair and the denial of the truth and meaning of causality. It assumes that there is no continuity at all within the flow of conditions and therefore negates the law of cause and effect.

Dependent origination, then, is the teaching that things do have a provisional (though not intrinsic) existence based on causes and conditions. Therefore, one who is following the Middle Way will think in terms of causes and conditions, and not existence or non-existence. For the follower of the Middle Way there are no immutable categories or boundaries, nor is there any question of absolute identity or absolute difference between entities. Dependent origination is the awareness of cause and effect and the interdependence of all things that gives rise to an authentic sense of responsibility, genuine love and compassion.

Dependent origination applies to all phenomena, but the Buddha was specifically concerned with applying it to the human predicament. He wished to show the specific causes and conditions that bind people to an existence of suffering, and through understanding those causes, how to change them. To this end, the Buddha expounded the twelve-fold chain of dependent origination.

> *"With ignorance as condition, volitional formations [come to be]; with volitional formations as condition, consciousness; with consciousness as condition, name-and-form; with name-and-form as condition, the six sense bases; with the six sense bases as condition, contact; with contact as condition, feeling; with feeling as condition, craving; with craving as condition, clinging; with clinging as condition, becoming; with becoming as condition, birth; with birth as condition, aging-and-death, sorrow, lamentation, pain, displeasure, and despair come to be. Such is the origin of this whole mass of suffering. This, monks, is called dependent origination." (Ibid, p. 353)*

Admittedly, this formula may seem a little obscure. Nevertheless, it is the foundation upon which the Buddha's teachings rest and so deserves careful study. Through the ages Buddhists have understood and taught the twelve-fold chain in a variety of ways depending upon the social and historical context. The following explanation is based upon the Buddha's expanded analysis of this formula from another discourse, and also the traditional understanding derived from the abhidharma, the phenomenological treatises written by the early Buddhist monks in India as a systematic explanation of the sūtras.

In the traditional understanding, ignorance and volitional formations refer to past causes inherited from one's past life or lives. The cycle begins with ignorance of the true nature of reality. Specifically, the Buddha states that this link in the twelve-fold chain refers to ignorance of the four noble truths.

> *"And what, monks, is ignorance? Not knowing suffering, not knowing the origin of suffering, not knowing the cessation of suffering, not knowing the way leading to the cessation of suffering. This is called ignorance."* (Bodhi 2000, p. 535)

Due to ignorance, one is disposed to perform acts of thought, word and deed based upon the most selfish and short sighted of motives. These are the volitional formations.

> *"And what, monks, are the volitional formations? There are these three kinds of volitional formations: the bodily volitional formation, the verbal volitional formation, the mental volitional formation. These are called the volitional formations."* (Ibid, p. 535)

These actions are also called "karma" which is not destiny or fate, but intentional activity motivated by ignorance, and to the consequences of those actions upon the future life or lives of the one who performs them. Volitional formations are also a subset of the mental formations that are the fourth of the five aggregates that constitute human life. They are habit-patterns that condition both ourselves and our environment in accordance with the nature of our motivations.

The next five links of the chain spell out the consequences of past karma in terms of one's present life. They are the present effects of past causes. The first link is consciousness, which is the same as the fifth of the five aggregates.

> *"And what, monks, is consciousness? There are these six classes of consciousness: eye-consciousness, ear-consciousness, nose-consciousness, tongue-consciousness, body-consciousness, mind-consciousness. This is called consciousness." (Ibid, p. 535)*

According to Buddhism, the kind of person we are in this life is not simply the result of heredity and environment but is the outcome of karma. In other words, the kind of person that we are now has been determined by our own choices and the habits or dispositions that we have built up over many previous lives. These predispositions give rise to and condition conscious experience of various kinds (consciousness of the external world and the internal awareness of thoughts and feelings). According to the abhidharma, the perpetuation of consciousness carries over from the expiration of one sentient being to the conception of a new sentient being. At some point, whether instantaneously or after an "intermediate existence" (depending on which version of abhidharma one gives credence to), consciousness finds itself drawn to the most appropriate womb and environment wherein it's karmic inheritance can unfold. This transmigration of consciousness as a gandharva or "being to be reborn" is explained by the Buddha as follows:

> *"Monks, the conception of an embryo in a womb takes place through the union of three things. Here, there is the union of the mother and father, but it is not the mother's season, and the being to be reborn is not present – in this case there is no conception of an embryo in a womb. Here, there is the union of the mother and father, and it is the mother's season, but the being to be reborn is not present – in this case too there is no conception of an embryo in a womb. But when there is the union of the mother and father, and it is the mother's season, and the being to be reborn is*

present, through the union of these three things the
conception of an embryo in a womb takes place."
(Nanamoli & Bodhi 1995, p. 358)

Some might be misled into thinking that consciousness is a kind of self that transmigrates from one lifetime to another. This was the mistaken view of a monk named Sati, who believed that the same consciousness "runs and wanders through the round of rebirths." (Ibid, p. 349) The Buddha admonished Sati and in no uncertain terms stated that consciousness is not a fixed entity that transmigrates but is itself something that arises in accordance with conditions. Consciousness is more of a recurring pattern, like a wave, than a thing. In another discourse, the Buddha even says that the mutability and impermanence of consciousness is even more drastic than that of the body, and therefore one would be better off identifying the body as a self.

> *"It would be better, monks, for the uninstructed*
> *worldling to take as self this body composed of the four*
> *great elements rather than the mind. For what reason?*
> *Because this body composed of the four great elements*
> *is seen standing for one year, for two years, for three,*
> *four, five, or ten years, for twenty, thirty, forty, or fifty*
> *years, for a hundred years, or even longer. But that*
> *which is called 'mind' or 'mentality' and 'consciousness'*
> *arises as one thing and ceases as another by day and by*
> *night. Just as a monkey roaming through the forest*
> *grabs hold of one branch, lets that go and grabs*
> *another, then lets that go and grabs still another, so too*
> *that which is called 'mind' and 'mentality' and*
> *'consciousness' arises as one thing and ceases as*
> *another by day and by night." (Bodhi 2000, p. 595)*

Consciousness, then, is constantly changing to reflect the conditions that brought it about. As the Buddha explains to Sati, sometimes it is consciousness of something visual, or something auditory, or something tangible, or of some other sense. From moment to moment consciousness changes its focus and composition as often as a monkey jumping from branch to branch. Each moment of consciousness is therefore unique, dependent on conditions, impermanent, and not a candidate for any kind of permanent unchanging self.

Consciousness in turn gives rise to and is supported by the aggregates that make up name-and-form, the psychophysical personality.

> *"And what, monks, is name-and-form? Feeling, perception, volition, contact, attention: this is called name. The four great elements and the form derived from the four great elements: this is called form. Thus this name and this form are together called name-and-form." (Ibid, p. 535)*

Name-and-form in this case, encompasses four of the five aggregates – form, feeling, perception, and mental formations. "Name" is applied to feeling, perception, and mental formations as well as to contact and attention. These five always accompany consciousness as supportive functions that are involved in the recognition, or "naming," of experience. "Form" is constituted by the four primary elements that are elsewhere listed as earth, air, fire, and water. These four elements do not simply refer to earth, air, fire, and water as we commonly relate to them. Rather, the four primary elements are emblematic of our experience of the physical world – solidity, movement, temperature, and cohesion respectively.

When dependent origination is explained within the boundaries of a single lifetime, then the links of name-and-form and consciousness are shown to be mutually conditioning. Instead of consciousness arising due to the ignorance and volitional formations attributed to a previous lifetime, consciousness is said to arise depending on name-and-form and to in turn give rise to name-and-form. In another discourse, Śāriputra explains this through the simile of two sheaves of reeds that are able to stand up by leaning up against one another, thus providing mutual support (Ibid, pp. 608 – 609).

Upon birth, the psychophysical personality begins to utilize the six sense bases consisting of sight, sound, touch, taste, smell and cognition.

*"And what, monks, are the six sense bases? The eye
base, the ear base, the nose base, the tongue base, the
body base, the mind base. These are called the six sense
bases." (Ibid, p. 535)*

These six senses bring one into contact with the world. They are sometimes
called the six sense entrances because through them the world enters into our
awareness. They are also referred to as the six roots because through them
we are rooted in the world.

*"And what, monks, is contact? These are the six classes
of contact: eye-contact, ear-contact, nose-contact,
tongue-contact, body-contact, mind-contact. This is
called contact." (Ibid, p. 535)*

Contact naturally results in feelings based on that contact.

*"And what, monks, is feeling? There are these six
classes of feeling: feeling born of eye-contact, feeling
born of ear-contact, feeling born of nose-contact,
feeling born of tongue-contact, feeling born of body-
contact, feeling born of mind-contact. This is called
feeling." (Ibid, p. 535)*

These feelings constitute the second of the five aggregates. Again, these last
five links describe what one experiences in the present life; they are all givens
that are the fruits of one's own actions.

The next three links describe one's present actions in relation to the
circumstances that one experiences. They are the present causes that will
have future effects. The first is the craving that arises based upon feeling.

*"And what, monks, is craving? There are these six
classes of craving: craving for forms, craving for sounds,
craving for odors, craving for tastes, craving for*

tangibles, craving for mental objects. This is called
craving." (Ibid, p. 535)

One wishes to experience only pleasant feelings while avoiding the unpleasant at all costs. This craving leads to clinging to particular things, people, ideas and circumstances.

> *"And what, monks, is clinging? There are these four*
> *kinds of clinging: clinging to sensual pleasures, clinging*
> *to views, clinging to rules and vows, clinging to a*
> *doctrine of self. This is called clinging." (Ibid, p. 535)*

This results in "becoming," which is a way of summarizing the way in which we "become" hell-dwellers, hungry ghosts, animals, fighting demons, humans, and heavenly beings in the three realms. The three realms consist of the realms of desire (which takes in all existence from the hells up to the lower six heavens), form (the more refined heavens), and the formless (the most refined heavens). "Becoming" refers to the constant struggle for identity and happiness that characterizes the day-to-day life of most people.

> *"And what, monks, is becoming? There are these three*
> *kinds of becoming: sense-realm becoming, form-realm*
> *becoming, formless-realm becoming. This is called*
> *becoming. (Ibid, p. 535)*

The last two links of the chain explain the future effects of the present causes. In the Buddhist view, this constant struggle for a happy existence or even for a peaceful annihilation can never be achieved because life is characterized by the three marks of impermanence, suffering and non-self. One's desperate strivings and unrequited desires can only lead to a future birth.

> *"And what, monks, is birth? The birth of the various*
> *beings into the various orders of beings, their being*
> *born, descent [into the womb], production, the*

manifestation of the aggregates, the obtaining of the
sense bases. This is called birth." (Ibid, p. 534)

Birth will then lead to another round of old age and death, grief, lamentation, suffering, dejection and despair.

"And what, monks, is aging-and-death? The aging of
the various beings in the various orders of beings, their
growing old, brokenness of teeth, grayness of hair,
wrinkling of the skin, decline of vitality, degeneration of
the faculties: this is called aging. The passing away of
the various beings from the various orders of beings,
their perishing, breakup, disappearance, mortality,
death, completion of time, the breakup of the
aggregates, the laying down of the carcass: this is called
death. Thus this aging and this death are together
called aging-and-death." (Ibid, p. 534)

In short, the twelve-fold chain of dependent origination shows that human life is the outcome of a vicious circle of desire, karma and suffering. The only escape is to abolish ignorance and recognize the vicious circle for what it is. Once the chain is broken, liberation is at hand.

"But with the remainderless fading away and cessation
of ignorance comes cessation of volitional formations;
with the cessation of volitional formations, cessation of
consciousness; with the cessation of consciousness,
cessation of name-and-form; with the cessation of
name-and-form, cessation of the six sense bases; with
the cessation of the six sense bases, cessation of
contact; with the cessation of contact, cessation of
feeling; with the cessation of feeling, cessation of
craving; with the cessation of craving, cessation of
clinging; with the cessation of clinging, cessation of
becoming; with the cessation of becoming, cessation of
birth; with the cessation of birth, cessation of aging-

*and-death, sorrow, lamentation, pain, displeasure, and
despair cease. Such is the cessation of this whole mass
of suffering." (Ibid, p. 534)*

Who has achieved liberation? As discussed earlier, the twelve-fold chain is not concerned with the preservation or eradication of an individual person or entity. It is concerned with the way in which suffering is perpetuated and the way in which the conditions that give rise to suffering can be unraveled. The important thing is that suffering has ended and liberation has been achieved.

There is another way of understanding the twelve-fold chain of dependent origination, however, that does not need to assume the literal existence of many lifetimes. It can be said that from moment-to-moment we are renewing ourselves and enacting the cycle of birth and death, with all the suffering that it entails. From this point of view, ignorance and volitional formations refer to our inability to accept the life process on its own terms. We desperately search for some form of stability and lasting happiness and refuse to acknowledge the dynamic flow and interrelations that is the true reality of our lives.

Due to this misguided activity, we fall out of sync with the true rhythm of life and end up feeling self-conscious and threatened. We never see reality itself because it is clouded over with our expectations, regrets, frustration and all other manner of projection. At this point, the psychophysical personality, name-and-form, is consolidated and immediately begins interpreting the world encountered through the senses in terms of self and other. The contact between this self and the world outside it from moment-to-moment gives rise to the feelings that constitute our self-referential experience of the world.

At this point we begin craving for what is pleasant and constantly strive to be in the situations we do want. In this way, every moment becomes a new experience of transitory pleasure and pain.

Birth, then, refers not to an actual rebirth, but to the birth of a new self-concept or identity based on what we are experiencing in that single moment. Thus, from moment-to-moment we have a new idea about who we are in relation to our environment. We see ourselves variously as competent, kind, gentle, harsh, admirable, pitiable, uncertain, loving, loved, hateful, hated, indifferent, fascinated and so on as each moment arises. However, no matter how comfortable we are with these ideas of ourselves, they will all fade away as the next moment comes and the cycle renews itself. This is the momentary meaning of aging and death.

Looked at in this way, the abolishing of ignorance means that we cease living life in terms of self-reference. By not projecting our desires and expectations onto reality or bifurcating it into self and other, the actions and self-consciousness that lead to so much suffering ceases. Free of the chain, life can take on entirely new qualities that are no longer characterized by ignorance, craving, grasping or the myriad forms of suffering. The moment-to-moment unfolding of the life process continues, but now it is free of our erroneous and fearful interpretations, such as the idea of birth and death. Dependent origination teaches that since all entities are actually phases and configurations of the continuous unfolding of causes and conditions, there are no clear-cut lines that can be drawn between self and other, birth and death. Without such self-oriented projections, dependent origination can be seen just as it is – a dynamically relational unfolding of reality wherein every part contains the whole and is embraced by the whole.

The *Lotus Sūtra* states that the Buddha taught the twelve-fold chain of dependent origination for the sake of the pratyekabuddhas. "To those who were seeking Pratyekabuddhahood, he expounded the teaching of the twelve causes, a teaching suitable for them." (Murano 2012, p. 14) As with the four noble truths this would indicate that the twelve-fold chain of dependent origination is a Hīnayāna teaching, but once again Zhiyi, taught that the twelve-fold chain of dependent origination could be understood on increasingly profounder levels up to and including the perspective of the *Lotus Sūtra*. Just as the voice-hearers and privately awakened ones enter into the One Vehicle that takes them to buddhahood, so do the teachings associated with them blossom into the teaching of the One Vehicle.

Sources

Bodhi, Bhikkhu, trans. *The Connected Discourses of the Buddha: A New Translation of the Samyutta Nikaya*. Boston: Wisdom Publications, 2000.

_____, ed., *In the Buddha's Words: An Anthology of Discourses from the Pali Canon*. Boston: Wisdom Publications, 2005.

Gosho Translation Committee, editor-translator. *The Writings of Nichiren Daishonin*. Tokyo: Soka Gakkai, 1999.

Hori, Kyotsu, comp. *Writings of Nichiren Shonin: Doctrine Volume 2*. Tokyo: Nichiren Shu Overseas Propagation Promotion Association, 2002.

Murano, Senchu, trans. *The Lotus Sutra*. Hayward: Nichiren Buddhist International Center, 2012.

_____. *Kaimokusho or Liberation from Blindness*. Berkeley: Numata Center for Buddhist Translation and Research, 2000.

Nanamoli, Bhikkhu and Bodhi, Bhikkhu, trans. *The Middle Length Discourses of the Buddha: A New Translation of the Majjhima Nikaya*. Botson: Wisdom Publications, 1995.

Chapter 16 – Provisional Mahayana: The Perfection of Wisdom

Writings of Nichiren Shōnin Doctrine 2, pp. 35-37, 44, 48-50
Kaimoku-shō or Liberation from Blindness, pp. 14-17, 26-27, 32-33, 35-36
The Writings of Nichiren Daishonin I, pp. 224-226, 231-232, 235-237

The second of the five comparisons is that Mahāyāna Buddhism is superior to Hīnayāna Buddhism. I will say something about the origins of Mahāyāna Buddhism is another chapter, but for now the important thing to know is that beginning in the 1st century BCE a class of sūtras known as Mahāyāna or "Great Vehicle" began to appear that spoke of the bodhisattva vehicle. Those who eschewed the two vehicles of the śrāvakas and pratyekabuddhas as spiritually selfish took up the bodhisattva vehicle instead, aspiring to attain buddhahood for the sake of all sentient beings. These sūtras extolled this as the superior path. The earlier sūtras only take into account one buddha, the historical Śākyamuni Buddha of this world, and only one bodhisattva, his successor Maitreya Bodhisattva. They only deal with this era wherein the teaching of the Buddha Dharma is still extant. Most importantly, they only teach the way to attain arhatship or pratyekabuddhahood, both of which see liberation as the irrevocable abandonment of the six lower realms and the beings still transmigrating within them. Mahāyāna sūtras, however, have a grander scope that takes in the whole universe and unimaginably vast scales of time wherein there are countless buddhas inhabiting pure lands throughout the universe (the ten directions) with bodhisattva attendants who voluntarily take birth even in this Sahā world (the world of Endurance) in order to help liberate all beings and accumulate the merit and insight they would need to attain buddhahood and establish their own pure lands. According to the Mahāyāna sūtras, it is indeed possible to accomplish the greatest and most selfless goal of buddhahood itself. In *Kaimoku-shō*, Nichiren offered the following comparison between the Hīnayāna and Mahāyāna sūtras that highlights these differences:

> *The Great Assembly Sūtra, the Larger Perfection of*
> *Wisdom Sūtra, the Golden Splendor Sūtra, and the Pure*

Land Sūtra were expounded for the purpose of
criticizing adherents of the two vehicles who relied on
the Hīnayāna sūtras. In these Mahāyāna sūtras, the
Pure Lands of the Buddhas were established in the
worlds of the ten directions in order to encourage
ordinary men and bodhisattvas to be born there. This
troubled adherents of the two vehicles. There are some
differences between the Hīnayāna sūtras and the
Mahāyāna sūtras. In the Mahāyāna sūtras, it says that
the buddhas appear in the world of the ten directions;
that great bodhisattvas are dispatched from the worlds
of the ten directions; that these particular sūtras are
expounded in the worlds of the ten directions; that the
Buddhas assembled from the worlds of the ten
directions; that Śākyamuni, the World Honored One,
stretched his tongue over the one thousand million
Sumeru worlds; or that the Buddhas stretched their
tongues. All these statements are given, I believe, for
the purpose of criticizing the teaching of the Hīnayāna
sūtras that there is only one Buddha in the worlds of the
ten directions. (Murano 2000, pp. 26-27 adapted)

Furthermore, whereas the Hīnayāna sūtras and schools do not recognize that sentient beings universally possess the nature of buddhahood, the *Flower Garland Sūtra* states that right after his awakening the Buddha saw that all beings are capable of being buddhas also but do not realize it.

Then the Buddha, with the unimpeded, pure, clear eye
of knowledge, observes all sentient beings in the
cosmos and says, "How strange – how is it that these
sentient beings have the knowledge of the Buddha but
in their folly and confusion do not know it or perceive it?
I should teach them the way of sages and cause them
forever to shed deluded notions and attachments, so
they can see in their own bodies the vast knowledge of
buddhas, no different than the buddhas. (Cleary 1993,
p. 1003)

In the *Nirvāna Sūtra*, just before his final nirvāna the Buddha teaches that the essential nature of the Buddha is unborn and deathless and that all beings are endowed with this same buddha-nature.

> *"This is to say that the Tathagata is eternal and unchanging, that he is utmost peace itself, and that all beings have the Buddha Nature." (Yamamoto, Kosho, p. 143)*

Though the buddha-nature of all sentient beings is asserted, the Buddha stated in the passage from the *Flower Garland Sūtra* that sentient beings are ignorant of this and would need to be taught. In the *Nirvāna Sūtra*, Kāśyapa Bodhisattva points out:

> *"There surely is the Buddha Nature. But having not yet practiced the best expediency of the Way, he has not yet seen it. Having not seen it, there can be no attainment of the unsurpassed bodhi." (Ibid, p. 169)*

Having buddha-nature, then, is one thing, but actually arousing the aspiration to attain buddhahood and making efforts to realize and actualize buddha-nature is something else again. This aspiration and determination to dedicate all their efforts to attaining buddhahood for the sake of all beings is what differentiates a bodhisattva from the śrāvakas and pratyekabuddhas of the two vehicles. The following contrast is made in the *Perfection of Wisdom in Eight Thousand Lines Sūtra*:

> *For a bodhisattva should not train in the same way in which persons belonging to the vehicle of the śrāvakas or pratyekabuddhas are trained. How then are śrāvakas and pratyekabuddhas trained? They make up their minds that "one single self we shall tame, one single self we shall pacify, one single self we shall lead to nirvāna." Thus they undertake exercises that are intended to*

192

*bring about wholesome roots for the sake of taming
themselves, pacifying themselves, leading themselves to
nirvāṇa. A bodhisattva should certainly not in such a
way train himself. On the contrary, he should train
himself thus: "My own self will I place in suchness, and,
so that all the world might be helped, I will place all
beings into suchness, and I will lead to nirvāṇa the
whole immeasurable world of beings." With that
intention should a bodhisattva undertake all the
exercises that bring about all the wholesome roots. But
he should not boast about them. (Conze 1995, p. 163
adapted)*

The same sūtra also contains the following dialogue between the Buddha and
his disciple Subhūti about the bodhisattvas that describes their meeting with
good spiritual friends, their initial resolution, their practice of the six
perfections, and their dedication of their efforts to attaining perfect and
complete awakening in order to save all sentient beings:

*Subhūti: How should a bodhisattva who is only just
beginning stand in perfect wisdom, how train himself?*

*The Buddha: Such a bodhisattva should tend, love, and
honor the good friends. His good friends are those who
will instruct and admonish him in perfect wisdom, and
who will expound to him its meaning. They will expound
it as follows: "Come here, son of good family, make
endeavors in the six perfections. Whatever you may
have achieved by way of generous giving, guarding
morality, perfecting yourself in patience, exertion of
energy, entering into meditative absorptions, or
mastery in wisdom – all that dedicate to perfect and
complete awakening. But do not misconstrue perfect
and complete awakening as form, or any other
aggregate. For intangible is all-knowledge. And do not
long for the level of a śrāvaka or a pratyekabuddha. It is
thus that a bodhisattva who is just beginning should*

193

gradually, through the good friends, enter into perfect wisdom."

Subhūti: Doers of what is hard are the bodhisattvas who have set out to win perfect and complete awakening. Thanks to the practice of the six perfections, as described above, they do not wish to attain release in a private nirvāṇa of their own. They survey the highly painful world of beings. They wait to win perfect and complete awakening, and yet they do not tremble at birth and death.

The Buddha: So it is. Doers of what is hard are the bodhisattvas who have set out for the benefit and happiness of the world, out of pity for it. "We will become a shelter for the world, a refuge, the place of rest, the final relief, islands, lights, and leaders of the world. We will win perfect and complete awakening, and become the resort of the world," with these words they make a vigorous effort to win such a perfect and complete awakening. (Ibid, p. 188 adapted)

The bodhisattva's career begins with the arousal of the "awakening mind" (S. *bodhicitta*), the initial aspiration to attain perfect and complete awakening and save all sentient beings. The bodhisattva's determination is currently expressed in East Asian Buddhism by the four great vows from the *Bodhisattva Practice Jeweled Necklace Sūtra* (probably composed in China in the late fifth century) that were popularized by Zhiyi (538-597), the founder of the Tiantai school. The four great vows are the general vows that all bodhisattva's take, though some bodhisattvas in the sūtras are credited with more specific vows. These four great vows are as follows:

Sentient beings are innumerable:

I vow to save them all.

Our defilements are inexhaustible:

194

I vow to quench them all.

The Buddha's teachings are immeasurable:

I vow to know them all.

The Way of the Buddha is unexcelled:

I vow to attain the Path Sublime.

In order to fulfill these vows the bodhisattvas must transcend the insight and spiritual maturity of the two vehicles: "And if a bodhisattva is unable even to realize the level of a śrāvaka or pratyekabuddha, how much less can he know perfect and complete awakening!" (adapted from Conze 1984, p. 105) Though the bodhisattvas' training encompasses that of the two vehicles, the bodhisattvas must beware of grasping at the concepts the two vehicles use to analyze reality (like the four noble truths, the five aggregates, or the twelve links of the chain of dependent origination) as though they were actual things, nor should they fall into the individualized nirvāṇa of the two vehicles. Instead they must develop skillful means (S. *upāya*) and the six perfections (S. *pāramitā*) in order to attain buddhahood for the sake of all beings. Skillful means is essentially the same things as the perfection of wisdom. "But what is this skillful means of a bodhisattva? It is just this perfection of wisdom." (adapted from Conze 1995, p. 250) The perfection of wisdom is the insight that all phenomena (called dharmas in Buddhism) are empty of an unchanging independent selfhood or essence and therefore there is ultimately nothing to grasp and nothing to reject. "The non-appropriation and the non-abandonment of all dharmas, that is perfect wisdom." (Conze 1984, p. 102) This insight is the origin, guide, and culmination of the other five perfections: generosity, morality, patience, energy, and meditation. Under the direction of the perfection of wisdom the development and application of the other five perfections become skillful means for the sake of all beings rather than for the sake of gaining worldly benefit or the attainment of the Hīnayāna nirvāṇa that abandons the six worlds.

> *Buddha: [The bodhisattva] courses in all the six perfections. But it is the perfection of wisdom that controls the bodhisattva when he gives generously, or*

guards morality, or perfects himself in patience, or
exerts himself energetically, or enters meditative
absorption, or has insight into phenomena. One cannot
get at a distinction or difference between the six
perfections – all of them are upheld by skillful means,
dedicated to the perfection of wisdom, dedicated to all-
knowledge. (adapted from Conze 1995, p. 119)

To understand the six perfections and especially the perfection of wisdom is
to understand the bodhisattva-vehicle and the foundations of the Mahāyāna.
The following passage provides a brief review of them:

Here, Śāriputra, a bodhisattva, a great being, having
stood in the perfection of wisdom, by way of not taking
his stand on it, should perfect the perfection of
generosity, by way of seeing that no renunciation has
taken place, since gift, giver, and recipient have not
been apprehended. He should perfect himself in the
perfection of morality, through not transgressing into
either offense or non-offense. He should perfect the
perfection of patience and remain imperturbable. He
should perfect the perfection of energy and remain
indefatigable in his physical and mental energy. He
should perfect the perfection of meditation and derive
no enjoyment (from the absorptions). He should perfect
the perfection of wisdom, on account of the fact that he
apprehends neither wisdom nor foolishness. (Conze
1984, p. 45 adapted)

As the Mahāyāna tradition developed, the specific meaning of each of the six
perfections was also developed. The *Revealing the Profound and Secret Sūtra*
states that there are three kinds of each of the six perfections. Other passages
from the Perfection of Wisdom sūtras provide more detailed descriptions.
Let's take each of the six in turn and see what the sūtras had to say about each
one, starting with the perfection of generosity.

The three kinds of giving are giving of teaching, giving of goods, and giving of fearlessness. (Cleary 1995, p. 78)

The supramundane perfection of giving, on the other hand, consists in the threefold purity. What is the threefold purity? Here a bodhisattva gives a gift, and he does not apprehend a self, a recipient, or a gift; also no reward of giving. He surrenders that gift to all beings, but does not apprehend those beings, or himself either. And, though he dedicates that gift to supreme awakening, he does not apprehend any awakening. (Conze 1984, p. 199 adapted)

The perfection of generosity, therefore, consists in the teaching of the Dharma, the giving of material goods (including even one's own body and life), and even the giving of fearlessness. All of this, however, is done without any thought of clinging, or self-congratulation, or expectation of return. It is done with the insight that there is ultimately no giver, no gift, and no receiver.

The three kinds of discipline are the discipline of increasingly giving up what is not good, the discipline of increasingly developing what is good, and the discipline of increasingly benefiting sentient beings. (Cleary 1995, p. 78)

Moreover, the irreversible bodhisattva undertakes to observe the ten wholesome ways of action. He himself abstains from taking life, and also others he establishes in the abstention from taking life; he praises the abstention from taking life, and also those others who abstain from taking life; one acquiescent. And so for the abstention from: taking what is not given, sexual misconduct, intoxicants as tending to cloud the mind, lying speech, malicious speech, indistinct prattling, covetousness, ill will and wrong views. Endowed with these attributes, etc. Moreover, the irreversible bodhisattva even in his dreams commits no offense

197

against the ten wholesome ways of acting, how much
less when he is awake. (Conze 1984, p. 389 adapted)

The perfection of morality is stated in terms of what came to be known as the three categories of pure precepts to be followed by bodhisattvas (to give up what is evil, to do what is good, and to benefit all beings) and the ten courses of wholesome conduct that carried over into Buddhism from Brahmanism (though in this case abstention from intoxicants replaces abstention from abusive speech). Again, all of this is done without any attachment or aversion.

> *The three kinds of forbearance are the forbearance of*
> *bearing injury, the forbearance of serenity in suffering,*
> *and the forbearance of truthful observation of realities.*
> *(Cleary 1995, pp. 78-79)*
>
> *And when confronted with those who struggle to kill*
> *him, the bodhisattva renounces himself with supreme*
> *patience for the sake of those very beings and does*
> *them no harm. (Conze 1984, p. 622)*
>
> *No one can attain any of the fruits of the holy life, or*
> *keep it – from the stream-winner's fruit to perfect and*
> *complete awakening – unless he patiently accepts this*
> *elusiveness of the Dharma. (Conze 1995, p. 98 adapted)*

The perfection of patience is of course about being patient when suffering setbacks in life, physical or emotional harm, or even malice from other beings. They overcome anger and ill-will through their compassion and the insight that in the interplay of causes and conditions there is nothing ultimately personal about any of the injuries suffered. Again, this perfection is perfected as the bodhisattva overcomes attachment and aversion and the idea that there are ultimately real beings and objects to grasp or reject. The bodhisattva must also be patient with the Dharma itself. The teaching that all things are empty of any self-nature or essence can be quite disconcerting, and its subtleties are hard to understand. The bodhisattva must patiently continue to contemplate the perfection of wisdom until they see that in fact no unchanging independent essence can be found amidst causes and conditions and that the unobstructed true nature of reality is the groundless ground (so to speak) of the liberated selfless compassion of buddhahood.

> *The three kinds of diligence are diligence as armor, diligence of concerted effort to increasingly develop good qualities, and diligence of concentrated effort to help sentient beings. (Cleary 1995, p. 79)*

> *A bodhisattva is not armed with the great armor if he delimits a certain number of beings, and thinks, "So many beings will I lead to nirvāṇa, so many beings will I not lead to nirvāṇa; so many beings will I introduce to awakening, so many beings will I not lead to awakening!" But on the contrary, it is for the sake of all beings that he is armed with the great armor and he thinks, "I myself will fulfill the six perfections and also on all beings will I enjoin them." (Conze 1984, p. 138 adapted)*

The perfection of energy is the bodhisattva's tireless efforts to work for the liberation of all beings. It is like armor, because with it the bodhisattva is protected from any obstacles and will not fall prey to the lesser goals of the two vehicles. Like right effort of the eightfold path, the perfection of energy is about preventing the arising of unwholesome states, abandoning those that have arisen, generating positive states, and maintaining positive states that have arisen. Unlike right effort, the perfection of generosity is specifically dedicated to the benefit and liberation of all beings and again the bodhisattva does not hold the idea that either the unwholesome or the wholesome qualities have any essential nature to accept or reject. In this way the bodhisattva is without any undue anxiety over negative states or conceit over positive ones, they simply work unselfconsciously to assist all beings on the path to awakening.

> *The three kinds of meditation are meditation in a state of bliss without discriminating thought, still and silent, extremely tranquil and impeccable, thus curing the*

pains of afflictions; meditation that brings forth virtuous
qualities and powers; and meditation that brings forth
benefit for sentient beings. (Cleary 1995, p. 79)

If, although he enters into those meditative absorptions,
the infinite states of mind, and formless attainments, he
does not gain his rebirths through them, does not relish
them, is not captivated by them – then this is the
perfection of meditation of a bodhisattva who courses
in the unlimited. (Conze 1984, p. 134 adapted)

The perfection of meditation (S. *dhyāna*) is a development of right
concentration (S. *samādhi*) of the eightfold path. Meditation in a state of bliss
without discriminating thought refers to the second through fourth of the four
dhyānas (states of increasingly refined meditative absorption) wherein
discursive thought has been transcended. One way of entering into the
dhyānas would be through contemplating the four infinite virtues of loving-
kindness, compassion, sympathetic joy, and equanimity and extending those
feelings in one's regard to all beings in all directions. From the fourth dhyāna
one might also cultivate the four attainments that are increasingly subtle
formless objects of contemplation: space, consciousness, nothingness, and
neither perception nor non-perception. It is taught in Buddhism that entering
any of these states creates the karma to be reborn into a corresponding
heaven. The bodhisattva, however, does not practice meditation for the
purpose of attaining a heavenly rebirth or to selfishly abide in such pleasant
states. Instead, meditation is used to overcome the hindrances of sensual
desire, ill-will, drowsiness, agitation, and debilitating doubt. Meditation is also
the optimum way of developing the aforementioned four infinite virtues and
other wholesome qualities with which to help sentient beings. Finally,
meditation provides the calmness and clarity of mind that allows for the
insight into the true nature of reality. All of this is cultivated for the sake of all
beings, but again without holding onto any of these states as an object of
attachment or aversion.

The three kinds of insight are insight focused on
conventional worldly truth, insight focused on ultimate
truth, and insight focused on benefiting sentient beings.
(Cleary 1995, p. 79)

Furthermore, a bodhisattva who courses in the perfection of wisdom gives a gift which is threefold pure; with his attention centered on the knowledge of all modes, he dedicates to perfect and complete awakening that gift which he gives, after he has made that wholesome root common to all beings. This is the perfection of giving of a bodhisattva who courses in the perfection of wisdom. Similarly should one understand the perfection of morality, patience, energy, and meditation of a bodhisattva who courses in perfect wisdom. With regard to all perfections, and to all dharmas, he sets up the notion that they are an illusion, a dream, a reflected image, an echo, a reflection, a magical creation; with his attention centered on all-knowledge, he dedicates to perfect and complete awakening that wholesome root, after he has made it common to all beings. It is thus that a bodhisattva who courses in perfect wisdom, fulfills the perfection of wisdom. A bodhisattva is then called "armed with the great armor." It is thus that a bodhisattva, having stood firm in each single perfection, fulfills all the perfections. (Conze 1984, pp. 130-131 adapted)

The perfection of wisdom is the ability to deal with the conventional truth of the ordinary common-sense way of relating to the world as a multiplicity of persons, places, and things and at the same time be awakened to the ultimate truth that all things, all dharmas, are empty. This does not mean that things do not exist at all. That is not what "emptiness" means. Emptiness is another way of talking about how things that are caused and conditioned do not have an unchanging, independent self-nature. It is a deeper way of contemplating dependent origination that points to the flowing, composite, conceptual nature of the things that we experience. Things are empty because they are impermanent. So there is nothing to be permanently grasped. Things are empty because they are composite. So apart from the components (causes and conditions that are all in turn caused and conditioned ad infinitum) there is nothing to grasp. Things are empty because they are not what they seem to be as a result of our mind projecting categories and concepts onto the dynamic interdependent flow of causes and conditions. Apart from our mental concepts there is no singular thing to be grasped in the flow of causes and conditions. Emptiness is not meant to be a theory or belief that we should just subscribe to conceptually. It is meant to be something to observe directly by deeply contemplating the flowing, composite, and conceptual nature of phenomena. Emptiness is not so much a characteristic as a way of pointing out that things are not the solid permanent independent facts they seem to be. Nevertheless, they are contingent realities. By realizing that all things are empty, bodhisattvas overcome undue attachment towards them and also overcome any undue aversion towards them. Free of attachment and aversion, bodhisattvas deal with phenomena in a more graceful, fearless, and wholesome way. They can care about and deal with conditioned phenomena without falling into the trap of craving certain conditions and fearing others. This includes craving or fearing anything within the six lower realms, or even the peace attained in the higher realms of the two vehicles. This is why the perfection of wisdom is synonymous with skillful means and is the spirit that unites and guides the other five perfections.

According to the *Lotus Sūtra*, the Buddha specifically taught the six perfections for the bodhisattvas. "To bodhisattvas, he expounded the teaching of the six perfections, a teaching suitable for them, and caused them to attain perfect and complete awakening, that is, to obtain the knowledge of the equality and difference of all things." (Murano 2012, p. 14) It is the six perfections that differentiate the bodhisattva vehicle from the other two vehicles. The knowledge of the equality and difference of all things refers to the ability of the perfection of wisdom to deal both with the ultimate truth of the universal quality of emptiness and also the conventional truth that recognizes the different characteristics of conditioned phenomena in their transience and interrelationships.

By introducing the bodhisattva vehicle with its six perfections, expounding the teaching of the emptiness of all dharmas, and providing the assurance that all beings have the buddha-nature the Mahāyāna sūtras advanced beyond the limited aspirations and world view of the Hīnayāna teachings. According to Nichiren and his Tiantai predecessors, however, the Mahāyāna sūtras other than the *Lotus Sūtra* are only a provisional form of Mahāyāna with two important shortcomings.

The Flower Garland Sūtra, Large Perfection of Wisdom Sūtra, and the Mahāvairocana Sūtra conceal not only the possibility of attaining buddhahood by adherents of the two vehicles but also Śākyamuni Buddha's attainment of buddhahood in the remotest past. These sūtras have two faults. First, they still preserve the differences between the three vehicles; therefore, their teachings are merely expedient. They do not reveal the teaching of the three thousand worlds in one thought-moment expounded in the first fourteen chapters of the Lotus Sūtra. Second they hold that Śākyamuni Buddha attained Buddhahood during his life in this world. (Murano 2000, p. 32 adapted)

Zhiyi's teaching of the three thousand realms in a single thought-moment has already been discussed. How this teaching underlies the teaching of the One Vehicle of the Trace Gate and the attainment of buddhahood in the remotest past in the Original Gate will be discussed in a later chapter. For now, let's look at why Nichiren believed that the provisional Mahāyāna teachings were lacking in comparison with the teaching of the three thousand realms in a single thought-moment.

In 13th century Japan there were seven schools of Buddhism that were considered Mahāyāna: Dharma Characteristics school (J. Hossō-shū), Three Treatises school (J. Sanron-shū), Flower Garland school (J. Kegon-shū), Mantra school (J. Shingon-shū), Meditation school (J. Zen-shū), Pure Land school (J. Jōdo-shū), and the Japanese form of the Tiantai school (J. Tendai-shū). All of them based their teachings and practices upon the Mahāyāna sūtras or at least Mahāyāna commentaries in some manner (including Zen, rhetoric about a transmission beyond words notwithstanding). In upcoming chapters I will have more to say about the specific origins and teachings of these schools. Of these seven Mahāyāna schools, Nichiren considered six of them to be based upon sūtras that did not guarantee the attainment of buddhahood for all beings, particularly the adherents of the two vehicles. The Tiantai school was one exception in that they were ostensibly based upon the *Lotus Sūtra*, though Nichiren would accuse them of actually following Mantra teachings.

One would think that all Mahāyāna schools would recognize the ability of all people to attain buddhahood since they were based upon the Mahāyāna sūtras wherein the Buddha asserted at the beginning and the end of his teaching that all beings have the buddha-nature and are therefore capable of attaining buddhahood. In fact, the Mahāyāna sūtras did not always guarantee universal buddhahood for all beings. In particular, the arhats and

pratyekabuddhas who attained the Hīnayāna nirvāṇa were believed to be incapable of taking up the bodhisattva vehicle and attaining buddhahood, particularly since upon passing away they would never again be reborn in the six worlds or anywhere else. This is why Nichiren writes that, "The Hossō and Sanron schools established eight realms, but not ten. Needless to say, they did not know that the ten realms interpenetrate one another." (Adapted from ibid, p. 14) In other words, because the Dharma Characteristics and Three Treatises schools taught that the arhats and pratyekabuddhas have no realms of their own they simply become extinct upon their deaths and therefore these two schools only acknowledge eight of the ten realms. The Dharma Characteristics school also taught, based upon its own sūtras and commentaries, that people have one of five distinct natures: some people are incorrigible disbelievers (S. *icchantika*) who are incapable of ever leaving the six lower realms, some are capable of taking up the śrāvaka vehicle, some are capable of taking up the pratyekabuddha vehicle, some are capable taking up the buddha vehicle, and some are able to take up any one of the three

vehicles. In this scheme there are some who will never escape saṃsāra and very few who can or will attain buddhahood. Even though these people may have buddha-nature as the true nature of their lives, they do not have the wisdom or virtue to ever realize it. In the following passage from "A Letter to Lord Daigaku Saburō" (*Daigaku Saburō-dono Gosho*), Nichiren reiterates his estimation of the limitations of the Hīnayāna schools and the Dharma Characteristics and Three Treatises schools:

> *The three schools of Abhidharma Treasury, Completion of Reality, and Discipline schools are based on Hīnayāna sūtras and explain only the lower six worlds. Among Mahāyāna teachings, the Three Treatises school was brought to China from India before the Tiantai school. This sect discusses eight realms, not ten realms, [excluding the realms of śrāvaka and pratyekabuddha].*

> *The Dharma Characteristics school was originally*
> *founded in India as the Yogacara. It was brought over to*
> *China after the Tiantai school, during the reign of*
> *Emperor Taizong of Tang. This school, too, expounds*
> *only eight of the ten realms. Though a Mahāyāna*
> *school, the Dharma Characteristics school holds the*
> *doctrine of the "five mutually distinctive natures,"*
> *insisting that those without the nature of awakening*
> *will never become Buddhas. This seems to be similar to*
> *non-Buddhist teachings, and is a common concern*
> *among Buddhist schools. (Hori 2004, pp. 210 – 211*
> *adapted)*

The belief that the arhats and pratyekabuddhas disappear forever after their deaths and that some people are forever incapable of ever attaining buddhahood means that there are only eight realms and that for some beings the world of buddhahood is inaccessible to them. This view falls far short of the mutual possession of the ten realms wherein the world of buddhahood embraces and is embraced by the other nine realms, meaning that all beings, no matter their present state of being, are capable of buddhahood and that the buddhas never abandon the beings of the nine realms.

As for the other Mahāyāna schools, Nichiren does not discuss Zen or Pure Land until much later in the *Kaimoku-shō*, though they are also based upon provisional sūtras in Nichiren's view. Nichiren does, however, accuse the Flower Garland and Mantra schools of stealing the teaching of the three thousand realms in a single thought moment and making it a part of their own teachings.

> The Flower Garland and Mantra schools are essentially provisional Mahāyāna schools based on the sūtras of provisional Mahāyāna Buddhism... took the teaching of the three thousand realms in a single thought-moment from the Tiantai school and made it the core of their school. (Murano 2000, p. 16 adapted)

According to the argument Nichiren makes, neither the *Flower Garland Sūtra* that is the basis of the Flower Garland school, nor the *Mahavairochana Sūtra* and other esoteric sūtras that are the basis of the Mantra school guarantee

205

the attainment of buddhahood by the followers of the two vehicles. This would leave these schools in the same position doctrinally as the Dharma Characteristics and Three Treatises schools insofar as being unable to assert that all beings are capable of attaining buddhahood. In order to remedy the shortcoming of their teachings, the Flower Garland and Mantra schools both misappropriated the doctrine of the three thousand realms in a single thought-moment that was based upon Zhiyi's interpretation of the *Lotus Sūtra* in order to be able to compete successfully with the Tiantai school.

Sources

Cleary, Thomas, trans. *The Flower Ornament Scripture: A Translation of the Avatamsaka Sūtra*. Boston: Shambhala, 1993.

_____, trans. *Buddhist Yoga: A Comprehensive Course*. Boston: Shambhala, 1995.
Conze, Edward, trans. *The Large Sūtra on Perfect Wisdom*. Berkeley: University of California Press, 1984.

_____. *The Perfection of Wisdom in Eight Thousand Lines & It's Verse Summary*. San Francisco: Four Seasons Foundation, 1995.

Gosho Translation Committee, editor-translator. *The Writings of Nichiren Daishonin*. Tokyo: Soka Gakkai, 1999.

Hori, Kyotsu, comp. *Writings of Nichiren Shonin: Doctrine Volume 2*. Tokyo: Nichiren Shu Overseas Propagation Promotion Association, 2002.

_____. *Writings of Nichiren Shonin: Doctrine Volume 3*. Tokyo: Nichiren Shu Overseas Propagation Promotion Association, 2004.

Murano, Senchu, trans. *The Lotus Sūtra*. Hayward: Nichiren Buddhist International Center, 2012.

_____. *Kaimokusho or Liberation from Blindness*. Berkeley: Numata Center for Buddhist Translation and Research, 2000.

Yamamoto, Kosho, trans. *Mahaparinirvāna-Sūtra: A Complete Translation from the Classical Chinese Language in 3 Volumes*. Tokyo: Karinbunko, 1973.

Chapter 17 – Origins of the Buddhist Schools of East Asia

Writings of Nichiren Shōnin Doctrine 2, pp. 34-37
Kaimoku-shō or Liberation from Blindness, pp. 13-17
The Writings of Nichiren Daishonin I, pp. 224-226

When Nichiren begins his discussion of the different teachings of the Buddha in *Kaimoku-shō*, he does so in reference to ten schools of Buddhism that existed in Japan by the 13th century. Throughout the rest of *Kaimoku-shō* as well as in Nichiren's other writings, he refers to these schools and assumes that the reader is familiar with them. We, however, are not familiar with these schools, their origins, their founders, or their distinct teachings and practices. In this chapter I am going to present a brief overview of the history of Buddhism in India and East Asia in order to show how these schools arose and what they were about in order to provide the context for Nichiren's discussion of them.

I have already discussed the life of Śākyamuni Buddha and how scholars such as Hajime Nakamura believe that he passed away in 383 BCE. Though others might put forth other dates, I am going to go with that one. The traditional story (which can be found in chapters eleven and twelve of the Cullavagga section of the Theravādin Vinaya) is that during the rainy season retreat after the Buddha's final nirvāṇa the elder Mahākāśyapa convened a council of 500 arhats to recite the discourses (Dharma) and discipline (Vinaya) that had been taught by the Buddha so that they would not be forgotten or altered. Ānanda recited all the discourses (what became the Sūtra-basket) and Upāli recited all the precepts (what became the Vinaya-basket) on that occasion. In time, the Abhidharma-basket was added to the Sūtra-basket and Vinaya-basket to complete the *tripiṭaka* (lit. three baskets). The Abhidharma is a collection of works that present a systematic analysis of the teachings found in the other two baskets. The *tripiṭaka* was then passed on by oral transmission for several centuries in different languages and dialects. After just a few generations, however, many different versions existed of the Three Baskets. In regard to this first council Charles Prebish wrote:

> *The historicity of the council as described is questioned by almost all scholars. That a small group of Buddha's intimate disciples gathered after his death is not unlikely, but a council in the grand style described in the various texts is almost certainly a fiction. (Prebish, p. 23)*

In East Asian Buddhism, Mahākāśyapa's role in leading the Sangha after the Buddha's final nirvāṇa did not end with the conclusion of the first council (whatever that may or may not have been). He is viewed as the Buddha's successor and the heir of the Dharma. This claim is contradicted in the *Mahāparinibbāna Sutta* of the Theravādin version of the Buddha's teachings, wherein the Buddha flatly refused to designate a successor.

> *And the Lord said to Ānanda: "Ānanda, it may be that you will think: 'The Teacher's instruction has ceased, now we have no teacher!' It should not be seen like this, Ānanda, for what I have taught and explained to you as Dharma and discipline will, at my passing, be your teacher." (Walshe, pp. 269-270)*

Other accounts found in Indian sūtras did, however, portray the Buddha as designating Mahākāśyapa the first in what would become a lineage of successors.

> *Perhaps more to the point, in the Mūlasarvāstivādin vinaya, the Buddha explicitly confirms Mahākāśyapa as his legitimate successor. Similarly, when the convocation of the five hundred arhants occurs, we are given a picture of Mahākāśyapa presiding by acclamation. Mahākāśyapas's preeminent position is further defined in Northwestern texts; he is listed several times as the Buddha's successor, who in turn is*

to choose his own successor and even the successor of his successor. (Ray, p. 108)

In 472, a work called the *History of the Transmission of the Dharma Treasury* was translated into Chinese, though a Sanskrit copy has never been found and it may have been a Chinese creation. According to this work, after the Buddha's passing, Mahākāśyapa transmitted the "Dharma treasury" to Ānanda, who in turn transmitted it to Śānavāsa and Madhyāntika. Śānavāsa then transmitted it to Upagupta. The succession continues on from Upagupta until the twenty-third (or twenty-fourth if Madhyāntika is included) and final successor, Āryasimha who was martyred in the Kashmir by a king hostile to Buddhism. Included in this linage of twenty-four successors were the great

luminaries of Mahāyāna Buddhism as the eleventh successor Aśvaghoṣa (c. first or second century), the thirteenth successor Nāgārjuna (late second to early third century), and the twentieth successor Vasubandhu (c. fourth or fifth century). This lineage was accepted in the Tiantai school and listed by Guanding (561-632; also known as Zhang'an) in his introduction to the *Great Calming and Contemplation* of Zhiyi (538-597).

Leaving aside the matter of whether or not a lineage of patriarchs was established, traditional accounts are in agreement that a second council was held a century after the first council. This council was held at Vaiśālī, the capital of the Vriji confederation. The second council composed of seven hundred elder monks was called because of a disagreement over the precepts. According to the Theravādin account there were ten points at issue wherein the Vriji monks had become lax. For instance, they allowed for the acceptance of offerings of gold and silver on the part of the monks. By the council's end the ten points had been condemned. This was the last council universally recognized by all schools of Buddhism. Prebish says, "Almost all scholars agree that this council was a historical event." (Prebish, p. 25) The time of the council, however, is more likely to have been around middle of the fourth century BCE, if one accepts 383 BCE as the date of the Buddha's passing. (See William, p. 16)

Sometime after the second council (perhaps around 300 BCE) a new controversy arose when a monk named Mahādeva claimed that arhats were still fallible in a number of areas. According to some accounts, another council was held in Pāṭaliputra (the new capital city of Magadha) to resolve the issue.

There may also have been disagreements about the precepts between conservative and liberal factions of monks. The result of this controversy was the first major schism in the Sangha. The conservative group who held the arhat in higher regard came to be known as the Sthaviravāda (lit. School of the Elders). The more liberal group that saw the arhat as fallible came to be known as the Mahāsamghika (lit. Greater Sangha). These two groups split into even more factions over time until there were some eighteen or twenty major schools of Buddhism. These eighteen or twenty schools each had their own distinctive interpretation of the Abhidharma-basket so they are considered Abhidharma schools, but many of them had their own versions of the Vinaya-basket and the Sūtra-basket as well. After the aforementioned second council at Vaiśālī, there would no longer be any pan-Buddhist councils.

In 268 BCE, Aśoka became the emperor of the Mauryan dynasty that had conquered all but the southern tip of the Indian subcontinent. In 260 BCE, Aśoka was so conscience stricken by the bloody conquest of the Kalinga kingdom that he renounced warfare and became a Buddhist layman. Emperor Aśoka ruled peacefully until his death in 232 BCE. Among the many things he did to support Buddhism two are significant in terms of its development. One was that, according to the Theravādins, he convened a third council of Buddhism in 250 BCE in Pātaliputra, now the capital of the empire. One thousand Sthaviravādin monks attended this council in order to clarify the moral and doctrinal standards for the Sangha. Those who did not meet those standards were expelled. The second thing Aśoka did was to send missionaries to all parts of the known world, including sending his son Mahinda and his daughter Sanghamitta to Sri Lanka to spread Buddhism there. That branch of the Sthaviravāda later spread to Burma, Thailand, and other parts of SE Asia, where it is now known as Theravāda (the Pāli name for School of the Elders).

The Theravāda recension of the *tripiṭaka* was recorded in the Pāli language in Sri Lanka in the first century BCE and is often referred to now as the Pāli canon. Theravāda is now the only survivor of the pre-Mahāyāna schools of Buddhism.

In northwest India and the Kashmir, other branches of the Sthaviravāda flourished for a time. The most important of these was the Sarvāstivādin, whose later branches or sub-sects included the Dharmaguptakas (whose Vinaya lineage is still maintained by the monks and nuns of China, Korea, and Vietnam) and the Sautrāntikas (who did not consider the Abhidharma canonical). King Kanishka I (c. 128-151), third ruler of the Kushana dynasty that ruled much of central Asia, the Kashmir, and northern India, became a patron of the Sarvāstivāda and convened what that school considered the fourth Buddhist council wherein a treatise on Abhidharma called the *Great Exegesis of Abhidharma Treatise* (S. *Abhidharma-mahāvibhāṣā-śāstra*) was written (though scholars believe that it was actually compiled in the 3rd century during the reign of King Kanishka II). Sarvāstivāda as well as all other schools of Buddhism disappeared from central Asia and India by the end of the twelfth century due to the resurgence of Vedic religion and Muslim conquests. The *tripiṭaka* of the Sarvāstivāda was recorded in Sanskrit but today only a portion of it exists in its Chinese translation.

Beginning in the first century BCE, a new form of Buddhism called Mahāyāna (lit. Great Vehicle) arose within the existing Abhidharma schools, particularly within the Mahāsamghika and the Sarvāstivāda. Monks (and nuns) within those orders began to aspire to buddhahood and engage in contemplative practices that they hoped would grant them visions of buddhas and bodhisattvas who could give their blessings and even new teachings to these aspiring bodhisattvas. Apparently these Mahāyāna monks and nuns remained a minority within Indian Buddhism and because they did not have their own Vinaya-basket or (at least until the fourth century) an Abhidharma-basket, they remained members of the Sarvāstivāda, Mahāsamghika, or other schools that they were ordained in. Though Mahāyāna monastics may have been involved in the stūpa cults, wherein both lay Buddhists and even the monastics revered the relics of the Buddha and other great saints, Mahāyāna itself held that upholding the perfection of wisdom brought infinitely greater merit than stūpa veneration. A Mahāyāna monk or nun probably did not appear all that different from the non-Mahāyāna monastic, the difference was in their aspirations, the nature of their contemplations, and perhaps their private devotions. Tensions did arise eventually, but records from Chinese monks who traveled to India testified that Mahāyāna and non-Mahāyāna monastics coexisted within the same monasteries.

Over the following centuries, until the end of Buddhism in India and central Asia, the Mahāyānists compiled the Mahāyāna sūtras. These sūtras critiqued Abhidharma scholasticism for reifying its categories of analysis and what they saw as the limited and even spiritually selfish goal of becoming an arhat in order to escape saṃsāra by attaining nirvāṇa only for oneself. Instead, the early Mahāyāna sūtras taught the emptiness of all phenomena and upheld the bodhisattva-vehicle discussed in the last chapter. Later Mahāyāna sūtras emphasized the mind-constructed nature of experience and the purification of the mind to reveal the buddha-nature. Among the early Mahāyāna sūtras that appeared between the first century BCE and the second century CE were the *Flower Garland Sūtra*, the Pure Land sūtras, the *Vimalakīrti Sūtra*, the Perfection of Wisdom sūtras, and the *Lotus Sūtra*. Later Mahāyāna sūtras of the third and fourth centuries include the *Revealing the Profound Secrets Sūtra*, the *Lankāvatāra Sūtra*, and the *Nirvāṇa Sūtra*. Starting in the seventh century, tantric forms of practice began to appear within Buddhism that incorporated mantras, mudras, and mandalas. The purpose of tantric or esoteric Buddhist practice was to achieve the aims of both worldly benefit and the quick attainment of buddhahood. Esoteric themed sūtras like the *Mahāvairocana Sūtra*, the *Diamond Peak Sūtra*, and the *Act of Perfection Sūtra* appeared at this time.

The earliest Mahāyāna monk that we know of by name was supposedly Aśvaghoṣa, who was the court poet of either King Kanishka I or King Kanishka II. Aśvaghoṣa was the author of the earliest Sanskrit biography of the Buddha, the *Buddhacarita*. He is also credited with the *Awakening of Faith in the Mahāyāna Treatise*, a popular work in East Asian Buddhism that was probably composed in China in the 6th century and became very important in the Flower Garland school.

The most famous Indian Mahāyānist of all was the south Indian monk Nāgārjuna. According to legend, Nāgārjuna retrieved the Mahāyāna sūtras from the nāgas, who had hidden them until the world was ready. He was also the author of the *Root Verses on the Middle Way* (S. *Mūla-madhyamaka-kārikā*), and other works dealing with the perfection of wisdom teachings, the distinction but also interrelationship between conventional truth and ultimate truth, and the doctrine of emptiness. In China he was credited with the *Great Perfection of Wisdom Treatise* that Kumārajīva translated into Chinese. Nāgārjuna and his disciple Āryadeva were the founders of the Middle Way (S. *Madhyamaka*) school of Mahāyāna.

Vasubandhu is the next most prominent Mahāyāna teacher. He lived in northwest India in the fifth century. He was originally a Sarvāstivādin monk who authored the *Treasury of Abhidharma Treatise* (S. *Abhidharma-kośa-*

bhāshya), a poem with auto-commentary that summarizes the *Great Exegesis Treatise of Abhidharma Treatise* but also subjects it to a critique from the Sautrāntika perspective. His older brother Asanga later converted him to the Mahāyāna. Legend says that Asanga studied the Mahāyāna with Maitreya Bodhisattva. As a Mahāyānist, Vasubandhu helped his brother Asanga establish the Yoga Practitioners (S. *Yogācāra*) school of Buddhism (also known as the Consciousness-Only (S. *Vijñānavāda*) school. The Yoga Practitioners school is critical of the teaching of emptiness and its seeming nihilism, and instead focuses on the cultivation of consciousness in order to overcome subject-object dualism and thereby attain buddhahood. Other famous patriarchs of the Yoga Practitioners school who wrote commentaries on Vasubandhu's writings include Nanda (sixth century), Dharmapāla (530-651), and Śīlabhadra (529-645).

Now I will shift the focus to China and Japan. In a previous chapter I have already discussed how Buddhism came to China and how it was received. As we have just seen, however, Indian Buddhism was not a monolithic entity but a plethora of precept lineages, Abhidharma schools, devotional and philosophical movements, and even competing versions of the *tripiṭaka*. As various Hinayana and Mahāyāna works were translated into Chinese it became a challenge to make sense of it all. The Chinese began to wonder which teaching represented the true intentions of Śākyamuni Buddha. In time, ten major schools were established that were subsequently brought to Japan.

The *Great Exegesis of Abhidharma Treatise* of the Sarvāstivādins had been translated into Chinese as early as the late 4th century, giving rise to an Abhidharma school. That school was later replaced by the Abhidharma Treasury school that became recognized as the preeminent school of Sarvāstivādin teachings in East Asia. The Abhidharma Treasury school was based on the study of the *Treasury of Abhidharma Treatise* of Vasubandhu that was translated into Chinese by Paramārtha (499-569) between 563-567 and again by Xuanzang (602-664) between 651-654. Japanese monks who had gone to China to study with Xuanzang brought this school to Japan in 658. In Japan it was called the Kusha-shū. By 793, the Abhidharma Treasury school was merely a curriculum taught within the Dharma Characteristics school.

Another important Abhidharma school was the Completion of Reality school. This school focuses on the study of the *Completion of Reality Treatise* (S.

Satyasiddhi-śāstra) by an Indian monk named Harivarman (c. 4th century) that was translated by Kumārajīva between 411-412. It is considered a work of the Bahuśrutīya school of pre-Mahāyāna Buddhism, but it also teaches the emptiness of all dharmas and so is considered a good introduction to Mahāyāna teachings. The Korean monk Hyegwan brought the Completion of Reality school to Japan in 625, where it became known as the Jōjitsu-shū. By 806 it had become no more than a curriculum taught within the Thee Treatises school.

The Discipline school was founded in China by Daoxuan (596-667) who instituted the Vinaya of the Dharmagupta school based on the *Four-part Discipline* translated in the early 5th century. From that time on, Mahāyāna monks and nuns in China, Korea, and Vietnam have all been ordained in the Dharmagupta precept lineage. The Discipline school was brought to Japan by Jianzhen (688-763) in 753 where it was called the Ritsu-shū. In 755, Jianzhen established a precept platform to confer the Dharmagupta precepts upon monks and nuns at Tōdaiji Temple in Nara, and two more precept platforms were established in 761 at Yakushiji Temple (in present day Tochigi prefecture) and Kanzeonji Temple (in present day Fukuoka prefecture). The Ritsu-shū's popularity declined after the 8th century. In Nichiren's day, Eizon (1201-1290) revived the school in conjunction with esoteric Buddhism, thereby establishing the Mantra-Discipline school (J. Shingon Risshū).

The Three Treatises School introduced the Middle Way school teachings to China. It was based on the study of three treatises translated by Kumārajīva. In 404 Kumārajīva translated the *One Hundred Verse Treatise* attributed to Nāgārjuna's disciple Āryadeva. In 409 he translated the *Middle Way Treatise* (a translation of Nāgārjuna's *Root Verses on the Middle Way*), and the *Twelve Gates Treatise* attributed to Nāgārjuna. Jizang (549-632) is considered the founder of the Three Treatises school because he was the one who systematized and refined its teachings. The Korean monk Hyegwan (the same monk who brought the Completion of Reality teachings) was a disciple of Jizang and he brought the Three Treatises school to Japan in 625, where it was called the Sanron-shū. The Sanron-shū died out as an independent school by the mid-twelfth century.

The aforementioned Chinese monk Zhiyi founded the Tiantai school when he established a teaching center on Mt. Tiantai in the latter half of the sixth century. He was later known as the Great Master Tiantai. Zhiyi was a great

215

scholar and meditator who wanted to systematize all the seemingly contradictory teachings that had been translated into Chinese. To do this, he classified the Buddha's teachings into five flavors and eight different types of teaching. Zhiyi was a practitioner as well as a scholar. He put equal emphasis on meditation practice and doctrine in order to create a balanced system whereby doctrine would inform practice and practice would actualize doctrine. The concept of the "three thousand realms in a single thought-moment" (covered in a previous chapter) was part of his explanation of the sudden and perfect method of calming and contemplation meditation. He also taught the unity of the threefold truth of emptiness, provisional existence, and the Middle Way in order to clarify the true meaning of the teachings of the Perfection of Wisdom sūtras and Nāgārjuna regarding emptiness, causality, and the Middle Way. The Tiantai school declined in prestige during the 7th and 8th centuries due to the rise of the Dharma Characteristics, Flower Garland, and Zen schools. These schools overshadowed the Tiantai school in terms of prestige and royal patronage. The Tiantai school was briefly revived during the time of Zhanran (711-782; aka Miaole), the school's sixth patriarch (if Zhiyi is considered the first). The Tiantai teachings were first brought to Japan by Jianzhen, who was also a Tiantai monk as well as a Vinaya master. Saichō (767-822; later known as Dengyō) later studied these teachings and was greatly intrigued by them. In 804, Saichō was able to travel to China to learn more about Tiantai Buddhism and other teachings and bring back more reliable texts. Saichō returned to Japan in 805 and began the establishment of the Japanese version of this school, known as the Tendai-shū, on Mt. Hiei.

Translations of the Yoga Practitioner teachings had begun to appear in China by the sixth century, but these earlier translations were not complete or reliable. In order to clarify the Buddhist teachings, the monk Xuanzang traveled to India where he studied with Śīlabhadra and other teachers. He also gathered sūtras and commentaries to translate upon his return to China. He and his disciple Kuiji (632-682; also known as Ci'en) then established the definitive form of the East Asian Yoga Practitioner school known as the Dharma Characteristics school. The Dharma Characteristics school was first brought to Japan by the Japanese monk Dōshō (629-700) who had traveled to China to study with Xuanzang and then returned in 661. In Japan it is called the Hossō-shū.

The *Flower Garland Sūtra* became the basis of its own school in China. The Flower Garland School was established by Dushun (557-640), though its third patriarch, Fazang (643-712) was the true founder of the school. The Chinese monk Daoxuan (702-760) introduced the Flower Garland school to Japan in 736, but its establishment as a school is credited to the Korean monk Simsang (d. 742), a student of Fazang who gave a lecture to the emperor on the Flower Garland teachings in 740. In Japan it is called the Kegon-shū.

Esoteric Buddhism was introduced to China when the Indian monk Śubhākarasimha (637-735)) came in 716 and translated the *Mahāvairocana Sūtra* with his disciple Yixing (683-727) in 725. At some point they also translated the *Act of Perfection Sūtra*. In 720, two more Indian masters of tantric Buddhism came to China, Vajrabodhi (671-741) and his disciple Amoghavajra (705-774). Amoghavajra translated the *Diamond Peak Sūtra* in 746. These sūtras were the basis of the Mantra school of esoteric Buddhism. Amoghavajra transmitted the Mantra teachings to Huiguo (746-805) who in turn transmitted them to Japanese monk Kūkai (774-835; later known as Kobo). Kūkai had gone to China in 804 and returned to Japan in 806 whereupon he founded the Japanese Mantra school, the Shingon-shū.

The Kusha, Jōjitsu, Ritsu, Sanron, Hossō, and Kegon schools are known collectively as the six schools of Nara, because all of them were established in Japan during the time when Nara was the capital of Japan (710-794). The next period of Japanese history is known as the Heian period (794-1192) because the capital was moved to Heian-kyo (the name was changed to Kyoto in the eleventh century). During this period the Tiantai and Mantra schools were brought to Japan.

In the Kamakuran period (1192-1333), Zen and Pure Land Buddhism began to become popular as distinctive Buddhist movements. Both were present in some form before that time. Pure Land devotions were known and practiced by members of all schools of East Asian Buddhism going back at least to the time of the monk Huiyuan (334-416) and his White Lotus Society that was dedicated to the practice of chanting the name of Amitābha Buddha and visualizing the buddha and his Pure Land of the West. The practice of reciting the name of Amitābha Buddha was also one of the methods utilized for calming and insight meditation by Zhiyi. After the persecution of Buddhism by the Emperor Wu in 845, only the Pure Land and Zen schools continued to flourish in China. The Zen school initially held itself aloof from and even criticized Pure Land Buddhism, but in the end Pure Land practice was even incorporated into the Zen school. The Pure Land Buddhism which survived the persecution of 845 and later attained mass appeal throughout East Asia was not, however, the same as that championed by Huiyuan or Zhiyi. Rather, it was a form of Pure Land Buddhism inspired by the three Pure Land sūtras. This form of Pure Land Buddhism deemphasized the visualization of Amitābha Buddha and the Pure Land of the West, and put much greater emphasis on the 18th vow of Amitābha Buddha, called the Original Vow, and the chanting of the name of Amitābha Buddha to the virtual exclusion of all other practices in order to be reborn in the Pure Land after death. Three teachers of Chinese Pure Land Buddhism in particular spread this kind of Pure Land Buddhism. These teachers were Tanluan (476-542), Daochuo (562-645), and Shandao (613-681). In Japan, the exclusive practice of Pure Land Buddhism was advocated by Hōnen (1133-1212) beginning in 1175. By the Kamakuran era, Pure Land Buddhism had become immensely popular, though it was considered a movement within the Tendai-shū and was not recognized as a separate school until the early 15th century.

Bodhidharma is credited with establishing the Zen school in China in the early 6th century. Bodhidharma was the legendary 28th patriarch of Indian Buddhism and 1st patriarch of the Zen school in China. Zen is actually the Japanese pronunciation of the Chinese word *chan*, which is in turn a transliteration of *dhyāna*, the Sanksrit word for meditative absorption. Zen, however, refers to the unity of *dhyāna* and *prajñā* (wisdom) and not meditative absorption alone. According to the Zen school the Dharma has been transmitted from person-to-person (or mind-to-mind) from Śākyamuni Buddha through his successors all the way to the present-day Zen Masters. In this way the true meaning of the Buddha's teachings has been passed on through the actual awakening of these successors and not just in the written teachings. By the tenth century there were five houses of Zen, but only two have survived: the Linji founded by Linji Yixuan (d. 866) and the Caodong founded by Dongshan Liangjie (807-869) and his disciple Caoshan Benji (840-901). Zen was actually brought to Japan before the Kamakura period, for instance, Saichō was given transmission in the Ox Head lineage while in China, but it was never promulgated. A monk named Dainichin Nōnin tried to establish a Bodhidharma School in 1189 after receiving a certificate of Zen transmission with a correspondent in China, but he was regarded as a fraud. Eisai (1141-1215) succeeded in introducing Linji (J. Rinzai) Zen to Japan 1191, after spending four years in China training with the Zen Masters there. Dōgen

(1200-1253) introduced Caodong (J. Sōtō) Zen to Japan after studying in China from 1223-1227. After the Sung dynasty fell to the Mongols, Zen Masters from China such as Lanxi Daolong (J. Rankei Dōryū) came to Japan and helped to spread Rinzai Zen.

I hope that this brief survey (by no means comprehensive) will help clarify who and what Nichiren is talking about as he discusses the other schools of Buddhism in relation to the teaching of the *Lotus Sūtra*. Further details about the teachings and history of these ten schools will be provided as needed as we proceed through the *Kaimoku-shō*.

Sources

Ch'en, Kenneth. *Buddhism in China: A Historical Survey*. Princeton: Princeton University Press, 1964.

Donner, Neal, and Stevenson, Daniel B., trans. *The Great Calming and Contemplation: A Study and Annotated Translation of the First Chapter of Chih-I's Mo-Ho Chih-Kuan*. Honolulu: Kuroda Institute, 1993.

Gosho Translation Committee, editor-translator. *The Writings of Nichiren Daishonin*. Tokyo: Soka Gakkai, 1999.

Hori, Kyotsu, comp. *Writings of Nichiren Shonin: Doctrine Volume 2*. Tokyo: Nichiren Shū Overseas Propagation Promotion Association, 2002.

Kasahara, Kazuo. *A History of Japanese Religion*. Tokyo: Kosei Publishing Co., 2002.

Kashiwahara, Yusen & Sonoda, Koyu. *Shapers of Japanese Buddhism*. Tokyo: Kosei Publishing Co., 1994.

Matsunaga, Alicia & Matsunaga, Daigan. *Foundation of Japanese Buddhism Vol. I & II*. Los Angeles: Buddhist Books International, 1988.

Mitchell, Donald W. Buddhism: *Introducing the Buddhist Experience*. New York: Oxford University Press, 2002.

Murano, Senchu, trans. *Kaimokusho or Liberation from Blindness*. Berkeley: Numata Center for Buddhist Translation and Research, 2000.

Prebish, Charles S., ed. *Buddhism: A Modern Perspective*. University Park: The Pennsylvania State University Press, 1978.

Pruden, Leo, trans. *The Essentials of the Eight Traditions*. Berkeley: Numata Center for Buddhist Translation and Research, 1994.

Ray, Reginald *A. Buddhist Saints in India: A Study in Buddhist Values & Orientations*. New York: Oxford University Press, 1994.

Takakusu, Junjiro. *The Essentials of Buddhist Philosophy*. Delhi: Motilal Banarsidass, 1978.

Tamura, Yoshiro. *Japanese Buddhism: A Cultural History*. Tokyo: Kosei Publishing Co., 2000.

Walshe, Maurice, trans. *The Long Discourses of the Buddha: A Translation of the Digha Nikaya*. Boston: Wisdom Publications, 1995.

Williams, Paul. *Mahāyāna Buddhism: The Doctrinal Foundations*. New York: Routledge, 1989.

Williams, Paul & Tribe, Anthony. *Buddhist Thought: A Complete Introduction to the Indian Tradition*. New York: Routledge, 2000.

Chapter 18 – Misappropriation of the Dharma

Writings of Nichiren Shōnin Doctrine 2, pp. 34-37, 78-80, 85
Kaimoku-shō or Liberation from Blindness, pp. 13-17, 74-76, 84
The Writings of Nichiren Daishonin I, pp. 224-226, 259-260, 264

After praising the Buddha and the teaching of the "three thousand realms in a single thought-moment" found in the *Lotus Sūtra*, Nichiren laments the misappropriating of the Dharma. He accuses the Abhidharma Treasury school and the Completion of Reality school of teaching Mahāyāna doctrines that are not found in their own texts. He then accuses Brahmanism, Taoism, and Confucianism of misappropriating Buddhist teachings in order to bolster their own. Finally, he accuses the Flower Garland and Mantra schools of using the Tiantai teaching of the "three thousand realms in a single thought-moment" to interpret their own sūtras. This may seem rather odd to us. Even in our age of "intellectual property" law, we do not usually think that this should apply to religious teachings. In fact, religious traditions have always mutually influenced and cross-fertilized one another when they have come into contact (even when that contact is antagonistic). What exactly is Nichiren concerned about? Is there any truth to his accusations?

Let's start with Nichiren's accusation against Brahmanism. Nichiren says:

> For instance, non-Buddhist teachings in India (gedō)
> before the time of the Buddha were shallow in theology.
> After the Buddha, however, they seemed to realize their
> own shortcomings as they learned from Buddhism and
> cunningly stole Buddhist concepts to make their own
> heretical teachings more sophisticated. These are cases
> of Buddhists assisting heretics and heretics stealing
> Buddhism. (Hori 2002, p. 35 adapted)

For over a thousand years the various schools of Indian thought, both orthodox (S. *āstika*) and heterodox (S. *nāstika*) debated their teachings with one another. Even in refuting another school of thought, one would have to take into account the good points made by one's rival. There also needed to be common terms of debate. It is no wonder that there are commonalities between the various schools of Indian thought. In addition, because it is very hard to date early Indian texts and those texts are themselves based on even older oral traditions, it becomes difficult, if not impossible, to tell who is borrowing from who. A case in point would be early Buddhism and the *Yoga Sūtras* of Patañjali, a collection of terse aphorisms on yoga practice that appeared after the time of the Buddha but before the fifth century CE. The presentation of the practice of yoga in the *Yoga Sūtras* deals with meditation practice (what is sometimes called "Rāja Yoga" or "Dhyāna Yoga") and has much in common with Buddhist methods. For instance, the Yoga Sūtras speak of the state of meditative absorption being preceded in the mind of the practitioner by faith, energy, mindfulness, concentration and wisdom (See *Yoga Sūtras* I.20). The Buddha spoke of these as five faculties and five powers that a practitioner should cultivate. The *Yoga Sūtras* also speak of cultivating an attitude of loving-kindness, compassion, sympathetic joy, and equanimity towards others (See *Yoga Sūtras* I.33). The Buddha taught these as the "four immeasurable minds" or as the "four divine abodes." Was Patañjali using Buddhist terminology and methods? Or did the Buddha draw upon the ancient tradition of yoga in his own teachings? He did, after all, study with two masters of yoga, Āḷāra Kālāma and Udraka Rāmaputra, before he attained awakening and began teaching the Buddha Dharma. So who borrowed from whom? Edwin Bryant, a translator of the *Yoga Sūtras* of Patanjali, says:

> *Scholars have long pointed out a commonality of vocabulary and concepts between the Yoga Sūtras and Buddhist texts. All this underscores the basic point that there was a cluster of interconnected and cross-fertilizing variants of meditational yoga – Buddhist and Jain as well as Hindu – prior to Patañjali, all drawn from a common but variegated pool of terminologies, practices, and concepts (and many strains continue to the present day). (Bryant, p. xxv)*

Chip Hatranft, another translator of the *Yoga Sūtras*, says:

*In any event, Patañjali's yoga evolved to a great extent
from a Buddhistic approach that itself had been a
development of brahmanical-Upanishadic yoga. This
interweaving of influences is a characteristic feature of
Indian philosophical thought. (Hartranft, p. 84)*

So it would seem that in the case of the Yoga school of Indian thought, the accusation of appropriating the teachings of another school may run both ways. In any case, it was not a matter of stealing someone else's ideas but of drawing from a common pool of methods relating to spiritual cultivation.

Advaita or Non-dual Vedānta presents a more clear-cut case of Buddhist teachings becoming the inspiration for a teaching that is not only non-Buddhist but even inimical to Buddhism. Vedānta deals with the ultimate meaning of the Vedas, specifically the Upanishads. It actually encompasses several different schools of interpretation ranging from non-dualism (or monism), to qualified non-dualism, and even to outright dualism. Vedānta begins with the *Brahma Sūtras* (also called the *Vedānta Sūtras*) of Bādarāyana. The author, Badarāyana, has been traditionally identified with the seer Vyasa, who is credited with being the compiler and editor of the Vedas and the Purānas. The *Brahma Sūtras* have been dated as early as the fourth century BCE and as late as the fifth century CE. Like the *Yoga Sūtras*, the *Brahma Sūtras* is a short collection of very terse aphorisms. These aphorisms are meant to provide a systematic explanation of the deepest meaning of the Upanishads, but they require a commentary in order to understand. The Upanishads, the *Bhagavad Gita*, and the *Brahma Sūtras* are together considered the triple basis of Vedānta. The non-dual form of Vedānta, called Advaita Vedānta, began with the teachings of Śankara (788-820), a brahmin who became a wandering mendicant (*sannyāsin*), wrote commentaries on the *Brahma Sūtras* and the Upanishads, and founded many monastic centers and orders of monks. Śankara's teacher's teacher was a brahmin named Gaudapada (eighth century) whose only extant work is a commentary on the *Māndukya Upanishad*. In that commentary, Gaudapada taught a form of non-dualism that Surendranath Dasgupta points out was obviously influenced by the Middle Way school (or *Śūnyavāda*) teachings about emptiness (*śunyatā*) and the Consciousness-Only (*Vijñānavāda*) teachings about the ultimate purity of consciousness once defilements have been overturned.

Gaudapada thus flourished after all the great Buddhist teachers Aśvaghoṣa, Nāgārjuna, Asanga, and Vasubandhu; and I believe that there is sufficient evidence in his kārikās for thinking that he was possibly himself a Buddhist, and considered that the teachings of the Upanishads tallied with those of Buddha.
(Dasgupta, p. 423)

It is so obvious that these doctrines are borrowed from the Madhyamika doctrines as found in Nāgārjuna's kārikās and the Vijñānavāda doctrines, as found in Laṅkāvatāra, that it is needless to attempt to prove it. Gaudapada assimilated all the Buddhist Śūnyavāda and Vijñānavāda teachings and thought that these held good of the ultimate truth preached in the Upanishads. It is immaterial whether he was a Hindu or a Buddhist, so long as we are sure that he had the highest respect for the Buddha and for the teachings that he believed to be his. Guadapada took the smallest Upanishad to comment upon, probably because he wished to give his opinions unrestricted by the textual limitations of the bigger ones. His main emphasis is on the truth that he realized to be perfect. He only incidentally suggested that the great Buddhist truth of indefinable and unspeakable vijñāna or vacuity would hold good of the highest ātman of the Upanishads, and thus laid the foundation of a revival of the Upanishads studied on Buddhist lines. How far the Upanishads guaranteed in detail the truth of Gaudapada's views it was left for his disciple, the great Śaṅkara, to examine and explain.
(Ibid, p. 429)

Śankara's teachings followed Gaudapada's non-dualism in identifying Brahman as the only reality that is also our true self or Ātman, all else is an illusion (*māyā*). His commentary on the *Brahma Sūtras* along these lines in particular became the foundation of Advaita Vedānta. Other schools of Vedānta arose later that refuted his work on the grounds that he had misread the *Brahma Sūtras* and the Upanishads. These later commentators accused Śaṅkara of being a crypto-Buddhist. Śaṅkara, however, did his best to obscure the Buddhist inspirations for his teachings and in fact he was quite opposed to Buddhism. Dasgupta made the following observations in regard to Śaṅkara and Advaita Vedānta:

> *The main difference between the Vedanata as expounded by Gaudapada and as explained by Śankara consists in this, that Śankara tried as best he could to dissociate the distinctive Buddhist traits found in the exposition of the former and to formulate the philosophy as a direct interpretation of the older Upanishad texts. In this he achieved remarkable success. He was no doubt regarded by some as a hidden Buddhist (pracchanna Bauddha), but his influence on Hindu thought and religion became so great that he was regarded in later times as being almost a divine person or an incarnation. (Ibid, p. 437)*

> *Śankara and his followers borrowed much of their dialectic form of criticism from the Buddhists. His Brahman was very much like the śūnya of Nāgārjuna. It is difficult indeed to distinguish between pure being and pure non-being as a category. The debts of Śankara to the self-luminosity of Vijñānavāda Buddhism can hardly be overestimated. There seems to be much truth in the accusations against Śankara by Vijñāna Bhikshu and others that he was a hidden Buddhist himself. I am led to think that Śankara's philosophy is largely a compound of Vijñānavāda and Śūnyavāda Buddhism with the Upanishad notion of the permanence of self superadded. (Ibid, pp. 493-494)*

According to Wendy Doniger, Buddhism also inspired Śankara's monastic system. This was displeasing to others brahmins and also caused some to accuse Śankara of being a crypto-Buddhist.

*While there had been renouncers in Hinduism since
before the time the Upanishads mapped out the path of
flame and Release, they lacked the institutional backing
to become a major force – until Śankara. But Śankara
took the idea of formal monastic orders and institutions
from Buddhism and reworked it for Hinduism, an action
that stirred up some Brahmins like a saffron flag waved
in front of a bull. Ramanuja called Śankara a "crypto-
Buddhist (prachanna-baudda). (Doniger 2009, p. 507)*

According to Gavin Flood, "The orders founded by Śankara were partly
instrumental in eradicating Jainism and Buddhism from south India and also
giving coherence and a sense of pan-Indian identity to orthodox, vedic
traditions." (Flood, pp. 92-93) So it would seem that Śankara had indeed
learned from Buddhism (at least through Gaudapada) and used what he
learned to strengthen the teachings and institutions of an important element
of the Hindu tradition at the expense of Buddhism. In the case of Śankara,
Nichiren's concern that others have misappropriated the Dharma to the
detriment of Buddhism seems accurate and justified.

Turning to the Chinese traditions, Nichiren said of them:

*The same can be said of those in China (geten).
Confucian and Taoist scholars before Buddhism was
introduced to China had been as simple and immature
as infants. However, in the Later Han dynasty, when
Buddhism came to China and gradually spread after the
initial controversies, some Buddhist monks returned
home because they could not keep Buddhist precepts or
chose to return to secular life. Some Buddhist monks
simply adopted Buddhist teachings into Confucianism
and Taoism in collaboration with secular men. (Hori
2002, p. 35)*

The Taoists were the first to adopt Buddhist ideas. In a previous chapter I
talked about how Taoism as a religion came about in the second century CE
with the enshrining of Laozi as the Great Lord on High, the appearance of the

scripture called the *Classic of Great Peace*, and the founding of the Celestial Masters or Central Orthodox School of Taoism. According to Kenneth Ch'en, religious Taoism from the beginning was modeled on Buddhism.

> *To begin with, the Taoists never had any idea of their system as a religion consisting of a body of doctrines and beliefs left behind by a master and preserved as a corpus of literature. It was only after Buddhism had come in and gained widespread acceptance that the Taoists took over from Buddhism the idea of a religion. Once having made the initial appropriation, the Taoists decided that they might just as well go all the way in imitating the foreign model. (Ch'en, p. 473)*

Ch'en goes on to say that beginning in the fifth century Taoists were using statues in imitation of Buddhism, were modeling their writings on Buddhist texts or even resorting to outright plagiarism, and took from Buddhism concepts such as karma, rebirth, and the bodhisattva ideal (Ibid, pp. 473-476).

Nichiren cites a passage from Zhiyi's *Great Calming and Contemplation* that speaks of former Buddhist monks returning to lay life, becoming Taoists, and using Buddhist teachings to bolster Taoism. "They appropriate the teachings of the Buddha and put them into their own texts. Thus, they pull higher teachings down to the level of lower teachings, nobler teachings down to the level of poor teachings, and make the two religions equal to each other." (Murano 2000, p. 15) Nichiren then cites a commentary on the above passage by Zhanran that specifically names Wei Yuansong (6th century) as an example of a Buddhist reverting to Taoism and attacking Buddhism. Wei Yuansong was a Buddhist novice from Sichuan who went to Chang'an, the capital of the Northern Zhou dynast, to seek his fortune. In 567, Wei Yuansong submitted a memorial to Emperor Wu (r. 561-577) claiming that the Buddhist Sangha should be purged of corrupt monks and nuns, that the building of stūpas was wasting the treasury of the empire and should be stopped, and that statues and images were not worthy of worship and should be destroyed. He went on to suggest that the distinction between monastic and householder should be abolished, that Buddhism and secular virtue were no different, and that the emperor should be considered to be the Buddha. Emperor Wu had been looking for an excuse to rein in the power of the Buddhist establishment, and

227

so the memorial was quite timely. Wei Yuansong was rewarded with the title Duke of Sichuan, and he left the Sangha and returned to the fold of Taoism. Wei Yuansong and a Taoist priest named Zhang Bin continued to advocate the suppression of Buddhism and in 574 Emperor Wu issued a decree proscribing Buddhism. Throughout the region ruled by the Northern Zhou, from 574 until Emperor Wu's death in 577, countless stūpas, statues, and shrines were destroyed, more than forty thousand temples were confiscated, and millions of monks and nuns were laicized. Ironically, Emperor Wu also proscribed Taoism because it had come to his attention how much the Taoists had modeled themselves on Buddhism. (To learn more about Wei Yunansong see Ch'en, pp. 187-194) Wei Yuansong certainly serves as a vivid example of a former monk returning to Taoism, using Buddhist teachings to further his own agenda, and then turning upon Buddhism itself.

Confucianism also adopted and adapted Buddhist insights and methods. During the Song dynasty (960-1279) a new form of Confucianism arose that is now known as Neo-Confucianism. Some of the founders were particularly influenced by Zen Buddhism, which had its golden age during the Tang dynasty (618-907). Zhou Dunyi (1017-1073) provided Neo-Confucianism with a metaphysical system in a short work entitled *An Explanation of the Diagram of the Great Ultimate* and in a commentary on the *Book of Changes* called *Penetrating the Book of Changes*. Shao Yong (1011-1077) also wrote about metaphysics inspired by the *Book of Changes* in his work *Supreme Principles Governing the World*. Zhang Zai (1020-1077) expressed the ethics of Neo-Confucianism in a short work called *The Western Inscription*. The Cheng brothers, the idealist Cheng Hao (1032-1085) and the rationalist Cheng Yi (1033-1107) are considered the founders of the two main branches of Neo-Confucianism, the School of Mind and the School of Principle respectively. The Cheng brothers were in fact the nephews of Zhang Zai, students of Zhou Dunyi, and friends with Shao Yong. Altogether, the five of them are known as the "Five Masters of the early Song." The greatest of the Neo-Confucians was Zhu Xi (1130-1200). He synthesized and systematized the work of the earlier Neo-Confucians, but in particular he carried forward the teachings of the School of Principle. Zhu Xi's commentaries on the *Analects of Confucius*, the *Book of Mencius*, the *Great Learning*, and the *Doctrine of the Mean* raised the status of these "four books" over and above the five classics (the six classics minus the lost *Book of Music*) of early Confucianism. The four books with Zhu Xi's commentaries became the basis of the civil service examination system in China from 1313 until 1905 when the system ended. His teachings also predominated in Korea during the time of the Yi dynasty (1392-1910) and in Japan during the Tokugawa period (1603-1867) where in both cases they became the official ideology of the state. Lu Xiangshan (1139-1192) carried forward the teachings of the School of Mind and was Zhu Xi's main intellectual rival.

None of these men had ever been monks, but many of them (particularly Zhang Zai and Cheng Hao) had studied Zen Buddhism in their youth. Zhou Dunyi's writings do not show much Buddhist influence, but he was a dedicated man of peace, loved lotus flowers, admired Buddhist teachings, and was teasingly called "that poor Zen fellow" by Cheng Yi. Their teachings were particularly concerned with the goodness of human nature, its cultivation, self-reflection, sincerity as the basis of good character, and the investigation of principle (C. *li*). By "principle" they meant that which makes things what they are, and it seems to encompass both the idea of natural law and morality. This is the same term that was used in the Flower Garland school of Buddhism to explain the interpenetration of principle and actuality (C. *shih*). As for the cultivation of sincerity, a term whose meaning includes such things as integrity, authenticity, and tranquility, the Neo-Confucians, especially the School of Mind branch, adopted the method of quiet sitting inspired by Zen and Taoist practices. Fung Yu-lan observed that the Neo-Confucians were particularly indebted to Zen (which he refers to by the Chinese name Ch'an using the Wade-Giles transliteration):

> *There are three lines of thought that can be traced as the main sources of Neo-Confucianism. The first, of course, is Confucianism itself. The second is Buddhism, together with Taoism via the medium of Ch'anism, for of all the schools of Buddhism, Ch'anism was the most influential at the time of the formation of Neo-Confucianism. To the Neo-Confucianists, Ch'anism and Buddhism are synonymous terms, and, as stated in the last chapter, in one sense Neo-Confucianism may be said to the logical development of Ch'anism. Finally, the third is the Taoist religion, of which the cosmological views of the Yin-Yang school formed an important element. The cosmology of the Neo-Confucianists is*

chiefly connected with this line of thought. (Yu-lan, p. 268)

Shu-hsien Liu made the following remarks about the influence of Buddhism (especially Hua-yen, the Flower Garland School) on Neo-Confucianism:

> *Ironically, the most important stimulation for the movement actually came from Buddhism and Taoism, as most Neo-Confucian thinkers drifted along for years before they returned to the Confucian Way. In fact, the most important concept in Sung-Ming Neo-Confucian philosophy – li (principle) – was barely mentioned in ancient Confucian philosophy. As Hua-yen first developed li as a philosophical concept, it was probable that Neo-Confucian thinkers took over the concept from Hua-yen and instilled new meaning into it. Neo-Confucians never made an attempt to conceal the fact that they were much indebted to Buddhism and Taoism for the introduction of new ideas; they supplied their own interpretations and in spirit were against the negativism they saw in Buddhism and Taoism. Thus, they developed sophisticated theories of metaphysics, cosmology and human nature in competition with Buddhism and Taoism, but in spirit they believe their theories were true to the teachings of Confucius and Mencius. (Liu, pp. 113-114)*

The Neo-Confucians were not friendly to Buddhism, however indebted they may have been. As Liu notes, they were against the negativism and quietism of Buddhism. This was probably a reaction to the otherworldly nature of Pure Land Buddhism and the austere monasticism of Zen and its emphasis on emptiness, which seemed to be the teaching of nihilism. They also saw Buddhism and Taoism as selfish in that both seemed to be seeking for their own spiritual liberation. Zhu Xi said of them: "The mistake of the Buddhists arises from their dislike [of the world] which is the result of their selfishness, and the mistake of the Taoists arises from their trickery which is the result of their selfishness. The mistake of the Buddhists is to dislike and take lightly human affairs and therefore wish to turn everything into void." (Chan, p. 646) Perhaps this is the impression Zhu Xi had of the Buddhists he knew, but his criticism of Buddhists selfishly rejecting the world were anticipated by Mahāyāna criticisms of the selfish Hīnayāna goals of the śrāvakas and pratyekabuddhas who reject the world and seek only their own liberation. Zhu Xi's criticisms of the teaching of emptiness as nihilistic were also anticipated by Tiantai teachings that similarly criticize wrong views of emptiness that fall into nihilism and lose sight of the Middle Way. It seems that the Neo-Confucians, however inspired by Buddhism they may have been, had only a shallow and distorted understanding of it.

Now let's look at the inter-sectarian misappropriation of teachings. According to Nichiren the three Hīnayāna schools in Japan all subscribed to Mahāyāna teachings. In fact, the Dharma Treasury school became part of the Dharma Characteristics school in 793, and the Completion of Reality school became part of the Three Treatises school in 806. So those two schools were no longer even independent entities but had become mere curricula of study within the Mahāyāna schools. The Discipline school actually considers itself a Mahāyāna school because the Dharmagupta vinaya, in their view, applied to both Hīnayāna and Mahāyāna monks. In addition, the school also administered the Mahāyāna precepts of the *Brahma Net Sūtra* and taught that all precepts should be followed with a Mahāyāna outlook. The Discipline school had long allied itself to Mahāyāna ideals and teachings. In Nichiren's day, the monk Eizon (1201-1290) and his disciple Ryōkan (1217-1303) led a revival of this school but ended up establishing a new school called the Discipline-Mantra school, as their teachings combined the precepts with Mantra school esotericism.

Nichiren's harsher accusations of misappropriation are actually leveled against the Flower Garland and the Mantra schools of Mahāyāna Buddhism. Of them he says:

> *Next the Flower Garland and Mantra schools were*
> *originally provisional schools based on provisional*
> *sūtras. Tripitaka Masters Śubhākarasimha and*
> *Vajrabodhi stole the "three thousand realms in a single*
> *thought-moment" concept from Tiantai using it as the*
> *basis for their own school. They added it to their mudrās*

231

and mantras to appear superior to others. Those
scholars who do not know this believe that the
Mahavairochana Sūtra had the "three thousand realms
in a single thought-moment" doctrine from its
beginning in India. At the time of Chengguan, the
Flower Garland school stole the doctrine and read it into
the words of the Flower Garland Sūtra asserting, "Mind
is like an artist." People do not realize this. (Hori 2002,
pp. 36-37 adapted)

Śubhākarasimha and Vajrabodhi were two of the Indian teachers who brought tantric Buddhism to China. Nichiren is accusing them of incorporating the Tiantai teaching of the "three thousand realms in a single thought-moment" into their translations and commentaries on the esoteric teachings in order to claim that, like the *Lotus Sūtra*, their teachings could lead all beings to buddhahood. Furthermore, in promoting the mudrās, mantras, and mandalas of the tantric teachings, they claimed that their methods were superior in terms of practice to the *Lotus Sūtra*. In fact, however, the esoteric sūtras do not explicitly teach that all beings, particularly the Hīnayāna practitioners of the two vehicles, can attain buddhahood. The esoteric sūtras are therefore not the Buddha's final teachings but a provisional understanding. This means that the esoteric methods, based as they are on a lesser point of view, are not comparable to the teaching and practice of the *Lotus Sūtra*.

Chengguan (737-820) was the fourth patriarch of the Flower Garland school. He traveled widely studying the teachings and practices of many schools, including the Tiantai teachings with Zhanran, its 6th patriarch. Apparently in his commentary on the *Flower Garland Sūtra*, Chengguan used the teaching of "three thousand realms in a single thought-moment" to explain the meaning of the passage in the sūtra that begins "Mind is like an artist" thereby claiming the Tiantai teaching for the Flower Garland school. To be fair, it should be pointed out that Zhiyi was the first one to make the connection between that passage in the *Flower Garland Sūtra* and the concept of "three thousand realms in a single thought-moment."

Nichiren also accused the Flower Garland schools' third patriarch, Fazang (643-712; aka Xianshou) of hiding the fact that he had been influenced by the Tiantai comparative classification of doctrines system when he came up with

232

his own system. This is a problematic accusation for two reasons. One is that the Flower Garland school's comparative classification system originated with the second patriarch Zhihyan (602-668), and the second problem is that Zhiyi himself was modifying earlier comparative classification schemes and using their terminology. Still, Nichiren did not approve of how the Flower Garland school presumed to improve upon the Tiantai comparative classification system and in doing so demoted the *Lotus Sūtra*. These comparative classification of doctrines systems will be discussed in later chapters of this commentary.

The misappropriation of the Dharma that Nichiren and his Tiantai predecessors were concerned about has to do with taking insights or methods from a rival to bolster one's own position and then attacking the rival as inferior. This does strike me as being ungrateful and dishonest. It is one thing to have a friendly rivalry and to learn and grow through dialogue and even civilized debate (in academic circles this is called "peer review"), but it is another to take another tradition's teachings and claim it as one's own while covering up the true source. It also doesn't seem right to take someone else's teachings out of context in order to attack it or to downplay it. From the above examples it would seem that Buddhism and the Tiantai school have had their teachings misappropriated by unfriendly rivals. It seems only fair to point this out and set the record straight.

Sources

Bryant, Edwin F., trans. *The Yoga Sūtras of Patanjali*. New York: North Point Press, 2009.

Chan, Wing-tsit, trans. *A Source Book in Chinese Philosophy*. Princeton: Princeton University Press, 1963.

Ch'en, Kenneth. *Buddhism in China: A Historical Survey*. Princeton: Princeton University Press, 1964.

Dasgupta, Surendranath. *A History of Indian Philosophy Volume 1*. New Delhi: Motilal Banarsidass, 1997.

Doniger, Wendy. *The Hindus: An Alternative History*. New York: The Penguin Press, 2009.

Flood, Gavin. *An Introduction to Hinduism*. New York: Cambridge University Press, 1996.

Gosho Translation Committee, editor-translator. *The Writings of Nichiren Daishonin*. Tokyo: Soka Gakkai, 1999.

Hartranft, Chip, trans. *The Yoga-Sūtra of Patanjali*. Boston: Shambhala, 2003.

Hori, Kyotsu, comp. *Writings of Nichiren Shonin: Doctrine Volume 2*. Tokyo: Nichiren Shu Overseas Propagation Promotion Association, 2002.

Kohn, Livia. *Early Chinese Mysticism: Philosophy and Soteriology in the Taoist Tradition*. Princeton: Princeton University Press, 1992.

Liu, Shu-hsien. *Understanding Confucian Philosophy: Classical and Sung-Ming*. Westport: Praeger Publishing, 1998.

Murano, Senchu, trans. *Kaimokusho or Liberation from Blindness*. Berkeley: Numata Center for Buddhist Translation and Research, 2000.

Prabhavananda, Swami. *The Spiritual Heritage of India: A Clear Summary of Indian Philosophy and Religion*. Hollywood: Vedānta Press, 1979.

Robinet, Isabelle auth. Brooks, Phyllis trans. *Taoism: Growth of a Religion*. Stanford: Stanford University Press, 1997.

Wong, Eva. *The Shambhala Guide to Taoism*. Boston: Shambhala Publications Inc., 1997.

Yao, Xinzhong. *An Introduction to Confucianism*. New York: Cambridge University Press, 2000.

Yu-lan, Fung. *A Short History of Chinese Philosophy*. New York: The Free Press, 1966.

Chapter 19 – A Brief History of the T'ien-t'ai School and Tendai Shu

Writings of Nichiren Shōnin Doctrine 2, pp. 36-37
Kaimoku-shō or Liberation from Blindness, pp. 16-17
The Writings of Nichiren Daishōnin I, pp. 225-226

Nichiren was ordained and trained as a Tendai monk, so much of his teachings and arguments are incomprehensible without at least a rudimentary understanding of Tiantai Buddhism. In this chapter I provide a brief history of the Tiantai school in China and Japan. In the next chapter I will cover the Tiantai teachings relating to the classification of the Buddha's teachings that Nichiren alludes to throughout his writings.

In the sixth century, the Chinese monk Zhiyi (538-597) established a teaching center on Mt. Tiantai. He was later known as the Great Master Tiantai, founder of the school of the same name. Zhiyi was a great scholar and meditator who wanted to systematize all the seemingly contradictory teachings that had been translated into Chinese. To do this, he classified the Buddha's teachings into five flavors and eight categories of teaching. As a practitioner, as well as a scholar, he put equal emphasis on meditation practice and doctrine in order to create a balanced system whereby doctrine would inform practice and practice would actualize doctrine. The concept of the "three thousand realms in a single thought-moment" (covered in a previous chapter) was part of his explanation of the sudden and perfect method of tranquility and insight meditation. He also spoke of awakening in terms of realizing the unity of the threefold truth of emptiness, provisional existence, and the Middle Way in order to clarify the true meaning of the teachings of the Perfection of Wisdom sūtras and Nāgārjuna's (second-third century) teachings regarding emptiness, causality, and the Middle Way. He derived the unity of the threefold truth from a line in Nāgārjuna's major work, Verses on the Middle Way:

"Whatever is dependently co-arisen

That is explained to be emptiness.

That, being a dependent designation,

Is itself the middle way." (Garfield, p. 304)

Zhiyi taught that the threefold truth could be realized through a "threefold contemplation" cutting through the "three categories of delusion" and giving rise to the "three kinds of knowledge." Ultimately, Zhiyi taught that the three truths of the threefold truth are simply different aspects of the one true nature of reality that can be realized in a single moment of insight.

Zhiyi lost his parents when he was seventeen years old, during the turbulent end of the Southern Liang Dynasty (502-557). Soon after, he sought ordination as a Buddhist monk. In 560 CE, Zhiyi visited Nanyue Huisi (515-577) on Mount Dasu, and studied the *Lotus Sūtra* under him, and, as a result of intense practice, he was said to have attained awaking through this phrase of "The Previous Life of Medicine King Bodhisattva" chapter of the *Lotus Sūtra*: "The Buddhas of those worlds praised him, saying simultaneously, 'Excellent, excellent, good man! All you did was a true endeavor. You made an offering to us according to the true Dharma.'" (Murano 1974, p. 301) His awakening was certified by Huisi. With the recommendation of Huisi, Zhiyi left Mount Dasu and went to Jinling and stayed at Waguansi Temple where he lectured to clergy and laity over a period of eight years. During this time, he greatly impressed the literati and monks whom he came in contact with.

> *There are several well-known monks that are associated*
> *with Chih-i, such as Fa-chi, who was skilled in*
> *meditation, Fa-lang, who was the great master in the*
> *San-lun tradition, and Pao-ch'iung and Ching-shao, who*
> *were distinguished monks in the capital Chin-ling. It is*
> *recorded in the Pieh-chuan that these monks either*
> *challenged Chih-i with the knowledge of contemplation*
> *or with engagement of doctrinal debate, but all of them*
> *ended up gaining great admiration and respect for Chih-*
> *i's knowledge and wisdom and his power of*
> *contemplation. (Shen Vol. I, p. 14)*

However, because of an anti-Buddhist movement by the Northern Zhou dynasty, Zhiyi retired to Mount Tiantai in 575 CE at the age of thirty-nine. He undertook *dhūta* practice at the Flower Peak of the mountain and lectured at Xiuchansi Temple. In 585 CE, at the age of forty-eight, Zhiyi returned to Jinling, the capital of the Chen dynasty, at the request of several district lords and governors. In 587 CE, he gave lectures on the *Lotus Sūtra*, which were later compiled as *The Words and Phrases of the Lotus Sūtra*. To avoid the conquest of the Chen dynasty by the Sui dynasty, Zhiyi stayed at Mount Lu and the town of Changsha. In 591 CE, he was invited by Prince Guang (later known as Yangdi) and went to Yangzhou. He granted bodhisattva precepts to the prince and received the honorific name "Zhihzhe" from him. He established Yuquansi Temple in Jingzhou and expounded *The Profound Meaning of the Lotus Sūtra* in 593 CE and *The Great Calming and Contemplation* in 594 CE. He returned to Mount Tiantai in 595 CE. Two years later, in 597 CE, while he was on the way to see Prince Guang, he became sick and died.

Zhiyi upheld the *Lotus Sūtra* as the most profound teaching of the Buddha. In terms of practice he emphasized the method of perfect and sudden calming and contemplation, but also utilized elaborate repentance ceremonies and devotional Pure Land practices. In his teachings, Zhiyi drew upon the *Great Perfection of Wisdom Treatise* attributed to Nāgārjuna that had been translated (or perhaps written) by Kumārajīva, the *Great Perfection of Wisdom Sūtra*, and the *Nirvāna Sūtra* in order to expound a comprehensive system of Buddhist teaching and practice. Zhiyi's three major works were the aforementioned *Words and Phrases of the Lotus Sūtra*, the *Profound Meaning of the Lotus Sūtra*, and the *Great Calming and Contemplation*. These three works were actually based on notes taken from his lectures that were compiled and edited by Zhiyi's disciple Guanding (561-632; aka Zhang'an).

Before Zhiyi there had been a lot of debate about the true meaning of the Buddha's teachings due to the contradictions found between the various sūtras and commentaries coming from India. Starting in the late fifth century, various attempts were made to reconcile the many teachings that were being translated. By Zhiyi's time there were the so-called three schools of the south and seven schools of the north that each presented a different system for classifying the sūtras. These were not schools in the sense of sects or monastic orders, but rather differing schools of thought propounded by different monks. These schools arranged the sūtras into such categories as sudden, gradual, and indeterminate. Many of these schools favored the *Flower*

Garland Sūtra or the *Nirvāna Sūtra* as the ultimate teaching of the Buddha. Zhiyi critiqued these systems and presented his own system in the *Profound Meaning of the Lotus Sūtra* of the five flavors and eight teachings that showed how the teaching and practice of the other sūtras all led up to the *Lotus Sūtra* as the definitive expression of the Buddha's ultimate teaching. This is what Nichiren is referring to in the following passage of the *Kaimoku-shō*:

> *The Buddhist texts, however, created three sects in*
> *South China and seven sects in North China. The*
> *controversies among them were furious. In the end,*
> *they were defeated by [T'ien-t'ai] Chih-che in the Ch'en*
> *(Chi) and Sui (Zui) dynasties. Accordingly, the priests of*
> *the ten sects stopped quarreling and resumed their*
> *mission to save the people. (Murano 2000, p. 16)*

The school Zhiyi founded was named the Tiantai school after the mountain where he resided. Though Zhiyi was the founder and first patriarch, Nāgārjuna is sometimes considered the honorary first patriarch because so much of the Tiantai teachings are based upon the *Great Perfection of Wisdom Treatise*. Huiwen (n.d.), the teacher of Huisi is then considered the second patriarch, Huisi the third, and Zhiyi the fourth. Sometimes it is Huiwen who is considered the honorary first patriarch of the school, making Huisi the second and Zhiyi the third. The Tiantai school declined during the seventh and eighth centuries due to the rise of the Dharma Characteristics, Flower Garland, and Zen schools that overshadowed the Tiantai school in terms of prestige and royal patronage. The Tiantai school was briefly revived during the time of Zhanran (711-782; aka Miaole), the school's sixth patriarch (if Zhiyi is considered the first). Zhanran wrote commentaries on Zhiyi's three major writings that Nichiren quoted almost as often as Zhiyi himself. Unfortunately, the persecution of Buddhism by the Emperor Wuzong in 845 was the end of the great scholastic schools of Buddhism in China. After that, the Zen and Pure Land Buddhism dominated Chinese Buddhism.

The Tiantai teachings were first brought to Japan by Jianzhen (J. Ganjin; 688-763), who was also a Tiantai monk as well as a Vinaya master. Saichō (767-822; known posthumously as Dengyō) later studied these teachings and was greatly intrigued by them. In 788 Saichō established a temple (later named Enryakuji by Emperor Saga in 823) on Mt. Hiei to study and practice away from the world. The world, however, came to him. In 794 the capital of Japan moved from Nara to Kyoto, right at the foot of Mt. Hiei. In 797, Saichō came to the attention of the emperor and he was given a post at court. Beginning in 798, Saichō gave annual lectures on the *Lotus Sūtra* at Mt. Hiei that were attended by monks from the Nara schools. His reputation grew and in 802, Saichō was invited to lecture on the three major works of Zhiyi at Takaosanji Temple in Kyoto attended by fourteen prestigious monks of the six schools of Nara. Paul Groner said of this occasion, "The many years which Saichō had devoted to the study of Tendai texts must have enabled him to make a strong and lasting impression at the lectures." (Groner, p. 36)

In 804, Saichō was able to travel to China to learn more about Tiantai Buddhism and other teachings and bring back more reliable texts. He could not speak Chinese but was able to read it and had to rely on interpreters. He was able to study with Daosui (n.d.), the seventh patriarch of the Tiantai school, and Xingman (n.d.), a monk who had been a student of Miaole. From the former, Saichō received the bodhisattva precepts of the *Brahma Net Sūtra* (allegedly translated by Kumārajīva though many scholars believe it is a Chinese creation). He also received the teachings of the minor Zen branch known as the Ox Head school from a monk named Xiuran (who may or may not have been a disciple of the Zen Master Mazu Daoyi (709-788). He also received esoteric Buddhist initiations and teachings from a monk named Shunxiao (n.d.) and other esoteric practitioners, though his study of these teachings was not as deep as he would have liked.

After only eight and a half months, Saichō returned to Japan in 805 and began the establishment of the Tendai-shū on Mt. Hiei. The Tendai-shū was originally set up to be a comprehensive school of Buddhism that utilized all teachings and methods of practice united by the perfect teaching of the *Lotus Sūtra* as taught by Zhiyi. This synthesis of teachings and practices was called "*enmitsuzenkai.*" "*En*" means "Perfect" and refers to the perfect teaching of the *Lotus Sūtra*. "*Mitsu*" means "esoteric" or "secret" and refers to esoteric Buddhism. "*Zen*" refers to the practice of meditation. "*Kai*" means "precepts" and refers to Saichō's concern with the establishment of the Mahāyāna precepts. Saichō established two tracks of practice: one track was for the practice of esoteric Buddhism, while the other was for the practice of the Tiantai method of calming and contemplation.

Saichō also worked to establish a Mahāyāna precept platform on Mt. Hiei for the conferral of Mahāyāna precepts from the *Brahma Net Sūtra* on his disciples so that Mahāyāna monastics could have a Mahāyāna precept lineage. Though the *Brahma Net Sūtra* precepts had been conferred upon monks and householders in both China and Japan before this, they had never been used in place of the Dharmagupta precepts, nor had there ever been a separate precept platform (*kaidan*) for their conferral. This was an unprecedented innovation that aroused the opposition of the six schools of Nara. The controversy raged throughout Saichō's life, but a week after his death in 822 the court finally granted permission for Mt. Hiei to have a Mahāyāna precept platform and it was finally constructed in 827.

Saichō also got involved in doctrinal controversies with monks of the Nara schools, in particular with a monk named Tokuitsu (c. 780-842) of the Dharma Characteristics school who insisted that the One Vehicle teaching of the *Lotus Sūtra* was only a provisional teaching whereas the three vehicles teaching was the definitive truth. Tokuitsu's rationale was based upon the teaching of the "five mutually distinct natures." In his view, not all people are capable of attaining buddhahood, so some should settle for the lesser goals of the two vehicles, while those who are able should take up the bodhisattva vehicle. The One Vehicle was taught for those who are able to take any of the three vehicles to encourage them to take up the buddha vehicle. Saichō vigorously argued that this was not the case. The Buddha taught the One Vehicle for all beings because all beings are capable of attaining buddhahood. This debate was carried out in the form of essays and treatises. According to Paul Groner, "Tendai scholars have often claimed that Saichō decisively won the debate." (Ibid, p. 95)

Something should also be said about the relationship between Saichō and Kūkai (774-835; known posthumously as Kōbō), the founder of the Mantra school in Japan. They first met when they were traveling to China together in 804. Kūkai returned to Japan in 806 after having studied and received the authority to teach esoteric Buddhism. He established the Shingon-shū or Mantra school on Mt. Kōya in 816. For many years Saichō and Kūkai were friends. In 809, Kūkai had gone to Mt. Hiei to learn about the Tiantai teachings from Saichō. In turn, Saichō inquired about the esoteric teachings, borrowing texts and even receiving an esoteric initiation from Kūkai in 812. Unfortunately, their relationship soured in later years, as one of Saichō's disciples defected to the Mantra school and Kūkai refused to lend texts and insisted that Saichō become his disciple if he wished to study Mantra teachings. They also had fundamental disagreements over the relative importance of the *Lotus Sūtra* and esoteric Buddhism. Not surprisingly, Kūkai compared the *Lotus Sūtra* and Tiantai teachings unfavorably with the Mantra sūtras, teachings, and practices. By 816, the two monks were no longer corresponding with each other.

After the passing of both Saichō and Kūkai, the successive patriarchs of the Tendai school on Mt. Hiei developed Tendai esotericism to bolster the popularity of their school. Ennin (794-864; aka Jikaku), the third chief priest, and Enchin (814-891; aka Chishō), the fifth, were particularly responsible for bringing esoteric Buddhism to the fore in the Tendai school and even for making it more important than the *Lotus Sūtra*. Because of this, Nichiren would in his later years accuse them of having turned the Tendai school into the Mantra school in all but name, thus leading to the neglect of the *Lotus Sūtra* within the Tendai school itself. Nichiren would express his critiques of Kūkai, Jikaku, and Chishō in his later writings such as *Selecting the Right Time* (*Senji-shō*)) and *Essay on Gratitude* (*Hōon-jō*).

Pure Land Buddhism also developed in the Tendai school. Saichō himself aspired to rebirth in the Pure Land, but it was Ennin who established the Jōgyō Zammai-dō (Hall for Walking Meditation) in 849. This hall was dedicated to the practice of the constant walking meditation taught in the *Great Calming and Contemplation* of Zhihyi which featured the chanting of nembutsu as discussed previously. After that, Pure Land devotion became an important part of Tendai Buddhism. By Nichiren's time, many Tendai temples had become centers for the practice of Hōnen's (1133-1212) exclusive nembutsu version of Pure Land Buddhism.

Zen Buddhism in Japan also had its origins in Tendai temples. Eisai (1141-1215) was a Tendai monk who tried to propagate Rinzai Zen practice as part of the Tendai School. He established Jufukuji Temple in Kamakura in 1200 and Kenninji Temple in Kyoto. These temples were initially meant to be Tendai temples where Rinzai Zen would be practiced. However, by Nichiren's day they had become pure Rinzai Zen temples run by monks such as Lanxi Daolong (1213-1278; J. Rankei Dōryū) who had come from Song China to Japan in 1246 at the invitation of Hōjō Tokiyori (1227-1263) and was installed as the abbot of Kenninji Temple in 1259.

Nichiren's rather triumphal summary of the careers of Zhiyi and Saichō and the prestige of the Tiantai school in China and Japan seem a bit exaggerated. Rather than engaging in formal debates, Zhiyi and Saichō gave lectures and wrote essays and corresponded with fellow monks. They did, nevertheless, win the respect of their contemporaries, both monks and literati, for their insightful scholarship and depth of spiritual cultivation. As a Tendai reformer, Nichiren was alarmed that Tendai temples were being converted into centers of Mantra, Pure Land, and Zen practice. He lamented what he saw as the neglect of the teachings of Zhiyi, Miaole, and Saichō and hoped to restore the heritage of the Tiantai school. More importantly, Nichiren was determined to carry forward the legacy of the Tiantai school by sharing the teaching and practice of the *Lotus Sūtra*, the Buddha's highest teaching, with all people.

Sources

Chappel, David, ed., and Masao Ichishima, comp. Trans. Buddhist Translation Seminar of Hawaii. *T'ien-t'ai Buddhism: An Outline of the Fourfold Teachings*. Tokyo: Shobo, 1983.

Ch'en, Kenneth. *Buddhism in China: A Historical Survey*. Princeton: Princeton University Press, 1964.

Garfield, Jay L., trans. *The Fundamental Wisdom of the Middle Way: Nāgārjuna's Mūlamadhyamikakārikā*. New York: Oxford University Press, 1995.

Gosho Translation Committee, editor-translator. *The Writings of Nichiren Daishonin*. Tokyo: Soka Gakkai, 1999.

Groner, Paul. Saichō: *The Establishment of the Japanese Tendai School*. Berkeley: Berkeley Buddhist Studies Series, 1984.

Hori, Kyotsu, comp. *Writings of Nichiren Shonin: Doctrine Volume 2*. Tokyo: Nichiren Shu Overseas Propagation Promotion Association, 2002.

Hurvitz, Leon. *Chih-i: An Introduction to the Life and Ideas of a Chinese Buddhist Monk*. Melanges chinois et bouddhiques 12 (1960-62): 1-372. Brussels: l'Institute Belge des Hautes Etudes Chinoises.

Kasahara, Kazuo. *A History of Japanese Religion*. Tokyo: Kosei Publishing Co., 2002.

Kashiwahara, Yusen & Sonoda, Koyu. *Shapers of Japanese Buddhism*. Tokyo: Kosei Publishing Co., 1994.

Matsunaga, Alicia & Matsunaga, Daigan. *Foundation of Japanese Buddhism Vol. I & II*. Los Angeles: Buddhist Books International, 1988.

Mitchell, Donald W. *Buddhism: Introducing the Buddhist Experience*. New York: Oxford University Press, 2002.

Murano, Senchu. *Kaimokusho or Liberation from Blindness*. Berkeley: Numata Center for Buddhist Translation and Research, 2000.

Pruden, Leo, trans. *The Essentials of the Eight Traditions*. Berkeley: Numata Center for Buddhist Translation and Research, 1994.

Shen, Haiyan. *The Profound Meaning of the Lotus Sutra: T'ien-t'ai Philosophy of Buddhism volumes I and II*. Delhi: Originals, 2005.

Stone, Jacqueline. *Original Enlightenment and the Transformation of Medieval Japanese Buddhism*. Honolulu: Kuroda Institute, 1999.
Swanson, Paul. *Foundations of T'ien-tai Philosophy: The Flowering of the Two Truths Theory in Chinese Buddhism*. Berkeley: Asian Humanities Press, 1989.

_____, trans. *The Collected Teachings of the Tendai School*. Berkeley: Numata Center for Buddhist Translation and Research, 1995.

Takakusu, Junjiro. *The Essentials of Buddhist Philosophy*. Delhi: Motilal Banarsidass, 1978.

Tamura, Yoshiro. *Japanese Buddhism: A Cultural History*. Tokyo: Kosei Publishing Co., 2000.

Williams, Paul. *Mahayana Buddhism: The Doctrinal Foundations*. New York: Routledge, 1989.

Wright, Arthur F. *Buddhism in Chinese History*. Stanford: Stanford University Press, 1959.

Chapter 20 – The Comparative Classification of Doctrines of the T'ien-t'ai School

Throughout *Kaimoku-shō*, Nichiren takes for granted the Tiantai system of comparative classification of doctrines. In this chapter, I hope to provide an overview of this classification system. I think it is important to be familiar with it in order to understand Nichiren's evaluation of the Buddha's teachings. In addition, I believe that Zhiyi's classification system is valuable in its own right as a coherent system of step-by-step reflections on the nature of reality leading to deeper and deeper insights.

 We have covered the origins of the sūtras earlier in this commentary. Textual scholars and even Buddhist practitioners today recognize that not all of the sūtras are verbatim accounts of Śākyamuni Buddha's discourses. The Mahāyāna sūtras in particular are looked upon as works that originated in later times and were the products of inspired practitioners who were attributing their teachings to either the historical Buddha or to an idealized manifestation of the Buddha. Zhiyi and his contemporaries, however, believed that all of these were the actual words of the Buddha. Because of this belief they had to find a way to reconcile the seeming differences in doctrine, practice, or at least shifts of emphasis between the so-called Hīnayāna sūtras and the Mahāyāna sūtras, and also the differences between the various Mahāyāna sūtras.

Even before the time of Zhiyi (at least as early as the fifth century), Chinese Buddhists created various systems of dividing up the sūtras according to the periods in the Buddha's life and by their relative profundity in order to reconcile the seemingly contradictory teachings of the Buddha. In this way it could be shown that the Buddha gave different teachings to different people at different times and what may have been relevant for some would not be for others, and what was taught early on was by way of preparing his disciples for deeper insights and greater aspirations later on. Zhiyi tried to improve upon these earlier systems with two interlocking systems known as the eight teachings and the five flavors that would have a long-lasting influence on East Asian Buddhism, though rival systems would often overshadow it.

It was Zhiyi's system of the comparative classification of doctrines in the sūtras that Nichiren believed had the most credibility. It was his belief that it adhered most closely to the evidence provided in the sūtras. Nichiren discusses this system in detail in the *Treatise on Protecting the Nation* (*Shugo Kokka-ron*), *Outline of All the Holy Teachings of the Buddha* (*Ichidai Shōgyō Tai-i*), *Genealogical Chart of the Buddha's Lifetime Teachings in Five Periods* (*Ichidai Goji Keizu*) and in other works. It also formed an important part of Nichiren's five principles for propagation that he would explain in later writings such as *Treatise on the Teaching, Capacity, Time and Country* (*Kyōki Jikoku-shō*).

Let's begin our own examination of this system with the eight teachings and then move on to the five flavors/periods.

The Eight Teachings

Zhiyii taught that the Buddha's teachings could be categorized into four doctrinal teachings of deepening profundity and four methods of teaching.

The Four Doctrinal Teachings:

The Tripitaka Teaching – this corresponds to pre-Mahāyāna teachings as found in the Chinese Āgamas or the Pāli Canon and is directed to the śrāvakas (voice-hearers) who strive to become arhats (those who escape from this world of birth and death and do not return). It emphasizes emptiness and approaches it through analysis of the aggregates and the links of dependent origination. In other words, this teaching aims to reveal the emptiness of the self by examining the components of existence such as the five aggregates of form, feeling, perception, mental formations, and consciousness. It is shown that each of these is impermanent, subject to suffering, and cannot be the basis of an abiding independent self either alone or together. The links of dependent origination reveal the succession of causes and effects that make up existence and likewise reveal that an abiding self cannot be found therein. By doing this, the śrāvakas will realize the contingent nature of the self and thereby extinguish greed for what could satisfy the "self," anger in regard to what threatens such a "self," and ignorance regarding the selfless nature of the aggregates. In this way they will realize nirvāṇa and free themselves from birth and death. It might be asked: "What are the aggregates if they are not a self?" Do they somehow exist in their own right in some manner? And who is it that is free of birth and death and who enters nirvāṇa if there is no self? These are questions that are taken up in the following teachings.

The Shared Teaching – this corresponds to the Perfection of Wisdom sūtras and is directed to the more advanced śrāvakas and those just starting out on the bodhisattva path. Because these teachings are directed at both śrāvakas and bodhisattvas it is called the teaching they share in common. This level of discourse approaches emptiness more immediately or intuitively because it does not involve analysis. Rather, one learns not to impute substance or a fixed nature onto things in the first place. It is also more thoroughgoing in its application of emptiness in that it applies it not just to the self but also to all dharmas (phenomena). In answer to the above question, the aggregates not only do not provide a self either together or in part to an individual, but they themselves have no abiding substance or fixed nature. Each aggregate depends upon causes and conditions, which are also dependent on causes and conditions and so on ad infinitum. Emptiness in this teaching is the emptiness of any fixed nature or substance whatsoever. In response to the question as to who is saved, this teaching asserts that the bodhisattvas vow to save all sentient beings but do not cling to the idea that there are beings at all. It is all an empty show, but a show manifesting suffering or liberation depending upon the flow of causes and conditions. The question might then be asked: "How should bodhisattvas deal with causes and conditions if they know that they are all ultimately empty and have no basis, origin, or goal and no real self or entity abides anywhere?"

The Distinct Teaching – this corresponds to the *Flower Garland Sūtra* that is directed specifically to those who are firmly established bodhisattvas, so it is distinct from the teachings for śrāvakas. At this point, one needs to see that emptiness is not a dead-end but just the beginning. This requires an appreciation for contingent phenomena and thus the truth of provisional existence. While continuing to recognize that all things are empty, the bodhisattvas also see that this emptiness is not a blank void or nothingness. Rather, the lack of a fixed or independent nature is what allows all things to flow and move, change and grow, and ultimately interrelate so thoroughly that all things affect all other things like a web that quivers all at once when any one strand is touched. All things, all beings, are provisional manifestations of this interpenetrating dynamic process. Realizing this, bodhisattvas negate the negation of emptiness. They are free to reengage the world and appreciate all things without clinging or attachment. Gradually they realize the Middle Way that integrates peaceful detachment with compassionate involvement. Zhiyi called the empty, the provisional, and the Middle Way aspects of reality the threefold truth. In this teaching they are approached dialectically. Emptiness is the thesis, provisional existence is the antithesis, and the synthesis is the Middle Way. This is not the final teaching however, because an even greater integration lies ahead. Finally, one might ask: "If the tripitaka and shared teachings negate the self and all phenomena, and the distinct teaching negates that negation, is there any explicitly affirmative teaching in Buddhism at all?"

The Perfect Teaching – this corresponds to the *Lotus Sūtra* and the *Nirvāna Sūtra* and it is considered perfect or well rounded (the Chinese character 圓 used for this teaching holds both meanings) because it presents the integration of all three truths – the empty, the provisional, and the Middle Way – into a seamless whole. Each of these, if properly understood, immediately leads to an understanding of the other two in this teaching. For instance, what is empty is provisionally existent and therefore exemplifies the Middle Way. While the earlier teachings negate the world of birth and death through an analytical or intuitive approach to emptiness or negate a one-sided emptiness by affirming the provisional existence of all things; the perfect teaching affirms the total unity of the threefold truth of the empty, the provisional, and the Middle Way. In this teaching, the affirmative aspects of the earlier negations are made explicit. Negative and limiting aspects are emptied, positive and boundless phenomena are provisionally affirmed, and all manifests the liberation of the Middle Way. For instance, previously the vehicles of the śrāvakas and pratyekabuddhas (privately awakened ones) were condemned in favor of the bodhisattva vehicle, but now all the provisional vehicles are shown to be none other than the unfolding of the One Vehicle leading all to buddhahood. In previous teachings the historical Śākyamuni Buddha was shown to be a finite provisional manifestation of the cosmic principle of buddhahood that is sometimes personified as a cosmic buddha named Vairocana who is said to transcend birth or death. The *Lotus Sūtra*, however, portrays Śākyamuni Buddha himself as the one who reveals the unborn and deathless nature of buddhahood through his timeless spiritual presence and skillful activity. Previous teachings compared and contrasted the empty, the provisional and the Middle Way, but here the intrinsic unity of the freedom of emptiness, the creative responsiveness of the provisional, and the sublimity of the Middle Way is fully revealed.

The Four Methods of Teaching

The Sudden Method – the Buddha teaches directly from his own awakening without any preliminaries. This is usually identified with the *Flower Garland Sūtra*. The *Flower Garland Sūtra*, however, is more of a presentation of the Buddha's awakened state than a discursive teaching by the Buddha.

The Gradual Method – the Buddha begins at a very basic common-sense level and then gradually cultivates the understanding of his disciples. Beginning with the tripitaka teachings, the Buddha gradually introduced Mahāyāna teachings up to and including the Perfection of Wisdom sūtras. In this way, the disciples' understanding, and aspiration matured until they could appreciate and benefit from the Buddha's highest teaching in the *Lotus Sūtra*. The *Lotus Sūtra* itself is held to transcend any of the four methods because it is the goal of all of them.

The Secret Method: the Buddha teaches some people who can benefit by a specific teaching, but others are not aware of this because they are not ready and would misunderstand or even misuse the teaching. For instance, the Buddha might give advanced teachings on emptiness to bodhisattvas unbeknownst to the śrāvakas who might misinterpret it as nihilistic if they were to hear it.

The Indeterminate Method: the Buddha teaches one doctrine but the various people who hear it understand it in different ways. For instance, the four noble truths might be taught and understood by śrāvakas as referring to existing states of suffering or liberation that actual beings can reside. Bodhisattvas, however, would understand that the four noble truths lead beyond grasping at existing states and that no actual beings reside anywhere outside of the interdependent flow of causes and conditions.

The Five Flavors / Periods

Zhiyi taught that the four doctrinal teachings were combined like ingredients into five different flavors of Dharma. The perfect teaching by itself was the best, but other flavors and periods made concessions to those who were not ready for the perfect teaching by combining it with other teachings, or in the case of the Deer Park period excluding it altogether. While Zhiyi believed that the Buddha used these different flavors throughout his fifty years of teaching, he also indicated that certain sūtras exemplified particular flavors. The seventh century Tiantai patriarch and reformer Zhanran later identified these flavors and their corresponding sutras more rigidly with a chronological scheme of the Buddha's teachings called the five periods. In *Treatise on Protecting the Nation*, Nichiren provides citations from various sūtras to justify this time scheme of the five periods. These five flavors or periods were then made to correspond to certain analogies used in the sūtras. One analogy comes from the *Nirvāna Sūtra* and relates the teachings to milk and its products – cream, curds, butter, and clarified butter. This analogy was Zhiyi's inspiration for the five flavors. Another analogy relates the teachings to the process by which an estranged son is reconciled with his father and given his birthright as related in the parable of wealthy man and his poor son in the fourth chapter of the *Lotus Sūtra*. Yet another analogy comes from the *Flower Garland Sūtra* and relates the teachings to the progression of the sun from dawn to high noon.

The Flower Garland – This lasted for the first three weeks after the Buddha's awakening and as such was not perceived by anyone but the gods and advanced bodhisattvas. This period combines the perfect teaching with the specific teaching. This means that while the *Flower Garland Sūtra* presents the final goal of Buddhism, many parts are aimed only at the bodhisattvas and so exclude those who do not share their aspirations or insight. This period is compared to fresh milk before it undergoes any further refinement; or to the time when the prodigal son is frightened to death by the magnificent wealth and power of the father whom he has forgotten; or the sun at dawn that illuminates only the highest peaks of the mountains.

The Deer Park – for the next twelve years beginning with the Deer Park discourse, the Buddha exclusively taught the tripitaka doctrine for the śrāvakas. At this stage the Buddha taught the four noble truths and the twelvefold chain of dependent origination in order to free people from worldly attachments and to overcome self-centeredness. This period is compared to the cream derived from milk; or the time when the father sends servants to employ the son for menial labor and later visits the son dressed as a fellow worker; or the sun when it has risen high enough to illuminate the deepest valleys.

The Expanded (*Vaipulya*) – for the next eight years the Buddha taught preliminary Mahāyāna teachings in order to castigate the śrāvakas for their complacency and to inspire the novice bodhisattvas by teaching the six perfections, the emptiness of all phenomena, and the existence of the buddhas in the pure lands of the ten directions. The *Vimalakīrti Sūtra*, the three Pure Land sūtras, and those pertaining to Consciousness-Only and later the esoteric teachings are all lumped into this catch-all category which contains all four teachings by content that are taught depending on how they correspond to the needs of the audience at any given time and place. This period is compared to the production of curds; or the time when the son and the father develop mutual trust and the son enters his father's mansion freely on business; or the sun at breakfast time.

The Prajna or Perfection of Wisdom (*Prajñā-pāramitā*) – for the next twenty-two years the Buddha taught the Perfection of Wisdom sūtras which included the common, specific and perfect teachings, but not the tripitaka teachings. This period emphasized the emptiness of all phenomena and negated all the distinctions and dichotomies set up in the previous teachings so the way would be clear for the Buddha's ultimate teaching in the following period. This period is compared to the production of butter; or the time when the father entrusts the son with his storehouses of gold, silver, and other treasures; or the sun late in the morning.

The Lotus and Nirvāṇa – in the last eight years of the Buddha's life he taught only the unadulterated pure teaching in the *Lotus Sūtra* and reiterated it in the *Nirvāṇa Sūtra*. This was the period which not only comes full circle back to the Buddha's own point of view but brings along all those who were gradually prepared by the last three periods and who did not understand or felt left out of the sudden teaching of the Flower Garland period. In this teaching the eventual attainment of buddhahood by all beings and the timeless nature of the Buddha's awakening are affirmed. This period is compared to the production of clarified butter or ghee; the time when the father reveals that he is the son's true father and bestows all his wealth upon the son; or the sun at high noon.

Flower Garland	combining	milk	fright	illumination of high peaks
Deer Park	exclusive	cream	menial labor	illumination of deep valleys
Expanded	corresponding	curds	entering mansion	sun at breakfast
Perfection of Wisdom	inclusive	butter	entrusting storehouses	sun late in the morning
Lotus and Nirvāna	pure	clarified butter or ghee	inheritance	sun at noon

Sources

Chappel, David, ed., and Masao Ichishima, comp. Trans. Buddhist Translation Seminar of Hawaii. *T'ien-t'ai Buddhism: An Outline of the Fourfold Teachings*. Tokyo: Shobo, 1983.

Hurvitz, Leon. *Chih-i: An Introduction to the Life and Ideas of a Chinese Buddhist Monk*. Melanges chinois et bouddhiques 12 (1960-62): 1-372. Brussels: l'Institute Belge des Hautes Etudes Chinoises.

Pruden, Leo, trans. *The Essentials of the Eight Traditions*. Berkeley: Numata Center for Buddhist Translation and Research, 1994.

Shen, Haiyan. *The Profound Meaning of the Lotus Sutra: T'ien-t'ai Philosophy of Buddhism volumes I and II*. Delhi: Originals, 2005.

Stone, Jacqueline. *Original Enlightenment and the Transformation of Medieval Japanese Buddhism*. Honolulu: Kuroda Institute, 1999.

Swanson, Paul. *Foundations of T'ien-tai Philosophy: The Flowering of the Two Truths Theory in Chinese Buddhism*. Berkeley: Asian Humanities Press, 1989.

_____, trans. *The Collected Teachings of the Tendai School*. Berkeley: Numata Center for Buddhist Translation and Research, 1995.

Chapter 21 – Trace Gate: Obtainment of Buddhahood by the Two Vehicles

Writings of Nichiren Shōnin Doctrine 2, pp. 37-45, 48
Kaimoku-shō or Liberation from Blindness, pp. 18-28, 33
The Writings of Nichiren Daishōnin I, pp. 224-233, 235

Now we come to the part of the *Kaimoku-shō* where Nichiren reveals the unique teachings of the *Lotus Sūtra* that puts it in a category beyond all the others sūtras, including other Mahāyāna sutras. As discussed previously, according to the five periods of Tiantai Buddhism, Śākyamuni Buddha taught the *Lotus Sūtra* during the last eight years of his life. All the teachings prior to those last eight years were preparation for this final teaching of the *Lotus Sūtra*. One could speak of the *Lotus Sūtra* in terms of the twenty wonders consisting of the ten wonders of the Trace Gate and the ten wonders of the Origin Gate, or in terms of the three thousand realms in a single thought moment that Zhiyi derived from his understanding of what awakening to the truth of the *Lotus Sūtra* means. What Nichiren chose to focus on are the two teachings of the One Vehicle and the Eternal Lifespan of the Buddha, also known as (1) the teaching of the attainment of buddhahood by the people of the two vehicles and (2) Śākyamuni Buddha's attainment of buddhahood in the remotest past. Nichiren begins:

> I studied the teachings of the Buddha and found that
> there are many differences between the Buddha's
> teachings expounded during the first forty and more
> years and those expounded during his last eight years.
> The most important difference, however, which is
> pointed out by many scholars today, and which I also
> agree with, is that the Buddha taught during his last
> years the two teachings that: (1) adherents of the two
> vehicles, the pratyekabuddha vehicle and the śrāavaka
> vehicle, can become buddhas, and (2) Śākyamuni
> Buddha attained awakening in the remotest past.
> (Murano 2000, p. 18 slightly modified)

In this chapter I will discuss the meaning of the first teaching, how the One Vehicle enables those of the two vehicles to obtain buddhahood. This is clearly the main point of the Trace Gate, or first half of the *Lotus Sūtra*. In chapter two of the *Lotus Sūtra*, the Buddha begins the teaching of the One Vehicle. In the very first part of that chapter he speaks of the "ten suchnesses" which are the "ten factors" in Zhiyi's teaching of the "three thousand realms in a single thought-moment." As discussed in a previous chapter, these ten factors show what the ten realms have in common that allows them to contain one another as different states in the ongoing dynamic process of interdependent becoming. Since they contain one another, the realm of buddhahood is embraced by and embraces the other nine realms. This means that buddhahood is an integral part of all and is realizable by all. Knowing this, the Buddha used various skillful means to teach people how to realize the different goals that appealed to them, but his true intention was that all those he taught would realize their own buddhahood. After being requested to do so three times by Śāriputra, the Buddha then clarifies that the three vehicles of the śrāvakas, pratyekabuddhas, and bodhisattvas were taught as a form of skillful means and that in fact there is only the One Vehicle that leads all to buddhahood. From chapter two to chapter nine the One Vehicle is expounded in terms of the parable of the burning house, the parable of the wealthy man and his poor son, the simile of the herbs, and others. In chapter seven, the Buddha tells the assembly how he has been teaching them the *Lotus Sūtra* in his capacity as a bodhisattva as long ago as "three thousand dust mote eons." In these chapters, the Buddha gave predictions of buddhahood to major śrāvaka disciples such as Śāriputra, Maudgalyāyana, Mahākāśyapa, and many others, including his son Rāhula. In chapter thirteen he predicted buddhahood for his wife Yaśodharā, and his aunt Mahāprajāpatī who were also śrāvakas. Many of those the Buddha gave predictions too were arhats, those who had already cut off any ties to the world of birth and death and who therefore were not ever going to be reborn again. Throughout the Trace Gate the Buddha makes it very clear through plain statement, the use of parables, a past life story, and specific prophecies that even those who are following the way of the two vehicles will also attain buddhahood.

We might also wonder about the exact relationship between the three vehicles and the One Vehicle. The Buddha makes this clear in chapter two of the *Lotus Sūtra* where he says, "I also expound various teachings to all living beings only for the purpose of revealing the One Buddha Vehicle. There is no other vehicle, not a second or third." (Murano 2012, p. 33) Some interpreters of the *Lotus Sūtra* think that there are three or four vehicles because they look at the parable of the burning house in chapter three where a wealthy old man entices children out of a burning house by promising them carts drawn by sheep, deer, or oxen, but in the end gives them all a great cart drawn by white oxen. The first three carts represent the three vehicles of the śrāvakas, pratyekabuddhas, and bodhisattvas whereas the great white ox cart represents the One Vehicle. For some reason some interpreters believe that there are in fact four carts, with the white ox cart being the fourth alternative; or they say that the ox cart initially promised and the great white ox cart are actually one and the same, and so there are three vehicles after all with the first two simply being replaced by the third. All of this ignores the fact that the Buddha has already said there is not a second or third vehicle and that in the parable itself the first three ox carts are purely rhetorical. The carts that are initially promised, including the regular ox cart, do not appear in the parable except as imaginary goals. Likewise, the limited forms of awakening imagined by those who take up one of the three vehicles are not real, only the perfect and complete awakening of the One Buddha Vehicle is the real awakening.

The three vehicles are limited aspects of the One Buddha Vehicle taught by the Buddha to motivate the disciples in accordance with their inclinations and limited understanding and aspirations. The śrāvakas are viewed as the most limited in terms of ability and aspiration so they are taught the four noble truths and eightfold path as it is the most straightforward form of instruction for those wishing to escape suffering. The pratyekabuddhas wish to gain a deeper insight, so they contemplate the twelve-fold chain of dependent origination in their forest hermitages. The bodhisattvas aspire to save all beings, so they practice the six perfections. The One Vehicle encompasses these teachings and practices but also goes beyond them. Unlike the first two vehicles it directs the teaching of the four noble truths and insight into dependent origination to the attainment of buddhahood and not mere escape from the cycle of birth and death. The bodhisattva vehicle of the provisional Mahāyāna teachings exhort the bodhisattvas to make vows and practice the six perfections for many ages and cautions them to never fall back into the lesser goals of the two vehicles. The One Vehicle, however, reveals that ultimately the distinction between the two vehicles and the bodhisattva vehicle is merely rhetorical for the purpose of spurring on those capable of immediately raising their aspirations and making greater efforts. When the śrāvakas, pratyekabuddhas, and bodhisattvas mature in their practice they find that their limited motivations and preconceived ideas fall away. In taking faith in the One Vehicle they realize that all authentic practitioners have been traveling in it all along. Providing that they do not cling to their former ideas based on imaginary goals and dichotomies, the śrāvakas, pratyekabuddhas, and bodhisattvas of the provisional teachings realize that they are all actually bodhisattvas of the One Vehicle. As the Buddha says, "Śāriputra! Some disciples of mine who think that they are arhats or pratyekabuddhas, will not be my disciples or arhats or pratyekabuddhas if they do not hear or know that the buddhas, the tathāgatas, teach only bodhisattvas." (Ibid, p. 34)

However it is interpreted in relation to the other three vehicles, the teaching of the One Vehicle is a radical contradiction of the assumptions made by all the earlier teachings that arhats and pratyekabuddhas could never arouse the aspiration to attain buddhahood for the sake of all beings because they had cut off all those desires and inclinations that perpetuates the cycle of birth and death. Because their body is cremated upon death and their consciousness does not go on to a new rebirth the goal of those attaining liberation through the two vehicles is to "reduce the body to ashes and annihilate consciousness." This sounds extremely negative, but the point is to quickly put a stop to the painful cycle of birth and death by eradicating greed, hatred, and delusion even if it means that nothing will follow. Those who attain such a goal would be liberated from suffering, but also irrevocably past caring about the world and the suffering multitudes left behind. To arouse the aspiration to attain buddhahood and voluntarily participate in the painful cycle of birth and death for innumerable eons to build up the merit needed to become a buddha in order to liberate others is viewed by the two vehicles as a super-heroic path above and beyond what anyone might be expected to give of themselves and also an unrealistic goal for the vast majority of spiritual seekers who have a hard enough time liberating themselves. The way of the two vehicles taught in the tripitaka teaching of the Deer Park period (in the Tiantai system of comparative classification of doctrines) presents itself as the most realistic way and efficient way for each person to attain liberation from suffering.

The Mahāyāna sūtras, however, view the way of the two vehicles as spiritually selfish. Nichiren cites passages from the *Flower Garland Sūtra*, the *Great Assembly Sūtra*, the *Vimalakīrti Sūtra*, the *Expansive Dhāranī Sūtra*, the *Larger Wisdom Sūtra*, the *Heroic Valor Sūtra*, and the *Golden Splendor Sūtra* to show that up until the time of the teaching of the One Vehicle the Buddha had condemned those following the two vehicles as being incapable of attaining buddhahood. Their buddha-nature is likened to a tree that cannot grow in a burning pit or poisonous water, or like seeds that have been burned and cannot grow again, or a tree that has withered, and many other analogies. The people of the two vehicles are also unable to repay the debt of gratitude that they owe their parents and others because they have fallen into the "pit of liberation." These passages also say that while the people of the two vehicles have destroyed the seeds of buddhahood, those who still have the three poisons of greed, hatred, and delusion or who have committed the five rebellious sins of killing one's father, killing one's mother, killing an arhat, injuring a buddha, or causing a schism in the Sangha may still attain buddhahood. The *Vimalakīrti Sūtra* even goes so far as to have Mañjuśri Bodhisattva say that greed, hatred, delusion, and other defilements are themselves the seeds of buddhahood:

> *Vimalakīrti then asked Mañjuśri, "What may act as the seeds of the Tathāgata?"*
>
> *Mañjuśri said, "The body is the seed, ignorance and partiality are the seeds, greed, hatred, and delusion are the seeds." (Watson, p. 95 adapted)*

Going by these passages, it would seem that once one has opted for the two vehicles and eradicated one's attachments to the world of birth and death one can no longer opt for the bodhisattva-vehicle and strive to attain buddhahood. Of course, the idea here is that an arhat or pratyekabuddha would not even want to attain buddhahood, they have no more desires or aspirations of any kind. A worldly person still enmeshed in the painful cycle of birth and death, perhaps even the "incorrigible disbeliever" (S. *icchantika*), still has the possibility of someday aspiring to attain perfect and complete awakening. Their own defilements and the suffering caused by those defilements may even be what spur them on to purify themselves and overcome suffering not just for their own sakes but for all beings. Their selfish passions may someday be transmuted into the selfless aspiration of the bodhisattva, especially if they encounter the Mahāyāna teachings, are warned against falling into the trap of the two vehicles and follow the bodhisattva-vehicle to its conclusion. As discussed in a previous chapter, Nichiren states that these provisional Mahāyāna sūtras were taught for the purpose of overturning the narrow view of the Hīnayāna sūtras that Śākyamuni Buddha was the only buddha in the ten directions and that aspiring to buddhahood was not a realistic goal.

The Mahāyāna sūtras taught the way to buddhahood for all those took up the bodhisattva vehicle. There were, however, some who were not capable of doing this according to these sūtras. Some sūtras, catering to patriarchal misogyny and puritanism, taught that women could not attain buddhahood in their present forms or that incorrigible disbelievers could never attain buddhahood. Other Mahāyāna sūtras did allow that women and incorrigible disbelievers could attain buddhahood, such as the *Śrīmālā Sūtra* or the *Vimalakīrti Sūtra* in the case of women or the *Nirvāṇa Sutra* in the case of the incorrigible. Chapter twelve of the *Lotus Sūtra* also addresses the issue of incorrigible disbelievers and women, and this will be discussed in a later chapter. The most fixed rule of all, however, in both the Hīnayāna and Mahāyāna sūtras is that those who attain nirvāṇa on the path of the two vehicles have cut off all ties with the world of birth and death and so are no longer eligible to take up the bodhisattva vehicle. They are the hardest cases of all, and if it could be shown that if even they can attain buddhahood, than buddhahood can truly be said to be universal.

In the *The Differences Between Hīnayāna and Mahāyāna Teachings* (*Shōjō Daijō Fumbetsu-shō*) Nichiren points out what is at stake if the attainment of buddhahood were not open to all.

> To tell the truth, if attaining awakening by the people of the two vehicles had not been revealed, then all beings in the nine realms would never be able to become buddhas. The essence of the Lotus Sūtra, as a reasonable teaching, is that each sentient being in the ten realms contains the ten realms within itself. For example, each person is composed of the four elements of earth, water, fire, and air. If one of these elements is missing, there will be no human being. It is true that not only human beings but also all other sentient and non-sentient entities such as grasses, plants, and dust particles throughout the ten realms each possess the

ten realms. If the beings of the realms of the two
vehicles are not able to become buddhas, then no one in
the eight realms can become buddhas either. (Hori
2002, p. 194 adapted)

Buddhahood is a part of the integral whole of each being according to the teaching of the mutual possession of the ten realms. If the realm of the buddha is missing from some, it would have to be missing from all, because the mutual possession of the ten realms describes the full range of subjective experience and objective expression inherent in everyone and everything. So buddhahood is either a possibility for everyone or it is closed to everyone. Furthermore, Nichiren recognized that if the people of the two vehicles are excluded, then the bodhisattvas can never lead all people to buddhahood and their four great vows will go unfulfilled, leaving them unable to attain buddhahood as well. If the bodhisattva vehicle cannot be fulfilled then no one in any of the other realms will attain buddhahood.

All bodhisattvas make the four great vows. If a
bodhisattva does not accomplish the first vow, how can
he attain the fourth? All sūtras preached prior to the
Lotus Sūtra state that bodhisattvas and ordinary people
are able to attain buddhahood, but never the people of
the two vehicles. Thinking that they can become
buddhas while the people of the two vehicles cannot,
wise bodhisattvas and ignorant people throughout the
six worlds felt happy. The people of the two vehicles
plunged into grief and thought, "We should not have
entered Buddha Way." Now in the Lotus Sūtra it is
guaranteed that they can attain buddhahood, so not
only the people of the two vehicles, but also the people
of the nine realms will all become buddhas. Upon
hearing this teaching, bodhisattvas realized their
misunderstanding. As stated in the pre-Lotus sūtras, if
the people of the two vehicles cannot attain
buddhahood then the four great vows cannot be
accomplished. Consequently, bodhisattvas would also
be unable to become buddhas. When it was preached
that people of the two vehicles were unable to attain

buddhahood, they should not have been left alone in
sadness; bodhisattvas should have joined them in grief.
(Ibid, pp. 194-195 adapted)

Nevertheless, it would seem as though the main teaching of the Buddha is that those following the two vehicles cannot attain buddhahood. The *Lotus Sūtra* is the only sūtra to say otherwise. The *Lotus Sūtra* itself says that it is difficult to understand and hard to believe. Nichiren cites several passages from the *Infinite Meanings Sūtra* (a prologue to the *Lotus Sūtra*) and the second chapter of the *Lotus Sūtra* where the Buddha acknowledged that this teaching is different than anything he had taught in the forty previous years and that he is casting aside all expedients and revealing the truth.

> *I used the power of skillful means to teach the Dharma*
> *in various ways. And after more than forty years the*
> *truth has not yet been revealed. (Reeves 2008, p. 36*
>
> *Now is the time to say it.*
>
> *I will expound the Great Vehicle definitely. (Murano*
> *2012, p. 36)*
>
> *I have laid aside all expedient teachings.*
>
> *I will expound only unsurpassed enlightenment to*
> *bodhisattvas. (Ibid, p. 49)*

In chapter eleven of the *Lotus Sūtra*, a buddha from the past named Many Treasures Tathāgata appeared in his stupa of treasures and testified to the truth of Śākyamuni Buddha's teaching of the One Vehicle.

> *"Excellent! Excellent! You, Śākyamuni, the World*
> *Honored One, have expounded to this great multitude*
> *the Sūtra of the Lotus Flower of the Wonderful Dharma,*
> *the Teaching of Equality, the Great Wisdom, the*
> *Dharma for Bodhisattvas, the Dharma Upheld by the*
> *Buddhas. So it is, so it is. What you, Śākyamuni, the*

World Honored One, have expounded is all true." (Ibid, pp. 186-187)

In chapter twenty-one, the buddhas from the pure lands of the ten directions who are the emanations of Śākyamuni Buddha stretched out their tongues, emitted rays of light, coughed, and snapped their fingers together as a way of endorsing Śākyamuni Buddha's new teachings.

The buddhas who were sitting on the lion-like seats under the jeweled trees also stretched out their broad and long tongues and emitted innumerable rays of light. Śākyamuni Buddha and the buddhas under the jeweled trees displayed these supernatural powers of theirs for one hundred thousand years. Then they pulled back their tongues, coughed at the same time, and snapped their fingers. (Ibid, pp. 298-299)

Nichiren and his contemporaries accepted all this as a record of actual events in India at Vulture Peak. Today, we might have a little trouble accepting this testimony as valid simply because we do not view the *Lotus Sūtra* as a historical event or the verbatim record of a talk given by the historical Śākyamuni Buddha. Many people today may not even believe in rebirth, and so the dilemma of the two vehicles who cannot become bodhisattvas because they have cut themselves off from the cycle of birth and death may seem to be an imaginary or at least purely hypothetical problem. So what can we make of all of this if we do not accept these basic assumptions regarding the Mahāyāna sūtras as being the record of actual teachings and events or the metaphysical assumptions involved in the distinctions (or non-distinction) between the two vehicles and the One Vehicle?

I am of the opinion that those who wrote the *Lotus Sūtra* had themselves awakened to the highest truth that the Buddha had awakened to through their own faith and practice. They were monks (and perhaps nuns) who had awakened to a selfless compassion that went far beyond what they expected. Perhaps they had been striving to become arhats, or perhaps they were Mahāyānists who aspired to attain buddhahood in some distant time and place. In any case, when they attained awakening they realized that it cut through all their dualistic ideas, including the division between Hīnayāna and Mahāyāna. They knew for themselves that all the teachings of the Buddha did not lead to lesser goals but to the very same awakening the Buddha had realized. I believe that the *Lotus Sūtra* is the literary expression of their insight and the supreme joy that they felt in the form of a great drama in which the Buddha reveals the One Vehicle teaching. When the sūtra says that Śāriputra "felt like dancing for joy" (Ibid, p. 52) or that Śāriputra declares to the Buddha, "Today I have realized that I am your son, that I was born from your mouth, that I was born in [the world of] the Dharma, and that I have obtained the Dharma of the Buddha." (Ibid, pp. 52-53) I hear the voice of those anonymous Mahāyāna monks (and perhaps nuns as well) voicing their joyful surprise at how they had awakened to the same truth to which the Buddha had awakened. All of the rhetorical flourishes and fantastic events of the *Lotus Sūtra* are by way of underscoring how momentous this awakening was, and how, for them, it surpassed any other teaching, whether Hīnayāna or Mahāyāna, that they had heard. It does not worry me that the historical Buddha might not have spoken the exact words attributed to him in the *Lotus Sūtra*, nor do I worry that the Assembly in Space might not have literally occurred. What I think is marvelous is that more than 2,000 years ago the Buddha's followers realized that all people were capable of attaining perfect and complete awakening of a Buddha and that all who heard the Dharma would embark upon the One Vehicle enabling them to do so. When we read, recite, ponder, and share the *Lotus Sūtra* I believe that we are reading, reciting, pondering and sharing the testimony of those long ago practitioners who had such a surprising and joyful awakening that surpassed every expectation and who furthermore had the conviction that their awakening was available to all people. More than two thousand years later the *Lotus Sūtra* enables us to share their faith, hope, and conviction regarding the true meaning of the Buddha's teachings.

In Nichiren's time, however, not all agreed that what the *Lotus Sūtra* taught was so unique or important. Nichiren acknowledges that is difficult to trust the Buddha since he spoke first one way for over forty years and then another for the last eight according to the Tiantai school's five period chronology of the Buddha's teachings. Because of this, those who followed other sūtras believed that their sūtras taught what was most important and either accounted for or overruled the teachings in the *Lotus Sūtra*. The Flower Garland school believed that what the *Flower Garland Sūtra* taught about interdependence was more important; the Mantra school believed that what the *Mahavairochana Sūtra* taught about using mudrās, mantras, and mandalas was more important; the Pure Land Buddhists believed that what the three Pure Land sūtras taught about rebirth in the Pure Land by calling upon the name of Amitābha Buddha was most important. Nichiren states that in the seven hundred years since Buddhism was introduced to Japan until his own time, only Saichō (aka Grand Master Dengyō) understood the true import of the *Lotus Sūtra*. This is because Saichō's successors, the patriarchs and teachers of the Tendai school who should have been upholding the uniqueness and preeminence of the *Lotus Sūtra*, turned their attention to esoteric practices or Pure Land piety instead. It may have been the members of the Tendai school who paid lip service to the *Lotus Sūtra* but based their actual practice upon the views and methods of other sūtras that Nichiren was thinking of when he wrote, "Also it appears today that everyone seems to put their faith in the *Lotus Sūtra*, but their faith is superficial, not from the bottom of their hearts." (Hori 2002, p. 44, modified as per Murano 2000, p. 28)

In Nichiren's view, people needed to go back to the teachings of Saichō and the great Tiantai patriarchs Zhiyi and Zhanran who all upheld the uniqueness and preeminence of the insights presented in the *Lotus Sutra*. Nichiren realizes how difficult this will be, however. He cites the *Lotus Sūtra* to the effect that it is easier to throw Mt. Sumeru than to expound the *Lotus Sūtra* in the evil world after the Buddha's extinction. He also cites the *Nirvāṇa Sūtra* that says, "The slanderers of the True Dharma in the latter age of decay are countless in number just as the soil of all the worlds in the universe is immeasurable. Those who keep the True Dharma are few in number just like the bit of soil on a fingernail." (Ibid, p. 45) Despite the difficulties, Nichiren argues that it is of utmost importance to uphold the *Lotus Sūtra*, because otherwise the teaching of the universality of attaining buddhahood will be obscured or even lost.

> *It seems that the sūtras expounded before the Lotus Sūtra are more attractive than the first fourteen chapters of the Lotus Sūtra. But if the earlier sūtras are more attractive [and more valuable], Śāriputra and other adherents of the two vehicles will have lost their chance to become buddhas forever. How sad it would be for them! (Murano 2000, p. 28 adapted)*

There is more to the teaching of the *Lotus Sūtra* and the Tiantai interpretation of the true import of the sūtra than just the One Vehicle taught in the Trace

Gate. Zhiyi, I believe, awakened to the same truth that the creators of the *Lotus Sūtra* did. He expressed it in terms of the "three thousand realms in a single thought-moment." However, the full import of what the creators of the *Lotus Sūtra* and Zhiyi realized will not be revealed until we discuss the Original Gate and the Buddha's attainment of buddhahood in the remotest past. The One Vehicle teaching was only the relatively shallow beginning of what they realized. As Nichiren says a little further on in *Kaimoku-shō*:

> *The second chapter, "Expedients," in the Trace Gate of the Lotus Sūtra makes up for one of the two faults of the pre-Lotus sūtras by revealing the teachings of the 'three thousand realms in a single thought-moment' and 'attainment of buddhahood by the people of the two vehicles.' Yet, since the chapter has not yet revealed the Original and Eternal Buddha by 'outgrowing the provisional and revealing the essential,' it does not show the real concept of the "three thousand realms in a single thought-moment." Nor does it establish the true meaning of 'attainment of buddhahood by people of the two vehicles.' They are like the reflections of the moon in the water, or rootless grass floating on waves. (Hori 2002, p. 48, slightly modified) adapted)*

Sources

Gosho Translation Committee, editor-translator. *The Writings of Nichiren Daishonin*. Tokyo: Soka Gakkai, 1999.

Hori, Kyotsu, comp. *Writings of Nichiren Shonin: Doctrine Volume 2*. Tokyo: Nichiren Shu Overseas Propagation Promotion Association, 2002.

Murano, Senchu, trans. *The Lotus Sutra*. Hayward: Nichiren Buddhist International Center, 2012.

_____. *Kaimokusho or Liberation from Blindness*. Berkeley: Numata Center for Buddhist Translation and Research, 2000.

Reeves, Gene, trans. *The Lotus Sutra*. Boston: Wisdom Publications, 2008.

Watson, Burton, trans. *The Vimalakirti Sutra*. New York: Columbia University Press, 1997.

Chapter 22 – The Almost Perfect Flower Garland Sutra

Writings of Nichiren Shōnin Doctrine 2, pp. 38-39, 43-51, 64-66
Kaimoku-shō or Liberation from Blindness, pp. 19-20, 26-37, 57-59
The Writings of Nichiren Daishonin I, pp. 227-228, 231-238, 248-249

It may come as a surprise to some that Nichiren praises the *Flower Garland Sūtra* so extravagantly in the *Kaimoku-shō*. Of course, his rhetorical strategy is to build up the *Flower Garland Sūtra* so that when he points out that the *Lotus Sūtra* is even more profound the latter assertion will have even more impact. Basically he is saying, "If you think the *Flower Garland Sūtra* is great, and in many respects it is, then you will be even more impressed by the *Lotus Sūtra*." Another reason for his praise of the *Flower Garland Sūtra* is because Nichiren sees it as containing all the best aspects of the sūtras other than the *Lotus Sūtra* (according to the Tiantai school system of the five flavors or periods). If the *Lotus Sūtra*, in teaching the attainment of buddhahood by the people of the two vehicles and the attainment of buddhahood in the remote past, surpasses the *Flower Garland Sūtra*, then it certainly surpasses all other sūtras. Before moving on to the teaching of the attainment of buddhahood in the remotest past, let's take a closer look at the *Flower Garland Sūtra*. Why does Nichiren praise it? And what teachings does the Flower Garland school based upon it convey that are a part of the common heritage of East Asian Mahāyāna Buddhism, including Nichiren Buddhism?

As is evident in *Kaimoku-shō*, Nichiren believes that the *Flower Garland Sūtra* expresses the Buddha's vision of perfect and complete awakening beneath the Bodhi Tree. The sūtra, after all, begins, "Thus have I heard. At one time the Buddha was in the land of Magadha, in a state of purity, at the site of awakening, having just realized true awareness." (Cleary 1993, p. 55 slightly modified) The scene of the Buddha's awakening is soon transformed into the Hall of Awakening and the Buddha becomes the cosmic Vairocana Buddha of the Lotus Repository World, while the teachings are given by a host of celestial bodhisattvas led by Dharma Wisdom. Though considered the first teaching of the Buddha, it is really more of a record of visionary transformations and teachings witnessed by Śākyamuni Buddha as he sat beneath the Bodhi Tree immediately after his perfect and complete awakening.

According to the Tiantai school system, the Flower Garland period of the Buddha's teachings represents the Sudden method of teaching and conveys the distinct and perfect teachings for advanced bodhisattvas. In fact, as Nichiren points out in *Kaimoku-shō*, Śākyamuni Buddha does not actually teach anything in the *Flower Garland Sūtra*. Rather, advanced bodhisattvas such as Dharma Wisdom and numerous others are the ones who actually teach the Dharma. Nichiren even says that until the Buddha taught the *Lotus Sūtra*, he did not actually teach anything that was not derived from the teachings of Dharma Wisdom and the other bodhisattvas. Nichiren even goes so far as to say that in the *Flower Garland Sūtra* and all the other sūtras prior to the *Lotus Sūtra* the Buddha was the student and Dharma Wisdom and the other bodhisattvas were the teachers.

> Therefore, during the time when the pre-Lotus sūtras were preached Lord Śākyamuni was not the teacher who revealed what others did not know, but he was rather a student of such bodhisattvas as Dharma Wisdom. Likewise, it is said in the first chapter on the "Introduction" of the Lotus Sūtra that Bodhisattva Mañjuśrī was a teacher of Śākyamuni Buddha for nine generations. In various sūtras preached before the Lotus the Buddha is quoted as having said that he, 'never preached even one word.' It means that his preaching did not go beyond what was preached by such bodhisattvas as Dharma Wisdom. (Hori 2002, p. 66)

Nichiren states that the *Flower Garland Sūtra* can be seen as the root source of the teachings in the other sūtras with the exception of the *Lotus Sūtra*.

> An assertion in the sūtra that 'there is no distinction among the mind, the Buddha, and the unawakened' is said to be the theoretical foundation of not only the Flower Garland, but also the Dharma Characteristics, Three Treatise, Mantra, and Tiantai schools. (Ibid, p. 46 adapted)

The actual origins of the *Flower Garland Sūtra* are apparently in Central Asia or even China, centuries after the Buddha's passing. Only two chapters, the "Ten Grounds" and the "Entry into the Realm of Reality" are extant in Sanskrit, and they date as late as the second century CE. Those two chapters were originally considered sūtras in their own right. At some point before the middle of the 5th century these two sūtras, several other independent sūtras, and perhaps some newly generated sūtras to fill the gaps, were edited and compiled in the form of the *Flower Garland Sūtra*. (See Cook, pp. 21-22)

In China, the *Flower Garland Sūtra* inspired the creation of two schools. The first was the short-lived Ten Grounds school (C. Ti-lun) based upon a commentary on the "Ten Grounds" chapter of the *Flower Garland Sūtra* attributed to Vasubandhu and translated into Chinese in the sixth century. The second school, the Flower Garland school (C. Hua-yen), subsumed this earlier school in the seventh century. The Flower Garland school is considered to have five great patriarchs: Dushun (557-640), Zhiyan (602-668), Fazang (643-712; aka Xianshou), Chengguan (738-820 or 838), and Zongmi (780-841). Dushun is honored as the first patriarch, but Fazang was the one who systematized its teachings and was the actual founder of the school. Zongmi was both a patriarch of the Flower Garland school and also a Zen Master. The persecution of Buddhism in China by the Emperor Wu from 845-847 were disastrous for the Flower Garland, Dharma Characteristics, Tiantai, and other schools that relied upon patronage and scholarly apparatus. They faded away in China as independent schools, and only Pure Land and Zen continued to flourish in China thereafter. Still, the influence of the Flower Garland school continued to be felt long after as it became the doctrinal foundation for Zen Buddhism in China, Korea, and Vietnam and some of its terminology and insights were assimilated by Neo-Confucianism.

During its heyday, the Flower Garland school tried to account for all the Buddha's teachings. Among the teachings it assimilated were those emphasizing the tathāgatagarbha or buddha-nature. Its primary sources were translations of Indian Mahāyāna works by the Indian scholar-monk Paramārtha (499-569). Among several other works, Paramārtha translated the *Summary of the Mahāyāna* (S. *Mahāyāna-samgraha*) by Asanga, a work that gave rise to the short-lived Summary of the Mahāyāna school (C. She-lun) that faded away when the Dharma Characteristics school was established based upon the newer translations of Yogācāra works by Xuanzang (602-664).

Paramārtha is also credited with translating the *Awakening of Faith in the Mahāyāna Treatise* attributed to Aśvaghosha. How Paramārtha's buddha-nature oriented teachings differed from the later teachings of Xuanzang's Dharma Characteristics school will be explained momentarily.

Like the Tiantai school before it, the Flower Garland school organized the Buddha's lifetime of teachings into a five-part classification system: Hīnayāna, Initial Mahāyāna, Fnal Mahāyāna, Sudden, and Perfect. Its patriarchs conveyed the main points of the *Flower Garland Sūtra* itself in terms of the ten mysteries and six characteristics that are alluded to by Nichiren. By explaining these, I will be able to provide a brief summary of the teachings of the Flower Garland school. This will hopefully provide both a summary of the common assumptions held by a majority of East Asian Buddhists (including Nichiren) up to the present-day but will also show why the Flower Garland teachings are held in such high regard. I will then discuss why Nichiren felt that there was a flaw or even a crack in the gem that is the *Flower Garland Sūtra*.

The Five Teachings

Hīnayāna – This is identical to the tripitaka teaching or the Deer Park period of the Tiantai system. The purpose of this period is to teach the śrāvakas that there is no self, only the five aggregates, the twelve sense bases (the five physical sense plus mind and their respective objects), or the eighteen elements (the twelve sense bases plus the respective consciousness for each pair of sense and sense-object), or the twelve-fold chain of dependent origination. In keeping with the teachings of the Abhidharma Treasury school or the Completion of Reality school, the method of these teachings is to show that what we take to be a permanent, independent, unchanging self is actually nothing more than the causal and conditioned flow of the actual building blocks of reality called dharmas. The dharmas are just momentary phenomenal expressions of bare consciousness, various types of mental activities, and basic material elements like earth (resistance, solids), air (pressure, gases), fire (temperature, chemical reactions), and water (cohesiveness, liquids).

According to the Abhidharma Treasury school, the Hīnayāna followers traverse five paths: (1) the path of accumulating merit and meditative stability, (2) the path of preparation through insight meditation, (3) the path of seeing wherein they overcome the defilements and get their first genuine

271

glimpse of nirvāṇa and become stream-winners, (4) the path of cultivation whereby they deepen their realization and attain the fruits of the once-returner and non-returner, and finally (5) the path of no-more-learning whereby they attain nirvāṇa and become arhats and after death, according to this level of teaching, they reduce the body to ashes and annihilate consciousness. They are never reborn in the six lower realms (or anywhere else) ever again.

The focus here is on what the Flower Garland school calls the realm of phenomena or actualities (C. *shih*; J. *ji*). By looking past our assumptions that there are graspable things like tables, chairs, animals, or people, we see that underlying these things is nothing but the impersonal flow of dharmas, the real actualities. Awakening to the dharmas, one lets go of the idea of self and loses one's attachment and aversion for conditioned phenomena.

Initial Mahāyāna (Consciousness-Only) – This teaching is roughly equivalent to the shared teaching and also many elements of the Expanded and Prajna periods. It actually has two parts, the first of which is the teachings of the Yogācāra or Consciousness-Only school as expounded by the Dharma Characteristics school. In this teaching the Buddha explains that there is more to us than just our five sensory consciousnesses and the mind that constitute our conscious life. There are two other forms of consciousness whose activities we would today call the subconscious. There is a seventh consciousness that constantly clings to the idea of a self that acts and is acted upon. This defiled consciousness constantly reinforces our egocentrism. The object of the seventh consciousness, what it takes to be a "self," is the eighth consciousness that is actually the storehouse of all our memories and the seeds sown by our karmic activities (which is to say our intentional thoughts, words, and deeds both wholesome and unwholesome). The storehouse consciousness is actually the source of the other seven consciousnesses and their respective experiences because the seeds in the storehouse produce them. The activities of the first seven consciousnesses in turn are said to perfume the storehouse consciousness by planting new seeds and further conditioning (for better or worse) the seeds that are already there, thereby perpetuating their phenomenal existence or allowing them to ripen into conscious experience and activity. So the experiences we have in terms of the first six consciousnesses and our reactions to them create and condition the seeds in the storehouse and the seeds in the storehouse give rise to further experiences and activities when conditions allow them to ripen. This process of mutual conditioning between the seeds in the storehouse consciousness and the activities of the first seven forms of consciousness is what is known as the simultaneity of cause and effect. All of this helps to account for the continuity of memory and more importantly the continuous flow of karma and one's sense of a stable identity even when the sixth consciousnesses drops away due to unconsciousness, deep sleep, or at the moment of death. It is also used to show how consciousness conditions experience and gives rise to our experience of the duality of subject and object. According to this teaching there are no objects apart from how they are experienced in consciousness and no fixed independent subject apart from the delusion of the ego-consciousness that falsely takes the conditioned flow of the storehouse consciousness to be such a subject or self.

According to this teaching there are three natures. The flow of causes and conditions that makes up the storehouse consciousness is called the dependent nature because the misperception of the duality of subject and object depends upon it as its basis. The subject-object duality superimposed upon the dependent nature is called the imagined nature. The Buddha's clear perception that there are no subjects or objects within the dependent nature is called the perfected nature. The three natures are often explained using the analogy of a man seeing a rope in the dark. At first the man thinks he sees a snake. This is the imagined nature. Then he sees that what he took to be a snake in the dark is just a rope. This is to recognize the dependent nature upon which the illusion of the snake depends. Upon further examination he sees that even the common object called a rope is really just a mass of fibers twisted together and there is no real objective rope. This is the perfected nature that no longer falsely attributes a fixed self or self-nature to the flow of causes and conditions. Through the teaching of the three natures, the Consciousness-Only teachings point out that all objects including the dharmas of the previous teaching are just misperceptions of the flow of consciousness and that to overcome these delusions consciousness must be purified through Buddhist practice.

The problem is that in order to purify oneself through authentic practice one must have pure seeds within the storehouse consciousness that can give rise to such practices and their corresponding fruit. This led to a Buddhist theory of five mutually distinct natures covered previously. In this theory, some have the seeds to become arhats, some have the seeds to become pratyekabuddhas, some have the seeds for buddhahood, some have all three types of seeds, and some have no pure seeds at all and can only hope to attain temporary respite in the human or heavenly realms. Accordingly, the Consciousness-Only school teaches that the three vehicles are the ultimate teaching of the Buddha and that the One Vehicle is only to encourage those with all three kinds of seeds to aspire to buddhahood. This is the teaching that Saichō (767-822) refuted in favor of the One Vehicle teaching of the *Lotus Sūtra* as applying to everyone equally because of the universality of buddha-nature.

Those who can attain buddhahood, according to this teaching, must still spend three innumerable eons (S. *asamkhya kalpas*) cultivating their store of merit and wisdom as bodhisattvas practicing the six perfections. During this time they also traverse five paths except that for them the path of no-more learning is the attainment of buddhahood. At that point they undergo a revolution at the base of consciousness (i.e. the eighth), so that all eight consciousnesses are purified. The eighth or storehouse consciousness is transformed into the great mirror-like knowledge that reflects reality just as it is, the seventh transforms into the equality knowledge that perceives the non-dual true nature, the sixth transforms into the distinguishing knowledge that correctly perceives differences between conditioned phenomena, and the first five consciousnesses transform into the all-performing knowledge of unrestricted activity that guides compassionate action.

Initial Mahāyāna (Middle Way) – In India the Consciousness-Only School arose as a reaction to the seemingly nihilistic rhetoric of the Madhyamika or Middle Way school. The Middle Way school had set up two levels of truth. The first was the conventional (S. *samvirti*) whereby one can speak in terms of self, others, and everyday objects. The other was the ultimate (S. *paramārtha*) whereby self, other, and all things (including the dharmas) are empty of any self-nature. The teaching of emptiness has been covered previously. The problem for some people was that if even the dharmas were empty then there was no solid basis for anything at all. There was nothing for the conventional truth to be based upon except a fathomless emptiness. To correct this, the Consciousness-Only School claimed that consciousness was the actual basis of reality as discussed above. The Flower Garland school, however, saw this as a mistake, in that consciousness was also a causal process even according to the Consciousness-Only school teachings and therefore also empty of self-nature. Because the Middle Way teachings, such as taught by the Three Treatises school, are seen as more consistent in applying emptiness to all dharmas without excepting consciousness, the Flower Garland school judged them to be profounder than the Consciousness-Only teachings.

The focus in the Initial Mahāyāna is on what the Flower Garland school calls the realm of principle (C. *li*; J. *ri*). The principle of all phenomena is that they are all empty of any kind of self-nature. The Consciousness-Only teachings indicate this by pointing out how all things are just transformations of consciousness. The Middle Way teachings are then used to point out how all conditioned things, including consciousness, cannot have an unchanging independent self-nature and are therefore empty. Awakening to the principle of emptiness, one is free of all clinging because there is nothing to cling to and no one to do any clinging. Fazang, however, taught that principle is not merely emptiness but the buddha-nature itself, which is taught in the Final Mahāyāna.

Final Mahāyāna – The teaching of the tathāgatagarbha or buddha-nature constitutes the third kind of teaching and is derived from the *Awakening of Faith in the Mahāyāna Treatise*, and sūtras that emphasize the tathāgatagarbha such as the *Revealing the Profound Secrets Sūtra*, the *Laṅkāvatāra Sūtra*, and the *Queen Śrīmālā Sūtra*. While the previous teachings explained that reality is empty of self-nature, this teaching explains that reality is not empty of buddha-qualities. The true reality is in fact buddha-nature, which is empty of defilement. Another term for this is tathāgatagarbha. "Tathāgata" is another term for a buddha, and it can mean either "thus-come-one" or "thus-gone-one." In other words, a buddha is one who comes and goes freely from the realm of truth. "Garbha" means either "womb" or "embryo" and perhaps it is best to translate it as "matrix." So "tathāgatagarbha" means "matrix of the thus-come-one." The tathāgatagarbha is the Dharma-kāya or reality-body of the Buddha when obscured by defilements. It is the unconditioned true nature of reality and therefore, unlike conditioned phenomena, is characterized as pure, blissful, eternal, and true self. It might seem a bit odd to call it a "true self" seeing as how so much effort was made to deny that anything has a self-nature, but in this case the term does not mean the "self-nature" of a conditioned self or dharma but the authenticity of the true nature of all reality. I must confess that I am not myself convinced of the wisdom or coherence of this kind of rhetoric, nevertheless it is the term used in sūtras like the *Queen Śrīmālā Sūtra*

275

and the *Nirvāṇa Sūtra*. The tathāgatagarbha is also the pure aspect of the storehouse consciousness even prior to its transformation into the perfect mirror wisdom consciousness. In fact, according to Paramārtha's translations and commentaries the tathāgatagarbha is the pure consciousness that is not just an aspect of the eighth consciousness but can be considered a ninth consciousness. There is no one who is bereft of this buddha-nature, the pure consciousness. Note that Paramārtha's interpretation was rejected by the Dharma Characteristics school but continued to be affirmed in the Tiantai school, the Flower Garland school, and the Mantra school. The teaching that there is a pure consciousness that must be cleared of adventitious defilements (such as those stored by the storehouse consciousness) is, however, something that can be found as far back as the teachings in the Pāli canon.

> *This mind, O monks, is luminous, but it is defiled by*
> *adventitious defilements. The uninstructed worldling*
> *does not understand this as it really is; therefore for him*
> *there is no mental development.*
>
> *This mind, O monks, is luminous, and it is freed from*
> *adventitious defilements. The instructed noble disciple*
> *understands this as it really is, therefore for him there is*
> *mental development. (Nyanaponika & Bodhi, p. 36)*

If this is indeed the case, and there is a pure consciousness in the depths of our being, then Buddhist practice is not about creating an awakened state of mind but of recovering or rediscovering the awakened state of mind that was there all along. This is what is taught in the *Awakening of Faith in the Mahāyāna Treatise*: "Grounded on the original enlightenment is non-enlightenment. And because of non-enlightenment, the process of actualization of enlightenment can be spoken of." (Hakeda, p. 38) How the pure consciousness came to be obscured by adventitious defilements in the first place seems to be an unanswerable question. The point of the teaching is that a pure awakened mind is always present and that our practice can wipe away the obscurations and allow it to shine like a bright mirror cleared of dust. Another analogy often used is of the ocean and its waves. The defilements that arise according to causes and conditions are like the waves that arise in the ocean when the wind blows. When the wind has died down and the waves have calmed, the ocean becomes still and calm and can reflect the clear blue sky. This analogy is the inspiration for what the Flower Garland school calls the Ocean Seal Samadhi wherein the mind, like a calm ocean, is restored to its original nature that is calm and serene and perfectly reflects reality as it is.

The initial and final Mahāyāna constitute what the Flower Garland school considers the Gradual teaching of the Buddha, because he gradually leads the bodhisattvas to perfect and complete awakening. According to sūtras like the *Bodhisattva Practice Jewel Necklace Sūtra* there are fifty-two stages of bodhisattva practice. These stages are spread out over the five paths enumerated in the Consciousness-Only teachings. The first ten are the ten degrees of faith for those on the path of accumulation. The next thirty are the ten abodes, ten kinds of practice, and ten dimensions of merit transference that belong to the path of preparation. Then come the ten grounds, the first of which corresponds to the path of seeing, and the next nine of which belong to the path of cultivation. Then there is a stage of preliminary awakening followed by supreme subtle awakening that is equivalent to the path of no-more learning. What is attained is not the nirvāṇa of the arhat that rejects saṃsāra, but rather the non-abiding nirvāṇa whereby through wisdom the Buddha does not dwell in saṃsāra, through compassion the Buddha does not abide in nirvāṇa either, but rather freely engages in liberating activities throughout saṃsāra. Actually the Buddha realizes that saṃsāra and nirvāṇa are not separate but simply reality when viewed from a deluded or awakened perspective respectively.

The focus here is on what the Flower Garland school calls the realm of the non-obstruction of principle and actuality (C. *li shih wu ai*; J. *riji muge*). The principle of emptiness and the actualities of conditioned phenomena are not separate. Unless phenomena are empty of self-nature they cannot be causal and conditioned phenomena, as they would just be permanently themselves, unalterable, permanent, and capable of neither influencing nor being influenced by any other phenomena. Apart from conditioned phenomena there is no such thing as emptiness, as emptiness is what we call the principle at work in the interdependent relations of conditioned phenomena. Principle and phenomena actually implicate each other. This is of course similar to the unity of provisional existence and emptiness in the Middle Way according to the Tiantai teachings. Awakening to the non-obstruction of principle and actuality, one is able to be both liberated due to emptiness and simultaneously compassionately engaged with the actualities of the world.

Sudden – The Sudden teaching does not add any new content but differs in the manner of presentation. It is indicative of a direct presentation of reality instead of a gradual teaching by way of concepts or a series of reflections. Chengguan associated this kind of teaching with the Zen school. The following scene from the *Vimalakīrti Sūtra* is an example of it in action:

> When the various bodhisattvas had finished one by one giving their explanations, they asked Mañjuśrī, "How then does the bodhisattva enter the gate of nondualism?"
>
> Mañjuśrī replied, "To my way of thinking, all dharmas are without words, without explanations, without purport, without cognition, removed from all questions and answers. In this way one may enter the gate of nondualism."
>
> Then Mañjuśrī said to Vimalakīrti, "Each of us has given an explanation. Now, sir, it is your turn to speak. How does the bodhisattva enter the gate of nondualism?"
>
> At that time Vimalakīrti remained silent and did not speak a word.
>
> Mañjuśrī sighed and said, "Excellent, excellent! Not a word, not a syllable – this truly is to enter the gate of nondualism!" (Watson, pp. 110-111)

Perfect – This level of teaching is identified by Zhiyan as the One Vehicle teaching and therefore with both the *Lotus Sūtra* and the *Flower Garland Sūtra*. According to Zhiyan, the Hīnayāna, Gradual Mahāyāna, and Sudden Mahāyāna teachings are the three vehicles taught by the Buddha in accordance with the capacities of his disciples. In the *Lotus Sūtra* all these former teachings merge into the single identity of the One Vehicle. Zhiyan called this the Shared Doctrine wherein the One Vehicle is an expression of the common thread shared by the three vehicles. By contrast, the *Flower Garland Sūtra* teaches what Zhiyan called the Distinct Doctrine that expresses the Buddha's own perspective that transcends the three vehicles and is only accessible to those who also attain perfect and complete awakening. Zhiyan, naturally, claimed that the One Vehicle of the Distinct Doctrine taught in the *Flower Garland Sūtra* is superior to all the other perspectives and teachings based on them. Fazang, even demoted the One Vehicle teaching of the *Lotus Sūtra* to the category of the Final Mahāyāna to emphasize the contrast he saw between the two sūtras.

The focus here is on what the Flower Garland school calls the realm of the non-obstruction of actuality and actuality (C. *shih shih wu ai*; J. *jiji muge*). What this means is that if all actual phenomena are empty of a fixed, unchanging self-nature because they are dependent on causes and conditions, then their true nature is nothing but causes and conditions. Those causes and conditions are themselves actualities dependent on causes and conditions. Therefore, any actuality is part of a vast network of other actualities all of which are mutually supporting and mutually containing and contained. This being the case, actualities not only do not obstruct one another but require each other in a holistic network of interpenetration where all things are one with all other things and yet able to retain their own distinct phenomenal actuality. For instance, grapes depend upon sunlight, rain, soil, and a myriad other climatic conditions; these contributing factors all enter into the composition of the grapes that then express all these contributing factors in a unique way through the color, consistency, flavor, and quality of the wine that the grapes produce. As the *Flower Garland Sūtra* teaches, "Thus does infinity enter into one, yet each unit's distinct, with no overlap." (Cleary 1993, p. 200) Awakening to the non-obstruction of actuality and actuality, one realizes that all is one and one is all. In terms of practice, this means that the first stage of the fifty-two stages of practice contains all the other stages within it.

In order to expound the interpenetration of all phenomena or actualities the Flower Garland school teaches it in terms of the ten mysterious gates and six characteristics. There are different versions of the ten mysterious gates. The following is how they are listed according to Fazang in his *On the Golden Lion Treatise* (the brief explanations are my own):

1. Simultaneous complete correspondence – This gate is another way of expressing the mutual interdependence of all phenomena as per the

279

teaching of the non-obstruction of actuality and actuality. All the other gates are derived from this one.

2. Purity and mixture of the stores containing all qualities – This means that every single phenomenon retains its own pure identity or wholeness but can also be seen as the mixture of the qualities of the causes and conditions of the whole.
3. Mutual inclusion and differentiation of one and many – Each phenomenon or actuality contains all others as its causes and conditions but without losing its own distinct identity.
4. Mutual identity of all phenomena in freedom – Each actuality freely expresses itself but at the same time it is identified with all other phenomena that it supports and is supported by.
5. Simultaneous establishment of disclosure and concealment – A single actuality that is focused on expresses, in its own unique way, all of its causes and conditions but in doing so obscures them as well.
6. Peaceful coexistence of the minute and the subtle – Even the most seemingly small and insignificant actuality contains and is contained by the whole without interfering with its own unique expression.
7. Realm of Indra's net – The mutual interpenetration of all things can be likened to the net of the god Indra wherein the interstices of the net each hold a jewel and each jewel reflects all the others and is reflected in all the others.
8. Creation of understanding by revealing the Dharma through facts – One can take any actuality as an example of the teaching of mutual interpenetration.
9. Differentiation of the ten time periods – The actualities of past, present, and future also mutually implicate one another and are not separate though they remain distinct.
10. Universal accomplishment through the projection of consciousness only – The mutual interpenetration of all actualities is none other than the activity of the One Mind, the absolute understood as pure consciousness.

In the same treatise, Fazang gives the following explanation of the six characteristics of wholeness, diversity, universality, particularity, formation, and disintegration possessed by phenomena in their interrelations using the analogy of a golden statue of a lion:

The lion represents the character of wholeness, and the
five organs, being various and different, represent
diversity. The fact that they are all of one dependent-
arising represents the character of universality. The
eyes, ears, and so on remain in their own places and do
not interfere with one another; this represents the
character of particularity. The combination and
convergence of the various organs makes up the lion;
this represents the character of formation. The fact that
each remains at its own position represents the
character of disintegration. (Chang, p. 230)

All of this only provides a bit of a taste of the way the Flower Garland school explains interpenetration. It would take many more pages to clarify the meaning of the ten mysterious gates and the six characteristics and this would stray from my intention of simply presenting a brief overview of the *Flower Garland Sūtra* and the teachings of the Flower Garland school. The important thing to know is that the Flower Garland school felt that the highest teaching of Buddhism was that every single phenomena exists only by virtue of the totality of all causes and conditions, which is to say by virtue of all other phenomena. This means that every single phenomenon contains and is contained by all others throughout the past, present, and future in a totality that is identified with the pure consciousness that is the buddha-nature when obscured but when cleared of defilement is the One Mind of the Buddha.

The Flower Garland school presents a marvelous and inspiring vision of reality as a single organic system whose basis is the purity of the buddha-nature that is empty of an unchanging independent self-nature and the defilements but not empty of the qualities of buddhahood. Nichiren, however, insists that *Flower Garland Sūtra* itself is lacking in comparison with the *Lotus Sūtra*.

How can it be that the Buddha kept his teachings
unrevealed in such a wonderful sūtra? The Buddha said
in this sūtra, however, that adherents of the two
vehicles and the incorrigible disbelievers cannot become
buddhas. This statement of the Buddha is like a flaw in
a precious stone. He also said as many as three times in
this sūtra that he attained awakening for the first time

281

during his life in this world. He never revealed in this
sūtra that he attained buddhahood in the remotest past
as he did in the "Chapter of the Duration of the Life of
the Tathagata" in the Lotus Sūtra. From this we must
say that the Flower Garland Sūtra is like a broken gem,
the moon covered with clouds, or the eclipsed sun. It is
very strange. (Murano 2000, pp. 29-30 adapted)

Let's examine these two points. Earlier in *Kaimoku-shō*, Nichiren cited a
passage of the *Flower Garland Sūtra* that compared the two vehicles to a tree
in a burning pit and the incorrigible disbelievers to a tree in poisonous water,
in neither case will their buddha-nature ever be able to flower just as a tree in
a burning pit or poisonous water cannot flower. (See Hori 2002, pp. 38-39)
This passage is not in the *Flower Garland Sūtra* as translated by Thomas
Cleary. Still, it is true that the *Flower Garland Sūtra* does not have any
passages that would assure the arhats or pratyekabuddhas of someday
attaining buddhahood. On the other hand there are passage like the
following: "The very first thought to seek buddhahood the worldly, or even
those of the two vehicles cannot know – much less the other virtuous
practices." (Cleary 1993, p. 399 slightly modified) Both the *Lotus Sūtra* and the
Flower Garland Sūtra teach that the bodhisattva vehicle is beyond the
comprehension of the followers of the two vehicles and that the Buddha uses
skillful means to teach, but it would seem that Nichiren is correct in that only
in the *Lotus Sūtra* does the Buddha explicitly affirm that even the major
disciples who were already arhats will attain buddhahood, going so far as to
give them predictions of their attainment of buddhahood.

As for the attainment of buddhahood in the remote past, the *Flower Garland
Sūtra* does affirm that the true nature of the buddhas is unborn and deathless.
"Just as space itself is unborn and unperishing, so is the truth of the buddhas,
ultimately birthless and deathless." (Ibid, p. 521) The problem for Nichiren is
that this affirmation is usually taken to only apply to the Dharma-body of the
Buddha, who is called Vairocana or Mahāvairocana. Śākyamuni Buddha is
usually viewed as a mere emanation of Mahāvairocana who was born on a
certain date, attained buddhahood under the Bodhi Tree at the age of thirty

(or thirty-five), and passed away when he entered final nirvāṇa at the age of
eighty. As cited above, the *Flower Garland Sūtra* opens by stating that
Śākyamuni Buddha had just attained awakening under the Bodhi Tree. A little

further on in the sūtra the bodhisattvas say to the Buddha, "Countless eons of practice complete, you've become truly awake under the enlightenment tree: you appear universally to liberate beings, like clouds filling all to the end of time." (Ibid, p. 150) This passage also asserts that Śākyamuni Buddha had just attained buddhahood while sitting under the Bodhi Tree. Again, Nichiren is correct in that only in chapter sixteen of the *Lotus Sūtra* does Śākyamuni Buddha himself speak of his attainment of buddhahood as happening in the remote past and of his life as being unborn and deathless. What this means will be covered next.

Sources

Chang, Garma C. *The Buddhist Teaching of Totality: The Philosophy of Hwa Yen Buddhism*. University Park: The Pennsylvania State University Press, 1989.

Ch'en, Kenneth. *Buddhism in China: A Historical Survey*. Princeton: Princeton University Press, 1964.

Cleary, Thomas. *Entry Into the Inconceivable: An Introduction to Hua-Yen Buddhism*. Honolulu: University of Hawaii Press, 1983.

_____, trans. *The Flower Ornament Scripture: A Translation of the Avatamsaka Sūtra*. Boston: Shambhala, 1993.

Cook, Francis H. *Hua-yen Buddhism: The Jewel Net of Indra*. University Park: The Pennsylvania State University, 1991.

Gosho Translation Committee, editor-translator. *The Writings of Nichiren Daishonin*. Tokyo: Soka Gakkai, 1999.

Gregory, Peter N., trans. *Inquiry Into the Origin of Humanity*. Honolulu: Kuroda Institute, 1995.

Hakeda, Yoshito S., trans. *The Awakening of Faith: Attributed to Ashvaghosha*. New York: Columbia University Press, 1967.

Hori, Kyotsu, comp. *Writings of Nichiren Shonin: Doctrine Volume 2*. Tokyo: Nichiren Shu Overseas Propagation Promotion Association, 2002.

Murano, Senchu, trans. *Kaimokusho or Liberation from Blindness*. Berkeley: Numata Center for Buddhist Translation and Research, 2000.

Nyanaponika, Thera and Bodhi, Bhikkhu trans. & ed., *Numerical Discourses of the Buddha: An Anthology of Suttas from the Anguttara Nikaya*. Walnut Creek: AltaMira Press, 1999.

Odin, Steve. *Process Metaphysics and Hua-Yen Buddhism: A Critical Study of Cumulative Penetration vs. Interpenetration*. Albany, State of New York Press, 1982.

Watson, Burton, trans. *The Vimalakīrti Sūtra*. New York: Columbia University Press, 1997.

Chapter 23 – Original Gate: Attainment of Buddhahood in the Remote Past

Writings of Nichiren Shōnin Doctrine 2, pp. 45-49
Kaimoku-shō or Liberation from Blindness, pp. 29-35
The Writings of Nichiren Daishonin I, pp. 233-236

Now we come to where Nichiren says, "In the second place, let us discuss the concept of the attainment of buddhahood by Śākyamuni Buddha in the remote past revealed in the Original Gate of the *Lotus Sūtra*." (adapted from Hori 2002, p. 45) What exactly does this mean? Why does it matter when the Buddha attained buddhahood? Why did Nichiren put so much importance on this teaching? I hope to make all of this clear in the following pages.

The first thing Nichiren does, as we have seen, is to stress how all of the sūtras prior to the *Lotus Sūtra* (according to the five periods system of Tiantai) state that Śākyamuni Buddha attained buddhahood while sitting under the Bodhi Tree as a young man. The *Flower Garland Sūtra* that presents the most sublime teachings of Mahāyāna Buddhism does not challenge this, let alone any of the lesser Mahāyāna sūtras. The *Infinite Meanings Sūtra*, the first part of the so-called Threefold Lotus Sūtra, does not deny this. This is significant because the *Infinite Meanings Sūtra* specifically takes account of the Buddha's forty years of teaching including the Hīnayāna teachings, the basic Mahāyāna teachings, the Perfection of Wisdom teachings and the *Flower Garland Sūtra* (See Reeves p. 37) and includes them all as teachings given during the time when the truth had not yet been revealed (Ibid, p. 36). The Buddha also says of the teaching of the infinite meanings that it leads to awakening quickly and is the "great direct way" (Ibid, p. 42). Despite all of this the Buddha also says in the *Infinite Meanings Sūtra*, "Good sons, after sitting upright for six years under the bodhi tree at the place of the Way, I could attain supreme awakening." (Ibid, p. 36) I'd like to note that the translator Gene Reeves says of this sūtra, "Some believe that it may have been originally composed in China." (Ibid, p. 4) If that is so, then the *Infinite Meanings Sūtra* may have deliberately been composed as a prologue to the *Lotus Sūtra* as translated by Kumārajīva to account for and subsume the teachings of the other sūtras extant in China at that time. Even so, the composers accepted that the Buddha attained awakening as a young man forty years or so before teaching the *Lotus Sūtra*. Finally, even in the Trace Gate and the majority of the chapters of the Original Gate the Buddha speaks of attaining buddhahood under the Bodhi Tree as in the following passage, "I for the first time sat at the place of enlightenment." (Murano 2012, p. 46) Nichiren points out that it is only in chapters fifteen and sixteen of the *Lotus Sūtra* that the Buddha speaks of his attainment of buddhahood as occurring in the remote past.

In chapter fifteen a vast multitude of bodhisattvas appeared from the space beneath the ground and Śākyamuni Buddha tells Maitreya Bodhisattva and the assembly that he had been the teacher of these bodhisattvas for the past innumerable eons. Maitreya Bodhisattva then asks how this could be possible since the Buddha had only been a buddha for forty years. (See Ibid, p. 243 for Maitreya's questions) The Buddha gives the following response in chapter sixteen:

> "The gods, men, and asuras in the world think that I, Śākyamuni Buddha, left the palace of the Śākyas, sat at the place of enlightenment not far from the City of Gaya, and attained Anuttara-samyak-sambodhi [some forty years ago]. To tell the truth, good men, it is many hundreds of thousands of billions of nayutas of kalpas since I became the Buddha." (Ibid, p. 247)

This is the teaching of the attainment of buddhahood in the remotest past (J. *kuon jitsujō*). In chapter sixteen, the Buddha provides an analogy for how long it has been since he attained awakening. The analogy had to do with smashing a practically countless number of worlds to dust and then depositing single particles of dust on other worlds that are vast distances apart until all the dust is gone and then smashing to dust all the worlds in the space covered by that distribution whether or not they received a dust particle and then counting all of that dust and multiplying that figure by an astronomical amount to figure out how many eons (S. *kalpas*) it has been since the Buddha attained buddhahood. This mind-boggling analogy is referred to as the "five hundred dust-particle kalpas" (J. *gohyaku jinden-go*). Some English translations even insert "million" into this figure, as in "five hundred (million) dust-particle kalpas" though even this only hints at the amount indicated in the analogy.

The point of all this, is to get across the idea that the Buddha, as he says of himself, "became the Buddha in the remotest past" (Ibid, p. 243).

In the same chapter, the Buddha also says that he would not actually enter final nirvāṇa, the complete nirvāṇa that is the passing away of an arhat, pratyekabuddha, or buddha. "The duration of my life is innumerable, asamkhya kalpas. I am always here. I shall never pass away." (Ibid, p. 243) He also says, "The duration of my life, which I obtained by the practice of the Way of Bodhisattvas, has not yet expired. It is twice as long as the length of time as previously stated." (Ibid, p. 249) It is because of this open-endedness of the Buddha's awakened life span that Śākyamuni Buddha as he presents himself in chapter sixteen, the "Duration of the Life of the Tathāgata" chapter, is called the "Eternal Buddha." In fact, the analogy of "five hundred (million) dust particle kalpas" has been understood to indicate that there is in fact a duration with a beginning and an end, even though it is so vast as to defy calculation. On the other hand, the analogy would also seem to indicate something that is so vast as to suggest timelessness, or at least the lack of any-thing that can be measured in terms of beginning or ending, birth or death. The Buddha actually states explicitly in chapter sixteen that there is no birth or death in his way of viewing the world.

> *"All that I say is true, not false, because I see the triple world as it is. I see that the triple world is the world in which the living beings have neither birth nor death, that is to say, do not appear or disappear, that it is the world in which I do not appear or from which I do not disappear, that it is not real or unreal, and that it is not as it seems or as it does not seem. I do not see the triple world in the same way as [the living beings of] the triple world do. I see all this clearly and infallibly." (Ibid, p. 249)*

All of this is very much in line with the profound understanding of emptiness in Mahāyāna Buddhism, whereas no phenomena appear or disappear because no phenomena have a substantial independent nature that can appear or disappear. In chapter two of the *Lotus Sūtra* the Buddha says, "All things are from the outset in the state of tranquil extinction." (Ibid, p. 40) In chapter fourteen he says, "All things are insubstantial. They are as they are. ... They are not born. They do not appear. They do not arise." (Ibid, p. 217) So throughout the *Lotus Sūtra* the teaching of emptiness is used to indicate that, on the ultimate level, no phenomena is a thing that has birth or death. In chapter sixteen, this teaching is applied to the Buddha's awakening and the Buddha's life or work in the world of birth and death.

The application of Buddhist insight into the insubstantiality or selflessness of phenomena to show that the Buddha should not be thought of in terms of birth and death can also be found in the teachings recorded in the Pāli canon and not only in Mahāyāna sūtras. For instance, at one time the wanderer Vacchagotta questioned the Buddha about what happened to the Tathāgata after death. Did he reappear in some other existence or not or both or neither? By asking this question, Vacchagotta assumed that there was some fixed entity that corresponded to the label Tathāgata. The Buddha however, used the simile of a fire to show that one should not think of the Tathāgata as a fixed being that can be said to appear or disappear.

> *"What do you think, Vaccha? Suppose a fire were burning before you. Would you know: `This fire is burning before me'?"*
>
> *"I would, Master Gautama."*
>
> *"If someone were to ask you, Vaccha: `What does this fire burning before you burn in dependence on?' – being asked thus, what would you answer?"*
>
> *"Being asked thus, Master Gautama, I would answer: `This fire burning before me burns in dependence on grass and sticks.'"*
>
> *"If that fire before you were to be extinguished, would you know: `This fire before me has been extinguished'?"*
>
> *"I would, Master Gautama."*
>
> *"If someone were to ask you, Vaccha: `When that fire before you was extinguished, to which direction did it*

*go: to the east, the west, the north, or the south?' –
being asked thus, what would you answer?"*

*"That does not apply, Master Gautama. The fire burned
in dependence on its fuel of grass and sticks. When that
is used up, if it does not get any more fuel, being
without fuel, it is reckoned as extinguished."*

*"So too, Vaccha, the Tathāgata has abandoned that
material form by which one describing the Tathāgata
might describe him; he has cut it off at the root, made it
like a palm stump, done away with it so that it is no
longer subject to future arising. The Tathāgata is
liberated from reckoning in terms of material form,
Vaccha, he is profound, immeasurable, unfathomable
like the ocean. The terms `reappears' does not apply,
the term `does not reappear' does not apply, the term
`both reappears and does not reappear' does not apply,
the term `neither reappears nor does not reappear'
does not apply. The Tathāgata has abandoned that
feeling by which one describing the Tathāgata might
describe him...has abandoned that perception by which
one describing the Tathāgata might describe him...has
abandoned those formations by which one describing
the Tathāgata might describe him...has abandoned that
consciousness by which one describing the Tathāgata
might describe him; he has cut it off at the root, made it
like a palm stump, done away with it so that it is no
longer subject to future arising. The Tathāgata is
liberated from reckoning in terms of consciousness,
Vaccha; he is profound, immeasurable, unfathomable
like the ocean. The term `reappears' does not apply, the
term `does not reappear' does not apply, the term `both
reappears and does not reappear' does not apply, the
term `neither reappears nor does not reappear' does
not apply." (Nanamoli & Bodhi, pp. 593 – 594)*

The Buddha made this point again and again throughout his teachings. The
Buddha did not think of himself in terms of a fixed identity that depended

upon impermanent and contingent phenomena such as the five aggregates of form, feeling, perceptions, mental formations, or even consciousness. The Buddha did not even try to identify a self apart from phenomena. It is not that the Buddha negated or extinguished his self-hood, it was that the Buddha had awakened to the true selfless nature of reality that transcends the limitations of such self-conscious views and the finite reference points upon which such self-reference depends. One might say that before awakening, arbitrary boundaries between the self and the rest of reality create a false view of self and that after awakening these boundaries are recognized as arbitrary and not ultimately significant. The boundaries of the self do remain insofar as they are needed to function in the world of conventional reality, but they no longer have any hold over those who have seen through them and realize that these fixed boundaries between self and other, beginning and end, inside and outside have no real substance. Free of these boundaries, the Buddha saw that there was no fixed, independent or definable self that can undergo birth or death in the first place. For this reason, the Buddha spoke of himself as the Tathāgata, the "Thus Come/Thus Gone One." In other words, he was able to operate both in the realm of conventional reality in order to teach and impart liberation as the "one who comes from the realm of Truth" and in the realm of freedom from the fixed, independent and finite self as the "one who goes to the realm of Truth." The Tathāgata, therefore, did not think of himself in terms of existence or non-existence, both, neither, or any other form of classification. Again and again, he pointed his disciples back to his pragmatic teachings concerning suffering and the end of suffering and away from idle speculation as to the nature of his existence as in the following passage:

> "But Anuradha, when the Tathāgata is not apprehended by you as real and actual here in this very life, is it fitting for you to declare: 'Friends, when a Tathāgata is describing a Tathāgata – the highest type of person, the supreme person, the attainer of the supreme attainment – he describes himself apart from these four cases: 'The Tathāgata exists after death,' or 'The Tathāgata does not exist after death,' or 'The Tathāgata both exists and does not exist after death,' or 'The Tathāgata neither exists nor does not exist after death'?"

"No, venerable sir."

"Good, good, Anuradha! Formerly, Anuradha, and also now, I make known just suffering and the cessation of suffering." (Bodhi 2000, pp. 937 – 938)

It must be understood that the Buddha was not saying that people do not really exist, or that the Tathāgata has escaped existence or that birth and death are not actual events. What he realized for himself and tried to share with others was the insight into the selfless nature of all events and phenomena. There are definitely experiences of birth and death, suffering and joy, and on rare occasions awakening to the Truth and going on to teach the Truth. However, those who do know the Truth, the Dharma, no longer view or experience these things from the point-of-view of self-reference. For them, their views of such dichotomies as self and other, suffering and joy, birth and death or even existence and non-existence have changed. In fact, the viewpoint of the Buddha changed so radically that for him, these terms have become wholly inadequate and misleading.

Getting back to the *Lotus Sūtra*, the Buddha went further than just denying that birth and death apply to the Tathāgata. The Buddha said that his talk of awakening under the Bodhi Tree and his imminent final nirvāṇa were also examples of skillful methods of teaching, and that in fact it might be better to think of the Buddha as a constant presence leading all beings to awakening. Chapter sixteen of the *Lotus Sūtra* is unique in that the Buddha spoke of his life itself as a skillful means, and that these skillful means have no beginning or end. Here the denial of birth and death is turned into an affirmation of the constant awakening presence of the Eternal Śākyamuni Buddha who is always thinking, "How shall I cause all living beings to enter into the unsurpassed Way and quickly become Buddhas?" (Murano 2012, p. 255)

Nichiren saw the attainment of buddhahood in the remote past as a teaching of supreme importance that was not revealed in any other sūtra or even the other chapters of the *Lotus Sūtra*. It is important to understand that he was not relating to this teaching simply as a way of deifying Śākyamuni Buddha or setting up some eternal supreme being in a theistic manner. Rather, he saw this teaching as confirming and providing the underlying rationale for the teaching of the two vehicles being able to obtain buddhahood. More importantly, Nichiren saw the Eternal Buddha of chapter sixteen as the living actualization of the three thousand realms in a single thought-moment, the doctrine that makes buddhahood possible for all people. After reviewing the deficiencies of all the other sūtras and even of the Trace Gate in regard to this teaching, Nichiren says:

> In the Original Gate of the Lotus Sūtra, it was revealed that the Buddha had attained perfect and complete awakening in the remote past, making it untenable to assert that he attained buddhahood for the first time in this world. Thus the Eternal Buddha doctrine destroyed the buddhahood resulting from the four teachings. As the buddhahood resulting from the four teachings became untenable, the way leading to buddhahood shown in those four teachings proved to be invalid. Thus the ten realms doctrine preached in the pre-Lotus sūtras and the Trace Gate of the Lotus Sūtra was destroyed and the doctrine of causal relationship among the eternal ten realms was established in the Origin Gate of the Lotus Sūtra. This is the doctrine of "original cause and original effect." In this relationship the nine realms are all included in the realm of the Eternal Buddha, and the realm of the Buddha is in each of the eternal nine realms. This is truly the "mutual possession of the ten realms," "one hundred realms and one thousand factors" and "three thousand realms in a single thought-moment." (Hori 2002, pp. 48-49 adapted)

In this passage, Nichiren sums up his thoughts about the significance of the attainment of buddhahood in the remote past and the "eternal" life of the Buddha. He does so in terms of Tiantai doctrine and terminology, so at this point I would like to unpack what he means by all of this.

To begin with, Nichiren tells us that when the Buddha revealed his attainment of buddhahood in the remote past the buddhahood resulting from the four teachings was destroyed and the way to buddhahood they taught was thereby invalidated. The four teachings that Nichiren refers to here are the tripitaka, shared, distinct, and perfect teachings that comprise the category of four doctrinal teachings according to the Tiantai system. Each of these four doctrinal teachings had its own system of stages of practice leading either to arhatship, pratyekabuddhahood, or buddhahood. For instance, in the distinct teaching the bodhisattva would traverse fifty-two stages of practice before attaining buddhahood as taught in the *Flower Garland Sūtra*. What these systems had in common was that each of them taught that one must first make causes to attain awakening and those causes would later ripen into the effect of awakening. This perspective assumed that the ten realms did not co-exist for the individual but would be experienced sequentially as causes were sown and effects later ripened. As an example, an animal that died and had the karma to ripen as a human would be reborn as a human. That human being might take up the Mahāyāna teachings and aspire to buddhahood. Upon dying such a person might then be reborn in a pure land as a bodhisattva serving one of the many celestial buddhas. After three innumerable eons of accruing merit the bodhisattva might then attain buddhahood. Each of the ten realms would only come into being as the ripening of previous causes. This vision of the ten realms also means that buddhahood, the unconditioned, would come about as the result of causes and conditions. However, if Śākyamuni Buddha attained buddhahood in the remote past, then that means he was a buddha during all the times that he was appearing throughout the six worlds of birth and death as a bodhisattva. This means that the ten realms can co-exist in various ways, and that it is incorrect to say that the realm of buddhahood only appears after causes sown in the other nine realms have ripened. Instead, the nine realms wherein the causes of buddhahood are sown and the realm of buddhahood that is the ripening of those effects both exist simultaneously. This is the wonder of "original cause and original effect" (the first two of the ten wonders of the Original Gate), wherein the cause and effect of buddhahood express a non-dual whole without beginning or end, a more appropriate way of talking about the unconditioned true nature.

The doctrines of the "mutual possession of the ten realms" and "three thousand realms in a single thought-moment" are thereby validated if it is indeed true that the Buddha's buddhahood co-existed with his bodhisattvahood that in turn manifested throughout the other eight realms. In the Trace Gate, the arhats and other beings of the nine realms were given predictions of buddhahood and so related to the world of buddhahood as something to be realized in the future. In the Origin Gate, the Eternal Śākyamuni Buddha states that buddhahood has no beginning or end and therefore is not something separate from whatever realm is being experienced here and now. In other words, buddhahood is always underfoot, always actively at work in and through whatever causes and conditions may be prevailing at the moment. It is not something lost to the past or a remote future possibility but the true reality of the present. It is not some other realm, a distant pure land or abstract ideal, but the total all-embracing reality of wherever one happens to be. The immanence of buddhahood within the lives of all beings is what the mutual possession of the ten realms is all about and what the Eternal Śākyamuni Buddha of the Original Gate embodies and expresses.

The three thousand realms in a single thought-moment and the mutual possession of the ten realms also shed light on other doctrines that have been mentioned in relation to the provisional teachings. For instance, the total interrelation and interpenetration of all phenomena taught in the ten mysterious gates of the Flower Garland school can now be seen as ten different ways of explaining and appreciating the total interpenetration of the phenomenal expressions of buddhahood with the phenomena of the other nine realms. The gate of the differentiation and mutual implication of the ten time periods is another way of stating that the time of Śākyamuni Buddha's awakening is not separate from the present moment. The Flower Garland school's teaching that the first stage of bodhisattva practice contains all subsequent stages including final awakening is now expressed as the Buddha's own experience of the co-existence of his awakening in the remote past and the bodhisattva practices demonstrated through the subsequent ages culminating in his skillful method of attaining buddhahood beneath the Bodhi Tree. The teaching in the *Awakening of Faith in the Mahāyāna Treatise* that original awakening is the basis of acquired awakening is revealed to be actualized by the Eternal Buddha who, though already a buddha, demonstrates the practice and realization of buddhahood in age after age for the sake of all sentient beings. The world of buddhahood is the buddha-nature, the ninth or pure consciousness. The other nine realms are the fluctuations of the wholesome and unwholesome seeds in the eighth or storehouse consciousness that obscure the unconditioned reality of buddhahood. It can now be understood that from the perspective of the Eternal Buddha, buddhahood is in a sense acquired based on practice but in a deeper sense this acquiring is really the full manifestation of something that is already unconditionally present. The realm of buddhahood in the depths of life is not something that is sometimes absent and sometimes present. One does not need to get it or to get rid of the other nine realms. Rather, the realm of buddhahood expresses itself in and through the delusions and awakening practices of the other nine realms until the time is right for buddhahood to be clearly realized and fully actualized in those realms.

Nichiren does not clarify what this will mean in terms of our daily life and practice of Buddhism. At this point he is only establishing the importance of the attainment of buddhahood in the remote past by Śākyamuni Buddha and the uniqueness of the Original Gate of the *Lotus Sūtra* in expounding it. In *Kaimoku-shō* as a whole, Nichiren is more concerned with establishing the preeminence of the *Lotus Sūtra* and questioning his own role as its practitioner and whether the persecutions he has faced invalidate or validate the role he has taken upon himself. For that matter, there is still one more comparison to go, in which even the teaching of the Original Gate is made subordinate to the "three thousand realms in a single thought-moment" doctrine that Nichiren identifies as the actual seed of buddhahood.

Sources

Bodhi, Bhikkhu, trans. *The Connected Discourses of the Buddha: A New Translation of the Samyutta Nikaya*. Boston: Wisdom Publications, 2000.

Gosho Translation Committee, editor-translator. *The Writings of Nichiren Daishonin*. Tokyo: Soka Gakkai, 1999.

Hori, Kyotsu, comp. *Writings of Nichiren Shonin: Doctrine Volume 2*. Tokyo: Nichiren Shu Overseas Propagation Promotion Association, 2002.

Murano, Senchu, trans. *The Lotus Sūtra*. Hayward: Nichiren Buddhist International Center, 2012.

_____. *Kaimokusho or Liberation from Blindness*. Berkeley: Numata Center for Buddhist Translation and Research, 2000.

Nanamoli, Bhikkhu and Bodhi, Bhikkhu, trans. *The Middle Length Discourses of the Buddha: A New Translation of the Majjhima Nikaya*. Botson: Wisdom Publications, 1995.

Reeves, Gene, trans. *The Lotus Sūtra*. Boston: Wisdom Publications, 2008.

Chapter 24 – The Eternal Shakyamuni Buddha as the Focus of Devotion

Writings of Nichiren Shōnin Doctrine 2, pp. 49, 76-77
Kaimoku-shō or Liberation from Blindness, pp. 35, 72-73
The Writings of Nichiren Daishonin I, pp. 236, 257-258

The "Original Buddha" (J. *honbutsu*) or "Eternal Buddha" of chapter sixteen of the *Lotus Sūtra* represents the unity of the three bodies (S. *trikāya*) of the Buddha in the Tiantai and Nichiren traditions. I have already discussed the concept of the three bodies of the Buddha in connection with the three virtues of ruler, teacher, and parent. Briefly, they are the accommodative-body (S. *nirmanakāya*) that is the historical Buddha, the reward-body (S. *sambhogakāya*) that is the idealized Buddha who presides over a pure land, and the Dharma-body (S. *dharmakāya*) that is the universal truth that the Buddha awakens to as the true nature of life. Many times, the three bodies are considered to be three different kinds of buddhas, but they really should be seen as three different aspects of buddhahood. The doctrine of the three bodies is actually something that developed in later Mahāyāna sūtras and does not appear in the *Lotus Sūtra*. Still, the Eternal Buddha of chapter sixteen was viewed by Zhiyi as embodying all three and Nichiren also saw this as an important point. In fact, it was one reason that Nichiren saw the Eternal Śākyamuni Buddha as uniquely worthy of being the focus of devotion (J. *honzon*) in that he embodied all three aspects of buddhahood.

Unfortunately, the writings in which Zhiyi explained his views about the three bodies in relation to the Eternal Śākyamuni Buddha have not been translated into English. I must rely upon what scholars have stated about his teaching. In the following passage from her book *Original Enlightenment*, Jacqueline Stone summarizes Zhiyi's interpretation (Note that she calls the *sambhogakāya* the "recompense body" and the *nirmanakāya* the "manifested body"):

> Elsewhere, in a dynamic synthesis, he interpreted
> Śākyamuni Buddha of the "Fathoming of the Lifespan"
> chapter as embodying all three bodies in one. When the

Buddha's wisdom grasps the ultimate reality, that
which is realized is the Dharma body; and the wisdom
that realizes it is the recompense body. For the sake of
living beings, this wisdom manifests itself in physical
form as the human Buddha who teaches in the world;
this is the manifested body. Since the recompense body
both realizes the truth that is the Dharma body and
responds to aspirations of the beings in the form of the
manifested body, Chih-i regarded it as central. However,
he also rejected any notion of hierarchy among the
three bodies, denying that one can be seen as prior to
the others. (Stone, p. 26)

Preeminence is usually assigned to the Dharma-body of the Buddha as it is the unconditioned true nature of reality that is unborn and deathless. The tathāgatagarbha or buddha-nature is the Dharma-body when it is obscured by defilements, and the Dharma-body is the buddha-nature when it is fully realized and actualized by a Buddha. The reward-body and accommodative-bodies are usually seen as subordinate temporal emanations of the Dharma-body that appear in particular times and places. Basically, the Dharma-body is aligned with the ultimate truth that is emptiness, and the other two bodies are aligned with the conventional truth that is phenomenal existence. Zhiyi, however, attempted to go beyond dualistic interpretations of emptiness and phenomenal existence. He taught that the truths of emptiness and provisional existence are both united in the truth of the Middle Way so that all three are a single integral truth. The unity of the threefold truth thereby undercuts any duality between the ultimate and the conventional. Applying this to the three bodies of the Buddha means that three bodies are also to be viewed as three constant aspects of an integral whole.

If the three bodies are three aspects of an integral whole then that means that it is not just the Dharma-body that is unborn and deathless, but that the reward-body and the accommodative body must also be unborn and deathless. All three are empty of birth and death, all three are ungraspable, and all three are unconditioned. In the last chapter I pointed out how even in the Pāli canon the Buddha did not identify with conditioned phenomena, such as the five aggregates that appear and disappear. In Mahāyāna Buddhism, the aggregates themselves are asserted to be ultimately empty and are not independent substances that come into or out of being. In the *Lotus Sūtra*, it is asserted that all phenomena are of the nature of nirvāṇa. In chapter sixteen of the Lotus Sūtra, Śākyamuni Buddha speaks of his own awakened lifespan as beyond calculation both in terms of its beginning and its end and from his point of view there is no birth or death in the triple world. Zhiyi understood all of this to mean that not just the Buddha's true nature, but also his ideal qualities and his concrete presence in the world all transcend birth and death.

This is exactly the point that Nichiren highlights in *Kaimoku-shō*. Nichiren says that while other sūtras do teach that the Dharma-body of the Buddha (sometimes called Vairocana or Mahāvairocana) is without beginning or end, only chapters fifteen and sixteen of the *Lotus Sūtra* suggest that the Buddha as an integral whole transcends birth and death.

> *The beginningless and endless Dharma-body is expounded in the Nirvana Sūtra compiled in forty volumes, which was expounded by the Buddha on his deathbed between two trees, and also in other Mahayana sūtras expounded before the Lotus Sūtra. But the eternity of the reward-body and accommodative-body of the Buddha is not expounded in those sūtras. The eternity of the three bodies of the Buddha is expounded only in the two chapters of the Lotus Sūtra. (Murano 2000, p. 35 adapted)*

Further on in *Kaimoku-shō*, Nichiren criticizes the other schools of Buddhism for having an incorrect focus of devotion (J. *honzon*). He says this because they all chose to revere a Buddha that only represents one or another of the three bodies of the Buddha.

> *Nevertheless, all Buddhist schools except for the Tiantai are confused about the focus of devotion. The Abhidharma Treasury, Completion of Reality, and Discipline schools make the focus of devotion Śākyamuni Buddha, who attained buddhahood by going through the 34 steps of fighting against the delusions of*

views and attitudes. This is like a crown prince of a
world-honored sovereign, who, confused, thinks of
himself as a son of an ordinary subject. (Hori 2002, p. 76
adapted)

Here Nichiren is saying that the three Hīnayāna schools are only looking at the Buddha from the perspective of the accommodative-body. In other words, they only relate to the Buddha as an historical teacher who passed away long ago. So though they are heirs of the Eternal Buddha, they only think of themselves as the latter day disciples of a long dead Indian sage.

The four schools of Flower Garland, Mantra, Three
Treatises, and Dharma Characteristics schools are of
Mahāyāna Buddhism, among which the Dharma
Characteristics and Three Treatises schools worship as
their focus of devotion a buddha similar to the superior
accommodative-body of Mahāyāna Buddhism. It is just
like the crown prince of a heavenly king thinking of
himself as the son of a warrior. (Ibid, p. 76 adapted)

The superior accommodative-body is the Buddha as viewed by advanced bodhisattvas who are able to perceive the Buddha's meritorious qualities that set him apart from other sages. It is still a view of the Buddha that sees him as no longer present in the world. This is why Nichiren compares the superior accommodative-body to a warrior and not just a mere commoner.

The Flower Garland and Mantra schools establish
Vairocana and Mahāvairocana instead of Śākyamuni
Buddha as the focus of devotion respectively. It is like a
king's son despising his father while respecting a
nameless person who acts as though he were the king
of the Dharma. (Ibid p. 76 adapted)

Vairocana Buddha is name given to the reward-body of Śākyamuni Buddha in the *Flower Garland Sūtra*, the *Brahma Net Sūtra*, and the *Contemplation of the Universal Sage Bodhisattva Sutra*. Mahāvairocana is the name of the

Buddha who teaches the *Mahāvairocana Sūtra* and who is sometimes viewed as the reward-body and other times as the Dharma-body. When Vairocana and Mahāvairocana are viewed as buddhas separate from Śākyamuni Buddha, Nichiren regards them as abstractions and compares them to strangers who have no real connection to our lives.

> *The Pure Land school considers Amitābha Buddha, who is merely an emanation of Śākyamuni in the Pure Land to the West, to be the lord of this world and abandons Śākyamuni, who is the real lord of this world. (Ibid, pp. 76-77 adapted)*

Amitābha Buddha, the Buddha of Infinite Light (a.k.a. Amitāyus, Infinite Life), is the reward-body that presides over the Pure Land of the West and is revered by the Pure Land schools who chant his name as their primary practice so that they can be reborn in his pure land after death. Nichiren calls Amitābha Buddha an "emanation" of Śākyamuni Buddha in reference to the events of chapter eleven of the *Lotus Sūtra*, in which the buddhas of the ten directions come to this world and are revealed to all be emanations of Śākyamuni Buddha. Nichiren laments the fact that so many Buddhists revere this otherworldly buddha and neglect Śākyamuni Buddha, the actual lord of the Dharma of this world.

> *The Zen School, just like a lowly man with little virtue despising his parents, despises the Buddha and his sūtras. (Ibid, p. 77)*

The polemical target here were those Zen iconoclasts in Nichiren's day that rejected the sūtras and traditional Buddhist devotional practices. Nichiren viewed them as rejecting the teachings of Śākyamuni Buddha out of arrogance. I will explain more about the Zen School and what it was like in Nichiren's time in another chapter.

In these other schools, the focus of devotion was a buddha who only represented one of the three bodies and not the integrated whole that the Eternal Śākyamuni Buddha represented for the Tiantai school and Nichiren. As far as Nichiren was concerned, these other schools of Buddhism were underestimating the true significance of Śākyamuni Buddha whose true nature, virtues, and skillful means of teaching are all without beginning or end. Nichiren cites Zhanran (711-782; aka Miaole), the Tiantai school's sixth patriarch, who argues that the other schools are like children who do not know the age of their father and therefore will not be able to know his pure land.

> Throughout all the sūtras expounded by the Buddha, the eternity of the Buddha is not revealed anywhere else than in the "Chapter on the Duration of the Life of the Tathāgata." We should know the duration of the lives of our parents. If we do not know the duration of the life of the Buddha, who is our father, we shall not be able to know his Pure World. The teachers of these schools are clever but inhuman because they do not know that they should be dutiful to their father, that is, the Buddha. (Murano 2000, pp. 72-73 adapted)

This argument may sound a bit odd, so I am going to attempt to explain it by reference to things already covered in this commentary. To begin with, recall that in the Tiantai tradition the Buddha is considered to possess the three virtues of ruler, teacher, and parent. Throughout the *Lotus Sūtra* the Buddha is said to be like a father whose only thought is for the welfare of his children, and his disciples are considered the heirs of the Buddha Dharma. Teachers such as Zhanran and Nichiren therefore considered it our filial duty to deeply understand and appreciate the true role and status of the Buddha. To know the Eternal Śākyamuni Buddha deeply is to know and appreciate the Buddha's original cause, original effect, original land, and the rest of the ten wonders of the Original Gate of the *Lotus Sūtra*. These ten wondrous teachings make it clear that the Buddha is not just a transient presence in this world, but that from the beginningless past to the present and on into the endless future Śākyamuni Buddha's awakening activities unfold in this world, and that the true land of this Buddha is in fact this world that is actually the Pure Land of Tranquil Light where the Original Buddha's original disciples attain awakening. So what Zhanran is saying is that the Eternal Śākyamuni Buddha should be viewed as our father in the Dharma, that our filial duty is to truly understand and appreciate the true wonder of the Buddha's constant awakening presence, and thereby to understand and appreciate that the Eternal Buddha's true Pure Land is right here and now and that we are his heirs.

In *Genealogical Chart of the Buddha's Lifetime Teachings in Five Periods* (*Ichidai Goji Keizu*), Nichiren writes of these same critiques and also the comments of Zhanran. He then proceeds to explain how the Tiantai school regards the Eternal Śākyamuni Buddha as the focus of devotion.

> *The focus of devotion of the Tiantai School is Śākyamuni Buddha, who had actually practiced the bodhisattva way and attained buddhahood in the remote past. The buddhas such as Vairocana Buddha, the lord preacher of the Flower Garland Sūtra, and Mahāvairocana, lord preacher of the Mantra School, are retainers of this Eternal Śākyamuni Buddha.*

> *Except for the Eternal Buddha revealed in the Original Gate of the Lotus Sūtra, buddhas all attained buddhahood for the first time in this life and possess the three kinds of bodies. Accommodative-body buddhas are finite buddhas who appear in this world, showing both beginning (attaining buddhahood) and ending (entering nirvāṇa). The reward-body is obtained as the reward of completing the bodhisattva practice and having mastered the wisdom of the buddha. Buddhas in this body therefore have a beginning (attaining buddhahood) but no end (entering nirvāṇa). The Dharma-body is the body of fundamental truth, the Dharma to which the Buddha is awakened, which is immaterial and has no beginning or ending. The Vairocana Buddha of the Flower Garland school and Mahāvairocana of the Mantra school are claimed to be buddhas of the reward-body and Dharma-body respectively.*

> *The Buddha as revealed in the Original Gate of the Lotus Sūtra is the one who attained buddhahood in the remote past. He, too, possesses the three kinds of*

buddha-body. In this Eternal Buddha, the three bodies
are fused in one, having no beginning and no ending,
and he lives forever from the eternal past to the infinite
future to guide the people. (Hori 2004, p. 250 adapted)

In the above passage, Nichiren makes it very clear that the true focus of devotion of the Tiantai School is none other than the Eternal Buddha of Original Gate of the *Lotus Sūtra* who embodies the unity of the three bodies of a Buddha and who is in all respects unborn and deathless. For Nichiren, this is the most integrated and complete view of Śākyamuni Buddha and therefore provides us with the most complete and integrated view of buddhahood, including our own. Nichiren will have more to say about this in *Kanjin Honzon-shō*, where the Eternal Śākyamuni Buddha as the true focus of devotion for Buddhism in the latter age of the Dharma is the main topic.

One final thought. It is not hard to think of the true nature of reality as having no beginning or end. We might even be able to imagine that the glorified Buddha presiding over a pure land has no beginning or end. But how can we say that the accommodative-body or historical Buddha (whom we tentatively assign the dates 463-383 BCE) is without a beginning or end? Of course, the physical frame and historically conditioned personality of Siddhārtha Gautama was born on a certain date and died eighty years later, but this is to speak in terms of the aggregates that the Buddha did not identify as a "self." If we change our focus we will see that the historical Buddha was a temporary formation in a flow of causes and conditions that express the skillful means of the Eternal Buddha, it is this flow of concrete skillful activity in the world that is the true accommodative-body of the Buddha, and like any other conditioned phenomena it is ungraspable and not a matter of a fixed independent substance that appears and then disappears. It is a beginningless and endless process with no boundaries, though it gives rise to phenomena that we conventionally ascribe boundaries to – like the life of an Indian prince who became an ascetic and then an awakened teacher, or the compilation of a text and its many iterations and translations that we relate to as the *Lotus Sūtra*. I won't pretend that I fully understand the meaning of saying that the accommodative-body too is unborn and deathless, but I am sure it does not mean that the historical Siddhārtha Gautama is now to be viewed as an eternal ghostly presence or spirit much less that he is still physically alive. I do get the sense that it means that the Eternal Buddha is a real constant presence in the world: as the true nature of reality (the Dharma-body); as the virtuous qualities of buddhahood in the depths of our lives and communicated to ourselves and others in and through our Buddhist practice (reward-body); as the concrete manifestations of Buddha Dharma in the form of our teachers and fellow practitioners; as the text of the *Lotus Sūtra* that can guide and inspire us; as the Omandala that depicts our focus of devotion (J. *gohonzon*); and as the sound of the Odaimoku as the seed of buddhahood that we sow in our lives and the lives of others.

Sources

Gosho Translation Committee, editor-translator. *The Writings of Nichiren Daishonin*. Tokyo: Soka Gakkai, 1999.

_____. *The Writings of Nichiren Daishonin Volume II*. Tokyo: Soka Gakkai, 2006.

Hori, Kyotsu, comp. *Writings of Nichiren Shonin: Doctrine Volume 2*. Tokyo: Nichiren Shu Overseas Propagation Promotion Association, 2002.

_____. *Writings of Nichiren Shonin: Doctrine Volume 3*. Tokyo: Nichiren Shu Overseas Propagation Promotion Association, 2004.

Murano, Senchu, trans. *Kaimokusho or Liberation from Blindness*. Berkeley: Numata Center for Buddhist Translation and Research, 2000.

Stone, Jacqueline. *Original Enlightenment and the Transformation of Medieval Japanese Buddhism*. Honolulu: Kuroda Institute, 1999.

Chapter 25 – Slanderers of the Lotus Sutra

Writings of Nichiren Shōnin Doctrine 2, pp. 49-52
Kaimoku-shō or Liberation from Blindness, pp. 35-39
The Writings of Nichiren Daishonin I, pp. 236-238

After establishing the uniqueness of the attainment of buddhahood in the remote past that is taught in chapters fifteen and sixteen of the *Lotus Sūtra*, Nichiren stresses how difficult it is to believe in this teaching because all the other sūtras and even the greater part of the *Lotus Sūtra* take the former view that Śākyamuni Buddha attained buddhahood as a young man under the Bodhi Tree. Why should anyone go along with what these two chapters alone are teaching about the actual extent of the Buddha's awakened lifespan? He then proceeds to review how the other schools of Buddhism dismiss the *Lotus Sūtra*.

Nichiren begins by reviewing the lineage and teachings of the Dharma Characteristics school, the only major East Asian Mahāyāna school that denies that all people can attain buddhahood. In the chapter on the "History of the Schools" I reviewed their history. In the chapters on "Provisional Mahāyāna: The Perfection of Wisdom" and "A Brief History of the Tiantai School and Tendai Shū" I reviewed the Dharma Characteristic school's teaching that each sentient being has one of five mutually distinct natures, and how they assert that some beings do not have the seeds for buddhahood in the depths of their lives and so cannot transcend the six worlds of birth and death at all. According to this teaching, some people just do not have what it takes to attain buddhahood. Saichō refuted this teaching in Japan after he established the Tendai school, and that too was discussed.

Nichiren then reviews the lineages and claims of the Flower Garland school and the Mantra school. I have also already covered the origins of those schools in the "Origins of the Ten Buddhist Schools" chapter and the history and teachings of the Flower Garland school in particular in the chapter "The Almost Perfect Flower Garland Sūtra." Nichiren lumps these two schools together here and elsewhere because both schools claimed that their teachings already accounted for and surpassed the teachings of the *Lotus*

Sutra and the Tiantai school. This was discussed in the chapter "Misappropriation of the Dharma." One thing I will add here is that Nichiren cites the *Mahāvairocana Sūtra* as saying, "I am the origin of everything." I have not found any statement like that in the current English translation of that sūtra, but the sūtra does say, "Yet all the actions of Vairocana's body, all the actions of his speech, and all the actions of his mind proclaim everywhere and always in the realms of sentient beings the Dharma of the words of the mantra path." (Giebel 2005, p. 4) I can see where a passage like this sounds similar to the teaching that the Buddha is always present. However, as with such passages in the *Flower Garland Sūtra*, it only applies to the Dharma-body or perhaps the reward-body. The *Mahāvairocana Sūtra* does not make the radical claim that is made in chapter sixteen of the *Lotus Sūtra* wherein Śākyamuni Buddha says that his attainment of buddhahood was in the

remote past and that he will not actually enter final nirvāṇa but will always be present teaching all sentient beings. The sūtras that the Flower Garland and True Word schools are based on do not explicitly teach that Śākyamuni Buddha, not just the Dharma-body, is the Eternal Buddha. If these two schools teach that all three bodies of buddhahood are unborn and deathless aspects of the Eternal Buddha, then it is because they are trying to pass off the teachings of the Tiantai school as their own as far as Nichiren is concerned.

Making the point that mistakes about Buddhism were already being made even in India in the first thousand years after the Buddha's teaching, Nichiren cites the examples of Vātsīputrīya and Vaipulya. "Even the clever teachers of the Vātsīputrīya and the Vaipulya schools did not know the difference between Mahāyāna and Hīnayāna." "Vaipulya" means "Expansive" and is another word for Mahāyāna sūtras. In the *Great Perfection of Wisdom Treatise*, Vaipulya refers to those who take a one-sided or even nihilistic view of emptiness. The Vātsīputrīya was an Abhidharma school that appeared in the third century BCE and taught that there was in fact an entity that can be called a person who transmigrates and is neither the same as nor different from the five aggregates. This school was condemned as non-Buddhist for asserting the existence of a substantial self. Nichiren also makes reference to Vimalamitra and Madhava. The former was a Sarvāstivādin monk who lived sometime after Vasubandhu and who tried to refute the Mahāyāna, the latter was a teacher of Sāṃkhya (See Gosho Translation Committee 1999, p. 238 and p. 292 footnote 59). Nichiren concludes:

"From this we can see that the teachings of the Buddha were misunderstood even in their birthplace not so long after the extinction of the Buddha. People who were born long after the extinction of the Buddha in remote countries such as China and Japan, where languages are different, are less clever, die younger, and have more greed, more anger, and more stupidity. There is no wonder that none of them understands the Buddhist sūtras correctly." (Murano 2000, p. 38)

Nichiren quotes again what the *Nirvāṇa Sūtra* said about the scarcity of those who can uphold the True Dharma being like the soil on a fingernail compared to the soil of all the worlds in the universe. He also quotes the *Decline of the Dharma Sūtra* that says, "Slanderers of Buddhism are as numerous as the sands of the Ganges River, while those who uphold the True Dharma as just a pebble or two." (Hori 2002, p. 52) Nichiren concludes this part of the *Kaimoku-shō* by drawing upon both of these passages to make an analogy concerning how the primary wrongdoings of his time were not secular but religious in nature.

Those who fall into the evil worlds because of their worldly crimes are just as few as a bit of soil on a fingernail, while those who fall there because of crimes against Buddhism are as numerous as the soil of the entire worlds in the universe. More monks than laymen, more nuns than laywomen fall into the evil worlds. (Ibid, p. 52 adapted)

This means that while most people obey the secular laws of land, many people completely misunderstand and violate the Dharma, or spiritual law. In this case, the Dharma is the universality and immediacy of buddhahood as taught by the *Lotus Sūtra* in terms of the One Vehicle and the Eternal Buddha. We should probably pause here and consider what "slandering" the Dharma means. The answer is actually provided in the *Lotus Sūtra*:

Those who do not believe this sūtra

But slander it,

Will destroy the seeds of Buddhahood

Of all living beings of the world.

Some will scowl at this sūtra

And doubt it,

Listen! I will tell you

How they will be punished.

In my lifetime or after my extinction

Some will slander this sūtra,

And despise the person who reads or recites

Or copies or keeps this sūtra.

They will hate him,

Look at him with jealousy,

And harbor enmity against him.

Listen I will tell you how they will be punished.

When their present lives end,

They will fall into the Avīci Hell.

They will live there for a kalpa,

And have their rebirth in the same hell.

This rebirth of theirs will be repeated

For innumerable kalpas. (Murano 2012, pp. 82-83)

So it would appear that slander refers to looking down upon the sūtra and doubting it, or despising, hating, being jealous of, and bearing enmity towards those who uphold the sūtra. In chapter thirteen of the *Lotus Sūtra*, it states that the enemies of the sūtra will accuse the practitioners of having "made up the sūtra by themselves" and of "expounding the teaching of heretics." It also says: "They will speak ill of us, or frown at us, or drive us out of the monasteries from time to time." (Ibid, p. 214) In chapter twenty, Bodhisattva Never Despise's assurances of the future buddhahood of all he meets is disbelieved and he is both verbally and even physically abused in just the way that chapter thirteen describes.

In his *A Clarification of Slandering the True Dharma* (*Ken Hōbō-shō*), Nichiren relies upon the definitions of Zhiyi and Vasubandhu in responding to the question, "What does slandering the Dharma mean exactly?" Nichiren writes:

> *Grand Master Tiantai explains in his Commentary on the Brahmā Net Sūtra, "the term slander means to go against." We may say slandering the True Dharma means to go against the teaching of the Buddha. Vasubandhu's Treatise on the Buddha-nature preaches, "Hate means to go against principle." It means that to slander the True Dharma equals to cause people to abandon it. (Hori 2004, p. 115)*

Nichiren and his contemporaries believed that the sūtras were the actual words of Śākyamuni Buddha. So if a sūtra taught that if you slander the Wonderful Dharma you will fall into the Avīci Hell for doing so then that was all that needed to be said. Furthermore, realms like the Pure Land or the Avīci Hell were taken to be actual places where one could be reborn, though they were also understood more metaphorically as well. Since most modern Buddhist do not believe that these sūtras were verbatim discourses of the Buddha and many do not believe in literal heavens and hells and some seriously question even the doctrine of rebirth, it must be asked what possible meaning any of this has for us. As discussed earlier, the Mahāyāna sūtras were the inspired products of later followers of the Buddha who felt that it would be better to express the true intent of the Buddha's teachings through myth, poetry, and paradox. So the question is – what was really intended by these warnings not to engage in slander of the *Lotus Sūtra*?

As Nichiren has explained, the *Lotus Sūtra*'s two unique teachings concern the One Vehicle whereby even those who would seem to be excluded from attaining buddhahood are promised its attainment and the revelation that Śākyamuni Buddha had in fact been the Buddha since the remote past even before his awakening beneath the Bodhi Tree. Women, evildoers like Devadatta, and those disciples who were believed to have become arhats who would no longer return to the world after their passing, are all told that they will in fact return to the world and attain buddhahood. This was in seeming contradiction to the earlier teaching that only a very few could aspire to and attain buddhahood. The revelation of the attainment of buddhahood in the remote past means that even during the Buddha's innumerable past lifetimes as an ordinary human being, or an animal, or some other form of sentient being striving to attain buddhahood the Buddha had been a buddha all along. And now even though the Buddha is going to appear to pass away for good, he asserts that he will still be present. In light of these two teachings, buddhahood should be understood as inclusive of all beings, all time, and all space. It is a constant and active presence even when it is not apparent or seems to be absent in the lives of those who strive for it. Throughout the *Lotus Sūtra* these ideas are put forward as the fullest expression of the Dharma and to embrace them with faith and joy is to embrace the Wonderful Dharma and to reject them is to reject the Wonderful Dharma. The Wonderful Dharma is held to be even more worthy of respect and offerings than the Buddha himself because it is through the Wonderful Dharma that one attains buddhahood. It is for this reason that rejection means a total alienation from what is truly of value in life, and therefore leads to rebirth in hell. It is for this reason that a single moment of faith and rejoicing in the Wonderful Dharma of the *Lotus Sūtra* is said to bring unequalled merit, rivaled only by the merit brought by the perfection of wisdom itself which is none other than buddhahood itself.

It would seem that the most important thing is to revere the Wonderful Dharma and to awaken to its full significance. This is why the *Lotus Sūtra* describes the vast demerit incurred or merit made by those who slander or praise it respectively. Whether the Buddha directly taught these sūtras or not, and whether or not there are literal rebirths in a Pure Land or an Avīci Hell, the point seems to be that we create our own misery to the extent that we deny the Wonderful Dharma whereas we can attain awakening through upholding the Wonderful Dharma. And what is this Wonderful Dharma? It is not simply a formula, text, or even a creed that one must believe without evidence. It is none other than the true nature of all existence, the reality of all things. This is what all buddhas awaken to, praise, and point out to all sentient beings using many skillful methods so that they too may realize that they are buddhas as well.

The stated intent of the other sūtras and teachings upheld by the other schools of Buddhism is to provide people with a way to attain buddhahood or at least liberation from the cycle of birth and death. The *Lotus Sūtra* directly teaches that all beings can attain buddhahood and that buddhahood is beginningless and endless and therefore realizable here and now. The *Lotus Sūtra*'s teaching is that all beings are worthy of the most profound respect because all beings are destined for buddhahood and in fact the world of buddhahood already resides in the depths of their life, already embraces them. To denigrate this message is to denigrate the true value of life. The other sūtras and schools of Buddhism should not be trying to obscure or denigrate the message of the *Lotus Sūtra* but uphold it because the sūtra expresses the fulfillment of their own true intentions. Nichiren laments that this is not the case, and that on the contrary people find the lesser teachings to be easier to embrace and uphold.

Sources

Giebel, Rolf W., trans. *The Vairocanabhiambodhi Sūtra*. Berkeley: Numata Center for Buddhist Translation and Research, 2005.

Gosho Translation Committee, editor-translator. *The Writings of Nichiren Daishonin*. Tokyo: Soka Gakkai, 1999.

_____. *The Writings of Nichiren Daishonin Volume II*. Tokyo: Soka Gakkai, 2006.

Hori, Kyotsu, comp. *Writings of Nichiren Shonin: Doctrine Volume 2*. Tokyo: Nichiren Shu Overseas Propagation Promotion Association, 2002.

_____. *Writings of Nichiren Shonin: Doctrine Volume 3*. Tokyo: Nichiren Shu Overseas Propagation Promotion Association, 2004.

Murano, Senchu, trans. *The Lotus Sūtra*. Hayward: Nichiren Buddhist International Center, 2012.

_____. *Kaimokusho or Liberation from Blindness*. Berkeley: Numata Center for Buddhist Translation and Research, 2000.

Chapter 26 – Persecutions in the Latter Age of the Dharma

Writings of Nichiren Shōnin Doctrine 2, pp. 51-58, 64, 94-96
Kaimoku-shō or Liberation from Blindness, pp. 38-48, 56, 99-100
The Writings of Nichiren Daishonin I, pp. 238-243, 247-248, 271-272

Nichiren writes, "It was difficult to believe the *Lotus Sūtra* even when it was first expounded. It is more difficult in this Age of Degeneration, when saints and sages are decreasing in number, and when deluded people are increasing instead." (Murano 2000, p. 38 modified) Nichiren is referring here to the Latter Age of Degeneration (J. *mappō*, lit. final dharma), the last of three periods of time that follow the appearance of a Buddha. Nichiren refers to these three ages and particularly to the Latter Age of Degeneration throughout *Kaimoku-shō*. In addition, he cites many passages from the *Lotus Sūtra* where the Buddha seems to make prophetic remarks about the kinds of troubles that will be faced by those who try to uphold the *Lotus Sūtra* in the dark times of the Latter Age.

> *Many people hate it with jealousy even in my lifetime,*
> *Needless to say, more people will do so after my*
> *extinction. (Murano 2012, p. 180)*
>
> *In my lifetime or after my extinction some will slander*
> *this sūtra, and despise the person who reads or recites*
> *or copies or keeps this sūtra. They will hate him, look at*
> *him with jealousy, and harbor enmity against him. (Ibid,*
> *p. 83)*
>
> *This sūtra leads all living beings to the knowledge of all*
> *things. I did not expound it before because, if I had done*
> *so, many people in the world would have hated it and*
> *few would have believed it. (Ibid, p. 228)*
>
> *Ignorant people will speak ill of us, abuse us, and*
> *threaten us with swords or sticks." (Ibid, p. 212)*

They will say to kings, ministers, and brahmins, and also to householders and other monks, "They have wrong views. They are expounding the teaching of heretics."
(Ibid, p. 213 modified).

The will speak ill of us, or frown at us, or drive us out of our monasteries from time to time. (Ibid, p. 214)

When he said this, people would strike him with a stick, a piece of wood, a piece of tile or a stone. He would run to a distance and say in a loud voice from afar, "I do not despise you. You will become buddhas." (Ibid, p. 293)

Nichiren follows the citations from the *Lotus Sūtra* with a passage from the *Nirvāṇa Sūtra* recounting how even the Buddha's own contemporaries spread evil rumors about him. There are certainly many passages in the Mahāyāna sūtras and the Pāli canon that show that not everyone loved the Buddha even during his life. Nichiren next cites the testimony of the great past teachers of the Tiantai school who also faced slander and abuse. Nichiren reviews all of this because he and his followers were questioning why they were faced with so much abuse and so many persecutions for upholding the *Lotus Sūtra*. They had expected that they would receive protection and blessings for making such a good cause, but in fact their lives had become harder.

It has already been more than twenty years since I began speaking for this sūtra, and my troubles have been increasing day-by-day, month-by-month, and year-by-year. Small troubles are incalculable while severe ones are four in number. Not speaking of two of them, I have already been twice the target of royal persecution, and my life now is in jeopardy. Moreover, my disciples and lay supporters, including those laymen who had just come to hear me speak, were punished severely as though they had been rebels. (Hori 2002, pp. 53-54)

317

The four major persecutions that Nichiren speaks of are as follows: 1) The first was the riot at Matsubagayatsu on August 27, 1260, when an angry mob attacked Nichiren's hut at Matsubagayatsu in Kamakura in reaction to the *Risshō Ankoku-ron*. Nichiren escaped, but his hut was burned down and he was forced to flee the city. 2) The second was the exile to the Izu peninsula on May 12, 1261. This was the first of the two persecutions by the Kamakuran shogunate. Nichiren was pardoned in February of 1263 and allowed to return to Kamakura. 3) The third was the ambush in the woods at Komatsubara on November 11, 1264. The local steward of Awa, Tōjō Kagenobu, who hated Nichiren for various secular and religious reasons, ambushed Nichiren and his followers who were on their way to visit a Kudō Yoshitaka, the lord of Amatsu. In the ambush, Nichiren was wounded on the forehead, two of his disciples were wounded and one killed. Both Tōjō Kagenobu and Kudō Yoshitaka died from wounds sustained during the fighting. 4) The fourth persecution and the second of those inflicted by the shogunate was the attempted execution of Nichiren at Tatsunokuchi and the subsequent exile to Sado Island as described in the introduction to this commentary. By reviewing the predictions that those who uphold the *Lotus Sūtra* in the Latter Age will be faced with persecution, Nichiren was reassuring his followers that these things were only to be expected, and that in fact their persecutions were validating the Buddha's teachings. If they were living proof of the predictions of persecution, then doubtless they would also prove that those who uphold the *Lotus Sūtra* would also receive incalculable merit and attain buddhahood. As Nichiren says, "Though my sufferings today are difficult to bear, I am happy for in the future I will be free from the evil realms. (Ibid, p. 58)

A few remarks need to be made about the sūtra passages. These, and many others Nichiren cites, certainly do sound as though they are prophecies. However, they should not be understood to be predictions of the future made by an omniscient Buddha, though that is how Nichiren and others in past ages understood them. The three ages of the Dharma in particular are often taken either too literally or too easily dismissed out of hand. I think it is important to understand the nature of these "prophecies."

There are two reasons these prophecies appear in the sūtras. The first is that Śākyamuni Buddha had a keen understanding of human nature and he also seemed to accept (at least to a certain extent) the cyclic nature of the Vedic worldview. Śākyamuni Buddha understood that while the Dharma itself is incorruptible and in a sense eternal (having no beginning or end but simply being the way things actually are) its historical expressions and the institutions set up to uphold and pass them along are not. Eventually, these constructed phenomena will themselves come to an end after a period of corruption and decline. The teachings will be obscured, misunderstood, and fought over. People will lose the true spirit of the teachings and either follow the empty form or twist the forms to suit their own ends once the actual Dharma is forgotten. The Sangha as an institution will either fade away, or face oppression as social and political circumstances change, or it will rot from within due to the actions of those who use religion for their own aggrandizement. The Buddha did not need to see the future to make such a "prediction." His own deep understanding of human weakness and the impermanent and contingent nature of all phenomena caused him to realize that even his own teachings and the Sangha he was creating were not immune to the process of change and loss.

The other reason these prophecies appear is because the Mahāyāna sūtras themselves were the artistic and inspired creation of monks living many generations after the time of the Buddha. Putting their own insights and observations into the mouth of the historical Buddha or a glorified Buddha or disciple or bodhisattva or god in imaginary discourses, these monks described the circumstances of corruption and persecution that they themselves were facing in the form of "prophecies" given by the Buddha, his contemporaries, and mythic figures who were supposedly present to hear the Buddha's teaching many centuries before.

The three ages of the Dharma appear in the Pāli canon and in the Mahāyāna sūtras as a way of summarizing the teaching that even the Dharma itself (as a conceptual teaching and historical phenomena) will decline. It fits in very well with the common Vedic motif of the cycle of creation, maintenance, decline, and destruction. According to the teaching of the three ages, the Former Age of the True Dharma begins with the first rolling of the Wheel of the Dharma by the Buddha at the Deer Park. It will continue for a thousand years to be followed by the Middle Age of the Semblance of Dharma. After a thousand years of the Middle Age of Semblance the ten thousand years of the Latter Age of the Degeneration of Dharma will begin. During the first age, those with a strong affinity for the Buddha and the Dharma will be born during the lifetime of the Buddha or soon enough afterwards to be able to benefit from the True Dharma and thereby attain awakening. Those with a weaker karmic affinity will be born in the Semblance Age when the true spirit of Buddhism has been lost and only the outwards forms remain more or less intact. But even they are able to make some progress, and according to Mahāyāna teachings they can be reborn in the pure lands of the celestial buddhas and bodhisattvas after their deaths and thereby attain awakening in those happier circumstances. Those born in the Latter Age of Degeneration, however, have no good roots or genuine karmic affinity for the Dharma, so they are born into an age when even the outward forms are disappearing and rather than practice the Dharma people will only fight over it. It is also taught that the Latter Age will be the time of the five degenerations. The five degenerations are: 1) the decay of the age due to famine, plagues, and war; 2) the decay of views as people take up wrong views; 3) the decay of evil passions as people's greed, hatred, and ignorance increase; 4) the decay of living beings as their physical and spiritual strength ebbs; and 5) the decay of lifespan as people live shorter lives.

When the teaching of the three ages is taken too literally, people start trying to affix dates so they can definitively state when one age has ended or begun. As noted previously, in East Asia, it was believed that the Buddha lived from 1029 to 949 B.C.E. due to the attempts of Chinese Buddhists to show that the Buddha predated Laozi and the Taoist teachings. Assuming these dates for the life of the Buddha they, and Nichiren, believed that the Latter Age had begun in 1052 C.E. However, modern scholars believe the Buddha's actual dates were five hundred years or more later than that. The Japanese Buddhist scholar Hajime Nakamura set the dates as late as 463-383 B.C.E. What all this means is that if the dates of the three ages are taken literally, then Nichiren's belief that he was living in the Latter Age is completely off the mark since the Latter Age would not actually begin until the sixteenth or seventeenth century. In addition, the idea that the world suddenly shifts gears spiritually like clockwork when a particular calendar date comes around should strike us as naive and entirely too arbitrary.

The three ages of the Dharma should not be dismissed, however. It is a teaching that shows an awareness of the contingent and corruptible nature of the historical manifestations of the Dharma. It is a recognition that existentially, if not historically and geographically, we are indeed alienated from the true spirit of the Buddha's teachings and that we should listen to the Dharma as if hearing it for the first time (which many of us are) and not take it for granted. It is a recognition that Buddhism as a historical phenomena cannot remain static but must meet new challenges in every age.

Furthermore, the three ages teach us to never be complacent about the Three Treasures – the Buddha, Dharma, and Sangha. This teaching challenges us to try to renew the Dharma in the face of all corruption, deceit, oppression, and misunderstanding. It should not be taken in a way that causes us to be cynical or to despair that we are living in an age too corrupt to practice Buddhism. Nichiren did not take it in a pessimistic way – rather he saw the Latter Age as an opportunity to spread the Dharma in a new way through the Odaimoku. Other Buddhists might point to Nichiren's way as just a further symptom, or even cause, of the corruption and loss of the true spirit and original form of the Dharma. Nichiren Buddhists, however, should have confidence that Nichiren did not misinterpret the true intent of the many sūtra passages he marshaled to show the correct way to practice in the Latter Age. He may have taken these passages more literally than we might, but I do believe he saw the actual intent of these teachings – to spur us out of our complacency and despair and to renew our commitment to the Dharma and its efficacy in new ways for a new age. This is an argument that Nichiren will make in more detail in his later more mature writings on the subject (particularly the *Senji-shō*, the *Selection of the Time*) but for now he simply wants to show that the conditions which these sūtras speak of are the conditions that he and his contemporaries were facing.

Sources

Gosho Translation Committee, editor-translator. *The Writings of Nichiren Daishonin*. Tokyo: Soka Gakkai, 1999.

Hori, Kyotsu, comp. *Writings of Nichiren Shonin: Doctrine Volume 2*. Tokyo: Nichiren Shu Overseas Propagation Promotion Association, 2002.

Murano, Senchu, trans. *The Lotus Sūtra*. Hayward: Nichiren Buddhist International Center, 2012.

_____. *Kaimokusho or Liberation from Blindness*. Berkeley: Numata Center for Buddhist Translation and Research, 2000.

Sasaki, Konen. "When Did Life of Sakyamuni Begin and End?" [Part 1]. Nichiren Shu News, April 1, 2000, p. 1.

_____. "When Did Life of Sakyamuni Begin and End?" [Part 2]. Nichiren Shu News, June 1, 2000, p. 1.

Chapter 27 – Nichiren's Self-Questioning

Writings of Nichiren Shōnin Doctrine 2, pp. 52-53
Kaimoku-shō or Liberation from Blindness, pp. 41-43
The Writings of Nichiren Daishonin I, pp. 238-240

At this point in the *Kaimoku-shō*, Nichiren turns from a review of the teachings and the primacy of the *Lotus Sūtra* to a reflection on his own life in light of these teachings. This self-inquiry is spurred by the opposition and persecutions he has faced in trying to uphold the teaching of the *Lotus Sūtra*, and the questions of his disciples and followers as to why so many misfortunes have befallen them. As we have seen, only the Tiantai school had ever championed the *Lotus Sūtra* as containing the Buddha's most important teachings. In Nichiren's time, even the Tendai school had turned away from the *Lotus Sūtra* to focus on esotericism or Pure Land piety. In championing the *Lotus Sūtra* over the other teachings and practices, Nichiren had aroused the ire of the religious establishment, of the popular movements of his day like Zen and Pure Land Buddhism, and of the shogunate whose handling of religious affairs Nichiren had dared to criticize. Both he and his followers wondered if they were indeed doing the right thing, or if they were being punished for somehow going against the Dharma or being too confrontational about promoting the *Lotus Sūtra*.

From this point on in the *Kaimoku-shō* the essay begins to circle around back to themes that have already been covered but in different ways and from different angles. I have actually already drawn on later parts of the text in dealing with some of the themes treated up to this point. This circling around the same themes is what makes *Kaimoku-shō* a particularly difficult text to study. If one confines oneself to commenting on things as they arise, one will end up having to repeat oneself and also missing out on what is said about the same subject later in the text. If one deals with a subject in terms of what is said about it throughout the text, then one must jump around the text. I have dealt with this by dealing with each subject as they arise according to the whole text (and some statements by Nichiren in other writings that provide clarify and amplify what he means). From this point on we will be moving past some sections where the subjects and themes were already dealt with in an earlier chapter of this commentary.

Now would be a good time to review the structure of *Kaimoku-shō* as it relates to Nichiren's self-inquiry. The entire *Kaimoku-shō* is concerned with the question as to whether Nichiren and his followers are doing the right thing and, if so, why they are facing such hardships. However, it is not until this point in the essay that Nichiren explicitly raises the question. The *Kaimoku-shō* itself has no chapters, but Kyotsu Hori's translation and Senchu Murano's translation both divide it into chapters, though their divisions differ. *Kaimoku-shō* is divided into two parts, but that is because the length of it required two volumes, it is not a division of the content. For convenience, I will now refer to Kyotsu Hori's division of the text into chapters. In the first five chapters, Nichiren has been making the case that the Buddha's teachings are the most comprehensive and profound of religious teachings, and that among the Buddha's teachings the *Lotus Sūtra* contains two teachings that are of supreme importance: the attainment of buddhahood by people of the two vehicles that guarantees the universality of buddhahood, and the attainment of buddhahood in the remote past by Śākyamuni Buddha, that shows that the Eternal Śākyamuni Buddha of the Original Gate is our true or original teacher and that buddhahood is not bound in terms of time (or space) but is always here and now. Both of these are expressions of the underlying insight that Zhiyi called the "three thousand realms in a single thought-moment." Nichiren points out in chapter seven that the *Lotus Sūtra* itself says that it is unique, that it will be hard to believe, and that those who uphold it will face persecution and hardship in the Latter Age. The issues and the situation have now been set up. Now Nichiren can begin to discuss the role he believes himself to be performing in light of it all.

In chapter six, Nichiren states that he was born in a remote country place and is a poor monk with no social status. He wonders about his past lives and whether he had failed to hear the Buddha's teachings in the past or if he had heard it and sowed the seed of buddhahood but then fallen away. He speaks of his realization that false teachers have turned people away from the *Lotus Sūtra*. Knowing that he will be persecuted and face many hardships, including opposition from the "three obstacles and four devils," if he speaks out about this situation, Nichiren makes the determination to do so anyway, inspired by the analogy of the "six difficult and nine easier acts" in the eleventh chapter of the *Lotus Sūtra*. Nichiren comes to the conclusion that in his present lifetime he will not fail in his efforts to uphold the *Lotus Sūtra* and teach it to others. "... it is not easy to uphold even a word or phrase of the *Lotus Sūtra* in the Latter Age of Degeneration. This must be it! I have made a vow that this time I will have an unbending aspiration to buddhahood and never fall back!" (Hori 2002, p. 53) The rest of *Kaimoku-shō* is an elaboration and clarification of this section.

In chapter seven, Nichiren speaks of how his four persecutions are the fulfillment of the predictions of the hardships to be faced in the Latter Age. This has already been discussed. Nichiren also speaks of the three kinds of enemies that a practitioner of the *Lotus Sūtra* will face according to chapter thirteen of the *Lotus Sūtra*. He identifies the three formidable enemies as the teachers and followers of the Zen, Discipline, and Pure Land schools. Nichiren believes that the events of his life are the fulfillment of the prophecies in the *Lotus Sūtra*, and furthermore that he has had to face even greater persecutions than any before him in his attempts to teach the *Lotus Sūtra*. Yet he still wonders on behalf of himself and his followers whether he really is the practitioner of the *Lotus Sūtra* because has not received the heavenly protection the sūtra also promises.

In chapter eight, Nichiren continues this line of questioning as to why the gods have not protected him from persecution and furthermore as to why the śrāvaka disciples of the Buddha, who were granted predictions of buddhahood in the *Lotus Sūtra*, have not protected him. He also discusses the hardships faced by the Buddha and his disciples.

In chapter nine, Nichiren talks about the *Flower Garland Sūtra* as we have seen. As sublime as the *Flower Garland Sūtra* teaching was, it wasn't until the *Lotus Sūtra* that the Buddha taught the perfect teaching of the attainment of buddhahood by people of the two vehicles and the attainment of buddhahood in the remote past. It wasn't until the *Lotus Sūtra* that the Buddha could say that his original vow to make all beings equal to himself was fulfilled. These teachings are all connected with the "three thousand realms in a single thought-moment."

In chapter ten, Nichiren recounts the events of chapters twelve through sixteen in the *Lotus Sūtra*, culminating in Śākyamuni Buddha's revelation that his awakened life span has no beginning or end. Because of this teaching the true importance of Śākyamuni Buddha as the preeminent teacher who is the source or original of all the other buddhas and the teacher of all the bodhisattvas is established.

In chapter eleven, Nichiren criticizes the other schools for only revering buddhas who represent only partial aspects of buddhahood. This has already been discussed in a previous chapter of this commentary.

In chapter twelve, Nichiren speaks of the "three thousand realms in a single thought-moment" as the seed of awakening. He talks about the process of awakening or attaining buddhahood in terms of sowing this seed, cultivating it, and harvesting it. He once again accuses the Flower Garland and Mantra schools of plagiarizing this teaching, but also explains that other rivals of the Tiantai school secretly agreed with the Tiantai teachings. Nichiren asserts that all beings only attain buddhahood through the *Lotus Sūtra* and reasserts that the vows made by all buddhas are only fulfilled by the *Lotus Sūtra*.

In chapter thirteen, Nichiren again asks why he has not yet received protection from the buddhas, bodhisattvas, and gods who have vowed to protect the practitioner of the *Lotus Sūtra*. He again insists that the Zen and Pure Land Buddhists are the enemies predicted in the sūtras and that only he and Saichō have correctly taught the *Lotus Sūtra* in Japan. Nichiren elaborates on what he calls the five proclamations found in chapters eleven and twelve of the *Lotus Sūtra*, and this includes a discussion of the six difficult and nine easier acts and the attainment buddhahood by Devadatta and the dragon king's daughter. There is also a long section in which Nichiren examines the claims made by other sūtras wherein they each insist that they are the "king of sūtras." He also discusses the four reliances that are the four things to rely on in order to properly understand the Buddha's teachings. In this section Nichiren self-confidently asserts, "It is I, Nichiren, who is the richest person in Japan today, because I sacrifice my life for the sake of the *Lotus Sūtra* and leave my name for posterity." (Ibid, p. 90)

In chapter fourteen, Nichiren discusses in detail the three kinds of enemies the practitioner of the *Lotus Sūtra* will face according to chapter thirteen of the *Lotus Sūtra*. Here he identifies these enemies with the teachers of the Zen, Discipline, and Pure Land schools who are his rivals in Kamakura.

In chapter fifteen, Nichiren offers explanations for why he and his followers have had to face such persecutions and other hardships if they are indeed the practitioners of the *Lotus Sūtra* and why those who slander the *Lotus Sūtra* do not seem to be facing any punishments. He explains that he and his followers are expiating the transgressions they committed in their past lives; that those who are incapable of correction in this life may have it easy now but will fall into hell in their next life; and that the gods who are supposed to protect the practitioners of the *Lotus Sūtra* may have already abandoned the country. Regardless of the reasons for the persecutions and hardships, Nichiren makes a vow to uphold the *Lotus Sūtra* no matter what he is faced with.

In chapter sixteen, Nichiren elaborates on the theme of expiating past transgressions, and speaks again of the three obstacles and four devils that arise to obstruct practice. He also explains a parable from the *Nirvāṇa Sūtra* about a poor woman and her child that Nichiren relates to their practice and the attainment of buddhahood. He also speaks of the *Lotus Sūtra* in terms of the "three thousand realms in a single thought-moment" that alone leads to buddhahood.

In chapter seventeen, Nichiren explains the two methods of propagation, *shoju* (the gentle way of embracing good) and *shakubuku* (the confrontational way of subduing evil). He also once again directs criticism at the founders of the Zen and Pure Land schools in Japan.

In chapter eighteen, Nichiren brings the *Kaimoku-shō* to its conclusion and restates his determination to prevent evil and spread the *Lotus Sūtra* in spite of any persecutions he may have to face.

As can be seen from this outline, there are several themes and topics that Nichiren returns to again and again, such as the three kinds of enemies, his identification of them with his rivals in Kamakura, the protection of heavenly beings, the uniqueness of the *Lotus Sūtra*, the "three thousand realms in a single thought-moment" as the seed of buddhahood, the hardships a practitioner can expect to face, the expiation of past karma, and the vows that Nichiren makes and the mission he determines to undertake on behalf of all beings to uphold and spread the teaching of the *Lotus Sūtra*. In the following chapters of this commentary, I will make an attempt to explain each of these topics in the hope that we can understand each of them in terms of its original context and reflect on how these topics may or may not speak to us today.

Sources

Gosho Translation Committee, editor-translator. *The Writings of Nichiren Daishonin*. Tokyo: Soka Gakkai, 1999.

Hori, Kyotsu, comp. *Writings of Nichiren Shonin: Doctrine Volume 2*. Tokyo: Nichiren Shu Overseas Propagation Promotion Association, 2002.

Murano, Senchu, trans. *Kaimokusho or Liberation from Blindness*. Berkeley: Numata Center for Buddhist Translation and Research, 2000.

Chapter 28 – The Seed of Buddhahood

Writings of Nichiren Shōnin Doctrine 2, pp. 52-53, 58-80, 107-109
Kaimoku-shō or Liberation from Blindness, pp. 41-43, 49-77, 117-120
The Writings of Nichiren Daishonin I, pp. 238-240, 243-261, 282-283

Nichiren places great importance on the concept or analogy of "sowing the seed of buddhahood." In fact, while other forms of Mahāyāna Buddhism stress that all beings have buddha-nature, Nichiren tends to say very little about buddha-nature. Instead, he emphasized the act of sowing the seed of buddhahood in one's present lifetime. In terms of the five comparisons, the last of the five is that sowing the seed of buddhahood is superior to even the preaching of the Original Gate of the *Lotus Sūtra*. I have already mentioned, in my brief survey of the five comparisons, that Nichiren equates the seed of buddhahood with the doctrine of the "three thousand realms in a single thought-moment" and in turn identifies that doctrine with the Odaimoku. These ideas are further developed in the *Treatise on Spiritual Contemplation and the Focus of Devotion* (*Kanjin Honzon-shō*) and other writings, but the beginnings of Nichiren's thoughts in this direction are clearly evident in *Kaimoku-shō*, as I hope will be made clear.

As Nichiren begins his self-inquiry he wonders whether he had ever sown the seed of buddhahood by taking faith in the *Lotus Sūtra* in a past life, or if he had done so but then fallen away.

> *According to the "Parable of the Magic City" chapter of the Lotus Sūtra there were three categories of people who had an opportunity to listen to the sūtra and sow the seed of buddhahood during the time of Great Universal Wisdom Buddha in the past. They all were to obtain buddhahood eventually with the third and last group being guaranteed to be future buddhas upon listening to Śākyamuni Buddha preach the Lotus Sūtra. I wonder whether or not I was excluded from the third category of people. Or, am I one of those who, while*

*having listened to the Lotus Sūtra and sowed the seed
of buddhahood 500 dust-particle kalpas in the past,
have kept falling back till today without eventually
getting it? (Hori 2002, pp. 52-53 adapted)*

In chapter seven, "Parable of the Magic City," of the *Lotus Sūtra*, the Buddha
tells the story of a buddha who lived long ago named Great Universal Wisdom
Excellence Buddha. This buddha had been a king who had sixteen sons before
he left the palace to attain buddhahood. These sixteen princes also left home
to become disciples of their father who was now a buddha. Together, Great
Universal Wisdom Excellence Buddha and his sixteen sons preached the *Lotus
Sūtra*. According to the T'iantai interpretation of the story the śrāvakas who
heard this teaching of the *Lotus Sūtra* could be divided into three groups:
those who heard it, took faith, and attained buddhahood; those who heard it
and took faith but then fell away from their initial faith to follow lesser
teachings; and finally those who did not take faith. Śākyamuni Buddha reveals
that he was the sixteenth prince in that remote age, and that his present-day
disciples are those who first heard the *Lotus Sūtra* taught by him in that past
age. Of those who initially took faith and fell away, they will be able to recover
that faith and attain buddhahood upon hearing the *Lotus Sūtra* that he,
Śākyamuni Buddha, is presently teaching. Of those who did not take faith at
that time, Śākyamuni Buddha's present teaching of the *Lotus Sūtra* provides
them with another chance to sow the seed of faith so that they may enjoy the
harvest of buddhahood in the future. Nichiren wonders, on behalf of himself
and his followers, if he (and they) were excluded from these groups. In other
words, he wonders if in their past lives he and his followers were either not
present during these past occasions when the *Lotus Sūtra* was taught or if
they had been there but had rejected the sūtra, thus failing to sow the seed of
buddhahood. Similarly he wonders if he had heard the *Lotus Sūtra* in the
remote past five hundred million dust-particle kalpas ago (the remote past
when Śākyamuni Buddha attained buddhahood according to chapter sixteen)
and had sown the seed of buddhahood but had continually fallen away from
that initial moment of taking faith in the *Lotus Sūtra* ever since.

Further on in *Kaimoku-shō*, Nichiren stresses the importance of understanding
that the seed of buddhahood must be sown, nurtured, and harvested. He also
identifies it with the doctrine of the "three thousand realms in a single
thought-moment."

As for the three steps for obtaining buddhahood – its sowing, nurturing, and harvesting – those terms are not mentioned in the canons of the Mantra and Flower Garland schools, not to speak of its true meaning. They maintain that one is able to reach the first of the ten stages of bodhisattvahood and obtain buddhahood within the present lifetime. However, as provisional sūtras they do not preach the planting of the seeds in the past. Thus they talk about attaining buddhahood without planting seeds, which is like Jiaogao of Qin China or Yuge no Dōkyō of Japan trying to usurp the throne without any right.

These schools of Buddhism fight with one another for superiority, but I, Nichiren, do not jump into the scramble, leaving the matter to sūtras. Based on the concept of the seed of buddhahood preached in the Lotus Sūtra, Bodhisattva Vasubandhu insisted on the "supremacy of the seed" in his Lotus Sūtra Treatise. This later became the "three thousand realms in a single thought-moment" doctrine of Grand Master Tiantai. The seed of the various venerables appearing in such Mahāyāna sūtras as the Flower Garland and the Mahavairochana Sūtra is without exception this "three thousand realms in a single thought-moment" doctrine. It was Grand Master Tiantai alone who perceived this in the history of Buddhism. (Ibid, pp. 77-78 adapted)

In bringing up the three categories of people in chapter seven of the *Lotus Sūtra*, Nichiren equates the seed of buddhahood with hearing and taking faith in the *Lotus Sūtra*. Here, Nichiren stresses that the seed must be sown, nurtured, and harvested or else it will remain undeveloped, or even lost. He then identifies the seed with the doctrine of the "three thousand realms in a single thought-moment." So the seed of buddhahood is not simply about hearing and believing in the *Lotus Sūtra*, it is about hearing it, taking its unique teachings to heart, and contemplating the true nature of reality that Zhiyi taught in terms of the "three thousand realms in a single thought-moment."

For Nichiren, everything comes back to the doctrine of the "three thousand realms in a single thought-moment" that was one of the ways Zhiyi explained the perfect teaching of Śākyamuni Buddha in the *Lotus Sūtra*. Though it is a conceptual model based on Buddhist cosmology, we should not forget for a moment that its purpose is to express the Buddha's insight and help us see things as the Buddha sees things.

Previous to the above passage, Nichiren reviewed the life and teachings of Śākyamuni Buddha up to the expounding of the Trace Gate and Origin Gate to show how the *Lotus Sūtra* alone revealed the "three thousand realms in a single thought-moment." Nichiren writes in more detail about the hardships faced by the śrāvakas, and how the Buddha had castigated them for their Hīnayāna mindsets that did not aspire to buddhahood for the sake of all beings. He talks about how the great bodhisattvas led by Dharma Wisdom did the actual expounding of the *Flower Garland Sūtra* and how all the sūtras up to (but not including) the *Lotus Sūtra* were derived from the teachings give by those bodhisattvas. In the *Lotus Sūtra*, however, the Buddha finally began to teach things that had not been said in any other sūtra, including the *Flower Garland Sūtra*. He first taught the One Vehicle in place of the previous teaching that there were three different vehicles for śrāvakas, pratyekabuddhas, and bodhisattvas. By teaching the One Vehicle, Śākyamuni Buddha made it clear that all beings have the world of buddhahood within their lives. Nichiren equates this with a brief glimpse of the ultimate truth of the "three thousand realms in a single thought-moment" that whetted the appetite of those who heard it for the perfect teaching.

> *In revealing the single path to awakening replacing the three kinds of teaching for bodhisattvas, śrāvakas, and pratyekabuddhas in the second chapter on "Expedients" of the Lotus Sūtra, the Buddha briefly expressed the "three thousand realms in a single thought-moment" doctrine held in his bosom. Since it was the first time for the Buddha to reveal the truth, it sounded to his disciples as faint as the voice of a nightingale heard by the half-asleep or the moon rising halfway over a mountain covered by a thin cloud. Surprised by the words of the Buddha, Śāriputra and other disciples called on the gods, dragons, and great bodhisattvas,*

and together they petitioned the Buddha. Gods and dragons as numerous as sand of the Ganges River, eighty thousand bodhisattvas trying to attain buddhahood, and wheel-turning noble kings in ten thousands, hundred millions of lands all respectfully held hands together in gasshō and wished to hear the perfect teaching. In other words, they requested him to preach the doctrine that they had never heard during his preaching in more than forty years of the pre-Lotus sūtras, expounding four of the five flavors and three of the four teachings. (Ibid, p. 66 adapted)

Referring to the Tiantai classification of the Buddha's teaching we can see that what is being said here is that the tripitika, shared, and distinct teachings, and the four flavors of the Flower Garland, Deer Park, Expanded, and Perfection of Wisdom, taught prior to the *Lotus Sūtra* had not made it clear that all beings could attain buddhahood and that the world of the buddha resides within all beings. All of those assembled together in the *Lotus Sūtra* to hear the Buddha teach were now ready to hear the undiluted perfect teaching that had not been given by the bodhisattvas of the *Flower Garland Sūtra* or anyone else in any other sūtra. Though some aspects of the perfect teaching may have appeared in the *Flower Garland Sūtra* and other Mahāyāna sūtras, the unequivocal assertion that even arhats and pratyekabuddhas would attain buddhahood had not been made before, and now something even more marvelous was going to be taught by Śākyamuni Buddha.

In response to the request by Śāriputra and others to know how to fulfill the six perfections, Śākyamuni Buddha declares in the second "Expedients" chapter of the Lotus Sūtra that all buddhas hope to open the gate to the wisdom of the Buddha for all people. The people here refer to the men of the two vehicles such as Śāriputra, who had been considered unable to obtain buddhahood, men of incorrigible disbelief lacking the buddha-nature, and all those in the nine realms (except the realm of the Buddha). Therefore, his vow to save all the numerous people was at last fulfilled in preaching the Lotus Sūtra. That is what he meant in declaring in

333

the same second chapter of the Lotus Sūtra: "I had vowed to make everyone exactly like myself. The original vow of mind has already been fulfilled."

Upon hearing this, great bodhisattvas and gods expressed their understanding in the third chapter on "A Parable" of the Lotus Sūtra, "We have often listened to the Buddha preach, but have never heard of the Dharma as deeply as this." Grand Master Dengyō, founder of the Tendai school in Japan, interprets this as follows: "That they had often listened to the Buddha preach means that they had listened in the past to such great teachings as the Flower Garland Sūtra before they listened to the Lotus Sūtra. And that they have never heard of the Dharma as deeply as this means that they never heard of the teaching of the Lotus Sūtra, in which all are assured of obtaining buddhahood." That is to say, they said that while listening to various Mahāyāna sūtras as numerous as the grains of sand in the Ganges River such as the Flower Garland Sūtra, Expanded sūtras, Perfection of Wisdom sūtras, Revealing the Profound and Secret Sūtra, and the Mahavairochana Sūtra, they had never heard of the attainment of buddhahood by men of the two vehicles or eternity in the life of the Buddha, the two doctrines that constitute the basis of Buddhism and the backbone of the "three thousand realms in a single thought-moment" doctrine. (Hori 2002, p. 68 adapted)

Nichiren then describes the ceremony in the air as it occurs in the *Lotus Sūtra*, wherein the Stūpa of Treasures rises up out of the ground and into the air in chapter eleven and within it the ancient buddha known as Many Treasures Tathāgata speaks out to testify to the truth of what Śākyamuni Buddha had been teaching. Śākyamuni Buddha then purifies the Sahā world (this world whose name means "Endurance") and recalls the buddhas of the ten directions who are his emanations to gather around him. Śākyamuni Buddha then opens the Stūpa of Treasures. Many Treasures Tathāgata invites Śākyamuni Buddha to sit beside him in the stūpa. Śākyamuni Buddha does so and then uses his power to allow the entire assembly to float into the air, thus beginning the Assembly in Space. Śākyamuni Buddha then exhorts those present to teach the *Lotus Sūtra* after his passing. After exhorting them three times, the Buddha tells the story of Devadatta and then Mañjuśrī Bodhisattva appears and introduces the dragon king's daughter who attains buddhahood immediately after offering the Buddha a precious gem. Inspired by all this, the bodhisattvas agree to teach the *Lotus Sūtra* even in the face of persecution, but Śākyamuni Buddha tells them that there are other bodhisattvas who will do it. That is when, in chapter fifteen, the bodhisattvas appear from the space beneath the ground, and the Buddha asserts that these are his original disciples. This leads to the questions of Maitreya Bodhisattva that lead to Śākyamuni Buddha explaining for the first time, in chapter sixteen, that he actually attained awakening in the remote past. This has been covered previously. Nichiren goes over all this again to make two important points. If Śākyamuni Buddha is the Eternal or Original Buddha, then that means he has been in this world all along, not just for a few decades, and that therefore this world is the true pure land of the Eternal Buddha. Nichiren puts it this way, "He now declared that this world is the land of the Original Buddha and what had been said to be pure lands throughout the universe are defiled lands of manifestations." (Ibid, p. 75) Furthermore, this means that the Eternal Buddha is the real source of the buddhas throughout the universe who are his emanations and has been since the remote past, which means that all those buddhas, all their bodhisattva attendants, and all the gods are not the teachers of Śākyamuni Buddha but the disciples of the Eternal Śākyamuni Buddha. "Since Śākyamuni is eternal and all other buddhas in the universe are his emanations, then those great bodhisattvas who were taught by the emanation buddhas and who are from other worlds are all disciples of Lord Śākyamuni Buddha." (Ibid, p. 75)

The true status and preeminence of the Eternal Śākyamuni Buddha is therefore established in chapter sixteen of the *Lotus Sūtra*. The Eternal Śākyamuni Buddha's eternal connection with this world and with those of us who live in it is thereby established. This also means that the Eternal Śākyamuni Buddha's teachings regarding the universality of buddhahood and his own constant efforts from the beginningless past and on into the endless future to help all beings attain buddhahood is given preeminence. In terms of the "three thousand realms in a single thought-moment" this teaching means that in addition to the deluded beings of the nine realms containing the realm of buddhahood, the Buddha is now asserting that he is always active in the other nine realms. He does not appear or disappear within them, but is always present, though sometimes the presence is subtle and hard to notice. Sometimes the Buddha appears in different guises or forms other than human or even other than sentient, and sometimes the Buddha seems to be absent. These different ways of being present, or even present as an absence, are the Buddha's skillful means of awakening all beings. It is not just that sentient beings have the potential to become buddhas. More importantly, the Buddha is an eternally active presence in the lives of all sentient beings. The nine realms contain buddhahood and buddhahood contains the nine realms. This is the radical claim of the teaching of the mutual possession of the ten realms. Knowing this, the "three thousand realms in a single thought-moment" can be fully understood.

After identifying the doctrine of the "three thousand realms in a single thought-moment" with the seed of buddhahood, Nichiren returns to his previous theme concerning how the other schools of Buddhism tried to misappropriate this teaching or at least how they publicly put down the *Lotus Sūtra* but privately acquiesced to the Tiantai teachings. He again berates the patriarchs of the Flower Garland and Mantra schools for stealing the doctrine of the "three thousand realms in a single thought-moment" when interpreting their own sūtras, though those sūtras did not say anything about the attainment of buddhahood by people of the two vehicles or Śākyamuni Buddha attaining buddhahood in the remotest past. Nichiren also claimed that such men as Jizang (549-632), the founder of the Three Treatises school; Kuiji (632-682; also known as Cien), the founder of the Dharma Characteristics School; and Kūkai (774-835; also known as Kōbō), the founder of the Japanese branch of the Mantra school (Shingon Shū) were all at least privately in agreement with the Tiantai teachings and revered the *Lotus Sūtra*.

Having pointed out that even the patriarchs and teachers of other schools all tried to lay claim to the perfect teaching of the *Lotus Sūtra*, Nichiren states that only the *Lotus Sūtra* actually enables anyone to attain buddhahood.

> *Therefore we say that, although buddhas, bodhisattvas, men, and gods appearing in various sūtras seem to have obtained buddhahood through their respective sūtras, in reality they were truly enlightened because of the Lotus Sūtra. The four great vows of Śākyamuni and other buddhas such as saving a countless number of*

336

people were fulfilled in this sūtra of the Lotus. In the second chapter, it is stated [by the Buddha], "My wishes are all fully satisfied." (Ibid, p. 80)

Nichiren returns to this idea that buddhahood is only possible through the *Lotus Sūtra* further on in the *Kaimoku-shō* after he explains a parable from the *Nirvāna Sūtra*. In the parable a poor homeless woman wanders about from place to place begging. She then has a child and is kicked out of the inn where she was staying. She faces many hardships due to cold, hunger, insects, and bad weather. Finally, she is caught in a flood. She does all she can to hold on to her baby, but both are drowned. The parable concludes that due to her compassion for her child and her attempts to save it she is reborn in the Brahmā Heaven. The sūtra interprets the parable in the following way:

If a good man wishes to uphold the True Dharma, (...) he must do the same as the poor woman in sacrificing her own life in the Ganges because of her love for her child. Good man! Bodhisattvas upholding the Dharma should also be ready to sacrifice their lives. (...) Such people will be able to attain buddhahood without seeking it, just as the poor woman will be reborn in the Brahmā Heaven without seeking it. (Ibid, p. 107)

Nichiren interprets this parable in terms of his own life. What is of interest here is that he says the child in the story "refers to faith in the *Lotus Sūtra*, which is the seed of buddhahood." (Ibid, p. 108) Nichiren interprets the end of the story as follows: "The drowning of the mother and her baby refers to Nichiren being almost beheaded at Tatsunokuchi for his unwavering faith in the *Lotus Sūtra*. Rebirth in the Brahmā Heaven means his attainment of buddhahood. (Ibid, p. 108) Nichiren goes on to cite an interpretation of this parable by Zhiyi's disciple Zhang'an Guanding (561-632). According to this interpretation the mother was able to be reborn in the Brahmā Heaven because her single-minded thought for her baby's safety and welfare was like those forms of meditative absorption that focus on loving-kindness and compassion. To concentrate the mind on boundless loving-kindness, compassion, sympathetic joy, or equanimity is said in Buddhism to enable one to have a mind like the god Brahmā, and is a cause for rebirth in the Brahmā

337

Heaven. In bringing up this interpretation, Nichiren is saying that like this poor homeless woman who did not study any deep teachings or take up any formal meditative practice, we too can naturally attain buddhahood if we deeply focus on and cherish the *Lotus Sūtra* and particularly the doctrine of the "three thousand realms in a single thought-moment" even if we do not fully understand it at first. Nichiren says:

> Also, many ways are claimed for leading to buddhahood, such as the "mind-only" doctrine of the Flower Garland school, the Three Treatises doctrine of "the Middle Way of the eight negations," the "consciousness-only" doctrine of the Dharma Characteristics school, and the Mantra doctrine of the "five wheels," but none of these seem to work in actuality. The only way seemingly that leads to buddhahood is the "three thousand realms in a single thought-moment" doctrine of the Tiantai. However, we in the Latter Age of Degeneration do not possess the intelligence to understand it; nevertheless, among all the sūtras preached by Śākyamuni during his lifetime, only the Lotus Sūtra embodies the gem of the "three thousand realms in a single thought-moment" doctrine. Doctrines of other schools may look like gems, but in actuality they are merely yellow rocks. Just as, no matter how hard you squeeze sand, you will not get oil, or barren women will never have children, even wise men will not be able to attain buddhahood by means of other sūtras. As for the Lotus Sūtra, even ignorant persons will be able to plant the seed of buddhahood. The above citation from the Nirvāṇa Sūtra stating "Such people would be able to obtain buddhahood without seeking it" must have meant this attainment of buddhahood by the means of the Lotus Sūtra.
>
> Not only I Nichiren, but also my disciples will reach the land of the Buddha unfailingly so long as we hold on to unwavering faith no matter what difficulty confronts us. (Ibid, pp. 108-109 adapted)

How does one hold to unwavering faith in the *Lotus Sūtra* and particularly the doctrine of the "three thousand realms in a single thought-moment"? The answer is through chanting Namu Myōhō Renge Kyō, "Devotion to the Sūtra of the Lotus Flower of the Wonderful Dharma." Nichiren does not identify the "three thousand realms in a single thought-moment" with the Odaimoku in *Kaimoku-shō*, but he does call it a gem that the *Lotus Sūtra* embodies. In an earlier passage, Nichiren explains the etymology of the Odaimoku and especially emphasizes how the character *myō* refers to the perfect teaching, the fulfillment of the six perfections of bodhisattva practice, and the mutual possession of the ten realms. (See Ibid pp. 66-68) Nichiren will explicitly bring all of this together in the *Kanjin Honzon-shō*.

> *For those who are incapable of understanding the truth of the "three thousand realms in a single thought-moment," Lord Śākyamuni Buddha, with his great compassion, wraps this jewel with the five characters of myō, hō, ren, ge, and kyō and hangs it around the necks of the ignorant in the Latter Age of Degeneration. (Ibid, p. 164 adapted)*

Another theme further developed in *Kanjin Honzon-shō* is that the teaching of the Original Gate as a discourse given by the historical Śākyamuni Buddha was for the sake of his contemporaries who would attain buddhahood upon hearing it and bring to fruition the seeds sown in the distant past. In the Latter Age of Degeneration, the teaching of the Original Gate will be the Odaimoku that will act as the seed of buddhahood for those who have either not received any seed or who have neglected or destroyed the seeds that had been sown in the past.

On closer examination, however, the Original Gate differs from the Trace Gate. That is to say, the Original Gate, all through the preface, the main discourse, and the epilogue, was preached for those people in the beginning of the Latter Age of Degeneration. The teaching of the Original Gate during the lifetime of Śākyamuni Buddha and what would spread in the beginning of the Latter Age are likewise absolutely perfect. However, the former is for attaining enlightenment, whereas the latter is for sowing the seed of buddhahood. While the former is crystallized in the 16th chapter, "The Life

339

Span of the Buddha," with half a chapter each preceding and following it, the latter is solely embodied in the five characters of *myō*, *hō*, *ren*, *ge*, and *kyō*, the title of the *Lotus Sūtra*. (Ibid, p. 154 adapted)

Having surveyed what Nichiren has to say in the *Kaimoku-shō* and also *Kanjin Honzon-shō*, we can see that Nichiren insists that to attain buddhahood one must sow the seed of buddhahood through encountering and taking faith in the *Lotus Sūtra*. This seed of buddhahood is specifically identified as the doctrine of the "three thousand realms in a single thought-moment" that is about the mutual possession of the ten realms, meaning that all beings possess the world of the Buddha (expressed in the Trace Gate as the attainment of buddhahood by the people of the two vehicles); and that the Buddha is an active presence in all ten realms enabling people to realize and actualize their own buddhahood (as expressed in the Origin Gate as the attainment of buddhahood in the remotest past). Furthermore, one must nurture this seed and bring it to harvest, it cannot be taken for granted. Nichiren states that it is possible to fall away having once received the seed of buddhahood, and he insists that one must maintain unwavering faith even in the face of hardships and persecution. This seed of buddhahood is identified with the five characters of the Chinese title of the *Lotus Sūtra* preceded by "*Namu*," a word which expresses faith and devotion to the sacred title or Odaimoku of the *Lotus Sūtra*. According to Nichiren, Śākyamuni Buddha preached the Original Gate in the form of a discourse in the Former Age of the Dharma to bring to harvest the buddhahood whose seeds had been sown in the distant past. The Odaimoku is the same perfect teaching but in a form suitable for sowing the seed of buddhahood in the lives of the people in the Latter Age of the Dharma.

Now all of this talk about seeds can be more than a little confusing. How can a complex doctrine like the "three thousand realms in a single thought-moment" or the Odaimoku be considered a seed of buddhahood? Is Nichiren's talk of seeds a rejection of teachings, such as found in the *Awakening of Faith in the Mahāyāna Treatise* or the *Nirvāna Sūtra*, that assert that all beings have buddha-nature and can therefore realize buddhahood? Is buddhahood possible only if the right seeds are sown in our lives? Can these seeds be neglected, lost, or destroyed, as Nichiren seems to suggest? And of course, Nichiren was not the first to speak of seeds of buddhahood. According to the Consciousness-Only School, the seeds of arhatship, pratyekabuddhahood, or buddhahood are innate, but not everyone has all three types of pure seeds, and some people have none at all. The *Expansive Dhāranī Sūtra* teaches that the seeds of buddhahood of the followers of the two vehicles had been burnt. Conversely, the *Vimalakīrti Sūtra* states that even greed, hatred, and delusion can act as the seeds of buddhahood. Is Nichiren rejecting the idea that all beings have buddha-nature in favor of the idea that one must have the seed of buddhahood and that it is possible that one has not received such a seed, or, having once received it, has destroyed or lost it?

First of all, Nichiren definitely does not reject the concept of buddha-nature and in fact positively asserts the Tiantai view of it. In *Kanjin Honzon-shō*, Nichiren criticizes the *Flower Garland Sūtra* and *Mahavairochana Sūtra* in the following terms: "They fail to preach the three causes of buddhahood inherent in all living beings: the buddha-nature, wisdom to see it, and the right actions to develop the wisdom. How can they decide what the seed of buddhahood is?" (Ibid, p. 145) This is said in the context of a discussion of the three thousand realms in a single thought-moment as the basis of the seed of buddhahood. What Nichiren is referring to is the threefold buddha-nature taught by the Tiantai school as taught in the following passage Nichiren cites from one of the three major writings of Zhiyi:

> The Words and Phrases of the Lotus Sūtra, fascicle ten, preaches: "The 'proper cause buddha-nature' is possessed by the Dharma-kāya Buddha, and it is innately possessed by all the people throughout all their past, present, and future lives. By nature they are endowed also with the seeds of 'discerning cause' and 'assisting cause buddha-nature'; these buddha-natures are not acquired as a result of practicing Buddhism. (Ibid, p. 17 modified)

The threefold buddha-nature is composed of three causes innate in all beings that lead to the three bodies of the Buddha. The first is the 'proper cause buddha-nature' (J. *shōin busshō*) that is the true nature of all phenomena. When it is obscured and unrecognized by defilements it is buddha-nature in the most general meaning of the term, but when it is realized it is the Dharma-body. The second is the 'discerning cause' that is the seed of wisdom that realizes or awakens to the real true nature. This seed of wisdom blossoms into the reward-body of the Buddha. The 'assisting cause' is the seed of wholesome actions and practice that actualizes the true nature. This is the seed that blossoms into the accommodative-body. These three kinds of buddha-nature are called the seeds of similarity because they are pure causes that lead to effects of a similarly pure nature. In the teachings of Tiantai and Nichiren Buddhism, the buddha-nature is viewed in terms of three kinds of innate seeds that all beings possess that lead to buddhahood.

> *The Profound Meaning of the Lotus Sūtra comments on the seeds of similarity thus: "Anyone with a mind possesses the seeds of innate buddha-nature. If one hears but a phrase of the sūtra, they have the seed of wisdom to realize buddha-nature. Should one put one's hands together and bow in prayer towards the Buddha, that is the seed of right actions to advance towards buddhahood. (Ibid, p. 246)*

The Tiantai teaching also speaks of the seeds of opposition:

> *The seeds of opposition means opening and merging the three paths of defilements, karma, and suffering into the three merits of the Dharma-body, wisdom, and liberation respectively. (Ibid. p. 246 modified)*

According to Tiantai and Nichiren Buddhism, the teaching and practice of the *Lotus Sūtra* is so transformative that it can enable even the cycle of suffering to become their opposites: the three merits of the Dharma-body, wisdom, and liberation. The three merits are actually just a variation on the theme of the three bodies of the Buddha. So what we have here is the assertion that through the teaching and practice of the *Lotus Sūtra* a person can turn the raw material of life, even its most painful or sordid aspects, into seeds of buddhahood. The confusion and pain of ordinary life can motivate us to reflect more deeply in order to develop the wisdom to overcome suffering, begin living in a more constructive and wholesome way, and ultimately see that even confusion and pain manifest the true nature of reality. In this way the three paths become the three merits.

Now if everyone has the innate seeds of similarity and if even the negative or painful aspects of our life are the seeds of opposition, then why is it that attaining buddhahood is so difficult? Why does it seem like some have lost or destroyed the seed of buddhahood, and why must we sow the seed of buddhahood anew through the Odaimoku? The answer is that seeds will not grow without the proper causes and conditions. In this view, buddhahood is not some fixed self-nature but is itself a dynamic interdependent process. This is what the *Lotus Sūtra* in fact teaches, "All things are devoid of substantiality. The seed of buddhahood comes from dependent origination." (Murano 2012, p. 44) While the unconditioned selfless true nature of reality may not be caused or conditioned, that true nature is nothing other than how conditioned phenomena really are: empty of any fixed, independent self-nature; arising, transforming, and passing away in accord with causes and conditions; and manifesting the Middle Way that transcends the concepts of the eternity or annihilation of any substantial phenomena. In turn, buddhahood is an awakening to the unconditioned nature that communicates itself in and through skillful means, which are the utilization of causes and conditions by a perfect wisdom that never loses sight of the unconditioned true nature of the conditions it engages.

The seeds of buddhahood do require the whole process of sowing, nurturing, and harvesting. But once again, what do we mean by sowing, nurturing, and harvesting a doctrine or the chanting of the title of a sūtra? Here we must remember that Nichiren cited Vasubandhu as the one who spoke of the "supremacy of the seed." Vasubandhu was one of the founders of the Consciousness-Only tradition, so it is this school of thought that can provide us with the context for the idea of a "seed of buddhahood." As discussed previously, in the Consciousness-Only School it is taught that all one's thoughts, words, and deeds leave an impression in the storehouse consciousness, a deep subconscious that records everything that we do and experience. When such impressions are made, they do two things. The first thing is that these karmic activities are the causes that become seeds which are stored in the storehouse consciousness until such time as the appropriate causes and conditions come together that allow them to ripen into an effect that is consciously experienced. The second thing is that these karmic activities condition or "perfume" the seeds that are already stored in the storehouse consciousness, mitigating some and enhancing others, perhaps even allowing some to ripen. In this way of understanding the mind, it is entirely possible to have seeds that lie undeveloped for long periods of time. It is also possible to do things that will have a negative effect on the seeds in the storehouse consciousness, for instance, the *Lotus Sūtra* says, "Those who do not believe this sūtra, but slander it, will destroy the seeds of buddhahood of all living beings in the world." (Ibid, p. 81) This is why Nichiren wonders whether he had once had the seed sown in his life but had afterwards lost them.

Fortunately, the Eternal Śākyamuni Buddha in chapter sixteen has asserted that he is always present and always teaching the Dharma. In every age he provides sentient beings with a chance to once again hear the Dharma, take faith in it, and thereby sow, nourish, and bring to harvest the seeds of buddhahood. This is actually another reason why the attainment of buddhahood and the doctrine of the "three thousand realms in a single thought-moment" is so important. What these teachings are saying, according to Nichiren and the Tiantai school, is that the Buddha is always present from the beginningless past to the endless future, but not merely as our innate buddha-nature, which on its own may never be realized or actualized as we indefinitely perpetuate our neglect of the seeds of buddhahood. As the Eternal Śākyamuni Buddha, the reward-body that is the Eternal Buddha's wisdom, and the accommodative-body that is the Eternal Buddha's awakened activity in the world are both beginningless and endless as well, and so always involved in our lives in one form or another. This is why the "Verses for Opening the Sūtra" used in Nichiren Shū says, "Expounding is the Buddha's wisdom. Expounded is the Buddha's truth. The letters composing this sutra are the Buddha's manifestation." What the Verses for Opening the Sūtra are asserting is that the Eternal Śākyamuni Buddha is present whenever we receive and keep, read, recite, copy, or expound the Lotus Sūtra. The Buddha's three bodies are present and active whenever we chant the Odaimoku and in fact are none other than the practice of chanting the Odaimoku.

I hope it is clear that the "seed of buddhahood" is not a concrete thing, nor does it mean having a conceptual understanding of the "three thousand realms in a single thought-moment." Rather, it is an impression made within the depths of our lives when we hear this teaching of the *Lotus Sūtra* that assures us that all beings can attain buddhahood and that the Buddha is always present in our lives, working through myriad skillful means to awaken us. In Nichiren Shū, the practice of Odaimoku chanting is how we bring this teaching and its assurances into our hearts and keep them ever in mind. If we are to truly benefit from this practice, we must appreciate that chanting Namu Myōhō Renge Kyō is a way to enter into the presence of the Eternal Śākyamuni Buddha and receive the seed of buddhahood into our lives as if for the first time. Every time we chant Namu Myōhō Renge Kyō, therefore, is a precious opportunity, the one thought-moment in which the world of buddhahood is manifestly present to us and within us.

Sources

Gosho Translation Committee, editor-translator. *The Writings of Nichiren Daishonin*. Tokyo: Soka Gakkai, 1999.

Hori, Kyotsu, comp. *Writings of Nichiren Shonin: Doctrine Volume 2*. Tokyo: Nichiren Shu Overseas Propagation Promotion Association, 2002.

Murano, Senchu, trans. *The Lotus Sutra*. Hayward: Nichiren Buddhist International Center, 2012.

_____. *Kaimokusho or Liberation from Blindness*. Berkeley: Numata Center for Buddhist Translation and Research, 2000.

Chapter 29 – The Four Admonitions

Nichiren is known primarily for his advocacy of the *Lotus Sūtra* as the Buddha's highest teaching and for the practice of chanting its Odaimoku (lit. sacred title) in the form of Namu Myōhō Renge Kyō (lit. Devotion to the Sūtra of the Lotus Flower of the Wonderful Dharma). He is also known for his denunciation of other schools of Buddhism. This denunciation is often summarized in the form of the "four admonitions" (J. *shika no kakugen*):

> *Pure Land Buddhism is a way leading to the Hell of*
> *Incessant Suffering; Zen Buddhism is the act of heavenly*
> *devils, who hinder the Buddhist way; Mantra (Shingon)*
> *Buddhism is an evil teaching leading to the destruction*
> *of our nation; and Discipline (Ritsu) Buddhism is a false*
> *teaching by traitors. (Hori 1992, p. 178 adapted)*

The four admonitions in the form in which they are cited above are from a letter allegedly written by Nichiren to the Zen Master Lan-ch'i Tao-lung (1213-1278; J. Rankei Dōryū) of Kenchōji Temple. This letter is one of eleven letters that were supposedly written to the political and religious leaders in Kamakura on October 11, 1268 after envoys from the Mongol Empire arrived in Japan demanding tribute. Nichiren viewed this as the threat of foreign invasion that he had predicted in the *Treatise on Spreading Peace Throughout the Country by Establishing the True Dharma* (*Risshō Ankoku-ron*). It is plausible that he wrote such letters to remind the political and religious leaders that his predictions were coming true, but scholars have cast doubts upon the authenticity of the eleven letters. Nevertheless, those same admonitions can be found scattered throughout other writings of Nichiren's, including authenticated works, though not always together or in that particular order. There is no doubt that Nichiren condemned Pure Land, Zen, Mantra (J. Shingon), and the Discipline (J. Ritsu) schools using the very words found in the letter to Tao-lung.

Why did Nichiren condemn these four schools of Buddhism? Nichiren explains why very succinctly in a letter written in 1275 to the Mantra school monk Gōnin:

> *Startled by the great earthquake in the first year of the Shōka Era (1257) and the huge comet in the first year of the Bun'ei Era (1264), I examined all the Buddhist scriptures. They preach that the two calamities that had never happened in Japan would occur: domestic disturbance and foreign invasion. These serious calamities were induced by the fallacies of Hīnayāna and provisional Mahāyāna teachings of Mantra, Zen, Pure Land, and Discipline Buddhism destroying the True Dharma of the Lotus Sūtra in Japan. (Hori 2003, p. 254 adapted)*

In the *Risshō Ankoku-ron*, Nichiren had blamed the exclusive nembutsu movement begun by Hōnen for causing the disastrous earthquakes, plagues, and famines that had struck Japan because it had turned people away form the *Lotus Sūtra*. In subsequent writings, Nichiren made it clear that he blamed any school that turned people away from, or slandered, the *Lotus Sūtra* and not just the Pure Land Buddhism of Hōnen. Zen, Mantra, and the Discipline schools soon joined Pure Land as the targets of Nichiren's critiques. This is because he saw these four schools as actively slandering the *Lotus Sūtra* and causing people to turn away from it. Instead of embracing the teaching that could enable all people to attain buddhahood and transform this world into a pure land, the rulers, religious leaders, samurai, and common people were taking up teachings that Nichiren saw as debilitating to the individual and to society as a whole, thus bringing about natural and social disasters.

Nichiren's polemics against the Kamakuran religious establishment brought about harsh reprisals, such as the four major persecutions discussed in a previous chapter. Even Nichiren's own disciples apparently felt that Nichiren's condemnations were either unnecessary or too aggressive. In a writing from 1280 called the *Remonstration with Bodhisattva Hachiman* (*Kangyō Hachiman-shō*), Nichiren responds to the criticism of his own disciples regarding his admonitions and explains that he must speak out because these four schools will not respond positively to the teaching to uphold the *Lotus*

Sūtra and practice the Odaimoku, but will consider it inferior to their own teachings and practices.

> *My ignorant disciples think: "Our master [Nichiren] propagates the Lotus Sūtra; however, not only is he unsuccessful but also he often encounters great difficulties. This is because he uses the subduing means of propagation declaring that Mantra Buddhism is the evil dharma that destroys the country, the nembutsu is the teaching that leads people into the Hell of Incessant Suffering, Zen is the teaching of heavenly demons, and Discipline priests are national traitors. This is like mixing your reasoning with abuse when presenting a lawsuit."*

> *I will cross-examine such ignorant disciples of mine by asking, "Why don't you try urging all those Mantra priests, Pure Land believers and Zen Buddhists to chant the daimoku, Namu Myōhō Renge Kyō?" Those Mantra priests would probably say, "Our teacher, Grand Master Kōbō, writes that the Lotus Sūtra is a joke and Śākyamuni Buddha is in the realm of ignorance, who does not amount to a palanquin bearer or a sandal-carrier. Rather than reading the Lotus Sūtra, which is useless, it is better to recite our short magic spell just once."*

> *Pure Land Buddhists all would say: "Our Venerable Shan-tao speaks of the Lotus Sūtra as incapable of causing even one out of 1,000 to attain buddhahood; Hōnen Shōnin advises us to 'abandon, close, set aside, and cast away' all buddhas and sūtras except those of the nembutsu; and the Meditation Master Tao-ch'o declares, 'Nobody has ever attained buddhahood except through the nembutsu.' Your Namu Myōhō Renge Kyō will be an obstacle to our nembutsu, so we will never chant the daimoku even if it means creating evil karma.*

> *Followers of the Zen school all would maintain: "Zen is the supreme Dharma transmitted directly from mind to*

mind, without committing to the writings of all the Buddhist sūtras. For instance, Zen is like the moon in the sky while all the Buddhist sūtras are like a finger pointing at the moon. Ignorant masters such as Grand Master T'ien-t'ai regard the expedient finger as more important than the moon itself. The Lotus Sūtra is a finger while Zen is the moon. After finding the moon, what is the use of the finger?"

When believers of the Buddhist schools thus slander the Lotus Sūtra, how can we induce them to take the excellent medicine of Namu Myoho Renge Kyo? (Ibid, pp. 273-274 adapted)

In the following chapters, I will explain the origins and teachings of each of these four schools. I will then revisit in more detail Nichiren's criticisms of them. In this way, I hope to put Nichiren's four admonitions into the context of his times. By doing this I hope to show why Nichiren singled out these four schools throughout the *Kaimoku-shō*. It must be admitted, however, that to our ears the four admonitions sound very negative and sectarian. However, in reading the record of the Buddha's last days in the Pāli Canon I believe that I have found statements corresponding to the four admonitions in the teachings of the historical Śākyamuni Buddha. According to the *Mahāparinibbāna-sutta* of the *Long Discourses of the Buddha*, the Buddha spent his last year giving final instructions to Ānanda and his other followers to make sure that the Dharma would be taught correctly after his passing. Let's examine them one by one.

On their last teaching tour together, Ānanda noticed how weak the Buddha had become due to old age and illness. He remarked that he was sure the Buddha would make some statement about the Sangha regarding a successor. The Buddha told him that he had no statement to make and that in fact they had already been taught all that they needed to know. He said, "I have taught the Dharma, Ānanda, making no inner and outer: the Tathāgata has no teacher's fist in respect of doctrines." (Walshe, p. 245) By this the Buddha meant that he had held nothing back or concealed in a closed fist. There were to be no secret teachings to be doled out by any successor. There were no further revelations. This basically undercuts the claims of any group that would claim that in order to practice Buddhism one needs not just the

Buddha's teachings but special initiations or empowerments, or to be taught special esoteric rituals. This was the essence of Nichiren's critique of Mantra, or esoteric Buddhism: in the *Lotus Sūtra* we have been taught everything that we need to know, nothing is missing. Through our faith in the *Lotus Sūtra* we are initiated directly into buddhahood and empowered to actualize the qualities of the Buddha's insight and virtue in our daily lives.

The Buddha then said, "Therefore, Ānanda, you should live as islands unto yourselves, being your own refuge, with no one else as your refuge, with the Dharma as an island, with the Dharma as your refuge, with no other refuge." (Ibid, p. 245) Here the Buddha is saying that we will find the Dharma, the true nature of things, within our own lives by putting his teachings into practice for ourselves. It is not something that will be given to us by some external savior. He says nothing here of having to die and be reborn in a pure land. Nichiren believed that to live one's life alienated from the chance to realize the *Lotus Sūtra*'s teaching that this world itself is the true pure land where buddhahood is actualized would in fact lead to a hellish existence. In saying that the practice of nembutsu or calling upon Amitābha Buddha will lead to hell, Nichiren is pointing out that true refuge is found in the Dharma within our own lives here and now.

On his deathbed beneath the Sala trees, the Buddha said, "Ānanda, it may be that you will think: 'The Teacher's instruction has ceased, now we have no teacher!' It should not be seen like this, Ānanda, for what I have taught and explained to you as Dharma and discipline will, at my passing, be your teacher." (Ibid, p. 269-70) According to this account the Buddha did not appoint a successor or patriarch. He believed that the teachings he gave were sufficient guidance. In fact, earlier the Buddha stated that after his passing any teaching put forward as the Dharma, even those by elder monks, should be verified by comparing it to the Buddha's actual discourses. In calling Zen the school of heavenly devils, Nichiren was criticizing what he perceived as the arrogant claims made by some Zen Masters that their own personal enlightenment superseded the Buddha's teachings in the sūtras. The point made is that in Buddhism we have the objective criteria of the sūtras to determine what Buddhism actually teaches and we do not have to rely on middlemen. In fact, in Nichiren Buddhism it is taught that we each inherit the Dharma directly from the scrolls of the *Lotus Sūtra*. This is not to say that we should not seek teachers and mentors for guidance and encouragement, but it means that in the end we cannot go by hearsay. We must discern for ourselves what the Dharma is through our own reading of the sūtras and we must validate the teachings for ourselves through our own practice.

The Buddha also told Ānanda, "If they wish, the Sangha may abolish the minor rules after my passing." (Ibid, p. 270) Unfortunately Ananda was too distraught to ask the Buddha which of the precepts were to be considered minor rules. At the first Buddhist council, it was decided to keep all the precepts in place because a) circumstances had not changed so there was no reason to change anything, b) changing them would cause the householder supporters of the Sangha to accuse them of laxness after the Buddha's passing, c) they could not agree on which precepts could be considered minor. In Nichiren's time the Ritsu or Discipline school championed the practice of all the precepts just as they had been laid down in fourth century BCE India. Nichiren could see that this was no longer appropriate to the time and place, and that such external observance was in any case to miss the true point of Buddhism as taught in the *Lotus Sūtra*. As we can see, the historical Buddha did not want Buddhism to become a religion bound up in the external observance of increasingly irrelevant rules. As Nichiren Buddhists we do not formally take precepts, but we endeavor to live in the spirit of Namu Myōhō Renge Kyō. This is actually a more demanding course than simply following a list of rules. We must be honest with ourselves, attentive to our actual circumstances, and always try to find the best way to bring the spirit of our devotion to the *Lotus Sūtra*'s teaching of universal and immanent buddhahood into our work, family, and other significant relationships, in fact into every aspect of our lives.

To sum up, the Buddha's final admonitions, and Nichiren's four admonitions describe the responsibility and the empowerment of authentic Buddhist practice. We do not seek or require external saviors, or special initiations, or gurus, or external rules. Instead we are empowered by the Dharma itself to find within our lives the Buddha's merits and awakening. This is also a great responsibility as well because it also means that we will have no one to blame but ourselves if we do not look within and live in accord with our true nature as awakened beings. Fortunately, through the practice of Odaimoku we have a simple yet powerful way of reminding ourselves to look to the Wonderful Dharma itself, the Wonderful Dharma of the *Lotus Sūtra* that assures us that not only are we all buddhas-in-the-making, but we are in fact buddhas actualizing buddhahood. Looking nowhere but to our own awakening for awakening is the true meaning of the Buddha's final admonitions and the four admonitions of Nichiren. Here is the continuity between the Buddha's passing, Nichiren's taking up the banner of the Buddha's teaching in the Latter Age, and our own reception of the banner of Namu Myōhō Renge Kyō here and now.

Sources

Gosho Translation Committee, editor-translator. *The Writings of Nichiren Daishonin*. Tokyo: Soka Gakkai, 1999.

_____. *The Writings of Nichiren Daishonin Volume II*. Tokyo: Soka Gakkai, 2006.

Hori, Kyotsu, trans. St. Nichiren's *Rissho Ankoku-ron and Letters and Tracts Concerning It*. Tokyo: Nichiren Shu Overseas Propagation Promotion Association, 1992.

Hori, Kyotsu, comp. *Writings of Nichiren Shonin: Doctrine Volume 2*. Tokyo: Nichiren Shu Overseas Propagation Promotion Association, 2002.

_____. *Writings of Nichiren Shonin: Doctrine Volume 1*. Tokyo: Nichiren Shu Overseas Propagation Promotion Association, 2003.

Murano, Senchu, trans. *Kaimokusho or Liberation from Blindness*. Berkeley: Numata Center for Buddhist Translation and Research, 2000.

Walshe, Maurice, trans. *The Long Discourses of the Buddha: A Translation of the Digha Nikaya*. Boston: Wisdom Publications, 1995.

Chapter 30 – Brief Overview of Pure Land Buddhism

Writings of Nichiren Shōnin Doctrine 2, pp. 37, 53, 57-58, 64, 76-77, 81, 94, 96-98, 101-102, 105-106, 109, 112-114

Kaimoku-shō or Liberation from Blindness, pp. 17, 42, 47, 56, 72, 79, 98, 101-104, 108-109, 114, 120, 123-125

The Writings of Nichiren Daishonin I, pp. 226, 239, 242, 247, 258, 261, 271, 273-275, 277, 280, 283, 286-287

The tradition of Pure Land Buddhism in East Asia that Nichiren refers to throughout the *Kaimoku-shō* was very well known. Nichiren did not have to provide any background but took it for granted that his audience knew what he was talking about. In our case, however, we need to become familiar with the larger context in which Nichiren was writing, starting with the very beginnings of Pure Land Buddhism.

I have previously explained the origins of the Buddhist canon, including the Mahāyāna sūtras. Three Mahāyāna sūtras dealing with Amitābha Buddha (aka Amitāyus) and the Pure Land of the West became known as the three Pure Land sūtras in East Asia where they became the basis of Pure Land piety. These three sūtras are: the *Buddha of Infinite Life Sūtra*, the *Contemplation of the Buddha of Infinite Life Sūtra*, and the *Amitāyus Buddha Sūtra*.

The *Buddha of Infinite Life Sūtra* (aka the *Larger Sukhāvatīvyūha Sūtra*, J. *Muryōju-kyō*) originated in India and was first translated into Chinese in the second century CE. It tells the story of a bodhisattva named Dharma Treasury (S. Dharmākara) who made forty-eight vows to create the best of all pure lands in the western region of the universe beyond all known worlds wherein all beings could attain awakening. In fulfilling his vows he became a buddha known either as Infinite Light (S. Amitābha) or Infinite Life (S. Amitāyus). The eighteenth vow in particular became known in the Pure Land tradition as the Original Vow that expressed his true intention for all beings. The eighteenth vow states:

"If, when I attain buddhahood, sentient beings in the lands of the ten directions, who sincerely and joyfully entrust themselves to me, desire to be born in my land, and call my name even ten times, should not be born there, may I not attain perfect awakening. Excluded, however, are those who commit the five gravest offenses and abuse the Wonderful Dharma." (Inagaki 1995, p. 243 adapted)

Alternatively, the part that is usually translated as "call my name" could be translated as "are mindful of my name." The Japanese term "nembutsu" which refers to the chanting of the name of Amitābha Buddha could mean either "calling on" or "being mindful of the Buddha."

The exclusionary clause in this vow refers to those who "commit the five gravest offenses" which are: (1) killing one's father, (2) or mother, (3) or an arhat, (4) injuring the Buddha (since it is believed that a buddha cannot be murdered), and (5) creating a schism in the Sangha. These five acts are so heinous that one who commits them is said to be reborn in hell immediately upon dying. "Abusing the Wonderful Dharma" refers to the same "Wonderful Dharma" (S. *saddharma*) that also appears in the full title of the *Lotus Sūtra*. Abusing the Wonderful Dharma means to disparage, misrepresent, or neglect the true intent of the Buddha's teachings as expressed, for instance, in the *Lotus Sūtra*. Pure Land Buddhists sometimes claim that this "exclusionary clause" was just a warning and that Amitābha Buddha in fact excludes no one. Nichiren, however, took this passage at its word and pointed out that those who slandered the Dharma would in fact be excluded from rebirth in the Pure Land of the West.

Later on Śākyamuni Buddha, who is relating the story of Amitābha Buddha, states that this teaching will outlast all the others:

"I have expounded this teaching for the sake of sentient beings and enabled you to see Amitāyus and all in his land. Strive to do what you should. After I have passed into nirvāṇa, do not allow doubt to arise. In the future, the Buddhist scriptures and teachings will perish. But,

*out of pity and compassion, I will especially preserve
this sūtra and maintain it in the world for a hundred
years more. Those beings that encounter it will attain
deliverance in accord with their aspiration." (Ibid, p.
312)*

The *Contemplation of the Buddha of Infinite Life Sūtra* (J. *Kammuryōju-kyō*)
was allegedly translated into Chinese from the Sanskrit in the fifth century but
no extant Sanskrit or even Tibetan copy of it has been found. It opens with the
story of Prince Ajātaśatru's palace coup. At the urging of Devadatta who had
ambitions to take over the Sangha, Prince Ajātaśatru imprisoned his father,
King Bimbisāra, and tried to starve him to death. Queen Vaidehī, however,
smuggled food and drink on her person when visiting her husband in the
dungeon and thereby kept him alive. When Ajātaśatru found out about this he
threatened to cut her down himself with his sword but was restrained by one
of his ministers and the physician Jīvaka. Instead, he had her locked away in
the palace. Filled with despair she looked to Vulture Peak and called out for
the Buddha to send his disciples to comfort her with the teaching of the
Dharma. Miraculously, the Buddha appeared himself along with Ānanda and
Mahāmaudgalyāyana. Queen Vaidehī then asked the Buddha what she had
done to deserve such an evil son, and also why was it that the Buddha also
had such an evil cousin as Devadatta. Apparently these questions were taken
as rhetorical because they are not answered in this sūtra (though the Buddha
does discuss his past karmic relations with Devadatta in the *Lotus Sūtra*).
Queen Vaidehī then asks if there is a land where she can be reborn where she
will be free of sorrow and afflictions. The rest of the sūtra is the Buddha's
response as he teaches a total of sixteen subjects for contemplation. The first
thirteen deal with various aspects of the Pure Land of the West and of
Amitābha Buddha and his attendants Avalokiteśvara Bodhisattva and
Mahāsthāmaprāpta Bodhisattva. The last three deal with contemplations
involving those of high, middle or low spiritual capacity and their response to
the saving power of Amitābha Buddha. The power of simply hearing and
saying the name of Amitābha Buddha is especially stressed towards the end of
this sūtra.

The Amitayus Buddha Sūtra (aka the *Smaller Sukhāvatīvyūha Sūtra* J. *Amida-
kyō*) was translated into Chinese by Kumarajiva in the fifth century. In it, the
Buddha expounds on the benefits of calling on the name of Amitābha or

Amitayus and also the advantages of aspiring to birth in the Pure Land of the West.

There are a multitude of pure lands with resident celestial buddhas distributed throughout the universe according to the Mahāyāna sūtras, Amitābha Buddha and his Western Pure Land became the most popular because it was believed that Amitābha Buddha and his pure land manifested all the virtues of all the others. Best of all was the fact that one needs only call upon Amitābha's name to be reborn there. Because these three sūtras in particular emphasized the power of simply calling upon Amitābha Buddha's name, they soon eclipsed all other Pure Land sūtras, including even those about Amitābha Buddha. As we shall soon see, they even threatened to eclipse the rest of the Buddha Dharma altogether.

Pure Land Buddhists in East Asia often point to the great Indian Mahāyāna patriarchs Nāgārjuna (c. 150-250) and Vasubandhu (c. 320-400) as advocates for the practice of Pure Land Buddhism. Nāgārjuna, the founder of the Mādhyamika school of Indian Mahāyāna Buddhism, is credited with writing the *Ten Grounds Sūtra Treatise* (a sūtra which is considered a chapter in the *Flower Garland Sūtra*) in which it is said that there is a difficult way of attaining awakening through self-cultivation and an easy way of attaining awakening by thinking of and calling upon the names of the buddhas of the ten directions. , Devotion to Amitābha Buddha is especially recommended. The practice of keeping in mind and visualizing Amitābha Buddha in this treatise is not based upon the aforementioned three Pure Land sūtras but rather upon another early Mahāyāna sūtra called the *Buddha-encountering Samadhi Sutra* (S. *Pratyutpanna Samādhi Sūtra*), which was translated into Chinese in the second century CE. As we shall see, the *Pratyutpanna Sūtra* would come to have a great influence on Chinese Buddhist practice, but would eventually lose its place to the three Pure Land sūtras within the Pure Land Buddhist tradition.

Vasubandhu, one of the founders of the Indian Yogācāra school of Buddhism, is credited with writing the *Verses on the Vow for Rebirth and the Exposition of the Limitless Life Sutra*, which is also known as the *Pure Land Treatise* when its auto-commentary is included. The *Pure Land Treatise* is a commentary on the The *Buddha of Infinite Life Sūtra* and it emphasizes the visualization of Amitābha Buddha, the merit contained in his name, and the saving power of his eighteenth vow.

In China, the monk Huiyuan (334-416) is regarded as the founder of the Pure Land tradition. According to the traditional account, in the year 402 he gathered together one hundred and twenty-three fellow monks, hermits, and literati together on Mt. Lu and founded the White Lotus Society. The White Lotus Society was dedicated to the practice of the *Pratyutpanna Sūtra*. Their practice consisted of chanting the name of Amitābha Buddha and visualizing the buddha and his Pure Land of the West. They also rigorously observed the precepts and their aim was to retire from the world and aspire to rebirth in the Pure Land. They did not try to spread this teaching among the masses and Huiyuan's group passed away along with its founders. However, it was to serve as an inspiration for later Pure Land practitioners and other groups going by the name of the White Lotus or Lotus Society in later times.

The practice of devotion to Amitābha Buddha also became a part of the Tiantai school from its inception. The founder, Zhiyi (538-597), made Pure Land Buddhism an integral part of his system of meditative practice. Zhiyi's major work, the *Great Calming and Contemplation*, describes four samādhis, which are four kinds of meditation practice: (1) constant sitting, (2) constant walking, (3) half-walking and half-sitting, and (4) neither walking nor sitting. The constant walking meditation practice was based upon the *Pratyutpanna Sūtra*. It consisted of circumambulating a statue of Amitābha Buddha while chanting that Buddha's name and visualizing him.

Pure Land Buddhism quickly became a major feature of just about all forms of Chinese Buddhism. After the persecution of Buddhism by the Emperor Wu in 845, only the Pure Land and Zen schools continued to flourish in China. The Zen school initially held itself aloof from and even criticized Pure Land Buddhism, but in the end Pure Land Buddhism was even incorporated into the Zen school by Zen Masters such as Yongming (904-975) and Zhu Hong (1535-1615).

The Pure Land Buddhism which survived the persecution of 845 and which attained mass appeal throughout East Asia was not, however, the Pure Land Buddhism of the *Pratyutpanna Sūtra* championed by Huiyuan or Zhiyi. Rather, it was the form of Pure Land Buddhism inspired by the three Pure Land sūtras. This form of Pure Land Buddhism deemphasized the visualization of Amitābha Buddha and the Pure Land of the West, and put much greater emphasis on the eighteenth vow, called the Original Vow, and the chanting of the name of Amitābha Buddha to the virtual exclusion of all other practices.

Three teachers of Chinese Pure Land Buddhism in particular should be noted because they provided the major source of inspiration for the Pure Land movement of Hōnen (1133-1212) in Japan. These teachers are Tanluan (476-542), Daochuo (562-645), and Shandao (613-681).

Tanluan started out as a monk in the Four Treatise school of Chinese Mādhyamika Buddhism. When stricken with a grave illness, however, he turned to Taoism in order to discover a way to prolong his life. He then met an Indian monk named Bodhiruci who converted him to Pure Land Buddhism by presenting him with translations of the *Contemplation of the Buddha of Infinite Life Sūtra* and the *Pure Land Treatise* attributed to Vasubandhu. Tanluan subsequently wrote a very influential commentary on Vasubandhu's treatise. In his commentary, Tanluan emphasized the distinction between the easy way and the difficult way of attaining awakening discussed in the *Ten Grounds Sūtra Treatise* attributed to Nāgārjuna, the chanting of the name of Amitābha Buddha as a way of eradicating karmic evil, the importance of the mind of faith, and reliance upon the Other-power of Amitābha Buddha as opposed to reliance upon our own limited self-power. These and other teachings of Tanluan would become important elements in Pure Land Buddhism.

Daochuo considered himself a disciple of Tanluan even though the latter had passed away long before Daochuo was even born. Daochuo was originally a teacher of the *Nirvāna Sūtra*; but at age forty-eight, inspired by Tanluan's teachings and the *Contemplation of the Buddha of Infinite Life Sūtra*, he became a fervent practitioner and popularizer of Pure Land Buddhism. In particular he taught that the Latter Age of Degeneration had already begun (according to his calculations wherein the age of the True Dharma was believed to have lasted only five hundred years) so the difficult Path of Sages was no longer a viable practice for people who should turn instead to the easy Path of Rebirth in the Pure Land.

Shandao was the direct disciple of Tanluan and came to enjoy even greater esteem than his master. He wrote the *Annotations on the Contemplation of the Buddha of Infinite Life Sūtra* that would have an enormous impact on Pure Land Buddhism. Shandao divided all Buddhist practice into those practices that were based upon the three Pure Land sūtras and all those that were not. He termed the former the correct, and the latter the miscellaneous practices.

Shandao then selected the practice of chanting the name of Amitābha Buddha as the practice that would assure rebirth in the Pure Land and referred to four other devotional practices as auxiliary practices. Shandao also expounded the three kinds of faith discussed in the *Contemplation of the Buddha of Infinite Life Sūtra* as essential for rebirth: sincere faith, deep faith, and the faith that aspires to rebirth in the Pure Land. Finally, Shandao provided a very graphic depiction of the way of Pure Land Buddhism in terms of his famous parable of the two rivers and the white path wherein a man chased by bandits (representing the elements of life entangled in suffering) crosses over a white bridge (representing nembutsu practice) over a river of fire and a river of raging waters (representing greed and hatred respectively) in order to cross to the other shore (representing rebirth in the Pure Land). All of these ideas and images would appear prominently in the teachings of the Japanese Pure Land movement begun by Hōnen.

Pure Land Buddhism was a ubiquitous feature of Japanese Buddhism right from the start. The Pure Land Buddhism of the Nara period (710-794) and the Heian period (794-1185) that followed was not the sole practice of reciting the name of Amitābha Buddha nor was it a separate school of Buddhist practice. Rather, as in Chinese Buddhism, nembutsu was a practice utilized by all schools as a form of meditation. The term "nembutsu" in fact means "thinking of the Buddha" and does not exclusively mean the vocal recitation of "Namu Amida Butsu," but includes the various forms of contemplation and visualization associated with Amitābha Buddha. Many Buddhist clergy of all schools and their aristocratic patrons aspired to be reborn in the Pure Land of Amitābha Buddha. Lectures were given on the The *Buddha of Infinite Life Sūtra*, copies of the three Pure Land sūtras and the *Pratyutpanna Sūtra* abounded; and many statues, paintings and mandalas of Amitābha Buddha, his attendants, and the wonders of his Pure Land were made. Many monks and nuns took up the meditative practices of visualizing Amitābha Buddha and the Pure Land, contemplating his wisdom and virtues, as well as keeping his name in mind or even reciting it out loud.

The simple practice of reciting the name of Amitābha Buddha was spread among the common people by wandering holy men like Gyōgi (668-749) and later Kūya (903-972) in spite of laws which forbade the unauthorized propagation of Buddhism outside the aristocracy and the official government sponsored temples, whose sole job was to pray for the peace of the nation. However, even this early popularization of vocal nembutsu was not taught as

361

an exclusive practice, and both Gyōgi and Kūya and others like them were devoted to the study and practice of Buddhism as a whole. They also dedicated themselves to building bridges, digging wells, clearing roads, setting up hospices and other social welfare projects of practical benefit for the people.

Pure Land practice was also given further impetus by the Tendai school. The founder, Saichō (767-822), himself aspired to rebirth in the Pure Land, but it was Ennin (794-864), the third chief priest on Mt. Hiei, who established the Hall for Walking Meditation (J. Jōgyō Zammai-dō) in 849. This hall was dedicated to the practice of the constantly-walking samādhi taught in the *Great Calming and Contemplation* of Zhiyi which featured the chanting of nembutsu as discussed previously. After that, Pure Land devotion became an important part of Tendai Buddhism.

The Tendai monk Genshin (942-1017) made an especially important contribution to the development of Pure Land Buddhism in Japan when he wrote his *Essential Collection Concerning Rebirth in the Pure Land* (J. *Ōjō-yōshū*) in 985. The *Ōjō-yōshū* was a compilation of passages compiled to warn the reader about the sufferings of the six lower worlds (hells, hungry ghosts, animals, fighting demons, humanity, and the heavens). In particular, the book's gruesome descriptions of the torments awaiting wrongdoers in the hell realms was intended to cause people to aspire to rebirth in the Pure Land of Amitābha Buddha. This work became immensely popular in Japan and even gained acclaim in China. However, even though Genshin had been inspired by Shandao, he did not advocate the exclusive practice of vocal nembutsu. In fact, he remained an orthodox Tendai monk who was equally, if not more, devoted to the *Lotus Sūtra* as he was to the Pure Land teachings and practices. In fact, Genshin advocates the simple practice of vocal nembutsu only for those whose capacities are so weak that they are incapable of the more disciplined and rigorous practices of the Tendai school encompassing everything from the specifically Pure Land practice of visualizing Amitābha Buddha to the more general Mahāyāna practice of the six perfections.

This by no means exhausts the many different teachers or approaches to Pure Land Buddhism during the Nara and Heian periods of Japan. Other notable Pure Land practitioners include: Yōkan (1033-1111) of the Three Treatises (J. Sanron) school who wrote a work called the *Ten Reasons for Rebirth in the Pure Land* which emphasized the vocal recitation of nembutsu as a primary practice; Ryōnin (1072-1134) of the Tendai school who developed the "nembutsu of mutual interpenetration" (J. *yūzū nembutsu*) wherein it is taught that the nembutsu contains the merits of all other practices and one person's practice becomes the practice of all; and Kakuban (1095-1143) of the Mantra (J. Shingon) school who provided an esoteric explanation for the nembutsu and set the stage for the later development of the New Doctrine (J. Shingi) school of Mantra in the late thirteenth century. However, none of these earlier teachers ever tried to establish a separate school or argue for the exclusive practice of vocal nembutsu. Nor did the practice of vocal nembutsu ever become the basis of a powerful mass movement outside the purview of the government authorized schools of Buddhism until Hōnen inaugurated his Pure Land movement and wrote the *Collection of Passages on the Nembutsu Chosen in the Original Vow* (J. *Senjaku hongan nembutsu-shū*).

Hōnen, the first of the Kamakuran reformers, was the founder of the Pure Land (J. Jōdo) school. He was born in Mimasaka Province (modern day Okayama Prefecture) as the son of a local samurai. Unfortunately, in the year 1141, the local estate manager for the retired emperor murdered Hōnen's father over a land dispute. Hōnen was only eight years old at the time. It is said that, as he lay dying, Hōnen's father begged Hōnen not to desire revenge or resort to violence but rather to renounce the world and seek awakening instead. It is not known what happened to his mother. What is known is that he went to the local Bodaiji temple to live with his uncle, his mother's younger brother, who was the resident monk there. At age thirteen, in the year 1145, the talented young man was sent to study at Mt. Hiei, where he was ordained as a Tendai monk two years later. In 1150, disillusioned by the worldliness and brutal power struggles of the warrior monks (J. *sōhei*) at Enryakuji, the main temple at Mt. Hiei, he moved to the Kurodani area in the western part of the mountain. In Kurodani he studied with Eikū, a disciple of Ryōnin, and took the name Hōnen. There, except for occasional excursions to study in Kyoto or Nara, he spent the next twenty-five years deeply immersed in the Pure Land teachings and practices that were popular there, especially those of Genshin taught in the *Ōjō-yōshū*. It is said that during this time he read the entire Buddhist canon multiple times (Nichiren says seven) in order to determine the best means of salvation in the Latter Age of the Dharma.

In 1175, at the age of forty-two, Hōnen chanced upon a passage in Shandao's *Annotations on the Contemplation of the Buddha of Infinite Life Sūtra* that he felt clarified everything. The passage asserted that one should simply chant the nembutsu, Namu Amida Butsu, single-mindedly at all times, and that this was the practice that accorded with the original vow, or eighteenth vow, of Amitābha Buddha. This became the inspiration for Hōnen's insistence on the exclusive practice of nembutsu. It was even claimed that Hōnen received confirmation of this new form of Pure Land practice from Shandao himself in a dream. Hōnen soon left Kurodani and moved to the city of Kyoto. He eventually settled in the district known as Ōtani. There he began to teach all who would listen about the exclusive practice of nembutsu that he insisted could save all people in the Latter Age of the Dharma. According to Hōnen, all people, without any qualification except faith in Amitābha Buddha, could become assured of rebirth in the Pure Land. In 1186, Hōnen was given the chance to present and defend his teachings before the leading Buddhist scholars of his day in what is referred to as the Ōhara Debate. From that point on his popularity increased and even many of the aristocracy became his followers, including the Fujiwara Regent, Kujō Kanezane (1148-1207). Though Kanezane was deposed in 1196, he continued to be a powerful patron and defender of Hōnen. Hōnen's major work, the *Senjaku hongan nembutsu-shū*, was supposedly written at his request in 1198.

Not everyone was impressed by Hōnen's teachings. The growing popularity of Hōnen's movement and the excesses of some of his followers particularly distressed the monks of Enryakuji on Mt. Hiei. In 1204 they petitioned Emperor Gotoba (1180-1239) to have Hōnen's exclusive nembutsu movement suppressed. The Tendai monks were especially disturbed by the antinomian tendencies of Hōnen's disciples Gyōkū and Junsai (aka Anraku). Gyōkū had achieved notoriety by teaching that one need only say the nembutsu once in order to be saved, and that any practice beyond that was superfluous. Junsai had the dubious reputation of being the handsomest monk in Japan and was quite popular with the noble ladies of Kyoto. Hōnen and his movement had the sympathy of many at court, so no action was taken against him or his followers at that time. Hōnen himself repudiated the doctrine of "once-calling" and supposedly expelled Gyōkū. He also refuted the idea that by relying on the nembutsu one could continue to indulge in wrongdoing. However, both these ideas seemed to be implied in his teachings on the saving power of even a single recitation of nembutsu. In order to rein in the excesses of some of his disciples, Hōnen had them sign a seven-article pledge. The pledge is interesting in that it reveals the kinds of abuses of the Pure Land teachings that his followers were prone to, such as getting into rancorous disputes with followers of the Mantra and Tendai schools or deriding the precepts. This did not stop the abuses and excesses, however. Nor did it quell the criticisms from the Buddhist establishment.

In 1205 a new petition requesting the suppression of Hōnen and his disciples was presented to Retired Emperor Gotoba (he had retired in the past year) from Kōfukuji Temple. Once again, the imperial court did nothing. Unfortunately, the indiscretion of two of his monks, Jūren and the aforementioned Junsai, brought about a new crisis in 1206. While Retired Emperor Gotaba was away on a pilgrimage to the Kumano shrine, these two monks held an all-night service at the palace at the invitation of some ladies of the court, two of whom were said to have been ordained without permission. It is not certain that anything untoward occurred, but to have monks staying overnight at the palace and ordaining court ladies without any supervision or permission was too much of a scandal to ignore. The enemies of the Pure Land movement finally got their wish in 1207 as the court ordered the execution of Jūren, Junsai, and two other disciples, and the laicization followed by exile of Hōnen and seven of his disciples. Thanks to his influential friends, like the former regent Kujō Kanezane, Hōnen's exile was comparatively mild. He was sent to the province of Tosa on the island of Shikoku and by the end of the year he was pardoned. He was not allowed to return to the capital however, and so he lived just outside Osaka for four years. In 1211 he was allowed to return to Ōtani in Kyoto, where he died the following year in 1212.

In 1212, the very year that Hōnen passed away, his main work, the *Senjaku hongan nembutsu-shū*, was published for the first time. Now the teachers of the established schools of Buddhism were truly outraged, and this time at Hōnen himself. Prior to his death, Hōnen may have had his enemies, but most viewed him as an orthodox Tendai monk with a single-minded focus on vocal nembutsu practice and the desire to share it with as many people as possible. In this sense, he fit the mold of earlier Pure Land popularizers like Gyōgi or Kūya. Aside from that, he continued to uphold the precepts, he was well known as an ordination master, he participated in the rites of esoteric Buddhism, and he even kept a record of his deep meditative experiences and visualizations which were like those taught in Genshin's *Ōjō-yōshū*. With the publication of the *Senjaku-shū*, however, it became clear that the excesses of his disciples might actually have been in accord with the more radical ideas that Hōnen had kept to himself and his inner circle. Even those who had formerly held Hōnen himself in high esteem for his scholarly acumen and personal integrity, though looking askance at the Pure Land movement he had inspired, roundly condemned the *Senjaku-shū*.

The first serious critique of Hōnen was by Kōin (1145-1216) of the Onjōji Temple of the Tendai school. He wrote *Discerning the Meaning of the Pure Land* (J. *Jōdo Ketsugi-shō*) in which he critiqued Hōnen for saying that only the nembutsu could lead to rebirth in the Pure Land. Kōin asserted that the *Lotus Sūtra* led to instant rebirth in the Pure Land and that even the *Contemplation of the Buddha of Infinite Life Sūtra* spoke of attaining rebirth in the Pure Land through the recitation of the Mahāyāna sūtras in addition to the nembutsu. Pure Land hagiographies of Hōnen claim that Hōnen himself convinced Kōin that he was in error, converted him to the Pure Land cause, and that Koin then burned the *Jōdo Ketsugi-shō* himself.

A more substantial critique came from Myōe Kōben (1172-1232) of the Kegon school (the older Nara school of Buddhism based on the *Flower Garland Sūtra*). The very year of the publication of the *Senjaku-shū* he produced *Refuting the Evil Dharma* (J. *Zaijarin*) to refute it, and one year later he wrote *Supplementary Writing to Refuting the Evil Dharma* (J. *Zaijarin Shōgon-kī*). Myōe's critique was reinforced in 1225 in the Tendai monk Jōshō's work *Denouncing the Collection of Passages on the Nembutsu* (J. *Dan Senjaku*). A summary of these critiques is given in *A History of Japanese Religion*:

> *Kōben's main grievances were that Hōnen had ignored the 'aspiration to enlightenment' (bodaishin), which Kōben considered to be fundamental to all Buddhism, and that Hōnen had outrageously compared the Gate of the Holy Path – the Tendai, Shingon, and Kegon sects – to a band of robbers. (The doctrine of the aspiration to enlightenment implies that all living things possess the potential for enlightenment and that they need to arouse and realize that potential.) Kōben also claimed that Hōnen rejected the attainment of enlightenment in this life as a Difficult Practice and insisted that the nembutsu alone was sufficient to ensure rebirth in the Pure Land, there being no need for the aspiration to enlightenment. Yet for Kōben, there could be no Buddhism without the aspiration to enlightenment.*

Kōben described Hōnen as 'chief destroyer of the Law in the present age,' 'the greatest enemy of Buddhism in the three worlds of the past, present, and future,' and 'a great misleader of sentient beings.' In their objections and the vehemence of their rhetoric, the writings of Kōin and Jōshō resembled those of Kōben; together these works fueled the controversy surrounding nembutsu practice and the community of nembutsu believers. (Kasahara 2002, p. 176)

Ryūkan (1148-1227), one of Hōnen's closest disciples, rose to the challenge of countering these refutations. In response to Jōshō's *Dan Senjaku*, he wrote *Revealing the Collection of Passages on the Nembutsu* (J. *Ken Senjaku*). The response of Jōshō and the Tendai school in 1227 was to destroy Hōnen's tomb and burn the wood blocks used to print the *Senjaku-shū*. This was done with the consent of the imperial court. In addition, the court exiled Ryūkan and many other members of the Pure Land movement. Though Ryūkan himself did not advocate it, the court especially wanted to get rid of those disciples of Hōnen who taught the radical doctrine of "once-calling," like Jōkakubō Kōsai (1163-1247).

These refutations and persecutions did not put a stop to Hōnen's Pure Land movement. His disciples continued to spread his teachings and gain sympathizers both among the common people and the nobility, and in time even many of the temples of the established schools, such as the Tendai and Mantra schools, became centers of Pure Land practice and devotion following the teachings of Hōnen.

The mainstream of Hōnen's Pure Land School is considered to be the Chinzei branch of Shōkōbō Benchō (1162-1238). He met Hōnen in Kyoto in 1197 and became his disciple in 1199. From 1204 until his death he propagated Hōnen's teachings in northern Kyushu. Unlike the more radical disciples of Hōnen, Benchō taught that one should continue to chant the nembutsu throughout one's life as opposed to relying on the single recitation of nembutsu, or once-calling. In addition, he taught that it was possible to attain rebirth in the Pure Land through other practices besides the nembutsu in accordance with the other vows of Amitābha Buddha. Because his teaching was not so radical or exclusive, he had an easier time gaining support from the Tendai establishment. He is considered to be the second patriarch of the Pure Land school after Hōnen.

Nen'a Ryōchū (1199-1287) was a Tendai monk who became Benchō's disciple in 1236. He later moved to Kamakura and received the patronage of Hōjō Tsunetoki, the fourth regent, and established the Kōmyōji Temple there in 1243. He is considered the third patriarch of the Pure Land school. Ryōchū and his disciple Gyōbin would later come into conflict with Nichiren in Kamakura. Gyōbin in particular made several accusations against Nichiren to the shogunate that led to Nichiren's near execution at Tatsunokuchi in 1271.

There were many other disciples of Hōnen who also succeeded in spreading his teachings. Zenne Shōkū (1177-1247) is notable for bringing about the acceptance of Hōnen's teaching among the aristocracy in Kyoto and for founding the more Tendai oriented Seizan branch of the Pure Land school. One of his grand disciples was Ippen (1239-1289) the founder of the Timely (J. Ji) school of Pure Land Buddhism that was one of the strongest of the Pure Land schools until the sixteenth century. Shinran (1173-1262), the founder of the True Pure Land school (J. Jōdo Shin-shū), was also a disciple of Hōnen. In fact, he was among those exiled in 1204. From the sixteenth century on the True Pure Land school became the most powerful and influential of all the Pure Land schools and one of the largest of all the schools of Japanese Buddhism to this day.

It should be pointed out, however, that until the time of Shōgei (1340-1420), the seventh successor of Hōnen in the Chinzei branch, the Pure Land school was considered a sub-sect of Tendai and was not able to ordain it's own monks or maintain temples not affiliated with Tendai. From the point of view of Nichiren, the Pure Land movement had not been successfully refuted since its followers abounded and the movement lived on, now hosted by the Tendai and Mantra temples themselves who had gone from critiquing it to accommodating it.

In the Treatise on *Spreading Peace Throughout the Country by Establishing the True Dharma* (J. *Risshō Ankoku-ron*), Nichiren summarizes Hōnen's *Senjaku-shū*, and launches into his own critique of that work. He points out that Hōnen had lumped together all the sūtras, teachings, and practices of Buddhism outside of the three Pure Land sūtras and recommended that they be "abandoned, closed, set aside, and cast away." Nichiren's four-word summary of Hōnen's intent seems to be justified. In the *Senjaku-shū*, Hōnen does indeed say to "reject" and "set aside" the difficult Path of Sages that would include the teaching and practice of the *Lotus Sūtra*; and to "cast aside" and "abandon" all other practices besides nembutsu, which would again include the teaching and practice of the *Lotus Sūtra*. Hōnen also asserts that the Buddha "closed" the gateway to all teachings and practices other than the nembutsu. So it would appear that Hōnen does indeed use the phrases that Nichiren accuses him of using in reference to the entire Buddhist canon and the teachings and practices of Buddhism outside the exclusive practice of nembutsu. In *Risshō Anokoku-ron* and now once more in *Kaimoku-shō*, Nichiren argues that it does not make sense to reject the ultimate teaching of the *Lotus Sūtra* in favor of the provisional teaching of the three Pure Land sūtras.

In the *Kaimoku-shō*, Nichiren points out that Hōnen and the other Pure Land teachers argued that even though the teachings of what they called the "Path of Sages" was profound and worthy of respect they were also beyond the capacity of most people in the Latter Age of the Dharma to understand and put into practice. For instance, in the *Senjaku-shū*, Hōnen argues that, "the ultimate principle is profound while man's understanding is shallow." (Augustine & Tessho 1997, p. 12) He exhorts people to cast aside all other "miscellaneous" practices, and to take up the "exclusive and right practice" of nembutsu. "Why should anyone cast aside the exclusive and right practice, by which a hundred out of a hundred attain rebirth, and stubbornly cling to the miscellaneous practices, by which not even one out of a thousand attain rebirth?" (Ibid, p. 28) Hōnen believed that the nembutsu alone was suited to the capacities of people like himself in the Latter Age. "Hence, one should know that it is because the Pure Land teaching corresponds to the human capacity and the times, that it is now an opportune practice." (Ibid, p. 140) So even if the *Lotus Sūtra* is the more profound teaching and a direct path to buddhahood, it is unable to help people who cannot make sense of it or practice it. Nichiren counters this with a citation from Zhiyi's *Great Calming and Contemplation*, "Those without faith in the *Lotus Sūtra* consider it to be only for sages and to be too difficult for ignorant people like themselves. Those without wisdom become self-conceited considering themselves equal to the Buddha." (Hori 2002, p. 96) In other words, one should have trust and confidence that the *Lotus Sūtra* is for all people and not just for sages. Nichiren then cites Zhanran who said, "Those who would misunderstand the *Lotus Sūtra* perhaps do not know how meritorious acts of beginners can be. They give credence to those of high rank and despise the beginners." (Ibid, p. 97) He then cites Saichō who stated that the Latter Age is precisely the time when the *Lotus Sūtra* would save the people. "It is exactly the time now for all people to be saved by the One Vehicle teaching of the *Lotus Sūtra*." (Ibid, p. 97) Finally, Nichiren even cites Genshin, who had written, "The whole of Japan is ready to believe in the perfect teaching of the *Lotus Sūtra*." (Ibid, p. 97) The point is that the *Lotus Sūtra* is in fact intended precisely for ordinary people in the Latter Age of Degeneration, who will gain incalculable merit as beginners who take faith in the *Lotus Sūtra*. Nichiren dismissed Hōnen's pessimism in regard to people's spiritual capacity, and instead he encouraged all people to have confidence that by taking faith in the *Lotus Sūtra* and practicing the Odaimoku all people in the present age can sow the seed of buddhahood in the depths of their lives and thereby come to realize that the only true pure land is this world wherein buddhahood is a universal possibility and in fact, for those able to perceive it by faith, a present actuality.

Sources

Augustine, Morris & Tessho, Kondo, translators. *Senchaku Hongan Nembutsu Shu: A Collection of Passages on the Nembutsu Chosen in the Original Vow.* USA: Numata Center for Buddhist Translation and Research, 1997.

Ch'en, Kenneth. *Buddhism in China: A Historical Survey.* Princeton: Princeton University Press, 1964.

Coates, Harper H. & Ishizuka, Ryugaku. *Hōnen the Buddhist Saint: His Life and Teachings.* Kyoto: The Society for the Publication of Sacred Books of the World, 1949.

Gosho Translation Committee, editor-translator. *The Writings of Nichiren Daishonin.* Tokyo: Soka Gakkai, 1999.

Hori, Kyotsu, comp. *Writings of Nichiren Shonin: Doctrine Volume 2.* Tokyo: Nichiren Shu Overseas Propagation Promotion Association, 2002.

_____. *Kaimokusho or Liberation from Blindness.* Berkeley: Numata Center for Buddhist Translation and Research, 2000.

Inagaki, Hisao. *The Three Pure Land Sūtras.* Kyoto: Nagata Bunshodo, 1995.

Kasahara, Kazuo. *A History of Japanese Religion.* Tokyo: Kosei Publishing Co., 2002.

Kashiwahara, Yusen & Sonoda, Koyu. *Shapers of Japanese Buddhism.* Tokyo: Kosei Publishing Co., 1994.

Matsunaga, Alicia & Matsunaga, Daigan. F*oundation of Japanese Buddhism Vol. I & II.* Los Angeles: Buddhist Books International, 1988.

Tamura, Yoshiro. *Japanese Buddhism: A Cultural History.* Tokyo: Kosei Publishing Co., 2000.

Williams, Paul. *Mahāyāna Buddhism: The Doctrinal Foundations.* New York: Routledge, 1989.

Wright, Arthur F. *Buddhism in Chinese History*. Stanford: Stanford University Press, 1959.

Chapter 31 – Zen Buddhism in China

Writings of Nichiren Shōnin Doctrine 2, pp. 37, 57-58, 64, 77, 79, 81, 91, 94, 99-102, 109, 112-114

Kaimoku-shō or Liberation from Blindness, pp. 17, 47-48, 56, 72, 75, 79, 93, 98, 106-109, 120, 123-125

The Writings of Nichiren Daishonin I, pp. 226, 242-243, 247, 258, 259, 261, 269, 271, 275-277, 283, 286-287

The name "Zen" is the Japanese pronunciation of the Chinese name of the school, which is "Chan." In turn, "Chan" is short for "*channa*," the Chinese transliteration of the Sanskrit word for "meditative absorption," which is "*dhyāna*." Because "Zen" is the more familiar term, I will continue to use it in reference to this school of Buddhism. Though its name refers to meditative absorption, and silent sitting meditation is its main practice, Zen is more than simply a school valuing meditation above all else. In fact, Zen does not have a monopoly on the practice of silent sitting meditation. Beginning in the second century there were many teachers of meditation who were not considered to be Zen Buddhists in the sectarian sense of the word, and even after the Zen school appeared in China there were Buddhist teachers of meditation who were not Zen Buddhists. What is it that makes Zen Buddhism different? The following verse composed by an anonymous author can perhaps help point to what distinguishes Zen from other schools of East Asian Buddhism:

> *A special transmission outside the scriptures,*
>
> *Not founded upon words and letters;*
>
> *By pointing directly to [one's] mind*
>
> *It lets one see into [one's own true] nature and [thus] attain Buddhahood.*
>
> *(Dumoulin 1994, p. 85)*

This description of Zen in four phrases is attributed to Bodhidharma (c. fifth – sixth century) the legendary first patriarch of Zen in China but they were composed many centuries later. D.T. Suzuki wrote that a Tiantai historian named Zongjian had attributed the verses to the Zen master Nanquan Puyan (748-835) in a history of Buddhism the Tiantai scholar wrote in 1257 (See Suzuki 1949, p. 176). They appear altogether for the first time in the *Garden of Matters from the Patriarch's Hall* (C. *Zuting shiyuan*) compiled in 1108 (See Foulk 1999, p. 265). Not all Zen masters have accepted these verses. Dōgen (1200-1253), the founder of the Sōtō school in Japan, was in fact very critical of them. However, they do provide a good starting point for understanding how the Zen tradition as a whole perceives and presents itself. Earlier, I spoke of a list of twenty-four successors to the Buddha listed in a fifth century Chinese work called the *History of the Transmission of the Dharma Treasury*. This was accepted in the Tiantai and other schools. The Zen school would later add four additional successors to the list making Bodhidharma the twenty-eighth. The earliest extant list appears in the *Baolin Monastery Record* (C. *Baolin zhuan*) compiled in 801 (see Foulk 1999, p. 222). The reason they did this was because Zen teaches that the transmission of the Dharma is necessarily a mind-to-mind transmission that must occur face-to-face. According to Zen, there can be no second or third hand transmission of the Dharma through writings, commentaries, or hearsay. Rather, the Dharma must be realized through a direct perception of the true nature of mind while in a state of meditative absorption united with perfect wisdom, and a previously awakened master must then authenticate that realization in a face-to-face encounter so as to help the disciple root out complacency and self-deception.

The stories and anecdotes that make up the legendary history of Zen can be found in the various collections of *kōans* or "case studies" that were compiled in China during the Song dynasty (960-1279). The story of the beginning of Zen with a non-verbal transmission of the Dharma from Śākyamuni Buddha to Mahākāśyapa can be found in the kōan collection called the *Gateless Gate* (J. *Mumon-kan*; C. *Wumen guan*). The *Gateless Gate* was compiled by the Zen master Wumen Huikai (1183-1260) and published in 1229. The story, however, was based on accounts given in the *Extensive Record of the Lamp* (C. *Tiansheng guandeng lu*) written in 1036 (See Foulk 1999, p. 253). Here is the story as it appears in the *Gateless Gate*:

*When the World Honored One long ago was at a
gathering on Vulture Peak, he held up a flower to
instruct the assembly. At that time, everyone in the
assembly was silent; only the venerable Mahākāśyapa
broke into a faint smile. The World Honored One said, "I
have the collection of the eye of the true dharma, the*

*wonderful mind of nirvāṇa, the subtle dharma gate that
in its true form is formless. Not setting up scriptures, as
a separate transmission apart from the teachings, I pass
it on to Mahākāśyapa." (Foulk 1999, p. 280)*

Here we find a dramatization of the transmission of the Dharma that transcends words and concepts, though of course the tradition of this wordless transmission is itself being passed down through stories and in written works.

According to the legend, the twenty-eighth successor of the Buddha was Bodhidharma about whom not much of any certainty is known. The earliest account of him is by a non-Buddhist named Yang Xuanzhi who claimed to have met him in Luoyang, the capital of the Northern Wei dynasty (386-534), during the height of its glory (sometime between 516-526). According to Yang's Record of the Buddhist Monasteries of Luoyang, Bodhidharma was a Persian who claimed to have been one hundred and fifty years old. Yang says that the old monk was admiring the Yongning Temple at the time of their meeting and that he chanted nembutsu. He says nothing about Bodhidharma being a Zen master. Another early account is a short biography by a former disciple of Bodhidharma named Tanlin (fl. 506-574) that appears as a preface to a short work entitled the *Two Entrances and Four Practices* attributed to Bodhidharma. According to Tanlin, Bodhidharma was the third son of a king in southern India who became a Mahāyāna monk, came to China to teach the true Dharma, had two disciples named Daoyu and Dazu Huike (487-593), and taught a form of meditation called "wall gazing." A century later, Daoxuan (d. 667) incorporated Tanlin's short biography into his *Continued Biographies of Eminent Monks*. According to Daoxuan's version Bodhidharma had been a brahmin before becoming a monk, came to southern China by sea during the reign of the Liu-Song dynasty (420-479), journeyed into north China during the reign of the Northern Wei dynasty, and died at the age of one hundred and fifty (no time or place is given). Another biography, incorporating material from the previous two, appeared in the *Chronicle of the Lankāvatāra Masters* by Jingjue (683-750) written between 713-716. Jingjue's account also posits Bodhidharma as the third son of a south Indian king. In this biography, Bodhidharma handed on the *Lankāvatāra Sūtra* to his disciple Huike telling him, "If you practice according to it, you will naturally be liberated." (Cleary 1986, p. 32) Ironically, it is the *Lankāvatāra Sūtra* that is the source of the expression often used in Zen that sutras are like a finger pointing to the moon of awakening, and that when one sees the moon there is no longer any need to regard the finger. "As the ignorant grasp the finger-tip and not the moon, so those who cling to the letter, know not my truth." (Suzuki 1994, p. 193)

The legend of Bodhidharma as it eventually coalesced by the tenth century is as follows: The twenty-seventh patriarch Prajñātara goes to south India and takes Bodhidharma as his disciple. He transmits the "treasury of the eye of the True Dharma" to Bodhidharma and urges his disciple to go to China. Bodhidharma finally sails to China in 527 and thereupon has a meeting with Emperor Wu (r. 502-549) of the Liang dynasty (502-557). In that meeting, Bodhidharma answered the emperor's questions in accord with the emptiness teachings of the Perfection of Wisdom sūtras, leaving the emperor nonplussed.

> *Emperor Wu of Liang asked the great master Bodhidharma, "What is the highest teaching of the holy truths?" Bodhidharma said, "Empty, without holiness." The Emperor said, "Who is facing me?" Bodhidharma replied, "I don't know." The Emperor did not understand. After this Bodhidharma crossed the Yangtze River and came to the kingdom of Wei. (Cleary 1992, p. 1)*

According to legend, Bodhidharma crossed over the Yangtze River on a reed. He then travels to Mount Song near Luoyang. At Mount Song he meditates for nine years in a cave near the Shaolin Temple and is called the "Wall Gazing Brahmin." He is also credited with teaching Indian martial arts to the monks there. It was during this time that Bodhidharma met Huike, the monk who would become his successor. Bodhidharma at first ignored Huike, until the latter took a rather drastic step to get his attention.

As the founder of Zen faced a wall, his future successor stood in the snow, cut off his arm, and said, "My mind is not yet at peace. Please pacify my mind." The founder said, "Please bring me your mind, and I will pacify it for you." The successor said, "I have looked for my mind, and cannot find it." The founder said, "I have pacified your mind for you." (Cleary 1997, p. 181)

According to the *Blue Cliff Record*, Bodhidharma came into conflict with the Vinaya Master Guangtong and the translator Bodhiruchi because he criticized formalism and the study of scriptures and instead advised practitioners to directly perceive the true nature of the mind. The *Blue Cliff Record* then claims that Guantong and Bodhiruchi tried to poison Bodhidharma six times. The sixth attempt succeeded. Bodhidharma is said to have passed away at the age of one hundred and fifty around the year 532. A legend claims that a Chinese diplomat later met him on the road returning to India wearing only one shoe. Later, when Bodhidharma's reliquary was opened, they found it contained only the other shoe.

The *Two Entrances and Four Practices* attributed to Bodhidharma describe his "wall gazing" form of meditation as the entrance to the Way by principle and furthermore expounds four practices as the entrance to the Way by practice.

The noble enter the Way by many paths, but essentially there are but two of which I speak. One is by principle and one is by practice. Those who enter by principle avail themselves to the teaching of the enlightened doctrine that all beings possess the same true nature, though it is obscured and not apparent due to worldly attachments and delusion. If one forsakes delusion and returns to the true, fixing one's gaze on a wall and forsaking thoughts of self and other, sacred and profane, and so on, then, by not moving and not chasing after scriptures or teachings, one is in accord with principle. [When one undertakes] silent, non-discriminating non-action it is called entering the Way through principle.

Entering by practice entails four essential practices that encompass all others. What four types of practice are these? The first is enduring the result of past actions. The second is the practice of acting according to conditions. The third practice is seeking nothing, and the fourth is known as practicing the Dharma.
(Ferguson 2000, p. 18)

The essay goes on to explain that "enduring the result of past actions" means accepting hardships and suffering as the inevitable fruition of past transgressions; "acting according to conditions" means to face all situations with equanimity; "seeking nothing" is to be content; and "practicing the Dharma" means to recognize the emptiness of all phenomena, which is the perfection of wisdom, and yet to continue to practice the first five perfections out of compassion. There is nothing unprecedented in this essay, nothing that cannot already be found in the Pāli canon or the Mahāyāna sūtras, particularly the Perfection of Wisdom sūtras, or the *Laṅkāvatāra Sūtra* that Bodhidharma is credited with passing on to Huike. As for the unique method of "wall gazing," there is disagreement as to whether this means that one should literally gaze at a wall or if it is just a metaphor for how one should sit still and immobile without making judgments.

In 534, Huike, the second patriarch of Zen in China, went to Yecheng, the capital of the Eastern Wei dynasty (534-550). He taught there until it was conquered by the Northern Chou dynasty (557-581). He hid in the mountains from the persecution of Buddhism during the years 574-577 by Emperor Wu (r. 561-577) of the Northern Zhou. He was able to return to Yecheng in 579. According to Andy Ferguson he spent the last years of his life as a wanderer. "Sometimes he would go to wine houses, sometimes to butcher shops, and sometimes he would mingle in the bustling lanes of the city. He also was found among the ranks of household servants." (Ferguson 2000, p. 22) In 593 a jealous monk reported Huike to the authorities because his lectures on the *Nirvāṇa Sūtra* had been disrupted by Huike's own lecture on the Dharma outside the gate of his temple. The second Zen patriarch was then executed on trumped up charges.

The third patriarch was Jingzhi Sengcan (d. 606) who met Huike when they were both hiding in the mountain from the persecution of Emperor Wu of the

Northern Zhou. Nothing much is known about Sengcan though a teaching poem called *Faith in Mind* was later attributed to him. The poem is all about overcoming attachment and duality. The opening verses are often cited:

> *Attaining the Way is not difficult*
>
> *Just avoid picking and choosing.*
>
> *If you have neither aversion nor desire,*
>
> *You'll thoroughly understand.*
>
> *A hair's breadth difference*
>
> *Is the gap between heaven and earth.*
>
> *(Ibid, p. 461)*

Dayi Daoxin (580-651) met Sengcan in 592 at the age of fourteen and practiced with him for nine years. He received the transmission of the Dharma from Sengcan and became the fourth patriarch. After that, he spent ten years at Great Woods Temple on Mt. Lu and there studied the teachings of the Tiantai and Three Treatises schools and also practiced nembutsu. He later settled down and taught for three decades at the East Mountain Temple on the eastern peak of Mount Shuangfeng. At East Mountain Temple the Zen monks under Daoxin's direction followed the precepts, farmed and performed other chores to maintain the temple, recited and studied not just the *Laṅkāvatāra Sūtra* but also the *Heart Sūtra* and *Diamond Sūtra*, and also incorporated the chanting of nembutsu along with sitting meditation practice.

Niutou Farong (594-657) was one of the disciples of Daoxin, though it is uncertain as to whether he received transmission of the Dharma from him. He later formed his own lineage at Niutou or Ox Head Mountain. Because of that, his lineage came to be known as the Ox Head School of Zen. It did not survive past the tenth century, however Saichō (767-822), the founder of Tendai in Japan, did receive transmission in this lineage of Zen when he was in China.

Daman Hongren (601-674) is the disciple of Daoxin who became the fifth patriarch. He continued to teach at the East Mountain Temple, though he moved its location to Mt. Fengmao. He had many disciples who established lineage of their own, but the two main disciples that we shall be concerned with here were Yuquan Shenxiu (605-706) and Dajian Huineng (638-713). Shenxiu became a disciple of Hongren in 656 and practiced with him until 661. He received the transmission of the Dharma and retired to a hermitage. In 676 he moved to a hermitage near the Yuquan Temple near Luoyang. He attracted many disciples and then the attention and patronage of Empress Wu (624-705) who invited him to teach in the capital in the year 700. Shenxiu was awarded the title "National Teacher" and he greatly contributed to the popularity and prestige of Zen Buddhism, though his own lineage was to be overshadowed by that of Huineng's. He wrote an explanation of the practice of Zen called the *Treatise on the Contemplation of the Mind* (C. *Guanyin lun*; J. *Kanjin-ron*) that shows the influence of Tiantai teachings and makes extensive use of Mahāyāna sūtras and teachings. He is known to have taught the following verses:

> *All Buddha-dharmas come forth fundamentally from mind.*
>
> *If you waste effort seeking it outside,*
>
> *It's like rejecting your father and running away from home.*
>
> *(Ibid, p. 43)*

In 732, a disciple of Huineng named Shenhui (670-762) appeared in Luoyang and began disparaging the lineage of Shenxiu (with whom he had briefly studied before going south to study with Huineng). Shenhui claimed that Huineng and not Shenhui was the true sixth patriarch of Zen. He accused Shenhui and his successors of being primarily interested in imperial patronage. Furthermore, he claimed that the "sudden enlightenment" taught in Huineng's Southern School of Zen were superior to the "gradual enlightenment" approach taught by the Northern School of Shenhui and his successors. Shenhui claimed that there is no need to engage in the kind of expedient practices to subdue and calm the mind advocated by the Northern School. Rather, one should simply and directly realize the true nature of mind as Buddha. Shenhui's unscrupulous polemics caused the authorities to banish him in 753. In 756, after the devastating An Lushan rebellion destroyed the twin capitals of Luoyang and Chang'an, he was recalled to help the government raise money by selling ordination certificates. At that time, he heartily accepted the patronage of the Tang dynasty (618-907). In his own teaching, Shenhui also resorted to skillful means or "expedients" to help those who did not become suddenly enlightened. (See Doumoulin 1994, pp. 330-331), thus making him either a hypocrite or reducing his differences with his rivals to a matter of semantics. In any case, the Northern School suffered greatly from the An Lushan rebellion and disappeared in the ninth century due to the persecution of 845. Shenhui's own lineage did not survive past that persecution either. The result of Shenhui's campaign, however, was that the legend of Huineng, the sixth patriarch of Zen and the teacher of the Southern School of "sudden enlightenment" became known far and wide.

An "autobiography" of Huineng is given in the *Platform Sutra of the Sixth Patriarch*, a work that was compiled towards the end of the eighth century in the form of a record of sermons and teachings of Huineng. According to the *Platform Sutra*, Huineng was an illiterate woodcutter from southern China who sold firewood in the marketplace to support his widowed mother. One day he overheard someone reciting the *Diamond Sūtra*. Huineng says, "Upon hearing it my mind became clear and I was awakened." (Yampolsky 1967, p. 127) Huineng asked the man about where he had studied the *Diamond Sūtra* and learned that Hongren had been giving lectures on it. He then found a way to provide for his mother and left to find Hongren. Upon meeting him, Hongren asked Huineng how he could expect to become a buddha since he was from the less civilized southern region of China. Huineng replied, "Although people from the south and people form the north differ, there is no north or south in buddha-nature. Although my barbarian's body and your body are not the same, what difference is there in buddha-nature?" (Ibid, p. 128) Hongren saw that the young man had talent and sent him to work in the threshing room of the temple. Eight months later, Hongren told the monks of East Mountain Temple that whoever could present him with verses expressing awakening would inherit from him the robe of the Dharma and become the sixth patriarch of Zen. According to the *Platform Sūtra*, Shenxiu was still residing at the temple and though he had no ambition to become the sixth patriarch, he was the head monk and he knew the other monks expected him to write a verse. In addition, he wished to express his understanding so that he could have it tested by Hongren. So he wrote the following verse anonymously on the eastern wall of the south corridor:

Our body is the Bodhi tree,

And our mind a mirror bright.

Carefully we wipe them hour by hour,

And let no dust alight.

(Price 1985, p. 15)

The wall was to have had a scene from the *Laṅkāvatāra Sūtra* painted on it, but when Hongren saw it he dismissed the painter and said, "It would be best to leave this verse here and to have the deluded one's recite it. If they practice in accord with it, they will not fall into the three lower worlds. Those who practice by it will gain great benefit." (Yampolsky 1967, p. 130 modified). Privately, however, he told Shenxiu that he had not yet awakened, though he was close. Later, Huineng learned of these verses and had someone read them to him. He then had that person write verses of his own on the western wall of the south corridor:

There is no Bodhi-tree,

Nor stand of a mirror bright.

Since all is empty,

Where can the dust alight?

(Price 1985, p. 18 adapted)

When Hongren saw these verses, he erased them and then secretly invited Huineng to see him at midnight. That night Hongren taught Huineng the *Diamond Sūtra* and Huineng became fully awakened. Here is what Huineng said of this awakening and what happened next:

"Who would have thought," I said to the Patriarch,
"that the Essence of Mind is intrinsically pure! Who
would have thought that the Essence of Mind is
intrinsically free from becoming or annihilation! Who

would have thought that the Essence of Mind is intrinsically self-sufficient! Who would have thought that the Essence of Mind is intrinsically free from change! Who would have thought that all things are the manifestation of the Essence of Mind!"

Knowing that I had realized the Essence of Mind, the Patriarch said, "For him who does not know his own mind there is no use learning Buddhism. On the other hand, if he knows his own mind and sees intuitively his own nature, he is a Hero, a 'Teacher of gods and men,' 'Buddha'."

Thus to the knowledge of no one, the Dharma was transmitted to me at midnight, and consequently I became the inheritor of the teaching of the 'Sudden' School as well as of the robe and begging bowl.

You are now the Sixth Patriarch," said he. "Take good care of yourself, and deliver as many sentient beings as possible. Spread and preserve the teaching, and don't let it come to an end. Take note of my stanza:

Sentient beings who sow the seed of awakening

In the fields of causation will reap the fruit of buddhahood.

Inanimate objects void of buddha-nature

Sow not and reap not.

He further said, "When the Patriarch Bodhidharma first came to China, most Chinese had no confidence in him, and so this robe was handed down as a testimony from one Patriarch to another. As to the Dharma, this is transmitted from mind to mind, and the recipient must realize it by his own efforts. From time immemorial it has been the practice of one Buddha to pass to his successor the quintessence of the Dharma, and for one Patriarch to transmit to another the esoteric teaching

383

from mind to mind. As the robe may give cause for
dispute, you are the last one to inherit it. Should you
hand it down to your successor, your life will be in
imminent danger. Now leave this place as quickly as you
can, lest someone should do you harm." (Ibid, pp. 18-20
adapted)

Hongren then helped Huineng sneak away from the temple that night.
Huineng returned to the south and according to some accounts lived as a
layperson among hunters and merchants for some sixteen years. He then
reappeared in 676 and finally received ordination as a monk from a master of
the Discipline school named Yinzong (627-713). After that Huineng settled and
taught at Baolin Temple on Mt. Caoxi until his death.

There are several things to note about this story. Huineng is presented as an
illiterate nobody who is not even a monk when he attains awakening and
becomes the sixth patriarch of Zen. This makes the point that anyone can
attain the intuitive insight into the true nature of mind that Zen aims for, it
does not dependent on worldly status or education, and even a layperson can
achieve it. On the other hand, the story and the subsequent teachings of
Huineng in the *Platform Sūtra* is full of references to the sūtras and even
Huineng's first awakening and his more complete awakening later are inspired
by hearing the teaching of the *Diamond Sūtra*. There are also many references
in this work to the *Lankāvatāra Sūtra*, the *Nirvāna Sūtra*, and even the *Lotus
Sūtra*. While the *Platform Sūtra* champions a mind-to-mind transmission, its
teachings do not actually contradict the sūtras and cites them frequently. Also,
eventually Huineng did accept ordination by a monk of the Discipline school.
This shows that while Zen did consider all the traditional trappings and
institutions secondary to direct insight into one's true nature it did not entirely
dispense with them either. Also, it shows that Zen did not yet have a distinct
institutional identity at that time.

In the discourses and teachings that Huineng gives in the rest of the *Platform
Sūtra* he provides a Zen take on traditional Buddhist teachings and practices.
In regard to meditation he stresses the unity of wisdom and concentration. In
regard to the practice of Pure Land Buddhism he stresses that the pure land is
to be found here and now in the purity of our minds. When asked about
Bodhidharma's statement that Emperor Wu had gained no merit from all his

charitable practices, Huineng explains that the impermanent blessings brought about by such wholesome activity is incomparable to the true merit of the Dharma-body realized when one awakens to the true nature. Meeting a haughty monk whose pride is based on his many recitations of the *Lotus Sūtra*, Huineng chides the monk for reciting the sūtra without any understanding of its true meaning. Interestingly, Huineng even teaches that in Buddhism there is no "sudden" or "gradual" except insofar as some people are able to realize the truth more easily than others. This would seem to undercut the sectarian polemics between the Northern School and Southern School, but a story is then told of how Shenxiu sent a monk to Huineng's temple to spy on him and learn about his superior "sudden" method. All in all, the *Platform Sūtra* presents a teaching that is critical of how Buddhism is too often reduced to formalities and external trappings, to pious conduct aimed at worldly benefits or rebirth in a pure land after death, or to rote learning or even mere recitation of the sūtras. In place of these things, it offers a form of Buddhism that is more egalitarian, immediate, earthy, free of unnecessary preliminaries and expedients, able to be inspired by the sūtras without being caught by the surface meaning, and ultimately directed to an intuitive insight into the true nature of one's mind and thus of all reality.

Huineng's Southern School of Zen survived and flourished after the persecution of Buddhism in 845 at the hands of Emperor Wu of the Tang dynasty. There were many prominent teachers after Huineng, but I shall only mention a few here whose contributions to the Zen School explain its later development.

Mazu Daoyi (709-788) was the grand disciple of Huineng. He was an imposing figure and it was he who started the tradition of shouting and striking out with his staff as a means of jolting people into a direct awakening to their true nature. He is known for teaching that "this very mind is buddha mind." (Ferguson 2000, p. 67) His own teacher Nanyue Huairang (677-744) had taught Mazu that sitting in meditation to become a buddha is like trying to polish a tile until it shines like a mirror, in other words it is a wasted effort. Instead, one must not grasp at sitting meditation as a practice to become something other than what one is but should directly know the mind-ground. (See Ibid, pp. 46-47)

Baizhang Huaihai (720-814) was a disciple of Mazu. He is known for establishing a monastic rule specifically for Zen monasteries. At his temple, he had a special hall built where monks could meditate, and during times of rigorous training even sleep and eat. This became a model for Zen monasteries from that point on. Huaihai also made sure that the monks did their own work and raised their own food. In this way, Zen became an independent school with its own self-sufficient monastic life. According to a story, in his old age, Huaihai's disciples hid his work tools so that he would rest. He then retreated to his room and refused to eat until his tools were returned. He told his disciples, "A day without work is a day without eating." In regard to the sūtras, Huaihai taught that an awakened person "knows that all teachings with words are only a reflection of the immediacy of self-nature and are just meant to guide you." (Ibid, p. 79) He also said, "If you don't understand in this manner and just go on chanting the Vedic scriptures, then you're just making matters worse, and moreover you're slandering Buddha." (Ibid, p. 80) By this, Huaihai meant that monks who recite the sūtras without understanding their true meaning are no better than the brahmins who recite the Vedas for blessings.

By the middle of the Tang dynasty there were five prestigious lineages that came to be known as the Five Houses of Zen, all descended from the Southern School of Huineng. The first was the Guiyang established by Huaihai's disciple Guishan Lingyu (771-853) and his disciple Yangshan Huijhi (807-853). This lineage was known for its use of esoteric symbols, especially circles, but it died out in the tenth century. The second was the house of Linii Yixuan (d. 866), a grand disciple of Huaihai. Linji was especially known for shouting at and hitting his disciples. He is also the one who said, "If you meet the Buddha, kill the Buddha." (Schloegl 1976, p. 43) In context, what was meant was that monks should not cling to anything – even sacred images, saints, or family members – in their efforts to realize their own true nature. Linji's house later became a champion of the *kōan* method of Zen practice that I will explain below. It survives to the present day, and most abbots of temples and monasteries in China, Korea, and Vietnam belong to this school. Linji's lineage also came to Japan where it is called Rinzai. Dongshan Liangjie (807-869) and his disciple Caoshan Benji (840-901) established the house of Caodong. This school later became the champion of the "silent illumination" method of practice that will also be described below. The house of Caodong continues to be an important lineage of Zen in Japan, where it is known as Sōtō. Yunmen Wenyan (864-949) established the fourth house. He was renowned for using a single word to answer questions. For instance, "a monk asked, 'What is Tao' Yunmen said, 'Attain.'" (Ferguson 2000, p. 262) This house did not survive past the twelfth century. Fayan Wenyi (885-968) established the fifth, and last house. Fayan drew upon the teachings of the Flower Garland school more than his predecessors, but his disciple Tiantai Deshao (891-972) was more influenced by Tiantai teachings and even helped the Tiantai school restore texts that had been lost by getting new copies from writings that had survived in Korea. Deshao's disciple Yongming Yanshou (904-975) continued this syncretic tradition by promoting the recitation of the *Lotus Sūtra* and nembutsu practice along with Zen meditation (he was considered to also be the sixth patriarch of Pure Land Buddhism in China). Another disciple of Deshao, Daoyuan (n.d.) wrote an important collection of biographies of the Zen masters of the various lineages called the *Transmission of the Lamp* in 1004. The house of Fayan died out during the Song dynasty.

Zen is usually thought of as a form of silent sitting meditation. As Mazu learned, there is more to Zen than just quietly sitting, but it is true that the silent meditation exemplified by the "wall gazing" practice of Bodhidharma when he sat facing the wall of the cave near the Shaolin temple is central to the actual practice of Zen. Hongzhi Zhengjue (1091-1157) of the Caodong house of Zen called this simple unadorned practice "silent illumination." The method (if it can be called a method) of "silent illumination" has been defined as "clear awareness in the tranquility of no-thought." (Chang 1959, p. 47) In other words, the practitioner simply remains upright and attentive in the midst of all things without any attachment or aversion to whatever thoughts, feelings, or sensations may arise and, in this way, realizes and actualizes his or her own true nature.

During the Song dynasty (960-1279) a new method of Zen practice began to be used, especially within the Linji schools by teachers such as Dahui Zonggao (1089-1163). This was the *kōan* (C. *kung-an*) method. A *kung-an* is a "public case" and in Zen usage it refers to the old stories and anecdotes of the Zen patriarchs that are used as subjects for intense contemplation. Oftentimes only a single word or a short phrase from the kōan may be used. Such a word or short phrase is called the *huatou* in Chinese (J. *wato*), which literally means "word's head" and refers to the stillness of the mind before it is disturbed by speech. The point of *kōan* or *huatou* introspection was to get beyond the words to the inner meaning of the story, phrase, or word and directly perceive the true nature of mind. One famous example that is also a *kōan* often given to beginners is this one: A monk asked Zhaozhou, "Does a dog have buddha-nature?" Zhaozhou replies, "No!" In this case, Zhaozhou's "No!" (C. *wu*; J. *mu*) is the *huatou* that becomes the actual subject of contemplation. Before long, collections of these stories were compiled such as the *Blue Cliff Record*, the *Book of Serenity*, and the *Gateless Gate*.

Zen eventually became the dominant tradition of Chinese Buddhism. The warfare and persecution of previous centuries had devastated those schools of Buddhism that relied upon scholarship, large temples, and imperial patronage. Zen survived because its temples and monasteries were in the mountains away from the cities and had become fairly self-sufficient. By the end of the Song dynasty, the abbots of most temples were Zen masters of either the Linji or Caodong houses of Zen. These temples also accommodated the teachings of the earlier schools such as the Flower Garland school or the Tiantai school. They also catered to the practice of Pure Land Buddhism for the common people, though some Zen masters used the nembutsu as a kind of *huatou* practice in its own right. The temples continued to ordain people using the Dharmaguptaka Vinaya of the Discipline school, though Baizhang's rules were also used to organize and regulate the life and routines of Zen monastic life. The primary practice of the Zen monks had become either the *kōan* or *huatou* introspection of the Linji school or the silent illumination of the Caodong, though even the latter utilized *kōans* at times. This eclectic, but ultimately Zen affiliated, form of Buddhism, continues to be the standard form of Buddhism in China, Korea, and Vietnam to this day.

Sources

Broughton, Jeffrey L. *The Bodhidharma Anthology: The Earliest Records of Zen*. Berkeley: University of California Press, 1999.

Chang, Cheng-chi. *The Practice of Zen*. Westport: Greenwood Press, 1978.

Cleary, J.C. *Zen Dawn: Early Zen Texts*. Translated from Tun Huang. Boston: Shambhala, 1986.

Cleary, Thomas. *Unlocking the Zen Koan: A New Translation of the Zen Classic Wumenguan*. Berkeley, North Atlantic Books, 1997.

Cleary, Thomas and Cleary, J.C. *The Blue Cliff Record*. Boston: Shambhala, 1992.

Dumoulin, Heinrich. *Zen Buddhism: A History, Volume I India and China*. New York: MacMillian, 1994.

Ferguson, Andy. *Zen's Chinese Heritage: The Masters and Their Teachings*. Boston: Wisdom Publications, 2000.

Foulk, T. Griffith. "Sung Controversies Concerning 'Separate Transmission' of Ch'an." In *Buddhism in the Sung*. Ed. by Gregory, Peter N. and Getz, Daniel A. Jr. Honolulu: University of Hawai'i Press, 1999.
Gosho Translation Committee, editor-translator. *The Writings of Nichiren Daishonin*. Tokyo: Soka Gakkai, 1999.

Hori, Kyotsu, comp. *Writings of Nichiren Shonin: Doctrine Volume 2*. Tokyo: Nichiren Shu Overseas Propagation Promotion Association, 2002.

Mitchell, Donald W. *Buddhism: Introducing the Buddhist Experience*. New York: Oxford University Press, 2002.

Murano, Senchu. *Kaimokusho or Liberation from Blindness*. Berkeley: Numata Center for Buddhist Translation and Research, 2000.

Price, A.F. and Mou-lam, Wong. *The Diamond Sutra and the Sutra of Hui Neng*. Boston: Shambhala, 1985.

Schloegl, Irmgard. *The Zen Teachings of Rinzai*. Berkeley: Shambhala, 1976.

Suzuki, D.T. *The Lankavatara Sutra: A Mahayana Text*. Taipei: SMC Publishing Inc., 1994.

_____. *Essays in Zen Buddhism*. New York: Grove Press, 1949.

Yampolsky, Philip B. *The Platform Sutra of the Sixth Patriarch*. New York: Columbia University Press, 1967.

Chapter 32 – Establishment of Zen in Japan

Writings of Nichiren Shōnin Doctrine 2, pp. 37, 57-58, 64, 77, 79, 81, 91, 94, 99-102, 109, 112-114

Kaimoku-shō or Liberation from Blindness, pp. 17, 47-48, 56, 72, 75, 79, 93, 98, 106-109, 120, 123-125

The Writings of Nichiren Daishonin I, pp. 226, 242-243, 247, 258, 259, 261, 269, 271, 275-277, 283, 286-287

One the earliest transmissions of Zen teachings to Japan occurred when Saichō (767-822) went to China in 804 to learn more about Tiantai Buddhism. While there, he also received the teachings of the Ox Head School of Zen Buddhism from a monk named Xiuran, who may or may not also have been a disciple of the Zen master Mazu Daoyi (709-788). After only eight and a half months, Saichō returned to Japan in 805 and began the establishment of the Tendai school on Mt. Hiei. Under the umbrella of the Tendai school he propagated a synthesis of teachings and practices called *"enmitsuzenkai."* *"En"* means "Perfect" and refers to the perfect teaching of the *Lotus Sūtra.* *"Mitsu"* means "esoteric" or "secret" and refers to esoteric Buddhism. *"Zen"* refers to the practice of meditation. *"Kai"* means "precepts" and refers to Saichō's concern with the establishment of the Mahāyāna precepts, which at that time Zen was not taught or practiced independently of the *enmitsuzenkai* system.

There were other attempts to establish an independent Zen lineage in Japan, but none of them had any lasting success until the Kamakura period (1185-1336). At that time there was more traffic between Japan and Song China, and Japanese monks traveled to China to learn about Zen, and eventually several Chinese Zen masters came to Japan as they fled the instability caused by the fall of the Song dynasty due to the coming of the Mongols and sometimes at the invitation of the Hōjō regents. By the end of the Kamakura period, both Rinzai (C. Linji) and Sōtō (C. Caodong) forms of Zen Buddhism were established and thriving in Japan. The Hōjō regents and the samurai class as a whole were particularly enamored of Zen as it provided them with a new form of Buddhism that seemed simple and direct and was set apart from the court intrigues of the Tendai and Shingon establishment back in Kyoto.

During the Kamakura period, Zen received its warmest reception among the warrior class – the samurai. According to a popular saying of the time, "Tendai is for the imperial court, Shingon for the nobility, Zen for the warrior class, and Pure Land for the masses. (Doumoulin 1990, p. 31)

One of the first to meet some success in establishing an independent Zen school was the notorious Dainichi Nōnin (12th century), founder of the Daruma Shū or Bodhidharma school. Nōnin was a Tendai monk who had read about Zen and practiced it on his own until he attained an awakening. In 1189, he sent two disciples to China to meet with a Zhuoan Deguang (1121-1203), a Dharma heir of Dahui Zonggao (1080-1163). The disciples showed Deguang a letter expressing his realization. Deguang approved and sent back a certification of Nōnin's enlightenment, a *kesa* (Dharma robe), an inscribed portrait of himself, and a picture of Bodhidharma. The initial success of Nōnin's Daruma Shū aroused the wrath of the jealous Tendai establishment. In 1194, the Tendai school made an appeal to the imperial court to prohibit the Daruma Shū. The court agreed and prohibited it for "being 'incomprehensible' and circulating nonsense." (Matsunaga Vol. II 1988, pp. 187-188) There is a story that his own nephew murdered Nōnin, though there is nothing to substantiate this claim. His disciples, led by Kakuan, continued the Daruma Shū for a time after his death until they dispersed to study with other Zen masters. Nichiren's criticisms of Zen in the *Kaimoku-shō* singles out Dainichi Nōnin, but in fact many of the early Japanese Zen masters such as Eisai (1141-1215) and Dōgen (1200-1253) were also extremely critical of Nōnin. Here is a critique of him by Eisai in his *Treatise on Letting Zen Flourish to Protect the State* (*Kōzen Gokoku-ron*):

Question: Some people falsely call the Zen school the Daruma school (Bodhidharma school) and insist as follows: "We make no practice or any cultivation, for originally being free from self-afflicting passions, one is basically awakened. Therefore, there is no use for any particular precept or practice. There should only be use for lying down. Why should one take the trouble of making such practices as the nembutsu, worshipping the Buddha's relics by making offerings, practicing a longtime observance of taking one meal a day before noon, being moderate in one's consumption of food, and so forth? What do you think about this?"

Answer: That person is to be counted among those who have no wrongs that they would never commit. It is to this kind of person that the holy teachings refer to as a holder of fixed views on emptiness. No one can sit and talk with such a person. One should keep a hundred yojanas' distance away from them. (Tokiwa 2005, p. 118)

Nōnin's naturalism and antinomianism certainly seem to have precedent in the rhetoric of Zen masters like Yongming Yanshou (904-975) whose work, the *Zong jing lu* (J. *Sogyoroku*) was a great influence on Nōnin. Despite having received transmission in the lineage of Rinzai Zen, his Zen seems to have been quite unique to himself. Based on the writings of the Daruma Shū, here is Dumoulin's assessment of Nōnin's form of Zen:

Nōnin did not adopt Ta-hui's form of Zen. His own style came from the Zen meditation practiced in Tendai, which resonates with the early Zen of the Northern school first introduced from China by its founder Saichō. He drew copiously from the Sogyoroku, which was studied zealously on Mt. Hiei. In this way he fused Zen and the teachings of the sūtras (zenkyo itchi). He also incorporated into his doctrine and practice elements of Tendai esotericism (taimitsu). He did not engage in the practice of kōan. The Zen of the Daruma school, as its texts show, distinguished itself in this way from the Rinzai Zen of the Sung period in the line of Ta-hui. (Dumoulin 1990, p. 12)

The aforementioned Eisai was another Tendai monk who made efforts to propagate Zen, though in the end he was not able to establish a school of Zen separate from the *enmitsuzenkai* system. He did, however, prepare the ground for later Zen masters who did succeed in establishing the Rinzai School of Zen in Japan. In 1168, Eisai made his first trip to China and spent less than six months there. He brought back many Tiantai writings with him but also an interest in the teaching and practice of Zen. He was finally able to return to China in 1187. On that trip he was able to learn and practice Zen under the instruction of Xu'an Huaichang (n.d.) of the house of Linji and received transmission. Eisai returned to Japan in 1191 and founded the first Zen temple, Hōonji Temple, the next year. At Hōonji Temple he gave ordinations in accord with the Zen monastic precepts. He found, however, that the animosity of the Tendai monks towards Zen was quite fierce due to Nōnin's Daruma Shū as just discussed. The 1194 prohibition against the Daruma Shū also applied to Eisai's activities as well, though Eisai argued that he had not been trying to create a Zen School separate from the Tendai School. In 1195 he was given a chance to defend his views before the imperial court, probably due to the assistance of his patron, the Fujiwara Regent Kujō Kanezane (1148-1207). In his defense, Eisai explained that what he was teaching was already a legitimate part of Tendai Buddhism.

> *Eisai replied that Zen was nothing new: "Saichō, the*
> *patriarch of the Tendai school, has already taught Zen;*
> *if the Zen school is void, then so is Saichō, and the*
> *Tendai school has no meaning." (Ibid, p. 17)*

The Tendai monks were not convinced by Eisai's explanation because the Rinzai form of Zen taught by Eisai was different than that of the Ox Head Zen that Saichō had brought to Japan. Seeing that he was getting nowhere, Eisai returned to Kyūshū and with the patronage of the shogun Minamoto Yoritomo (1147-1199) he established Shōfukuji Temple in 1195. In 1198 he wrote the *Kōzen gokoku-ron* in order to defend the practice of Zen and recommend it to the country's rulers. This work only further aroused opposition from the monks of Mt. Hiei, so in 1199 Eisai moved to Kamakura. In Kamakura, he received the patronage of Hōjō Masako (1156-1225), the widow of the first shogun Minamoto Yoritomo (1147-1199). She was the daughter of the ruler of the Hōjō clan, Hojo Tokimasa (1138-1215), who became the first regent of the Kamakura shogunate from 1199-1205). She was also the mother of the second and third shoguns Minamoto Yoriie (1182-1204) and Minamoto Sanetomo (1192-1219) who were both murdered. She was also the sister of Hōjō Yoshitoki (1163-1224) who became the second Hōjō regent after Tokimasa was forced to retire. After her husband's death, Masako was ordained as a nun by Gyoyu (1163-1241), a leading disciple of Eisai, but she did not retire from public life, and instead became a negotiator for the shogunate with the imperial court. She established the Jufukuji Temple in Kamakura in 1200 as a memorial for her late husband and his father and made Eisai its founding abbot. At the request of the second shogun Yoriie, Eisai was then invited back to Kyoto in 1202 to establish Kenninji Temple. Both Jufukuji and Kenninji were affiliated with Tendai, as Eisai was not yet able to promote Zen independently of the *enmitsuzenkai* system. Eisai's position in society rose with the help of his Hōjō patrons and in 1206 he was given the job of restoring the Tōdaiji Temple in Kyoto, and a year later was assigned to restore the Hosshōji Temple's pagoda. He completed the latter task in 1213 and began to seek the position of high priest or even the title "great master" from the imperial court. This aroused the opposition of the Tendai monks and many in the imperial court who felt the Eisai was being presumptuous and vain. Others have argued that he sought such titles in order to be in a better position to promote Zen Buddhism. In the end he was only granted the title of provisional high priest. (See Kashiwahara & Sonoda 1994, pp. 84-85) Though Eisai never succeeded in his lifetime in establishing an independent Zen school, he did succeed in gaining support for Zen among the Hōjō regents and in establishing temples that would later become major centers for the teaching and practice of Zen Buddhism. In the *Kōzen Gokoku-ron*, Eisai correctly predicted that Zen would someday flourish in Japan:

> *Turning my thoughts to the future, I am convinced that the principle of the Zen school will never diminish or die out. Fifty years after I leave the world, this school will certainly flourish most vigorously. (Tokiwa 205, p. 190)*

Though he remained fairly obscure during his own lifetime, the efforts of Dōgen to establish a pure Zen School in Japan was more successful in the long term. Dōgen was originally ordained as a Tendai monk in 1213 at Mt. Hiei. He soon became disillusioned with the corruption and spiritual complacency he saw there. He then visited Kenninji in 1214 in hopes of learning about Zen from Eisai. Eisai, however, was too old and too busy managing the Kenninji in Kyoto and Jufukuji in Kamakura, so Dōgen studied with Eisai's successor at Kenninji, Myōzen (1184-1225). Myōzen and Dōgen both hoped to learn more about authentic Zen practice, so in 1223 they both went to China. In China, Dōgen finally met the man he felt was the teacher he had been looking for, Tiantong Rujing (1162-1228), a Zen master of the Caodong (J. Sōtō) lineage. Dōgen returned to Japan in 1227 and taught for a time at Kenninji. Fearing attack by the ever-jealous Tendai establishment, he moved to Fukakusa near Kyoto in 1230. In 1233 he established Kōshō Hōrinji Temple. A monk named Ejō (1198-1280), a grand disciple of Nōnin, joined Dōgen there in 1234 and later became Dōgen's successor. Other members of the Daruma Shū would also join Dōgen over the following years. In 1243, Dōgen wrote *The True Dharma as the Protection of the Nation* (*Gokoku Shōbō Gi*) and submitted it to the court as a defense of his teachings. This aroused the anger of the Tendai monks who accused Dōgen of abandoning the Mahāyāna and teaching the way of the pratyekabuddhas. Dōgen also faced heavy competition from the Rinzai monk Enni Bennen (1202-1280), a grand disciple of Eisai, who had established Tōfukuji Temple near Kōshō Hōrinji in 1243. In the fall of 1243, Dōgen moved again to the estate of a lay follower in Echizen province, deep in the mountains and far from the intrigues of Kyoto and Kamakura. There he established Eiheiji Temple in 1244. In the winter of 1247-1248, Dōgen left for Kamakura at the request of the fifth regent of the Kamakura shogunate, Hōjō Tokiyori (1227-1263) who wished to make him the abbot of a new temple there, but Dōgen declined and returned to Eiheiji. Dōgen passed away in 1253. Today, Dōgen is very well known, and in particular his *Treasury of the Eye of the True Dharma* (*Shōbōgenzō*) is widely studied and praised as one of the great works of Zen literature. In Nichiren's time, however, Dōgen was not widely known. The Sōtō school of Zen that he established did not become popular until the time of Keizan (1268-1325) who established Sōjiji Temple in 1322, also far from Kyoto and Kamakura, and popularized Sōtō Zen by utilizing esoteric practices that were appealing to ordinary people.

Enni Ben'en (1202-1280), Dōgen's competitor on the outskirts of Kyoto, was a Tendai monk who became a disciple of Eichō (d. 1247), who was a disciple of Eisai. In 1235, Ben'en went to China and received transmission from Wuzhun Shifan (1178-1249) of the Rinzai lineage. He returned to Japan in 1241 and in 1243, with the patronage of a member of the prestigious Fujiwara clan, was made the founding abbot of Tōfukuji Temple in Kyoto. The Tōfukuji was not a pure Zen temple, however, but taught the *enmitsuzenkai* tradition of Tendai Buddhism, though Rinzai Zen was emphasized. Tōfuku-ji was completed in 1255. During his time in Kyoto, Ben'en was able to win over the imperial court and even the members of the other schools of Buddhism who ceased their opposition to Zen. He eventually became the tenth abbot of Kenninji. In 1257, Hōjō Tokiyori invited Ben'en to Kamakura to restore monastic discipline at Jufukuji. Enni Ben'en was given the posthumous name Shōichi in 1312. He had many disciples who in turn founded or became the abbots of important Zen temples in Japan who collectively constituted the Shōichi-ha.

Lanxi Daolong (1213-1278) was a Rinzai lineage monk from China who was invited to Japan by Hōjō Tokiyori in 1246. In Japan he was called Rankei Dōryū. He first resided at Jōrakuji Temple in Kamakura, but in 1253 Tokiyori had the Kenchōji Temple built for him. In 1259 he went to Kyoto and became the eleventh abbot of Kenninji. During his tenure at Kenninji he converted the temple from the *enmistuzenkai* tradition to the pure Rinzai Zen as practiced in China. In 1265 he was briefly exiled under suspicion of being a spy for the Mongols, but he was soon returned to favor. Hōjō Tokimune (1251-1284), the eighth regent of the Kamakura shogunate, even began the construction of a new temple, the Engakuji, for Daolong, but the Zen master died before it was completed. He was given the posthumous name Daikaku, and his many disciples in Kamakura constituted the Daikaku-ha.

Due to the efforts of Zen masters like Daolong who came from China at the request of the Hōjō regents, Rinzai Zen was finally successfully transplanted to the cities of Kyoto and Kamakura. By the end of the fourteenth century there were five temples each in Kyoto and Kamakura that would become known as the Five Mountains. The Five Mountains became the head temples of the various Rinzai Zen lineages of Japan. The Five Mountains of Kamakura were Kenchōji, Engakuji, Jufukuji, Jōchiji, and Jōmyoji. The Five Mountains of Kyoto were Tenryūji, Shōkokuji, Kenninji, Tōfukuji, and Manjuji. In the deep mountains of the north, Dōgen's Sōtō Zen was also quietly gaining strength at Eiheiji and Sōjiji. Just as Eisai had predicted, within fifty years of his passing Zen had in fact become established in Japan.

Sources

Dumoulin, Heinrich. *Zen Buddhism: A History, Volume II Japan*. New York: MacMillian, 1990.

Gosho Translation Committee, editor-translator. *The Writings of Nichiren Daishonin.* Tokyo: Soka Gakkai, 1999.
_____. *The Writings of Nichiren Daishonin Volume II*. Tokyo: Soka Gakkai, 2006.

Hori, Kyotsu, comp. *Writings of Nichiren Shonin: Doctrine Volume 2*. Tokyo: Nichiren Shu Overseas Propagation Promotion Association, 2002.

_____. *Writings of Nichiren Shonin: Doctrine Volume 3*. Tokyo: Nichiren Shu Overseas Propagation Promotion Association, 2004.

Kasahara, Kazuo, ed. McCarthy & Sekimori, Gaynor, trans. *A History of Japanese Religion*. Tokyo: Kosei Publishing Company, 2002.

Kashiwahara, Yusen and Sonoda, Koyu. *Shapers of Japanese Buddhism*. Tokyo: Kosei Publishing Company, 1994.

Matsunaga, Alicia & Matsunaga, Daigan. *Foundation of Japanese Buddhism Vol. I & II*. Los Angeles: Buddhist Books International, 1988.

Mitchell, Donald W. *Buddhism: Introducing the Buddhist Experience*. New York: Oxford University Press, 2002.

Murano, Senchu. *Kaimokusho or Liberation from Blindness*. Berkeley: Numata Center for Buddhist Translation and Research, 2000.

Tokiwa, Gishin, trans. *A Treatise on Letting Zen Flourish to Protect the State*. In Zen Texts. Berkeley: Numata Center for Buddhist Translation and Research, 2005.

Chapter 33 – Nichiren's Critique of Zen

Writings of Nichiren Shōnin Doctrine 2, pp. 37, 57-58, 64, 77, 79, 81, 91, 94, 99-102, 109, 112-114

Kaimoku-shō or Liberation from Blindness, pp. 17, 47-48, 56, 72, 75, 79, 93, 98, 106-109, 120, 123-125

The Writings of Nichiren Daishonin I, pp. 226, 242-243, 247, 258, 259, 261, 269, 271, 275-277, 283, 286-287

Nichiren is very critical of Zen, the alleged teaching "outside the scriptures," in the *Kaimoku-shō*. He specifically mentions the infamous self-enlightened Dainichi Nōnin (twelfth century) and the Chinese Rinzai Zen master Shōichi, otherwise known as Lanxi Daolong (1213-1278). Nichiren does not seem to have known of or been concerned with either Dōgen (1200-1253) or Eisai (1141-1215). From Nichiren's perspective, Nōnin was the monk responsible for introducing Zen as an independent school of Buddhism in Japan. Nōnin is even put on a par with Hōnen, insofar as being the founder of a movement that Nichiren believed was to the detriment of the Tendai school and leading people to neglect and even denigrate the *Lotus Sūtra*.

> *During the era of Kennin (1201-1203) two monks named Hōnen and Dainichi emerged to establish the schools of Pure Land and Zen respectively. Hōnen declared that in the Latter Age of Degeneration not even one out of one thousand could obtain Buddhahood by means of the Lotus Sūtra, whereas Dainichi maintained that Zen is the essence of Buddhism transmitted specially outside the written scriptures and verbal preaching. These two false teachings spread all over Japan. (Hori 2002, p. 112)*

Nichiren complains that together with Pure Land, Zen was subverting the Tendai school. "The movement was gradual at first, but in the end even revered high priests all left Tendai for those sects of Zen and Pure Land to strengthen them." (Ibid, p. 37) In surveying the history of Zen in Japan one can see why Nichiren would say this. The Japanese monks who were propagating Zen had originally been Tendai monks. The Kenninji, Tōfukuji and other temples originally established as Tendai temples in the *enmitsuzenkai* tradition were, under the direction of the Hōjō sponsored Zen masters like Daolong, being converted into Rinzai Zen temples. The Hōjō regents like Tokiyori (1227-1263) and Tokimune (1251-1284) were enthusiastic patrons of Zen. They invited more and more Zen masters to come from China, established temples for them, and looked to them for spiritual guidance. This was happening at the same time that many Tendai temples were becoming bastions of Hōnen's exclusive nembutsu movement. Between the popularity of Pure Land Buddhism and the Hōjō support of Zen in both Kamakura and Kyoto, Nichiren could see that the Tendai and Shingon establishment was going to lose its power and prestige, just as the Nara schools had previously lost their power and prestige when the capital was moved to Kyoto and the Tendai and Shingon schools were being newly established. Nichiren mentions repeatedly that the scholar monks of the Tendai and Shingon schools no longer even tried to defend their own teachings from the claims of Zen and Pure Land.

High monks of the Tendai and Shingon schools enjoy high reputation within their respective schools without knowing what their own schools are. Being greedy and afraid of court nobles and warriors in power, they approve and even praise what the Pure Land and Zen schools claim. (Ibid, p. 102)

Scholars of Tendai and Shingon Buddhism are afraid of the Pure Land and Zen followers and try to cater to their whims, just like a dog wagging its tail in front of its master and mice terrified by a cat. Preaching in the service of kings and generals, they themselves speak of what would lead to the destruction of Buddhism and the country. Such scholars of Tendai and Shingon Buddhism will fall into the realm of hungry spirits in this life and the Hell of Incessant Suffering in future lives. (Ibid, pp. 112-113)

What Nichiren found most upsetting about Zen was that its proponents claimed that "truth cannot be expressed in writing and, therefore, the *Lotus Sūtra* is not the truth." (Ibid, p. 64) In *Kaimoku-shō*, Nichiren summarizes his understanding of Zen claims in the following passage:

> *The Lotus Sūtra is a finger pointing to the moon while the Zen School is the moon itself. After grasping the moon there is no need for the finger to point at it. Zen is the heart of the Buddha while the Lotus Sūtra is merely his words. Having finished preaching all the sutras, including the Lotus, the Buddha picked up a bunch of flowers and gave it to Kāśyapa because he alone understood what the Buddha meant. As proof the Buddha entrusted him with his kesa (patchwork robe), which had been handed down through twenty-eight patriarchs of Buddhism in India to six patriarchs of Buddhism in China. (Ibid, pp. 101-102 adapted)*

After reviewing the history and teachings of Zen in China and Japan this would certainly seem to be a fair characterization of how Zen presents itself. The Zen masters would usually not single out the *Lotus Sūtra*, but certainly the *Lotus Sūtra* would also be included among the sūtras that would be considered a "finger pointing to the moon." If Nichiren had ever had any discussions with Zen Buddhists about the comparative merits of the *Lotus Sūtra* and Zen, they may have actually said something like this to him. It is certainly true that the iconoclasm and even rhetorical disdain for the Buddha, the sūtras, and even the Zen patriarchs used by some Zen masters could become quite extreme, such as when Linji (d. 866) told his monks that if they should meet the Buddha they should kill him, or in the following statement by Deshan Xuanjian (819-914):

> *Deshan entered the hall and addressed the monks saying, "I don't hold to some view about the ancestors. Here, there are no patriarchs and no buddhas. Bodhidharma is just an old stinking foreigner. Śākyamuni is a dried piece of excrement. Mañjuśrī and Samantabhadra are dung carriers. What is known as*

'realizing the mystery' is nothing but breaking through to grab an ordinary person's life. 'Bodhi' and 'nirvāṇa' are a donkey's tethering post. The twelve divisions of scriptural canon are devil's texts; just paper for wiping infected skin boils. The four fruitions and the three virtuous states, original mind and the ten grounds, they are just graveyard guarding ghosts. They'll never save you. (Ferguson 2000, p. 199 adapted)

There may be a time and a place where such harsh and disrespectful rhetoric might be an effective skillful means. In the context of monastery life where normally the sūtras are studied and the various daily and seasonal ceremonies are reverently observed, and the Buddhas, lineage founders, and successive teachers are looked upon with faith and gratitude it is very possible that the monastics might become complacent and come to believe that they will attain awakening through their study or piety. In such a context, this kind of rhetoric can shock them out of their complacency so that they will cease clinging to mere ceremony or conceptual learning and strive to realize for themselves the true nature of reality. Outside of the context of serious practice and apart from a competent teacher who knows when to be shocking and when to uphold traditional practices and teachings, this kind of rhetoric becomes an excuse for antinomianism and leads to an utter disregard for the Three Treasures, the teachings of the sūtras, and even the precepts. It is because of this kind of extreme rhetoric that Nichiren states, "The Zen Sect, just like a lowly man with little virtue despising his parents, despises the Buddha and his sūtras." (Hori 2002, p. 77) Even other Zen masters like Dōgen felt that this was going too far and harshly condemned such attitudes, as in the following passage from his essay *Buddhist Sūtras* (*Bukkyō*):

In great Sung [China] today such people sign their names under masters' titles and occupy positions of temple master. Without shame before the past and present, they stupidly make nonsense of the Buddha's truth. It is difficult to permit that the Buddha-Dharma is present in them. Old veterans like these, down to the last person, say: "Buddhist sūtras are not the original intention of the Buddha's truth; the Patriarch's transmission is the original intention. In the Patriarch's transmission the mysterious, the profound, and the fine have been transmitted." Words like these are stupid in the extreme; they are the talk of madmen. There is no mystery in the authentic transmission from the ancestral Master that differs from the Buddhist sūtras, or even from a single word or half a word therein. Both the Buddhist sūtras and the Patriarch's truth have been authentically transmitted and have spread from Śākyamuni Buddha. The Patriarch's transmission has been received only by rightful successors from rightful successors, but how could [rightful successors] not know, how could they not clarify, and how could they not read and recite the Buddhist sūtras? A past Master says, "You deluded yourself with the sūtras. The sūtras do not delude you." There are many stories about past masters reading sūtras. I would like to say to the unreliable as follows: If, as you say, the Buddhist sūtras should be discarded, then the Buddha's mind should be discarded and the Buddha's body should be discarded. If the Buddha's body-mind should be discarded, the Buddha's disciples should be discarded. If the Buddha's disciples should be discarded, the Buddha's truth should be discarded. If the Buddha's truth should be discarded, how could the Patriarch's truth not be discarded? If you discard both the Buddha's truth and the Patriarch's truth, you might become one person with a shaved head among a hundred secular people. Who could deny that you deserved to taste the stick? Not only would you be at the beck and call of kings and their retainers; you might be answerable to Yama-rāja. (Nishijima and Cross Book 3 1997, pp. 110-111)

By the last few lines, Dōgen means that those who say such things are just secular people with shaved heads that will eventually fall into the power of King Yama, the stern judge of the hell realms. Dōgen is quite unequivocal in his condemnation of those who would dismiss the sūtras. In fact, in the essay

Taking Refuge in the Three Treasures (*Kie-Sanbō*), Dōgen particularly singled out the *Lotus Sūtra* for praise.

> *The Lotus Sūtra is the one great purpose of the buddha-tathāgatas. Of all the sūtras preached by the Great Teacher Śākyamuni, the Lotus Sūtra is the great king and is the great teacher. Other sūtras and other Dharmas are all the subjects and the retinue of the Lotus Sūtra. What is preached in the Lotus Sūtra is just the truth; what is preached in other sūras always includes skillful means, which are not the Buddha's fundamental intention. If we evoked preaching contained in other sūtras in order to compare and appraise the Lotus Sūtra, that would be backwards. Without being covered by the influence of the merit of the Lotus Sūtra, other sūtras could not exist. Other sūtras are all waiting to devote themselves to the Lotus Sūtra. (Ibid Book 4, p. 178 modified)*

So it is evident that not all Zen masters would agree with Deshan's apparent dismissal of the sūtras. Dōgen's insistence on the importance of the sūtras even goes against the saying that Zen is a "special transmission outside the scriptures," a saying that Dōgen even described as "fallacious" in his essay *The Buddha's Teachings* (*Bukkyō*) (see Ibid Book 2, p. 57). Dōgen's praise of the *Lotus Sūtra* even sounds very much like something Nichiren might have written. On the other hand, even Dōgen upheld the idea of a one-to-one transmission of the Dharma that guarantees its authenticity and of the supremacy of the practice of Zen meditation over all other practices, as in this passage from *A Talk About Pursuing the Truth* (*Bendōwa*):

> *In the authentic transmission of [our] religion, it is said that this Buddha-Dharma, which has been authentically and directly transmitted one-to-one, is supreme among the supreme. After the initial meeting with a [good] counselor we never again need to burn incense, to do prostrations, to recite Buddha's name, to practice*

> *confession, or to read sūtras. Just sit and get the state*
> *which is free of body and mind. (Ibid Book 1, p. 4)*

Actually, common practices like burning incense, doing prostrations, and the reading of sūtras were done by Dōgen and the monks at Eiheiji, but not for the sake of attaining buddhahood. As Dōgen explains in regard to upholding precepts, such things should be done because that is the lifestyle of Buddhist monks.

> *[You] should maintain the precepts and eating*
> *regulations (one meal a day before noon, etc.). Still, it is*
> *wrong to insist upon them as essential, establishing*
> *them as a practice and expect to be able to gain the*
> *Way by observing them. We follow them just because*
> *they are the activities of Zen monks and the lifestyle of*
> *the Buddha's children. Although keeping them is good,*
> *we should not take them as the primary practice. I don't*
> *mean to say, however, that you should break the*
> *precepts and become self-indulgent. Clinging to such an*
> *attitude is an evil view and not that of a Buddhist*
> *practitioner. We follow the precepts or regulations*
> *simply because they form the standard for a Buddhist*
> *and are the tradition of Zen monasteries. While I was*
> *staying at Chinese monasteries, I met no one who took*
> *them as the primary concern. (Okumura 1998, p. 21)*

Dōgen was particularly critical of practices like the reading of sūtras, trying to attain awakening through conceptual understanding, or the chanting of nembutsu and other pious practices. He saw nothing to be gained by such practices, especially in comparison with the practice of Zen meditation under the guidance of a Zen master who had received the mind-to-mind transmission.

> *Further, do you know for yourself any virtue that is*
> *gained from practices such as reading sūtras and*
> *reciting names of buddhas? It is very unreliable to think*

that only to wag the tongue and raise the voice has the virtue of the Buddha's work. When we compare [such practices] with the Buddha-Dharma, they fade further and further into the distance. Moreover, we open sūtras to clarify the criteria that the Buddha taught of instantaneous and gradual practice, and those who practice according to the teaching are invariably caused to attain the state of real experience. This is completely different from aspiring to the virtue of attainment of bodhi by vainly exhausting the intellect. Trying to arrive at the Buddha's state of truth [only] through action of the mouth, stupidly chanting thousands of tens of thousands of times, is like hoping to reach [the south country of] Etsu by pointing a carriage towards the north. Or it is like trying to put a square peg into a round hole. Reading sentences while remaining ignorant of how to practice [is like] a student of medicine forgetting how to compound medications. What use is that? Those who chant endlessly are like frogs in a spring field, croaking day and night. In the end it is all useless. It is still more difficult for people who are deeply disturbed by fame and gain to abandon these things. The mind that craves gain is very deep, and so it must have been present in the ancient past. How could it not be present in the world today? It is most pitiful. Just remember, when a practitioner directly follows a master who has attained the truth and clarified the mind, and when the practitioner matches that mind and experiences and understands it, and thus receives authentic transmission of the subtle Dharma of the Seven Buddhas, then the exact teaching appears clearly and is received and maintained. This is beyond the comprehension of Dharma-teachers who study words. So stop this doubting and delusion and, following the teaching of a true master, attain in experience the buddha's samādhi of receiving and using the self, by sitting in Zazen and pursuing the truth. (Ibid, pp. 7-8)

406

Dōgen made sure that his community did not discard the sūtras and his understanding of the transmission of the Dharma included the transmission of the sūtras and the maintaining of the precepts and other common practices, but he still insisted that the transmission brought by Bodhidharma (fifth - sixth century) and passed on through the Chinese patriarchs of Zen was more authentic than any other lineages based on the study of the sūtras, or the precepts, or based on devotional practices. Though Dōgen actually argues in *Bendōwa* that the term Zen school is not correct, and that what is being taught is simply authentic Buddhism, it is clear that Dōgen's view is that only in the transmission of the Zen patriarchs will one find authentic Buddhism, and that only Zen meditation is the authentic practice.

Before getting into Nichiren's response to these kinds of claims in the *Kaimoku-shō* and some other writings, I'd like to point out that the tension between those Buddhists dedicated to meditation practices and those who concentrated on keeping, maintaining, learning, understanding, and passing on the teachings of the Buddha can even be found in the Pāli canon. For instance, in the following passage from the *Numbered Discourses* (P. *Anguttara Nikāya*) an elder monk laments the arguments between the meditators and the *Dhamma*-experts (*Dhamma* is the Pali word for Dharma) and advises reconciliation and mutual respect.

> *Thus have I heard. On one occasion the Venerable Mahācunda was dwelling at Sahājāti among the Cetic people. There he addressed the monks thus:*
>
> *"Friends, there are monks who are keen on Dhamma and they disparage those monks who are meditators saying: 'Look at those monks! They think, "We are meditating, we are meditating!" And so they meditate to and meditate fro, meditate up and meditate down! What, then, do they meditate about and why do they meditate?' Thereby neither these monks keen on Dhamma nor the meditators will be pleased, and they will not be practicing for the welfare and happiness of the multitude, for the good of the multitude, for the welfare and happiness of devas and humans.*

"Then, friends, there are meditating monks who disparage the monks who are keen on Dhamma, saying: 'Look at those monks! They think, "We are Dhamma-experts, we are Dhamma experts!" And therefore they are conceited, puffed up and vain; they are talkative and voluble. They are devoid of mindfulness and clear comprehension, and they lack concentration; their thoughts wander and their senses are uncontrolled. What then makes then Dhamma-experts, why and how are they Dhamma-experts?' Thereby neither these meditating monks nor those keen on Dhamma will be pleased, and they will not be practicing for the welfare and happiness of the multitude, for the good of the multitude, for the welfare and happiness of devas and humans.

"There are Dhamma-experts who praise only monks who are also Dhamma-experts but not those who are meditators. And there are meditators who praise only those monks who are also meditators but not those who are Dhamma-experts. Thereby neither of them will be pleased, and they will not be practicing for the welfare and happiness of the multitude, for the good of the multitude, for the welfare and happiness of devas and humans.

"Therefore, friends, you should train yourselves thus: 'Though we ourselves are Dhamma-experts, we will praise also those monks who are meditators.' And why? Such outstanding men are rare in the world who have personal experience of the deathless element (Nibbāna).

"And those other monks, too, should train themselves thus: 'Though we ourselves are meditators, we will praise also those monks who are Dhamma-experts.' And why? Such outstanding persons are rare in the world who can by their wisdom clearly understand such a difficult subject." (Nyanaponika and Bodhi 1999, pp. 163-164)

Nichiren's critique of Zen in the *Kaimoku-shō* actually consists of a series of citations of earlier Tiantai criticisms of Zen. The first citation directed at Zen is from Zhiyi's (538-597) *Great Calming and Contemplation*, "Those without faith in the *Lotus Sūtra* consider it to be only for sages and to be too difficult for ignorant people like themselves. Those without wisdom become self-conceited considering themselves equal to the Buddha." (Hori 2002, p. 96) Nichiren applies the first part of this statement to the Pure Land patriarchs who claimed that the *Lotus Sūtra* was too advanced for the people of the Latter Age of Degeneration. The second half of Zhiyi's statement would seem to apply to those in the Zen school who consider themselves equal to the Buddha and who therefore have no need of the sūtras. We have already seen how even other Zen masters like Dōgen criticized the view that would discard the Buddha, or the Dharma taught in the sūtras.

The next series of citations criticizing Zen are from Zhihyi's *Great Calming and Contemplation* and Zhanran's (711-782) *Supplemental Amplifications on the Great Calming and Contemplation*. Zhiyi, the Tiantai founder, sets out ten things that Buddhist monks should keep in mind when teaching and practicing Buddhism. Roughly these ten are to:

1. Clarify that the principle of the path is the quiescent and inconceivable true nature of reality.
2. Establish the structure and framework of the sūtras, particularly in terms of the eight kinds of teachings that include four types according to content and four according to method.
3. Reconcile seeming contradictions with the four aims of teaching in order to meet people's worldly desires, individual strengths, therapeutic needs, or to directly teach the ultimate truth.
4. Eliminate wrong views and attitudes.
5. Practice in a way that is appropriate to one's ability and without pride.
6. Deeply understand the meaning of the teachings both broadly and deeply.
7. Unfold the meaning of the sūtras gradually with attention to context and in coordination with the meanings in other sūtras.
8. Gradually settle the interpretation of the sūtras in agreement with what they actually say.
9. Make sure to match meanings and connotations when translating sūtras.

10. Fully assimilate the meaning of the sūtras through contemplation.

Zhiyi claims to maintain nine of these practices, with the exception of translation of Buddhist texts, and criticizes those monks who only study but do not practice meditative contemplation on the one hand, and on the other hand criticizes those who only meditate but do not study.

> Except for translation, in nine out of ten ways I am vastly different from those monks in the world who study only the writings or those Zen monks who are concerned with formality. Some Zen monks concentrate on meditation, but their meditation is either shallow or false. They practice none of the remaining nine except for meditation. This is not idle talk. Wise men in the future who have eyes should consider this seriously. (Hori 2002, p. 100)

Zhiyi is making the point that the true practitioner maintains a balance between the study of the Buddha's teachings to inform practice and the putting into practice of the teachings through meditation. In this he is not only saying that those who study the sūtras and those who meditate should have mutual respect, as the Venerable Mahācunda advised, but that a true practitioner will engage in both in order to have authentic practice and understanding. Zhanran clarifies the above passage in his *Supplemental Amplifications*, saying that:

> Monks who study only the writings refer to those who are concerned only with letters but do not engage in introspection of the mind; and Zen monks who are concerned only with formality refer to those who are concerned only with concentration on the nose or lower belly without experiencing the true state of meditation. This is the same as the meditation of brahmins, who will never gain complete freedom from delusions and passions. Tiantai's statement that some Zen monks concentrate only on meditation is an understatement sympathetic to them. In actuality, they lack both

410

*practice in meditation as well as wisdom to understand
the doctrine. Those who practice Zen consider only
meditation important and pay little attention to the
study of doctrines. (Ibid, p. 100 adapted)*

What Zhanran means is that the Zen monks are only practicing "calming" or
"tranquility" (S. *śamatha*, C. *chih*, J. *shi*) meditation that leads to the states of
meditative absorption (S. *dhyāna*, C. *chan*, J. *zen*). He specifically mentions the
techniques of concentrating on the tip of one's nose or the lower belly
(actually the point called the *tanden* in Japanese is an inch and a half below
the navel) as one is breathing that are the very basic forms of "calming" or
"tranquility" meditation taught in Tiantai Buddhism. In and of themselves,
they do not lead to "insight" (S. *vipaśyanā*) or "contemplation" (C. *guan*, J.
kan). Authentic meditation as taught in Tiantai consists of both *śamatha* and
vipaśyanā, both calming and contemplation (C. *zhiguan*, J. *shikan*). To only
practice for the sake of meditative absorption without introspection into the
true nature of mind is to do what the pre-Buddhist brahmins and yogis did,
which was to attain pleasant states of mind that correlated to various
heavenly realms but did not lead to the insight that puts an end to the three
poisons of greed, hatred, and delusion and the cycle of rebirth. From another
passage by Zhiyi (who does not actually provide any names) and its
amplification by Zhanran it is clear that it is Bodhidharma and his followers
who are the Zen masters that are being criticized.

Is this a fair characterization of Zen Buddhism? Does Zen actually ignore the
sūtras and teach a form of meditation that focuses only on attaining
meditative absorption through elementary concentration practices? After
surveying the teachings of the Zen masters from Bodhidharma to Huineng
(638-713) to Dōgen, it would appear that Zen claims to go far beyond any such
preliminary practices to a direct apprehension of the true nature of mind. In
his *Two Entrances and Four Practices* Bodhidharma taught, "If one forsakes
delusion and return to the true, fixing one's gaze on a wall and forsaking
thoughts of self and other, sacred and profane, and so on, then, by not
moving and not chasing after scriptures or teachings, one is in accord with
principle." (Ferguson 2000, p. 18) This would suggest that simply by dropping
all mental preoccupations one immediately comes to know the truth. This
would imply a simultaneous practice of calming and contemplation. Huineng

later explicitly taught that samādhi (concentration) and prajñā (wisdom) are united and that to truly attain the one is to attain the other.

> *"Learned audience, in my system (dhyāna) samādhi and prajñā are fundamental. But do not be under the wrong impression that these two are independent of each other, for they are inseparably united and are not two entities. Samādhi is the quintessence of prajñā while prajñā is the activity of samādhi. At the very moment that we attain prajñā, samādhi is therewith; and vice versa. If you understand this principle, you understand the equilibrium of samādhi and prajñā." (Price and Mou-lam 1985, p. 42)*

The unity of calming and contemplation is not unique to Huineng, for it is taught in the *Nirvāna Sūtra*, "As one practices samādhi on all things abiding in a good samādhi, there is the form of good wisdom. One sees no discrimination between samādhi and wisdom. This is equanimity." (Yamamoto 1973, p. 754) The unity of concentration and wisdom as the optimum method of meditation is of course the basis of the "perfect and sudden" method of "calming and contemplation" in Tiantai Buddhism. Zhiyi taught, "If a person perfects the two dharmas of meditative absorption and wisdom, then this amounts to the complete fulfillment of the dharma of benefiting both oneself and others." (Dharmamitra 1992, p. 31) Despite the rhetoric of the Zen masters about teaching a unique way of meditation, and the accusations of Zhiyi and Zhanran that the Zen masters are doing no more than teaching concentration on the breath, it would seem that both were trying to teach a form of meditation that balances or unifies concentration and wisdom as per the teachings contained in the Mahāyāna sūtras.

Dōgen's instructions for meditation have many similarities with what was taught by Zhiyi. Here is one example:

> *Therefore we should cease the intellectual work of studying sayings and chasing words. We should learn the backward step of turning light and reflecting. Body and mind will naturally fall away, and the original*

*features will manifest themselves before us. If we want
to attain the matter of the ineffable, we should practice
the matter of the ineffable at once. (Nishijima and Cross
1997 Book 1, p. 280)*

Compare that with Zhiyi:

*As for the cultivation of turning, once one has realized
that contemplation itself arises from the mind and once
one has also understood that, if one continues to follow
along with analysis of the objective sphere, this does
not by itself directly bring about convergence with the
original source, one should then turn back the direction
of one's contemplation so that one now contemplates
the very mind that is engaged in contemplation.
(Dharmamitra 2001, p. 43)*

The above description of "turning" is actually only the fifth of "six wondrous
Dharma-gates," taught by Zhiyi, with the sixth being the most direct and
profound, while the first five are of a more preliminary nature.

It is my impression that Zen meditation was either influenced by the teachings
of Zhiyi at some point, or that Zen and Tiantai Buddhism were both drawing
upon a common well of meditative methods and approaches that were being
brought to China from India in the form of instructions found in the sūtras and
practitioners who had personally mastered those techniques. In the case of
the Zen school, Bodhidharma not only gave personalized instruction, but
according to some accounts passed on the *Lankāvatāra Sūtra* as well to
provide further guidance for his disciples. The successive Zen masters also
utilized sūtras such as the *Diamond Sūtra*, the *Śūrangama Sūtra*, the *Perfect
Enlightenment Sūtra*, and others, which Nichiren points out in his *Questions
and Answers Regarding Other Schools* (*Shoshū Mondō-shō*) and *Genealogical
Chart of the Buddha's Lifetime Teachings* (*Ichidai Goji Keizu*). While Zen
obviously relies on personalized instruction and realization over the
conceptual study of the sūtras, it cannot be denied (by either its proponents
or critics) that the Zen tradition as a whole does in fact utilize the sūtras, their
meditation instructions are consistent with what the sūtras teach, and despite

413

their rhetoric to the contrary, many of the Zen masters had formerly been trained in the Discipline, Tiantai, Flower Garland, or other schools and were knowledgeable of and quite able to draw upon the Buddhist canon when needed.

In the case of the Tiantai school, it quite clear that Zhiyi was not trying to set up an academic school, but rather a school that equally valued study and practice, or rather practice informed by study and study put into practice. In addition, the Tiantai school and Nichiren himself were well aware that a superficial or deluded understanding of the sūtras is not sufficient. This is the reason why Nichiren frequently cites the four reliances from the *Nirvāna Sūtra*: "One should rely on the Dharma, and not upon persons; one should rely on the meaning and not upon words; one should rely on wisdom and not upon knowledge; one should rely on the sūtra that completely reveals the truth and not upon sūtras that do not reveal the whole truth." (See Yamamoto 1973, p. 153) What is interesting about the four reliances is that they not only caution against taking the literal words over the deeper meaning, and conceptual knowledge over wisdom, but they also caution practitioners to follow the Dharma (presumably the teachings of the Buddha) over subjective opinions and personality cults, and in following the Dharma one must be sure to discern what teaching contains the all-embracing ultimate intention of the Buddha.

In *Establishing the Right Way of Contemplation* (*Risshō Kanjō*), Nichiren raises concerns about the practice of meditation among his contemporaries in the Tendai Shū that clarifies his specific concerns about Zen Buddhism. He writes:

> *Recently monks of the Tendai school are inclined to appreciate practicing contemplation of the mind, ignoring the valuable teaching expounded in the first and second halves of the Lotus Sūtra, namely the Trace Gate and the Original Gate.*
>
> *Now I ask you. Is their way of practicing contemplation of the mind based on the unique doctrines of "threefold contemplation in a single thought" or the "three thousand realms in a single thought-moment," which the Grand Master Tiantai practiced and experienced for*

himself and expounded in the Great Calming and Contemplation? Or is it the way of contemplation of the Zen school propagated by Grand Master Bodhidharma? If it is the Zen way of contemplation advocated by Grand Master Bodhidharma, I should say it is an unreliable and expedient way based on the Laṅkāvatāra Sūtra and the Śūraṅgama Sūtra expounded before the truth was revealed in the Lotus Sūtra. When the wondrous meditation of the Lotus Sūtra is expounded, that way of Zen should be discarded as expedient, for it is stated, "All expedients should be discarded and the truth will be revealed." If it is the Zen of Grand Master Bodhidharma as founder based on the idea that there is a special transmission other than the teaching expounded by Śākyamuni Buddha, than it is an idea as heretical as that conceived by a heavenly devil. Both are unreliable types of meditation by which one cannot accomplish the way of the Buddha. They should not be adopted. (Hori 2002, pp. 218-219 adapted)

Nichiren presents two alternatives here. Either Zen is based on the teachings of provisional sūtras, or it is a transmission apart from the sūtras. If the former, then Zen is the provisional practice of provisional teachings. As he says in *Kaimoku-shō*, "Compared to the *Lotus Sūtra*, teachings of such schools as Mantra, Zen, Flower Garland, and Three Treatises are expedients leading to the true teaching of the *Lotus Sūtra*. (Ibid, p. 79 modified) If the latter, then it is claiming to be something not found in the Buddha's teachings that are found in the sūtras, though of course the claim is itself based on written records, such as the apocryphal story of Mahākāśyapa smiling when Śākyamuni Buddha held up a flower. For Nichiren, the correct practice of contemplation is that which is directly based upon the teaching of the *Lotus Sūtra*. Nichiren goes on to say in *Risshō Kanjō* that if meditation practice is in fact based upon the "calming and contemplation" practice taught by Zhiyi (specifically referring to the contemplation in a single thought of emptiness, provisional existence, and the Middle Way), then it will not go against the *Lotus Sūtra* but will instead be fulfilled by the *Lotus Sūtra*.

If they claim that their contemplation of mind is based on the "threefold contemplation in a single thought" expounded by Grand Master Tiantai in his Great Calming and Contemplation, they should not be against his intention made clear in his writing regarding what should be discarded and what should be maintained. If their way is based on the way stated in the Great Calming and Contemplation, they should not be against the Lotus Sūtra. Since the Great Calming and Contemplation preaches the way of practicing contemplation of mind according to the doctrine of "three thousand realms in a single thought-moment" in the Lotus Sūtra, the way to practice the "threefold contemplation in a single thought" is nothing but recognizing the Wonderful Dharma to be beyond conceptual understanding. Therefore, the monks who belittle the Lotus Sūtra and make too much of contemplation of mind commit the grave offense of slandering the True Dharma, are men of false view, or are as devilish as a heavenly devil. This is because, according to Grand Master Tiantai's "threefold contemplation in a single thought," "calming and contemplation" means the unique state of mind in which the Lotus Sūtra awakens one to the truth of the One Buddha teaching through steadily maintaining the mind in tranquility. (Ibid, p. 219 adapted)

Nichiren's conviction is that the highest form of meditation is not found in a special transmission confined to an elite lineage of Zen masters or any other select group of people. Rather, it is to be found expressed by Śākyamuni Buddha himself in the *Lotus Sūtra*, but the sūtra's teaching must come alive for us in and through actual contemplation of the Wonderful Dharma, here expressed in terms of the "threefold contemplation in a single thought" and the "three thousand realms in a single thought-moment." This goes beyond any conceptual teaching or otherworldly piety. This points to actual contemplation of the true nature of mind, as Nichiren will write about in more length in *Kanjin Honzon-shō*.

The connection between this kind of contemplation based on the *Lotus Sūtra* and the practice of Odaimoku is stated in the *Treatise on the Ten Chapters* (*Jisshō-shō*):

> *What we should chant all the time as the practice of the perfect teaching is 'Namu Myōhō Renge Kyō,' and what we should keep in mind is the way of meditation based on the truth of 'three thousand realms in a single thought-moment.' Only wise men practice both chanting 'Namu Myōhō Renge Kyō' and meditating on the truth of 'three thousand realms in a single thought-moment.' Lay followers of Japan today should recite only 'Namu Myōhō Renge Kyō.' As the name has the virtue of reaching the body that it represents, when one chants 'Namu Myōhō Renge Kyō,' one will not fail to receive all the merit of the Lotus Sūtra. (Ibid, p. 4 adapted)*

Namu Myōhō Renge Kyō fulfills the same function as calming and contemplation practice in Nichiren's view, as it allows anyone to contemplate the Wonderful Dharma and receive the merit of the Buddha's highest teaching. In Nichiren's time, very few lay people would have had the opportunity to study the Tiantai teachings or had the time to engage in meditation practice. It was very important that a way of practice suitable to ordinary working people be provided if Buddhism was truly to be a Great Vehicle for all beings. Though Nichiren encouraged those who could to practice the Tiantai method of meditation, he clearly saw it as practically superfluous compared to the great merit of chanting Namu Myōhō Renge Kyō, which Nichiren and his disciples and followers found could itself calm the mind and open it to the great insight of the Buddha.

Sources

Dharmamitra, Bhikshu, trans. *The Essentials of Buddhist Meditation*. Seattle: Kalavinka Press, 1992-2008.

_____. *The Six Dharma Gates to the Sublime*. Seattle: Kalavinka Press, 2001-2008.

Dumoulin, Heinrich. *Zen Buddhism: A History, Volume II Japan*. New York: MacMillian, 1990.

Ferguson, Andy. *Zen's Chinese Heritage: The Masters and Their Teachings*. Boston: Wisdom Publications, 2000.

Gosho Translation Committee, editor-translator. *The Writings of Nichiren Daishonin*. Tokyo: Soka Gakkai, 1999.

_____. *The Writings of Nichiren Daishonin Volume II*. Tokyo: Soka Gakkai, 2006.

Hori, Kyotsu, comp. *Writings of Nichiren Shonin: Doctrine Volume 2*. Tokyo: Nichiren Shu Overseas Propagation Promotion Association, 2002.

_____. *Writings of Nichiren Shonin: Doctrine Volume 3*. Tokyo: Nichiren Shu Overseas Propagation Promotion Association, 2004.

Murano, Senchu. *Kaimokusho or Liberation from Blindness*. Berkeley: Numata Center for Buddhist Translation and Research, 2000.

Nishijima, Gudo and Cross, Chodo, trans. *Master Dogen's Shōbōgenzō Books 1-4*. London: Windbell Publications, 1997.

Nyanaponika Thera and Bodhi, Bhikkhu, trans. *Numerical Discourses of the Buddha: An Anthology of Suttas from the Anguttara Nikaya*. Walnut Creek: AltaMira Press, 1999.

Okumura, Shohaku, trans. *Shobogenzo-zuimonki: Saying of Eihei Dōgen Zenji recorded by Koun Ejo*. Tokyo: Soto-shū Shumucho, 1998.

Price, A.F. and Mou-lam, Wong. *The Diamond Sutra and the Sutra of Hui Neng*. Boston: Shambhala, 1985.

Yamamoto, Kosho, trans. *Mahaparinirvana-Sutra: A Complete Translation from the Classical Chinese Language in 3 Volumes*. Tokyo: Karinbunko, 1973.

Chapter 34 – Mantra or Tantric Buddhism from India to Japan

Writings of Nichiren Shōnin Doctrine 2, pp. 34, 36-37, 44, 46, 50-51, 67, 75-81, 84-85, 88-89, 102, 108, 112, 114
Kaimoku-shō or Liberation from Blindness, pp. 13, 16-17, 27, 29, 36-37, 60, 70, 72-77, 83-85, 89-91, 109, 119, 123, 126
The Writings of Nichiren Daishonin I, pp. 224, 225-226, 232, 233, 237-238, 250, 256-261, 263-264, 267-268, 277, 283, 286-287

Throughout the *Kaimoku-shō* Nichiren refers to the Mantra (J. Shingon, C. Zhenyan) school of Buddhism. He accuses those who brought Mantra Buddhism to China from India of misappropriating the teachings of the Tiantai school, and throughout makes critical comments about this form of Buddhism. He does not, however, write a sustained critique of the Mantra school in *Kaimoku-shō*, as he will in later works such as *Selection the Right Time* (*Senji-shō*) or *Essay on Gratitude* (*Hōon-jō*). This does not mean that he considered Mantra Buddhism less of a problem then Zen or Pure Land Buddhism. On the contrary, he seemed to have considered Mantra Buddhism to be the underlying cause for the displacement of the *Lotus Sūtra* in Japanese Buddhism, but he also saw it as a much more difficult school of Buddhism to critique. For one, it was much more strongly entrenched than either the Pure Land or Zen movements. Secondly, Nichiren himself used many of its methods and shared many of its concepts. Finally, Mantra Buddhism had become intertwined with the Tendai school, and Nichiren for a long time held out hope that the Tendai school would listen to his call for reform and he probably did not want to alienate potential allies unless it was necessary. In *A Letter to Lords Toki and Soya* (*Soya Nyūdō-dono Gosho*), Nichiren states that his criticisms of the Zen and Pure Land schools were just a warmup for his criticism of Mantra Buddhism.

> *The false teachings of Buddhism refer to the false opinions regarding the comparative superiority between the Mantra and Lotus schools. The reason for my criticism of the Zen and Pure Land schools is for the*

purpose of clarifying this point. (Hori 2004, p. 195 adapted)

What is Mantra Buddhism? "Zhenyan" in Chinese or "Shingon" in Japanese is a translation of the Sanskrit word *"mantra"* as Mantra Buddhism is the practice of the "mantra path." What then is a mantra? According to Adrian Snodgrass the word mantra means "the thought (*man*) that liberates (*tra*)" or as "a receptacle, a container (*tra*) of thought (*man*)" (Snodgrass 1988, p. 45) As an example, the *Heart Sūtra* ends with the mantra *"Gate gate paragate parasamgate bodhi svaha."* Related to a mantra is a dhāranī. The word dhāranī is synonymous with mantra, though it often refers to a longer formula. Snodgrass says that that dhāranī "means a 'support, that which sustains': it is a support for meditation." (Ibid, p. 44) In the *Lotus Sūtra*, dhāranī are found in both chapters twenty-six and twenty-eight. The word *vidyā* is also synonymous with dhāranī, and it means "knowledge" or "spell," the latter in the sense of mystic knowledge. Mantra Buddhism is the path of using these special incantations (almost always in Sanskrit or transliterations of Sanskrit) as a form of meditative practice and a primary focus of ritual whereby one can attain buddhahood and even worldly goals or "success" (S. *siddhi*).

Mantranaya, the "Mantra Path" or Mantrayāna, the "Mantra Vehicle" is what this early ritualistic and magical form of Buddhism in India was called, and how it came to be known in East Asian Buddhism. It was also given the name "esoteric" or "secret teaching" (J. *mikkyō*). Esoteric Buddhism presents itself as a quicker and more efficient path to buddhahood than the slower path of the six perfections, which is said to take three innumerable eons to complete. Originally the ritual texts of Esoteric Buddhism were called sūtras, but in time they came to be called tantras, and they were contrasted with the sūtras containing doctrine.

> *The Sanskrit word tantra, meaning "warp," was used to refer to texts dealing primarily with ritual practice. In contrast, the sūtras were the woof, setting forth basic religious principles. Because of its emphasis on tantras, later esoteric Buddhism (and sometime esoteric Buddhism in general) is often termed Tantric Buddhism. (Yamasaki 1988, pp. 10-11)*

By the eighth century, Esoteric Buddhism in India was called Vajrayāna, the Vajra Vehicle. "Vajra" is a Sanskrit term for "diamond" or "thunderbolt" or even "adamantine." (See Williams and Tribe 2000, pp. 196-197) The vajra is the weapon of the Vedic thunder god Indra, and also the weapon of a spirit named Vajrapāni who acts as a protector of the Buddha is the Pāli canon.

The use of mantras in Indian religion goes back to the time of the Vedas and the rituals and sacrifices of Brahmanism. Even the Pāli canon contains *parittas* or "protective verses" that are still used today in Theravada Buddhism. By the second or third century mantras and dhāranī were already beginning to appear in Mahāyāna sūtras such as the aforementioned *Heart Sūtra* and the *Lotus Sūtra*. By the fourth century, Mahāyāna Buddhism began to borrow from popular religious practices and from Brahmanism to create a variety of rituals aimed at averting disaster, attracting prosperity, and even subduing enemies. Keishō Tsukamoto explains some of the reason for this:

> *King Aśoka strictly suppressed religious rituals using incantations and magical practices (Rock Edict 9). After the collapse of the Mauryan dynasty, however, Brahmanism was revived under Pushyamitra, and its magical incantatory tendencies increased apace. In the process of forming Hinduism, native beliefs were subsumed into Brahmanic religious ritual, influencing Mahāyāna Buddhism to no small degree. In Mahāyāna scriptures we find a strong, ritualistic, magical, and mystical element. When the western Roman Empire fell in 475, trade with western India stopped, causing the ruin of the Indian monetary economy and bringing about the downfall of the commercial society that patronized Buddhism. This aided the growth of Hinduism, with its base in rural villages; to hold out against Hinduism, Buddhism took on a stronger mystical and ritualistic hue, providing benefits to believers in this life. (Tsukamoto 2007, pp. 389-390)*

Taikō Yamasaki, a Mantra priest and professor of esoteric studies, provides the following description of how early esoteric Buddhism evolved within the Mahāyāna in his book *Shingon: Japanese Esoteric Buddhism*:

Shingon, setting these developments within the framework of Mikkyō history, tends to see Mahāyāna thought as representing an increasingly philosophical, academic superstructure of Buddhism. In contrast, the evolving esoteric sub-stream of Buddhism is understood as representing the concerns of the common people.

Even the sūtras coming out of the priestly academies, however, all dealt with some type of incantation. On the popular level, esoteric texts were increasingly concerned with devotional ritual and magical practices for worldly benefit. Techniques to cause and stop rain, for example, had become an important part of Buddhist ritual by the fourth or fifth centuries. When these two currents of Buddhism, the philosophical and the magical (whose separation is somewhat overstated here), were systematically combined in the seventh century, esoteric Buddhism came into its flowering.

About 320 C.E., King Chandragupta I founded the Gupta dynasty, which would unite northern and southern India. Under this dynasty, Brahmin culture again came to dominate India, beginning the so-called Hindu period. During this period Sanskrit became the common language of Buddhism, which incorporated much Brahmin terminology. The Gupta dynasty supported Hinduism, but did not suppress Buddhism, whose main patrons were merchants and members of the court. Although the Mahāyāna schools continued to develop during this period, they seem to have been active mostly within the confines of their temple compounds.

Esoteric Buddhism seems to have maintained its strong appeal among the populace, and Buddhist ritual continued to be elaborated during the Gupta dynasty.

One sūtra of this period, for example, describes worship rituals to be performed for various Hindu deities in order to fulfill a petitioner's particular wish. It records detailed techniques for establishing a sacred space in which the practitioner invited the deity to manifest himself and receive the offering, methods for constructing altars, techniques for making entreaties to the deities, and rituals for offering incense, flowers, and light to different deities.

From around the time of Chandragupta I, too, esoteric Buddhist ritual texts (giki) were written prescribing the rules and forms of ritual. Modeled after similar texts in Brahmanism, these were related to specific sūtras, whose doctrinal import they expand on in terms of actual practice. Already by the fourth century, therefore, Buddhism had a wealth of magical rituals. As well as the above worship and meditation practices, techniques existed for summoning the powers of particular deities to achieve such purposes as making and stopping rain, healing, and so on.

The fire ritual (Skt., homa; Jap., goma) is another example of Brahmanistic ritual taken into esoteric Buddhism. This practice, adopted whole, appears as a Buddhist form of offering around the third century. Later sūtras describe three types of fire ritual (for averting misfortune, increasing good fortune, and subduing baneful influences), illustrating how it had become established as an important esoteric Buddhist practice. Although the fire ritual's Brahmanistic format remained more or less intact, the practice was given Buddhist symbolic significance. (Yamasaki 1988, pp. 9-10)

The rituals and magical practices of this early period were not very systematic, and their goals were, for the most part, worldly benefits. Starting in the seventeenth century these came to be known in Japan as the "miscellaneous" (J. *zobu*) form of esotericism. The later forms of esotericism that developed in

India were more refined and had the swift attainment of buddhahood as their goal (though worldly benefits were not lost sight of). These were distinguished from the former type as pure (J. *shojun*) esotericism. A more precise five-fold division of Tantric Buddhism was used in India that was carried over into Tibet in a modified form. The five-fold classification divides Tantric Buddhism into Kriyā, Caryā, Yoga, Mahāyoga (or Yogottara), and Yogini (or Yoganiruttara) tantras. In a four-fold Tibetan classification that is more widely known today, Mahāyoga and Yogini are considered the Father Tantra and Mother Tantra subdivisions of a single category called Anuttarayoga. (See Williams and Tribe 2000, pp. 203-204)

In the five-fold classification the early form of esotericism that appeared from as early as the second to as late as the sixth century is called Kriyā, which means "Action." A Kriyā text that came to be highly esteemed in Japanese Tendai Buddhism was the *Act of Perfection Sūtra* (S. *Susiddhikāra-sūtra*) that was translated into Chinese by Śubhakarasiṃha (C. Shanwuwei, 637-735) in 726. In this sūtra, many of the elements of Esoteric Buddhism are already in place. The sūtra not only features the use of mantras, but also mudrās (hand signs) and mandalas (circular platforms that later become painted diagrams). It also describes and explains the Buddhist version of the Vedic fire ritual (J. *goma*), the invocation of deities, initiations or empowerments, and the three purposes of esoteric rites (averting disaster, attracting prosperity, and subduing enemies). The sūtra also states the importance of the ācārya, the teacher of esoteric rites who is to be regarded on the same level as the Three Treasures or as a veritable buddha by his disciples. A disciple of an ācārya is sworn to secrecy and must never discuss any faults of the ācārya. Here we see the roots of what would later become guru-yoga in Tibetan Buddhism, wherein the guru represents the Buddha himself for the disciple. As far as the practice of mantra goes, the sūtra points out that ultimately "recitation is entirely dependent upon the mind." (Giebal 2001, p. 194)

The next type of esotericism to appear was Caryā, which means, "Practice." The *Mahāvairocana Sūtra* that was probably composed in the middle of the seventh century is representative of Cārya tantra. In India, the Mahāvairocana was actually called a tantra. It was translated into Chinese and called a sūtra in 725 by Śubhakarasiṃha and his Chinese disciple Yixing (638-727). This sūtra holds the primary place in Mantra Buddhism. The *Mahāvairocana Sūtra* is basically the instruction of Vairocana Buddha to Vajrapāni the Lord of

Mysteries in regard to the Mahāyāna path of mantra. In response to Vajrapāni's question about the cause, root, and culmination of the Buddha's omniscient knowledge, Vairocana Buddha says, "The mind that aspires to awakening is its cause, contemplation is its root, and skillful means is its culmination. Lord of Mysteries, what is awakening? It means to know one's mind as it really is." (Giebel 2005, p. 6 modified). In the rest of the sūtra, Vairocana explains how to fulfill the cause, root, and culmination of awakening in terms of esoteric practices. This includes such practices as the contemplation of the Sanskrit letter "A," which he states is the essence of all mantras; and deity yoga, wherein the practitioner generates the image of a deity and identifies himself with that deity. The sūtra also sets forth three different types of mandalas: those that use images of the beings composing them, those that use seed-syllables (S. *bīja*) of the beings, and those that use symbolic objects. These are the different types of Womb-realm Mandala that depict Vairocana Buddha at the center of an array of buddhas and bodhisattvas and other deities. In the sūtra, Vairocana Buddha states that all these esoteric practices and forms are of a provisional nature.

> *"The Dharma is free from differentiation and all false conceptions. If one eliminates false conceptions and the workings of the mind and thought, the supreme and perfect awakening that I attained is ultimately like empty space, but unknown to ordinary foolish beings, who are wrongly attached to the objective realm. That they hanker after auspicious times, directions, signs, and so on is because they are enveloped by ignorance, and it is in order to liberate them that they are taught in conformity with them as an expedient." (Ibid, p. 23)*

On the other hand, Vairocana Buddha also says, "If one dwells in this mantra practice, one will most certainly become a buddha." (Ibid, p. 82) Not only that, but Vairocana Buddha goes on to say that the skillful method of mantra practice enables its practitioners to attain all the desire, presumably including buddhahood, in a single lifetime.

> *"Lord of Mysteries, the Tathāgatas of the present [age] and so on in all world-systems, worthy of [worship] and*

perfectly and fully awakened, have mastered the
perfection of skillful means, and although these
Tathāgatas know that all differentiation is originally
empty by nature, by means of the power of the
perfection of skillful means they bring to the fore the
conditioned in the unconditioned. Responding in turn
[to the circumstances of beings], they appear
throughout the Dharma realm for the sake of beings,
causing them to see the Dharma, dwell in happiness,
and generate a joyful mind, or else they obtain long life,
enjoy themselves by disporting among the five desires,
and make offerings to the world honored buddhas. No
worldly people are able to believe the realization of such
a state, but because the Tathāgatas perceive its
purpose, with a joyful mind they teach these procedural
rules for the bodhisattva's path of mantra practice.
Why? [Because] that which cannot be obtained were
one to seek it diligently for immeasurable eons,
cultivating ascetic practices, those bodhisattvas who
practice the path via the gateway of mantras will
achieve in this lifetime." (Ibid, p. 92)

There are some disturbing elements in the *Mahāvairocana Sūtra* that I feel should be pointed out. The *Mahāvairocana Sūtra* on the whole encourages wholesome action and abiding by the precepts, but in chapter eighteen. "Receiving the Code of Training with Skillful Means," the sūtra also advocates the breaking of precepts by bodhisattvas as a form of skillful means. This opens the door to all kinds of rationalizations and antinomian interpretations. For instance, in that chapter there is the following explanation of the precept against taking life:

Then the World-honored One again gazed upon the
realm of beings with eyes of great compassion and
addressed the bodhisattva Vajrapāni, saying, "Lord of
Mysteries, those bodhisattvas keep the precept of not
taking life for as long as they live. They should forsake
the sword and the rod, be free from murderous intent,
and guard the life of another as if it were their own.

427

There is [also] another skillful means: in order to liberate some kinds of beings from retribution for evil deeds in accordance with their deeds, [the taking of life] is [on occasion] carried out, but without thoughts of enmity or animosity." (Ibid, p. 188)

In chapter thirty-one, "Entrustment," a criteria for determining who these teachings should be given to includes such things as the disciple having been born at an auspicious time and a physical description that probably only applies to certain high caste brahmins. (See Ibid, p. 225). I can't help but think that the *Mahāvairocana Sūtra* is an example of Mahāyāna Buddhism not just assimilating elements of Brahmanism but being itself submerged in Brahmin ideas and attitudes that aren't consistent with the Buddha Dharma.

The third type of esotericism to appear was Yoga or the tantra of "Union." The representative text of this class is the *Diamond Peak Sūtra* (S. *Vajraśekhara-sūtra*). The *Diamond Peak Sūtra* was written in South India in the latter half of the seventh century. It is actually a portion of a much larger collection of texts that continued to be written into the eighth century. Vajrabodhi (671-741; C. Jingangji) completed an initial translation into Chinese in 723. His disciple Amoghavajra (705-774; C. Bukong) translated it again in 746, and that is the version used in the Mantra School. The sūtra opens with a description of Vairocana, or Mahāvairocana as he is also called, in terms that equate him with the awakened-mind of all beings. The sūtra then retells the story of Śākyamuni Buddha's attainment of perfect complete awakening in terms of an esoteric initiation in which he is ultimately transformed into Mahāvairocana residing at the center of the Diamond-realm Mandala. The practice of this sūtra puts less emphasis on ritual and worldly aims then earlier esoteric teachings, though they are by no means absent, and more emphasis on an interior contemplative identification with the buddhas and bodhisattvas of the mandala and on the attainment of buddhahood.

After the Yoga tantras, the Mahāyoga (or Yogottara or Father tantras) developed in the late eighth century. The Yogini (or Yoganiruttara or Anuyoga or Mother tantras) developed in the tenth and eleventh centuries. There is also a third category called Non-dual (or Atiyoga) tantras that combines the Father and Mother tantras. These last three types of tantra in Tibetan Buddhism are considered the three sub-divisions of what is called

Anuttarayoga. These tantras shifted the attention from Mahāvairocana Buddha to Akshobhya Buddha, introduced the fierce wrathful forms of the buddhas and bodhisattvas, and also used so called "father-mother" (S. *yab-yum*) images of buddhas in sexual union with female consorts to represent the union of skillful means (represented by the buddha or father) and wisdom (represented by the consort or mother). These later types of tantra were not transmitted into China during the eighth century and so were not transmitted into Japan by Kūkai (744-835) and did not contribute to the teachings or practices of the Mantra school in Japan. Later translators tried to introduce these forms of tantra into China, but they did not catch on. During the Yuan dynasty (1271-1368), the Mongols introduced Tibetan Vajrayana into China. This had a more lasting, though minor, influence on Chinese Buddhism. None of this was of any concern to Nichiren and so will not be dealt with in this commentary.

According to Mantra Buddhism, the transmission of Mantra Buddhism begins with Mahāvairocana Buddha who gave the teachings to Vajrasattva. Vajrasattva is another name for Vajrapāni, the Lord of Mysteries, in the *Mahāvairocana Sūtra*. As an emanation of Mahāvairocana Buddha, Vajrasattva personifies the awakening mind (S. *bodhichitta*) within all beings that aspires to buddhahood. Vajrasattva is sometimes called a bodhisattva, but he is more properly a *vajradhara* or "Vajra-holder," which is to say a tantric practitioner as distinct from those who simply cultivate the six perfections. There is a legend that Vajrasattva then hid inside an iron tower in southern India where he resided until Nāgārjuna (c. 150-250) unlocked the tower and received the transmission of the *Mahāvairocana Sūtra* and the *Diamond Peak Sūtra* from him. Nāgārjuna then became the third patriarch in the transmission of Mantra Buddhism. Nāgārjuna is said to have passed the teachings on to the fourth patriarch Nāgabodhi (n.d.), about whom little is known other than that he had to have been living in the eighth century in order to have been the teacher of Vajrabodhi. So either Nāgārjuna or Nāgabodhi lived hundreds of years according to this story. This part of the transmission is obviously allegory not history.

The fifth patriarch was Vajrabodhi. He was a monk from southern India who studied at the famous Buddhist university of Nālandā in central India. He received transmission of the esoteric teachings from Nāgabodhi in 702. Vajrabodhi later sailed to China and arrived in 720 and spent the rest of his life there translating and propagating Esoteric Buddhism with the help of the

Chinese monk Yixing and another Indian monk named Amoghavajra, who would become the sixth patriarch of True Word Buddhism. Amoghavajra was from Sri Lanka and met Vajrabodhi in China when he was still only a novice (S. *śrāmanera*). He remained with Vajrabodhi until his death in 741. Amoghavajra then returned to Sri Lanka to learn more about Esoteric Buddhism there and in India. According to some version of the story he was also able to study with Nāgabodhi. He returned to China in 746 whereupon he translated the *Diamond Peak Sūtra*. He also transmitted the Mantra teachings to a Chinese monk named Huiguo (746-805), the seventh patriarch. Huiguo in turn transmitted them to the Japanese monk Kūkai (774-835; also known as Kōbō).

An alternate list of Mantra patriarchs leaves out Mahāvairocana Buddha and Vajrasattva Bodhisattva and begins with Nāgārjuna as the first so that the second is Nāgabodhi, the third is Vajrabodhi, and the fourth is Amoghavajra.

The fifth in this system is Śubhakarasiṃha, the sixth is his assistant Yixing, the seventh is again Huiguo, and the eighth is again Kūkai. This list of patriarchs is considered to consist of those who propagated the esoteric teachings in the world.

Śubhakarasiṃha was an Indian prince who had renounced his throne to become a monk. He also studied at Nālandā. He arrived in China in 716 and translated the *Mahāvairocana Sūtra* with his disciple, the Chinese monk Yixing in 725. They also translated the Act of Perfection Sūtra in 726. There were apparently stories circulating about Śubhakarasiṃha that portrayed him as a practitioner of the *Lotus Sūtra*. Nichiren refers to two of these in *Kaimoku-shō*. In one story he discovers a mantra expressing the gist of the *Lotus Sūtra* in an iron tower in southern India. In another, he falls sick and almost dies but recovers when is able to recite the title of the *Lotus Sūtra* and then a passage from chapter two. This story is recounted in more detail in Nichiren's *Treatise on Śubhakarasiṃha* (*Zemmui-shō*).

Yixing had studied the teachings of the Zen, Discipline, and Tiantai schools before being introduced to esoteric Buddhism by Vajrabodhi. He subsequently helped both Vajarabodhi and Śubhakarasiṃha with their work of translating and propagating esoteric Buddhism. He also wrote an important commentary with Śubhakarasiṃha on the *Mahāvairocana Sūtra* in which he incorporated many of the teachings he had learned from the Tiantai school. This was the basis for Nichiren's complaint that the Mantra school has misappropriated the teachings of the Tiantai school to make it appear that the *Mahāvairocana Sūtra* contained the same teachings as the *Lotus Sūtra* but was superior in that it provided for the esoteric practice utilizing mudrās, mantras, and mandalas that the *Lotus Sūtra* did not.

The eighth patriarch on both lists is the Japanese monk Kūkai. Kūkai was born into Japanese nobility. At the age of eighteen he entered the imperial university to study Confucianism in order to prepare for a career as a government official. However, he soon dropped out and become a self-ordained monk. He retreated into the mountains to practice the Morning Star meditation (J. *Kokūzō gumonji no hō*) that involved the recitation of the mantra of Space Store Bodhisattva (S. Ākāśagarbha; J. Kokūzō). This was based on an esoteric manual that had been translated in 717 by Śubhakarasiṃha and had been brought to Japan in 718 by the Japanese monk Dōji (d. 744). This practice was intended to help one memorize and understand the Buddhist sūtras, and was later practiced by Nichiren during his youthful studies at Seichōji. It was this practice that apparently whetted the appetite of the young Kūkai for esoteric Buddhism. He found, however, that while the *Mahāvairocana Sūtra* had been brought to Japan, there was no one who could explain how to put its teachings into practice. Kūkai then determined to go to China to find a master who could teach him. Somehow (probably through family connections) he was able to get officially ordained and assigned to travel to China as part of an official delegation in 804. One of the other members of that delegation was Saichō (767-822; also known as Dengyō), the future founder of the Tendai school. In the capital of Chang'an he met Huiguo and became his disciple. Huiguo was apparently very impressed by Kūkai and transmitted to him the practices relating to both the Womb-realm Mandala and the Diamond-realm Mandala. Though Huiguo died in the twelfth month of 805, Kūkai was able to study with other teachers of esoteric Buddhism in China, such as Prajñā (734-819) and he collected many texts and ritual implements. Kūkai returned to Japan in 806 to begin propagating the teachings and practices of Mantra Buddhism. Kūkai received the patronage and friendship of Emperor Saga (r. 809-823). His base of operations was Takaosanji Temple in the suburbs of Kyoto where he stayed until 823, but from 810-813 he was appointed the administrative head of the prestigious Tōdaiji Temple in Nara.

Something should also be said about the relationship between Saichō and Kūkai during this time. They may have first met when they were traveling to China together in 804, but others say they only met later back in Japan in 809 or 810. For many years Saichō and Kūkai were friends. When he had returned to Japan, Saichō had even performed esoteric initiations at the request of the imperial court in 805 and he was eager to learn more about esoteric Buddhism. In 809, Kūkai had gone to Mt. Hiei to learn about the Tiantai teachings from Saichō. In turn, Saichō borrowed texts from Kūkai and even received esoteric initiations (S. *abhishekha*) into the practices of the Womb-realm Mandala and Diamond-realm Mandala from him in 812 at the Takaosanji. Unfortunately, their relationship soured in later years, as one of Saichō's disciples defected to the Mantra school and Kūkai refused to lend texts he had requested and insisted that Saichō become his disciple if he wished to study Mantra teachings. They also had fundamental disagreements over the relative importance of the *Lotus Sūtra* and esoteric Buddhism. Not surprisingly, Kūkai compared the *Lotus Sūtra* and Tiantai teachings unfavorably with the Mantra sūtras, teachings, and practices. By 816, the two monks were no longer corresponding with each other.

The esoteric initiations performed by Kūkai at Takaosanji in 812 for Saichō and almost two hundred leading monks and nobles of Nara established Kūkai as the master of esoteric Buddhism in Japan. In 816, Kūkai requested and was granted permission to establish a training center on Mt. Kōya. Actual construction did not begin until 819 and it would not be completed until after Kūkai's death. In 823, Kūkai was appointed the head of Tōji Temple in the new imperial capital of Kyoto that was still under construction. Up until that time, the temples in the capital did not belong to a single school of Buddhism, but the Tōji became the headquarters of Mantra Buddhism during Kūkai's lifetime. When Emperor Saga retired, Kūkai continued to receive the patronage of the two subsequent emperors. Unlike Saichō, Kūkai also became popular among the monks of the other schools of Nara Buddhism and he rose high in the ranks of the state-controlled Buddhist bureaucracy. In 834 he was given permission to establish a chapel in the imperial palace where esoteric rites for the peace and security of the nation were held for a week in the beginning of each year following a week of Shintō rites. In 835 the Mantra School was officially recognized as a state sponsored school of Buddhism alongside the six schools of Nara Buddhism and the Tendai school. Two months later, Kūkai passed away on Mt. Kōya, though the Mantra school maintains that he has actually entered a state of samādhi and that he lives still on Mt. Kōya.

Esoteric Buddhism was also brought to Japan by Saichō, though he had not focused on it the way Kūkai had. Saichō's successors at Mt. Hiei traveled to China throughout the ninth century to learn more about esoteric Buddhism from the successors of Hui-kuo and in time two rival traditions of Esoteric Buddhism were well established in Japan. The first was the Tōmitsu (Tōji Esotericism) of the Mantra School, and the second was the Taimitsu (Tendai Esotericism) of the Tendai School. Nichiren does not take up the story of Taimitsu in the *Kaimoku-shō*, though it becomes a major theme of subsequent writings. Consequently, I will not deal with it here.

Sources

Abe, Ryuichi. *The Weaving of Mantra: Kūkai and the Construction of Esoteric Buddhist Discourse*. New York: Columbia University Press, 1999.

Giebel, Rolf W., trans. *Two Esoteric Sūtras*. Berkeley: Numata Center for Buddhist Translation and Research, 2001.

_____ & Todara, Dale. *Shingon Texts*. Berkeley: Numata Center for Buddhist Translation and Research, 2004.

_____. *The Vairocanabhiambodhi Sūtra*. Berkeley: Numata Center for Buddhist Translation and Research, 2005.

Gosho Translation Committee, editor-translator. *The Writings of Nichiren Daishonin*. Tokyo: Soka Gakkai, 1999.

Hakeda, Yoshito S. *Kūkai: Major Works*. New York: Columbia University Press, 1972.

Hori, Kyotsu, comp. *Writings of Nichiren Shonin: Doctrine Volume 2*. Tokyo: Nichiren Shu Overseas Propagation Promotion Association, 2002.

_____. *Writings of Nichiren Shonin: Doctrine Volume 3*. Tokyo: Nichiren Shu Overseas Propagation Promotion Association, 2004.

_____. *Writings of Nichiren Shonin: Faith and Practice Volume 4*. Tokyo: Nichiren Shu Overseas Propagation Promotion Association, 2007.

Murano, Senchu. *Kaimokusho or Liberation from Blindness*. Berkeley: Numata Center for Buddhist Translation and Research, 2000.

Snodgrass, Adrian. *The Matrix and Diamond World Mandalas in Shingon Buddhism. 2 Volumes*. New Delhi: Rakesh Goel on behalf of Aditya Prakashan, 1988.

Tsukamoto, Keisho. *Source Elements of the Lotus Sūtra: Buddhist Integration of Religion, Thought, and Culture*. Tokyo: Kosei Publishing Co., 2007.

Williams, Paul & Tribe, Anthony. *Buddhist Thought: A Complete Introduction to the Indian Tradition*. New York: Routledge, 2000.

Yamasaki, Taiko. *Shingon: Japanese Esoteric Buddhism*. Boston: Shambhala, 1988.

Yi-Liang, Chou. "Tantrism in China." In *Tantric Buddhism in East Asia*. Ed. by Payne, Richard K. Boston: Wisdom Publications: 2006.

Chapter 35 – Mantra Principles and Practices

Writings of Nichiren Shōnin Doctrine 2, pp. 34, 36-37, 44, 46, 50-51, 67, 75-81,
84-85, 88-89, 102, 108, 112, 114
Kaimoku-shō or Liberation from Blindness, pp. 13, 16-17, 27, 29, 36-37, 60, 70,
72-77, 83-85, 89-91, 109, 119, 123, 126
The Writings of Nichiren Daishonin I, pp. 224, 225-226, 232, 233, 237-238, 250,
256-261, 263-264, 267-268, 277, 283, 286-287

What is it that distinguishes Mantra or esoteric Buddhism from the other
forms of Buddhism that had previously been brought to Japan? According to
Taikō Yamasaki, Kūkai (774-835; also known as Kōbō) emphasized the
following four key differences the exoteric and esoteric (J. *mikkyō*) teachings:

> *1. Mikkyō is the direct teaching of the highest Buddha,
> the Dharma Body, the all-pervading body of universal
> enlightenment.*
>
> *2. Enlightenment can be manifested in this world and
> can be communicated.*
>
> *3. Mikkyō teachings stress immediate attainment of
> Buddhahood in this life.*
>
> *4. The esoteric tradition contains a great wealth of
> teachings for many purposes and includes methods of
> practice suited to all predilections and abilities.
> (Yamasaki 1988, pp. 58-59)*

Let's examine each of these points to get an overview of Mantra Buddhist
principles and practice, beginning with the special status given to
Mahāvairocana Buddha, the personification of the Dharma-body revered as
the "focus of devotion" (J. *honzon*) of the Mantra school. Who is
Mahāvairocana Buddha? In the Mahāyāna sūtras, the name Vairocana (lit.
Illuminator) is used to indicate Śākyamuni Buddha in a glorified or cosmic

aspect that can only be perceived by advanced bodhisattvas. It is Vairocana Buddha who is the Buddha of the *Flower Garland Sūtra*, the *Brahmā Net Sūtra*, the *Mahāvairocana Sūtra*, and the *Diamond Peak Sūtra*. The *Contemplation of the Universal Sage Bodhisattva Sutra*, the closing sūtra of the *Threefold Lotus Sūtra*, says, "Śākyamuni Buddha is called Vairocana, the Omnipresent. His dwelling place is called Always Tranquil Light." (Reeves 2008, p. 416) Sometimes the name Mahāvairocana (lit. Great Illuminator, but in Japanese he is called Dainichi, which means Great Sun) is used interchangeably with Vairocana Buddha. In the Tiantai school, Mahāvairocana Buddha is taken to be the Dharma-body, while Vairocana Buddha is understood to be the reward-body (S. *sambhoga-kāya*) aspect of Śākyamuni Buddha. (See Stone 1999, p. 26)

Kūkai agreed with the identification of Vairocana Buddha of the Pure Land of Eternally Tranquil Light as the reward-body and the Buddha representative of the *Lotus Sūra*. (See Giebel 2004, p. 195) Kūkai also identified Mahāvairocana Buddha as the Dharma-body, but he also identified him as the teacher of the sūtras that comprise the Mantra teachings. "The esoteric teachings are the Dharma expounded by the own-nature Dharma body, the Tathagata Mahāvairocana, together with his attendants for his own enjoyment of Dharma bliss. This corresponds to the so-called mantra vehicle." (Ibid, p. 169) Based on this differentiation, Kūkai insisted that the esoteric sūtras taught by Mahāvairocana Buddha were more profound than those taught by Śākyamuni Buddha or even Vairocana Buddha. In his essay *On the Differences Between the Exoteric and Esoteric Teachings*, Kūkai sets out this distinction.

> *The Buddha has three bodies, and the teachings are of two kinds. The sermons of the response and transformation [bodies] are called the exoteric teaching; their language is plain, cursory, and accommodated to the religious capacity [of the listener]. The discourses of the Dharma-Buddha are called the esoteric treasury; their language is secret, recondite, and veridical. (Giebel 2004, p. 17)*

Of course, Nichiren did not accept this. In *Kaimoku-shō*, Nichiren criticizes the Mantra School for ignoring Śākyamuni Buddha in favor of Mahāvairocana Buddha. He says, "It is like a king's son despising his father while respecting a

437

nameless person who acts as though he were the King of the Dharma." (Hori 2002, p. 76). His arguments against the Dharma-body alone being considered the "focus of devotion" has already been discussed previously. To briefly reiterate his position, the Dharma-body by itself in an abstraction, which is why he uses the analogy of a prince revering a nameless stranger rather than his own father. The Eternal Buddha of chapter sixteen of the *Lotus Sūtra*, however, is considered in Tiantai Buddhism and by Nichiren to represent the unity of the three bodies of the Buddha. The concrete historical Śākyamuni Buddha, the idealized Śākyamuni or Vairocana Buddha, and the universal truth called Mahāvairocana Buddha are all just aspects of the Eternal Śākyamuni Buddha. All three aspects are unborn and deathless because the Eternal Śākyamuni Buddha is the true nature of reality that is unborn and deathless and always trying to enable all beings to awaken to the true nature.

Kūkai did not see Mahāvairocana Buddha as an abstraction, however. He viewed him as a pantheistic supreme being. Mahāvairocana Buddha is the Dharma-body consisting of the six primary elements that compose all that is: earth, air, fire, water, space, and consciousness. Sometimes only the five primary physical elements (earth, air, fire, water, and space) that compose the world are spoken of as the physical body of Mahāvairocana Buddha. In this view, Mahāvairocana Buddha is all things and communicates through all things. He and his retinue, who personify various aspects of his wisdom and merit, communicate the Dharma not through conceptual or discursive teachings but through the mudrās, mantras, and mandalas used in Mantra Buddhism. These three correspond to the three mysteries of the mental, verbal, and physical activity of Mahāvairocana Buddha. Mudrās correspond to Mahāvairocana Buddha's actions. Mantras correspond to Mahāvairocana Buddha's words. Mandalas correspond to Mahāvairocana Buddha's mind or internal awakening. Various mudrās, mantras, and mandalas are associated with different buddhas, bodhisattvas, and deities but ultimately all of them are expressions of Mahāvairocana Buddha.

Now we can discuss the second distinguishing feature of Mantra Buddhism. The Dharma-body, Mahāvairocana Buddha, is not just an inert impersonal principle waiting to be discovered; rather, this Buddha is supposed to be the selfless true self that is always expressing itself in order to awaken all sentient beings. Let's now look at each of the three mysteries of Mantra Buddhism.

Mudrā means "seal." In Esoteric Buddhism it usually refers to certain ritual gestures or hand-seals of which there are many. Each mudrā communicates or embodies a different principle or activity of a Buddha, bodhisattva, or deity. A common mudrā is the gesture of putting one's palm together as if in prayer in front of one's heart. That is the Añjali mudra, known as *gasshō* in Japanese. Another mudrā is the Dharma-dhatu *dhyāna* mudrā used in meditation, wherein the hands are held in front of the abdomen palms up, one resting atop the other, with the thumb tips touching lightly to form a triangle. The triangle both represents the fire of concentration burning the defilements and also the Three Treasures of the Buddha, Dharma, and Sangha.

Mantras are verbal invocations found in many Mahāyāna sūtras, but it is in esoteric Buddhism that they really come into their own. They are believed to actually contain the power and merit of the buddha, bodhisattva, or deity that they are associated with. The mantras contain the Sanskrit seed syllables (S. *bīja*) that are the concentrated essence of the being they refer to. To recite a mantra and form mudrā is to invoke the actual presence of a buddha, bodhisattva, or deity. It is also a form of contemplation of and identification with the buddha, bodhisattva, or deity. Interestingly, Kūkai even wrote that the title of the *Lotus Sūtra* could be considered a mantra, a mandala in the form of letters, and that by reciting it and contemplating it one could attain awakening.

> *Kūkai often argued that in and of itself each letter of the sūtras, both in its form and in its sound, was already a manifestation of the wisdom and compassion of the Buddhas and bodhisattvas. In one of his commentaries on the Lotus Sūtra, for example, Kūkai wrote that the nine characters of the title of the sūtra written in Sanskrit in a script called Siddham (Jpn. Shittan) – Sa-Dhar-Ma-Pun-Da-Ri-Ka Sū-Tram (Sūtra of the Lotus, the Excellent Dharma) – were graphic symbols of the nine principal divinities of the gharba mandala described in the Mahāvairocana Sūtra: Mahāvairocana at the center and around him four Buddhas and four bodhisattvas, all seated on an eight-petaled lotus. Relying on the Mahāvairocana Sūtra and its ritual commentaries, Kūkai went on to declare that the sound of each of*

these letters was a manifestation of the powers of the divinities depicted, such as the powers to defeat evil, to purify the practitioner of all defilement, and to comfort sentient beings. (Abe 1999, p. 64; See also Hakeda 1972, pp. 65-66 and n. 8)

Related to mantras are the longer invocations called dhāranī. Here is a more detailed explanation of mantras and dhāranī that sheds a lot of light on how they came to be understood in Japanese Buddhism after Kūkai:

The word dhāranī, which derives from the Sanskrit verb root dhr, meaning to hold, keep, maintain, can roughly be translated as "that by which to sustain something." It is generally understood as a mnemonic device, containing within its short passages all the meanings of a section or chapter of a sūtra, or a particular teaching discussed therein. Dhāranī are also believed to be endowed with mystical power that protects those who chant it against malign influences such as demons, evil rulers, thieves, and diseases. As for mantra, there has been perennial, seemingly endless debate as to what the term means and how it can be defined. Many experts believe that it consists of two parts – the old Vedic root man, to think; and the action-oriented (krt) suffix –tra, indicating instrumentality. Thus it is possible to understand mantra as a linguistic device for deepening one's thought, and, more specifically, an instrument for enlightenment. However, it is also true that there are numerous mantras whose chanting is purported specifically to realize mundane effects, such as causing rain to fall, attaining health and long life, and eliminating political rivals.

It is often said that of the two forms of incantations, mantra tends to be shorter and more strongly contextualized in ritual procedures – that is, its chanting is associated with particular breathing, visualizing, and other meditative exercises. Yet from the point of view of linguistic structure alone, the distinction between dhāranī and mantra is not always clear. For example, both dhāranīs and mantras frequently contain a large number of unintelligible phonic fragments (which are often chanted in rhythmic refrain), such as phat, māṃ, trat, hāṃ, and hrīṃ, which have encouraged many to hold a view that mantras and dhāranīs are devoid of meaning: mumbo-jumbo.

By contrast, Kūkai distinguished mantra from dhāranī in their semantic and semiotic functions, i.e., in terms of the different manners through which they produced meaning or became meaningful. He defined mantra as a special class of dhāranī, capable of demonstrating that every syllable used in dhāranī was in fact a manifestation of the working of the Buddhist truth of emptiness. For example, Kūkai interpreted the syllables of the root mantra of the Buddha Mahāvairocana, A Vi Ra Hūm Kham, as representing the five essential forces of emptiness, respectively: stability (earth), permeating (water), purity (fire), growth (wind), and spacing (space). That is, even before syllables are put together to form a word, they are already the sources of countless meanings capable of illustrating the truth as it is explained in the writings of Buddhist scriptures. In other words, mantras show that dhāranīs are not devoid of meaning, but on the contrary, saturated with it. It is through their semantic superabundance that Kūkai attempted to explain why dhāranīs were impregnated with the power to condense the meaning of scriptures, to protect chanters, or to bring about supernatural effects. (Abe 1999, pp. 5-6)

A mandala is a "circle of blessings." The Womb-realm and Diamond-realm Mandalas used in Mantra Buddhism represent the realm of Mahāvairocana Buddha and the buddhas, bodhisattvas, and other deities who are his emanations and personifications of his wisdom and merit. Originally the mandalas were platforms into which the initiate and the initiator would actually enter. In China, such platforms were not used, and the mandala became a painting instead, though the practitioner is still supposed to enter into them through contemplative union with the buddhas, bodhisattvas, and deities represented in them.

> *The word mandala is composed of the Sanskrit root*
> *manda – meaning essence, center, true meaning, the*
> *purest flavor of clarified milk – with the suffix la,*
> *meaning accomplishment, possession. Mandala*
> *originally meant platform, essence, or circle in Sanskrit,*
> *and, by extension, that which is endowed with all power*
> *and virtue. In other words, mandala means that which*
> *has essence. The eighth-century Indian master*
> *Buddhaguhya wrote that in this case essence refers to*
> *the Buddha's enlightenment, and that the realm of this*
> *enlightenment is the mandala." (Yamasaki 1988, p. 123)*

In Mantra Buddhism, the mandala graphically portrays the five kinds of knowledge of the Buddha. Mahāvairocana Buddha in the center represents the ninth or pure consciousness, the essential nature of the Dharma-realm knowledge. The other four buddhas surrounding Mahāvairocana Buddha represent the transformation of the five consciousnesses of the five senses, the consciousness of mental phenomena (thought and feelings), the seventh or ego-consciousness, and the eighth or storehouse consciousness. When the storehouse consciousness is purified and ceases to be the unconscious source of delusions; it becomes the great mirror-like knowledge, an awareness that clearly reflects reality as it is without the projections of hidden biases or distortions. When the ego consciousness ceases to see the world in terms of self and other, it begins to function as equality knowledge, which recognizes the non-dual nature of reality. When the sixth consciousness ceases its mental chatter, it becomes the distinguishing knowledge that views all things with clarity and appreciation. The five sensory consciousnesses together become the all-performing knowledge that accomplishes all meritorious actions. Depending on the mandala, different buddhas represent the great mirror-like knowledge, the equality knowledge, the distinguishing knowledge, and the all performing knowledge. The five buddhas are also correlated with the five primary elements of earth, air, fire, water, and space.

There is a four-fold way of classifying different types of mandalas depending on how the buddhas, bodhisattvas, and deities within them are depicted. There is the mahā-maṇḍala or great mandala, which is a mandala depicting the various beings in the form of a painting. There is a samaya-maṇḍala or vow Mandala, which uses symbolic objects to represent the particular vows of the beings in the mandala. There is the dharma-mandala or truth mandala that uses Sanskrit seed syllables to represent the beings in terms of verbal or written expression. Finally, there is the karma-maṇḍala or action mandala, wherein the activities of the beings are represented using statues. Though these terms are not used in Nichiren Buddhism, Nichiren's Omandala Gohonzon is effectively a dharma-maṇḍala. In addition, temples such as Kuonji at Mt. Minobu use statuary to depict the Omandala, which would be of the karma-maṇḍala type; and illustrated or painted versions of the Omandala have also been made, and these would be maha-maṇḍala s.

The Womb-realm Mandala and Diamond-realm Mandala are central to the initiation ceremonies called abhiṣeka (J. *kanjo*), which means "sprinkling." Abhishekha is based upon the ancient Indian coronation ceremony, in which a newly consecrated king would be anointed with the waters of his kingdom. In Mantra Buddhism there are three levels of abhiṣeka associated with each of the two mandalas. The first is open to laypeople and is for establishing a basic connection with one of the beings in the mandala. The second is for those who will actually be taking up an esoteric practice. The third is for those who will become teachers of esoteric Buddhism. Each involves various preliminary rituals, purifications, and the taking of vows (S. *samaya*). The initiate (S. *sadhaka*) is then blindfolded, led into the practice hall upon which a mandala has been laid out on the floor, and then instructed to throw a flower onto the mandala, so that a connection is formed with whichever buddha, bodhisattva, or deity the flower lands upon. The master (S. *ācārya*) then sprinkles the head of the initiate. This is the five-fold empowerment (S. *adhisthāna*; J. *kaji*) by which Mahāvairocana Buddha compassionately transmits the five knowledges and the initiate faithfully receives them. The initiate will then be given practices appropriate to the connection formed.

The third distinction of Mantra Buddhism that Kūkai claims is the principle of "attaining buddhahood with one's present body" (J. *sokushin jōbutsu*). Both Kūkai and Saichō (767-822; also known as Dengyō) taught this principle, though Kūkai was inspired by apocryphal writings of Nāgārjuna and the esoteric teachings and practices while Saichō was inspired by the teachings of Zhanran (711-782; aka Miaole) and the story of the dragon king's daughter in the *Lotus Sūtra*. Kūkai's understanding was that all beings are originally enlightened or awakened, and that they only have to realize their intrinsic unity with Mahāvairocana Buddha. This realization can come about through the practice of the three mysteries. He explains it as follows in his essay *The Meaning of Becoming a Buddha in This Very Body*.

> *On the basis of this meaning it says, "When empowered by the three mysteries, [Buddhahood] is quickly manifested." "Empower" (lit., "add and hold") expresses the great compassion of the Tathāgata and the faithful minds of sentient beings: the reflection of the Buddha-sun appearing on the mind-water of sentient beings is called "adding" and the mind-water of the practitioner sensing the Buddha-sun is called "holding." If the practitioner contemplates well on this guiding principle, through the intercorrespondence of his three mysteries [with those of the Tathāgata] he will quickly manifest and realize in his present body the originally existent three bodies. Therefore it is said, "[Buddhahood] is quickly manifested." (Giebel 2004, p. 79)*

The thought that all beings are originally enlightened and possessed of the three bodies of the Buddha and only need to take faith in the Eternal Buddha (whether understood as the Dharma-body Mahāvairocana Buddha or the Eternal Śākyamuni Buddha of the *Lotus Sūtra*) and express buddhahood through ritual practices utilizing mudrās, mantras, and the contemplation of mandala images would later be incorporated into Tendai Buddhism and then into Nichiren Buddhism. The result was that practices such as meditative cultivation of the mind in order to perceive the truth were believed to be surpassed by practices in which the original enlightenment made itself immediately manifest in concrete ritual practices that would transform the practitioner into a buddha. Here is an explanation by Jacqueline Stone:

The valorization of the phenomenal world in Mikkyō thought was grounded in the bivalent meaning of the "three mysteries." On the one hand, the three mysteries are all forms, sounds, and thought, that is, the entire phenomenal world, equated with the body, speech, and mind of the cosmic buddha Mahāvairocana. On the other hand, the three mysteries are the concrete forms of esoteric practice by which identity with Mahāvairocana is realized: the intricate mudrās formed with the hands and body; the vocally recited mantras and dhāraṇīs; and the mental contemplations of the holy figures represented on the mandalas. In this connection, the categories of ri and ji, in addition to their earlier meanings of "principle" and "phenomena," assumed new connotations in the realm of esoteric practice, ri being the timeless paradigm to be contemplated in practice, and ji, its physical and temporal imitation or expression in actual practice. For example, ri is the mental visualization of the Buddha, while ji is the Buddha image standing on the altar. Hence the Taimitsu distinction between the Lotus, which is "esoteric in principle" (rimitsu) and the Mahāvairocana Sūtra, which, including as it does descriptions of mudrās and mantras, is "esoteric in concrete form" (jimitsu). Esoteric practice, with its ritual gestures, chanting of sacred formulas, and elaborate mandalas, was valorized as the secret language and gestures of the Buddha. Its strong sensory and aesthetic appeal, as well as its presumed efficacy in both soteriological and worldly matters, contributed greatly to its spread and patronage. Under its influence, one sees in the latter Heian period a general shift across Buddhist traditions away from silent, introspective contemplation toward practices having concrete form. This is evident, for example, in the way that the T'ien-t'ai contemplative methods introduced by Saichō were gradually supplemented and then surpassed in popularity by such tangible acts as reading, reciting, and copying the Lotus Sūtra, and in the way that the chanting of the nembutsu, the name of the Buddha Amitābha, emerged alongside, and eventually superseded, the silent contemplation or visualization of the Buddha. (Stone 1999, pp. 28-29 adapted)

In regard to Nichiren specifically, Stone wrote:

Where Chih-i's form of meditative discipline was that of "principle," or introspective contemplation to perceive the truth aspect of reality in one's mind, Nichiren's was that of "actuality," or the chanting of the daimoku, the title of the Lotus Sūtra, said to embody the reality of the Buddha's enlightenment and the seed of Buddhahood. Nichiren's usage reflects the strong influence of esoteric Buddhism, in which ri refers to formless truth that is contemplated inwardly, and ji, to its expression in outwardly manifest practices involving concrete forms. (Ibid, p. 68)

The fourth distinction that Kūkai made dealt with the variety of teachings and practices for people of different capacities. In the previous survey of the esoteric sūtras I have already mentioned the Buddhist versions of the Vedic fire rituals (J. *goma*) for the purposes of averting disaster, attracting prosperity, and subduing enemies. Fire rituals were also done for attracting love and prolonging life. I have also previously mentioned the relatively simple and austere practice of the contemplation of the Sanskrit letter "A." Nichiren would also criticize the use of Mantra ceremonies to eye-open statues of buddhas, rather than eye-opening ceremonies based on the *Lotus Sūtra*. Esoteric Buddhism, whether in its Tōmitsu form of the Mantra school or the Taimitsu form of the Tendai school basically provided Japanese Buddhism with a repertoire of rituals and ceremonies for sacred and secular purposes. In terms of Buddhist teachings, the Mantra school drew upon all the teachings of the schools of Buddhism that came before it. This was the basis of Nichiren's criticism that Śubhakarasiṃha (C. Shanwuwei, 637-735) and his Chinese disciple Yixing (638-727) had misappropriated Tiantai teachings in their commentary on the *Mahāvairocana Sūtra*. Kūkai did not just draw upon the earlier teachings, however, but he also set up his own system of classification of the teachings in terms of ten stages of the maturation of the mind. The ten are as follows:

1. The Mind of the Common Person, Like a Ram: this is the mind of ordinary people who follow their impulses without any self-restraint.
2. The Mind of the Foolish Child, Observing Abstinence: this is the mind of the followers of Confucius who take up self-discipline and self-cultivation.
3. The Mind of the Young Child, without Fear: this is the mind of the followers of the Vedas and other non-Buddhist teachings that lead to the temporary respite of the heavens.
4. The Mind of Aggregates-only and No-self: this is the mind of the śrāvakas who contemplate the five aggregates and realize no-self in order to escape the six worlds of rebirth.
5. The Mind That Has Eradicated the Causes and Seeds of Karma: this is the mind of the pratyekabuddhas who contemplate the twelve-fold chain of dependent origination in order break the bonds of karma and escape the six worlds of rebirth.
6. The Mind of the Mahāyāna Concerned for Others: this is the mind of the bodhisattvas who arouse the aspiration to attain buddhahood for the sake of all sentient beings. This mind is equated with the teachings of the Consciousness-Only School.
7. The Mind Awakened to the Non-birth of the Mind: this is the mind of the bodhisattvas who realize the truth of emptiness. It is equated with the teaching of the Middle Way school.
8. The Mind of the One Path As It Really Is: this is the mind that realizes the One Vehicle. This is the teaching of the *Lotus Sūtra*.
9. The Mind of Ultimate Own-naturelessness: this is the mind that realizes that nothing has its own nature apart from the total interpenetration of all phenomena. This is the teaching of the *Flower Garland Sūtra*.
10. The Mind of Secret Adornment: this is the mind that realizes the true nature of Mahāvairocana Buddha through the practice of Mantra Buddhism.

Kūkai insisted that the first nine do not represent the ultimate fruit of buddhahood and that the teaching of each stage of mind "when viewed in light of the subsequent [vehicles], it becomes a frivolous assertion." (Giebel 2004, p. 214) This is what Nichiren truly objected to in regard to the Mantra teachings, for Kūkai was saying that compared to the *Mahāvairocana Sūtra* and *Diamond Peak Sūtra* the *Lotus Sūtra* was just a frivolous assertion that did not truly allow anyone to realize buddhahood. From Nichiren's point of view, it was the *Mahāvairocana Sūtra* and *Diamond Peak Sūtra* that failed to fully reveal the One Vehicle and the eternal nature of Śākyamuni Buddha. This has already been discussed previously so I will not go into it again here. In other major writings, Nichiren provided a more extensive critique of Kūkai's teachings and the Tendai successors of Saichō who deemphasized the *Lotus Sūtra* in favor of Esoteric Buddhism. There is much more to say about Nichiren's criticism and selective assimilation of Esoteric Buddhism, but further discussion will have to wait for commentaries on the *Selecting the Right Time* (*Senji-shō*) and the *Essay on Gratitude* (*Hōon-jō*). One thing I would like to point out here is that Nichiren seems to have felt that the main underlying reason for the neglect of the *Lotus Sūtra* was due to the teaching of Mantra Buddhism, and that his vehement criticism of Zen and Pure Land Buddhism was in fact only a preparation for his later critiques of Mantra Buddhism.

Sources

Abe, Ryuichi. *The Weaving of Mantra: Kūkai and the Construction of Esoteric Buddhist Discourse*. New York: Columbia University Press, 1999.

Giebel, Rolf W., trans. *Two Esoteric Sūtras*. Berkeley: Numata Center for Buddhist Translation and Research, 2001.

_____ & Todara, Dale. *Shingon Texts*. Berkeley: Numata Center for Buddhist Translation and Research, 2004.

_____. *The Vairocanabhiambodhi Sūtra*. Berkeley: Numata Center for Buddhist Translation and Research, 2005.

Gosho Translation Committee, editor-translator. *The Writings of Nichiren Daishonin*. Tokyo: Soka Gakkai, 1999.
_____. *The Writings of Nichiren Daishonin Volume II*. Tokyo: Soka Gakkai, 2006.

Hakeda, Yoshito S. *Kūkai: Major Works*. New York: Columbia University Press, 1972.

Hori, Kyotsu, comp. *Writings of Nichiren Shonin: Doctrine Volume 2*. Tokyo: Nichiren Shu Overseas Propagation Promotion Association, 2002.

_____. *Writings of Nichiren Shonin: Doctrine Volume 3*. Tokyo: Nichiren Shu Overseas Propagation Promotion Association, 2004.

_____. *Writings of Nichiren Shonin: Faith and Practice Volume 4*. Tokyo: Nichiren Shu Overseas Propagation Promotion Association, 2007.

Murano, Senchu. *Kaimokusho or Liberation from Blindness*. Berkeley: Numata Center for Buddhist Translation and Research, 2000.

Reeves, Gene, trans. *The Lotus Sūtra*. Boston: Wisdom Publications, 2008.

Snodgrass, Adrian. *The Matrix and Diamond World Mandalas in Shingon Buddhism. 2 Volumes*. New Delhi: Rakesh Goel on behalf of Aditya Prakashan, 1988.

Stone, Jacqueline. *Original Enlightenment and the Transformation of Medieval Japanese Buddhism*. Honolulu: Kuroda Institute, 1999.

Tsukamoto, Keisho. *Source Elements of the Lotus Sūtra: Buddhist Integration of Religion, Thought, and Culture*. Tokyo: Kosei Publishing Co., 2007.

Williams, Paul & Tribe, Anthony. *Buddhist Thought: A Complete Introduction to the Indian Tradition*. New York: Routledge, 2000.

Yamasaki, Taiko. *Shingon: Japanese Esoteric Buddhism*. Boston: Shambhala, 1988.

Yi-Liang, Chou. "Tantrism in China." In *Tantric Buddhism in East Asia*. Ed. by Payne, Richard K. Boston: Wisdom Publications: 2006.

Chapter 36 – The Discipline for Laity, Monastics and Bodhisattvas

Writings of Nichiren Shōnin Doctrine 2, pp. 34-35, 57, 76, 91, 94, 99
Kaimoku-shō or Liberation from Blindness, pp. 13-14, 47-48, 72, 93, 98, 108.
The Writings of Nichiren Daishonin I, pp. 224, 242-243, 257, 269, 271, 275.

The Buddhist canon is often referred to as the *tripiṭaka*, a term that literally means "Three Baskets." These three baskets consist of the sūtra-basket that contains the Buddha's discourses, the vinaya-basket that contains all the precepts adhered to by the monks and nuns, and the abhidharma-basket that contains systematic treatises on the Dharma. The monk Upāli is credited with reciting the vinaya at the first Buddhist council after the Buddha's passing. In time, there came to be different recensions of the vinaya, all of them claiming to be identical to the vinaya recited at that first council. None of these were specifically designated as Mahāyāna, since even Mahāyāna monks and nuns in India considered the monastic vinaya to apply to themselves as well. For the most part, the precepts traditions do not vary too greatly, the differences amounting to nothing more than minor variations. In time, Mahāyāna sūtras did appear in India and China that set forth various bodhisattva precepts for both monastics and lay followers of the Mahāyāna teachings, but these were not intended to replace the vinaya.

By the fifth century, five different vinaya traditions were translated into Chinese, but it was the Dharmaguptaka tradition based on the *Four-part Discipline* that had been translated in 412 that eventually became the standard in China and from there throughout East Asia. This was due to the efforts of Daoxuan (596-667), who is regarded as the founder of the Discipline school. It must be emphasized that the Discipline school has always regarded itself as Mahāyāna. It also promulgates and confers Mahāyāna precepts to monastics and lay followers, and utilizes the teachings and practices taught in the Mahāyāna sūtras. Since the time of Daoxuan, Mahāyāna monks and nuns in China, Korea, and Vietnam have all been, and continue to be, ordained in the Dharmaguptaka precept lineage. This tradition was brought to Japan as well, but there the Dharmaguptaka ordination lineage has all but died out.

Now I would like to clarify a few terms and explain why the Buddha instituted the precepts. The term vinaya means "discipline" and refers generally to the rules, policies, and procedures of the monastic Sangha. Within the vinaya-basket will be found the "binding rules" (S. *prātimokṣa*) which are precepts for monks and nuns. The vinaya is also more than just rules, as it also includes the "collection of rules," (*skandhaka*) which are the procedures for ordinations, conducting meetings, resolving disputes, the proper distribution of materials donated to the Sangha, and many other matters.

Another terms that is associated with precepts is *śīla*, which means "morality" and is one part of the threefold training consisting of morality, concentration, and wisdom, and one of the six perfections of bodhisattva practice. What are generally called the five major precepts given to lay Buddhists are actually five forms of *śīla* or moral guidelines, they are not the same as the binding rules of the monastic prātimoksha. This is important to keep in mind. The five precepts against killing, stealing, sexual misconduct, lying, and using intoxicants that the Buddha taught to laypeople are broad and generalized. Laypeople that break them do so at their own peril, but there are no sanctions to be administered to laypeople by the monastics or any priestly class. Following the *śīla* is a matter for the conscience of the individual and the sanctions of civil society. In fact, the Buddha would often say to those lay followers who were excusing themselves after hearing his teaching, "Now is the time to do as you see fit." The binding rules are different from *śīla* in many ways. They are very specific and refer to concrete actions. They do not deal only with morality but also with issues of etiquette, humility, simple living, and maintaining harmony within the monastic community and between the monastics and the general society. Altogether they proscribe all those actions that are not in keeping with Buddhist monastic way of life. Finally, monks and nuns who break these rules do face sanctions, up to and including permanent expulsion from the monastic Sangha.

More comprehensive than the five precepts, are the ten courses of wholesome conduct (S. *daśa kuśala karmapatha*). The ten courses of wholesome conduct are to refrain from killing, stealing, engaging in sexual misconduct, lying, malicious speech, harsh speech, idle chatter (or gossip), covetousness, ill will, and holding wrong views. The ten courses of wholesome conduct describe how a person following the eightfold path of Buddhism lives.

In other words, such a person avoids these ten physical, verbal, and mental actions in an effort to develop right view, right intention, right action, and right speech. In East Asian Buddhism it is understood that following the five precepts is the cause for rebirth in the human realm, while following the ten courses of wholesome conduct is the cause for rebirth in the heavens of the desire realm (the higher heavens require the cultivation of meditative absorption).

Four times a lunar month come the *uposadha* or "fasting days." These are the days of the new moon, waxing half-moon, full moon, and waning half-moon. On the new and full moon *uposadha* days the Buddha instructed the monastic Sangha to come together to confess any transgressions against the precepts and then to recite the *pratimoksha*. On all four *uposadha* days the Buddha instructed the monastic Sangha to expound the Dharma to the lay followers. During *uposadha*, the lay followers might also observe eight precepts of abstinence in order to approximate the lifestyle of the arhats, those who are awakened by following the Buddha's teachings and completely free of birth and death. These eight precepts consist of the five precepts (though in this case the precept against sexual misconduct becomes a precept to refrain from all sexual relations) and in addition to a sixth to eat only one meal before noon, a seventh to refrain from secular entertainments and decorations, and an eighth to refrain from using luxurious furnishings (such as high beds and seats).

Novice monks or nuns (S. *śrāmaṇera* or *śrāmaṇerikā*; J. *shami* or *shamini*) were instructed by the Buddha to take up ten precepts for novices. These ten are almost identical to the eight precepts of abstinence except for the following differences: the seventh precept is divided into two so that the seventh novice precept is to abstain from dancing, singing, instrumental music, and unsuitable shows; and the eighth novice precept is to abstain from adorning themselves by wearing garlands and applying scents and ointments; the ninth novice precept is to abstain from high and luxurious bed and seats; and the tenth novice precept is to abstain from accepting gold and silver. The last precept is added because monks and nuns, including novices, were to live by begging for their necessities so they were not to collect money or otherwise get involved in buying or selling.

Upon full ordination, a monk or nun (S. *bhikṣu* or *bhikṣuṇī*) would take up the full *prātimokṣa* of the vinaya. According to the Theravādin tradition the Buddha set forth two hundred and twenty-seven precepts for monks and three hundred and eleven for nuns, but according to the Dharmaguptaka tradition used in East Asia the monks were given two hundred and fifty precepts and the nuns three hundred and forty-eight. These precepts are divided into eight categories. The first category deals with defeats or extreme offenses (S. *pārājika*) that require permanent expulsion of the offender from the monastic Sangha. The four offenses of defeat given for monks involve sexual intercourse, stealing, taking human life (includes abortion, euthanasia, and even simply encouraging someone to take their own life or another's life), and lying about one's spiritual attainments. Nuns have four more offenses of defeat, these four involve touching a man with lustful intent, allowing a man who has lustful intent to touch oneself, concealing another nun's misdeeds, and continuing to follow a monk expelled from the Sangha after one has been warned three times. The second category deals with probationary offenses that require a formal meeting of the Sangha (S. *saṃghāvaśeṣa*) to place an offender on probation and then again to fully reinstate them. The thirteen offenses for monks (seventeen for nuns) requiring a formal meeting include such things as masturbation, lewd conduct, false accusations, creating dissension within the Sangha, scandalizing the laity, and refusing to heed the admonitions of the Sangha after three warnings. The third category deals with offenses that require further consideration as to the actual severity of the offense because they are indeterminate (S. *aniyata*). There are two such offenses for monks (zero for nuns) and they involve being seen with a woman in suspicious circumstances either in private or in public. The fourth category deals with forfeiture offenses that require the relinquishing of misappropriated or inappropriate items and repentance (S. *naiḥsargika-pāyattika*). There are thirty of these offenses for both monks and nuns in the Dharmaguptaka vinaya and they include things like possessing too many robes or bowls or furnishings inappropriate for a monastery. The fifth category deals with expiatory offenses that require repentance (S. *pāyattika*). The Dharmaguptaka vinaya lists ninety such offenses for monks and one hundred and seventy-eight for nuns and include things like drinking alcohol, getting into fights with other monastics, killing animals, lying about matters other than spiritual attainments, and eating after noon. The sixth category deals with acknowledgment offenses that must be confessed (S. *pratideśanīya*). The

Dharmaguptaka vinaya lists four of these for monks and eight for nuns and they all involve improper means of obtaining food. The seventh category consists of etiquette training (S. *śaikṣa-dharma*) dealing with good manners and proper decorum. The Dharmaguptaka vinaya lists one hundred of these for monks and nuns and they include such things as not looking into the bowls of others when eating, not swinging one's arms excessively when walking, and other such minor matters. The eighth category consists of seven rules for settling disputes (S. adhikaraṇa-śamatha) concerning the precepts.

The Buddha did not present all these precepts at once. In fact, for some time after the establishment of the monastic Sangha there were no precepts to be followed. At one time, the Buddha explained that the dispensation of the teaching of other buddhas did not last long because they did not explain the Dharma in detail or set forth the training rules of the *prātimokṣa*. This prompted Śāriputra to ask for the *prātimokṣa*, but the Buddha declined to set them forth until "taint-producing things manifest themselves" which had not yet happened at the time Śāriputra requested the *prātimokṣa* because the monastic Sangha at that time consisted of monks who were at least stream-enterers. The Buddha assured Śāriputra that when taints did appear, the Buddha would make known the training rules to ward off those conditions causing the taints. (Ñānamoli, p. 126-129; see also Horner Part 1, pp. 18-19) This occurred when a monk named Sundinna was enticed by his family into impregnating his former wife so as to leave an heir. That an ostensibly celibate Buddhist monk had sired an heir created a scandal when it became known and the Buddha rebuked Sundinna in no uncertain terms for giving in to worldly passions, no matter the rationalization. The Buddha further pointed out that such scandalous conduct would impede others from taking faith in the Buddha's teaching and harm the faith of those who were already followers and supporters. The Buddha then gave the first of the precepts (the extreme offense regarding sexual intercourse by monks or nuns) and gave the reasons for doing so.

> *"I shall do so for ten reasons: for the welfare of the*
> *Sangha, for the comfort of the Sangha, for the restraint*
> *of the evil-minded, for the support of virtuous monks,*
> *for the restraint of taints in this life, for the prevention*

of taints in the life to come, for the benefit of unbelievers, for growth in believers, for the establishment of the Good Dharma, and for ensuring rules for restraint." (Ñānamoli, pp. 157-159; see also Horner Part 1, pp. 21-38)

From that point on it could not be taken for granted that the monks were at least stream-enterers, let alone once-returners, non-returners, or arhats. As time went on the Buddha found himself having to lay down more and more precepts to address wrong-doing and inappropriate behavior on the part of the monks and later the nuns. Each precept, then, was the result of a specific incident. At one point, Mahākāśyapa even asked the Buddha why there had come to be more training rules but fewer monks established in final knowledge of liberation. The Buddha responded, "That is how it is, Kāśyapa. When beings are degenerating and the Good Dharma is disappearing, there come to be more training rules and fewer monks become established in final knowledge." (adapted from Ñānamoli, p. 163) The Buddha went on to describe how the Good Dharma would eventually be replaced by the counterfeit Dharma and how the Good Dharma would disappear because monastics and lay followers would eventually become disrespectful and contemptuous of the Buddha, Dharma, and Sangha, and also of moral training and meditation practice. Even within the Buddha's lifetime the sanctity of the Sangha became so compromised that the Buddha stated that he would no longer participate in the *uposadha* day *prātimokṣa* recitals after one incident in which an unrepentant monk had to be forcibly expelled from the assembly of monks by Maudgalyāyana before the recital could begin. The Buddha stated as his reason that it was impossible that a Buddha should ever participate in any impure assembly. (Ibid, p. 160-163)

Once the precepts had been given, the Buddha assigned to them a value that put them on par with the teachings. Towards the end of his life, when Ānanda asked who would teach the Sangha after the Buddha's passing, the Buddha made it clear that the Dharma (the teachings given in the sūtras) and the discipline (the vinaya) should be seen as his only successors, at least according to the account given in the Mahāparinibbāna-sutta:

And the Lord said to Ānanda: "Ānanda, it may be that
you will think: 'The Teacher's instruction has ceased,
now we have no teacher!' It should not be seen like this,
Ānanda, for what I have taught and explained to you as
Dharma and discipline will, at my passing, be your
teacher." (Walshe, pp. 269-270 adapted)

In a passage from the vinaya-basket, the Buddha even states that his teachings can be considered to persist if at least the vinaya is preserved even if the baskets of the sūtras and abhidharma are lost. "Who does not understand cattle does not guard the herd, so not knowing moral habit, how can he guard restraint? Although the Suttantas and Abhidhamma be forgotten for all time, the teaching persists while Vinaya is not destroyed." (Horner Part 4, p. 127) Despite this, the Buddha did not have a rigid or narrow attitude about the precepts. To a monk who was having trouble remembering all the precepts the Buddha taught him to simply follow the three training rules of cultivating morality, concentration, and wisdom in order to eradicate greed, hatred, and delusion and thereby avoid all unwholesome acts. (Ñānamoli, p. 164)

Another monk, Kātyāyana, found it difficult to ordain new disciples because it was difficult to find even ten monks, the minimum needed to confer full admission into the Sangha. He also found that some of the precepts set forth by the Buddha were inappropriate for those living in Avanti where the environment and customs were different from those found in the kingdoms where the Buddha was teaching. To remedy this, Kātyāyana sent one of his students, whom he had ordained after finally managing to find enough monks for the ordination, to see the Buddha and ask if the rules could be changed to fit the local customs and environment. The Buddha agreed to this and stated that in the outlying kingdoms it would henceforth be permissible for only five monks to confer the full admission. He also allowed monks to wear shoes, bathe more frequently, use hides for coverings, and wear an extra robe for a longer period of time in order to suit the local customs and the harsher environment of the outlying kingdoms like Avanti. (Horner Part 4, pp. 260-267) This incident is important because it shows that the Buddha did allow for a certain amount of flexibility in the rules and regulation that he set forth, and that as long as the integrity of the Buddha Dharma was not harmed, he allowed for the adaptation of Buddhism to new situations. It was this principle of allowing the precepts to suit the local customs and circumstances that would allow Buddhism to grow into a world religion.

In the last few months of his life the Buddha even said to Ānanda, "If they wish, the order may abolish the minor rules after my passing." (Walshe, p. 270) So the Buddha did not even envision the entirety of the vinaya as something that should necessarily be maintained unchanged after his passing. Unfortunately, Ānanda did not ask the Buddha which of the precepts should be considered minor and which were more vital. For this he was duly chastised at the first Buddhist council. In the end, Mahākāśyapa proposed that in order not to scandalize the lay supporters of the Sangha they should retain all the precepts given by the Buddha.

> *"Let the Sangha hear me, friends; there are certain of our training rules that involve laymen, by which laymen know what is allowed to monks who are sons of the Śākyans and what is not. If we abolish these minor and lesser rules, there will be those who say: 'The training rules proclaimed by the monk Gautama to his disciples existed only for the period ending with his cremation; they kept his training rules as long as he was present, but now that he has attained final parinirvāna they have given up keeping his training rules.' If it seems proper to the Sangha, let not what is undeclared be declared, and let not what is declared by abolished; let the Sangha proceed according to the training rules as they have been declared." The resolution was placed before the Sangha and passed." (Ñānamoli, p. 339; see also Horner Part 5, pp. 399-400)*

As I mentioned above, Mahāyāna sūtras eventually appeared that put forth precepts specifically for bodhisattvas. One of the most popular of these in East Asia is the *Brahmā's Net Sūtra* allegedly translated by Kumārajīva (344-413) but believed to be an apocryphal sūtra produced in China in the fifth century. According to the *Brahmā's Net Sūtra*, Vairocana Buddha presented a set of ten major and forty-eight minor precepts for bodhisattvas. They were not originally intended to replace or provide an alternative to the vinaya for monastics. These bodhisattva precepts were, and continue to be, bestowed upon both lay followers and monastics to provide a code of conduct for aspiring bodhisattvas. The ten major precepts for bodhisattvas are in fact a slight variation on the ten courses of wholesome conduct. They prohibit the bodhisattva from killing, stealing, indulging lustfulness, speaking contrary to the truth, trafficking in intoxicants, speaking disparagingly of other Buddhists or gossiping about their actions that seem contrary to the precepts, praising oneself and demeaning others, being stingy with wealth or the Buddha Dharma, feeding anger and hardheartedness, and speaking ill of the Three Treasures. (Nearman, pp. 127-135)

The ten major precepts for bodhisattvas are described as offenses of defeat, meaning that those who break them disqualify themselves as bodhisattvas. This means that the ten major precepts are actually establishing a much stricter standard for bodhisattva conduct, as only the first four are considered offenses of defeat in the vinaya. However, unlike monastics who break one of the four offenses entailing defeat, a bodhisattva who breaks one of the ten major bodhisattva precepts can be rehabilitated if they sincerely repent (S. *pāpa-deśanā*; J. *sange*) by reciting the bodhisattva precepts and Mahāyāna sūtras in front of an image of the Buddha until such time as they receive a confirming vision that their defilements have been eradicated. This practice of repentance can take anywhere from a week to a year. A rather elaborate example of such a practice of repentance can be found in the *Contemplation of the Universal Sage Bodhisattva Sutra* that is the closing part of the *Threefold Lotus Sūtra*. The practice described in that sūtra is the basis of the Lotus Sūtra Penance Ceremony (J. *Hokke Sembō*) that is practiced by Nichiren Shū and other schools of East Asian Buddhism. Considering the high standards set by the bodhisattva precepts and the provisions for repentance when they are broken, it could be said that the Mahāyāna precept tradition is both more idealistic and more forgiving.

Based on the teachings of the Mahāyāna sūtras, the Discipline school taught that all the various formulations of precepts and practices, both Hīnayāna and Mahāyāna, are embraced by the three categories of pure precepts of the bodhisattva. These three are: the precepts for maintaining restraint that embrace all rules of discipline in order to put an end to all evil; the precepts that encompass all good deeds and teachings in order to cultivate all good; and the precepts for benefiting sentient beings so that they may all be liberated from suffering. (Pruden, pp. 14-15) By taking and living in accord with the three categories of pure precepts, bodhisattvas would fulfill the threefold training (morality, concentration, and wisdom), the six perfections, and all other practices needed to attain buddhahood and liberate all beings. Though the Discipline school focuses on the precepts, its vision of the three categories of pure precepts is so comprehensive as to take in all other teachings and practices, both Hīnayāna and Mahāyāna.

The precepts and the development of morality is a very fundamental part of the Buddhist path. The precepts lay the groundwork for the further mental and emotional development that will eventually lead to liberation. In taking up the precepts, the follower of the Buddha consciously affirms the most basic values that all people seem to know instinctively. Through the development of basic morality, we are protected from all manner of evil; whether the inner torment of a guilty conscience, the social and legal consequences of wrongdoing, or a future rebirth in unfortunate circumstances. Taking the precepts is also a sign of determination and sincerity. It shows that we are no longer willing to compromise our integrity or harm others for worldly gain, because we have aspired to the highest goal. The precepts also cause us to be more mindful of our daily activities; they provide a yardstick by which we can improve our character in every facet of life through exploring their implications in everyday situations.

The precepts are not just negative injunctions either; each of the precepts has a positive value as well. Those who truly follow the precepts against killing, stealing, sexual misconduct, lying and taking intoxicants will naturally develop the qualities of humility, love, compassion, generosity and honesty. Such people will not harm themselves or others; and instead, will seek to protect all beings. In being guided by the precepts, we can cultivate a character that is not only blameless, but also pure and worthy of respect.

Morality is an indispensable element of the Buddhist path, but moral discipline is not an end unto itself. Morality that is not supported by the practice of concentration and insight can easily wither away or degenerate into puritanical self-righteousness. It is only truly fulfilled when it acts as the basis for the cultivation of the mind that leads to perfect and complete awakening for the sake of oneself and all other beings. For the bodhisattva, morality functions as one of the perfections when it is guided by wisdom and thus accompanied by generosity, patience, energy, and meditation, all of which are practiced for the sake of all beings.

Sources

Ch'en, Kenneth. *Buddhism in China: A Historical Survey*. Princeton: Princeton University Press, 1964.

Gosho Translation Committee, editor-translator. *The Writings of Nichiren Daishonin*. Tokyo: Soka Gakkai, 1999.

Hori, Kyotsu, comp. *Writings of Nichiren Shonin: Doctrine Volume 2*. Tokyo: Nichiren Shu Overseas Propagation Promotion Association, 2002.

Horner, I.B., trans. *The Book of the Discipline Volumes 1-6*. Oxford: Pali Text Society, 1993.

Murano, Senchu. *Kaimokusho or Liberation from Blindness*. Berkeley: Numata Center for Buddhist Translation and Research, 2000.

Nanamoli, Bhikkhu, trans. *The Life of the Buddha*. Seattle: Buddhist Publication Society Pariyatti Editions, 2001.

Nearman, Hubert, translator. *Buddhist Writings on Meditation and Daily Practice: The Serene-Reflection Meditation Tradition*. Mount Shasta: Shasta Abbey, 1994.

Pruden, Leo, trans. *The Essentials of the Vinaya Tradition*. BDK English Tripitika 97-I, II. Berkeley: Numata Center for Buddhist Translation and Research, 1995.

Walshe, Maurice, trans. *The Long Discourses of the Buddha: A Translation of the Digha Nikaya*. Boston: Wisdom Publications, 1995.

Chapter 37 – The Discipline School in Japan

Writings of Nichiren Shōnin Doctrine 2, pp. 34-35, 57-57, 76, 91, 94, 99
Kaimoku-shō or Liberation from Blindness, pp. 13-14, 47-48, 72, 93, 98, 108.
The Writings of Nichiren Daishonin I, pp. 224, 242-243, 257, 269, 271, 275.

The Discipline school (J. Ritsu Shū) based upon the Dharmaguptaka recension of the vinaya found in the *Four-part Discipline* was brought to Japan by Jianzhen (J. Ganjin 688-763) in the year 753 after many trials and tribulations (eleven years of five unsuccessful attempts to cross over to Japan prior to the sixth successful trip and by that time Jianzhen had become partially blind and thirty-six of his companions had died due to shipwrecks, attacks by pirates, and other hardships). The Japanese imperial court and Buddhist clergy had eagerly sought this transmission from Jianzhen so that they could claim a legitimate transmission of the vinaya. In 755, Jianzhen established a precept platform (J. *kaidan*) at Tōdaiji Temple in Nara, and two more precept platforms were established in 761 at Yakushiji Temple (in present day Tochigi prefecture) and Kanzeonji Temple (in present day Fukuoka prefecture). In order to join the Sangha, candidates had to go to one of these three official precept platforms in order to take refuge in the Three Treasures and accept the Dharmaguptaka precepts.

Relations between Jianzhen and the Japanese government eventually broke down, however. Daigan and Alician Matsunaga summarize what occurred:

> *Unfortunately by the time Ganjin arrived, the Ritsuryō government had already formulated some definite ideas of its own concerning ideal priestly behavior, which were supported by certain senior monks serving as government officials. It was natural for Ganjin to presume that after all the difficulties he had experienced in reaching Japan at the express request of the government, that he should be solely in charge of matters concerning ordination. In the eyes of the government on the other hand, Ganjin may have been a*

great vinaya master, but he was not knowledgeable regarding either the language or situation in Japan. A Japanese system of ordination had already been devised by now and Ganjin's presence was viewed primarily as a formality to fulfill orthodox Buddhist requirements. If a candidate for ordination received government sanction, no need was visualized for the type of training Ganjin considered to be necessary; thus from the start the relationship between Ganjin and the government was strained. In 758 Ganjin resigned as an official of the Sōgō (Bureau of Priests) and placed his disciple Hosshin in charge of official ordinations. The Zoku Nihonji tactfully gave the reason for Ganjin's retirement to be that he found political affairs too confusing for his advanced age (he was 71). (Matsunaga, p. 51)

The imperial court in Japan was not at all interested in importing a system whereby itinerant mendicants would wander the countryside preaching the Dharma to all, subsisting on alms given by private citizens, and meditating in the forest. Rather, it was the case that Buddhism was viewed as something that could serve the state. Since Buddhism was accepted in Japan not out of respect for the Buddha's institution of the Sangha as an assembly of mendicants seeking liberation from birth and death but for the magical efficacy it was hoped Buddhist ceremonies could provide the state, it should not be surprising that, before long the Dharmaguptaka precepts were declared Hīnayāna and therefore obsolete. By the ninth century, the fortunes of the Discipline school in Japan had greatly declined.

Saichō (767-822), the founder of the Japanese Tendai school of Buddhism, was the one who initiated the move away from the Dharmaguptaka vinaya. He believed that it was inconsistent for Mahāyāna Buddhists to have to abide by what he saw as Hīnayāna precepts. According to Saichō, Mahāyāna Buddhists should accept the ten major and forty-eight minor bodhisattva precepts of the *Brahmā's Net Sūtra*, a sūtra that was allegedly translated by Kumārajīva. The conservative clergy of the older schools of Japanese Buddhism opposed this because they wished to maintain control over the ordinations of Buddhist monastics, but Saichō's efforts finally bore fruit after his death in 822 CE. According to Paul Groner:

*The Brahma's Net precepts were a set of Mahāyāna
rules compiled in China in the fifth century. They were
very popular in East Asia and often conferred on laymen
in order to strengthen their Buddhist ties. Jianzhen used
them in this manner when he performed Brahma's Net
ordinations shortly after his arrival in Japan. In addition,
the Brahma's Net precepts were also conferred on
monks and nuns, not to give them the status of monks
and nuns, but to reinforce the Mahāyāna quality of
their attitudes and practices. Most monks saw no
conflict between receiving the complete precepts
(upasampadā) of the Four-part Discipline first and the
Brahma's Net ordination second. (Groner, p. 9 adapted)*

Saichō reversed this. For his own Tendai trainees, he wished them to take the
precepts of the *Brahmā's Net Sūtra* first, and then train for twelve years on
Mt. Hiei as bodhisattva monks. At the end of that training they could then take
the Dharmaguptaka precepts taken by the other monks and nuns in Japan.
This would achieve two things: 1. It would remove the Tendai monks from the
jurisdiction of the Sōgō (Bureau of Priests) and 2. It would ensure that Tendai
monks were thoroughly Mahāyāna in their views and aspirations and would
not turn to more limited Hīnayāna views and aspirations by taking Hīnayāna
precepts during their initial training. Permission to build a new precept
platform at Mt. Hiei, the head temple of Saichō's Tendai School, for the sole
transmission of the Mahāyāna precepts of the *Brahmā's Net Sūtra* was finally
granted by the government after Saichō's death. After its construction in 827,
the Mahāyāna precepts of the *Brahmā's Net Sūtra* became the standard of
conduct for almost all Japanese Buddhists.

Saichō's plan of having Tendai monks live according to the lifestyle and aims
spelled out in the *Brahma's Net Sūtra* and also according to the lifestyle and
regulations of the Dharmaguptaka vinaya did not become a reality. For many
reasons that Paul Groner discusses in his book on Saichō, the Tendai monks
never did take the Dharmaguptaka vinaya. In fact, sometime between 823
and 828 and again in 877 the court actually issued edicts prohibiting the
Tendai monks and the monks of Nara from taking each other's precepts. From

that time on, the Tendai monks of Japan took only precepts of the *Brahmā's Net Sūtra*.

Even these were viewed as obsolete by later generations of Tendai monks. "Several centuries after Saichō's death, a movement began in the Tendai School to deemphasize the role of the *Brahma's Net* precepts as Tendai precepts in favor of the more ambiguous formless precepts of the *Lotus Sūtra*." (Ibid, p. 205) Japanese Buddhist monks were basically trying to find a set of precepts or, even better, a single precept that was at once the most profound and the least exacting and therefore the most flexible.

Part of the reason for this discomfort with the precepts was that it was believed that people were no longer capable of living up to specified codes of conduct, whether householder or monastic, because the Latter Age of Degeneration (J. mappō) had arrived. According to "prophecies" given by the Buddha (in both Pāli works and Mahāyāna sūtras) there would be a period of decline in the teaching and practice of the Buddha Dharma after the Buddha's passing. The first period would be the age of the True Dharma, which would last for five hundred or a thousand years (depending on the source text) during which it would be possible to hear the Dharma, practice it, and attain liberation. This would be followed by the period of the Semblance Dharma for another period of a thousand years during which time it would be possible to practice to some extent, but final liberation would no longer be possible. Then the Latter Age of Degeneration would begin, during which time even practice would become corrupted. According to an essay attributed to Saichō called the *Candle of the Latter Dharma* (J. *Mappō tōmyō ki*), in the Latter Age, it would no longer be possible to find pure monks so that one should instead respect and support the nominal monks. The *Candle of the Latter Dharma* says:

> *However, the point under discussion here concerns the fact that in the Latter Dharma, there are only nominal bhikshus. These nominal bhikshus are the True Treasures of the world. There are no other fields of merit where one can plant merit. Furthermore, if someone were to keep the precepts of the Latter Dharma, this would be exceedingly strange indeed. It*

would be like a tiger in the marketplace. Who would
believe it? (Rhodes, p. 9)

In Nichiren's day, Eizon (1201-1290) revived the Discipline school in conjunction with esoteric Buddhism, thereby establishing the Mantra-Discipline school (J. Shingon Ritsu Shū). Eizon began his efforts in 1236 when he and three other monks, inspired by Mahāyāna sūtras permitting self-ordination, conferred upon themselves the precepts at Tōdaiji Temple because there were no longer enough monks qualified as preceptors to do a formal ordination. Eizon taught at Saidaiji Temple in Nara and also traveled throughout the country. He soon won the support of the imperial court and the Hōjō rulers upon whom he bestowed the bodhisattva precepts. It is said that by the end of his life he had given the precepts to 97,710 people, from rulers to outcastes. In addition to promoting and conferring the precepts, Eizon also popularized the practices of chanting the name of Śākyamuni Buddha and the Mantra of Radiant Light. He also established 1,356 places of sanctuary for animals where hunting and fishing were prohibited. In 1300, the Retired Emperor Kameyama gave him the posthumous name Kōshō Bosatsu.

Ninshō (aka Ryōkan, 1217-1303) was Eizon's most successful disciple. He went to Kamakura in 1261 and there received the patronage of the Hōjō regents. He established the Kōsenji Temple at that time and went on to restore the Gokurakuji Temple in 1267. He lived a simple austere life and like his master devoted himself to social works such as the building of hospitals, bridges, and roads. He received many honors from the Hōjō regents and was considered one of the foremost practitioners of esoteric ceremonies for the protection of the nation. Consequently, he was assigned to be the abbot of several other temples in Kamakura and elsewhere in Japan, including the Daibutsuji in Kamakura, Tōdaiji in Nara, and Shitennnōji in Osaka. In 1328, Emperor Go-Daigo gave him the posthumous name Ninshō Bosatsu. Nichiren considered Ryōkan to be one of his primary adversaries in the political and religious establishment of Kamakura.

Nichiren himself did not emphasize adherence to the precepts. In fact, he referred to his contemporaries Eizon and Ryōkan as "national traitors" (Hori 2003, p. 273) because they were propagating the "Hīnayāna" precepts of the Dharmaguptaka vinaya. In the *Shimoyama Letter* (Hori 2008, pp. 71-75) Nichiren explained that in the Latter Age it was no longer appropriate to propagate the Hīnayāna precepts, as they would burden people who were not able to uphold them and whose delusions were too deep to be cured by them. He accused the precept masters of dishonesty and hypocrisy who were leading the nation of Japan to destruction by causing its rulers and people to rely on a teaching no longer appropriate to their own time and place.

In Nichiren's view, the Hīnayāna precepts had long since been replaced by the Mahāyāna precepts of the *Brahmā's Net Sūtra* instituted by Saichō (Grand Master Dengyō) at Mt. Hiei. Nichiren even refers to the *Candle of the Latter Age* attributed to Saichō. In his essay on spiritual practice appropriate to the people living in the Latter Age, *Four Depths of Faith and Five Stages of Practice*, Nichiren wrote:

> *Grand Master Dengyō said, 'I have discarded all 250 precepts.' Grand Master Dengyō was not the only one to do this. Jianzhen's disciples, Jubao and Dōchū, and the seven great temples (of Nara) all completely discarded the precepts as well. Grand Master Dengyo also cautioned future generations saying, 'In the Latter Age of Degeneration a person who can uphold the precepts will be as astonishing as a tiger in the marketplace. Who can believe this?'* (Hori 2007, p. 106 adapted)

In that same essay he also wrote:

> *Beginners should refrain from giving alms, observing the precepts, and the rest of the first five bodhisattva practices and for the present should instead take up the practice of Namu Myōhō Renge Kyō which is the spirit of the single moment of understanding by faith and the stage of rejoicing, This is the true intention of the Lotus Sūtra.* (Ibid, p. 104)

It is clear that Nichiren was no longer advocating even the Mahāyāna precepts of the *Brahmā's Net Sūtra*. He believed that the practice of revering the true spirit of the *Lotus Sūtra* by invoking its title transcended any precept codes or particular Buddhist practices or lifestyles inherited from the past as those were all just provisional methods based on provisional teachings that were no longer efficacious. The following statements of his in other writings also express his view that faith in the *Lotus Sūtra* is what leads to buddhahood and not the observance of precepts:

> *Speaking of Ajātaśatru and Devadatta: "I am convinced that ordinary people in the Latter Age of Degeneration commit sins more or less. Whether or not such a man can reach Buddhahood depends not on how serious his sin is but whether or not he believes in the Lotus Sūtra. (Hori 2002, p. 188)*

> *It is preached in the Lotus Sūtra, the "Appearance of the Stūpa of Treasures" chapter, 'Upholding this sūtra is what is called observing the precepts.' (Hori 2004, p. 214)*

In addition, Nichiren would occasionally refer to himself as a "monk without precepts." This may be because as a novice monk with no social standing from a country temple, he may never have been able to take the full Mahāyāna precepts from the precept platform at Mt. Hiei – there were, in fact, many monks at that time who were *shidosō*, or "privately ordained" who did not or even could not receive full ordination at any of the officially sanctioned precept platforms. Or it could be that in having been exiled (twice) by the government he had been defrocked as Shinran had been. Unlike Shinran, however, Nichiren continued to live the life of a Buddhist monk until the end of his life. He never married, remained a vegetarian, and only drank alcohol for medicinal purposes towards the end of his life. Yet, he makes no claims for himself on this basis. He sees upholding or rejecting the precepts as a matter of little to no import compared to his primary mission of upholding and teaching the *Lotus Sūtra* and particularly the practice of chanting its title as the supremely efficacious Buddhist practice for the Latter Age. Here are some passages from his writings that express this view:

> *Because I am a priest of no precepts who holds perverse views, the heavenly gods hate me and I am poor in both food and clothing. Nevertheless, I recite the Lotus Sūtra*

and from time to time preach it. It is exactly as if a huge snake were clasping a jewel in its mouth or sandalwood trees were growing amid the eranda groves. I throw away the eranda and offer the sandalwood, or cover the body of the snake and bestow the jewel. (Gosho Translation Committee 2006, p. 944)

I, Nichiren, do not observe the precepts with my body. Nor is my heart free from the three poisons. But since I believe in this [Lotus] sūtra myself and also enable others to form a relationship with it, I had thought that perhaps society would treat me rather gently. Probably because the world has entered into the latter age, even monks who have wives and children have followers, as do priests who eat fish and fowl. I have neither wife nor children, nor do I eat fish or fowl. I have been blamed merely for trying to propagate the Lotus Sūtra. Though I have neither wife nor children, I am known throughout the country as a monk who transgresses the code of conduct, and though I have never killed even a single ant or mole cricket, my bad reputation has spread throughout the realm. This may well resemble the situation of Śākyamuni Buddha, who was slandered by a multitude of non-Buddhists during his lifetime. (Gosho Translation Committee 1999, p. 42)

I, Nichiren, am not the founder of any school, nor am I a latter day follower of any older school. I am a priest without precepts, neither keeping the precepts nor breaking them. (Ibid, p. 669)

Now I am neither a sage nor a worthy man; I neither adhere to the precepts, nor am I without precepts; I neither possess wisdom nor lack it. Nevertheless, I was born some 2,220 years after the Buddha's passing, in the last five-hundred-year period, when the daimoku of the Lotus Sūtra is destined to spread. Before any other person of the various schools – whether here in Japan or in the far-off land of India and China – could begin to invoke the daimoku, I began chanting Namu Myōhō

*Renge Kyō in a loud voice and have continued to do so
for more than twenty years. (Ibid, p. 671)*

In order to reflect his new understanding of the Buddha and Buddhist practice, Nichiren believed that the time had come for the establishment of a new precept platform. Nichiren taught that it was impractical for the ordinary person in the Latter Age of the Dharma to attempt to approach awakening by merely adhering to a code of conduct. People no longer felt capable of living up to these various sets of precepts; many of those who did had come to realize that morality and ethics alone do not bring anyone closer to awakening. Of course, there were also hypocrites who strictly adhered to the letter of the precepts while violating their spirit. In order to remedy this, Nichiren taught that the true spirit of all the various sets of precepts is expressed in the *Lotus Sūtra*. Therefore, the most important thing is to simply strive to uphold the *Lotus Sūtra* in order to transcend one's imperfections and attain awakening. This is the true fulfillment of all the precepts.

The *Manual of Nichiren Buddhism* explains this as follows:

> *Nichiren claimed that the kaidan at Hieizan was
> established for the priests whose duty was to save the
> people of the semblance age of the Dharma and that a
> new kaidan should be established for the priests who
> would save those of the latter age of the Dharma. He
> also held that not only priests but also laymen should
> come to the Kaidan of the Essential Teaching and
> receive the Fundamental Precept of Nichiren Buddhism,
> that is to chant the Daimoku, which should be practiced
> by all living beings, priests or not. (Murano 1995, p. 62)*

Teaching, Practice and Proof, a writing attributed to Nichiren, refers to the "fundamental precept" of upholding the *Lotus Sūtra* as the "Diamond Chalice Precept." The following passage from the *Brahmā's Net Sūtra* is a possible source for this precept: "This precept of the diamond chalice is the source of all Buddhas, the source of all bodhisattvas and the seed of the Buddha nature." Nichiren realized that if the Wonderful Dharma of the Lotus Flower Teaching, Myōhō Renge Kyō, is the enlightenment of the Eternal Śākyamuni

470

Buddha and therefore the seed of buddhahood, then Myōhō Renge Kyō is itself the Diamond Chalice Precept. By chanting Namu Myōhō Renge Kyō, practitioners would be upholding the Diamond Chalice Precept that embraces all other precepts. Nichiren goes on to say in *Teaching, Practice and Proof*:

> Afterwards, [explain that] the core realization of Myōhō Renge Kyō, which is the main gate of the Lotus Sūtra, contains all the merits of the practices and virtues of all the buddhas of the past, present, and future, which manifests as the five characters. How could these five characters not contain the merits of all precepts? Once the practitioner has this comprehensive Wonderful Precept, even if he wants to destroy it, he cannot. This has been called the "Diamond Chalice Precept." All buddhas of the past, present, and future keep this precept. All the Dharma-bodies, reward-bodies, and accommodative-bodies become the buddhas of no beginning and no end. The Great Master Tiantai wrote: "[The Buddha] secretly put this into all the teachings and did not expound it." Now when all people, whether wise or foolish, householder or home-leaver, upper or lower class, of the present latter age of the Dharma train themselves in accord with the view of Myōhō Renge Kyō, why should they not obtain buddhahood? [The twenty-first chapter of the Lotus Sūtra states:] "Therefore, the man of wisdom who hears the benefits of these merits and who keeps this sūtra after my extinction will be able to attain the awakening of the Buddha definitely and doubtlessly." The people of the provisional schools who slip away from this decisive teaching of the three Buddhas (Śākyamuni, Many Treasures, and the emanation buddhas of the ten directions) will definitely end up in the Avici Hell. Similarly, if this precept is so excellent, then all the precepts of the previous provisional teaching will have no merit. Without any merit, the daily rules of abstention are useless. (Kyōgyōshō Gosho in the Shōwa

teihon p. 1488 as translated by Yumi and Michael McCormick)

Based on this understanding of the precepts, Nichiren Buddhism teaches that the Hīnayāna precept platform and the Mahāyāna precept platform are now obsolete: the time has arrived for the precept platform of the Diamond Chalice Precept that subsumes all other precepts. From this point of view, the practice of Namu Myōhō Renge Kyō ensures that morality and ethics are not unthinking, rigid adherence to any specific code of conduct. Rather, the moral and ethical life is based directly upon the wisdom and compassion of buddhahood. There is no need to go to a specially sanctioned place in order to receive the Diamond Chalice Precept. Wherever Namu Myōhō Renge Kyō is recited becomes the precept platform where all can dedicate their lives to the Wonderful Dharma and attain enlightenment. It is the place where all people of the world, lay or ordained, can receive the Wonderful Dharma of the Lotus Flower Teaching directly from the Eternal Śākyamuni Buddha, just as the bodhisattvas from beneath the earth received it during the Assembly in Space In a writing called *The Transmission of the Three Great Secret Dharmas*, Nichiren's position on the precept platform of the essential teaching [of the *Lotus Sūtra*] (J. *honmon no kaidan*) is clarified (at least for a medieval Japanese context):

> *Regarding the kaidan center for the practice of the Lotus Sūtra, should it not be established at the most outstanding place resembling the Pure Land of Mt. Sacred Eagle with the blessing of an imperial edict and a shogunal directive? Should it not be at such a time when the laws of the kingdom and Buddhist dharmas are in perfect accord with both king and his subjects all believing in the three great secret dharmas revealed in the Original Gate of the Lotus Sūtra, and the meritorious work of King Virtuous and the monk Virtue Consciousness in the past recur in the evil and corrupt world in the Latter Age of Degeneration? We have to wait for the opportune time for its realization. This is what we call the actual precept platform (ji-no-kaidan), where all the people of India, China, and Japan as well as of the Sahā World should repent their sins.*

472

Furthermore such heavenly beings as the great King of the Brahmā Heaven and Indra should come to assemble to practice the Lotus teaching.

After the establishment of this precept platform of the Original Gate of the Lotus Sūtra, the one on Mt. Hiei based on the Trace Gate of the sūtra would be useless. (Hori 2002, p. 290 adapted)

It would seem as though Nichiren were proposing that the celibate monastic lifestyle and the precepts that encoded that way of life were to be a thing of the past, an obsolete Hīnayāna practice. And yet, Nichiren never rejected that way of living the way Shinran had. In fact, he often exhorted his disciples to uphold Confucian and Buddhist standards of conduct even though they did not take such precepts formally or depend upon them for enlightenment. In the *Letter Sent with the Prayer Sūtra,* Nichiren states that one who upholds the *Lotus Sūtra* in the Latter Age should be especially dedicated to the celibate monastic lifestyle of those who live by the precepts.

But now you have cast aside the Nembutsu and the other beliefs of the provisional teachings and have put your faith in the correct teaching. Hence you are in truth among the purest of the observers of the precepts, a sage. To begin with, anyone who is a priest, even if he is a follower of the provisional schools of Buddhism, should be pure [in the observance of the precepts], and how much more one who is a votary of the correct teaching! Though one may have had a wife and family when one was a follower of the provisional schools, in a time of great trouble such as the present, he should cast all these aside and devote himself to the propagation of the correct teaching. And in your case you were a sage to begin with [because you observed the precepts]. How admirable, how admirable. (Gosho Translation Committee 2006, p. 461)

In the centuries after Nichiren's passing, the various lineages of Nichiren Buddhism continued to uphold the monastic way of living, even if they did not formally take either the Dharmaguptaka Vinaya or the Mahāyāna precepts of the *Brahmā's Net Sūtra*. I would like to note that in the seventeenth century a Nichiren monk named Gensei (1623-1668) did teach the importance of the precepts and advocated the Lotus Vinaya. A capsule biography on him can be found in the book *Shapers of Japanese Buddhism*, and I hope that someday some of Gensei's writings on the Lotus Vinaya and the value of precepts within the Nichiren Buddhist tradition will become available in English. Still, just knowing about him reveals to me that not only was the monastic lifestyle upheld by Nichiren Buddhist clergy (though probably no more or less strictly than the other monastic schools), but there were those who were especially interested in maintaining some form of precepts as part of their practice of the *Lotus Sūtra*.

Sources

Gosho Translation Committee, editor-translator. *The Writings of Nichiren Daishonin*. Tokyo: Soka Gakkai, 1999.

_____. *The Writings of Nichiren Daishonin Volume II*. Tokyo: Soka Gakkai, 2006.

Groner, Paul. Saichō: *The Establishment of the Japanese Tendai School*. Berkeley: Berkeley Buddhist Studies Series, 1984.

Hori, Kyotsu, comp. *Writings of Nichiren Shonin: Doctrine Volume 2*. Tokyo: Nichiren Shu Overseas Propagation Promotion Association, 2002.

_____. *Writings of Nichiren Shonin: Doctrine Volume 1*. Tokyo: Nichiren Shu Overseas Propagation Promotion Association, 2003.

_____. *Writings of Nichiren Shonin: Doctrine Volume 3*. Tokyo: Nichiren Shu Overseas Propagation Promotion Association, 2004.

_____. *Writings of Nichiren Shonin: Faith and Practice Volume 4*. Tokyo: Nichiren Shu Overseas Propagation Promotion Association, 2007.

_____. *Writings of Nichiren Shonin: Biography and Disciples Volume 5*. Tokyo: Nichiren Shu Overseas Propagation Promotion Association, 2008.

Kasahara, Kazuo. *A History of Japanese Religion*. Tokyo: Kosei Publishing Co., 2002.

Kashiwahara, Yusen & Sonoda, Koyu. *Shapers of Japanese Buddhism*. Tokyo: Kosei Publishing Co., 1994.

Matsunaga, Alicia & Matsunaga, Daigan. *Foundation of Japanese Buddhism Vol. I & II*. Los Angeles: Buddhist Books International, 1988.

Murano, Senchu. *Manual of Nichiren Buddhism*. Tokyo: Nichiren Shu Headquarters, 1995.

_____. *Kaimokusho or Liberation from Blindness*. Berkeley: Numata Center for Buddhist Translation and Research, 2000.

Nearman, Hubert, translator. *Buddhist Writings on Meditation and Daily Practice: The Serene-Reflection Meditation Tradition*. Mount Shasta: Shasta Abbey, 1994.

Pruden, Leo, trans. *The Essentials of the Vinaya Tradition*. BDK English Tripitika 97-I, II. Berkeley: Numata Center for Buddhist Translation and Research, 1995.

Rhodes, Robert, trans. *The Candle of the Latter Dharma*. BDK English Tripitika 107-I, III. Berkeley: Numata Center for Buddhist Translation and Research, 1994.

Chapter 38 – Divine Protection and Demonic Predations

Writing of Nichiren Shōnin: Doctrine Vol. 2, pp. 37, 53, 56, 58, 64, 80-81, 105, 107

Kaimoku-shō or Liberation from Blindness, pp. 17, 42, 46-47, 49, 56, 77, 113-114, 116

The Writings of Nichiren Daishonin I, pp. 226, 239, 242, 243, 247-248, 261, 280, 281

Throughout the *Kaimoku-shō*, Nichiren questions why he has not been protected from persecution and hardships by the buddhas, great bodhisattvas, the major śrāvaka disciples who had been given predictions of buddhahood, and other supernatural beings. Because he has upheld the *Lotus Sūtra* he expects such protection, and so the seeming lack of it is a cause of doubt for both himself and his supporters. This, he says, is in fact the main issue that *Kaimoku-shō* was written to address.

> *Nevertheless, people doubt me, and I myself wonder why gods and deities have not come to help me. They made vows to the Buddha to protect a practitioner of the Lotus Sūtra. I would think, therefore, that they should hurriedly come to his aid, calling him a practitioner of the Lotus Sūtra, even if they have suspicions about him, and carry out their promise to the Buddha. Yet, none has come to help me. Does this mean that I am not a practitioner of the Lotus Sūtra? Since this question is the basis of this writing and of cardinal importance in my life, I will take this up again and again in order to find a definitive answer. (Hori 2002, p. 58 adapted)*

Nichiren and his contemporaries wondered why the gods and other powerful spiritual beings had not come to Nichiren's rescue if he was indeed in the right. Skeptical people today would simply say that the absence of divine protection has nothing to do with the views or conduct of an individual or society but is simply because there is no such thing as supernatural beings and divine protection. Many educated modern people have trouble believing in even one God, let alone a whole pantheon of gods from another culture such as the Shintō kami or the Vedic devas that Nichiren and his contemporaries took for granted as actual beings who could be prayed to or even taken to task for not fulfilling their vows – such as to protect the practitioners of the *Lotus Sūtra*. Even today, however, there are those who believe that there may be such things as guardian angels or other ineffable but benevolent forces at work in and through the circumstances that make up our lives. This may be an authentic intuition or a delusion to stave off our insecurities, nevertheless the existence of such benevolent spiritual beings was the common sense of people in past ages and even the Buddha asserted their existence. I think that it is most honest to frankly admit that we (or at least I personally) do not know if there are such things as benevolent spiritual beings that can influence events in the material world. I have never seen or experienced anything that would offer concrete proof of such beings. For the moment, let's set aside the question of their actual existence or non-existence. Rather, I think it would be more helpful to first try to understand Nichiren's view of these beings within the context of his own time and place. With that understood, we can return to the question of how we can make sense of his doubts and his reflections on and response to those concerns.

In Japanese Buddhism, the heavenly gods and benevolent deities (J. *shoten zenjin*), are the guardian deities (J. *shugojin*) who protect the practitioners of Buddhism. The calligraphic mandala that Nichiren inscribed to represent the "focus of devotion" (J. *honzon*) of the Origin Gate of the *Lotus Sūtra* includes representatives of different types of guardian deities. There are the four leaders of the Bodhisattvas of the Earth from chapter fifteen and who are given the specific transmission to spread the *Lotus Sūtra* in the Latter Age in chapter twenty-one; there are the bodhisattvas who represent the provisional teachings such as Medicine King, Beautiful Lord (S. Mañjuśrī), Universal Good (S. Samantabhadra), and Loving One (S. Maitreya); there are the two Knowledge Kings (S. *vidyā-rājas*) Immovable Lord (S. Acalanātha, J. Fudō) and Desire King (S. Rāgāraja; J. Aizen); there are the arhats who have received predictions of buddhahood like Śāriputra and Mahākāśyapa; there are the Vedic deities (S. *deva*) Brahmā, Indra, Sūrya (the sun god), Candra (the moon god), and Aruna (the morning star), and the four heavenly kings who guard the four quarters of the world; and there are even the two major Shintō gods

(J. *kami*) Tenshō Daijiin (aka Amaterasu Ōmikami) and Hachiman (called the "Great Bodhisattva). In addition, other beings that are not as exalted as celestial bodhisattvas or gods can also be considered guardians. In *Kaimoku-shō*, Nichiren specifically mentions the ten *rākṣasī* (vampire like women of Indian mythology) who appear in chapter twenty-six of the *Lotus Sūtra*. In that chapter, these *rākṣasī* and their mother, Hārītī (J. Kishimojin) bestow *dhāraṇīs* for the protection of the practitioner of the *Lotus Sūtra*. On the calligraphic mandala, Nichiren also included the asura (a kind of titan or demon) and nāga (the dragons of Indian mythology) kings who appear in chapter one of the *Lotus Sūtra* among the congregation gathered to hear the Buddha's teaching. Traditionally in Buddhism there are eight kinds of supernatural beings that are considered to be disciples of the Buddha and guardians of the Dharma. These eight are *devas*, *nāgas*, *garudas* (giant birds who prey on the nāgas), *asuras*, *yakṣas* (nature spirits), *gandharvas* (anthropomorphic equines), *mahorāgas* (pythons), and *kiṃnaras* (anthropomorphic avians). This group of eight is mentioned throughout the *Lotus Sūtra*. These are the beings that Nichiren is thinking of when he asks why he has not received divine protection.

Previously I have discussed how the various Vedic deities are personifications of the forces of nature or aspects of life and death and how they appeared in the life story of the Buddha. There are a few other things I'd like to point out about them. Brahmā, in addition to being the Vedic creator deity, is also said to have infinite loving-kindness, compassion, sympathetic joy, and equanimity. Brahmā lives in the heaven reached by those who are able to attain meditative absorption by reflecting upon and cultivating those four positive affective qualities that came to be called *Brahmavihāras* or "abodes of Brahma." The name of the god Indra means "power" or "mastery" over the faculties of life (as represented by the other thirty-two gods who live atop Mt. Sumeru). Indra also appears in several sūtras in the guise of a demon (S. *rākṣasas*) or greedy brahmins who tests bodhisattvas by asking them to sacrifice body parts or even their lives for the sake of the Dharma, and who then rewards them when they are able to pass such tests with generosity and courageous perseverance. The sūtras also state that in the course of their many lifetimes of accumulating merit and working for the welfare of all being the celestial bodhisattvas can take on the role of Brahmā or Indra or any other god or spirit in this or any of a myriad other worlds. Examples of this are in the *Lotus Sūtra*, for instance in chapters twenty-four and twenty-five wherein it is stated that among the many forms that can be taken on by Wonderful Voice Bodhisattva and World Voice Perceiver Bodhisattva are Brahmā and Śakra (aka Indra) as well as many other types of beings and classes of people. It should be pointed out that Brahmā and Indra aren't so much unique individuals as they are roles or functions that can be taken on temporarily by various transmigrating beings. Every world system in the Vedic cosmology has an Indra ruling atop its respective Mt. Sumeru, and there are many Brahmās residing in many Brahmā heavens overlooking the all the worlds with their Mt. Sumerus and four continents. So really, there are many Indras and Brahmās who are actually celestial bodhisattvas who work to encourage and at times test other bodhisattvas and to uphold and protect the Dharma and its practitioners.

In *Kaimoku-shō*, Nichiren speculates that one reason the protection of these beings may not be forthcoming is because the heavenly gods and protective deities have left Japan. They have left because the Japanese people have neglected and even slandered the *Lotus Sūtra*.

> *Not having tasted the delicacy of the True Dharma, such great righteous guardian deities as Goddess Amaterasu, Shōhachiman and Sannō left the land, leaving room for demons to grow in power, and this country was about to crumble. (Ibid, p. 37)*

> *It could also be that the True Dharma has been slandered and guardian gods have abandoned this land of Japan. As a result, the slanderers of the True Dharma are not punished while those upholding it are left without divine assistance and are subjected to great difficulties. What is said in the Golden Splendor Sūtra: "The number of those who practice the True Dharma grows less by the day" refers to this land today, when the True Dharma is being slandered. I have explained this in detail in my Risshō Ankoku-ron. (Ibid, p. 105 adapted)*

Indeed, in *Risshō Ankoku-ron*, the traveler in the dialogue states, "As a result, sages and protective gods have abandoned our country, causing famine and epidemics to spread all over it." (Hori 2003, p. 137) This statement became a source of great controversy within Nichiren Buddhism after Nichiren's passing. According to this statement (as well as Nichiren's later statements such as in the passages of *Kaimoku-shō* cited above), one can no longer appeal to the heavenly gods and benevolent deities because they have abandoned the country that slanders the Dharma. In other writings, however, Nichiren continues to appeal to the kami and other deities in his prayers. In the *Kangyō Hachiman-shō*, Nichiren identifies Hachiman as a manifestation in Japan of Śākyamuni Buddha and explicitly states that the kami are still available to those who uphold the *Lotus Sūtra*.

> *Now, the Great Bodhisattva Hachiman's original substance, Śākyamuni Buddha, expounded the sole, true, Lotus Sūtra in India. As he manifested himself in Japan, he summarized the sūtra in two Chinese characters for honesty and vowed to live in the head of a wise man. If so, even if Hachiman burned his palace and ascended to heaven, whenever he finds a practitioner of the Lotus Sūtra in Japan, he will not fail to come down to reside where this practitioner is and protect him. (Ibid, p. 279 adapted)*

Later generations of Nichiren Buddhists would be divided by the question of whether Nichiren intended them to cease to venerate the kami because they were no longer available in a country that neglected and slandered the *Lotus Sūtra*, or whether they could continue to have confidence in and pay respects to the kami at their shrines because they were still protectors of the *Lotus Sūtra* and those who uphold and practice it. Considering that Nichiren included Amaterasu, Hachiman, and other gods and supernatural beings on his calligraphic mandala, perhaps it can be said that Nichiren believed that practitioners of the *Lotus Sūtra* could still venerate and appeal to the kami and other guardian deities and spirits. If the guardian deities are not entirely absent but still watching out for the welfare of the practitioners of the *Lotus Sūtra*, the question remains for Nichiren: why have they not spared Nichiren from his many persecutions?

In addition to the absence of benevolent deities, from Nichiren's perspective there may also be the presence of malign demonic powers actively trying to hinter the practitioner of the *Lotus Sūtra*. Describing his early considerations as to whether he should risk remonstrating against slander of the *Lotus Sūtra* Nichiren wrote, "If I spoke out, I realized, the three obstacles and four devils would overtake me." (Hori 2002, p. 53; see also 106-107) The "three obstacles and four devils" (J. *sanshō-shima*) are described in the writings of Tiantai Zhiyi (538-597). The following passage is a good example of Nichiren's citing of this teaching and his explanation of it:

> Therefore, it is stated in the Great Calming and Contemplation, fascicle five, "As practice and understanding of 'calming and contemplation' progress, the three obstacles and four devils compete to interfere with the practitioner... Do not follow them or fear them. When one follows them, one will fall into the evil realms; and if one is afraid of them, one will be unable to master the True Dharma." This is exactly what I have experienced with my own body. Also, this should be a clear mirror for my disciples and followers to reflect upon. Please practice with reverence, thereby producing nourishment for the future practitioners of the Lotus Sūtra.
>
> The "three obstacles" in this citation refer to defilements, evil karma, and painful retributions. The defilements are the obstacles arising from the three poisons of greed, hatred, and delusion; evil karma refers to the obstructions arising from wives and children; and the painful retributions are obstructions caused by the rulers of a country, parents, and others. Among the "four devils" that cause hindrances is the king of devils in the sixth heaven in the ream of desire. (Hori 2010, p. 83 adapted)

The three obstacles and the four devils were Zhiyi's way of cataloging all the various phenomena that can keep us from practicing Buddhism. The three obstacles consist of self-centered desires or defilements, the karma or unwholesome habits that arise from those defilements, and the painful consequences of such activity. In the passage above, Nichiren identifies the obstacle of evil karma with obstructions arising from family life. I believe this means that our worldly activity in this life can bind us to work and family so strongly that they become distractions keeping us from taking up Buddhism and/or maintaining our practice. Nichiren identifies the painful retributions that are the effects of past karma with obstructions to our practice brought about by parents or rulers. In other words, the fruition of our past unwholesome actions may now take the form of ridicule or even persecution by those who have power over us and/or by other circumstances outside our immediate control. Encountering such hardship can arouse our defilements, causing us to again perform unwholesome actions that will once more lead to difficulties down the line. The three obstacles describe the vicious circle created by our usual self-centered way of interacting with the world. They describe the way in which we bring unnecessary suffering upon ourselves and others, leading to further frustration and anxiety that leads to even more selfishly motivated activities and so on, ad nauseam... All of this keeps us mired in our own problems. If we are not careful, the three obstacles can prevent us from putting into practice the very teachings that can break the vicious cycle.

The four devils consist of the devil of the five aggregates, the devil of the defilements, the devil of death, and the devil king of the sixth heaven. The devil of the aggregates refers to the inherent insecurity, anxiety, and outright suffering which results from trying to identify with the five aggregates of form, feeling, perception, mental formations, and consciousness. The devil of the defilements refers to the ways in which self-centered desires inevitably arise based upon the needs of the body and mind for nourishment, security, pleasurable stimulation, and self-aggrandizement. The devil of death refers to the dread, fear, and terror that arise in the face of the inevitable dissolution of the body and mind upon death. The devil king of the sixth heaven, or Mara, refers to those things in life that tempt us to forget about Buddhist practice and live only for worldly goals and aspirations. The devil king of the sixth heaven personifies all those people, situations, and inner impulses which tempt or threaten us to forsake Buddhism and return to the old cycle of unthinking habit, fleeting pleasures and familiar pains. One could say that the other name for the devil king of the sixth heaven is "the devil we know" who attempts to frighten or cajole us away from the unfamiliar territory of liberation back into the vicious cycle of our self-centeredness. Interestingly, the devil king of the sixth heaven is also included on the calligraphic mandala, probably to show that even he is not outside the power of the Eternal

Śākyamuni Buddha, and that ultimately even the devilish functions can be turned to the realization of buddhahood.

What can all this mean for us? I believe that the heavenly gods and benevolent deities and the three obstacles and four devils serve to remind us that there are many inner forces that work within the subconscious mind. These forces may either help or hinder us. Past memories, good and bad associations, built up prejudices, habits or predispositions – all can serve to darken our vision or dampen our aspirations. On the other hand, we also have leaps of intuition or bursts of enthusiasm. In times of crises, many of us may also discover hidden reserves of courage, compassion and determination that we didn't even know we had. There may even be actual spiritual entities at work. In *The Varieties of Religious Experience*, William James points out that if in fact there are spiritual forces at work in our lives, then it would be through just such subconscious phenomena that they would make themselves felt.

> *But just as our primary wide-awake consciousness throws open our senses to the touch of things material, so it is logically conceivable that if there be higher spiritual agencies that can directly touch us, the psychological condition of their doing so might be our possession of a subconscious region which alone should yield access to them. (The Varieties of Religious Experience, p.198.)*

In addition, outside events and opportunities seem to have an uncanny way of corresponding to the necessities of our inner life, providing us with the needed catalysts to facilitate our growth as human beings. C.G. Jung called these meaningful coincidences "synchronicity." Whatever the name or explanation for these internal and external forces, they are a factor in many people's lives, especially those who are perceptive or sensitive enough to realize it. The gods and devils and other supernatural beings that populate the Buddhist cosmos remind us that there is more at work in our lives than just our conscious decisions and the seeming randomness of outside events.

Over the course of *Kaimoku-shō*, Nichiren provides the reader with several possible answers as to why he has seemingly not received the divine protection from hardship and persecution that he and his followers may have expected. It could be because the guardian deities have abandoned the country. It could be because they are testing his compassion, patience, and resolve. It could be because his practice has aroused the three obstacles and four devils. It could be because the predictions of the *Lotus Sūtra* and other Mahāyāna sūtras need to be fulfilled, or because it is inevitable that the practitioner of the *Lotus Sūtra* must meet hardship, or because the practitioner must expiate his or her past transgressions, and even the buddhas, bodhisattvas, gods, and other beings cannot make the task any easier because of these factors. Curiously, Nichiren never does give a definitive single answer to this question in *Kaimoku-shō*. In fact, he seems to dismiss the question as not so important after all. He says, "In the final analysis, no matter how I am abandoned by gods and how much difficulty I encounter, I will uphold the *Lotus Sūtra* at the cost of my own life." (Hori 2002, p. 105) For Nichiren, what matters is his mission, not whether he will receive divine blessings and protection. A bodhisattva is not daunted by difficulty or hardship but strives to realize the Wonderful Dharma and to help other beings realize it as well, no matter what the cost.

Sources

Gosho Translation Committee, editor-translator. *The Writings of Nichiren Daishonin*. Tokyo: Soka Gakkai, 1999.

Hori, Kyotsu, comp. *Writings of Nichiren Shonin: Doctrine Volume 2*. Tokyo: Nichiren Shu Overseas Propagation Promotion Association, 2002.

_____. *Writings of Nichiren Shonin: Doctrine Volume 1*. Tokyo: Nichiren Shu Overseas Propagation Promotion Association, 2003.

_____. *Writings of Nichiren Shonin: Followers Volume 6*. Tokyo: Nichiren Shu Overseas Propagation Promotion Association, 2010.

James, William. *The Varieties of Religious Experience*. New York: Collier Books, 1961.

Murano, Senchu, trans. *The Lotus Sutra*. Hayward: Nichiren Buddhist International Center, 2012.

_____. *Kaimokusho or Liberation from Blindness*. Berkeley: Numata Center for Buddhist Translation and Research, 2000.

Chapter 39 — Five Proclamations and Four Reliances

Writing of Nichiren Shōnin Doctrine 2: pp. 53, 68, 81-91
Kaimoku-shō or Liberation From Blindness: pp. 42-43, 62, 79-93
Writings of Nichiren Daishonin I: 239-240, 251, 261-269
Lotus Sūtra: 192-208

Five Proclamations

In considering whether or not to give public witness to the *Lotus Sūtra*, even though he knew he might face persecution, Nichiren found encouragement and confirmation of his chosen course of action in the simile of the "six difficult and nine easier actions" given by the Buddha in chapter eleven of the *Lotus Sūtra*.

> *Vacillating between whether I should speak out or whether I should not if I were to back down in the face of royal persecutions, I hit upon the "six difficult and nine easier actions" mentioned in the eleventh chapter, "Appearance of the Stūpa of Treasures," in the Lotus Sūtra. It says that even a man as powerless as I can throw Mr. Sumeru, even a man with as little superhuman power as I can carry a stack of hay on his back and survive the disastrous conflagration at the end of the world, and even a man as ignorant as I can memorize various sūtras as numerous as the sands of the Ganges River. Even more so, it is not easy to uphold even a word or phrase of the Lotus Sūtra in the Latter Age of Degeneration. This must be it! I have made a vow that this time I will have an unbending aspiration to buddhahood and never fall back! (Hori 2002, p. 53 adapted)*

The passage that Nichiren is referring to can be found in the verses of chapter eleven. Further on in *Kaimoku-shō*, Nichiren cites what he calls the "five proclamations" of the Buddha in chapters eleven and twelve, of which the "six difficult and nine easy actions" are a part of the third proclamation. The five proclamations refer to the "three proclamations" of chapter eleven and two exhortations of buddhahood in chapter twelve – the prediction of buddhahood for Devadatta and the attainment of buddhahood by the dragon king's daughter. The three proclamations are the three times in chapter eleven in which the Buddha exhorts those gathered to receive and keep, protect, read, and recite the *Lotus Sūtra* in the world after the passing of the Buddha. The first time is at the end of the prose section:

> "Who will expound the Sūtra of the Lotus Flower of the
> Wonderful Dharma in this Sahā-World? Now is the time
> to do this. I shall enter into Nirvāna before long. I wish
> to transmit this Sūtra of the Lotus Flower of the
> Wonderful Dharma to someone so that this sutra may
> be preserved." (Murano 2012, p. 192)

In the verse section, this request is reiterated:

> (The Buddha said to the great multitude.)
>
> Who will protect
>
> And keep this sūtra,
>
> And read and recite it
>
> After my extinction?
>
> Make a vow before me to do this!
>
> (Ibid, p. 194)

Further on in the verse section, the Buddha again repeats his request, though this third time he uses the simile of the six difficult and nine easier actions to contrast how difficult it will be to teach the *Lotus Sūtra* in the Latter Age compared to teaching any of the other sūtras. The six difficult actions consist of doing the following things in the evil world after the Buddha's passing:

1. *Expounding the Lotus Sūtra.*

2. *Copying and keeping the Lotus Sūtra.*

3. *Reading the Lotus Sūtra even for a while.*

4. *Keeping the Lotus Sūtra and expounding it to even one person.*

5. *Hearing and receiving the Lotus Sūtra and asking about its meaning.*

6. *Keeping the Lotus Sūtra.*

(Ibid, pp. 196-197)

By contrast the nine easier actions consist of teaching any of the other sūtras or any of a variety of astoundingly impossible superhuman feats. The implication being that teaching the other sūtras may be as difficult as the Herculean acts listed, but nowhere near as difficult as teaching the *Lotus Sūtra*. The nine easy actions are:

1. *Expounding all other sūtras.*

2. *Grasping and hurling Mr. Sumeru.*

3. *Hurling a thousand million worlds with the tip of one's toe.*

4. *Expounding innumerable sūtras in the highest heaven of the realm of form.*

5. *Grasping the sky and wandering about with it.*

6. *Putting the great earth on one's toenail and going up to the Brahma Heaven.*

7. Bearing a load of hay unscathed in an apocalyptic fire.

8. Keeping all the other sūtras and expounding them to the śrāvakas so they are able to attain the six supernatural powers.

9. Expound the Dharma to thousands and billions of people so that they are able to become arhats and attain the six supernatural powers.

(Ibid, pp. 195-197)

Nichiren regards these three proclamations as an assessment by Śākyamuni Buddha, Many Treasures Tathāgata, and the emanation buddhas of the ten directions who are all gathered together of the greater value of *Lotus Sūtra* in comparison to the value of the other sūtras. Certainly the passage concerned would seem to be saying that the One Vehicle teaching of the *Lotus Sūtra* that leads all beings to buddhahood, the main theme of the *Lotus Sūtra* up to that point, is of far greater value and will prove far more difficult to teach than any of the other sūtras that only lead to the comparatively modest goal of arhatship. One might ask if other Mahāyāna sūtras could also be considered difficult as opposed to easy, since they also teach the way to buddhahood. In fact, Nichiren goes on to cite statements of the teachers of the *Flower Garland School*, the Dharma Characteristics school, the Three Treatises school, and the Mantra school that their own Mahāyāna sūtras should be included with the *Lotus Sūtra* as among the six difficult actions. Nichiren even goes so far as to cite passages from a variety of sūtras, wherein each sūtra claims that it is in fact the most profound of sūtras. How, then, can Nichiren continue to insist that the *Lotus Sūtra* is the only sole sūtra that is difficult to receive and keep, read, recite, expound, and copy in the Latter Age after the Buddha's passing?

In order to evaluate these claims, Nichiren refers to the first and last of the "four reliances" taught by the Buddha in the *Mahāyāna Mahaparinirvāna Sūtra* as a guide for discerning the meaning of Buddhist teachings. The four reliances are to: "Rely on the Dharma and not upon persons; rely on the meaning and not upon the words; rely on wisdom and not upon discriminative thinking; rely on sūtras that are final and definitive and not upon those which are not final and definitive." (see Yamamoto, p. 153)

Nichiren takes the four reliances to mean that one should not trust the word of even great bodhisattvas like Samantabhadra or Mañjuśrī unless they are preaching with the sūtras in hand. Nichiren cites Nāgārjuna (late second to early third century), Zhiyi (538-597), Saichō (767-822; also known as Dengyō), and even Enchin (814-891; aka Chishō) who all state that one should only follow commentaries that accord with what is taught in the sūtras and furthermore that one should not believe in oral transmissions. All of these teachers are considered to be patriarchs of the Tiantai/Tendai school and therefore Nichiren is showing that the interpretations of the Tiantai school can be relied upon because they follow the principles of the four reliances. Nichiren's contention is that the other schools of Buddhism were straying from these principles, because of sectarian pride in their own particular doctrines and methods. Though it might seem ironic to those who believe that Nichiren was himself a sectarian polemicist, he wrote, "Surely, those who aspire to enlightenment should not be biased, stay away from sectarian quarrels, and not despise other people." (Hori 2002, p. 85) Nichiren did not see himself as trying to promote his own narrow view, or even the particular views of the Tiantai school. Rather, Nichiren was trying to find in the sūtras themselves the criteria for judging the relative merits of various Buddhist teachings. He believed that he had found such a criteria in the four reliances and in the statements of the *Lotus Sūtra* regarding its own supremacy. Nichiren's conviction was that in China only the Tiantai school had upheld what the sūtras actually teach, and that in Japan, only Saichō and himself had properly passed on this teaching without distorting or compromising it.

Four Reliances

Before moving on, let's consider the four reliances a little further. Though Nichiren cites the *Mahāyāna Mahaparinirvāna Sūtra* (where they are listed in the order given above), they appear in other Mahāyāna sūtras as well, such as the *Vimalakīrti Sūtra*. The source of the four reliances (or "four refuges") is the *Four Refuges Sūtra* (S. *Catuḥpratiśaraṇa-sūtra*) according to Étienne Lamotte.

> *The Catuḥpratisaraṇasūtra posits, under the name of*
>
> *refuges (pratisaraṇa), four rules of textual*
> *interpretation: (1) the dharma is the refuge and not the*
> *person; (2) the spirit is the refuge and not the letter; (3)*

*the sūtra of precise meaning is the refuge and not the
sūtra of provisional meaning; (4) (direct) knowledge is
the refuge and not (discursive) consciousness. As will be
seen, the aim of this sūtra is not to condemn in the
name of sound assessment certain methods of
interpretation of the texts, but merely to ensure
subordination of human authority to the spirit of the
dharma, the letter to the spirit, the sūtra of provisional
meaning to the sūtra of precise meaning, and discursive
consciousness to direct knowledge. (Lamotte, p. 12)*

What exactly does it mean to follow the Dharma and not the person? Isn't the
Dharma the teachings of Śākyamuni Buddha in the sūtras, and therefore the
teaching of a person? For that matter, there is the question of whether the
sūtras, particularly the Mahāyāna sūtras, are in fact verbatim records of the
Buddha's teaching. So how can we know whether we are following the
Dharma or just some person's opinion, whether the person of the Buddha or
the opinion of some anonymous person(s) attributed to the Buddha? Though
perhaps a bit circular, the Buddha's reply to the question asked of him by
Mahāprajapatī as to what is the Dharma may be worth considering.

*Then the Gautamī, Mahāprajapatī, approached the
Lord; having approached, having greeted the Lord, she
stood at a respectful distance. As she was standing at a
respectful distance, the Gautamī, Mahāprajapatī said to
the Lord: "Lord, it were well if the Lord would teach me
the Dharma in brief so that I, having heard the Lord's
Dharma, might live alone, aloof, zealous, ardent, self-
resolute."*

*"Whatever are the states, of which you, Gautamī, may
know: these states lead to passion, not to
passionlessness, they lead to bondage, not to the
absence of bondage, they lead to the piling up (of
rebirth), not to the absence of piling up, they lead to
wanting much, not to wanting little, they lead to
discontent, not to contentment, they lead to sociability,
not to solitude, they lead to indolence, not to the*

492

putting forth of energy, they lead to difficulty in
supporting oneself, not to ease in supporting oneself –
you should know definitely, Gautamī: this is not
Dharma, this is not discipline, this is not the Teacher's
instruction. But whatever are the states of which you,
Gautamī, may know: these states lead to
passionlessness, not to passion … (the opposite of the
preceding) … they lead to ease in supporting oneself,
not to difficulty in supporting oneself – you should know
definitely, Gautamī: this is Dharma, this is discipline, this
is the Teacher's instruction." (Horner 1992 volume V, p.
359 adapted)

The Dharma, then, is that which leads away from further deluded entanglement in our attachments and aversions for conditioned phenomena and toward liberation, the unconditioned. The Dharma is not the Dharma because the Buddha taught it. The Buddha is the Buddha, an "awakened one," because he awakened to the Dharma, which is the true nature of reality. Any teaching that is in accord with how things really are can be considered the Dharma. This is why anything that conforms to the "three seals of the Dharma" can be considered the word of the Buddha. The three seals are the observations that (1) conditioned phenomena are impermanent, (2) without a self-nature, and (3) that true peace can only be found in the unconditioned, which is nirvāṇa. Sometimes another seal is added, the observation that conditioned things are ultimately unsatisfactory, for a total of four seals.

Any verbalized expression of the Dharma, however, can only be relative and conditional, dependent upon the limitations of language and the particular context of the time and place in which it originated. That is why the second of the four reliances reminds us that we must look to the meaning and not just to the words. In speaking of his own usage of terms like "self" in certain contexts, the Buddha said, "… these are merely names, expressions, turns of speech, designations in common use in the world, which the Tathāgata uses without misapprehending them." (Walshe, p. 169) In the *Lankāvatāra Sūtra*, the following simile is used, "As the ignorant grasp the finger-tip and not the moon, so those who cling to the letter, knowing not my truth." (Suzuki, p. 193; see also pp. 168-169) The point being that words can only convey so much, but as for awakening to reality – you really have to be there.

493

The third reliance given by Lamotte from the *Four Refuges Sūtra* is the fourth according to the *Mahāyāna Mahaparinirvāna Sūtra*. This reliance tells us to rely upon sūtras that are definitive and not those that are provisional. The two terms actually used are *nītārtha* and *neyārtha*. The first term, *nītārtha*, means that the teachings in the sūtra in question is direct, clear, and precise and require no further interpretation. The second term, *neyārtha*, means that the teachings in the sūtra in question use figures of speech or otherwise accommodate the limited understandings and/or aspirations of the Buddha's audience and therefore the sūtra does require further interpretation if the Buddha's ultimate intention is to be understood. What is provisional and what is the Buddha's true intention has, however, been a subject for debate as we have seen.

 Ultimately, we must come to know the Dharma through our own practice and realization. This is what the fourth reliance (or third in the *Mahāyāna Mahaparinirvāna Sūtra*) is about. We must rely on direct knowledge (S. *jñāna*) of the truth, and not merely our discursive consciousness (S. *vijñāna*), which is always second hand, after the fact, and dualistic in that it can't help but bifurcate experience into the two poles of subject and object. From the very beginning, the Buddha taught people to come and see the truth for themselves, and not to rely on external authorities, hearsay, or even personal speculation. As the Buddha taught the Kālāmas:

> *"It was for this reason, Kālāmas, that we said: Do not go by oral tradition, by lineage of teaching, by hearsay, by a collection of scriptures, by logical reasoning, by inferential reasoning, by a reflection on reasons, by the acceptance of a view after pondering it, by the seeming competence of a speaker, or because you think: 'The ascetic is our teacher.' But when you know for yourselves, 'These things are wholesome, these things are blameless; these things are praised by the wise; these things, if undertaken and practiced lead to welfare and happiness', then you should engage in them." (Nyanaponika & Bodhi, p. 66)*

Nichiren took the first of the four reliances to mean that in determining the true meaning of Buddhism he should rely primarily on the Dharma taught in the sūtras by the Buddha, because the Buddha was testifying to his own direct knowledge of the Dharma. For Nichiren, the later commentators were unreliable because their own knowledge was second-hand and speculative, dependent upon a proper interpretation of the sūtras. Likewise, according to the reliance stating that one must rely on definitive sūtras and not provisional sūtras, Nichiren needed to determine which sūtra was the most definitive according to the Buddha himself and not according to the later sectarian writers of commentaries. In this, Nichiren found that in the *Lotus Sūtra* the Buddha had already clarified the matter. "It is said in the tenth chapter on the "Teacher of the Dharma" of the *Lotus Sūtra* that among the sūtras that had already been preached, are now being preached, and will be preached, the *Lotus Sūtra* is supreme. (Hori 2002, p. 85) Looking at the passage Nichiren is concerned with and the one following it we find several important points being made.

> *"I have expounded many sūtras. I am now expounding this sūtra. I also will expound many sūtras in the future. The total number of the sūtras will amount to many thousands of billions. This Sūtra of the Lotus Flower of the Wonderful Dharma is the most difficult to believe and the most difficult to understand."*

> *"Medicine King! This sūtra is the store of the hidden core of all the Buddhas. Do not give it to others carelessly! It is protected by the Buddhas, by the World Honored Ones. It has not been expounded explicitly. Many people hate it with jealousy even in my lifetime. Needless to say, more people will do so after my extinction." (Murano 1991, p. 180)*

Here the Buddha says that of all the sūtras the *Lotus Sūtra* is the most difficult to believe and the most difficult to understand. He also states that it is the hidden core of the Buddha and has not ever before been taught explicitly. Furthermore, people hate it and are jealous of it even during the Buddha's lifetime and will feel even more strongly opposed to it after the Buddha's passing. These are all themes that Nichiren raises many times in his writings.

All of this would certainly point to the *Lotus Sūtra* as the most definitive statement of the inner meaning of the Buddha's entire body of teachings. The other sūtras may be sovereign in respect to a particular teaching, such as the expounding of emptiness or in explaining the six perfections, but the *Lotus Sūtra* alone states the underlying purpose or intent of all the other sūtras. Nichiren cites the Tiantai patriarch Miaole Zhanran (711-782) as saying, "Besides the *Lotus Sūtra*, some sūtras claim to be king of sūtras, but they are not really the first among sūtras as they do not claim to be first among those which have already been preached, are being preached, and will be preached." (Hori 2002, p. 85 adapted)

Using the four reliances as his standard for evaluating Buddhist teachings and going by the statements made by the Buddha in the *Lotus Sūtra*, Nichiren believed that the evidence conclusively pointed to the *Lotus Sūtra* as the Buddha's most challenging and therefore most subtle and profound teaching. Because of the Buddha's own testimony, he did not even feel that it would be necessary to go into a point-by-point comparison of the teachings of the other sūtras with those contained in the *Lotus Sūtra*, though of course he does that earlier in the *Kaimoku-shō*. Convinced of the superiority of the *Lotus Sūtra* to all the other sūtras, Nichiren was certain that the path he had chosen to uphold it against all opposition must be correct.

> *It is I, Nichiren, who is the richest in Japan today, because I sacrifice my life for the sake of the Lotus Sūtra and leave my name for posterity. Gods of rivers take orders from the master of a great ocean, and gods of mountains follow the king of Mt. Sumeru. Likewise, when one knows the meaning of the "six difficult and nine easier actions" and "scriptures preached in the past, are preached at present, and will be preached in the future" in the Lotus Sūtra, one will automatically know the comparative merits of all Buddhist scriptures without reading them. (Ibid, p. 90 adapted)*

There is a problem here, however, for the modern Buddhist. Can we really base our own certainty of the superior status of the *Lotus Sūtra* upon this same process of evaluation? Earlier, I raised the question as to whether the Buddha couldn't be considered just a person in comparison to the Dharma that we must come to know for ourselves. The response to that question may be that the Buddha was one who claimed to know the Dharma for himself, and that he was not simply teaching his own personal opinions. If we take faith in his teachings and put them into practice, we may awaken ourselves. Through our own awakening we can confirm the truth of the Buddha's words. But what if the sūtras are not the actual words of the Buddha? What if the sūtras are literary fictions? What if they are the work of later monks who wished to express their own insights into the Dharma and did so using the form of Mahāyāna sūtras? The *Lotus Sūtra* even anticipates that the opponents of the Mahāyāna will say, "They made that sūtra by themselves in order to deceive the people of the world." (Murano 2012, p. 213) But are they wrong? Paul Williams, in his book on the origins and development of the Mahāyāna, summarizes the position of modern scholarship on the origins of the Mahāyāna sūtras.

> *Most Mahāyānists consider that the Mahāyāna sūtras were preached in one way or another by Śakyamuni Buddha, the 'historical' Buddha, and the sūtras themselves almost invariably start with Ānanda's phrase 'Thus have I heard at one time', plus the geographical location of the discourse. However, source-criticism and historical awareness has made it impossible for the modern scholar to accept this traditional account. Nevertheless, it is not always absurd to suggest that a Mahāyāna sūtra or teaching may contain elements of a tradition which goes back to the Buddha himself, which was played down or just possibly excluded from the canonical formulations of the early schools. (Williams 2009, p. 39)*

This returns us to the question as to when something can be considered Dharma, which is what Mahāprajapatī asked the Buddha. Paul Williams cites a translation of a passage from Śāntideva's *Śikṣāsamuccaya* that is itself a citation from a Mahāyāna sūtra wherein the criteria is given for when a teaching can be considered the word of the Buddha:

Through four factors is an inspired utterance the word
of the Buddhas. What four? (i) ... the inspired utterance
is connected with truth, not untruth; (ii) it is connected
with the Dharma, not that which is not the Dharma; (iii)
it brings about the renunciation of moral taints [kleśa]
not their increase; and (iv) it shows the laudable
qualities of nirvāṇa, not those of the cycle of rebirth
[saṃsāra]. (Ibid, p. 41)

The Mahāyāna response, therefore, to the question as to when a teaching can
be considered to have been taught by the Buddha is that it does not matter
whether or not it was taught by the historical Buddha, but whether it
conforms to the truth, to those teachings we know the historical Buddha did
teach, to the renunciation of defilement, and to revealing the praiseworthy
qualities of nirvāṇa, the unconditioned. Of course, this criteria comes down to
the subjective judgment of those who are evaluating a given teaching, but this
is certainly in line with the Buddha's advice to the Kālāmas when he told them
that they should not depend upon external authorities, traditions, or even
their own speculations, but rather to depend upon what they come to know
for themselves directly is wholesome and praiseworthy and to be put into
practice. Mahāyānists may consider the Śākyamuni Buddha who speaks in the
Mahāyāna sūtras as the personification of a wisdom tradition whose initial
inspiration is found, but not limited to, the life and teachings of the historical
Gautama Buddha.

In the case of Nichiren and those who follow him, there is certainly the
conviction that the *Lotus Sūtra* is an inspired teaching, and furthermore that it
expresses the ultimate intent of the Buddhist tradition as a whole – the
buddhahood or perfect and complete awakening of all people without
exception. To bring this point home, Nichiren adds to the three proclamations
two additional proclamations from chapter twelve of the *Lotus Sūtra*: the
prediction of buddhahood given to Devadatta and the transformation of the
dragon king's daughter into a buddha. Based on these two exhortations or
additional proclamations, Nichiren asserts that the *Lotus Sūtra* guarantees
that all men and women can attain buddhahood. This universal guarantee of
buddhahood is where Nichiren, basing himself on the *Lotus Sūtra*, believes
that all the teachings of all the other sūtras, Mahāyāna and pre-Mahāyāna,

are leading. It is, therefore, up to us to accept this with trust and joy, put it into practice, and find out for ourselves.

Sources

Gosho Translation Committee, editor-translator. *The Writings of Nichiren Daishonin*. Tokyo: Soka Gakkai, 1999.

Hori, Kyotsu, comp. *Writings of Nichiren Shonin: Doctrine Volume 2*. Tokyo: Nichiren Shu Overseas Propagation Promotion Association, 2002.

Horner, I.B., trans. *The Book of the Discipline Volume V*. Oxford: Pali Text Society, 1992.

Lamotte, Etienne, "Assessment of Textual Interpretation in Buddhism" In Lopez, Donald S. Jr. *Buddhist Hermeneutics*. Honolulu: University of Hawaii Press, 1988.

Murano, Senchu, trans. *The Lotus Sutra*. Hayward: Nichiren Buddhist International Center, 2012.

_____. *Kaimokusho or Liberation from Blindness*. Berkeley: Numata Center for Buddhist Translation and Research, 2000.

Nyanaponika, Thera and Bodhi, Bhikkhu trans. & ed., *Numerical Discourses of the Buddha: An Anthology of Suttas from the Anguttara Nikaya*. Walnut Creek: AltaMira Press, 1999.

Suzuki, D.T. *The Lankavatara Sūtra: A Mahāyāna Text*. Taipei: SMC Publishing Inc., 1994.

Walshe, Maurice, trans. *The Long Discourses of the Buddha: A Translation of the Digha Nikaya*. Boston: Wisdom Publications, 1995.

Williams, Paul. *Mahāyāna Buddhism: The Doctrinal Foundations Second Edition*. New York: Routledge, 2009.
Yamamoto, Kosho, trans. *Mahaparinirvana-Sūtra: A Complete Translation from the Classical Chinese Language in 3 Volumes*. Tokyo: Karinbunko, 1973.

Chapter 40 – The Three Kinds of Enemies [of the Lotus Sutra]

Writing of Nichiren Shōnin Doctrine 2: pp. 54-58, 91-104
Kaimoku-shō or Liberation From Blindness: 43-48, 95-112
Writings of Nichiren Daishonin I: 240-243, 269-280
Lotus Sūtra: 212-215

In the *Kaimoku-shō*, Nichiren states that the twenty stanzas of verses from chapter thirteen, "Encouragement for Keeping this Sūtra," of the *Lotus Sūtra* was being fulfilled by the actions of some of his contemporaries. In those verses, a host of bodhisattvas describe the persecutions and difficulties the practitioners of the sūtra will face in the evil world after the passing of the Buddha The Tiantai patriarch Zhanran Miaole (711-782) interpreted these verses as referring to three kinds of enemies who would appear in the Latter Age of the Dharma. The three are: (1) the ignorant laity who are deceived by the false and hypocritical monks and elders and will abuse the true monks, (2) the false monks who are deceitful and claim to be enlightened when in fact they are not, and (3) the respected elder monks who are revered as arhats but who in fact are simply better at hiding their ulterior motives of greed and contempt. Nichiren equated these three formidable enemies with those people in Japan who were trying to suppress the teaching and practice of the *Lotus Sūtra*.

The verses in chapter thirteen of the *Lotus Sūtra* are spoken by a host of eighty thousand bodhisattvas who are reiterating in verse the vow they have made to Śākyamuni Buddha to appear in any and all worlds after his passing in order to cause all beings to perform the five practices of keeping, reading, reciting, copying, and expounding the *Lotus Sūtra*, and also to memorize the sūtra and act according to its teachings. As they say to the Buddha in the first stanza: "Do not worry! We will expound this sūtra in the dreadful, evil world after your extinction." (Murano 2012, p. 212) In the following stanzas they acknowledge the many hardships that they will have to face. I have already spoken in a previous chapter about the origin and meaning of these kinds of prophecies in Mahāyāna sūtras, but there is another general point that should be made before looking at each of the three kinds of enemies. What these verses speak of is probably a description of the controversies that arose when the Mahāyāna sūtras began to appear around the first century BCE. Those monastics that were not part of the Mahāyāna movement rejected the Mahāyāna sūtras as spurious. To this day, the Theravāda, the sole remaining pre-Mahāyāna school of Buddhism, does not accept the Mahāyāna sūtras as part of the canon that contains the discourses of the historical Śākyamuni Buddha. The contention should not be exaggerated, however. There are Theravādin Buddhists, including monastics, who do find great inspiration in Mahāyāna sūtras or teachings, even though they will not admit them as canonical. Also, it would appear from the records of Chinese travelers to India before the disappearance of Buddhism that Mahāyāna and non-Mahāyāna monks coexisted in many monasteries and Buddhist universities like Nālanda. Finally, textual scholarship shows that the Mahāyāna sūtras are not verbatim records of discourses given by the historical Buddha, but are literary fictions created by anonymous Mahāyānists in order to express their own understanding of awakening and the full implications of the Buddha's teachings. It would be pointless, therefore, to try to revisit these ancient controversies. Nevertheless, the verses do describe the kinds of hardships faced by those trying to challenge established ideas and the set ways of their contemporaries.

Ignorant laypeople are the first kind of powerful enemy. They are described in a single stanza that reads, "Ignorant people will speak ill of us, abuse us, and threaten us with swords and sticks. But we will endure all this." (Ibid, p. 212) According to the commentators that Nichiren cites, these are the followers of the second and third kinds of powerful enemies, and they will be the ones who will slander the practitioner of the *Lotus Sūtra* to the authorities as it says in the stanzas: "In order to speak ill of us, in order to slander us in the midst of the great multitude, in order to say that we are evil, they will say to kinds, ministers, brahmins, and also to householders and other monks, 'They have wrong views. They are expounding the teaching of heretics." (Ibid p. 213) They will also mock the *Lotus Sūtra*'s claim that all people will be able to attain buddhahood. "They will despise us, saying to us [ironically], 'You are buddhas'." (Ibid, p. 213) The ignorant laypeople, then, are those who blindly follow the teachings of others and who do not do their own research or reflect on the meanings of the teachings for themselves. They cynically dismiss the teaching of the *Lotus Sūtra* as a pipe dream taught by those who are trying to gain some monetary profit or other advantage from such a message of hope.

In the time when the *Lotus Sūtra* first appeared, these people might have been the supporters of the more conservative schools like the Sarvāstivādins. In Nichiren's time, they would have been the followers of Hōnen's exclusive nembutsu who did not believe it was possible to attain buddhahood in this world. These people would include the mob who burned down Nichiren's hut at Matsubagayatsu, the steward Tōjō Kagenobu and his followers who ambushed Nichiren at Komatsubara, and the Hōjō regents who exiled Nichiren to Izu, attempted to have him executed at Tatsunokuchi, and who then exiled him to Sado Island. It is important to note that the ignorant laypeople are Buddhists. This is not about the persecutions that may come about at the hands of those belonging to other religions or ideologies. The ignorant laypeople are a powerful enemy precisely because they are Buddhists who support wrong views and who help to oppress those teachers who uphold the *Lotus Sūtra*. Today, ignorant laypeople would be those who claim to be Buddhists but who do not actually know for themselves the teachings of the Buddha taught in the sūtras and who base their understanding on the views and opinions of their teachers, who themselves may not have a deep understanding of the teachings of the Buddha but who present their own ideas as Buddhism. These people then close their minds to any who try to point out what the sūtras actually teach and instead cling to what they have read in secondary sources or to teachings given by whatever charismatic teacher they have chosen to follow. Because of this, Buddhism in the modern world has all too often been associated with psychedelic drugs, nationalism, and exploitive authoritarian teachers who use their power for personal aggrandizement, financial gain, and even sexual predation. The standards for ethical conduct and the criteria for what is or is not in keeping with the teachings set forth by the sūtras become obscured and lost when laypeople uncritically accept popular misconceptions and the biased teachings of charismatic authorities over what the Buddha taught. In this way, Buddhism is greatly misrepresented, its reputation tarnished, and its ability as a tradition to liberate people and lead them to buddhahood is greatly impeded.

Now it could be pointed out that if we are going to set up Śākyamuni Buddha's teachings in the sūtras as the ultimate criteria of what is or is not authentic Buddhism, we have a problem in regard to the Mahāyāna sūtras. I have already mentioned that these sūtras are not verbatim records of the historical Buddha's teaching. In fact, even the Pāli canon is a later redaction that as a whole cannot be taken as a verbatim record of the historical Buddha's teachings, though certainly they are the closest we can get to what the historical Buddha taught. I would propose that Śākyamuni Buddha, as a literary figure in the sūtras, is a personification of the ideals and insights of the Buddhist tradition. The Eternal Śākyamuni Buddha of the Original Gate therefore personifies what those Mahāyāna Buddhists who have given credence to the *Lotus Sūtra* believe is the ultimate message of Mahāyāna Buddhism. Nichiren believed that this message was one of the universal and immediate accessibility of buddhahood, and that this message was what the Tiantai school had been championing until it had become obscured by other messages that Nichiren saw as departures from what is taught in the Mahāyāna sūtras and particularly the *Lotus Sūtra*. For Nichiren, fidelity to Buddhism is fidelity to the tradition expressed in the sūtras that had inspired and guided Mahāyāna Buddhists for well over a millennium at the time he wrote *Kaimoku-shō*. In our present time and circumstances I think that to avoid falling into the category of "ignorant laypeople" we who wish to be inspired and guided by the Mahāyāna teachings should read these teachings for ourselves so that we will be in a position to judge whether or not a particular Buddhist group or a particular teacher is authentically representing that tradition or distorting it due to biased ideas or for less than worthy goals.

Evil or corrupted monastics are the second kind of powerful enemy. They are described in the stanza that reads, "Some monks in the evil world will be cunning. They will be ready to flatter others. Thinking that they have obtained what they have not, their minds will be filled with arrogance." (Ibid, p. 212) In chapter two, "Expedients," of the *Lotus Sūtra*, five thousand monastics and laypeople left the assembly before the Buddha could expound the Dharma that Śāriputra had requested to hear. Of them, it was said, "They were so sinful and arrogant that they thought that they had already obtained what they had not yet, and that they had already understood what they had not yet. Because of these faults they did not stay." (Ibid, p. 32) The arrogant monks of the *Lotus Sūtra* are those who are self-satisfied with their own limited understanding of the Dharma. Specifically, they are those who believe they have attained awakening and liberation, when in fact they have not yet attained true awakening because they have not yet aroused the heart of compassion that strives for the liberation of all beings. Nichiren applies this description to those who choose teachings of lesser profundity over those of greater profundity as per Nichiren's five comparisons or the Tiantai system of comparative classification of doctrines. Nichiren specifically singles out Hōnen and his followers as fitting this description, for they had chosen the provisional teachings of the Pure Land sūtras over the *Lotus Sūtra*. Another group that

Nichiren mentions who would match the description of evil and corrupted monks would be the armed monks of the Tendai School. In medieval Japan the large monasteries possessed large estates and used bands of warrior monks or *sōhei* to protect their lands, put pressure on the government, and on occasion to attack their rivals.

The evil monks who are the second of the powerful enemies are worse than ignorant laypeople in that they represent the Buddhist clergy who are supposed to be upholding Buddhist standards of teaching and conduct. It goes without saying that it is a dire situation when the Buddhist clergy themselves are misrepresenting Buddhism with superficial and biased teachings, tarnishing its reputation through their misconduct, and even physically attacking the true teachers of the Dharma. It is not unheard of, even in our day, for Buddhist clergy to be viewed as disreputable or suspect in many areas of the world, so it is incumbent upon those who are Buddhist clergy to hold themselves to a high standard of conduct so as to allow the Dharma to shine clearly in their teaching and in their conduct. It is also incumbent upon the Buddhist laity to make sure that those who are ordained clergy or authorized teachers are held accountable to the Buddha Dharma. The relationship between the laity and the clergy (or authorized teachers) should be a mutual partnership in which both sides are helping each other learn and live the Dharma to the best of their ability.

The false arhats are the third powerful enemy. As monks who are respected authorities on the Dharma, they are the ones in a position to do the most damage to Buddhism. They are described in three stanzas as those who live in hermitages in the forest and are greatly respected as arhats who are liberated from the world of birth and death and possessed of supernatural powers even though they are still full of worldly attachments and look down on others.

> *Some monks will live in forest hermitages or retired places,*
>
> *And wear patched pieces of cloth.*
>
> *Thinking that they are practicing the true Way,*
>
> *They will despise others.*

Being attached to worldly profits,

They will expound the Dharma to men in white robes.

They will be respected by people of the world

As the arhats who have the six supernatural powers.

They will have evil thoughts.

They will always think of worldly things.

Even when they live in forest hermitages,

They will take pleasure in saying that we have faults.

(Ibid, pp. 212-213 adapted)

Unlike the second kind of enemy, the false arhats are able to conceal their faults from their supporters. These are not just ordinary clergy, but teachers with great personal charisma who have acquired the kind of prestige that makes it very hard to challenge their teachings if they are not in accord with the Dharma as taught in the sūtras. Of his contemporaries, Nichiren identifies two people by name, Shōichi, also known as Enni Bennen (1202-1280), and Ryōkan, also known as Ninshō (1217-1303). The former was a Zen Master of the Rinzai lineage, whereas the latter was a teacher of the Mantra-Discipline school. In addition to Nen'a Ryōchū (1199-1287) of the Pure Land school that Nichiren mentions further on, these monks were the ones that Nichiren believed were behind the persecutions he and his followers had suffered at the hands of the Kamakuran shogunate and therefore they were the respected teachers who constituted the third powerful enemy of the *Lotus Sūtra* in his day.

In the present day there are several Dharma teachers (some are Buddhist clergy, and some are laypeople) who have acquired a kind of celebrity status, even outside the members or followers of their own respective lineage. Some teachers have been tainted by scandals and controversy, but others have not. In any case, we should always keep in mind that celebrity status (deserved or not) does not guarantee that the teacher's teachings are in accord with the Dharma as taught in the sūtras. We must always remember that we must read the Buddha's teachings for ourselves and personally reflect and apply the teachings if we are to have an authentic practice and realization of Buddha Dharma. It is no longer an age in which false arhats can command the government to persecute authentic teachers, but we must still be wary of turning over our own good sense and conscience over to any charismatic personality, institutional authority, or celebrity teacher. We should certainly be respectful of and learn from those who have many years of practice and study and who have been entrusted as teachers by their respective Sanghas, but ultimately we cannot relinquish our own personal responsibility to them or think that their knowledge and practice of the Dharma can stand in for our own.

Nichiren takes the twenty stanza verse section of chapter thirteen as a prediction of the situation that he and his followers have had to face. In response to the question as to why he has had to face such bitter opposition and persecutions for upholding the *Lotus Sūtra* and criticizing those who have obscured or denigrated its teaching, Nichiren can reply that this was only to be expected because the *Lotus Sūtra* itself predicted such things. In fact, the enmity of the other Buddhists, the physical assaults, and Nichiren's two exiles should be viewed as a fulfillment of the sūtra's predictions. If the three kinds of enemies of the *Lotus Sūtra* have appeared as the teachers of the Pure Land, Zen, Mantra, and Discipline schools and their followers, then, Nichiren asks, it must also mean that the practitioners of the *Lotus Sūtra* must also be present. Nichiren, naturally, offers himself as the candidate for that position. Instead of casting doubt on Nichiren and his mission to uphold the *Lotus Sūtra*, the persecutions should instead be viewed as a vindication of Nichiren and of the veracity of the *Lotus Sūtra*.

> *Exactly as the Buddha predicted, there are "three kinds of enemies of the Lotus Sūtra" all over Japan. Does this mean that the words of the Buddha have been proven untrue? Could this be? After all, who has been abused and despised by the ignorant people for the sake of the Lotus Sūtra? What monk has been brought to the attention of the court nobles and warriors in power? Which monk has been exiled as predicted in the sūtra? No such man exists in Japan, except for Nichiren. (Hori 2002, p. 102)*

Nichiren takes the description of the three kinds of enemies as a prophecy that vindicates his mission even as his persecutions fulfill the prophecy, but what should we make of this in our own lives and practice? Some people have interpreted this teaching to mean that one is only practicing the *Lotus Sūtra* correctly if one is arousing opposition. Consequently, these people believe that they must either identify who their enemies are or else preach the *Lotus Sūtra* so stridently that they will be sure to make enemies. I am not convinced that this is what the *Lotus Sūtra* really intends, even if it might appear to be the way Nichiren did things. If we look at chapter twenty, "Never Despising Bodhisattva," of the *Lotus Sūtra* we will find a story that illustrates what the sūtra intends. In that chapter the Buddha tells a story of a past life when he was known as the Never Despising Bodhisattva. That bodhisattva's whole practice consisted of bowing to all he met and greeting them with the words, "I do not despise you because you can become buddhas." (Murano 2012, p. 292) This practice of showing respect to all people and assuring them that they could attain buddhahood aroused the opposition of the arrogant monastics and laity who did not believe that ordinary people could attain buddhahood. They mocked him and even attempted to strike him with sticks and to throw stones at him. Never Despising Bodhisattva, however, did not return their abuse but moved to a safe distance and continued to regard them with respect and to assure them of their future buddhahood. This story seems to be a dramatization of the description given in the twenty stanzas of chapter thirteen. This story tells us two important things. The first is that Never Despising Bodhisattva did not seek to make enemies. All he did was respectfully share the message of the *Lotus Sūtra*, even if it contradicted the preconceived ideas of those who believed they had nothing more to learn about Buddhism. The second is that even when he was abused, he continued to maintain a respectful attitude and did not compromise his mission to preach the *Lotus Sūtra*. Nichiren himself equates his mission to teach Odaimoku with that of Never Despising Bodhisattva in *Testimony to the Prediction of the Buddha* (*Kembutsu Mirai-ki*):

> *Nevertheless, if there is a man after the death of the Buddha who breaks the attachment to the false doctrines of the "four tastes and three teachings" of the pre-Lotus sūtras and puts faith in the True Dharma of the Lotus Sūtra, all the virtuous gods and numerous bodhisattvas who sprang up from underground will*

protect such a practitioner of the Lotus Sūtra. Under such protection, this practitioner would be able to spread over the world the focus of devotion (honzon) revealed in the Original Gate and the five-word daimoku of Myō, Hō, Ren, Ge, and Kyō," the essence of the Lotus Sūtra.

He is just like Never Despising Bodhisattva, who, in the Age of the Semblance Dharma after the death of Powerful Voice King Buddha, spread in the land of this Buddha the twenty-four character passage in the Lotus Sūtra (chapter twenty) saying: "I respect you deeply. I do not despise you. Why is this? It is because you all will practice the way of bodhisattvas and will be able to attain buddhahood." With such propagation, the bodhisattva was severely persecuted by all the people in the land, who beat him with sticks and threw stones at him.

Although the twenty-four characters of Never Despising Bodhisattva differ in wording from the five characters which I, Nichiren, spread, they are the same in meaning. We both appeared in the world under the same conditions: he toward the end of the Age of the Semblance Dharma after the death of Powerful Voice King Buddha, and I at the beginning of the Latter Age after the death of Śākyamuni Buddha. (Hori 2002, p. 174 adapted)

The teaching of the three kinds of enemies of the *Lotus Sūtra* is the sūtra's way of warning us that if we present the teaching of the *Lotus Sūtra* we should not be surprised if we meet opposition from ignorant laypeople, corrupted clergy, and even respected teachers who are regarded as saints. We must not let this discourage us. Nor should we look for enemies or return abuse with abuse. From beginning to end we must treat all beings as future buddhas, whether they are presently acting as such or not. Another lesson we can take from this teaching is that we must be careful to not become one of the three kinds of enemies ourselves. We must not uncritically accept the teachings of others without checking things out for ourselves, like the ignorant laypeople.

We should not become arrogant and greedy like the evil monks, especially if we are put in a position of authority. We should not, like the false arhats, become self-righteous and pretend to be awakened when we are still tainted by greed, hatred, and delusion. Nor should we persecute others just because their opinions and views are different than our own, as the three kinds of enemies are said to do. Again, the humble, straightforward, and respectful practice of the *Lotus Sūtra* as exemplified by Never Despising Bodhisattva can serve as the model that will keep us from becoming one of the three kinds of enemies and enable us to deal in a firm but kind manner with them, should they confront us, so that we can eventually overcome all enmity and sow the seeds of buddhahood in their hearts.

Sources

Gosho Translation Committee, editor-translator. *The Writings of Nichiren Daishonin*. Tokyo: Soka Gakkai, 1999.

Hori, Kyotsu, comp. *Writings of Nichiren Shonin: Doctrine Volume 2*. Tokyo: Nichiren Shu Overseas Propagation Promotion Association, 2002.

Murano, Senchu, trans. *The Lotus Sutra*. Hayward: Nichiren Buddhist International Center, 2012.

_____. *Kaimokusho or Liberation from Blindness*. Berkeley: Numata Center for Buddhist Translation and Research, 2000.

Chapter 41 – Expiating Karma

Writing of Nichiren Shōnin Doctrine 2: pp. 103-107,
Kaimoku-shō or Liberation From Blindness: pp. 111-117
Writings of Nichiren Daishonin I: 278-282

Despite the predictions in the *Lotus Sūtra* that the practitioners of the sūtra will face hardships and persecutions, there are also passages that promise blessings, protection, and a life of ease in this and future lives for the practitioners while dire afflictions will be visited upon those who persecute them.

"Having heard these teachings, they became peaceful in their present lives. In their future lives, they will have rebirths in good places, enjoy pleasures by practicing the Way, and hear these teachings again." (Murano 2012, p. 109)

Anyone who reads this sūtra

Will be free from grief,

Sorrow, disease or pain.

His complexion will be fair.

He will not be poor,

Humble or ugly.

All living beings will wish to see him

Just as they wish to see sages and saints.

Celestial pages will serve him.

He will not be struck with swords or sticks.

He will not be poisoned.

If anyone speaks ill of him,

The speaker's mouth will be shut.

(Ibid, p. 230)

Anyone who does not keep our spells

But troubles the expounder of the Dharma

Shall have his head split into seven pieces

Just as the branches of the arjaka-tree [are split].

(Ibid, pp. 335-336)

"Universal Sage! Anyone who keeps, reads and recites this sūtra [in the later five hundred years] after [my extinction], will not be attached to clothing, bedding, food or drink, or any other thing for living. What he wishes will not remain unfulfilled. He will be able to obtain the rewards of his merits in his present life. Those who abuse him, saying, 'You are perverted. You are doing this for nothing,' will be reborn blind in successive lives in retribution for their sin. Those who make offerings to him and praise him, will be able to obtain rewards in their present life. Those who, upon seeing the keeper of this sūtra, blame him justly or unjustly, will suffer from white leprosy in their present life." (Ibid, p. 347)

Nichiren's followers wondered why, if these passages were true, did Nichiren face such hardships and persecutions. If he was truly a practitioner of the *Lotus Sūtra* then why wasn't he shielded from harm and why haven't his enemies been struck down as the sutra promises? Of course, they were also wondering why they had to face hardship themselves, even though they had taken up the *Lotus Sūtra* that promised protection and a life of ease for its practitioners.

Nichiren points out that many practitioners of the *Lotus Sūtra* in the past faced persecution and hardships. He also reminds his followers, once again, of the persecutions that will face the practitioners predicted by the *Lotus Sūtra* and of the abuse endured by Never Despising Bodhisattva in chapter twenty. He reminds them that many of the great teachers of the past, not even excepting Śākyamuni Buddha, faced great difficulties. In fact, the East Asian tradition speaks of nine hardships faced by the Buddha:

1. The female ascetic Sundarī claimed to have had an affair with the Buddha at the instigation of jealous brahmins. The brahmins then murdered her and attempted to frame the Buddha for the crime. (See Ñānamoli, pp. 139-141; also Numata Center, p. 130)

2. Brahmins mocked Buddha when a maidservant gave him stinking rice gruel. (I have not found the source for this story yet)

3. The brahmin Agnidatta invited the Buddha and Sangha to Vairanjā and then forgot to feed them during a famine. The Buddha and Sangha had only horse fodder to eat for the duration of their stay in Vairanjā. (See Ñānamoli, pp. 126-127)

4. After taking the throne in a palace coup, King Virūdhaka massacred the Śākya clan. (See Ñānamoli, p. 345; also Numata Center pp. 610-614)

5. The king of a brahmin city forbids people from giving offerings to Buddha or to listen to him. (I have not found the source for this story yet)

6. The daughter of a brahmin, Ciñchā, pretended to have been impregnated by the Buddha. (See Numata Center, pp. 129-130)

7. The Buddha's treacherous cousin, Devadatta, attempted to kill the Buddha with a boulder after the assassins sent to kill the Buddha failed to do so. (See Ñānamoli pp. 258-262; also Numata Center, pp. 558-559)

8. The Buddha spent the night outside in the middle of winter. It was on this occasion that he determined that three robes were enough to keep warm. (See Ñānamoli, pp. 164-165)

9. The drunken elephant sent by King Ajātaśatru (See Ñānamoli, pp. 262-264; also Numata Center, pp. 559-560)

Even the Buddha was subject to exposure to the elements, frame-ups, the massacre of his clan, and assassination attempts. His disciples also faced extreme hardships. One of his foremost disciples, Maudgalyāyana, was actually lynched by a band of false ascetics. (See Numata Center, p. 637) Nichiren also refers to the murders of the Indian patriarchs Kānadeva and Simha (or Āryasimha as he is sometimes called); the exile of Daosheng (d.

434), who insisted that even the incorrigible disbelievers (S. *icchantika*) have buddha-nature; and the branding and exiling of the monk Fadao (1086-1147), who dared to remonstrate with a Chinese emperor who was persecuting Buddhism. Nichiren also refers to two secular heroes, Suguwara Michizane (845-903) and Bai Juyi (772-846) who were persecuted and banished by their political enemies because they spoke out against corruption. Nichiren's point is that not even awakened beings or people of great virtue can escape hardships and even persecution.

What, then, of the promises of protection and ease in the *Lotus Sūtra*? Does the fact that no one, no matter how virtuous, can escape hardship mean that these statements are false? Nichiren finds the answer in the teaching of Tiantai Zhiyi (538-5097): "Our troubles and sufferings in this world are all due to our sins in our past lives, and rewards for our meritorious acts in this life will be received in our future lives." (Hori 2002, p. 104) He finds it in the teaching of the *Contemplation of the Mind Ground Sūtra* (J. *Shinjikan-gyō*): "If you want to know the cause in the past, see the effect in the present. If you want to know the effect in the future, see the cause in the present." (Murano 2000, p. 112) He also finds it in the *Lotus Sūtra*'s statement, "Thus he expiated his sin." (Murano 1991, p. 289) These teachings indicate that the abuse undergone by Never Despising Bodhisattva was a result of past misdeeds. Nichiren understands all this to mean that the hardships faced in this life are not because of, or in spite of, the good deeds one is currently doing. Rather, it is because past misdeeds are coming into fruition. In addition, one must have confidence that the good one is doing now will come to fruition in the future. Conversely, those who commit evil deeds will inevitably face the fruition of their actions in a future life. Severe misdeeds in particular will take time to come to fruition. In the meantime, according to the *Nirvāna Sūtra*, those who slander the Dharma will have nightmares that may cause them to reflect upon their conduct. The idea is that calamity does not come immediately, and that people will be given a chance to repent of their misdeeds. The promises of the *Lotus Sūtra* apply to those who have no past offenses to expiate and is a guarantee that upholding the *Lotus Sūtra* will sow the seeds of great benefit both for the present life and for the future, though they may not come to fruition immediately.

Nichiren applies this interpretation to his own life. In further support of this, he cites a passage from a six-fascicle version of the *Nirvāna Sūtra* that explains that those who committed evil deeds in the past will face many forms of retribution, though it will not be so bad if one protects the Dharma:

> *"Good men! The person who committed innumerable crimes and did various evil karmas in his previous existence will have his retribution in his present life. He will be despised by others. His appearance will be ugly. He will be short of clothing. His food and drink will be scanty. He will not be able to get profits although he seeks fortune. He will be born poor and to a family with wrong views. He will be persecuted by the government. He will also suffer in many other ways. He will receive these retributions in his present life. But his retributions will be less than the retributions he will receive if he does not protect the Dharma." (Murano 2000, p. 115)*

Nichiren examines himself in the light of this passage and concludes that, in fact, he was despised, ugly, short of clothing, poor, and persecuted by the government. Therefore, he must have committed many evil deeds in the past. He speculates that in the past he may have been a wicked ruler who persecuted the followers of the *Lotus Sūtra* by depriving them of the necessities of life or even executing them. Nichiren is saying that what others are inflicting upon him is what he used to do to others. By enduring exile and the near execution at Tatsunokuchi for the sake of the *Lotus Sūtra*, Nichiren is lessening or even eliminating his karmic debt. He says, "I may have already expiated some of these serious sins. But even the sins that I think I have already expiated may not have been expiated satisfactorily. In order to eliminate the bonds of birth and death, I must completely expiate all the sins I have committed." (Ibid, p. 116) So it is not that Nichiren has not received any blessings or protection, but that the blessings and protection have taken the form of allowing him to expiate his past karma in a mitigated form and that he has been protected from worse hardships and even death. In *A Letter to the Ikegami Brothers* (*Kyōdai-shō*) he explains the sūtra passages about the expiation of past misdeed as follows, "These scriptural statements mean that because we persecuted the practitioner of the True Dharma in a past life, our destiny is to fall into the Hell of Incessant Suffering. However, by strongly upholding the True Dharma in this life, we absolve the major torment of the future by suffering the comparatively minor torments in this life." (Hori 2010,

p. 77 adapted) In the *Testimony to the Prediction of the Buddha* (*Kembutsu Mirai-ki*) Nichiren wrote: "How lucky I am to be able to extinguish within one life my sin of slandering the True Dharma ever since the eternal past!" (Ibid, p. 178) In the *Differences Between the Lotus School and Other Schools Such as the Mantra School* (*Shingon Shoshū Imoku*) he wrote a clear and concise statement about his belief that he had both expiated his past misdeeds and received divine protection:

> *The sun and moon are clear mirrors shining on all the worlds in the universe, but do they know about Nichiren? I am sure that they know me. So, we should not doubt or worry about the protection of various heavenly beings. Nevertheless, I, Nichiren, have been persecuted because the sins that I committed in my past lives have not been completely eradicated. As I have been exiled because of my faith in the Lotus Sūtra, some of my sins may have been atoned so the Buddha may protect me under his robe. It was the protection of the Buddha that saved me from near death at Tatsunokuchi at midnight on the twelfth of the ninth month last year. Grand Master Miaole said in his Supplemental Amplifications on the Great Calming and Contemplation that the stronger our faith is, the greater the divine protection will be. Do not doubt this. You should firmly believe in and do not doubt that there always is divine protection. (Ibid, p. 125 adapted)*

Another aspect of the expiation of karma is that the very strength of one's practice is what brings about resistance both within ourselves and from the people around us, and allows hidden flaws within ourselves to arise where they can be seen, recognized, and resolved. Nichiren cites Zhiyi who wrote, in regard to the practice of calming and contemplation meditation, "The merit of trivial acts of practicing Buddhism without calming the mind and contemplation of the truth is not strong enough to bring out our past sins hidden in ourselves. Only when we practice calming the mind and contemplation of the truth under any circumstances can we bring our past sins out to the surface." (Hori 2002, pp. 106-107 adapted) Zhiyi also warned that, "We will then be confronted at once by the three obstacles and four devils." (Ibid, p. 107 adapted) The three obstacles and four devils have been discussed previously in this commentary.

Nichiren speaks of the power of practice to reveal the hidden seeds of past evil karma in terms of two analogies – the forging of iron and the collection of hemp oil. "It is like forging iron, for instance. Unless you hit it and forge it hard, hidden scars will not be seen. They appear only when the iron is hit hard many times on an anvil. Or it is analogous to squeezing hemp seeds. Unless squeezed hard, there is little oil." (Ibid, p. 107) Nichiren states that he would not have faced any resistance if he had remained content to teach the provisional sūtras that others were already teaching. "Ever since I, Nichiren, strongly condemned those who slander the True Dharma in Japan, I have been persecuted. It must be that grave sins in my past lives are revealed through my merits in defending the Dharma in this life." (Ibid, p. 107) From this perspective, to encounter resistance and even persecutions is proof that one's practice is valid, that it is making a real difference in one's life and the lives of others. I think it is true that if we challenge ourselves in our Buddhist practice, we will find ourselves coming up against latent forces of ego and the power of unwholesome habit patterns. We may even find ourselves having to stand up to and confront the people around us who are invested in an unwholesome or unjust status quo. Substance abusers, for instance, who try to break their addictions and change their way of living will meet resistance from "friends" and sometimes even family or co-workers when they try to change their habits and accustomed ways of doing things, and needless to say they will also have to confront their own inner demons. On the other hand, sometimes the resistance we meet in others is not because we are cultivating a more liberated, wholesome, and compassionate way of living but because we are acting out in ways that are needlessly provocative, arrogant, belligerent, and/or paranoid and mistaking that for taking a revolutionary or prophetic stance for everyone's good. We must be very wary of the view that resistance automatically proves we are right or that we are expiating karma. Sometimes it can be proof that we are on the wrong track, that we are hardening our ego instead of realizing selfless compassion, and actually sowing the seeds of conflict rather than harmony due to our belligerent self-righteousness.

What of those who were persecuting Nichiren and his followers? Why have they seemingly escaped harm? In *Kaimoku-shō*, Nichiren asserts that even though his persecutors have not faced any punishment in this life it is certain that they will fall into the Hell of Incessant Suffering. In other writings he speaks of four kinds of karmic retribution that can be observed unfolding in the world: general, individual, conspicuous, and inconspicuous. In the writing called *Persecutions Befalling the Sage* (*Shōnin Gonan Ji*), he wrote of the fates of three men who had once been followers but then turned upon other followers of Nichiren in 1279 in the village of Atsuwara (resulting in the arrest of twenty peasants and the execution of three of them) and of Japan in general in terms of these four kind of punishment:

> The deaths of Ōta Chikamasa, Nagasaki Jirō Hōe'nojōnTokisuna, and Daishimbō by falling off their horses could be interpreted as punishment for the sin of despising the Lotus Sūtra. There are four kinds of punishment: general punishment, individual punishment, conspicuous punishment, and inconspicuous punishment. The widespread epidemic and famine in Japan today, the fighting within the Hōjō clan, as well as the Mongol invasions are general punishments. A plague is an inconspicuous punishment. The case of Ōta and others are both conspicuous and inconspicuous. (Hori 2008, p. 119 adapted)

Based upon the teachings of the sūtras and the classic treatises explaining Buddhist cosmology and the working of karma, Nichiren believed that the fruition of karma was not just an individual matter but also something that unfolded in terms of whole societies, even nations. This is what we would today call "collective karma." He also believed that the effects of karma could occur in conspicuous or obvious ways, such as when there are wars or tragic accidents; however, it could occur in more subtle and inconspicuous ways, such as the slow and quiet progress of an illness. Nichiren also taught that the effects of karma can unfold in the present life, in the next life, or even be deferred to some other future lifetime. The intertwining of wholesome and unwholesome karmic seeds, the intermingling of individual and collective karma, and the uncertainty of when causes and conditions will bring about the karmic effects of past deeds all combine to make the unfolding of the karmic law of cause and effect quite subtle and complex.

I would now like to turn to a discussion of the challenges to this view that hardship is necessarily the effect of past-life misdeeds, and that those who commit misdeeds in the present will necessarily suffer for it in the future. In previous chapters we have discussed the Buddhist critique of those views that deny or, from the Buddha's perspective, misrepresent the karmic law of cause and effect. Currently, the alternatives to the Buddhist teaching of karma and rebirth boil down to one of two views, the materialistic or the theistic. In the materialistic view, there is no necessary connection between the moral intentionality of actions and the way the lives of beings unfold. Furthermore, nothing of the psyche carries over past brain death since mind is only the epiphenomenon of the brain. The theistic view insists that everything that happens does so according to God's plan, or because he wills it to happen, or at the very least allows it to happen. As discussed in the previous chapters, either of these views denies the law of karma whereby one's intentional actions (which is what "karma" means) is a determining or even decisive factor in how the lives of beings will unfold over time and over lifetimes. The Buddha claimed to have verified through his experience of recalling his own past lives as well as an extrasensory perception of the karmic unfolding of the lives of other beings that rebirth and the law of karma are realities and on that basis he refuted the materialists and theists of his day. He also repudiated those views by pointing out that the denial or misrepresentation of the law of karma undermines the motivation for morality and spiritual cultivation.

Materialists and theists counter that there is no proof that there is such a thing as rebirth or the law of karma. The testimony of the Buddha given in the sūtras that beings are reborn and that the quality of their lives is determined by the nature of their own actions is only valid if one accepts that testimony or if one is also able to verify it by experiencing past-life recall. On the other hand, the metaphysical views that there is nothing more than material interactions or that there is a God who created everything and is ultimately responsible for all that happens are also claims that cannot be proven or disproven, at least at this time. So in terms of which belief is the most credible or makes the most sense – the materialistic, theistic, or karmic – that will have to be determined by each person for him or herself.

There is another argument against the law of karma that does need to be carefully considered. It is the argument that the law of karma teaches us to blame the victim and therefore it is a teaching that is almost inherently inhumane and unjust. Unfortunately, even some Buddhists seem to believe that every bad thing that happens to individuals or even whole groups must necessarily be the result of past karma and that on some level the tragedies are therefore deserved. In the rest of this chapter I want to respond to this misunderstanding – and it is a misunderstanding – of the Buddhist teaching of the law of karma to show that it is not in accord with what the Buddha taught. Nichiren's explanation that his hardships and the hardships faced even by the Buddha and other great sages were a case of expiating karma does not mean that all hardships are necessarily the result of the sufferer's misdeeds.

The Buddha rejected the view that everything is the result of karma on several occasions. In one such instance the wanderer Sīvaka asks the Buddha about this:

> "Master Gautama, there are some ascetics and brahmins who hold such a doctrine and view as this: 'Whatever a person experiences, whether it be pleasant or painful or neither-painful-nor-pleasant, all that is caused by what was done in the past.' What does Master Gautama say about this?"

> "Some feelings, Sīvaka, arise here originating from bile disorders: that some feelings arise here originating from bile disorders one can know for oneself, and that is considered to be true in the world. Now when those ascetics and brahmins hold such a doctrine and view as this, 'Whatever a person experiences, whether it be pleasant or painful or neither-painful-nor-pleasant, all that is caused by what was done in the past,' they overshoot what one knows by oneself and they overshoot what is considered to be true in the world. Therefore I say that this is wrong on the part of those ascetics and brahmins.

> "Some feelings, Sīvaka, arise here originating from phlegm disorders ... originating from wind disorders ... originating from an imbalance [of the three] ... produced by change in climate ... produced by careless behavior ... caused by assault ... produced as the result of karma: how some feelings arise here produced as the

result of karma one can know for oneself, and that is considered to be true in the world. Now when those ascetics and brahmins hold such a doctrine and view as this, 'Whatever a person experiences, whether it be pleasant or painful or neither-painful-nor-pleasant, all that is caused by what was done in the past,' they overshoot what one knows by oneself and they overshoot what is considered to be true in the world. Therefore I say that this is wrong on the part of those ascetics and brahmins." (Bodhi 2000, pp. 1278-1279)

In his reply to Sīvaka, the Buddha asserts a variety of other causes and conditions besides karma that contribute to what is experienced in the present. In his book, *Exploring Karma & Rebirth*, Nagapriya explains the later analysis of this discourse in the commentarial tradition and how it places karma in the larger context of several different types of causality:

While the schema outlined in the Moliyasīvaka Sutta is a bit obscure, Buddhist scholastic philosophy (known as Abhidhamma) classified five modes – technically known as niyamas – of dependent origination. These modes are (1) physical inorganic (utu-niyama), (2) biological (bīja-niyama), (3) non-volitional mental (mano- or citta-niyama), (4) ethical (kamma- or karma-niyama), and (5) spiritual (dhamma- or dharma-niyama).

Examination of these niyamas can give us a better understanding of the scope and importance of Karma in human life. The utu-niyama embraces natural laws such as those of physics and chemistry. For example, when seeking an explanation for the occurrence of an earthquake we may be served better by the theory of plate tectonics than by the theory of Karma. The bīja-niyama governs the physical organic order, including the laws of biology. For example, if I catch a cold it would seem more sensible to explain this by supposing the presence of a virus rather than by supposing 'moral' causes. The mano- or citta-niyama governs the laws of the mind and to some extent relates to psychology. The phenomenon of shock or post-traumatic stress may, for example, be best explained under this heading. The karma-niyama governs the sphere of volitional human conduct (including body, speech, and mind). In practice, it does not seem easy to separate the non-volitional and volitional mental spheres. The exact meaning of dharma-niyama and what it governs is not clear. A traditional account links it to miraculous events in the Buddha's life, but it can also be thought of as the principle that underlies spiritual evolution. Seen in this way, the dharma-niyama explains the process by which we can transcend our selfishness, hatred, and ignorance and achieve generosity, compassion, and understanding. In traditional terms, it explains how it is that we can break free from the determining influence of Karma and rebirth and so put a stop on the wheel of perpetual re-becoming. It underlies the dynamics of spiritual development.

A further way of thinking about the dharma-niyama is to see it as the 'undeserved' compassionate influence that someone may exert on our life. In other words, it is the impact of the saint on the world. The saint does not act towards others in accordance with their karma but deals compassionately with everyone, regardless of merit. (Nagapriya, pp. 36-38)

The Buddha's general theory of dependent origination is as follows: "When this exists, that comes to be; with the arising of this, that arises. When this does not exist, that does not come to be; with the cessation of this, that ceases." (Bodhi 2000, p. 575) This means that all things come to be only due to causes and conditions and have no inherent existence in and of themselves. These causes and conditions operate according to these five *niyamas* or categories of natural law, of which the law of karma is only one of the five, and all five interact with each other in order to bring about life as we experience it. As Nagapriya so eloquently explains:

The five niyama analysis of experience shows that Karma is just one application of the general principle of dependent origination and, therefore, many circumstances and outcomes are likely to be governed by conditions only very indirectly related to Karma itself. But we should beware of seeing these different orders of conditionality as completely discrete. In reality, they are not five distinct orders of conditionality. This is only a map of what happens. Every experience comprises a vast network of conditions; our previous moral conduct will often have a bearing on our present experience, but in many situations non-moral factors may well exert a more decisive influence. The teaching of the five niyamas thus presents a more complex and subtle account of why things happen as they do than the crude view of Karma criticized above. We need also to remember that the actions of other people may be more decisive in any given situation that our own karmic stream; it may be their evil or their goodness that causes us to suffer or benefit, rather than our own. (Nagapriya, p. 39)

Each situation we are faced with in life is brought about by many forces, in each present moment it us up to us to determine whether we will act in that situation in a wholesome or unwholesome way – mentally, verbally, and physically. We have the freedom to make a good cause or a bad cause in relation to whatever situation we are faced with. In each moment, our mental, verbal, and physical actions will change the way we relate to, interact with, and experience the situation for better or worse. The causes we freely make will also have an effect on the future, whether they come to fruition later in life or in some future life. While not all is determined by karma, karma is our own particular responsibility and a decisive factor in shaping the course of our lives.

Nichiren also acknowledged that karma was not the only cause of misfortunate and hardships such as illness. In a letter to a sick lay follower he cited the teaching of Zhiyi that there are six causes of illness:

The Great Calming and Contemplation also lists the six
causes of sickness: 1. lack of harmony among the four
primary elements of the material world (of the earth
element, the water element, the fire element, and the
air element); 2. lack of moderation in eating and
drinking; 3. inconsistent practice of sitting meditation;
4. problems caused by a demon; 5. actions of a heavenly
demon; and 6. karmic retribution. (Hori 2010, p. 33
adapted)

We might come up with different ways of classifying or naming the factors
that bring about illness as opposed to medieval scholastic Buddhist categories
(we might talk about stress or toxins in the environment rather than demons
for instance), but the point is that Zhiyi and Nichiren recognized that
phenomena have a variety of causes and conditions of which karma is just
one. Of course, it may be the decisive one and the most relevant in many
cases, but that would not be something we should presume to judge without
the insight of a sage, an advanced bodhisattva, or a buddha.

As can be seen from the Buddha's teachings and also in Nichiren's writings,
the varieties and permutations of karma and the ways in which karma comes
to fruition can be quite complex. In fact, the Buddha listed "the precise
workings out of the results of karma" as one of the four things that could bring
about "madness or frustration" to those presuming to speculate about them
without direct knowledge.

"Bhikkhus, there are these four inconceivable matters
that one should not try to conceive; one who tries to
conceive them would reap either madness or
frustration. What four? (1) The domain of the Buddhas
is an inconceivable matter that one should not try to
conceive; one who tries to conceive it would reap either
madness or frustration. (2) The domain of one in jhāna
is an inconceivable matter… (3) The result of kamma is
an inconceivable matter… (4) Speculation about the
world is an inconceivable matter that one should not try
to conceive; one who tries to conceive it would reap
either madness or frustration. These are the four

inconceivable matters that one should not try to conceive; one who tries to conceive them would reap either madness or frustration." (Bodhi 2012, p. 463)

The law of karma is not simply a tit for tat system of rewards and punishments but an organic system whereby the circumstances and even body and mind of beings are the fruits of karmic seeds that they themselves have sown and continue to sow as they are confronted by and then react to the causes and conditions of life from moment to moment and lifetime to lifetime. While the givens of present circumstances have been, at least partially, determined by past actions, in each moment beings are free to either reinforce old patterns or forge new ones for better or worse. It is with this freedom to determine present actions that beings can bind themselves more closely to unwholesome patterns of cause and effect, or cultivate wholesome patterns of cause and effect, or attempt to free themselves from being bound by such karmic patterns altogether.

I'd like to conclude by sharing some passages about the metaphoric value of these teachings. As discussed above there are many who are skeptical of the teaching of karma and rebirth because it conflicts with their current belief system or because it seems scientifically implausible. Even many contemporary Buddhists may find themselves wondering if all this talk of past lives has any validity. There are even arguments between Buddhists about whether the teachings about karma and rebirth are or are not integral to the Buddha Dharma. I do not want to enter into that complex argument here, but I would like to remind people that the Buddha never expected anyone to blindly accept his word but instead to practice his teachings and find out for themselves what is or is not the case. He did not say, "Believe me," he said, "Come and see." So perhaps it would be more fruitful to consider the metaphorical value of these teachings, because the metaphorical value can hold true even if the facticity of karma and rebirth cannot be scientifically verified or personally verified at present.

Let's start with a statement made by Joseph Campbell in *The Power of Myth*. The interviewer, Bill Moyers, asked Campbell what the idea of reincarnation suggests. Campbell replied:

It suggests that you are more than you think you are.
There are dimensions of your being and a potential for
realization and consciousness that are not included in
your concept of yourself. Your life is much deeper and
broader than you can conceive it to be here. What you
are living is but a fractional inkling of what is really
within you, what gives you life, breadth, and depth. But
you can live in terms of that depth. And when you can
experience it, you suddenly see that all other religions
are talking of that. (Campbell, pp. 58)

Around the same time that Joseph Campbell gave that response, some psychiatrists and psychotherapists were using hypnotic regression to help their patients recover the past life dramas that were the alleged causes of present life psychological issues. One of these psychiatrists, Raymond Moody Jr., M.D., wrote a book about his experiences using this type of past-life regression therapy called *Coming Back: A Psychiatrist Explores Past-Life Journeys*. In that book Dr. Moody reflects on the facticity and meaning of the past-life memories recovered by his patients.

Are these regressions really memories of past lives? I
don't know. Later in this book I will offer several
possible explanations for the existence of so-called past
lives. But as a medical doctor who has dealt with the
mysteries of the mind, I must say that I can neither
refute nor support regressions as proof of reincarnation.

Some psychologists and psychiatrists believe that the
mind is creating dramas to help it cope with different
situations. I like to call this the language of the
unconscious. It is a language in which problems are
dealt with metaphorically rather than directly. To create
these metaphors, the mind draws upon all of its
available resources – memories thought to be long
gone, images from books and television, pieces of
conversation, even events daydreamed and "forgotten"
a long time ago.

> *When it needs to face dilemmas, the unconscious mind creates drama from the material at hand. Under hypnosis, these become memories as real as yesterday's lunch date. (Moody, p. 76)*

Further on he writes:

> *Past-life regressions can also help us tap a vast storehouse of knowledge that many of us don't even know we have. This is knowledge that is picked up randomly or learned in school and "forgotten" (but really hidden in a fold of gray matter). The experience of tapping knowledge is called "cryptomnesia" or "xenoglossia."*
>
> *If I were to say that I was too much a scientist to believe in reincarnation, then I would also have to add that regressions are valuable because they can help people understand themselves. They can help us to understand our fears, our desires, our hidden needs. They can justify us to ourselves. Because of that, past-life regressions are an enormously wonderful tool for self-discovery. They are a way of experimenting with various identities, modes of being, temperaments, personalities, and certainly a way of examining our psychological roots to explore the type of person we are.*
>
> *Where does this stream of images come from? And what is its purpose? This wellspring of imagery is one of the enduring mysteries of the mind. But thankfully its benefits are readily available. (Ibid, pp. 104-105)*

I'd also like to share the following statement by Nagapriya, the author of the book *Exploring Karma & Rebirth* that was cited above. Nagapriya writes:

> *So rebirth could be understood as a metaphor that communicates how our conduct can have implications*

far into the future, perhaps way beyond what we might have imagined." (Nagapriya, p. 127)

In this sense, rebirth can be used as a 'thought experiment': we imagine the implications of our actions into the future having a kind of domino effect on the world, even beyond our death. What kind of legacy do we want to leave the world? What kind of example are we offering to other beings? Making this kind of imaginative journey into the future may enable us to gain a better perspective on any action we are proposing to undertake, or even on our life as a whole. While few of us will be as influential as Shackleton or Heidegger, all of us will, nevertheless, exert a significant influence on at least some people; our lives will resound through theirs like the reverberations of a bell. They will then pass on that influence on to others. The more we consider this, the more we become aware of the gravity of the present moment — how our conduct irrevocably contributes to the creation of the future, for better or worse, and the more we realize the tremendous responsibility we have by virtue of participating in the world. And there is no way out of this, since even if we commit suicide this itself would have implications for others. (Ibid, p. 128)

Finally, I'd like to conclude with a statement attributed to the great European humanist Desiderius Gerhard Erasmus (1466 – 1536). I find this statement to be a powerful and concise explanation for how the law of karma works and a great reflection on how we are responsible for the unfolding of our lives for good or ill.

We sow our thoughts, and we reap our actions;

We sow our actions, and we reap our habits;

We sow our habits, and we reap our characters;

We sow our characters, and we reap our destiny.

Sources

Bodhi, Bhikkhu, trans. *The Connected Discourses of the Buddha: A New Translation of the Samyutta Nikaya*. Boston: Wisdom Publications, 2000.

_____. *The Numerical Discourses of the Buddha: A Translation of the Anguttara Nikāya*. Boston: Wisdom Publications, 2012.

Campbell, Joseph with Moyers, Bill, *The Power of Myth*. New York: Doubleday, 1988.

Gosho Translation Committee, editor-translator. *The Writings of Nichiren Daishonin*. Tokyo: Soka Gakkai, 1999.

_____. *The Writings of Nichiren Daishonin Volume II*. Tokyo: Soka Gakkai, 2006.

Hori, Kyotsu, comp. *Writings of Nichiren Shonin: Doctrine Volume 2*. Tokyo: Nichiren Shu Overseas Propagation Promotion Association, 2002.

_____. *Writings of Nichiren Shonin: Biography and Disciples Volume 5*. Tokyo: Nichiren Shu Overseas Propagation Promotion Association, 2008.

_____. *Writings of Nichiren Shonin: Followers Volume 6*. Tokyo: Nichiren Shu Overseas Propagation Promotion Association, 2010.

Moody, Raymond A. Jr., *Coming Back: A Psychiatrist Explores Past-Life Journeys*. New York: Bantam Books, 1991.

Murano, Senchu, trans. *The Lotus Sutra*. Hayward: Nichiren Buddhist International Center, 2012.
_____. *Kaimokusho or Liberation from Blindness*. Berkeley: Numata Center for Buddhist Translation and Research, 2000.

Nagapriya, *Exploring Karma & Rebirth*. Birmingham: Windhorse Publications, 2004.

Nanamoli, Bhikkhu, trans. *The Life of the Buddha*. Seattle: Buddhist Publication Society Pariyatti Editions, 2001.

Numata Center for Buddhist Translation and Research Editorial Staff. *Buddha-Dharma: The Way to Enlightenment (Revised Second Edition)*. Berkeley: Numata Center for Buddhist Translation and Research, 2003.

Chapter 42 – Nichiren's Vows

Writing of Nichiren Shōnin Doctrine 2: pp. 53, 105-106
Kaimoku-shō or Liberation From Blindness: pp. 43, 114,
Writings of Nichiren Daishonin I: 240, 280-281

Twice in *Kaimoku-shō*, Nichiren expresses his determination in the form of vows. Roughly one third of the way into the work he states, "... it is not easy to uphold even a word or phrase of the *Lotus Sūtra* in the Latter Age of Degeneration. This must be it! I have made a vow that this time I will have an unbending aspiration to buddhahood and never fall back!" (Hori 2002, p. 53) Towards the end of *Kaimoku-shō*, Nichiren again states his determination in the form of vow or perhaps series of vows to continue to uphold the *Lotus Sūtra* no matter what; furthermore, he vows to be like a pillar, a pair of eyes, or a great vessel for Japan. I think it could be said that this vow is the real climax of the *Kaimoku-shō*.

> *I have made a vow. Even if someone says that he would make me the ruler of Japan on the condition that I give up the Lotus Sūtra and rely upon the Contemplation of the Buddha of Infinite Life Sutra for my salvation in the next life, or even if someone threatens me saying that he will execute my parents if I do not say "Namu Amida-butsu," and no matter how many great difficulties fall upon me, I will not submit to them until a man of wisdom defeats me by reason. Other difficulties are like dust in the wind. I will never break my vow to become the pillar of Japan, to become the eyes of Japan, and to become the great vessel for Japan. (Hori 2002, pp. 105-106 adapted)*

This passage from *Kaimoku-shō* is sometimes cited in survey books dealing with Japanese Buddhism as an example of Nichiren's fiery determination. Unfortunately, this passage is also used to make the case that Nichiren was a megalomaniac, a fanatic, and a nationalist. Edward Conze summed up Nichiren in the following way in his book *Buddhism: It's Essence and Development*:

> *It is customary to reckon the sect of Nichiren (1222-82) as one of the schools of Amidism. It would be more appropriate to count it among the offshoots of nationalistic Shintoism. Nichiren suffered from self-assertiveness and bad temper, and he manifested a degree of personal and tribal egotism which disqualify him as a Buddhist teacher. He did not only convince himself that he, personally, was mentioned in the Lotus of the Good Law, but also that the Japanese were the chosen race which would regenerate the world. The followers of the Nichiren sect, as Suzuki puts it: 'even now are more or less militaristic and do not mix well with other Buddhists'. (p. 176)*

There are so many things wrong with that mischaracterization (originally published in 1951) that it is hard to know where to begin. How could Nichiren ever be confused with Amidism when that is the very school that Nichiren was most critical of? To this day, though, writers of introductory books on Buddhism continue to characterize Nichiren Buddhism as a form of Pure Land Buddhism simply because it also features chanting as its main practice. This is sheer laziness, however, since anyone who has read this far into this commentary or any of Nichiren's writings will already know that Nichiren Buddhism is no more related to Pure Land Buddhism than is Zen, and in fact it would be fairer to characterize Nichiren Buddhism as a streamlined form of Tiantai Buddhism. In addition, Edward Conze cites D.T. Suzuki (1870-1966) in confirmation of his opinion, but D.T. Suzuki was himself a rather chauvinistic proponent of Rinzai Zen and the uniqueness of the Japanese spirit (to the point where D.T. Suzuki has been accused of Japanese nationalism by modern critics like Robert Sharf and Brian Victoria). At the very least, D.T. Suzuki was no expert on Nichiren Buddhism and was not predisposed to give a fair or unbiased opinion. Aside from the ridiculous lumping in of Nichiren Buddhism with Pure Land Buddhism and the ludicrous appeal to D.T. Suzuki's opinions about it, I can see where some people might take some of Nichiren's statements, such as the above vows, out of context and misconstrue them to support the idea that Nichiren was a megalomaniac (what is today called more clinically a narcissistic personality disorder), a nationalist, and a violent fanatic. It is this that I want to address, because I think the above vows should not be interpreted in such a perverse manner and that in fact they are the high point of the *Kaimoku-shō*.

Let's begin with the charge of nationalism. It is certainly true that Nichiren was concerned with the welfare of Japan and its people. This, however, just makes Nichiren a concerned or even a patriotic citizen, it does not make him a nationalist. Now "nationalism" can mean different things. It seems to me that those accusing Nichiren of nationalism are claiming that he believed in the ideology of "my nation right or wrong," or that Nichiren valued the Japanese nation above all else, or that he believed the Japanese people were somehow unique and superior to all other nations and ethnicities. There is, however, absolutely no basis for such ideas in Nichiren's writings. Nowhere does Nichiren state that Japan is superior to other nations in any political, economic, or ethnic sense. In fact, he sometimes refers to Japan as a remote and tiny island nation far removed from India, the land of the Buddha (see the beginning of *Shugo Kokka-ron* on p. 3 of Hori 2003). He refers to the Hōjō regents as "mere rulers of a small island kingdom." (Hori 2008, p. 24) He even states that the two most important Shintō gods (whom Nichiren included on his calligraphic mandala) are inferior to the Vedic gods of India. "Such deities as Goddess Amaterasu and Great Bodhisattva Hachiman are highly esteemed in Japan, but they are merely minor gods compared to the King of the Brahmā Heaven, Indra, the sun and moon, and the Four Heavenly Kings." (Ibid, p. 37) Nichiren could in fact be quite critical of Japan. A rather blunt example of this can be found in the *Letter from Sado* (*Sado Gosho*) that is attributed to Nichiren. The following is not what one would expect to find in the body of works of a nationalist.

> *According to the Nirvāṇa Sūtra, the Buddha emitted a radiant light that illuminated the 136th hell underground and revealed that not a single offender remained there. This was because they had all achieved buddhahood through the "Life Span" chapter of the Lotus Sūtra. What a pity, however, that the icchantikas or persons of incorrigible disbelief, who had slandered the correct teaching, were found to have been detained*

there by the wardens of hell. They proliferated until they became the people of Japan today. (Gosho Translation Committee 1999, p. 304)

Nowhere in his writings does Nichiren suggest that his concern for the power or prestige of Japan, or its Shintō deities, or even the Japanese emperor overshadow that of Buddhism. In fact, to the contrary, Nichiren suggests the opposite: the nation's welfare depends upon the Dharma. This is the major theme of his *Treatise on Spreading Peace Throughout the Country by Establishing the True Dharma* (*Risshō Ankoku-ron*). If Nichiren was a nationalist, then so were Elijah, Isaiah, Jeremiah, and all the other Hebrew prophets who risked their lives to warn the nation of Israel that the conduct of their ruling elites was leading it into disaster.

When it comes to religious or spiritual considerations, Nichiren did view Japan as being in a unique position as a nation predisposed to Mahāyāna teachings and the *Lotus Sūtra* in particular and having a responsibility to return the True Dharma to the rest of Asia and even to India, the homeland of Buddhism. Nichiren comes by these ideas quite honestly. Mahāyāna Buddhism had in fact been introduced to Japan from the very beginning, as has been discussed. In the *Testimony to the Prediction of the Buddha* (*Kembutsu Mirai-ki*), Nichiren cites reports from China that Buddhism has disappeared from India and was on the verge of disappearing in China as well. He then quotes the Chinese Tiantai monk Zunshi who said, "Buddhism at first spread eastward to Japan from China, just as the moon rises in the west shining on the east. Now it comes back from Japan to China just as the sun rises in the east and sheds light on the west." (Hori 2002, p. 176) It was not nationalism that led Nichiren to believe that Japan's experience with Buddhism had been Mahāyāna in orientation from its inception and that it had been preserved (so far) in Japan while disappearing or deteriorating on the mainland. It was simply an observation. Furthermore, Japan's privileged (from Nichiren's point of view) position as a Mahāyāna nation and responsibility to restore the Dharma to the mainland was entirely conditional upon Japan upholding the true Dharma, otherwise Japan would itself be destroyed by invasion from without and civil war within. This is not nationalism. This is simply calling one's country to task for failing to live up to its potential and fulfill its responsibilities. This is the work of a prophet delivering messages of hope to those who will listen and warnings to those who will not.

Nichiren is also portrayed as an aggressive and even violent fanatic. The extravagant vows that he makes are sometimes cited as evidence of this. For instance, Nichiren vows to never give up the *Lotus Sūtra* even if someone offered to make him ruler of Japan or threatened to kill his parents. Is this unreasoning aggressive fanaticism, however? Or is it simply a refusal to cave in to bribes or threats? I would note that Nichiren's parents had already passed away when he wrote this, so this was a bit of rhetoric on Nichiren's part. What is often overlooked is Nichiren's caveat: "… I will not submit to them until a man of wisdom defeats me by reason." Was this empty rhetoric? Why even put that caveat in there? In fact, the whole of the *Kaimoku-shō* up to the point where Nichiren expresses this vow is a marshaling of texts to support Nichiren's case that the *Lotus Sūtra* is the ultimate teaching of the Buddha that should not be neglected, derided, or subordinated to lesser teachings. Now we may or may not accept Nichiren's reasoning, and may or may not find his proof-texts and the presumption of scriptural authority they rested upon convincing, but I do think Nichiren put in quite a lot of effort to present a well-reasoned case and that as far as he was concerned no one had provided him with any adequate response to the case he was making for the *Lotus Sūtra* (and against its detractors). Instead, he had been physically attacked on several occasions, banished twice, and almost been executed. Who exactly was being unreasonable and fanatical about their beliefs? Nichiren, who wrote long essays citing the Buddha's teachings in order to clarify the Buddha's true intention? Or those who were trying to silence and even kill him? And what was Nichiren advocating as the ultimate teaching based on the *Lotus Sūtra*? I rather like the way it is put in *Reply to Hoshina Goro Taro* (*Hoshina Goro Taro-dono Gohenji*), a letter attributed to Nichiren.

> *In Buddhism that teaching is judged supreme that*
> *enables all people, whether good or evil, to become*
> *Buddhas. Surely anyone can grasp so reasonable a*
> *standard. By means of this principle we can compare*
> *the various sūtras and ascertain which is superior.*
> *(Gosho Translation Committee 1999, p. 156)*

I, for one, am satisfied that Nichiren was not a nationalist, though certainly a patriot and even a prophetic figure. I am also satisfied that Nichiren was not unreasonable. I would even say that according to the standards of his time

Nichiren provided ample evidence and plentiful reasons for his advocacy of the *Lotus Sūtra*, and that it was his opponents who were responding to reasoning with violence. The question then remains as to whether Nichiren was a megalomaniac in vowing to become the pillar, eyes, and great vessel of Japan – as if all depended upon him. Doesn't such an attitude betray megalomania or narcissism on Nichiren's part? I, for one, do not think so. I believe that Nichiren's vows need to be understood in the context of the Mahāyāna tradition of bodhisattva vows, which are often quite grandiose in their attempts to inspire a heroic and even cosmic sense of selfless compassion. In light of this tradition, Nichiren's vows are actually quite humble and circumscribed.

In the previous chapter dealing with provisional Mahāyāna, I introduced the concept of the arising of the "thought of awakening" (S. *bodhicitta*), the initial aspiration to attain perfect and complete awakening and save all sentient beings. I also discussed the four great vows of bodhisattvas that are used in most East Asian religious services, including the Nichiren Shū. The four vows are one way of expressing the initial aspiration of a bodhisattva. Another way of expressing the bodhisattva's initial aspiration in terms of a general vow can be found in the *Great Perfection of Wisdom Treatise* attributed to Nāgārjuna.

> *One who seeks the Path of the Buddha, from the time of first bringing forth the resolve [to realize complete enlightenment], makes a vow, "I vow that I will become a Buddha and cross the beings over to liberation, that I will succeed in realizing all of the Buddha dharmas, that I will practice the six pāramitās, that I will smash the hordes of demon armies as well as of all the afflictions, that I will gain the knowledge of all modes, that I will realize the Buddha Path, and that I shall ultimately gain entry into nirvāṇa without residue. (Dharmamitra 2008, p. 731)*

I also mentioned previously that bodhisattvas also make specific vows. For instance there are the forty-eight vows of Bodhisattva Dharmākara who became Amitābha Buddha and who is particularly known for his eighteenth vows that enables anyone who calls upon his name to be reborn in his pure land as long as they have not committed any of the five grave offenses or slandered true Dharma. The *Flower Garland Sūtra* also contains many long passages wherein bodhisattvas express their vows and determination to save all beings. The vows and dedications of Bodhisattva Diamond Banner in the *Flower Garland Sūtra* are particularly interesting, as are the vows expressed by Śāntideva (c. 685-763) in his *Guide to the Buddhist Path of Awakening* (*Bodhicaryāvatāra*). They both hold much in common with Christian ideas about Jesus as a savior who took up the cross in order to spare others from suffering and who often compares himself in the gospels to bread, water, light, and a way for others. Here are a couple of selections from the vows expressed by Bodhisattva Diamond Banner:

> *I should be a light for all sentient beings, to enable them to attain the light of knowledge to annihilate the darkness of ignorance. I should be a torch for all sentient beings, to destroy all darkness of nescience. I should be a lamp for all sentient beings, to cause them to abide in the realm of ultimate purity. I should be a guide for all sentient beings, to lead them into the truth. I should be a great leader for all sentient beings, to give them the great knowledge. (Cleary 1993, p. 532)*

> *I should accept all sufferings for the sake of all sentient beings, and enable them to escape from the abyss of immeasurable woes of birth and death. I should accept all suffering for the sake of all sentient beings in all worlds, in all states of misery, forever and ever, and still always cultivate foundations of goodness for the sake of all beings. Why? I would rather take all this suffering on myself than to allow sentient beings to fall into hell. I should be a hostage in those perilous places – hells, animal realms, the nether world, etc. – as a ransom to rescue all sentient beings in states of woe and enable them to gain liberation. (Ibid, pp. 534-535)*

The following are Śāntideva's verses expressing the dedication to the welfare of all beings:

With the good acquired by doing all this as described, may I allay all the suffering of every living being.

I am medicine for the sick. May I be both the doctor and their nurse, until the sickness does not recur.

May I avert the pain of hunger and thirst with showers of food and drink. May I become both drink and food in the intermediate eons of famine.

May I be an inexhaustible treasure for impoverished beings. May I wait upon them with various forms of offering.

See, I give up without regret my bodies, my pleasures, and my good acquired in all three times, to accomplish good for every being.

Abandonment of all is Enlightenment and Enlightenment is my heart's goal. If I must give up everything, better it be given to sentient beings.

I make over this body to all embodied beings to do with as they please. Let them continually beat it, insult it, and splatter it with filth.

Let them play with my body; let them be derisive and amuse themselves. I have given this body to them. What point has this concern of mine?

Let them have me to do whatever brings them pleasure. Let there never be harm to anyone on account of me.

Should their mind become angry or displeased on account of me, may even that be the cause of their always achieving every goal.

Those who will falsely accuse me, and others who will do me harm, and others still who will degrade me, may they all share in Awakening.

I am the protector of the unprotected and the caravan-leader for travelers. I have become the boat, the causeway, and the bridge for those who long to reach the further shore.

May I be a light for those in need of light. May I be a bed for those in need of rest. May I be a servant for those in need of service, for all embodied beings.

For embodied beings may I be the wish-fulfilling jewel, the pot of plenty, the spell that always works, the potent healing herb, the magical tree that grants every wish, and the milk cow that supplies all wants.

Just as earth and the other elements are profitable in many ways to the immeasurable beings dwelling throughout space,

So may I be sustenance of many kinds for the realm of beings throughout space, until all have attained release.

In the same way as bygone Sugatas took up the Awakening Mind, in the same way as they progressed on the Bodhisattva training,

So too, I myself shall generate the Awakening Mind for the welfare of the world; and just so shall I train in those precepts in due order. (pp. 20-22)

In such a tradition, there is nothing odd about Nichiren making a vow to be a pillar, eyes, and a great vessel for the people of Japan. If anything, it is perhaps odd that Nichiren doesn't vow to be the pillar, eyes, and great vessel for the whole world, or for all sentient beings. Here, perhaps, Nichiren is being humble in restricting his concern to that which he can immediately address through his remonstrations with the rulers of Japan. Also, remember, that Nichiren believed that if the Japanese people took faith in the true Dharma of the *Lotus Sūtra*, then they would be in a position to restore Buddhism to India, thus returning the favor to those countries that initially transmitted Buddhism to Japan. Nichiren's far-reaching concern was actually for all sentient beings throughout the world in the Latter Age of the Dharma. It was his hope that all beings would awaken to Wonderful Dharma of the *Lotus Sūtra*. Nichiren's vows are not an expression of hubris, but the expression of the particular vows of a compassionate bodhisattva responding to his own unique historical situation with courage and determination to do what he can to help his fellow countrymen and women.

The *Kaimoku-shō* could very well end with these vows. They are the culmination of the rest of the whole work. Nichiren had addressed all his doubts and questions in regard to whether he was doing the right thing, whether he was interpreting the *Lotus Sūtra* and Śākyamuni Buddha's teachings correctly, and whether the persecutions and hardships he and his disciples and followers had faced and continued to face at the time of the writing of *Kaimoku-shō* were not somehow evidence that he was not in accord with the Buddha's teachings. In the end, he demonstrated that what he taught was not just his own biased view but was in accord with the teachings of the Buddha recorded in the sūtras, and that those sūtras had also predicted that there would be hardships and persecutions faced by those who would dare to uphold the true Dharma in the Latter Age. Having worked through his doubts, or perhaps just the doubts of those he was writing for, Nichiren reiterates his unwavering determination in the form of these vows. In this he expresses his bodhisattva spirit and aspiration to work for the liberation and awakening of all beings. The remainder of the *Kaimoku-shō* can be viewed as an epilogue in which Nichiren clarifies the methods that are to be used to propagate the *Lotus Sūtra*.

Sources

Cleary, Thomas, trans. *The Flower Ornament Scripture: A Translation of the Avatamsaka Sūtra*. Boston: Shambhala, 1993.

Conze, Edward. *Buddhism: It's Essence and Development*. Birmingham: Windhorse Publication, 2001.

Crosby, Kate and Skilton, Andrew, trans. *The Bodhicaryāvatāra*. New York: Oxford University Press, 1996.

Dharmamitra, Bhikshu, trans. *Nāgārjuna on The Six Perfection: An Ārya Bodhisattva Explains the Heart of the Bodhisattva Path*. Seattle: Kalavinka Press, 2008.

Gosho Translation Committee, editor-translator. *The Writings of Nichiren Daishonin*. Tokyo: Soka Gakkai, 1999.

Hori, Kyotsu, comp. *Writings of Nichiren Shonin: Doctrine Volume 2*. Tokyo: Nichiren Shu Overseas Propagation Promotion Association, 2002.

_____. *Writings of Nichiren Shonin: Doctrine Volume 1*. Tokyo: Nichiren Shu Overseas Propagation Promotion Association, 2003.

_____. *Writings of Nichiren Shonin: Biography and Disciples Volume 5*. Tokyo: Nichiren Shu Overseas Propagation Promotion Association, 2008.

Murano, Senchu, trans. *Kaimokusho or Liberation from Blindness*. Berkeley: Numata Center for Buddhist Translation and Research, 2000.

Chapter 43 – Shoju: Embracing Good

Writing of Nichiren Shōnin Doctrine 2: pp. 109-113
Kaimoku-shō or Liberation From Blindness: pp. 120
Writings of Nichiren Daishonin I: 283-286

Shōju and Shakubuku: Embracing Good and Subduing Evil

Nichiren now turns to the question of his method. Perhaps, though he is correct in upholding the *Lotus Sūtra*, it is his method that is wrong. In a letter written to his supporter Toki Jōnin during the Sado Exile but prior to the writing of *Kaimoku-shō*, Nichiren acknowledged the criticisms directed at him in regard to his way of presenting and teaching the Dharma.

> *Someone accusingly says that I, Nichiren, established a harsh doctrine high-handedly without considering the capacity of people to understand, resulting in persecutions. Others say that what is preached in the thirteenth chapter on the "Encouragement for Upholding This Sūtra" of the Lotus Sūtra about practitioners of the Lotus Sūtra encountering difficulties without fail is applicable to bodhisattvas of a high grade. A low grade practitioner like Nichiren, they maintain, ought to practice the tolerant way preached in the fourteenth chapter on the "Peaceful Practices" of the Lotus Sūtra, but he fails to follow it. Still others say, "I know it in principle, but dare not speak out." Some people say that Nichiren stresses only the theoretical study, neglecting the practice of meditation, and I have been fully aware of their criticisms. (Hori 2002, p. 12 adapted)*

In *Kaimoku-shō*, Nichiren also summarizes the criticisms of his followers and those sympathetic to him who wondered if his harsh rhetoric and condemnation of the other schools was unskillful, overly antagonistic, and bringing unnecessary troubles and persecutions down upon himself and those associated with him.

> *Some might say that Nichiren, who claims that*
> *followers of the Buddha of Infinite Life and Zen*
> *Buddhism will fall into the Hell of Incessant Suffering, is*
> *belligerent and therefore, will fall into the realm of*
> *fighting demons. Moreover, it is said in the "Peaceful*
> *Practices" (fourteenth) chapter of the Lotus Sūtra: "Do*
> *not try to expose the faults of other people or of other*
> *sūtras and do not despise other monks." So, they might*
> *wonder whether or not Nichiren has been abandoned by*
> *the gods because he has not been following these words*
> *of the Lotus Sūtra." (Ibid, p. 109 adapted)*

Their wish was that Nichiren would tone down his rhetoric, take a more humble approach, be more circumspect about the more radical and challenging claims he was making about the *Lotus Sūtra*, and put more emphasis on contemplative practices instead of polemics and doctrinal controversy. They suggested that Nichiren should follow the advice found in chapter fourteen of the *Lotus Sūtra* that its practitioners should not find fault with or despise others rather than trying to provoke the kind of persecutions described in chapters thirteen and twenty. Nichiren did not ignore such criticism. The final part of *Kaimoku-shō* contains one of his most considered responses to them. Nichiren begins by citing the Tiantai teachings about the two methods of *shōju* (摂受) and *shakubuku* (折伏) beginning with a passage from Zhiyi's *Great Calming and Contemplation*.

> *"In response, I would cite the following words of the*
> *Great Calming and Contemplation, fascicle ten: "There*
> *are two opposing ways of spreading Buddhism: shōju*
> *and shakubuku. Such statements in the 'Peaceful*
> *Practices' chapter as 'Do not be critical of others'*
> *represent shōju, while such words of the Nirvāna Sūtra*
> *as 'Arm yourselves with swords and sticks, and behead*
> *those who break the teaching of the Buddha' stand for*

shakubuku. Though these two ways are opposite in
nature, they both benefit the people." (adapted from
ibid, pp. 109-110)

The term *shōju* literally means, "to accept and receive" while *shakubuku* literally means, "to break and subdue." These are two different ways of teaching the Dharma, though I hope to also show they have implications for propagation and practice as well. *Shōju* is the way of provisionally "accepting and receiving" the views of others, even if they are limited or somewhat mistaken, in order to encourage them to progress in their practice and understanding of the Dharma. *Shakubuku* is to "break and subdue" the false views of those being taught in order to eliminate obstacles to practice and understanding and also to enable people to make a direct connection with the ultimate truth even if it challenges their present biases and misconceptions. These terms were not coined by Zhiyi, however. They were taken from the ninth of the ten vows of Queen Śrīmālā found in the following passage of the *Queen Śrīmālā Sūtra.*

"World-Honored One, from now until my attainment of
enlightenment, if I see anyone pursuing evil ways or
violating the pure precepts of the Tathāgata, [I will not
forsake him]. In the cities, towns, and villages under my
influence, I will subdue whoever should be subdued and
embrace whoever should be embraced. Why? Only by
subduing and embracing [sentient beings] will the true
Dharma endure. When the true Dharma endures, gods
and humans will thrive, the miserable places of
existence will diminish, and the Tathāgata's Dharma-
wheel will turn perpetually." (Chang, p. 366)

In the passage the characters for *shōju* are translated as "embrace" and the characters for *shakubuku* are translated as "subdue." I think this is a good way of translating those terms and so will speak in terms of embracing or subduing from here on.

Embracing as a method of teaching the Dharma

Nichiren cites passages from the commentaries of the grand masters of the Tiantai school that show that their understanding of teaching by accepting and embracing others was based upon the instructions found in chapter fourteen, the "Peaceful Practices" chapter of the *Lotus Sūtra*, and also those passages in the *Mahāyāna Mahāparinirvāna Sūtra* that speak of the bodhisattvas viewing sentient beings as parents love an only child.

The "Peaceful Practices" chapter of the *Lotus Sūtra* describes four peaceful practices for bodhisattvas who wish to expound the *Lotus Sūtra* in the evil world after the passing of the Buddha. Later interpreters understood these four peaceful practices to pertain to practices of the body, mouth, mind, and resolution. These practices, it should be noted, are directed to monks, that is to say celibate male mendicants and not to nuns or laypeople. Nevertheless, these four sets of practices do outline a way of life and a way of approaching the Dharma that is more widely applicable. They are pointers for all those who wish to promote the Dharma in a thoughtful, gentle, and kindly way conducive to promoting peace and understanding.

The peaceful practices of the body actually encompass much more than bodily action, though that does seem to be the focus. The Buddha explains them in terms of proper practices and the proper things to be approached. Proper practices involve being patient, gentle, and humble, and not impulsive, fearful, or driven by attachment. Curiously, the Senchu Murano's translation of the sūtra also reads, "He should see things as they are. He should not be attached to his non-attachment to anything. Nor should he be attached to his seeing things as they are." (Murano, p. 210) In other words, the bodhisattva should not be proud or conceited, and realizes that even attachment to the correct view or even the idea of non-attachment is still just attachment, and the whole point of spiritual liberation and the awakening of buddhahood is to be free of attachment. This does not mean that the bodhisattva should succumb to false views or fall back into attachment. What it means is that right views are held lightly and that non-attachment does not turn into aversion. The non-attachment of the bodhisattva is actually the ability to let go of what is unwholesome and to gracefully and unselfconsciously take up what is wholesome without clinging to it.

Before saying what the bodhisattva should approach, the Buddha lists those people the bodhisattva (in this case a male celibate monk or *bhikṣu*) should not approach. The bodhisattva-*bhikṣu* should not approach kings or powerful government officials from whom they might curry favor or patronage. They should not approach or associate themselves in an overly friendly way with the teachers of non-Buddhist philosophies or religious teachings, or the teachers and followers of anti-Mahāyāna forms of Buddhism as this might be taken as an indication of approval of their views. They should not approach or become associated with worldly people, including entertainers like dancers or wrestlers, or those like slaughterers, hunters, or fishermen who depend upon the killing of living beings for their livelihood, as this would signal approval of such activities. He should not approach much less become intimate with women, eunuchs, or young children and should not even visit homes alone to prevent temptation and scandal. The Buddha does say that the bodhisattva should expound the Dharma to these people if they approach him but should not wish to receive any compensation or other benefits. I cannot stress enough that the purpose of this passage listing those a bodhisattva should not approach is not a puritanical condemnation of any of these groups of people. Some of those listed are in fact quite respectable, such as kings and princes, brahmins and even Buddhist monks, nuns, and lay followers. Rather, the point of the passage is that a bodhisattva-*bhikṣu* should refrain from approaching anyone from whom they might gain (or be seen as trying to gain) some worldly benefit and those who follow teachings or ways of life that are inimical to Mahāyāna teachings and values. This does not mean that the bodhisattva-*bhikṣu* shuns such people. Rather, the bodhisattva-*bhikṣu* should remain courteous and professional and share the Dharma with them when asked but should not go beyond that by currying favor with the powerful, engaging in flirtation or seduction, or becoming close associates with those opposed to the Mahāyāna.

What should a bodhisattva-*bhikṣu* approach in order to expound the *Lotus Sūtra* in the evil world after the passing of the Buddha? The Buddha says that the first thing they should approach is a retired place where they can sit in meditative absorption (S. *dhyāna*; J. *zen*). The second thing they should approach is the truth of emptiness as described in the following passage:

All things are insubstantial. They are as they are. Things are not perverted. They do not move. They do not go. They do not turn. They have nothing substantial just as the sky has not. They are inexplicable. They are not born. They do not appear. They do not rise. They are nameless. They are formless. They have no property. They are immeasurable and limitless. They have no obstacle or hindrance. He should see all this. Things can exist only by dependent origination. (Ibid, pp. 211-212)

The verse section that follows and reiterates these instructions make it clear that the bodhisattva-*bhikṣu* who does sit in a retired place, concentrates his mind, and realizes the emptiness of all things will no longer be in danger of approaching people with ulterior motives in terms of their conditioned worldly roles. Rather, he has become able to lead kings, princes, common people, and brahmins by expounding the Dharma to them.

The peaceful practice of the mouth involves expounding the Dharma without putting down other people or sūtras. The bodhisattva-*bhikṣu* should not be a faultfinder nor despise or look down upon others, especially other teachers of the Dharma. He should not criticize or even praise others by name, as this makes things too personal and can lead to the forming of cliques and factions. Presumably if a criticism must be made in regard to the teaching or conduct of others it should be made in terms of generalities and principles and not in terms of specific individuals. The bodhisattva-*bhikṣu* who expounds the Dharma should always do so with a peaceful mind that is motivated by compassion for others and a wish to bring them the joy of the Dharma. When asked about the Dharma he should always answer in terms of the Mahāyāna and not the Hīnayāna so that the questioners will be able to "obtain the knowledge of the equality and differences of all things." (Ibid, p. 216) In other words, they should always teach from a Mahāyāna perspective. The sūtra also says, "He should expound the Dharma to them, wishing only two things: to attain the enlightenment of the Buddha and to cause them to do the same." (Ibid, p. 217) Those who take up this peaceful practice of the mouth will be free of sorrow, fear, quarrels and violence. They will truly be at peace.

The peaceful practice of the mind underscores the proper motivation that a bodhisattva-*bhikṣu* should have. He "should give up jealousy, anger, arrogance, flattery, deception, and dishonesty." (Ibid, p. 219) He should not despise others, get into fruitless arguments, or tell others that they will not be able to attain buddhahood because they follow the three vehicles rather than the One Vehicle. Instead, he "should be gentle, patient, and compassionate toward all living beings." (Ibid. p. 219) He should "look upon all the tathāgatas as his loving fathers, and upon all bodhisattvas as his great teachers" (Ibid, p. 218) and bow respectfully to all the great bodhisattvas from the bottom of his heart. He should also preach impartially to all living beings, not even spending more time with those who love the Dharma more as that would take away from time that could be spent teaching those who presently do not yet have such a deep appreciation. By following such a peaceful practice of the mind the bodhisattva-*bhikṣu* will earn the respect of others and attract a multitude to hear and receive the Dharma, and these people will in turn share it with others by performing the practices of keeping, reading, reciting, expounding, and copying the sūtra.

Finally, there is the peaceful practice of resolution that deals with the bodhisattva-*bhikṣu*'s determination and vow to teach the sūtra. The bodhisattva-bhikshu in the latter days of the Dharma when the teachings are on the verge of disappearing should have great compassion and loving-kindness towards all those who have not taken up the way of bodhisattvas and should think: "They do not know the Tathāgata expounded expedient teachings according to the capacities of all living beings. They do not hear, know or notice it, or ask a question about it or believe or understand it. Although they do not ask a question about this sūtra, or believe or understand it, I will lead them and cause them, wherever they may be, to understand the Dharma by my supernatural powers and by the power of my wisdom when I attain Anuttara-samyak-sambodhi." (Ibid, p. 220) By having such a resolution the bodhisattva-*bhikṣu* will be able to expound the Dharma flawlessly and all manner of people will seek him out to honor him and hear the Dharma. The gods who also wish to hear the Dharma will protect him and he will also receive the protection of the supernatural powers of all the buddhas of the past, present, and future.

After describing the four peaceful practices the Buddha delivers the parable known as the "gem in the topknot" wherein a king bestows a precious gem from his topknot upon a soldier of extraordinary merit just as the Buddha now bestows the teaching of the *Lotus Sūtra* upon those assembled before him now that they are finally ready for it. The Buddha repeats the parable in verse and then explains the benefits to be gained by those who read the sutra, expound it, and take up the four peaceful practices in the evil age after the Buddha's passing. He says that they "will be free from grief, sorrow, disease or pain." (Ibid, p. 224) They will not be poor, humble, or ugly. All living beings will wish to see them and they will be served by celestial pages and will be fearless because they will not be subject to violence, poisoning, or even people speaking ill of them. They will also dream of seeing the buddhas in their assemblies, of receiving a prediction of their own buddhahood, and finally of actually attaining buddhahood and expounding the Dharma themselves.

The aforementioned *Nirvāna Sūtra* takes as one of its major themes the assertion that the bodhisattva should see all beings with the same kind of love and compassion that a parent would for their children. In fact, the sūtra begins with the Buddha telling the assembly gathered at his deathbed that, "Today, the Tathāgata, the Alms-deserving, and the Perfectly Awakened One, pities, protects, and, with an undivided mind, sees beings as he does his son Rāhula. So, he is the refuge and house of the world." (Yamamoto, p. 3 adapted) Later on the Buddha elaborates:

> "O good man! If you say that the Tathāgata, for the
> sake of beings, talks about the superb virtue of the ten
> courses of wholesome conduct, this tells that he sees
> beings like his son Rāhula. How can you reproach him
> and ask if he really prevents beings from falling into
> hell? Should I see but one person falling into the Avici
> Hell, I shall, for the sake of this person, stay in the world
> for a kalpa or less than a kalpa. I have great compassion
> for all beings. How could I cheat one whom I see as my
> own son and let him fall into hell?" (Ibid, p. 96 adapted)

These passages from the *Lotus Sūtra* and the *Nirvāna Sūtra* reveal that the method of accepting and embracing is motivated by love and compassion, nurtured by meditation and contemplation, guided by insight into emptiness

550

and the knowledge of the difference and equality of all phenomena, eschews self-seeking and disputes, and enables those who take it up to attract others and guide them to the Mahāyāna and the *Lotus Sūtra* with gentle words and teachings that accept, embrace, and encourages the good in others.

Sources

Chang, Garma C. *A Treasury of Mahāyāna Sūtras: Selections form the Mahāratnakūta Sūtra*. University Park: The Pennsylvania State University Press, 1983.

Gosho Translation Committee, editor-translator. *The Writings of Nichiren Daishonin*. Tokyo: Soka Gakkai, 1999.

Hori, Kyotsu, comp. *Writings of Nichiren Shonin: Doctrine Volume 2*. Tokyo: Nichiren Shu Overseas Propagation Promotion Association, 2002.

Murano, Senchu, trans. *The Lotus Sutra*. Hayward: Nichiren Buddhist International Center, 2012.

_____. *Kaimokusho or Liberation from Blindness*. Berkeley: Numata Center for Buddhist Translation and Research, 2000.

Yamamoto, Kosho, trans. *Mahaparinirvana-Sutra: A Complete Translation from the Classical Chinese Language in 3 Volumes*. Tokyo: Karinbunko, 1973.

Chapter 44 – Shakubuku: Subduing Evil

Writing of Nichiren Shōnin Doctrine 2: pp. 109-114
Kaimoku-shō or Liberation From Blindness: pp. 120-125
Writings of Nichiren Daishonin I: 283-287

Subduing as a method of teaching the Dharma

Nichiren also cites passages from the Tiantai grand masters that show that their understanding of teaching by breaking and subduing was based upon passages in the *Mahāyāna Mahāparinirvāna Sūtra* (hereafter to be referred to simply as the *Nirvāna Sūtra*) that speak of kings defending Buddhist monks from corrupt monks and brahmin persecutors, and also the story of a doctor who had milk based medicines outlawed because they had been overprescribed by false doctor. They also cited the promises of spirit named Hārītī (J. Kishimojin) and her ten daughters to protect the practitioners of the *Lotus Sūtra* by splitting the heads of those who trouble them. Nichiren also refers to the story of Never Despising Bodhisattva from chapter twenty of the *Lotus Sūtra* as an example of the method of subduing.

In chapter five of the *Nirvāna Sūtra* a bodhisattva named Kāśyapa asks the Buddha how he obtained the adamantine and indestructible Dharma-body. The Buddha answers that those who uphold the True Dharma can obtain it. By upholding the True Dharma, he means that the secular authorities should protect the true monks. "One who upholds the True Dharma does not receive the five precepts and practice deportment but protects with the sword, bow, arrow, and halberd those monks who uphold the precepts and who are pure." (Yamamoto, p. 77 adapted)

In response to the Buddha's statement that the upholders of the True Dharma should protect the pure monks, Kāśyapa Bodhisattva points out that those monks "whose eyes turn to protection" (Ibid, p. 77-78) are usually considered false monks, just as in chapter fourteen of the *Lotus Sūtra* the monks are told to not approach kings and other authorities to gain influence. The Buddha replies by contrasting the precept abiding monk who basically minds his own business with the true monk who expounds the Mahāyāna sūtras and remonstrates with those monks who are breaking the precepts and in doing so incurs the wrath of the corrupt monks who may even violently attack the true monks.

"There may be a monk who goes where he will, is content, recites sūtras, sits, and meditates. Should any person come and ask about the Way, he will expound it. He will speak about giving, observing the precepts, virtuous acts, and say that one should covet little and be content. But he is not able to raise a lion's roar over the doctrine, is not surrounded by lion's, and is not able to subdue those who do evil. Such a monk cannot work out his own benefit, nor is he able to assist others. Know that this person is indolent and lazy. Though he may well uphold the precepts and stick to pure actions, such a one, you should know, can do nothing. Or there may be monks whose has all requisites, who upholds the prohibitive precepts, always raises a lion's roar, and delivers wonderful discourses on the sūtras, geya, assurances, gātha, utterances, fables, jātaka, expanded discourses, and marvelous events. He thus expounds all nine types of Buddhist sūtras. He gives benefit and peace to others. So he says, "Prohibitions are given in this Nirvāna Sūtra to monks saying that they should not keep menials, cows, sheep, or anything that goes against prohibitions. Should monks keep such defiled things, they must be taught not to. The Tathāgata has stated in the sūtras of various schools that any monk who keeps such things must be admonished just as kings correct ill acts and that they must be driven back to secular life." When a monk raises such a lion's roar, any who break the precepts, hearing this, will all be angered and harm that monk. If this person dies because of this, he is to be called one who upholds the precepts and who brings benefit to himself and others. Because of this, kings, ministers, prime ministers, and laymen protect those who deliver discourses. Any

person who protects the True Dharma should learn
things thus." (Ibid, pp. 77-78 adapted)

A true monk is one who not only strictly upholds the precepts but who also preaches the True Dharma, even in the face of persecution. Even in pre-Mahāyāna discourses, the Buddha made it clear that he intended for his monks (and even nuns and lay followers) to teach and even to refute false teachings. In the *Mahāparinibbāna-sutta* the Buddha tells Mara the following:

> *"Evil One, I will not take final nirvāṇa till I have monks*
> *and disciples who are accomplished, trained, skilled,*
> *learned, knowers of the Dharma, trained in conformity*
> *with the Dharma, correctly trained and walking in the*
> *path of the Dharma, who will pass on what they have*
> *gained from their Teacher, teach it, declare it, establish*
> *it, expound it, analyze it, make it clear; till they shall be*
> *able by means of the Dharma to refute false teachings*
> *that have arisen, and teach the Dharma of wondrous*
> *effect." (Walshe, p. 247 adapted)*

Nichiren also cites the following passage from the *Nirvāna Sūtra* that likewise emphasizes the duty of true monks to remonstrate with those who are violating the Dharma. The passage reads:

> *"If a good monk, seeing one who violates the Dharma,*
> *does not drive away, reproach, or impeach such a one,*
> *know that this monk is the enemy of the Buddha*
> *Dharma. If he drives away, reproaches, or impeaches*
> *such a one, he is my disciple, a true disciple."*
> *(Yamamoto, p. 67, adapted)*

We might recognize in this a Mahāyāna reiteration of the Buddha's statements in the *Mahāparinibbāna-sutta*. Nichiren cites a commentary on this passage by Zhiyi's disciple Guanding (561-632) that makes the point that a true friend will try to prevent a friend from committing evil and so it is more truly compassionate to correct them and in fact lacking in compassionate to remain silent. There are several examples in the Pāli canon of the Buddha remonstrating with monks who were found to be misrepresenting the Buddha Dharma to the detriment of themselves and others. He recognized that there may be times when one has to "be cruel to be kind" as we sometimes put it. There are times when one must speak the truth plainly to those who may not want to hear it. One occasion was when the Buddha denounced Devadatta in no uncertain terms, refusing to give him the leadership of the Sangha and making it clear that he did not consider him qualified to ever do so, even if the Buddha were to consider appointing a successor. The Buddha went so far as to say to Devadatta, "I would not hand over the Sangha of monks even to Śāriputra and Maudgalyāyana. How should I do so to such a wastrel, a clot of spittle, as you?" (Nanamoli, p. 258 adapted) Even if one takes the position that this incident is a story that arose after the death of the Buddha in order to vilify the schismatic Devadatta and his followers, it still seems to be so far out of character that one wonders how anyone could have attributed such words to the Buddha. And yet, there is a discourse in which the Buddha's rivals used this and later condemnations of Devadatta against him. Prince Abhaya, one of the sons of King Bimbisāra though not an heir, was a follower of Nirgrantha Jñātīputra, the founder of the Jains. According to the *Abhayarajakumara Sutta*, Nirgrantha Jñātīputra made the following request to Prince Abhaya:

> "Come Prince, go to the recluse Gautama and say:
> 'Venerable sir, would the Tathāgata utter speech that
> would be unwelcome and disagreeable to others?' If the
> recluse Gautama, on being asked thus, answers: 'The
> Tathāgata, prince, would utter speech that would be
> unwelcome and disagreeable to others,' then say to
> him: 'Then, venerable sir, what is the difference
> between you and an ordinary person? For an ordinary
> person would utter speech that would be unwelcome
> and disagreeable to others.' But if the recluse Gautama,
> on being asked thus, answers: 'The Tathāgata, prince,
> would not utter speech that would be unwelcome and
> disagreeable to others,' then say to him: 'Then,
> venerable sir, why have you declared of Devadatta:
> "Devadatta is destined for the states of deprivation,
> Devadatta is destined for hell, Devadatta will remain [in

*hell] for the eon, Devadatta is incorrigible"? Devadatta
was angry and dissatisfied with that speech of yours.'
When the recluse Gautama is posed this two-horned
question by you, he will not be able either to gulp it
down or to throw it up. If an iron spike were stuck in a
man's throat, he would not be able either to gulp it
down or to throw it up; so too prince, when the recluse
Gautama is posed this two-horned question by you, he
will not be able to gulp it down or to throw it up."
(Nanamoli & Bodhi, pp. 498-499)*

It is evident that Nirgrantha Jñātīputra is not being portrayed here as a
dispassionate observer. Nor is his inquiry sincere. In order to attack and
belittle the Buddha, he spitefully looked for a weak point to exploit. Again, this
is perhaps not an accurate portrayal of the founder of the Jains, but it may be
a historical fiction based on the kind of rancorous debates that may have
taken place between Buddhists and Jains after the passing of their founders.
In any case, the Buddha easily overcomes both horns of the dilemma and in
the course of doing so also provides an explanation for why he spoke so
harshly in regard to Devadatta. Prince Abhaya visits the Buddha and asks:

*"Venerable sir, would a Tathāgata utter such speech as
would be unwelcome and disagreeable to others?"*

"There is no one-sided answer to that, prince."

"Then, venerable sir, the Nirgranthas have lost in this."

*"Why do you say this, prince: 'Then, venerable sir, the
Nirgranthas have lost in this'?"*

*Prince Abhaya then reported to the Blessed One his
entire conversation with Nirgrantha Jñātīputra.*

*Now on that occasion a young tender infant was lying
prone on Prince Abhaya's lap. Then the Blessed One said
to Prince Abhaya: "What do you think, prince? If, while
you or your nurse were not attending to him, this child*

were to put a stick or pebble in his mouth, what would you do to him?"

"Venerable sir, I would take it out. If I could not take it out at once, I would take his head in my left hand, and crooking a finger of my right hand, I would take it out even if it meant drawing blood. Why is that? Because I have compassion for the child."

"So too, prince, such speech as the Tathāgata knows to be untrue, incorrect, and unbeneficial, and which is also unwelcome and disagreeable to others: such speech the Tathāgata does not utter. Such speech as the Tathāgata knows to be true and correct but unbeneficial, and which is also unwelcome and disagreeable to others: such speech the Tathāgata does not utter. Such speech as the Tathāgata knows to be true, correct, and beneficial, but which is unwelcome and disagreeable to others: the Tathāgata knows the time to use such speech. Such speech as the Tathāgata knows to be untrue, incorrect, and unbeneficial, but which is welcome and agreeable to others: such speech the Tathagata does not utter. Such speech as the Tathāgata knows to be true and correct but unbeneficial, and which is welcome and agreeable to others: such speech the Tathāgata does not utter. Such speech as the Tathāgata knows to be true, correct, and beneficial, and which is welcome and agreeable to others: the Tathāgata knows the time to use such speech. Why is that? Because the Tathagata has compassion for beings." (Ibid, pp. 499-500)

In other words, the Buddha only speaks what is true, correct, and beneficial; and whether or not it is welcome and agreeable or unwelcome and disagreeable he will only speak such things in the right time and place motivated solely by compassion. In the case of Devadatta, he was certain based upon his knowledge of Devadatta's character and activities and the law of cause and effect that Devadatta was heading for a fall. In some versions or translations of this event, the Buddha actually calls Devadatta a "lick-spittle"

557

with the implication that Devadatta's reliance on the very generous patronage of Prince Ajātaśatru is comparable to licking the spit of others. In other words, his reliance on Prince Ajātaśatru seems good, but is actually a degrading dependence that is leading him further and further away from the true good of liberation. All of this can be taken to rationalize the use of name-calling in a debate or disagreement, but I think the actual principles are quite clear. We should speak in a truthful and beneficial way, and whenever possible in a kind way; but also, in a timely and appropriate way, especially if what needs to be said will be unpleasant for others to hear.

Getting back to the *Nirvāna Sūtra*, the Buddha tells Kāśyapa Bodhisattva the story of King Virtuous, who was a past life of the bodhisattva who would become Śākyamuni Buddha. King Virtuous fought to his death against false monks who broke the precepts and were trying to kill the virtuous monk named Awakened to Virtue.

> *"The reward of protecting the True Dharma is extremely great and innumerable. O good man! Because of this, those laymen who protect the Dharma should take the sword and staff and protect such a monk who guards the Dharma. Even if one upholds the precepts, we cannot call this person one who upholds the Mahāyāna. Even if one has not received the five precepts, if one protects the True Dharma, such a one can well be called one of the Mahāyāna. One who upholds the True Dharma should take the sword and staff and guard monks. ... O good man! After I have entered nirvāna, the world will be evil-ridden and the land devastated, each pillaging the other, and the people will be driven by hunger. At such a time, because of hunger, men may make up their minds to abandon home and enter the Sangha. Such persons are false monks. Such, seeing those persons who strictly observe the precepts, correct in deportment, and pure in action, upholding the True Dharma, will drive such away or cause them harm. ... O good man! That is why I permit those who uphold the precepts to be accompanied by white clad laypeople with swords and staves. Although all kings, ministers,*

rich householders, and laymen may possess the sword
and staff for protecting the Dharma, I call this the
upholding of the precepts. You may possess the sword
and staff, but do not take life. If things go thus, we call
it the first-hand upholding of the precepts." (Yamamoto,
pp. 80-81 adapted)

The story shows that the protection and transmission of the True Dharma is the responsibility of the rulers and not just of the monastic Sangha because it is secular authorities who are charged with maintaining law and order and to protect the lives of the innocent through the use of, or at least threat of, deadly force if necessary. Intriguingly, the *Nirvāna Sūtra* states that the armed laypeople should not use their weapons to kill. In the story of King Virtuous it does not say that he actually killed any of the false monks attacking the monk Awakened to Virtue though he did apparently succeed in routing them. So even though the secular authorities are to take up weapons, they should refrain from actually using them to kill, but rather only to defend the innocent and drive off or subdue evildoers. The secular authorities therefore have a duty to protect innocent monks who live virtuously in accordance with the precepts and who teach the True Dharma by using force only when necessary and even then to refrain from actually killing.

Chapter nineteen of the *Nirvāna Sūtra* tells the story of King Sen'yo. According to the story in a past life Śākyamuni Buddha was a king who put to death several brahmins who slandered the Mahāyāna sūtras. Because he took such action to protect the Mahāyāna he never thereafter fell into hell in all his subsequent rebirths. I must note that the Yamamoto translates the passage in question so that the Buddha says: "I, at that time, greatly respected the Mahāyāna. I heard the brahmins slander the *vaipulya*. Having heard it, I made away with my life." (Ibid, p. 291, adapted) However, chapter twenty of the *Nirvāna Sūtra* makes it clear that in the story the king ended not his own life but that of the brahmins. I have looked at the passage in question in Chinese and a literal translation would read that the king "cut off the root of life." By context it would seem that he cut the root of life of the brahmin slanderers, not his own. I find it a curious expression and wonder if it is a kind of Buddhist pun, since from a Buddhist point of view the root or roots that keep us entangled in the sufferings of birth and death would be the three poisons of greed, hatred, and delusion. Did King Sen'yo kill himself? Or did he have the brahmins who slandered the Mahāyāna executed? Or did he cut off the roots of greed, hatred, and delusion of himself and the brahmins?

In chapter twenty, Kāśyapa Bodhisattva asks, "Why is it that the Tathāgata, when born a king, practicing the Bodhisattva Way, took the life of the brahmins of the palace?" (Ibid, p. 390, adapted) The Buddha says in reply, "You say that the Tathāgata, in days gone by, killed the brahmins. O good man! The bodhisattva-mahāsattva does not purposely kill an ant! How could he a brahmin?" (Ibid, p. 392, adapted). The Buddha explains that his killing of the brahmins does not really count as killing because he did it out of love so that the brahmins would be cast into hell wherein they would realize their error and then be reborn from there into the pure land of a Buddha and gain a life of ten eons. Therefore, the Buddha was actually giving them a life of ten eons. The Buddha explains that sometimes he has to take harsh measures to help people.

> "Should it be that beings slander the Mahāyāna, he applies kindly lashings in order to cure. Or he may take life in order that when happened in the past could be mended, thus to make it possible for the Dharma to be accorded with. The bodhisattva always thinks: 'How might I best make beings aspire to faith? I shall always act as best fits the occasion.'" (Ibid, p. 393)

The Buddha further explains that while there are three grades of killing: (1) those who kill animals, even an ant, will be reborn in the hells or as hungry ghosts or animals; (2) those who kill unenlightened people will also be reborn into those realms but will suffer even more; and (3) those who kill their parents, arhats, pratyekabuddhas or bodhisattvas will fall into the Avīci Hell. The killing of an *icchantika*, or incorrigible disbeliever, does not fit into any of those three and does not bring about any karmic recompense. The brahmins, in slandering the Mahāyāna teaching, had become *icchantika* and therefore King Sen'yo did not commit an evil act in killing them but a good one in fighting to protect the Mahāyāna and helping the brahmins to awaken. I find that the sūtra's explanation that the brahmins who were put to death were *icchantika* and therefore it was okay to kill them is even more disturbing to modern ears than the story it is attempting to explain. It basically amounts to saying that we do not have to value the lives of those who insult our religious convictions and that killing such people is in fact a meritorious deed that will ultimately benefit everyone – even those who have been killed. Today, not a day goes by without stories in the news of those willing to kill those who they feel do not share or respect their religious convictions. Every religiously motivated terrorist in the world feels that they are justified in killing those who do not share their convictions and that they will be given a free pass to heaven for doing so. So I find that this is a very unfortunate example of Mahāyāna rhetoric gone awry. Other passages in the *Nirvāna Sūtra* mitigate this story and its casuistic explanations, for they suggest that the *icchantika* may not always be what they appear, and that some might actually be bodhisattvas or else some may repent and cease to be *icchantika* and that in any case even the *icchantika* have buddha-nature that will someday come to fruition. Taking these other passages into account, the sūtra seems to be saying that killing even an *icchantika* is to kill a potential buddha, and therefore a grave crime that can only lead to rebirth in the Avīci Hell. I find these passages to be important warnings to not take the story of King Sen'yo literally.

Another parable cited in relation to the method of subduing is from chapter three of the *Nirvāna Sūtra*. The Buddha is asked why he now speaks of nirvāṇa as being pure, blissful, eternal, and the true self. This is confusing to his listeners because he had previously stressed that there is only non-self. The Buddha explains that it was because others had incorrectly attributed purity, bliss, eternity, and selfhood to contingent phenomena that he needed to stress impurity, suffering, impermanence, and non-self, but that nirvāṇa could properly be said to have these positive attributes. He then tells a parable wherein a king puts a doctor on his staff who is actually a charlatan. The charlatan doctor ignorantly prescribes milk-based medicines for every illness. An authentic doctor finds out about this and convinces the king to drive away the false doctor and hire him instead. The doctor then has the king outlaw milk-based medicines in order to break people's attachment to them. The king threatens to have anyone who takes such medicine beheaded. The day comes, however, when the king himself falls ill and can only be cured with milk-based medicine. The authentic doctor then reveals that in fact there are times when milk-based medicine is not ineffectual or harmful but in fact necessary and such is the case with the king's illness. In this story, at least, no one is actually beheaded. The parable uses the king's threat to underscore the strong measures needed to break the people of their attachment to the ineffectual and dangerous prescriptions of the charlatan so that they will take up the true doctor's remedies.

How did Nichiren understand these stories? In *Risshō Ankoku-ron*, Nichiren stated that while King Sen'yo and King Virtuous may have killed slanderers of the Dharma in the past, since the appearance of Śākyamuni Buddha the correct method is to simply deny them offerings. The *Nirvāna Sūtra* told those stories of the previous lives of Śākyamuni Buddha in order to emphasize the gravity of slandering the True Dharma and the great virtue of defending the True Dharma but such methods are not being advocated in the present. Instead, the withholding of alms and especially state support from corrupt monks and the support and protection of true monks should now be followed. In accordance with our current laws and the wise separation of church and state, I believe this means that each of us must discern what teachings or causes we should or should not support with our time and money and that the protection of the law should extend equally to all so that there will be no question of religious persecution arising from either the government or the actions of private individuals or institutions. Every religious or spiritual teaching should be free to stand or fall on its own merits or lack thereof.

In chapter twenty-six of the *Lotus Sūtra* various beings offer protective incantations called dhāranī to safeguard the practitioners of the *Lotus Sūtra*. One set of these is offered by a formerly malevolent spirit named Hārītī (J. Kishimojin) and her ten daughters and other children and attendants. Hārītī, whose name means "stealer of children," is a female yakṣa, or yakṣini, who originally came from the town of Rājagriha. The yakṣas are one of the eight kinds of supernatural beings who are said to revere and protect the Dharma. Originally the yakṣas appeared as the spirits of the trees and forests and even villages; but they had a fierce side as well, and in their more demonic aspect came to be called rākṣasas. According to legend, Hārītī was obsessed with eating the children of Rājagriha. Neither King Bimbisāra nor even the devas were able to stop her, so in desperation the townspeople turned to Śākyamuni Buddha. The Buddha visited her home while she was away and used his supernatural powers to hide her youngest son under his alms bowl. When Hārītī returned and could not find her son she was distraught and finally she herself sought out the Buddha. The Buddha then pointed out to her that if she felt so badly about missing even one child out of 500, she should consider how badly the parents of Rājagriha must feel when she takes away their children when they have so few to begin with. Hearing this, Hārītī felt remorse and compassion for those she had harmed. She repented of her actions; took refuge in the Buddha, Dharma, and Sangha; took the five precepts; and vowed to protect the people of Rājagriha. The Buddha then restored her youngest son to her. In return the Buddha had his monks, from that time on, make a symbolic offer of their food to the hungry ghosts. Hārītī came to be considered a protector of children and women giving birth as well as a protector of the Dharma, and her gentle image as a "giver of children" would sometimes cause her to be confused with Avalokiteśvara Bodhisattva. As can be seen in chapter twenty-six of the *Lotus Sūtra*, her fierce nature showed itself once more in her vow to protect the practitioners of the sūtra, for she and her children sang to the Buddha: "Anyone who does not keep our spells but troubles the expounder of the Dharma shall have his head split into seven pieces just as the branches of the *arjaka*-tree are split." (Murano 2012, p. 335) This statement is cited as one example of how the *Lotus Sūtra* also contains the method of subduing.

The threat requires some explanation. At face value a malevolent spirit converted to Buddhism is threatening to kill those who attack the practitioners of the *Lotus Sūtra*. This threat to split people's heads into seven pieces is an old one however, that even appears in the Pāli canon. In context, it would almost appear to be an idiom for how someone who has been cornered or defeated in an argument must feel. For instance, in the following passage the Buddha presses an arrogant brahmin to admit that his ancestors were not all of the brahmin caste. Because the brahmin is reluctant to answer he finds himself threatened with having his head split by a yakṣa.

> Then the Lord said to Ambattha: "Ambattha, I have a fundamental question for you, which you will not like to answer. If you don't answer, or evade the issue, if you keep silent or go away, your head will split into seven pieces. What do you think, Ambattha? Have you heard from old and venerable brahmins, teacher of teachers, where the Kanhāyans come from, or who was their ancestor?" At this, Ambattha remained silent. The Lord asked him a second time. Again Ambattha remained silent, and the Lord said: "Answer me now, Ambattha,

this is not a time for silence. Whoever, Ambattha, does not answer a fundamental question put to him by a Tathāgata by the third asking has his head split into seven pieces."

"And at that moment, Vajrapāni the yakṣa, holding a huge iron club, flaming, ablaze and glowing, up in the sky just above Ambattha, was thinking: 'If this young man Ambattha does not answer a proper question put to him by the Blessed Lord by the third time of asking, I'll split his head into seven pieces!' The Lord saw Vajrapāni, and so did Ambattha. And at the sight, Ambattha was terrified and unnerved, his hairs stood on end, and he sought protection, shelter, and safety from the Lord. Crouching down close to the Lord, he said: 'What did the Reverend Gautama say? May the Reverend Gautama repeat what he said!' 'What do you think, Ambattha? Have you heard who was the ancestor of the Kanhāyans?' 'Yes, I have heard it just as the Reverend Gautama said, that is where the Kanhāyans come from, he was their ancestor.'" (Walshe, pp. 115-116)

The *Sutta-nipāta* sheds further light on this metaphorical threat or idiom. A brahmin named Bāvari is cursed to have his head split in pieces by a vengeful beggar. So the monk Ajita asks the Buddha about this for the worried brahmin. The Buddha's reply indicates that the splitting of the head actually represents the destruction of ignorance. "Know ignorance to be 'the head'; clear knowledge is 'head-splitting' when conjoined with faith, mindfulness, concentration, desire, and energy." (Bodhi, p. 300) In other words, the threat of having one's head split into pieces may be an old idiomatic way of cursing someone with open-mindedness!

Finally, there is the story of Never Despising Bodhisattva in chapter twenty of the *Lotus Sūtra* that is cited by Nichiren as an example of the method of subduing evil. In the chapter the Buddha tells of a bodhisattva who lived during the age of the counterfeit Dharma of the Powerful-Voice-King Buddha. This bodhisattva's sole practice was to bow to all he met and say to them, "I respect you deeply. I do not despise you. Why is that? It is because you will be able to practice the Way of bodhisattvas and become buddhas." (Murano 2012, p. 292) Because of this he was called Never Despising Bodhisattva. The arrogant monks, nuns, laymen, and laywomen at that time felt that he was speaking falsely and so abused him and even threw things at him. Though forced to run away, Never Despising Bodhisattva did not relent and continued to assure people "in a loud voice from afar" (Ibid, p. 293) that they would become buddhas. In time, those who abused him became his followers and took faith in the teaching that they would be able to attain buddhahood. The Buddha goes on to say that Never Despising Bodhisattva was himself in a past life and that because he was able to lead so many people into the way to perfect and complete awakening he was able to meet many hundreds of thousands of millions of buddhas and expound the *Lotus Sūtra* and ultimately become a buddha himself. Those who abused him had to expiate their sins in the Avīci Hell but afterwards were able to become bodhisattvas themselves and meet many buddhas including Śākyamuni Buddha.

In the story of Never Despising Bodhisattva the method of subduing evil becomes clear. The bodhisattva does not berate or argue with others, nor does he resort to the coercive power of the state. Rather, he forthrightly proclaims the True Dharma that all beings can attain buddhahood in the face of disbelief, abuse, and even violence. Never Despising Bodhisattva is not only motivated by compassion, but his sole practice is a gesture of reverence and respect for the buddha-nature in all beings. When faced with abuse and violence he does not allow himself to be hurt but retreats to a safe distance. Instead of retaliating in kind he continues to voice his deepest conviction and reverence. The method of subduing therefore is about having the courage and compassion to stand up for what is right and to give voice to the True Dharma even though one may meet with derision or even persecution.

Sources

Bodhi, Bhikkhu, trans. *The Suttanipāta*. Boston: Wisdom Publication, 2017.

Gosho Translation Committee, editor-translator. *The Writings of Nichiren Daishonin*. Tokyo: Soka Gakkai, 1999.

Hori, Kyotsu, comp. *Writings of Nichiren Shonin: Doctrine Volume 2*. Tokyo: Nichiren Shu Overseas Propagation Promotion Association, 2002.

_____. *Writings of Nichiren Shonin: Doctrine Volume 1*. Tokyo: Nichiren Shu Overseas Propagation Promotion Association, 2003.

Murano, Senchu, trans. *The Lotus Sutra*. Hayward: Nichiren Buddhist International Center, 2012.

_____. *Kaimokusho or Liberation from Blindness*. Berkeley: Numata Center for Buddhist Translation and Research, 2000.

Nanamoli, Bhikkhu and Bodhi, Bhikkhu, trans. *The Middle Length Discourses of the Buddha: A New Translation of the Majjhima Nikaya*. Boston, Wisdom Publication, 1995.

Nanamoli, Bhikkhu, *The Life of the Buddha*. Kandy: Buddhist Publication Society, 1992.

Walshe, Maurice, trans. *The Long Discourses of the Buddha: A Translation of the Digha Nikaya*. Boston: Wisdom Publications, 1995.

Yamamoto, Kosho, trans. Mahaparinirvana-Sutra: A Complete Translation from the Classical Chinese Language in 3 Volumes. Tokyo: Karinbunko, 1973.

Chapter 45 – Choosing and Applying Shakubuku

Writing of Nichiren Shōnin Doctrine 2: pp. 109-114
Kaimoku-shō or Liberation From Blindness: pp. 120-125
Writings of Nichiren Daishonin I: 283-287

Choosing the Method

The two methods of embracing and subduing are said by Nichiren to be as incompatible as fire and water. "The way of embracing is as different from the way of subduing as water is from fire. Fire dislikes water. Water hates fire. Those who embrace laugh at those who subdue. Those who subdue feel sorry for those who embrace." (Murano 2000, p. 122 adapted). Nichiren quotes Guanding (562-632) as saying of Buddhist monks that in regard to the two methods of propagation: "When the world is not peaceful, they should carry staves. When the world is peaceful, they should observe the precepts. They should choose one or the other according to the needs of the time. They should not constantly cling to either of the two." (Ibid, p. 122 adapted) A choice is set up between the two contrasting methods. But how different, really, are the ways of embracing and subduing? Guanding's statement underscores the matter of the precepts – those who follow the way of embracing will follow the precepts including the precepts against killing and fighting, whereas those who follow the way of subduing are to set aside the precepts and take up arms to defend themselves. From examining the passages cited in the *Nirvāna Sūtra* and the *Lotus Sūtra* that are said to exemplify the ways of embracing and subduing it would appear that during a time when embracing is the correct method the laymen should follow the five precepts and the monastics should follow the monastic precepts and avoid violence of any kind. In addition, the monastics should stay away from people in power, refrain from criticizing others, practice meditation in seclusion, and only teach when approached by those respectfully seeking the Dharma. On the other hand, during a time when subduing is the correct method, the laypeople should set aside the five precepts (the first of which prohibits killing and violence) and take up arms to defend the True Dharma and the monastics who uphold it, while the true monastics are allowed to keep company with those who can defend them and, according to Guanding, even take up staves themselves. In addition, the true monastics should publicly roar the lion's roar by actively preaching the Dharma, denouncing false teachings and corruption in the Sangha, and expound the universality of buddha-nature even to those who refuse to listen and may even react violently. The watery method of embracing is therefore the way of seclusion, meditation, and non-violence; whereas the fiery method of subduing is the way of publicly preaching the True Dharma to those who may be violently opposed to it and it allows for the taking up of arms for defense. These two ways would indeed seem to be contradictory.

The ways of embracing and subduing, however, are not entirely opposed. They both have the same aim: the expounding of the True Dharma. They are both based on the compassionate motivation to teach people that all beings are capable of realizing buddhahood. The exemplar of the way of subduing in the *Lotus Sūtra* is Never Despising Bodhisattva and if one examines his practice it becomes evident that he does not actually do anything that would go against what is taught in chapter fourteen of the sūtra in regard to the four peaceful practices. Never Despising did not approach people in power but approached the four kinds of Buddhist devotees (monks, nuns, laymen, laywomen) and bowed respectfully while assuring them of their future attainment of buddhahood. He did not denounce or criticize anyone though his assurance contradicted the beliefs of those he greeted because they did not believe that anyone could attain buddhahood. He did not take up arms or even have armed guards though he did move away to a safe distance when people started to throw things at him. The crucial difference between the practice of Never Despising Bodhisattva and the four peaceful practices is that he does not seclude himself in meditation but actively expounds the True Dharma to those Buddhists who are, for whatever reasons, violently opposed to it. In addition, the passages in the *Nirvāna Sūtra* that endorse the taking up of arms also have passages that suggest that this should only be done to defend the pure monks and that one should even then refrain from actually using those arms to kill. I have not myself found passages where it permits monks to take up swords or bows and arrows, nor any passage that would recommend using coercion to force belief or compliance upon others (with the possible exception of the story of King Sen'yo previously discussed). The way of subduing is not about spreading the Dharma by way of the sword. Rather, it is about having the compassion and courage to correct those who are misrepresenting the Dharma, forthrightly giving public witness to the True Dharma, and if violent opposition is aroused to defend against it.

In *Kaimoku-shō*, Nichiren describes the circumstances that determine which method should be followed, making it clear that in the Latter Age of Degeneration both ways must be applied depending on the circumstances. His concern was which method to apply to Japan at that time.

> *"So, when the land is full of evil and ignorant people, the way of embracing should take precedence as preached in the 'Peaceful Practices' (fourteenth) chapter of the Lotus Sūtra. However, when there are many cunning slanderers of the True Dharma, the way of subduing should take precedence as preached in the 'Never Despising Bodhisattva' (twentieth) chapter.*
>
> *It is the same as using cold water when it is hot and fire when it is cold. Plants and trees are followers of the sun, so they dislike the cold moon. Bodies of water are followers of the moon, so they lose their true nature when it is hot. As there are lands of evil men as well as those of slanderers of the True Dharma in this Latter Age of Degeneration, there should be both embracing and subduing as means of spreading the True Dharma. Therefore, we have to know whether Japan today is a land of evil men or that of slanderers in order to decide which of the two ways we should use."* (Hori 2002, p. 111 adapted)

Nichiren further clarifies that according to Zhiyi (538-597) and Guanding, one must be sure of the conditions of the time and choose which method to use accordingly. What is the difference between "evil and ignorant people" and "cunning slanderers of the True Dharma"? By "evil and ignorant people" Nichiren means those who are ignorant of Buddhism and who commit unwholesome bodily, verbal, and mental actions without reference to Buddhist teachings. In a letter attributed to Nichiren, the author wrote of these kinds of people: "Paradoxical as it may seem, evil people who have not the least understanding of the principle of cause and effect and who are not dedicated to any Buddha whatsoever would appear to be the ones free from error with respect to Buddhism." (WND1, p. 173)

Slanderers, on the other hand, are those who have heard the Dharma and in fact have become Buddhists, but they choose provisional teachings over the True Dharma taught in the *Lotus Sūtra* and even reject the latter. For instance, as we have seen previously, they may reject the idea that all people can attain buddhahood or may reject the idea that women or seemingly incorrigible people could ever attain buddhahood, or that arhats or pratyekabuddhas could ever take up the Buddha-vehicle. They might insist that one can only begin cultivating the way to buddhahood after death, or that one must first undertake particular esoteric initiations or transmissions. The *Lotus Sūtra*, however, sets forth no such criteria and opens the way to buddhahood to all beings who hear and take faith in its teaching and this is why it surpasses the more limited views of the other sūtras. In a letter attributed to Nichiren, the following statement is made: "In Buddhism, that teaching is judged supreme that enables all people, whether good or evil, to become Buddhas. (Gosho Translation Committee 1999, p. 156) In *Kaimoku-shō*, Nichiren cites the widespread popularity of the teachings of Hōnen and Dainichi Nōnin that both reject reliance upon the *Lotus Sūtra* and the complicity of the Tendai and Mantra schools as evidence that Japan had become a land overrun by slanderers and so the method of subduing evil was called for.

Nichiren's argument for the need to use the way of subduing is developed further in the *True Way of Practicing the Teaching of the Buddha* (*Nyosetsu Shugyō-shō*).

> "All those who want to practice Buddhism should know that there are two ways of propagation, embracing and subduing. All Buddhist scriptures, sūtras and commentaries must be propagated through these two ways. However, scholars in Japan today, though they seem to have learned Buddhism in general, do not know how to meet the needs of the time. The four seasons differ from one another. It is warm in summer and cold in winter, flowers bloom in spring and trees bear fruit and nuts in autumn. How can we harvest crops in spring by planting seeds in the fall? Heavy clothes are for the cold winter, not the hot summer. A cool breeze is needed in the summer and not in the winter.

The same could be said of Buddhism. There are times when Hīnayāna teachings can be spread effectively, and times when provisional Mahāyāna teachings might be more effective. Still other times might call for the True Dharma to be disseminated for the attainment of buddhahood. The two thousand year period following the death of Śākyamuni Buddha, namely the Ages of the True Dharma and Semblance Dharma, is the time for the Hīnayāna and provisional Mahāyāna teachings to be spread. The five hundred year period at the beginning of the Latter Age of the Dharma is the time exclusively for the pure, perfect, only real teaching of the Lotus Sūtra to be disseminated. This is the time when quarrels and disputes are rampant, the True Dharma is hidden and the difference between the true and provisional teachings is blurred. It is said in the Nirvāna Sūtra: 'Arm yourself with swords, staves, and bow and arrows when there are enemies of the True Dharma; it is no use having them when there are no enemies.' Provisional teachings today are enemies of the True Dharma. If provisional teachings stand in your way as you try to spread the One Vehicle teaching of the Lotus Sūtra, you should thoroughly refute them. Of the two ways of propagation, this is the way of subduing of the Lotus Sūtra. Great Master Tiantai declares in his Profound Meaning of the Lotus Sūtra, fascicle nine: 'The Lotus Sūtra is the teaching of subduing, the denouncing of the provisional teachings.' How true this is!

In spite of this, suppose we perform the four peaceful practices today with the body, mouth, mind, and vows as preached in the 'Peaceful Practices' chapter of the Lotus Sūtra, is it not like trying to harvest crops in spring by planting seeds in winter? Roosters crow at dawn; if they crow in the evening, they are like strange ghosts. At the time when true and provisional teachings are confused, are not those who seclude themselves in mountain forests and practice the way of embracing,

571

without refuting the enemies of the Lotus Sūtra, like
ghosts who have missed the time for practicing the
Lotus Sūtra? Then is there anyone today, in the Latter
Age of the Dharma, who is practicing the way of
subduing as it is preached in the Lotus Sūtra? Suppose
someone cried out loudly without sparing his voice: No
sūtra except the Lotus Sūtra is the way leading to
buddhahood; others are the way to hell; the Lotus Sūtra
alone is the way leading to buddhahood.' Anyone who
proclaims these words and challenges the schools of
Buddhism, both their teachings and people, will without
fail encounter the three kinds of powerful enemies."
(Hori 2007, pp. 85-86 adapted)

What it means to say that the provisional teachings lead to hell when they
contradict the *Lotus Sūtra* and the reference to the three kinds of powerful
enemies has all been discussed previously in this commentary. I will not say
anything further about those issues here. What is of interest in this passage is
that it makes the point that the Tiantai tradition sees the *Lotus Sūtra* as the
sūtra of subduing evil because it forthrightly proclaims the teaching of the One
Vehicle and the eternity of the Buddha's lifespan, thus revealing the
shortcomings of the other teachings. Simply to proclaim the *Lotus Sūtra* as the
Buddha's supreme teaching is itself to take up the way of subduing because it
challenges the claims of the other sūtras that certain people cannot attain
buddhahood or that the Buddha is no longer present and active in our lives. In
refuting the provisional teaching, Nichiren felt that he was only following the
Buddha's example. In *A Letter to Buzen-kō at the Jissōji Temple* (*Jissōji Gosho*),
Nichiren wrote:

"Whenever Śākyamuni Buddha, the Buddha of Many
Treasures, and various buddhas from all over the
universe preach the Lotus Sūtra, they first refute the
provisional teachings by revealing the true teaching in
order to cut off the audience's attachment to the
provisional teachings before leading them into the true
teachings. Now, if you call me, Nichiren, who refutes the
provisional teachings by the true teaching, blind, is
Śākyamuni Buddha, too, blind? Are Tiantai and Dengyō

blind teachers? It is laughable indeed." (Hori 2008, pp. 187-188)

Furthermore, the method of subduing, of refuting the shortcomings of other Buddhist teachings is to be taken up at the time when the other teachings have become preferred to the *Lotus Sūtra*. In the past, the other teachings were laying the groundwork for what is taught in the *Lotus Sūtra*, but in the Latter Age of the Dharma they become themselves objects of clinging that distract from the *Lotus Sūtra* or even turn people away from it. When this happens the time has arrived to use the method of subduing rather than that of embracing.

Nichiren's Application of the Way of Subduing

At this point I would like to examine how Nichiren personally applied the way of subduing and what he taught his monastic and lay followers about applying it. One issue that I would like to address first is whether Nichiren was encouraging his followers to become belligerent and fight with those who refused to believe in the *Lotus Sūtra* in the same way they did. The answer is that he clearly did not. In fact, he even told them not to take up arms even if provoked. In response to the persecution of Nichiren's lay followers in the village of Atsuwara, he sent a letter called *Persecution Befalling the Sage* (*Shōnin Gonan Ji*) to his follower Shijō Kingo. In that letter he wrote: "Even if they cause a commotion by taking up arms against my followers, we should not act likewise. If any follower of mine tries to take up arms, please send me his name at once." (Hori 2008, p. 120) Nichiren was clearly opposed to violence on the part of his followers even in the face of provocation.

Another issue is the tone of Nichiren's rhetoric. He clearly was not following the peaceful practices of chapter fourteen of the *Lotus Sūtra* in his harsh criticisms of specific monks, both those who had passed away and those who were contemporaries. Nichiren was very conscious of the fact that people found his critical stance and the tone he sometimes took questionable. In *A Letter to Shōmitsu-bō* (*Shōmitsu-bō Gosho*) he responds to the following question:

> *Question: Is there any reason for you alone to speak ill of Kūkai and Śubhākarasimha?*

573

Answer: I am not criticizing them; I simply intend to
clarify any doubts about them. If you get angry with me,
I can't help it." (Ibid, p. 163)

People were, and continue to be, put off by Nichiren's prophetic warnings about the dire fate Japan faced of invasion by the Mongols if the Japanese people did not turn away from the provisional teachings and uphold the *Lotus Sūtra*. Nichiren was well aware that people thought he was just issuing hateful threats. His motivation was the compassionate one of correcting error so that people would not have to suffer such an invasion. To Shijō Kingo he wrote:

"When I say this, the ruler of the country might think
that I am issuing threats, but I do not say this out of
hatred. I say this out of compassion; I hope to save
them from the torment of the Hell of Incessant Suffering
in future lives by enduring light retribution in this life.
Great Master Zhang'an states in his Annotations on the
Nirvāna Sūtra, 'To remove the evil of another is to be
like a compassionate parent.' According to this I am the
mother and father of the ruler of the country and the
teacher for all the living beings." (Hori 2010, pp. 128-
129 adapted)

Nichiren felt that it was compassionate and kind to speak seemingly harsh words if it would get people to reconsider their positions, avoid slander, and embrace a more authentic path, whereas it was actually cruel to say only what is agreeable to the listener. In this Nichiren is in agreement with the Buddha who had advised that one should only speak in a timely manner what is true and beneficial, regardless of whether it is agreeable or not. What is agreeable should not be spoken if it is untrue or not of any benefit. In a letter attributed to Nichiren, the writer says:

Even though one may resort to harsh words, if such
words help the person to whom they are addressed,
then they are worthy to be regarded as truthful words
and gentle words. Similarly, though one may use gentle

words, if they harm the person to whom they are
addressed, they are in fact deceptive words, harsh
words. (Gosho Translation Committee 1999, p. 178)

People may question whether Nichiren was really compassionate or just dogmatic and self-righteous. That is something that no one can possibly judge. Obviously, those of us who are his modern-day followers give him the benefit of the doubt and take him at his word that his motivation was compassion, and that his denunciation of other monks was rooted in his earnest desire to correct error and proclaim the True Dharma. The important thing for us is to keep in mind that when we discuss Buddhism with others, we must always make sure that we are speaking out of compassion and not some lesser and more egotistic motivation.

Another issue to be addressed is the appropriateness of insisting on teaching the *Lotus Sūtra* to those who do not wish to hear it, or who are not able to really appreciate its significance. Isn't this unskillful? Wouldn't it be better to just let people learn and practice those Buddhist teachings that they find meaningful and encourage them in that, as the way of embracing suggests? Then, when they are ready they may come to the *Lotus Sūtra* on their own, and until then they will not feel any antagonism towards it because it has not been used to challenge their own beliefs and practices. Nichiren also addresses this issue in *Treatise on the Teaching, Capacity, Time and Country* (*Kyō Ki Ji Koku Shō*).

Question: How should we comprehend the statement in
chapter three, 'A Parable,' of the Lotus Sūtra, 'You
should not expound this sutra to ignorant people?'

Answer: This applies to wise masters, who are able to
discern the capacity of people, not to ordinary masters
in the Latter Age of Degeneration.

We should also solely expound the Lotus Sūtra to those
who slander the Dharma. This would establish the
connection of a poisonous drum between the unfaithful
people and the Lotus Sūtra as it is said that the sound of
a drum smeared with poison kills a man who hears

them. It is like the practice of Never Despising
Bodhisattva preached in the 'Never Despising
Bodhisattva' chapter of the Lotus Sūtra.

If a person has the capacity of a wise man, though, we
should teach him the Hīnayāna sūtras first of all, then
the provisional Mahāyāna sūtras, and finally the true
Mahāyāna sūtra, the Lotus Sūtra. If a man is deemed
ignorant, however, we should teach him the true
Mahāyāna sūtra from the start, as it can plant the seed
of buddhahood in both believers and slanderers. (Hori
2004, pp. 97-98)

Nichiren is saying that if one is a truly skillful teacher who is teaching someone
who has the ability to understand Buddhism on a very deep level and who is
open to learning then certainly Buddhism should be taught systematically
starting with the basics taught in the pre-Mahāyāna teachings, proceeding on
to the Mahāyāna developments, and finally arriving at the teaching of the
Lotus Sūtra. Nichiren assumes a very different set of circumstances, however.
He says that those who are not skillful teachers in the Latter Age of the
Dharma who is encountering people who are incapable of understanding
Buddhism on a deep level or who are even opposed to the *Lotus Sūtra*
because they cling to lesser teachings should simply proclaim the *Lotus Sūtra*
at the start so that people can at least make a connection with it, even if it
might initially be a negative one. Otherwise, they would lose their opportunity
to hear and connect with the sūtra at all. In support of this reasoning, Nichiren
alludes to the simile of the poison drum from the *Nirvāna Sūtra*. In the
Nirvāna Sūtra the teaching of the *Nirvāna Sūtra* is said to kill the ignorance of
even those who are opposed to it, in the same way that a drum smeared with
poison will kill those who hear the drum, even if they do not want to hear it.
The idea is that the poison smeared on the drum will spread outward with the
sound of the drum and kill those who hear it, likewise the sound of the
Dharma will ultimately defeat ignorance, even if those who hear it are initially
opposed to it. (See Yamamoto, p. 232)

Application of the Two Methods Today

Today, Nichiren Buddhists must decide for themselves whether to apply the
way of embracing or the way of subduing and also determine what that

means in our own circumstances. Are we living in a time when most people are Buddhists who are actively clinging to the provisional teachings and consciously rejecting the *Lotus Sūtra*? Or are we living in a time and in places where most people are not Buddhists, and are totally ignorant of any Buddhist teaching let alone the *Lotus Sūtra*? In fact, even in countries that have a long tradition of Mahāyāna Buddhism I think it could be said that most people are only nominally Buddhists and that far from clinging to one teaching over another they are mostly indifferent and regard all the sūtras and teachings as equally inexplicable and irrelevant to daily life in the modern world whose cosmology is based on materialistic science. Nichiren lived in an age when rival groups of Buddhists were neglecting or even actively rejecting the *Lotus Sūtra*. Most of us live in an age where Buddhism is itself unknown, neglected, or rejected and where even those who profess to be religious are more often than not those who follow consumerism and capitalism wherein the reigning ideology is to try to get the most while giving the least. This would seem to argue for the use of the method of embracing because if we go by the criteria set in the *Kaimoku-shō* the majority of people are ignorant of the Dharma while those who use provisional Buddhist teachings to argue for the neglect or rejection of the *Lotus Sūtra* are comparatively rare.

In addition, in countries wherein church and state are constitutionally separate and there is freedom of religion there is no need to have Buddhist laypeople take up arms to protect pure monks who preach the True Dharma. Many people in democratic industrialized nations enjoy freedom of religion and are free from oppression by the state. The police are expected to deal with any attacks or hate crimes perpetrated against those who are peacefully and lawfully practicing their religion. The question of whether or not one should take up arms or abide by the five precepts is rendered moot for most of us fortunate enough to be living in countries where we have freedom of religion. I suppose the question would still be relevant to Buddhists laypeople who are police officers or who have joined the armed forces. If one is indeed maintaining the security of the state and law and order within the state, then the *Nirvāna Sūtra* would seem to sanction laypeople taking up arms for that purpose. Still, the sūtra also warns that even the armed laypeople should refrain from killing. Certainly, there were kings, generals, and soldiers who were lay Buddhists even during the Buddha's lifetime. The Buddha did not demand that they become pacifists or quit their duties, but they did take the five precepts, and there are occasions in the sūtras wherein the Buddha counsels kings against holding animal sacrifices or from engaging in war of aggression or even administering capital punishment against criminals.

Also, in examining Nichiren's letters to lay followers and those monks who were helping him with propagation it becomes evident that even though he generally called for the way of subduing he still counseled his lay followers to be circumspect about their faith and he told his monks to refrain from getting into debates indiscriminately and when in a debate to behave with decorum. I think it is very important to review some of these passages of guidance.

In a letter to Shijō Kingo, Nichiren acknowledges that it is one thing for Nichiren, a celibate monk with no family whose whole life is dedicated to studying and practicing the Dharma, to provoke and endure persecution but quite another for laypeople with families to have to face persecution:

> "I myself may be able to endure attacks with sticks and pieces of wood, withstand rubble and debris thrown at me, vilification, and persecution by the ruler of a country, but how can lay believers who have a wife and children and no knowledge of Buddhism bear these difficulties? Wouldn't it have been better instead for such people not to have believed in the Lotus Sūtra? I have been feeling sorry for you thinking that if you couldn't carry through your faith, which is for temporary comfort, you would be mocked and ridiculed. However, it was wonderful that you showed the steadfastness of your faith throughout numerous persecutions including two banishments. Though you were threatened by your lord, you wrote this written pledge swearing to carry through your faith in the Lotus Sūtra even at the cost of fiefs in two places. Words cannot describe your commendable aspiration." (Hori 2010, p. 142)

In light of this, Nichiren advised his lay followers to be circumspect and careful about whom they speak with about Buddhism. For instance, he gave the following advice to Lord Misawa:

*"That all of you are not as versed in Buddhism as is
Nichiren, that you are secular, own property, have wives
and children, as well as men in your employ must make
it difficult for you to persevere in maintaining faith. So
being the case, I have long said that you may pretend
not to be believers of the Lotus Sūtra. As you all have
come to Nichiren's aid, I will not disown you under any
circumstance. I shall never neglect you." (Hori 2002, p.
241)*

This does not mean that Nichiren intended for anyone to deny the *Lotus Sūtra*
itself. He was simply saying that lay followers did not need to advertise their
faith and so bring trouble down on themselves. To the lay follower Nanjō
Tokimitsu he gave the following advise so as to avoid having people harass
him and try to talk him out of his faith in the *Lotus Sūtra*: "I advise you to get
to the bottom of the situation and not to show off your faith simply and
carelessly." (Hori 2007, p. 112) He also advises him to "always speak gently"
and to tell those who try to destroy his faith to mind their own business. He
does not tell him to try to argue back, much less to aggressively proselytize.
What Nichiren expected of his lay followers, especially those who were
uneducated or who had no deep understanding of Buddhism, was just this:
"Therefore ignorant people today should believe in Śākyamuni Buddha as the
focus of devotion, and they will automatically be able to avoid being unfilial to
the Buddha. If they, moreover, believe in the *Lotus Sūtra*, they will be able to
avoid unknowingly committing the sin of slandering the True Dharma. (Ibid, p.
54)

Nichiren gave the following advice to Toki Jōnin, an educated lay follower:
"The debate this time turned out to be victorious for you; however, you
should not engage in a polemic debate in Shimofusa Province (northern Chiba
Prefecture) again. By defeating such scholars as Ryōshō-bō and Shi'nen in a
debate, I am afraid, it would be beneath your dignity to meet with others in
debate." (Hori 2002, p. 279-280) So Nichiren did not discourage those who
were able to do so from participating in public debates (a kind of formal event
at the time in Japan), but advised against getting involved in useless debates.

Nichiren even advised fellow monks to be circumspect about the particular
teachings that he was sharing with them in his writings. In the cover letter to

the *Essay on Gratitude* (*Hōon-jō*) he said to the monk Jōken-bo: "I want you to remember not to speak about Buddhist doctrines to anyone who does not believe in them, regardless of how close he is to you." (Hori 2004, p. 64) He also said, "As for the writing of mine, *Hōon-jō*, it contains deeply significant doctrine, which should not be revealed to those who do not deserve to listen to it. Otherwise, it might bring about unexpected harm to you and to us if its content is revealed to many. (Ibid, p. 65) From this we can see that Nichiren did not intend for his teachings to be pushed onto others who do not care about Buddhism, and that he expected even his fellow monks to be tactful and reserved in regard to the particulars of his teaching and practice. Certainly Nichiren publicly called for his contemporaries to turn away from lesser teachings, uphold the *Lotus Sūtra*, and to take up the practice of chanting Odaimoku; but he apparently felt that the particulars of his teaching, such as the specific criticisms of other schools, or those teachings pertaining to the Eternal Śākyamuni Buddha as the true focus of devotion, or the precept platform of the Original Gate of the *Lotus Sūtra*, were things to be held in reserve for those who had already taken sincere faith in the *Lotus Sūtra* of for formal debates.

There were of course occasions when a formal public debate involving monks or even educated lay followers such as Toki Jōnin would occur. In a letter attributed to Nichiren, the writer advises a monk named Sammi-bo about what to say in a debate and just as importantly how to say it: "Say these things mildly but firmly in a quiet voice with a calm gaze and an even expression." (Gosho Translation Committee 1999, p. 478) At the end of the letter, the writer advises:

When in public debate, although the teachings that you advocate are perfectly consistent with the truth, you should never on that account be impolite or abusive or display a conceited attitude. Such conduct would be disgraceful. Order your thoughts, words, and actions carefully, and be prudent when you meet with others in debate. (Ibid, p. 483)

Though it is highly unlikely that anyone today would ever be involved in a formal religious debate such as were held in medieval Japan, the advice given would still make sense today whenever there is occasion to discuss Buddhism with friends, acquaintances, or inquirers. The attitude and tone of discussion should always be calm, respectful, and compassionate even when there is disagreement, whether the discussion is face-to-face or online.

Nichiren Shu's handbook for Nichiren Shu members, also discusses the two ways of embracing (shōju) and subduing (shakubuku). It does not come out and say whether today's situation calls for one or the other, though it does say, just as Nichiren says in *Kaimoku-shō*, that which we should use depends on the circumstances. The passage also cautions against using the method of subduing as an excuse for boorish or violent behavior, and states that those who would use the method of subduing should first have great self-discipline. All of this is in line with the passage from Nichiren's writings cited above.

> *Faith cannot be forced upon others, nor can we make someone believe through force. It is wrong to resort to intimidation and force, saying it is shakubuku, a means of spreading the Lotus Sutra.*
>
> *Shakubuku is a strict way of spreading Buddhism to awaken religious feeling in others so that they would be converted. On the other hand, shōju is a gentle way of persuasion according to the individual and circumstance. To resort to shakubuku as a way of persuasion, the person must strictly discipline himself first. By observing the life of our Founder, who risked his life to spread the teachings of the Buddha in order to repent and redeem his bad karma in his previous lives, we should know there are two ways of spreading the Lotus Sutra. Nichiren Shōnin said, 'Whether we should use the method of shakubuku or shōju depends in the circumstances.' (Hori 1986, p. 7)*

In this and the last two chapters of this commentary I have surveyed what has been said about the ways of embracing and subduing by Śākyamuni Buddha in the sūtras, by Zhiyi and other Tiantai patriarchs and teachers, by Nichiren, and by Nichiren Shū. I would now like to share my own personal understanding of the ways of embracing and subduing. It seems to me that the way of embracing is the way of peacefully minding one's own business and contemplating the Dharma in private while still being prepared and able to teach others if they ask about Buddhism in a way that will encourage them where they are in their own understanding and according to their own ability.

The way of subduing is the way of public witness to the truth, and that may include denouncing corrupt or false teachings and practices that are going by the name of Buddhism. The way of subduing does not cater to limited views and understandings of Buddhism but more forthrightly challenges or even goads fellow Buddhists to aim for the ultimate realization and actualization of buddhahood. It is a way based on compassion and courage that may provoke hostility in those who do not wish to have their views challenged. The way of subduing also allows for the legitimate and lawful defense of those who speak the truth from violence and oppression.

I feel that, going by Nichiren's criteria, the circumstances of today more often than not require the method of embracing as most people are simply ignorant about Buddhism and are not slanderers of the *Lotus Sūtra*, which is to say Buddhists who are trying to get people to neglect or reject the *Lotus Sūtra*. We are all now countries of "evil and ignorant people" who do not know enough about Buddhism to be considered slanderers, I would include countries that have historically been Buddhist but whose populations are nominally Buddhist at most. This is not to say that there are no people who are misrepresenting or slandering Buddhism because there certainly are. Some of these are people who think they know more than they do, some are atheists who take a reductionist view towards Buddhism (either because they decry it as a religion or because they think they are praising it for not being an atheistic philosophy), some are members of other religions who see Buddhism as a rival or false teaching that must be denounced, and some are Buddhists who are perpetuating some of the same errors and corrupt practices that Nichiren and other reformers before and after him have striven to correct. I do think it is important to address such distortions when they are encountered, especially those pertaining to the teaching and/or practice of the *Lotus Sūtra*. On the whole however, I feel it is better to not look for controversy or embark upon any reformist crusades but rather to try to exemplify the teachings in one's own life and to have a positive impact on the people one actually has personal interactions with.

When it comes to teaching the Dharma, I think it is very important to teach on the basis of personal experience with Buddhist practice under competent teachers. Teaching must be used to inform practice and practice is necessary to actualize the teachings. I think this is true whether one is following the way of embracing or subduing. And of course, both the ways of propagation are not simply to spread a sterile or abstract teaching but to lead the way to practice. How can we do this if we are not cultivating the practice ourselves?

Also, when teaching I think it is very important to keep in mind what both Nichiren and the Buddha taught: to only speak of what is true and beneficial, and to speak at the appropriate time – when the listener will be the most receptive to the message or at least when a warning must be given even if it will be rejected. While the truth may be agreeable or disagreeable to the listener, it is important that we make sure we are speaking out of compassion and not arrogance, egoism, or some misguided sectarianism. Really, I think the application of the ways of embracing and subduing come down to our own good sense. In the end, it is about embracing what is wholesome in others and in ourselves whenever we can, but also subduing what is unwholesome in ourselves and others when that is called for. It is about encouraging the cultivation of Buddhism until the fulfillment of its highest aim, but also subduing any complacence or other negative attitudes or unwholesome attachments that would prevent the realization and actualization of Buddhism's highest aim.

Sources

Gosho Translation Committee, editor-translator. *The Writings of Nichiren Daishonin*. Tokyo: Soka Gakkai, 1999.

_____. *The Writings of Nichiren Daishonin Volume II*. Tokyo: Soka Gakkai, 2006.

Hori, Kyotsu, trans. *Shingyō Hikkei: A Handbook for Members of the Nichiren Order*. Tokyo: Nichiren Order, 1986.

Hori, Kyotsu, comp. *Writings of Nichiren Shonin: Doctrine Volume 2*. Tokyo: Nichiren Shu Overseas Propagation Promotion Association, 2002.

_____. *Writings of Nichiren Shonin: Doctrine Volume 1*. Tokyo: Nichiren Shu Overseas Propagation Promotion Association, 2003.

_____. *Writings of Nichiren Shonin: Doctrine Volume 3*. Tokyo: Nichiren Shu Overseas Propagation Promotion Association, 2004.

_____. *Writings of Nichiren Shonin: Faith and Practice Volume 4*. Tokyo: Nichiren Shu Overseas Propagation Promotion Association, 2007.

_____. *Writings of Nichiren Shonin: Biography and Disciples Volume 5*. Tokyo: Nichiren Shu Overseas Propagation Promotion Association, 2008.

_____. *Writings of Nichiren Shonin: Followers Volume 6*. Tokyo: Nichiren Shu Overseas Propagation Promotion Association, 2010.

_____. *Kaimokusho or Liberation from Blindness*. Berkeley: Numata Center for Buddhist Translation and Research, 2000.

Yamamoto, Kosho, trans. *Mahaparinirvana-Sutra: A Complete Translation from the Classical Chinese Language in 3 Volumes*. Tokyo: Karinbunko, 1973.

Chapter 46 – Great Joy

Writing of Nichiren Shonin Doctrine 2: pp. 114-115
Kaimoku-shō or Liberation From Blindness: pp. 125-126
Writings of Nichiren Daishonin I: 287

Now we come to the conclusion of the *Kaimoku-shō*. Over the course of this writing Nichiren has reviewed all the reasons why he believes that the *Lotus Sūtra* alone allows all people to sow the seed of buddhahood and why he believes that it is necessary to refute all those teachings that would cause people to neglect or reject it. He has also addressed the reasons why he and his followers have to face many hardships if they are to uphold the *Lotus Sūtra* in the Latter Age of the Dharma. Nichiren concludes by reminding the reader that in chapter eleven of the *Lotus Sūtra* Śakyamuni Buddha, Many Treasures Tathāgata, and the buddhas throughout the universe all came together "for the purpose of making sure that the Lotus Sūtra would spread forever." (Hori 2002, p. 113) He says of them that "their compassion seems greater than that of parents who see their only child faced with great suffering." (Ibid, p. 113). Nichiren compares his own efforts to uphold the sūtra and refute those who would negate it to this great parental compassion of the buddhas saying, "I, Nichiren, am like a compassionate parent of everyone in Japan..." (Ibid, p. 114) In a later letter, Nichiren even said of himself that for the people of Japan he was a parent, teacher, and lord because of his efforts as the Buddha's messenger: "Though I am a fool, I have declared myself to be a messenger of the Buddha and a practitioner of the *Lotus Sūtra* so that peace and tranquility may be established in Japan. ... I am the father and mother of the people in Japan, their lord and their eminent teacher." (Hori 2010, p. 166) As the Buddha's messenger, Nichiren felt that he was sharing in the virtues of the Buddha as parent, teacher, and sovereign to those he was trying to correct and lead to the right path. In *Kaimoku-shō*, we see the thought process that Nichiren went through to come to his conviction that he was doing the right thing for the sake of the people of Japan and ultimately all beings.

Nichiren reminds the reader of the hardships faced by those who taught the *Lotus Sūtra* in the past, including Śakyamuni Buddha and the past Tiantai patriarchs. He states, "However, the masters had nothing to be ashamed of because they were abused for the sake of the *Lotus Sūtra*. Praise by the ignorant should be regarded as most dishonorable." (Ibid, p. 114) Nichiren is saying that neither should he or his followers feel that they are on the wrong path simply because they are being persecuted by those who are foolishly rejecting the *Lotus Sūtra*. In fact, such persecution is only to be expected.

Nichiren then reviews the great sacrifices made by Śākyamuni Buddha and other great teachers of Buddhism in the past. They are, he says, examples of those who were spreading the Dharma in the most appropriate manner according to the situations they faced. Likewise, Nichiren is sure that the hard course he has undertaken is also the correct one and therefore he has no regrets. In fact, he feels assured regarding the rewards and happiness he will reap in the future. He concludes the *Kaimoku-shō* saying: "Keep in mind that Buddhism must be spread according to the times. My exile is merely a trifle in this present life, which is not lamentable at all. Instead, I feel it is a great joy as I am sure I will be rewarded with great happiness in my future lives." (Ibid, pp. 114-115) In other words, Nichiren was not looking for worldly acclamation, comforts, or status. He was looking forward to ultimately attaining buddhahood for the sake of all beings.

Many people today, I think, are very casual about being either nominally religious, or vaguely spiritual, or openly disdainful of religious teachings and spiritual practice. Those who do investigate and take up Buddhism and Buddhist practice all too often are satisfied with the small rewards of worldly benefits like peace of mind gained through silent sitting practices, or perhaps good fortune in in their relationships or careers because they believe Buddhism can give them some kind of metaphysical control over their lives through ritual practices. I would not deny that sitting meditation or chanting can bring about peace of mind or help people gain the insight to refrain from bad and instead make good causes to help them make the most of life in a worldly sense. Even Śākyamuni Buddha gave discourses to lay followers to help them live wisely and thereby enjoy relatively happy lives in a worldly sense. However, what Nichiren is inviting us to do in *Kaimoku-shō* is to reflect more deeply about religious teachings including Buddhism and what they mean in terms of how we view life and our own role. Are we content to simply accept that this is the only life and that after death there is nothing at all? Or do we believe there may be some heavenly realm to hope for and that a virtuous life can lead us to it? Or do we wish to seek buddhahood – a life of selfless compassion that transcends small-minded concerns about personal happiness in this or some other lifetime? If we are really willing to engage the deepest teachings of Buddhism and try to realize and actualize them, what are we willing to put on the line? How much of ourselves are we willing to give? Are we only looking for protection and benefits? Or do we have the compassion and courage to give more and more of ourselves for the sake of all beings according to whatever the situation may demand? I cannot imagine that everyone will come to the same conclusions as Nichiren did, but I do think that if the *Kaimoku-shō* can inspire us to at least reflect on these questions than it will have been well worth taking the time to read and ponder its message.

Sources

Gosho Translation Committee, editor-translator. *The Writings of Nichiren Daishonin*. Tokyo: Soka Gakkai, 1999.

Hori, Kyotsu, comp. *Writings of Nichiren Shonin: Doctrine Volume 2*. Tokyo: Nichiren Shu Overseas Propagation Promotion Association, 2002.

_____. *Writings of Nichiren Shonin: Followers Volume 6*. Tokyo: Nichiren Shu Overseas Propagation Promotion Association, 2010.

Murano, Senchu, trans. *Kaimokusho or Liberation from Blindness*. Berkeley: Numata Center for Buddhist Translation and Research, 2000.

_____. *Kaimokusho or Liberation from Blindness*. Berkeley: Numata Center for Buddhist Translation and Research, 2000.

Bibliography

Abe, Ryuichi. *The Weaving of Mantra: Kukai and the Construction of Esoteric Buddhist Discourse*. New York: Columbia University Press, 1999.

http://www.accesstoinsight.org/tipitaka/an/an04/an04.077.than.html

Ames, Roger T. & Rosemont, Henry Jr., translators. *The Analects of Confucius: A Philosophical Translation*. New York: Ballantine Books, 1998.

Ames, Roger T. & Rosemont, Henry Jr., translators. *Dao De Jing "Making This Life Significant": A Philosophical Translation*. New York: Ballantine Books, 2003.

Augustine, Morris & Tessho, Kondo, translators. *Senchaku Hongan Nembutsu Shu: A Collection of Passages on the Nembutsu Chosen in the Original Vow*. USA: Numata Center for Buddhist Translation and Research, 1997.

Bodhi, Bhikkhu, trans. *The Connected Discourses of the Buddha: A New Translation of the Samyutta Nikaya.* Boston: Wisdom Publications, 2000.

_____, ed., *In the Buddha's Words: An Anthology of Discourses from the Pali Canon*. Boston: Wisdom Publications, 2005.

Bodhi, Bhikkhu, trans. *The Suttanipāta*. Boston: Wisdom Publication, 2017.

Broughton, Jeffrey L. *The Bodhidharma Anthology: The Earliest Records of Zen*. Berkeley: University of California Press, 1999.

Bryant, Edwin F., trans. *The Yoga Sutras of Patanjali*. New York: North Point Press, 2009.

Chan, Wing-tsit, trans. *A Source Book in Chinese Philosophy*. Princeton: Princeton University Press, 1963.

Chang, Cheng-chi. *The Practice of Zen*. Westport: Greenwood Press, 1978.

Chang, Garma C. *The Buddhist Teaching of Totality: The Philosophy of Hwa Yen Buddhism*. University Park: The Pennsylvania State University Press, 1989.

Chappel, David, ed., and Masao Ichishima, comp. trans. Buddhist Translation Seminar of Hawaii. *T'ien-t'ai Buddhism: An Outline of the Fourfold Teachings*. Tokyo: Shobo, 1983.

Ch'en, Kenneth. *Buddhism in China: A Historical Survey*. Princeton: Princeton University Press, 1964.

Christensen, J.A. *Nichiren: Leader of Buddhist Reformation in Japan*. Fremont: Jain Publishing, 2001.

Cleary, J.C. *Zen Dawn: Early Zen Texts*. Translated from Tun Huang. Boston: Shambhala, 1986.

Cleary, Thomas. *Entry Into the Inconceivable: An Introduction to Hua-Yen Buddhism*. Honolulu: University of Hawaii Press, 1983.

_____. *Unlocking the Zen Koan: A New Translation of the Zen Classic Wumenguan*. Berkeley, North Atlantic Books, 1997.

_____, trans. *The Flower Ornament Scripture: A Translation of the Avatamsaka Sutra.* Boston: Shambhala, 1993.

Cleary, Thomas and Cleary, J.C. *The Blue Cliff Record*. Boston: Shambhala, 1992.

Conze, Edward, trans. *The Large Sutra on Perfect Wisdom*. Berkeley: University of California Press, 1984.

_____. *The Perfection of Wisdom in Eight Thousand Lines & It's Verse Summary*. San Francisco: Four Seasons Foundation, 1995.

Conze, Edward. *Buddhism: It's Essence and Development*. Birmingham: Windhorse Publication, 2001.

Cook, Francis H. *Hua-yen Buddhism: The Jewel Net of Indra*. University Park: The Pennsylvania State University, 1991.

Crosby, Kate and Skilton, Andrew, trans. *The Bodhicaryāvatāra*. New York: Oxford University Press, 1996.

Danielou, Alain. *The Myths and Gods of India*. Rochester: Inner Traditions International, 1991

Dasgupta, Surendranath. *A History of Indian Philosophy Volume 1*. New Delhi: Motilal Banarsidass, 1997.

de Bar, Wm. Theodore and Bloom, Irene. *Sources of Chinese Tradition Volume One: From Earliest Times to 1600*. New York: Columbia University Press, 1999.

Dharmamitra, Bhikshu, trans. *Nāgārjuna on The Six Perfection: An Ārya Bodhisattva Explains the Heart of the Bodhisattva Path*. Seattle: Kalavinka Press, 1990-2008.

_____. *The Essentials of Buddhist Meditation*. Seattle: Kalavinka Press, 1992-2008.

_____. *The Six Dharma Gates to the Sublime*. Seattle: Kalavinka Press, 2001-2008.

Doniger, Wendy, trans. *The Rig Veda*. New York: Penguin Books, 1981.

_____. *The Laws of Manu*. New York: Penguin Books, 1991.

Doniger, Wendy. *The Hindus: An Alternative History*. New York: The Penguin Press, 2009.

Donner, Neal, and Stevenson, Daniel B., trans. *The Great Calming and Contemplation: A Study and Annotated Translation of the First Chapter of Chih-I's Mo-Ho Chih-Kuan*. Honolulu: Kuroda Institute, 1993.

Dumoulin, Heinrich. *Zen Buddhism: A History, Volume I India and China*. New York: MacMillian, 1994.

_____. *Zen Buddhism: A History, Volume II Japan*. New York: MacMillian, 1990.

Dundas, Paul. *The Jains*. New York: Routledge, 2002.

Feng, Gia-fu, and English, Jane trans. *Chuang Tsu: Inner Chapters*. New York: Vintage Books, 1974.

Feng, Gia-fu, and English, Jane trans. *Lao Tsu: Tao Te Ching*. New York: Vintage Books, 1972.

Ferguson, Andy. *Zen's Chinese Heritage: The Masters and Their Teachings*. Boston: Wisdom Publications, 2000.

Flood, Gavin. *An Introduction to Hinduism*. New York: Cambridge University Press, 1996.

Foulk, T. Griffith. "Sung Controversies Concerning 'Separate Transmission' of Ch'an." In *Buddhism in the Sung*. Ed. by Gregory, Peter N. and Getz, Daniel A. Jr. Honolulu: University of Hawai'i Press, 1999.

Giebel, Rolf W., trans. *Two Esoteric Sutras*. Berkeley: Numata Center for Buddhist Translation and Research, 2001.

_____ & Todara, Dale. *Shingon Texts*. Berkeley: Numata Center for Buddhist Translation and Research, 2004.

_____. *The Vairocanabhiambodhi Sutra*. Berkeley: Numata Center for Buddhist Translation and Research, 2005.

Gosho Translation Committee, editor-translator. *The Writings of Nichiren Daishonin*. Tokyo: Soka Gakkai, 1999.

_____. *The Writings of Nichiren Daishonin Volume II*. Tokyo: Soka Gakkai, 2006.

Gregory, Peter N., trans. *Inquiry Into the Origin of Humanity*. Honolulu: Kuroda Institute, 1995.

_____, *Tsung-mi and the Sinification of Buddhism*. Honolulu: Kuroda Institute, 2002.

Groner, Paul. *Saicho: The Establishment of the Japanese Tendai School*. Berkeley: Berkeley Buddhist Studies Series, 1984.

Hakeda, Yoshito S., trans. *The Awakening of Faith: Attributed to Ashvaghosha*. New York: Columbia University Press, 1967.

_____. *Kukai: Major Works*. New York: Columbia University Press, 1972.

Hartranft, Chip, trans. *The Yoga-Sutra of Patanjali*. Boston: Shambhala, 2003.

Hori, Kyotsu, comp. *Writings of Nichiren Shonin: Doctrine Volume 2*. Tokyo: Nichiren Shu Overseas Propagation Promotion Association, 2002.

_____. *Writings of Nichiren Shonin: Doctrine Volume 1*. Tokyo: Nichiren Shu Overseas Propagation Promotion Association, 2003.

_____. *Writings of Nichiren Shonin: Doctrine Volume 3*. Tokyo: Nichiren Shu Overseas Propagation Promotion Association, 2004.

_____. *Writings of Nichiren Shonin: Faith and Practice Volume 4*. Tokyo: Nichiren Shu Overseas Propagation Promotion Association, 2007.

_____. *Writings of Nichiren Shonin: Biography and Disciples Volume 5*. Tokyo: Nichiren Shu Overseas Propagation Promotion Association, 2008.

_____. *Writings of Nichiren Shonin: Followers Volume 6*. Tokyo: Nichiren Shu Overseas Propagation Promotion Association, 2010.

Horner, I.B., trans. *The Book of the Discipline Volume V*. Oxford: Pali Text Society, 1992.

Hurvitz, Leon. *Chih-i: An Introduction to the Life and Ideas of a Chinese Buddhist Monk*. Melanges chinois et bouddhiques 12 (1960-62): 1-372. Brussels: l'Institute Belge des Hautes Etudes Chinoises.

Inagaki, Hisao. *The Three Pure Land Sutras*. Kyoto: Nagata Bunshodo, 1995.

James, William. *The Varieties of Religious Experience*. New York: Collier Books, 1961.

Kasahara, Kazuo. *A History of Japanese Religion*. Tokyo: Kosei Publishing Co., 2002.

Kashiwahara, Yusen & Sonoda, Koyu. *Shapers of Japanese Buddhism*. Tokyo: Kosei Publishing Co., 1994.

Kohn, Livia. *Early Chinese Mysticism: Philosophy and Soteriology in the Taoist Tradition*. Princeton: Princeton University Press, 1992.

Lamotte, Etienne, "Assessment of Textual Interpretation in Buddhism." In Lopez, Donald S. Jr. *Buddhist Hermeneutics*. Honolulu: University of Hawaii Press, 1988.

Lau, D.C., translator. *Confucius: The Analects*. New York: Penguin Books, 1979.

_____. *Lao Tzu: Tao Te Ching*. New York: Penguin Books, 1963.

_____. *Mencius: A Bilingual Edition*. Hong Kong: The Chinese University Press, 2003.

Legge, James, translator. *The Four Books*. Taipei: Culture Books Co., 1992.

Le Mee, Jean Marie Alexandre, trans., *Hymns from the Rig Veda*. New York: Alfred A. Knopf, Inc., 1975.

Liu, Shu-hsien. *Understanding Confucian Philosophy: Classical and Sung-Ming*. Westport: Praeger Publishing, 1998.

Lynn, Richard John trans. *The Classic of Changes: A New Translation of the I Ching as Interpreted by Wang Bi*. New York: Columbia University Press, 1994.

Matsunaga, Alicia & Matsunaga, Daigan. *Foundation of Japanese Buddhism Vol. I & II*. Los Angeles: Buddhist Books International, 1988.

Mitchell, Donald W. *Buddhism: Introducing the Buddhist Experience*. New York: Oxford University Press, 2002.

Moody, Raymond A. Jr., *Coming Back: A Psychiatrist Explores Past-Life Journeys*. New York: Bantam Books, 1991.

Murano, Senchu, trans. *The Lotus Sutra*. Hayward: Nichiren Buddhist International Center, 2012.

_____. *Kaimokusho or Liberation from Blindness*. Berkeley: Numata Center for Buddhist Translation and Research, 2000.

_____. *Manual of Nichiren Buddhism*. Tokyo: Nichiren Shu Headquarters, 1995.

Nagapriya, *Exploring Karma & Rebirth*. Birmingham: Windhorse Publications, 2004.

Nanamoli, Bhikkhu and Bodhi, Bhikkhu, trans. *The Middle Length Discourses of the Buddha: A New Translation of the Majjhima Nikaya*. Botson: Wisdom Publications, 1995.

Nanamoli, Bhikkhu, trans. *The Life of the Buddha*. Seattle: Buddhist Publication Society Pariyatti Editions, 2001.

Numata Center for Buddhist Translation and Research Editorial Staff. *Buddha-Dharma: The Way to Enlightenment (Revised Second Edition)*. Berkeley: Numata Center for Buddhist Translation and Research, 2003.

Nyanaponika, Thera and Bodhi, Bhikkhu trans. & ed., *Numerical Discourses of the Buddha: An Anthology of Suttas from the Anguttara Nikaya*. Walnut Creek: AltaMira Press, 1999.

Odin, Steve. *Process Metaphysics and Hua-Yen Buddhism: A Critical Study of Cumulative Penetration vs. Interpenetration*. Albany, State of New York Press, 1982.

Olivelle, Patrick, trans. *Upanishads*. Oxford: Oxford University Press, 1996.

Palmer, Martin, trans. *The Book of Chuang Tzu*. New York: Penguin Books, 2006.

Plaks, Andrew, trans. *Ta Hsueh and Chung Yung*. New York: Penguin Books, 2003.

Prabhavananda, Swami. *The Spiritual Heritage of India: A Clear Summary of Indian Philosophy and Religion*. Hollywood: Vedanta Press, 1979.

Prebish, Charles S., ed. *Buddhism: A Modern Perspective*. University Park: The Pennsylvania State University Press, 1978.

Price, A.F. and Mou-lam, Wong. *The Diamond Sutra and the Sutra of Hui Neng*. Boston: Shambhala, 1985.

Pruden, Leo, trans. *The Essentials of the Eight Traditions*. Berkeley: Numata Center for Buddhist Translation and Research, 1994.

_____. *The Essentials of the Vinaya Tradition*. BDK English Tripitika 97-I, II. Berkeley: Numata Center for Buddhist Translation and Research, 1995

Ray, Reginald A. *Buddhist Saints in India: A Study in Buddhist Values & Orientations*. New York: Oxford University Press, 1994.

Real Life with Ryuei: https://www.nichirenbayarea.org/library

Reeves, Gene, trans. *The Lotus Sutra*. Boston: Wisdom Publications, 2008. Rhodes, Robert, trans. *The Candle of the Latter Dharma*. BDK English Tripitika 107-I, III. Berkeley: Numata Center for Buddhist Translation and Research, 1994.

Robinet, Isabelle auth. Brooks, Phyllis trans. *Taoism: Growth of a Religion*. Stanford: Stanford University Press, 1997.

Sadataka, Akira. *Buddhist Cosmology: Philosophy and Origins*. Tokyo: Kosei Publishing Co., 2004.

Sargeant, Winthrop. *The Bhagavad Gita*. New York: State University of New York Press, 1994.

Sasaki, Konen. "When Did Life of Sakyamuni Begin and End?" [Part 1]. Nichiren Shu News, April 1, 2000, p. 1.

_____. "When Did Life of Sakyamuni Begin and End?" [Part 2]. Nichiren Shu News, June 1, 2000, p. 1.

Schloegl, Irmgard. *The Zen Teachings of Rinzai*. Berkeley: Shambhala, 1976.

Shen, Haiyan. *The Profound Meaning of the Lotus Sutra: T'ien-t'ai Philosophy of Buddhism volumes I and II*. Delhi: Originals, 2005.

Simpkins, Alexander C. and Simpkins, Annellen. *Simple Confucianism: A Guide to Living Virtuously*. Boston: Tuttle Publishing, 2000.

Snodgrass, Adrian. *The Matrix and Diamond World Mandalas in Shingon Buddhism*. 2 Volumes. New Delhi: Rakesh Goel on behalf of Aditya Prakashan, 1988.

Stone, Jacqueline. *Original Enlightenment and the Transformation of Medieval Japanese Buddhism*. Honolulu: Kuroda Institute, 1999.

Suzuki, D.T. *The Lankavatara Sutra: A Mahayana Text*. Taipei: SMC Publishing Inc., 1994.

_____. *Essays in Zen Buddhism*. New York: Grove Press, 1949.

Swanson, Paul. *Foundations of T'ien-tai Philosophy: The Flowering of the Two Truths Theory in Chinese Buddhism*. Berkeley: Asian Humanities Press, 1989.

_____, trans. *The Collected Teachings of the Tendai School*. Berkeley: Numata Center for Buddhist Translation and Research, 1995.

Takakusu, Junjiro. *The Essentials of Buddhist Philosophy*. Delhi: Motilal Banarsidass, 1978.

Tamura, Yoshiro. *Japanese Buddhism: A Cultural History*. Tokyo: Kosei Publishing Co., 2000.

Tokiwa, Gishin, trans. *A Treatise on Letting Zen Flourish to Protect the State*. In *Zen Texts*. Berkeley: Numata Center for Buddhist Translation and Research, 2005.

Tsukamoto, Keisho. *Source Elements of the Lotus Sutra: Buddhist Integration of Religion, Thought, and Culture*. Tokyo: Kosei Publishing Co., 2007.

Walshe, Maurice, trans. *The Long Discourses of the Buddha: A Translation of the Digha Nikaya*. Boston: Wisdom Publications, 1995.

Watson, Burton, trans. *The Vimalakirti Sutra*. New York: Columbia University Press, 1997.

Williams, Paul. *Mahayana Buddhism: The Doctrinal Foundations Second Edition*. New York: Routledge, 2009.

Williams, Paul & Tribe, Anthony. *Buddhist Thought: A Complete Introduction to the Indian Tradition*. New York: Routledge, 2000.

Wong, Eva. *The Shambhala Guide to Taoism*. Boston: Shambhala Publications Inc., 1997.

Wright, Arthur F. *Buddhism in Chinese History*. Stanford: Stanford University Press, 1959.

Yamamoto, Kosho, trans. *Mahaparinirvana-Sutra: A Complete Translation from the Classical Chinese Language in 3 Volumes*. Tokyo: Karinbunko, 1973.

Yamasaki, Taiko. *Shingon: Japanese Esoteric Buddhism*. Boston: Shambhala, 1988.

Yampolsky, Philip B. *The Platform Sutra of the Sixth Patriarch*. New York: Columbia University Press, 1967.

Yao, Xinzhong. *An Introduction to Confucianism*. New York: Cambridge University Press, 2000.

Yasuo, Yamamoto. *The Structure of Oriental Values and Education*.

http://www.crvp.org/book/Series03/III-11/chapter_xxiii.htm

Yi-Liang, Chou. "Tantrism in China." In *Tantric Buddhism in East Asia*. Ed. by Payne, Richard K. Boston: Wisdom Publications: 2006.

Yu-lan, Fung. *A Short History of Chinese Philosophy*. New York: The Free Press, 1966.

Printed in Great Britain
by Amazon